M000077434

VENICE &
THE VENETIAN ARC

4th Edition

**Where to Stay and Eat
for All Budgets**

**Must-See Sights
and Local Secrets**

Ratings You Can Trust

Fodor's Travel Publications   New York, Toronto, London, Sydney, Auckland
www.fodors.com

FODOR'S VENICE & THE VENETIAN ARC

Editor: Matthew Lombardi

Editorial Production: Tom Holton
Editorial Contributors: Jeff Booth, Ruth Craig, Robin Goldstein, Cristina Gregorin, Michael Nalepa, Pamela Santini
Maps: David Lindroth, *cartographer;* Bob Blake and Rebecca Baer, *map editors*
Design: Fabrizio La Rocca, *creative director;* Guido Caroti, *art director;* Moon Sun Kim, *cover designer;* Melanie Marin, *senior picture editor*
Production/Manufacturing: Colleen Ziemba
Cover Photo: (canal scene, Venice): Travel Library/Robert Harding

Fourth Edition

ISBN: 1–4000–1585–5

ISBN-13: 978–1–4000–1585–6

ISSN: 1547–9269

SPECIAL SALES

This book is available at special discounts for bulk purchases for sales promotions or premiums. Special editions, including personalized covers, excerpts of existing books, and corporate imprints, can be created in large quantities for special needs. For more information, write to Special Markets/Premium Sales, 1745 Broadway, MD 6-2, New York, New York 10019, or e-mail specialmarkets@randomhouse.com.

AN IMPORTANT TIP & AN INVITATION

Although all prices, opening times, and other details in this book are based on information supplied to us at press time, changes occur all the time in the travel world, and Fodor's cannot accept responsibility for facts that become outdated or for inadvertent errors or omissions. So **always confirm information when it matters,** especially if you're making a detour to visit a specific place. Your experiences—positive and negative—matter to us. If we have missed or misstated something, **please write to us.** We follow up on all suggestions. Contact the Venice editor at editors@fodors.com or c/o Fodor's at 1745 Broadway, New York, New York 10019.

PRINTED IN THE UNITED STATES OF AMERICA

10 9 8 7 6 5 4 3 2 1

Be a Fodor's Correspondent

Your opinion matters. It matters to us. It matters to your fellow Fodor's travelers, too. And we'd like to hear it. In fact, we *need* to hear it.

When you share your experiences and opinions, you become an active member of the Fodor's community. That means we'll not only use your feedback to make our books better, but we'll publish your names and comments whenever possible. Throughout this guide, look for "Word of Mouth," excerpts of unvarnished feedback.

Here's how you can help improve Fodor's for all of us.

Tell us when we're right. We rely on local writers to give you an insider's perspective. But our writers and staff editors—who are the best in the business—depend on you. Your positive feedback is a vote to renew our recommendations for the next edition.

Tell us when we're wrong. We're proud that we update most of our guides every year. But we're not perfect. Things change. Hotels cut services. Museums change hours. Charming cafés lose their charm. If our writer didn't quite capture the essence of a place, tell us how you'd do it differently. If any of our descriptions are inaccurate or inadequate, we'll incorporate your changes in the next edition and will correct factual errors at fodors.com *immediately.*

Tell us what to include. You're bound to have some fantastic experiences not mentioned in this guide. Why not share them with a community of like-minded travelers? Maybe you chanced upon a palazzo or a trattoria that you don't want to keep to yourself. Tell us why we should include it. And share your discoveries and experiences with everyone directly at fodors.com. Your input may lead us to add a new listing or highlight a place we cover with a "Highly Recommended" star or with our highest rating, "Fodor's Choice."

Give us your opinion instantly at our feedback center at www.fodors.com/feedback. You may also e-mail editors@fodors.com with the subject line "Venice Editor." Or send your nominations, comments, and complaints by mail to Venice Editor, Fodor's, 1745 Broadway, New York, NY 10019.

You and travelers like you are the heart of the Fodor's community. Make our community richer by sharing your experiences. Be a Fodor's correspondent.

Buon viaggio! (Or simply: Happy traveling!)

Tim Jarrell, Publisher

CONTENTS

CLOSEUPS

ABOUT THIS BOOK

Our Ratings

Sometimes you find terrific travel experiences and sometimes they just find you. But usually the burden is on you to select the right combination of experiences. That's where our ratings come in.

As travelers we've all discovered a place so wonderful that its worthiness is obvious. And sometimes that place is so unique that superlatives don't do it justice: you just have to be there to know. These sights, properties, and experiences get our highest rating, **Fodor's Choice**, indicated by orange stars throughout this book.

Black stars highlight sights and properties we deem **Highly Recommended**, places that our writers, editors, and readers praise again and again for consistency and excellence.

By default, there's another category: any place we include in this book is by definition worth your time, unless we say otherwise. And we will.

Disagree with any of our choices? Care to nominate a place or suggest that we rate one more highly? Visit our feedback center at www. fodors.com/feedback.

Budget Well

Hotel and restaurant price categories from ¢ to $$$$ are defined in the opening pages of each chapter. For attractions, we always give standard adult admission fees; reductions are usually available for children, students, and senior citizens. Want to pay with plastic? **AE, D, DC, MC, V** following restaurant and hotel listings indicate whether American Express, Discover, Diners Club, MasterCard, and Visa are accepted.

Restaurants

Unless we state otherwise, restaurants are open for lunch and dinner daily. We mention dress only when there's a specific requirement and reservations only when they're essential or not accepted—it's always best to book ahead.

Hotels

Hotels have private bath, phone, TV, and air-conditioning unless we indicate otherwise. Hotels with the designation **BP** (for Breakfast Plan) at the end of their listing include breakfast in the rate; offerings can vary from coffee and a roll to an elaborate buffet. Those designated **EP** (European Plan) have no meals included; **MAP** (Modified American

Plan) means you get breakfast and dinner; **FAP** (Full American Plan) includes all meals. We always list facilities but not whether you'll be charged an extra fee to use them, so when pricing accommodations, find out what's included.

Many Listings	
★	Fodor's Choice
★	Highly recommended
♺	Family-friendly
✉	Physical address
✉	Branch address
✛	Directions
⌖	Mailing address
☎	Telephone
🖷	Fax
⊕	On the Web
✎	E-mail
🎟	Admission fee
◷	Open/closed times
V	Vaporetto stops
🖃	Credit cards
⇨	See also
Hotels & Restaurants	
🏨	Hotel
🛏	Number of rooms
♨	Facilities
❍❘	Meal plans
✗	Restaurant
✍	Reservations
🛆	Dress code
↘	Smoking
⛾	BYOB
✗🏨	Hotel with restaurant that warrants a visit

WHAT'S WHERE

VENICE	Seen from the window of a plane, Venice looks like a fish arranged on a blue tray, with Piazza San Marco located exactly at its belly. The tail consists of the picturesque neighborhood of Castello, where the workers of the Republic's legendary Arsenal once lived. The fins would correspond to the long Giudecca island to the south and the *sestieri* (neighborhoods) of San Polo and Santa Croce in the middle. The train station stands in place of the imaginary fish's eye, while the commercial harbor is where its mouth would be. On a clear day you can just catch a glimpse of the glittering ribbon of water drawing an inverted "S" across the city—the celebrated Grand Canal. The four dots of land swimming off the back of the fish are the islands of the northern lagoon: San Michele, Murano, Burano, and Torcello. Although Venice is smaller in size than most major Italian towns—you can walk from head to tail in about an hour—a warren of some 2,300 alleys multiplies your walking options, and the choice of itineraries is wide. An efficient water-transportation system led French architect Le Corbusier to conclude that Venice is the perfect city of the future, with two distinct networks of "streets," which allow for relaxed pedestrian circulation as well as speedy delivery of goods.
THE GRAND CANAL	Venice's incomparable main street testifies to the genius and expertise of its builders and architects and to the desires of its nobility, who had their showcase palaces built one after another. Among the landmarks you float by are the imposing facade of Palazzo Vendramin-Calergi, now the winter site of the town's casino; the finely wrought Ca' d'Oro, once covered in gold; and the baroque Santa Maria della Salute, built by Venetians to thank the Virgin Mary for having brought an end to a terrible plague. You'll pass under the Rialto Bridge and then the Ponte dell'Accademia, and as you catch sight of Palazzo Ducale you'll want to turn the boat around and do it all over again. But why not wait until nightfall, and sail across magic Venice under the moonlight?
PIAZZA SAN MARCO	No matter how you arrive in Venice, keep in mind that Piazza San Marco was the grand gateway of the Republic. It's easy to see why Napoléon called the square "Europe's stupendous drawing room." Almost nothing has changed since then—even the four Byzantine horses that the emperor stole from the Basilica's loggia were kindly returned to the city—and a bit

WHAT'S WHERE

	of the courteous atmosphere of the past comes back during Carnevale. An estimated 35,000 visitors a day come to this corner of the Mediterranean to admire the sights that made Venice world famous well before the days of mass tourism: the Basilica di San Marco, with its 42,985 square feet of glittering mosaics, built to treasure the relics of the Evangelist that were stolen from Alexandria in 828; and the exquisite Palazzo Ducale, the Gothic residence of the democratically elected doge and headquarters of the government.
SAN MARCO	The sestiere of San Marco is the most central of Venice's six districts, and one of the most expensive neighborhoods in Italy. It's no wonder high-fashion designers opened boutiques and shops here that rival the best in Rome and Milan. Art galleries, jewelry shops, and glass showrooms thrive as well. Some of the city's grandest hotels, all with a view of the Bacino di San Marco, are along the quarter mile between Campo Santa Maria del Giglio and San Zaccaria. Windows and the famous Piazza are not the only attractions of this busy sestiere. To start with, it claims one of the most-photographed bridges in the world, the Ponte di Rialto, heavy with history and souvenir stalls. Tucked away in an alley off Campo Manin is the Scala del Bovolo, perhaps the most graceful spiral staircase ever built. Nearby is the large Campo Santo Stefano, with cafés and usually a soccer match or two played up against the side of the church. The Teatro La Fenice, with a rich season of operas, concerts, and lectures, serves as Venice's center of musical culture. It was devastated by fire in 1996, but after countless delays it reopened to great fanfare in the fall of 2004.
DORSODURO	The sestiere of Dorsoduro was a favorite of American and English expatriates from the days of the Grand Tour. The one who made the most lasting impression was American heiress and art collector Peggy Guggenheim, who settled in a palace on the Grand Canal and got around in her private gondola. Her small but choice collection of modern art is now one of the most pleasant museums to visit in town. The engaging Gallerie dell'Accademia nearby contain many masterpieces of Western painting of the 14th through 19th centuries; and the Museo del Settecento Veneziano, housed in baroque Ca' Rezzonico, opens a dramatic window on the lifestyle of 18th-century Venice. As with the Grand Canal, it's hard to get enough

of the Zattere promenade, which skirts the wide Canale della Giudecca and at night offers some of Venice's most romantic views. Make a point of coming here for a cup of gelato or a glass of prosecco at one of the outdoor cafés. The city's prettiest budget hotels cluster along the silent *fondamente* (streets) of Dorsoduro. An array of artisans' shops, including mask workshops, book binderies, and wood carving shops, has sprouted in recent years to cater to the increasing numbers of independent tourists that explore the city at a relaxed pace.

SAN POLO & SANTA CROCE	Although attractions like the Frari, with two paintings by Titian, and the Scuola di San Rocco, lavishly decorated by Tintoretto, draw big crowds, the surrounding areas don't have the touristy feel or souvenir shops reserved for the main drag leading to the Rialto Bridge. A visit to the Rialto market, with its produce stalls and large *pescheria* (fish market), is an essential part of any visit to Venice. A few steps away are worthwhile sites: have a look at Palazzo Mocenigo, a Venetian noble apartment dating from the 18th century, the Renaissance Scuola Grande di San Giovanni Evangelista, and the San Giacomo dell'Orio. In the summer, the large Campo San Polo hosts the Cinema all'Aperto, with open-air shows of first-run movies (often international productions with Italian subtitles).
CANNAREGIO	A short distance from the bustle of the train station, Cannaregio offers some of the quietest and prettiest canal-side walks in town. You won't see any great-looking palaces, but the colorful boats and picturesque canals make up for the lack of architectural splendor. Too few visitors see the parish church of Renaissance painter Tintoretto, Chiesa della Madonna dell'Orto. And it seems only younger folks in search of wine and live music tread the Fondamenta della Misericordia after dark. The Jewish Ghetto has a fascinating history and tradition all its own. Here you can take a tour of some of the world's oldest synagogues and eat and drink kosher.
CASTELLO	For those who have been to Rome and visited the once working-class quarter of Trastevere, perhaps it makes sense to hear that the east side of Castello has been called "the Trastevere of Venice" for its lack of palaces and concentration of humble houses around which neighborhood life turns. Adventurous tourists who get out to Sant'Elena, San Pietro di Castello, and the Arsenale face an almost total absence of bars and shops, with the exception of Via Garibaldi and its tiny morning pro-

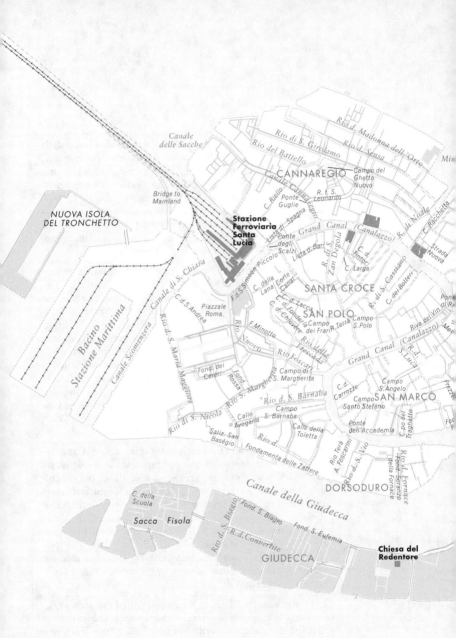

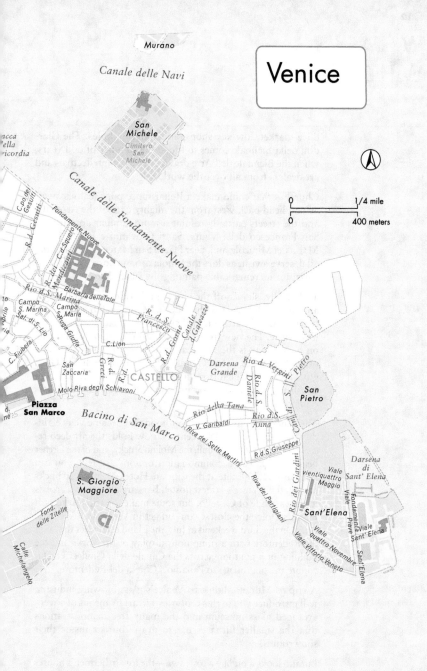

WHAT'S WHERE

duce market, low-key shops, and watering holes. The Giardini della Biennale comes to life in the summer of odd years, when the Biennale dell'Arte draws crowds of intellectuals and art dealers from all over the world.

Churches that could make a Renaissance pope jealous await as you head back west from the mighty gate of the Arsenale, and the streets partially resume a more familiar appearance. San Francesco della Vigna, Santi Giovanni e Paolo, Santa Maria dei Miracoli, and, near Piazza San Marco, San Zaccaria, all deserve a visit, as does the Scuola di San Giorgio degli Schiavoni for its remarkable paintings by Carpaccio.

SAN GIORGIO & THE GIUDECCA	Technically islands off the city's southern edge, San Giorgio and the Giudecca are within such an easy reach from San Zaccaria and the Zattere that they seem like extensions of central Venice. The view from the top of San Giorgio's Campanile on a clear day is the real reason to make the trip. The only other thing to see on San Giorgio is Palladio's church, San Giorgio Maggiore, which is rather bland on the inside, although worth a look for two important works by Tintoretto: *The Gathering of Manna* and *The Last Supper*. The Giudecca, a forlorn neighborhood that became Venice's industrial center in the 19th century, now holds the art deco remains of a gigantic flour mill, the Molino Stucky, and of the Dreher beer factory. The accommodation options are few: you can sleep in a $1,300 suite at the Cipriani Hotel, or spend 20 bucks for a bed in Venice's largest hostel. Bars are almost as scarce as in the east side of Castello, but some make the trip just to visit Harry's Dolci, the closest you can get in Venice to a Viennese café. On the third weekend in July, the island celebrates the Festa del Redentore with a sumptuous display of fireworks and the building of a pontoon across the Canale della Giudecca to facilitate the pilgrimage to Palladio's Chiesa del Redentore.
ISLANDS OF THE LAGOON	A trip to Murano, home to Venice's glass-blowing industry, will introduce you to this centuries-old art by means of a well-arranged glass museum and the many free demonstrations that the smaller furnaces use to draw tourists inside their showrooms. Burano looks a bit like a toy town—the low fishermen's houses are traditionally painted with the brightest colors possible to make them visible even in the thickest of the lagoon's fogs. The

Museo del Merletto contains paragons of antique lace made with threads as fine as cobwebs. They look nothing like the machine-made, often imported lace sold as "made in Burano" throughout Venice. The farther-flung Torcello was a lagoon power in the days before Venice was born; now its dreamlike atmosphere fosters legends like that of the Ponte del Diavolo, where the Devil, in the shape of a black cat, is believed to appear at the center of the unfenced arch every Christmas Eve at midnight.

The Lido is part of the narrow strip of land to the south that separates the Adriatic Sea from the lagoon, and since the beginning of the 20th century has served as Venice's fashionable beach resort. A sprinkle of stardust inebriates the island for the 10 days of the Biennale del Cinema in late August, the international film festival that rivals Cannes.

SOUTHERN VENETO

In the green plains to the west of the Venetian lagoon lie the art cities of Padua, Vicenza, and Verona, each with its own unique attractions, yet all bearing the Venetian patina of chic. Padua draws art lovers for the cycle of Giotto frescoes in the Scrovegni chapel, and Donatello's imposing bronze statue of *Il Gattamelata,* splendidly sited outside the Basilica di Sant'Antonio. Elegant Vicenza bears the hallmark of the 16th-century architect Andrea Palladio, as do the nearby Villa La Rotonda, Villa Pisani, and Villa Barbaro, where Venetian aristocrats vied with one another in the opulence of their holiday haunts. The most westerly city, Verona, is known the world over for its legendary lovers, Romeo and Juliet, though it's the breathtaking Roman arena that really steals the show—and still packs operagoers in for thrilling performances. Some of Italy's best shopping is concentrated here, with all the fashion names you could wish for. Verona is also the gateway to Lake Garda, with azure water and mountain vistas that provide some of the most stunning settings in Italy.

NORTHERN VENETO

The north of the region is presided over by the Dolomites, a magnet for connoisseurs of scenery attracted by the lush meadows of the valleys, the crystal waters of the lakes, and, most of all, the giant jagged teeth of the magnificent peaks. For others, this is the place to vaunt the latest Italian fashion accessories, for to be seen in Cortina d'Ampezzo is just as important as to ski here. But more enduring pleasures await a little further south—the Palladian bridge over the river at Bassano del Grappa, the en-

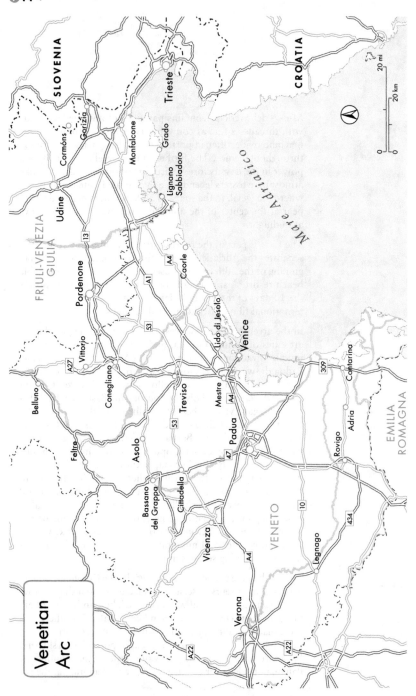

Venetian Arc

SLOVENIA

CROATIA

FRIULI-VENEZIA
GIULIA

Cormóns

Gorizia

Udine

13

Pordenone

Monfalcone

Grado

Trieste

Lignano
Sabbiadoro

A4

A1

53

Caorle

Vittorio

A27

Conegliano

Lido di Jesolo

Venice

Mare Adriatico

Belluno

Feltre

Asolo

53

Treviso

Mestre

A4

Padua

309

Contarina

Bassano
del Grappa

Cittadella

47

EMILIA
ROMAGNA

Rovigo

Adria

Vicenza

VENETO

10

Legnago

434

A4

Verona

A22

A22

20 mi

20 km

0

0

chanting vistas from Asolo, the perfectly preserved walls of Cittadella, and the checkerboard square of Marostica. All these are matched by the artistic delights of the region's capital, Treviso, whose medieval streets and churches are enlivened by striking frescoes from as early as the 13th century.

FRIULI-VENEZIA GIULIA	In the northeastern spur of Italy, sipping coffee in an art nouveau coffee house, swimming in the Adriatic, and visiting one of the oldest centers of Christianity is all possible in one day. The grand buildings of Trieste bear the imprint of Maria Theresa, empress of the Austrian Habsburg dynasty for which the city was the principal maritime outpost. Farther west, past the coastal haunts of Rilke and Dante and the salt-white castle of Miramare, stands Aquileia, whose basilica took shape in the early 4th century and contains the most extensive early Christian mosaics in the West. Due north, the Tempietto Longobardo in Cividale del Friuli is unique for its Lombard art. Udine boasts works by the Venetian master Tiepolo. After feasting the eye, feasts for the stomach await in Western Carnia, a mountainous zone of forests and tiny hamlets where wild game, herbs, and the freshest greenery are cooked over a heartening *fogolar* (central fireplace).

GREAT ITINERARIES

There are enough interesting things to see and do in Venice alone (not to mention the surrounding region) to fill weeks and even months of exploring. Assuming you don't have the luxury of that much time, you can use the plan below as an introduction to the world's most beautiful city.

If You Have Two Days

Start with a morning cruise along the **Grand Canal** from Piazzale Roma to San Zaccaria. You'll see **Piazza San Marco** for the first time from the water, as travelers before you have for hundreds of years. Spend the morning visiting the **Basilica** and **Palazzo Ducale,** allowing time to climb the **Campanile.** After lunch, take Salizzada San Moisè and Calle Larga XXII Marzo—lined with fashionable shops—to reach the *traghetto* (gondola ferry) in Campo Santa Maria del Giglio. Once across the Grand Canal, bear left and walk to the baroque **Chiesa della Madonna della Salute,** with several paintings by Titian. The Punta della Dogana, to the right as you come out of the church, opens to one of the best panoramas in town. Head for the **Peggy Guggenheim Collection,** home of first-rate 20th-century art, and then stretch your legs on the Zattere promenade while having a gelato.

On day two, start early to beat the crowds at the **Rialto Bridge** and market. Don't miss the lively pescheria, where fish have been sold for more than 1,000 years. Follow the main drag to Campo San Polo and the **Chiesa dei Frari,** with two important works by Titian. Visit the **Scuola Grande di San Rocco,** famous for a series of more than 50 paintings by Tintoretto—Venice's answer to the

Sistine Chapel. After lunch, jump into 18th-century Venice at **Ca' Rezzonico.** Finish your day with a visit to the **Gallerie dell'Accademia,** with masterpieces of Western painting dating from the 14th to 19th century.

If You Have Four Days

Start day three by exploring the sestiere of Castello. (On a clear morning, consider a stop first on the **Isola di San Giorgio,** with breathtaking views of the lagoon and the city. From Piazza San Marco, go to the church of **San Zaccaria,** with a famous altarpiece by Giovanni Bellini. Then visit the Greek church of **San Giorgio dei Greci,** lined with Byzantine icons. Time your walk to hit the **Scuola di San Giorgio degli Schiavoni** before it closes at midday. Take a glance at the graceful **Santa Maria Formosa,** then follow Calle del Paradiso via Campo Santa Marina toward a miracle born of marble, **Santa Maria dei Miracoli.** After a late lunch, visit **Campo Santi Giovanni e Paolo** and its Gothic abbey; then take Barbaria delle Tole to the **Campo dell'Arsenale.** Take vaporetto Line 82 from the Giardini della Biennale to the **Giudecca,** where you can have dinner, or return to Piazza San Marco along the Riva degli Schiavoni, particularly beautiful at sunset.

On your final morning, take a guided tour of the **Jewish Ghetto.** Board vaporetto Line 42 (Ponte delle Guglie landing) by 11 AM, cruising to the islands of the lagoon: **Murano** and its glass museum, where you should stop for lunch; **Burano** and its lace museum, where you should have a *merenda* (afternoon tea) with the local cookies called *buranelli*; and romantic **Torcello,** wrapped in the mists of the lagoon.

WHEN TO GO

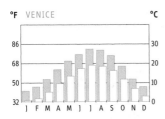

Venice is most crowded from April to October, during Christmas, and of course during Carnevale. If you're serious about your sightseeing, consider a winter visit. It's cooler and rainier, and you may encounter short periods of flooding, but the payoff is lower tourist density. You'll have less waiting in line, unhurried viewing of sights, substantial hotel discounts, and you'll find local people far less tourist-fatigued.

Climate

Weather-wise, the best sightseeing months are March, April, May, June, September, and October—generally pleasant and not too hot. In July and August, when southeasterly *scirocco* winds sweep Venice, days can get hot and sticky. Brief afternoon thunderstorms are common (and welcome) throughout the Veneto region. Venetian winters are relatively mild but always include foggy days, some rainy spells, and the risk of *acqua alta* (high water, when portions of the city flood). Inland towns are generally colder in winter and hotter in summer than Venice but less humid.

🔲 Forecasts **Weather Channel Connection** ☎ 900/932-8437 95¢ per minute from a Touch-Tone phone ⊕ www.weather.com.

ON THE CALENDAR

	Contact the Italian Government Tourist Board (⇨ Visitor Information, *in Smart Travel Tips*) for exact dates and further information on all the festivals held in Venice and the Venetian Arc.
WINTER January	Art movies from central and eastern Europe are shown at the Alpe-Adria Film Festival ⊕ www.alpeadriacinema.it/edizioneX/den.htm in Trieste.
January 6	For the Regata delle Befane, senior members of historical Bucintoro rowing club get dressed as the witch of the Befana to race along the Grand Canal.
10–12 days preceding Lent	Carnevale, dating from the Middle Ages, is celebrated in Venice with plays, masked balls, concerts, and fireworks.
SPRING Sun. in March or April	Su Zo per i Ponti. In this family fun run, you can choose the distance you'd like to cover while you join thousands of others climbing "up and down the bridges" as the race's name translates.
First weekend of Spring	FAI Day of Springtime ⊕ www.fondoambiente.it. Throughout Italy, monuments normally closed to the public are open for free visits.
April 25	For the Festa di San Marco a solemn Mass is held in the Basilica di San Marco to honor the city's patron saint, and red roses are sold.
Sun. in May (depends on tide)	Crews bring their own boats for La Vogalonga, an amateur rowing race.
May (coincides with Vogalonga)	Mediterranean wooden boats are celebrated at Navalis, held in Arsenale.
Last Sun. in May or 1st in June	The Sagra delle Ciliege (Cherry Festival) is held in the castle yard at Marostica.
6th Sun. after Easter	On Festa della Sensa (Ascension Day) a procession of boats leaves San Marco for the Lido, and the mayor, doge for a day, throws a golden ring in the water to celebrate the wedding of Venice and the Adriatic.
May & June	Vicenza's Teatro Olimpico hosts a concert season ⊕ www.olimpico.vicenza.it/it/festival.html. A Jazz Festival featuring internationally renowned performers is staged at various venues in Vicenza.
SUMMER June	The International Jazz Festival ☎ 0458077201 ⊕ www.estateteatraleveronese.it takes place in Verona. Classical, traditional, and contemporary musicians perform for Venezia Suono in dozens of campi around the city one Sunday in June.

2nd wk of June	Arquà Petrarca's Festa della Sacra Trinità features local food and wine tastings, theater performances, and music.
3rd wk of June	La Maciliana is celebrated in Chioggia with medieval fun and games.
Mid-June to early November	In even-numbered years, La Biennale brings together contemporary artists from around the world for an exhibition in Venice.
End of June	The Dama Castellana ⊕ www.dama.tv.it in Conegliano has a human chess match with processions, flag waving, and fireworks.
End of June to early September	Verona's Festival dell'Opera brings several spectacular productions to the city's historic arena.
3rd weekend of July	On the eve of the Festa del Redentore, commemorating the end of a 16th-century plague, *foghi* (fireworks) explode above the Giudecca and the following morning crowds of pilgrims cross the Canale della Guidecca over a pontoon bridge built for the event.
Third week of July	The Sagra del Pesce (Fish Festival) in Chioggia has fish tasting, music, poetry, and theater.
July & August	A Shakespeare Festival is staged at the Teatro Romano in Verona. The Festival Internazionale dell'Operetta is held at various venues in Trieste. Bassano del Grappa's Opera Estate Festival includes classical and jazz music, dance, opera, cinema, and theater.
1st weekend in August	The Palio di Feltre combines a series of medieval games with fine wine and good food.
Mid-August	Le Nozze Carsiche is a one-week reenactment of 19th-century weddings at Monrupino, near Trieste (held in odd-numbered years).
End of August– early September	Biennale del Cinema, Venice's international film festival, takes place on the Lido, where first runs of movies are shown in the Palazzo del Cinema.
FALL First Sun. of September	A procession of historic boats with crews in Renaissance costumes opens the Regata Storica rowing competition.
Second weekend in September	The *partita a scacchi* is a giant chess game played out by humans in Marostica in even-numbered years.
Sun. in September	A palio (horse race) with ten competing districts is run in Montagnana one Sunday in September.

ON THE CALENDAR

Second & third weekends in September	The Giostra della Rocca in Monselice relives medieval feasting games, climaxing with the *quintana* (medieval competition).
Third weekend in September	A palio run by Roman chariots takes place in the streets of Asolo.
September & October	The Teatro Olimpico in Vicenza hosts a classical drama season.
October	Watch from hills as nearly 2,000 boats compete in Trieste's annual Barcolana sailing regatta, the second weekend of October. On the last Sunday of October, the Venice Marathon begins in Stra and follows the Brenta River into Venice.
November 21	Festa della Madonna della Salute traditional thanksgiving pilgrimage to light candles at the Chiesa della Madonna della Salute.

The Art of Enjoying Art

Travel veterans will tell you that the endless series of masterpieces in Venice's churches, palaces, and museums can cause first-time visitors—eyes glazed over from a heavy downpour of images, dates, and names—to lean, Pisa-like, on their companions for support. After a surfeit of Tiepolo and Tintoretto and the 14th Titian, even the greatest of the Venetian masters may begin to pall. The secret, of course, is to act like a turtle—not a hare—and take your sweet time. Instead of trotting after briskly efficient tour guides, allow the splendors of the age to unfold—slowly.

Museums are only the most obvious places to view art; there are always the trompe l'oeil renderings of Assumptions that float across church ceilings and campo scenes that might be Carpaccio paintings brought to life. Of course, there may be many art treasures that will not quicken your pulse, but one morning you may see a Veronese so perfect, so beautiful, that your knees will buckle.

Carnevale

" . . . All the world repaire to Venice to see the folly and madnesse of the Carnevall . . .'tis impossible to recount the universal madnesses of this place during this time of licence," commented traveler John Evelyn in 1646. Indeed, Carnevale was once an excuse for all manner of carnal indulgence. In its 18th-century heyday, festivities began on December 26 and lasted two months; the festival has since traded some of its more outlandish flavor for commercialization and lasts only for the 12 days preceding Ash Wednesday.

If you plan to join the revelers, give some thoughts to your fancy dress, as even visitors there just to observe can feel quite naked without a costume. Do pack Grandma's Charleston dancing gown, spruce up your best Halloween suit, or cut and sew a brand-new garment—the more color and sparkles and out-of-this-worldness the better—but if you are short of time and can't pilfer from an attic, Venice has, of course, a bevy of costume rental shops (⇨ Specialty Shops *in* Chapter 6).

Concerts & Opera

Chances are you'll have to choose between concerts in Venice—most nights there are different performances in various theaters and churches. The love of Italian culture need not stop at Venice. Verona, Trieste, and Vicenza offer some of the most spectacular opportunities for indulging in a passion for open-air opera and concerts. An opera in the Roman arena at Verona is a spectacle overflowing with exuberance and flair. Stars of the opera world are regular fixtures—José Carreras and Placido Domingo have graced the stage in past years. Verona and Vicenza also have free concerts in the villas and churches, much lower-key affairs but still extravagantly performed. The festival season runs from July to August, when you can also attend the international operetta festival held in Trieste and jazz festivals in Verona and Vicenza.

Delicious Fish

The old Italian saying "Fish needs to swim three times: in water, in oil, and in wine" applies here, and although there is some meat to be found on local menus, con-

PLEASURES & PASTIMES

sider your trip to Venice in part an opportunity to eat local fish, much of it strange to foreign eyes—fried, baked, grilled, simmered, stewed, marinated, and even whipped. The average standard of Venetian restaurants has suffered from the effects of tourism, but fine restaurants are still to be found, and the kind of family-run trattoria called *bacaro con cucina* makes it possible to eat well at a fair price.

Getting Lost

There's no escaping the fact that Venice is a difficult place to navigate. Narrow, winding streets, a shortage of easily visible landmarks to orient yourself by, and near-meaningless address numbers all add to the confusion. Fortunately, getting lost in Venice can be a pleasure. You may not find the Titian masterpiece you'd set out to see, but instead you might come across an ageless bacaro or a charming shop that makes your afternoon; opportunities for such serendipity abound. And the city is nothing if not self-contained—sooner or later, perhaps with the help of a patient native, you can rest assured that you'll regain your bearings.

Shopping

You'll find all the style and quality you want in the streets of Venice and the main cities of the Veneto, lined with the heavyweight fashion names. Leather goods, shoes, clothing, jewelry, and ceramics of a superior quality are also specialties. In Venice look out for glassware, lace, and paper goods; in Bassano, colorful ceramics; in the Dolomites, hand-crafted wooden items. But take time to veer off the well-frequented tourist trails; for the best finds, let fate be your guide. Poking about in the narrow streets will often unearth original gift shops, where you might find that little item for the kitchen, or that lovely embroidered curtain or tablecloth that you admired in a restaurant the night before. Before buying any bulky or heavy items, check on how much it will cost to have them shipped home. Most pleasurable of all are the local markets, works of art in themselves, bulging with a vivid variety of greenery, mounds of rich red cherries, and sculptures of glittering fish. Every town also has a general market, which can be bargain-hunting grounds. On specific days of the week there's usually also an antiques-and-curios market.

Villas & Palazzos

Countless villas and palaces are sprinkled throughout the Venetian hinterland—none more notable than those designed by of Andrea Palladio, the Renaissance architect responsible for such masterpieces as Villa la Rotonda (near Vicenza) and Villa Barbaro (near Maser). The region's gracious country homes, Palladian or otherwise, give insight into how wealthy Venetians used to (and still do) get away from it all. Many of the villas are privately owned but are open to the public at certain times or by special request.

FODOR'S
CHOICE

The sights, restaurants, hotels, and other travel experiences on these pages are our editors' top picks—our Fodor's Choices. They're the best of their type in the area covered by the book—not to be missed and always worth your time. In the destination chapters that follow, you will find all the details.

LODGING	
$$$$	**Colombina**, Castello, Venice. A 16th-century palazzo has been converted into a quiet, romantic inn minutes from San Marco.
$$$$	**De la Poste**, Cortina D'Ampezzo, Northern Veneto. The owners make you feel like old friends at this chalet in the heart of one of Italy's poshest ski resorts.
$$$$	**Gabbia d'Oro**, Verona, Southern Veneto. Romanticism reigns at this historic hotel filled with antique furnishings and sumptuous fabrics.
$$$$	**Villa Cipriani**, Asolo, Northern Veneto. For old-word opulence, it's hard to beat the choice of Prince Phillip and Aristotle Onassis.
$$$–$$$$	**Ca' Maria Adele**, Dorsoduro, Venice. Five "concept rooms" mix classic and modern design at Venice's most elegant small hotel.
$$$	**Castello Formentini**, Cormòns, Venezia Giulia. Be the king of the castle—if only for a night—and sleep in modernized medieval splendor.
$$$	**Villa Pisani**, near Este, Southern Veneto. Staying in a grand 16th-century villa surrounded a 15-acre park makes for something more than a typical B&B experience.
$$–$$$	**Hotel Clocchiatti**, Udine, Friuli. The "Next" wing here mixes superior comfort and groundbreaking design.
$$–$$$	**Novecento**, San Marco, Venice. For the warm hospitality of a family-run hotel near Piazza San Maro, you can't do better.
$$–$$$	**Pensione Accademia Villa Maravege**, Dorsoduro, Venice. A garden with a view of the Grand Canal is just one of the pleasures at this exemplary Venetian villa.
$$	**Due Mori**, Marostica, Northern Veneto. The elegant, modern rooms here are an ideal base for visiting the hills of the northern Veneto.
$–$$	**La Calcina**, Dorsoduro, Venice. Impeccable, no-nonsense rooms with original art deco furnishings, a lovely reading room, and a floating deck all contribute to the experience here.
$	**Bernardi Semenzato**, Cannaregio, Venice. In a city markedly short on good budget options, this is a welcome exception.

FODOR'S
CHOICE

¢	Istituto San Giuseppe, Castello, Venice. Rooms are spartan at this convent, but the nuns maintain them with pride.
RESTAURANTS $$$$	Arquade, near Verona, Southern Veneto. Chef Bruno Barbieri creates nouveau Italian cuisine that's a pure pleasure.
$$$$	Osteria da Fiore, San Polo, Venice. A gastronomic temple that bloomed in the city's back streets, Da Fiore tops the list of Venice's fine fish restaurants.
$$$–$$$$	Al Bagato, Trieste, Venezia Giulia. You get the personal touch at this small seafood restaurant overseen by a dedicated and gifted chef.
$$$–$$$$	Alle Testiere, Castello, Venice. The food is as sophisticated as the atmosphere is informal at this tiny, five-table trattoria.
$$–$$$	Al Cacciatore de la Subida, Cormòns, Venezia Giulia. You're still in Italy, but you can taste the influence of Slovenia on the consistently delicious offerings of the tasting menu.
$$–$$$	Avogaria, Dorsoduro, Venice. A thoroughly modern attitude and fine Pugliese cuisine make a perfect change of pace from the Venetian norm.
$$	Antica Osteria al Cavallino, Treviso, Northern Veneto. The handwritten menu changes daily, but the classic northern Italian fare has maintained a standard of excellence for over a century.
$–$$	Osteria Terraglio, Bassano del Grappa, Northern Veneto. Come here for creative, modern cuisine that puts a premium on freshness.
$	Bancogiro, Santa Croce, Venice. This osteria with contemporary flair takes full advantage of its location next to the Rialto market.
$	Da Bastian, Maser, Northern Veneto. The changing menu here gives you the best of whatever is in season; you can take your meal in a pleasant garden when weather permits.
$	Trattoria Ca' d'Oro, Cannaregio, Venice. Settle at one of the long tables for a meal of Venetian specialties and hearty pastas.
¢	Cantina Do Mori, San Polo, Venice. Workers from the Rialto market have been refueling at this bacaro for more than 500 years.
¢	Cantinone già Schiave, Dorsoduro, Venice. The specialty here is *panini*—sandwiches made with top-quality meat and cheese.
¢	Enoteca la Mascareta, Castello, Venice. This bacaro is a favorite evening haunt for locals.

CHURCHES	**Cappella degli Scrovegni,** Padua, Southern Veneto. Brilliant frescoes by Giotto, impeccably restored and preserved, decorate Italy's second-most famous chapel.
	Basilica di San Marco, Venice. This one building above all others best defines the character of Venice.
	San Zeno Maggiore, Verona, Southern Veneto. The rose window and bronze doors are of special note at what is quite possibly the finest Romanesque church in Italy.
	Santa Maria dei Miracoli, Cannaregio, Venice. Renaissance master builder Pietro Lombardo created here a tiny marble gem.
	Santa Maria Gloriosa dei Frari, San Polo, Venice. The blazing colors of two of Titian's most spectacular altarpieces illuminate this monumental Gothic church.
MUSEUMS	**Ca' Rezzonico,** Dorsoduro, Venice. The Museum of 18th-Century Venice, housed in this palace, provides a fascinating glimpse into a world of elegant decadence.
	Gallerie dell'Accademia, Dorsoduro, Venice. During the French occupation of the city, Napoléon managed to found this incomparable collection of Venetian art.
ONLY IN THE VENETIAN ARC	**Arena di Verona,** Southern Veneto. Sit under the stars in this "second Colosseum" and enjoy world-class opera on a stage big enough for teams of horses.
	Castello di Miramare, Venezia Giulia. The Austrian influence over Trieste and the surrounding area is lavishly displayed at this castle built for the Archduke Maximilian of Habsburg.
	Cortina d'Ampezzo, Northern Veneto. You'll feel far from Venice as you soar in a different sort of gondola at this old-school ski resort.
	Piazza dell'Unità d'Italia, Trieste, Venezia Giulia. Trieste's main square rivals Venice's Piazza San Marco—with the added advantage that it opens directly onto the sea.
PALACES	**Ca' d'Oro,** Cannaregio, Venice. The most regal of the palaces lining the Grand Canal doubles as a fine art museum.
	Palazzo della Ragione, Padua, Southern Veneto. The highlight of this spectacular palace is Il Salone, one of Italy's most pleasing (and largest) halls.

FODOR'S CHOICE

	Palazzo Ducale, San Marco, Venice. The home of the doges stands as an awesome testament to a time when Venice was a great maritime power.
	Villa La Rotonda, Vicenza, Southern Veneto. A kind of Renaissance update of the Pantheon in Rome, Palladio's most famous villa was the inspiration for Thomas Jefferson's Monticello, as well as numerous capitol buildings.
QUINTESSENTIAL VENICE	**Biennale del Cinema**. Part of the grand Biennale series of art exhibits, this film festival may rank second to Cannes in prestige, but it's unequaled for fun.
	Festa del Redentore. The third Sunday in July marks Venice's most jubilant annual celebration, capped by fireworks over the Bacino di San Marco.
	Gondola Ride. From daybreak to the depths of a moonlit night, it's magical to ply Venice's surreal waterways, where fairytale palazzos waltz by, veiled in silvery mist.
	Ponte di Rialto. Climb Venice's most famous bridge for a classic view of the Grand Canal—then descend into the bustling markets that neighbor it.
SHOPPING	**Barbieri**, Castello, Venice. This has been *the* place for scarves and shawls in Venice since 1945.
	Giovanna Zanella Caeghera, Castello, Venice. Whimsical designs and exceptional caftsmanship make this Venice's most appealing place for shoes.
	Il Milione, Castello, Venice. The Fortuny-style lamps here are are both elegant and competitively priced.
	Le Forcole di Saverio Pastor, Dorsoduro, Venice. A walnut gondola oarlock from here is a masterpiece in engineering and a unique souvenir.
	Mondo Novo, Dorsoduro, Venice. The return of Carnevale has meant the revival of Venetian mask-making; designer Guerrino Lovato is a master of the craft.
	Venetia Studium, San Marco, Venice. The tradition of fine Venetian fabrics lives on at this shop, which, among other things, uses its wares to create Fortuny lamps.

SPORTS	**Biking on the Lido,** Venice. For a breath of fresh air, spend a day pedaling along the scenic (and flat) Lido.
	Regata Storica, Venice. With its parade and four races, this annual September event is the Olympics of Venetian rowing.
	Voga alla Veneta, Venice. If you're feeling adventurous, take a lesson in gondolier-style rowing, the lagoon's quintessential sport.

SMART TRAVEL TIPS

Finding out about your destination before you leave home means you won't squander time organizing everyday minutiae once you've arrived. You'll be more street-wise when you hit the ground as well, better prepared to explore the aspects of Venice and the Venetian Arc that drew you here in the first place. The organizations mentioned here can provide information to supplement this guide; contact them for up-to-the-minute details, and consult the A to Z sections that end the Southern Veneto, Northern Veneto, and Friuli-Venezia Giulia chapters for facts on the various topics as they relate specifically to the areas around Venice. Happy landings!

ADDRESSES

Venice addresses aren't much help when it comes to finding your way around. Instead of naming a street, an address gives the name of one of the city's six *sestieri*, or neighborhoods (San Marco, Cannaregio, Castello, Dorsoduro, Santa Croce, and San Polo) followed by a number. The hitch is that the numbers don't necessarily run in sequential order, so San Marco 3672 and 3673 might well be several streets away from each other. With that peculiarity in mind, Venetian addresses in this book include the nearest *campo* (square), bridge, vaporetto stop, *calle*, *riva* or a *fondamenta* (all terms for a street) when helpful. An invaluable Web resource is www.venicexplorer.net, which has a mapping function that will pinpoint any address in the city.

Yellow signs posted on many corners point toward the major landmarks—San Marco, Rialto, Accademia, etc.—but don't count on finding these once you're deep into residential neighborhoods. Even buying a good map at a newsstand—the kind showing all street names and vaporetto routes—won't insure you don't get lost. However, getting lost in Venice may mean you've also lost most of the other tourists; patience with yourself and the Venetians you ask for help can go a long way in making the experience part of the adventure.

Italian addresses outside of Venice are fairly straightforward: the street is followed by the street number. However, you might see an address with a number plus "bis" or "A" (e.g., Via Verdi 3/bis or Via Mazzini 8/A). This indicates that 3/bis or 8/A is the next entrance or door down from Via Verdi 3 and Via Mazzini 8, respectively.

In rural areas, some addresses give only the route name or the distance in kilometers along a major road (e.g. Via Fabbri, km 4.3), or sometimes only the name of the small village in which the site is located.

AIR TRAVEL

BOOKING
When you book, look for nonstop flights and remember that "direct" flights stop at least once. Try to avoid connecting flights, which require a change of plane. Two airlines may operate a connecting flight jointly, so ask whether your airline operates every segment of the trip; you may find that the carrier you prefer flies you only part of the way. To find more booking tips and to check prices and make online flight reservations, log on to www.fodors.com.

CARRIERS
When flying internationally, you must usually choose between a domestic carrier, the national flag carrier of the country you are visiting, and a foreign carrier from a third country. You may, for example, choose to fly Alitalia to Italy. National flag carriers have the greatest number of nonstops. Domestic carriers may have better connections to your home town and serve a greater number of gateway cities. Third-party carriers may have a price advantage.

Alitalia—in addition to other major European airlines and smaller, privately run companies such as Meridiana and Air One—has an extensive network of flights within Italy. Travel agents at home or in Italy can help find discounts for domestic trips, which may include a 50% family reduction and up to 30% off certain night flights.

There are fewer direct flights to Venice than to the more central travel hubs of Rome and Milan. Delta Airlines and Alitalia have direct flights to Venice from the United States. Direct service from Heathrow to Venice is provided daily by Alitalia and British Airways. One option is to fly into Milan and then go by train to Venice; the trip itself takes three hours, but getting from the airport to the station and catching your train can take an additional two or three hours.

To & From Italy **Air Canada** ☎ 888/247-2262 in U.S., 0870/524-7226 in U.K., 800/919091 in Italy ⊕ www.aircanada.com. **Air New Zealand** ☎ 800/262-1234 in U.S., 800/663-5494 in Canada, 0800/028 4149 in U.K., 13-24-76 in Australia, 0800/737 000 in New Zealand ⊕ www.airnz.com. **Alitalia** ☎ 800/223-5730 in U.S., 0870/544 in U.K., 61/292-44-2222 in Australia, 06/65641 in Rome, 848/865641 elsewhere in Italy ⊕ www.alitalia.it. **American Airlines** ☎ 800/433-7300 in U.S., 02/69682464 in Milan ⊕ www.aa.com. **British Airways** ☎ 800/403-0882 in U.S. and Canada, 0870/850-9850 in U.K., 1300/767-177 in Australia, 0800/274 847 in New Zealand, 06/52492800 in Italy ⊕ www.britishairways.com. **Continental Airlines** ☎ 800/231-0856 in U.S., 02/69633256 in Milan, 800/296230 elsewhere in Italy ⊕ www.flycontinental.com. **Delta Air Lines** ☎ 800/241-4141 in U.S., 06/65954406 in Italy ⊕ www.deltaairlines.com. **Lufthansa** ☎ 800/399-5838 in U.S., 800/563-5954 in Canada, 0870/8377 747 in U.K., 1300-655-727 in Australia, 0800 945 220 in New Zealand ⊕ www.lufthansa.com. **Qantas** ☎ 800/227-4500 in U.S., 06/52482725 in Rome ⊕ www.qantas.com. **Thai Airlines** ☎ 800/426-5204 in U.S., 61-1300-651-960 in Australia, 64-9-377-3886 in New Zealand ⊕ www.thaiair.com. **United Airlines** ☎ 800/241-6522 in U.S., 02/69633707 in Milan ⊕ www.ual.com. **US Airways** ☎ 800/428-4322 in U.S., 848/813177 in Italy ⊕ www.usairways.com.

Within Italy **Air One** ☎ 06/488800 in Rome, 848/848880 elsewhere in Italy ⊕ www.air-one.it. **Alitalia** ☎ 800/223-5730 in U.S., 020/7602-7111 in U.K., 06/65641 in Rome, 848/865641 elsewhere in Italy ⊕ www.alitalia.it. **Alpieagles** ☎ 041/599777 ⊕ www.alpieagles.com. **Meridiana** ☎ 020/7839-2222 in U.K., 06/478041 in Italy ⊕ www.meridiana.it.

CHECK-IN & BOARDING
Always find out your carrier's check-in policy. Plan to arrive at the airport about two hours before your scheduled departure time for domestic flights and 2½ to 3

hours before international flights. You may need to arrive earlier if you're flying from one of the busier airports or during peak air-traffic times. In Venice, only Delta insists that passengers arrive two hours before their international flight. Other airlines are more flexible and in fact, negotiating security is faster and simpler in Venice than in other cities. To avoid delays at airport-security checkpoints, try not to wear any metal. Jewelry, belt and other buckles, steel-toe shoes, barrettes, and underwire bras are among the items that can set off detectors.

Assuming that not everyone with a ticket will show up, airlines routinely overbook planes. When everyone does, airlines ask for volunteers to give up their seats. In return, these volunteers usually get a several-hundred-dollar flight voucher, which can be used toward the purchase of another ticket, and are rebooked on the next flight out. If there are not enough volunteers, the airline must choose who will be denied boarding. The first to get bumped are passengers who checked in late and those flying on discounted tickets, so get to the gate and check in as early as possible, especially during peak periods.

Always bring a government-issued photo ID to the airport; even when it's not required, a passport is best.

CUTTING COSTS

The least expensive airfares to Venice and other Italian destinations are priced for round-trip travel and must usually be purchased in advance. Airlines generally allow you to change your return date for a fee; most low-fare tickets, however, are nonrefundable. It's smart to call a number of airlines and check the Internet; when you are quoted a good price, book it on the spot—the same fare may not be available the next day, or even the next hour. Always check different routings and look into using alternate airports. Also, price off-peak flights, which may be significantly less expensive than others. Travel agents, especially low-fare specialists (⇨ Discounts and Deals), are helpful.

Consolidators are another option. They buy tickets for scheduled flights at reduced

rates from the airlines, then sell them at prices that beat the best fare available directly from the airlines. Sometimes you can even get your money back if you need to return the ticket. Carefully read the fine print detailing penalties for changes and cancellations, purchase the ticket with a credit card, and confirm your consolidator reservation with the airline.

🔳 Consolidators **AirlineConsolidator.com** ☎ 888/468-5385 ⊕ www.airlineconsolidator.com. **Best Fares** ☎ 800/880-1234 or 800/576-8255 ⊕ www.bestfares.com; $59.90 annual membership. **Cheap Tickets** ☎ 800/377-1000 or 800/652-4327 ⊕ www.cheaptickets.com. **Expedia** ☎ 800/397-3342 or 404/728-8787 ⊕ www.expedia.com. **Hotwire** ☎ 866/468-9473 or 920/330-9418 ⊕ www.hotwire.com. **Now Voyager Travel** ✉ 45 W. 21st St., Suite 5A New York, NY 10010 ☎ 212/459-1616 🖷 212/243-2711 ⊕ www.nowvoyagertravel.com. **Onetravel.com** ⊕ www.onetravel.com. **Orbitz** ☎ 888/656-4546 ⊕ www.orbitz.com. **Priceline.com** ⊕ www.priceline.com. **Travelocity** ☎ 888/709-5983, 877/282-2925 in Canada, 0870/876-3876 in U.K. ⊕ www.travelocity.com.

ENJOYING THE FLIGHT

State your seat preference when purchasing your ticket, and then repeat it when you confirm and when you check in. For more legroom, you can request one of the few emergency-aisle seats at check-in, if you are capable of lifting at least 50 pounds—a Federal Aviation Administration requirement of passengers in these seats. Seats behind a bulkhead also offer more legroom, but they don't have underseat storage. Don't sit in the row in front of the emergency aisle or in front of a bulkhead, where seats may not recline.

Ask the airline whether a snack or meal is served on the flight. If you have dietary concerns, request special meals when booking. These can be vegetarian, low-cholesterol, or kosher, for example. It's a good idea to pack some healthful snacks and a small (plastic) bottle of water in your carry-on bag. On long flights, try to maintain a normal routine, to help fight jet lag. At night, get some sleep. By day, eat light meals, drink water (not alcohol), and move around the cabin to stretch your legs. For additional jet-lag tips consult

Fodor's FYI: Travel Fit & Healthy (available at bookstores everywhere).

FLYING TIMES

The majority of flights available to Venice will be routed through another European hub, meaning your travel time can vary significantly. Direct flights from New York to Venice take about 9 hours, and to Milan 8½ hours. Flying time to Milan is 10–11 hours from Chicago, and 11½ hours from Los Angeles. It's 2½ hours to fly from London to Venice. It takes travelers from Sydney about 24 hours to reach Rome, and another hour from Rome to Venice.

HOW TO COMPLAIN

If your baggage goes astray or your flight goes awry, complain right away. Most carriers require that you file a claim immediately. The Aviation Consumer Protection Division of the Department of Transportation publishes *Fly-Rights,* which discusses airlines and consumer issues and is available on-line. You can also find articles and information on mytravelrights.com, the Web site of the nonprofit Consumer Travel Rights Center.

🛪 Airline Complaints **Aviation Consumer Protection Division** ⊠ U.S. Department of Transportation, Office of Aviation Enforcement and Proceedings, C-75, Room 4107, 400 7th St. SW, Washington, DC 20590 ☎ 202/366-2220 ⊕ airconsumer.ost.dot.gov. **Federal Aviation Administration Consumer Hotline** ⊠ for inquiries: FAA, 800 Independence Ave. SW, Washington, DC 20591 ☎ 800/322-7873 ⊕ www.faa.gov.

RECONFIRMING

Check the status of your flight before you leave for the airport. You can do this on your carrier's Web site, by linking to a flight-status checker (many Web booking services offer these), or by calling your carrier or travel agent. Always confirm international flights at least 72 hours ahead of the scheduled departure time. You should reconfirm by phone for flights out of Venice.

AIRPORTS & TRANSFERS

Venice's Aeroporto Marco Polo is served by domestic and international flights, including connections from 21 European

cities, plus direct flights from Moscow and New York's JFK. In addition, Treviso Airport, some 32 km (20 mi) north of Venice, receives daily arrivals from London's Stansted Airport.

A shuttle bus or 10-minute walk takes you from Marco Polo's terminal to a dock where public and private boats are available to deliver you direct to Venice's historic center. For €10 per person, including bags, Alilaguna operates regularly scheduled service from predawn until nearly midnight. It takes about an hour to reach the landing near Piazza San Marco, stopping at the Lido on the way. A *motoscafo* (water taxi) carries up to four people and four bags to the city center in a sleek, modern powerboat. The base cost is €80, and the trip takes about 25 minutes. Each additional person, bag, and stop costs extra, so it's essential to agree on a fare before boarding.

Blue ATVO buses take 20 minutes to make the nonstop trip from the airport to Piazzale Roma; from here you can get a vaporetto to the landing nearest your hotel. The ATVO fare is €3, and tickets are available on the bus when the airport ticket booth (open 9–7:30) is closed. Orange ACTV local buses (Line 5) leave for Venice at 10 and 40 minutes past every hour (hourly service after 11:10 PM) and take 30 minutes; before boarding, you must buy a €2 ticket at the airport tobacconist-newsstand, open 6:30 AM–9 PM, or from the ATVO/ACTV booth in the arrivals hall on the ground floor. During rush hour, luggage can be a hassle on the local bus. A land taxi from the airport to Piazzale Roma costs about €40.

🛪 Airport Information **Aeroporto Malpensa 2000** ⊠ 50 km [31 mi] north of Milan ☎ 02/74852200 ⊕ www.sea-aeroportimilano.it. **Aeroporto Marco Polo** ⊠ 10 km [6 mi] north of Venice, Tessera ☎ 041/2609260, 041/2609222 lost baggage ⊕ www.veniceairport.it. **Aeroporto Treviso** ⊠ 32 km [20 mi] north of Venice ☎ 0422/315131.
🛪 Taxis & Shuttles **Alilaguna** ☎ 041/5235775. **ATVO** ☎ 0421/383672. **Motoscafo** ☎ 041/5222303 airport transfers. **Radio Taxi** ☎ 041/5952080.

BEACHES

In the Veneto and Friuli regions, the tame landscape features sandy beaches with well-maintained facilities, catering mostly to crowds of locals and sunbathers from Austria and Germany. The lack of rocks and cliffs, and the shallowness of the sea, make them ideal for families with small children. As you go from south to north, the most popular sea resorts in the area are Venice beaches on the Lido; Jesolo (40 km [25 mi] from Venice), famous for its vibrant nightlife in summer; Lignano Sabbiadoro, named after the "golden sand" that attracts more than 100,000 visitors a day (located a few miles from the mouth of the Tagliamento River in Friuli); and the historic town of Grado, which makes a great day trip from Trieste. Inland, the shores of Lago di Garda bring together natural beauty with a low-key worldliness that includes discos, spas, and stylish restaurants; Torbole, to the north of Monte Baldo on the eastern shore, is a sailing and windsurfing center.

For most Italians who live along the coast, going to the beach is more a part of the regular summer routine than a vacation activity: locals head to the nearest beach during the long Italian lunch break and for the evening *passeggiata* (stroll). In Italy a healthy suntan is still much sought after, although awareness of the dangers of long-term overexposure is spreading. Creams and sunblocks are available, but read the labels carefully to make sure you are getting the protection you desire, and don't underestimate the scorching power of the Italian sun. The "tanning" season begins in early May, when bathing suits by the major designers begin to appear in the windows of Italian shops, and the beach season starts in earnest in early June, with the opening of beaches run by concessionaires.

It is essential to distinguish between the private and public beaches. The former are free and open to the public but offer no services. Although on the most popular public beaches it's sometimes possible to buy sandwiches and soft drinks from kiosks or roaming vendors, as a general rule you shouldn't expect such comforts, let alone pay telephones, toilets, or showers. Private beaches charge admission and range from spartan (cold showers and portable toilets) to luxurious (with gardens, stylish bars, fish restaurants, and private guest huts). Admission policies and prices vary accordingly: although most establishments offer day passes that cost €5–€30 per person and include a chaise lounge and an umbrella, some of the more exclusive places cater only to patrons who pay by the week or month. Inquire at local tourist offices for details.

The summer season ends on September 15. During weekends, holidays, and throughout August, sea resorts and beaches are very crowded, some posting no-vacancy signs by 10 AM. Nowhere in Italy, except in the rare nudist beach, is it common practice to walk around topless, and wearing beach attire (bare chests and thighs) in town can get you fined. Men or women pay a €40 fine for going topless in Venice, even aboard boats in the Grand Canal.

BIKE TRAVEL

Italians are great bicycling enthusiasts—in the flatlands and historical centers of the Veneto region, locals often commute by bike, and they are proud of it. Those who enjoy touring have fine bicycling itineraries at their disposal throughout Italy. One such itinerary is The Federazione Italiana Amici della Bicicletta's (FIAB) *Bicycle route of the Sun,* which runs from south to north Italy. The Web site www.cycling.it contains an interesting selection of articles (in Italian) from the publication *La Bicicletta,* with detailed descriptions of itineraries across national parks and areas of natural beauty.

Local Resources **FIAB** ⊠ Viale Col Moschin 1, 30170 Mestre ☎ 041/921515 ⊕ www.fiab-onlus.it.

BIKES IN FLIGHT

Most airlines accommodate bikes as luggage, provided they are dismantled and boxed; check with individual airlines about packing requirements. Some airlines sell bike boxes, which are often free at bike shops, for about $20 (bike bags can be considerably more expensive). International travelers often can substitute a bike for a piece of checked luggage at no charge; otherwise the cost is about $100.

Most U.S. and Canadian airlines charge $40–$80 each way.

BOAT & FERRY TRAVEL

You get around Venice by boat or by foot. These are your boat-going options.

BY GONDOLA

It's hard to believe that Venice could get any more beautiful, but as your gondola glides away from the fondamenta, a magical transformation takes place—you've left the huddled masses behind to marvel at the city as visitors have for centuries before you. To some it feels like a Disney ride, and some complain about flotsam, jetsam, and less than pleasant odors, but if you insist that your gondolier take you winding through the tiny side canals, you'll get out of the city's main salon and into her intimate chambers, where only private boats can go. San Marco is loaded with gondola stations, but to get off the circuit, and maybe even have a canal to yourself, try the San Tomà or Santa Sofia (near Ca' d'Oro) stations. The price of a 50-minute ride is supposed to be fixed at €73 for up to six passengers, rising to €91 between 8 PM and 8 AM, but these are minimums and you may have difficulty finding a gondolier who will work for that unless the city is empty. Bargaining can help, but in any case come to terms on cost and duration before you start, and make it clear that you want to see more than just the Grand Canal.

BY TRAGHETTO

Many tourists are unaware of the two-man gondola ferries that cross the Grand Canal at numerous strategic points. At €.50, they're the cheapest and shortest gondola ride in Venice, and they can save a lot of walking. Look for TRAGHETTO signs and hand your fare to the gondolier when you board.

Note that although there are several traghetti along the Grand Canal, only San Tomà and Santa Sofia operate every day (except on major holidays) from about 7 AM to 7 PM. Don't depend on the others, which might run only mornings or weekdays, or shut down due to rain, fog, strong currents, or even for lack of passengers.

Starting from the train station end of the Grand Canal, traghetto links include Ferrovia–S. Simeon Piccolo; Campo San Marcuola–Fondaco dei Turchia; Rialto Pescheria–Campo Santa Sofia (near Ca' d'Oro); Fondamenta del Vin–Riva del Carbon (near Rialto); Campo San Tomà–Calle del Traghetto (near Campiello dei Morti); San Samuele (Palazzo Grassi)–Ca' Rezzonico; Santa Maria del Giglio (Gritti Palace)–Calle Lanza (near Madonna della Salute); Dogana Point (Salute)–Calle Vallaresso.

BY VAPORETTO

ACTV water buses serve several routes daily and after 11 PM provide limited service through the night. Some routes cover the length of the Grand Canal, and others circle the city and connect Venice with the lagoon islands. Landing stages are clearly marked with name and line number, but check before boarding to make sure the boat is going in your direction.

Line 1 is the Grand Canal local, calling at every stop and continuing via San Marco to the Lido. The trip takes about 35 minutes from Ferrovia to Vallaresso, San Marco. Circular Line 41 (the odd number indicates it goes counterclockwise) will take you from San Zaccaria to Murano, and Line 42 (clockwise) makes the return trip. Likewise, take Line 42 from San Zaccaria to Giudecca's Redentore, but Line 41 to return. Line 51 (counterclockwise) runs from the station to San Zaccaria via Piazzale Roma, then continues to the Lido. From the Lido, Line 52 circles clockwise, stopping at San Zaccaria, Zattere, Piazzale Roma, the station, Fondamente Nuove (connect to northern lagoon islands), San Pietro di Castello, and back to the Lido. From San Zaccaria, Line 82 (same number both directions) loops past Giudecca and Zattere, then stops at Tronchetto (parking garage) on the way to Piazzale Roma and the station. From the station, Line 82 becomes the Grand Canal express to Rialto, with some boats continuing to Vallaresso (San Marco) and in summer going all the way to the Lido beaches. Line N runs from roughly midnight to 6 AM, stopping at the Lido, Vallaresso, Accademia, Rialto, the train station, Piazzale Roma, Giudecca, and San Zaccaria, then returning in the opposite direction.

An ACTV water bus ticket for all lines except the Grand Canal costs €3.50, or €6 round-trip (valid for 24 hours); a single ride on the Grand Canal line costs €5. (Children under four ride free.) Another option is Travel Cards: €10.50 buys 24 hours and €22 buys 72 hours of unlimited travel on ACTV boats and buses. A shuttle ticket allows you to cross a canal, one stop only, for €1.80

Line information is posted at each landing, and complete timetables for all lines are available for €.60 at ACTV/Vela ticket booths, located at most major stops. Buy tickets before getting on the boat and remember to validate them in the yellow time-stamp machines. Tickets are also sold on the boat; you must ask to buy one immediately upon boarding, which can be a hassle. When inspectors come aboard, ticketless riders are fined, as are those who haven't validated their tickets. Ignorance will not spare you; the fine is €40, and getting fined can be embarrassing. The law says you must also buy tickets for dogs, baby strollers left unfolded, and bags over 28 inches long (there's no charge for your bag if you have a Travel Card), but this is generally enforced only for very bulky bags. The telephone number for ferry information listed below has assistance in English. 🚢 **ACTV** ☎ 041/2424 ⊕ www.hellovenezia.it.

WATER TAXIS

A motoscafo isn't cheap; you'll spend about €55 for a short trip in town, €60 to the Lido, and €80 per hour to visit the outer islands. The fare system is convoluted, with luggage handling, waiting time, early or late hours, and even ordering a taxi from your hotel adding expense. Always agree on the price first.
🚢 **Motoscafi** ☎ 041/5222303. **Water taxis for airport transfers** ☎ 041/5415084.

BUSINESS HOURS

Religious and civic holidays are frequent in Italy. Depending on their local importance, businesses may close for the day (busi-

nesses do not close on a Friday or Monday if the holiday falls on the weekend).

BANKS & OFFICES

Banks are open weekdays 8:30 to 1:30 and 2:45 to 3:45. Venice's main post office, known as Fondaco dei Tedeschi, is open Monday through Saturday 8:15 to 7 for stamps and registered mail, until 6 for other operations.

GAS STATIONS

Gas stations are generally open Monday through Saturday from 7 to 7 with a break at lunch. Many stations have automatic self-service pumps that accept bills (some also take credit cards). Gas stations on autostrade are open 24 hours.

MUSEUMS & SIGHTS

In Venice, the 15 churches belonging to the Chorus Association are open Monday through Saturday 10 to 5 and Sunday 1 to 5 (with a few minor variations). Other churches usually open early in the morning, close at noon or 12:30, then reopen late in the afternoon until about 7 PM. The Basilica di San Marco closes at 4:30 from November through April; 5:30 the rest of the year. It opens Monday through Saturday at 9:45 and Sunday at 1 PM. Sightseeing in churches is discouraged during services, usually held at 7 AM, noon, and 6:30 PM.

Museum hours vary and change with the seasons. Venice's major museums (Museo Correr, Palazzo Ducale, and the Gallerie dell'Accademia) are open daily, but weekend visits can be crowded. Other museums are closed one day a week: always check ahead.

PHARMACIES

Most pharmacies are open weekdays 9 to 12:30 and 4 to 7:30 and Saturday 9 to 12:30. Pharmacists take turns being on call overnights and holidays; you'll find their names and addresses posted at pharmacies, or listed in local newspapers and tourist publications.

SHOPS

Shops generally open weekdays 9:30 to 1 and 3:30 to 7 and on Saturday morning. In Venice, tourist-oriented shops often stay open seven days a week and do not close at midday. Food shops open 8 to 1 and 5 to 7:30 and close Sunday and Wednesday afternoon, but butchers generally work only mornings. Bars and pastry shops usually close one day a week. Barbers and hairdressers, with some exceptions, are closed Sunday and Monday. Throughout the month of August, many businesses of all kinds close for holiday.

BUS TRAVEL TO & FROM VENICE

Frequent ACTV buses leave Piazzale Roma for Mestre and other destinations in the province. Line 5 runs to Aeroporto Marco Polo and Line 2 to Mestre train station.

ACTV buses from Venice to Padua (€3.50) leave at 25 and 55 minutes past each hour, and stop along the Brenta River. ATVO has daily buses from Venice to Cortina (€10.60) June–September and throughout the Christmas–New Year holidays. Buses leave Venice at 7:50 AM, and depart Cortina 3:15 PM. October–May service is available only on weekends.

◪ Bus Information **Bus Terminal** ✉ Piazzale Roma, across the Grand Canal from the train station, Santa Croce. **ACTV** ☎ 041/5287886 ⊕ www.actv.it ✉ Lost property; ACTV office, Piazzale Roma ☎ 041/2722179. **ATVO** ☎ 041/5205530 ⊕ www.atvo.it.

BUS TRAVEL ON THE LIDO

Buses on the Lido leave from the vaporetto landing at Santa Maria Elisabetta. Orange Line *A* goes to San Nicolò and back. Dark blue Line *B* goes to the Alberoni/Faro Rocchetta (Malamocco) and, in the opposite direction, to the Ospedale al Mare. Blue Line *C* serves long Via Sandro Gallo. Green Line *V* goes to Malamocco (Via Parri). Line 11 goes to Pellestrina.

Lido bus routes and schedules are included in the same guide that lists vaporetto information. You'll find these on sale at ACTV ticket sellers for €.60, and the staff there generally speaks English, French, and Spanish.

The driver does not sell tickets. Buy them at ticket offices or at tobacco shops before boarding. These tickets must then be validated when entering the bus.

The lost-property office is open daily 7:30 AM–8 PM.

◪ Bus Information **ACTV** ☎ 041/2424 ⊕ www.hellovenezia.it ✉ Lost property; ACTV office, Piazzale Roma ☎ 041/2722179.

CAMERAS & PHOTOGRAPHY

The *Kodak Guide to Shooting Great Travel Pictures* (available at bookstores everywhere) is loaded with tips. Taking photos is forbidden in many churches, and being the subject of a snapshot is a sore point with some Venetians. If you want to single someone out for a photo, ask permission first.

◪ Photo Help **Kodak Information Center** ☎ 800/242-2424 ⊕ www.kodak.com.

EQUIPMENT PRECAUTIONS

Silica gel packs may help keep gear free of moisture buildup during Venice's humid summers and winters. Cameras moved from air-conditioned rooms into humid weather may experience condensation problems and the lens may need drying. Fog and mist can also be dense enough to cause some electronic cameras to fail.

Don't pack film or equipment in checked luggage, where it is much more susceptible to damage. X-ray machines used to view checked luggage are extremely powerful and therefore are likely to ruin your film. Try to ask for hand inspection of film, which becomes clouded after repeated exposure to airport X-ray machines, and keep videotapes and computer disks away from metal detectors. Always keep film, tape, and computer disks out of the sun. Carry an extra supply of batteries, and be prepared to turn on your camera, camcorder, or laptop to prove to airport security personnel that the device is real.

FILM & DEVELOPING

In Venice and most major cities you'll see scores of photo developing shops, many with service in one hour (or less). One-hour shops will develop and print a 36-exposure roll for between €10–€15. Photography stores sell film starting at €4 (24-exposure Kodak ASA 100), but you'll pay much more at kiosks and souvenir shops.

VIDEOS

Although VHS videotapes and players are common, Italy, like other countries in Europe, uses a different video system than the one used in North America. This means you won't be able to play the videotapes you bring from home on Italian equipment, and tapes purchased in Italy won't work in an American VCR. This is also the case with DVDs: European players aren't compatible with American disks.

CAR RENTAL

Rates in Venice begin at €50 a day and €200 a week for an economy car with air-conditioning, a manual transmission, and mileage limited to 150 km (93 mi) a day. This includes the 20% IVA tax on car rentals. Most major American car-rental companies have offices or affiliates in Italy.

Fiats and Fords in a variety of sizes are the most typical rental cars. Most Italian cars have standard transmissions. If you want to rent an automatic, you must be specific when you reserve the car. Higher rates will apply.

Note that in Italy car-rental companies usually make it mandatory to purchase the collision-damage waiver, regardless of what coverage may be provided by your credit card.

▶ Major Agencies **Alamo** ☎ 800/522-9696 ⊕ www.alamo.com. **Avis** ☎ 800/331-1084, 800/879-2847 in Canada, 0870/606-0100 in U.K., 02/9353-9000 in Australia, 09/526-2847 in New Zealand ⊕ www.avis.com. **Budget** ☎ 800/527-0700, 0870/156-5656 in U.K. ⊕ www.budget.com. **Dollar** ☎ 800/800-6000, 0800/085-4578 in U.K. ⊕ www.dollar.com. **Hertz** ☎ 800/654-3001, 800/263-0600 in Canada, 0870/844-8844 in U.K., 02/9669-2444 in Australia, 09/256-8690 in New Zealand ⊕ www.hertz.com. **National Car Rental** ☎ 800/227-7368, 0870/600-6666 in U.K. ⊕ www.nationalcar.com.

CUTTING COSTS

Rates are generally better if you make a reservation from abroad rather than from within Italy. In Italy, you can save up to 30% by renting your car online using your home address. Weekend rates with limited mileage are usually good deals. It can often help to book through a travel agent, who will be aware of all your options and will shop around.

The price of rentals is uniform for each company throughout the country: you will not save money, for example, if you pick up a vehicle at a city rental office rather than at an airport.

▶ Local Agencies **Avis** ⊠ Piazzale Roma, Santa Croce ☎ 041/5225825 ⊠ Aeroporto Marco Polo ☎ 041/5415030 ⊕ www.avis.com. **Easy Car** ⊠ Aeroporto Marco Polo ☎ 041/5416557 ⊕ www.easycarspa.com. **Hertz** ⊠ Piazzale Roma, Santa Croce ☎ 041/5284091 ⊠ Aeroporto Marco Polo ☎ 041/5416075 ⊕ www.hertz.com. **Sixt Rent-a-Car** ⊠ Aeroporto Marco Polo ☎ 041/5415032 ⊕ www.sixt.com.

▶ Wholesalers **Auto Europe** ☎ 207/842-2000 or 800/223-5555 🖷 207/842-2222 ⊕ www.autoeurope.com. **Europe by Car** ☎ 212/581-3040 or 800/223-1516 🖷 212/246-1458 ⊕ www.europebycar.com. **Destination Europe Resources** (DER) ⊠ 9501 W. Devon Ave., Rosemont, IL 60018 ☎ 800/782-2424 ⊕ www.der.com. **Kemwel** ☎ 800/678-0678 🖷 207/842-2124 ⊕ www.kemwel.com.

REQUIREMENTS & RESTRICTIONS

In Italy your own country's driver's license is acceptable. An International Driver's Permit is nonetheless not a bad idea; it's available from the American or Canadian Automobile Association and, in the United Kingdom, from the Automobile Association or Royal Automobile Club. These international permits are universally recognized, and having one may save you a problem with the local authorities. In Italy you must be 21 years of age to rent an economy or subcompact car, and most companies require customers under the age of 23 to pay by credit card. Upon rental, all companies require credit cards as a warranty; to rent bigger cars (2,000 cc or more) you must often show two credit cards. Call local agents for details. There are no special restrictions on senior-citizen drivers.

Car seats are required for children under three and must be booked in advance. The cost ranges from €26 to €40 for the duration of the rental.

SURCHARGES

Before you pick up a car in one city and leave it in another, ask about drop-off charges or one-way service fees, which can be substantial. Also inquire about early-return policies; some rental agencies charge extra if you return the car before the time specified in your contract, whereas others give you a refund for the days not used. To avoid a hefty refueling fee, fill the tank just before you turn in the car, but be aware that gas stations near the rental outlet may overcharge. It's almost never a deal to buy the tank of gas that's in the car when you rent it; the understanding is that you'll return it empty, but some fuel usually remains.

The cost for an additional driver is about €5 per day.

CAR TRAVEL

Italy has an extensive network of *autostrade* (toll highways), complemented by equally well-maintained but free *superstrade* (expressways). All are clearly signposted and numbered. The ticket you are issued upon entering an autostrada must be returned when you exit and pay the toll; on some shorter autostrade, mainly connecting highways, the toll is paid upon entering. Viacards, on sale at many autostrada locations, make paying tolls easier and faster. You pass through the Viacard lane at toll booths, slipping the card into the designated slot.

Uscita means "exit." A *raccordo* is a connecting expressway. *Strade statali* (state highways, denoted by *S* or *SS* numbers) may be single-lane roads, as are all secondary roads; directions and turnoffs are not always clearly marked. Venice is on the east–west A4 autostrada, which connects with Padua, Verona, Brescia, Milan, and Turin.

Roads just outside of Venice are notoriously crowded and lines of 30–50 km are not uncommon during holiday weekends. Count on parking your car and leaving it during your stay in the city.

Automobil Club Italiano (ACI) gives travel tips and information in English about rules of the road, road conditions, and car insurance.

F ACI ☎ 06/49982389 ⊙ 8 AM–8 PM.

EMERGENCY SERVICES

It's advisable to call your rental company first—look for a free "numero verde" green number in the paperwork. If that fails, Automobil Club Italiano (ACI) has 24-hour emergency service.

F ACI emergency service ☎ 803116.

GASOLINE

Gas stations are located at frequent intervals along the main highways and autostrade. Usually on the periphery of towns and cities, they're rarely found in the center of municipalities. Gas stations on autostrade are open 24 hours. Otherwise, gas stations generally are open Monday through Saturday 7–7 with a break at lunchtime. Gas stations with an attendant take cash and credit cards. It's not customary to tip the attendant when full service is provided.

Many stations have automatic self-service pumps that accept only bills of 5, 10, 20, and 50 euros and don't give change or a receipt (*ricevuta*). The self-service pumps do not take credit cards.

In case you run out of gas along the toll roads and the main free superstrade, emergency telephones are provided. To find the phone, look on the pavement at the shoulder of the highway where painted arrows and the term "SOS" point in the direction of the nearest phone.

Gas (*benzina*) costs about €1.40 a liter. It's available in unleaded (*verde*) and super unleaded (*super*). Many rental cars in Italy take only diesel (*gasolio*) which costs about €1.10 a liter; ask about the fuel type when picking up your rental car.

PARKING

If you bring a car to Venice, you will have to pay for a garage or parking space. Warning: do not be waylaid by illegal touts, often wearing fake uniforms, who may try to flag you down as you approach Venice and offer to arrange parking and hotels; their activities have become a scandal in a city generally free of con men and criminals. Ignore them and continue on to one of the parking garages.

Parking at Autorimessa Comunale costs €19 for 24 hours. The private Garage San

Marco costs €20 for up to 12 hours and €26 for 12–24 hours. You can reserve a space in advance at either of these garages; you'll come upon both immediately after crossing the bridge from the mainland. Another alternative is Tronchetto parking (€18 for 1–24 hours); watch for signs for it coming over the bridge—you'll have to turn right before you get to Piazzale Roma.

Many hotels have negotiated guest discounts with San Marco or Tronchetto garages; get a voucher when you check in at your hotel and present it when you pay the garage. Line 82 connects Tronchetto with Piazzale Roma and Piazza San Marco and also goes to the Lido in summer. When there's thick fog or extreme tides, a bus runs to Piazzale Roma instead. Avoid private boats—they're a rip-off.

Do not leave valuables in the car. There is a luggage storage office, open 6 AM–9 PM, next to the Pullman Bar on the ground floor of the municipal garage at Piazzale Roma.

Parking space in most other cities of the Venetian Arc is at a premium, but in historic town centers where streets are closed to most traffic, peripheral parking areas are usually near capacity. Parking in an area signposted ZONA DISCO is allowed for limited periods (from 30 minutes to two hours or more—the limit is posted); if you don't have the cardboard disk, you can use a piece of paper to indicate what time you parked. The *parcometro,* the Italian version of metered parking, has been introduced in some major cities (not in Venice).

🚗 **Garages** **Autorimessa Comunale** ✉ Piazzale Roma, Santa Croce, end of S11 road ☎ 041/2727211 ⊕ www.asmvenezia.it. **Garage San Marco** ✉ Piazzale Roma 467/f, Santa Croce, turn right into bus park ☎ 041/5232213 ⊕ www.garagesanmarco.it. **Tronchetto** ☎ 041/5207555.

ROAD CONDITIONS

Autostrade are well maintained, as are most interregional highways. The condition of provincial (county) roads varies, but road maintenance at this level is generally good in Italy.

ROAD MAPS

Street and road signs are often challenging—a good map and patience are essential. Local road maps can be obtained at the point of rental pickup. Alternatively, most bookstores such as Feltrinelli sell them as do most highway gas stations. In major cities, look for the Touring Club Italiano's shop. They sell maps (road, bicycle, hiking, among others). Probably the best road maps are those produced by Michelin. The Michelin Web site is also good for driving instructions and maps (⊕ www.viamichelin.com).

RULES OF THE ROAD

Driving is on the right, as in the United States. Regulations are largely as in Britain and the United States, except that the police have the power to levy on-the-spot fines. In most Italian towns the use of the horn is forbidden in certain, if not all, areas; a large sign, ZONA DI SILENZIO, indicates where. Speed limits are 130 kph (80 mph) on autostrade and 110 kph (70 mph) on state and provincial roads, unless otherwise marked.

Handheld mobile phones are illegal while driving; fines can exceed €100. The blood-alcohol content limit for driving is 0.5 gr (lower than in the United States) with fines up to €5,000 for surpassing the limit and the possibility of six months' imprisonment. Though enforcement of laws varies depending on region, fines for speeding are uniformly stiff: 10 kph over the speed limit can warrant a fine of up to €500; over 10 kph, and your license could be taken away from you.

Nonetheless, Italians drive fast and are impatient with those who don't. Tailgating is the norm here—the only way to avoid it is to get out of the way. Drivers also honk a lot, often to alert other drivers of their moves. Right turns on red lights are forbidden. Headlights are not compulsory in cities when it rains or snows, but it's a good idea to turn them on. However, headlights are mandatory when driving on all roads outside city limits at all hours. Seat belts (front and back) and children's car seats are compulsory.

CHILDREN

Italians tend to love children and are generally very tolerant and patient with them, but there are few amenities provided specifically for them. Some discounts exist, such as children under 4 riding free on vaporetti, municipal buses, and trains, and children 4–12 paying 50% on Italian trains. It never hurts to ask about a *sconto bambino o studente* (child or student discount) before purchasing tickets. Certain museums and galleries may offer discounts only to students who are EU citizens, but in other places, any student might be eligible. Venice caters more to art and history lovers than people on family vacations.

If you are renting a car, don't forget to arrange for a car seat when you reserve. For general advice about traveling with children, consult *Fodor's FYI: Travel with Your Baby* (available in bookstores everywhere).

BABYSITTING

Most hotel concierges can help you locate a babysitter, often as not a young English-speaking woman with whom they may be personally acquainted. Prices range from €7–€25 per hour depending on the hotel. During holiday periods when the student population is vacationing, finding a sitter could prove difficult.

FLYING

If your children are two or older, ask about children's airfares. As a general rule, infants under two not occupying a seat fly at greatly reduced fares or even for free. But if you want to guarantee a seat for an infant, you have to pay full fare. Consider flying during off-peak days and times; most airlines will grant an infant a seat without a ticket if there are available seats. When booking, confirm carry-on allowances if you're traveling with infants. In general, for babies charged 10% to 50% of the adult fare you are allowed one carry-on bag and a collapsible stroller; if the flight is full, the stroller may have to be checked or you may be limited to less.

Experts agree that it's a good idea to use safety seats aloft for children weighing less than 40 pounds. Airlines set their own policies: if you use a safety seat, U.S. carriers usually require that the child be ticketed, even if he or she is young enough to ride free, because the seats must be strapped into regular seats. And even if you pay the full adult fare for the seat, it may be worth it, especially on longer trips. Do check your airline's policy about using safety seats during takeoff and landing. Safety seats are not allowed everywhere in the plane, so get your seat assignments as early as possible.

When reserving, request children's meals or a freestanding bassinet (not available at all airlines) if you need them. But note that bulkhead seats, where you must sit to use the bassinet, may lack an overhead bin or storage space on the floor.

SIGHTS & ATTRACTIONS

Places that are especially appealing to children are indicated in this guide by a rubber-duckie icon (🦆) in the margin. Feeding pigeons in San Marco is a favorite with kids, as is the view from atop the Campanile. Young ones might also enjoy the Scala Contarini del Bovolo—and you'll enjoy it, too, unless you happen to be carrying them up this long spiral climb. Watching glass come to life in Murano fascinates old and young alike. If the Museum of Naval History's collection of model ships doesn't interest your child, perhaps their collection of seashells will. Or you can take the child to the beach at Lido to start his or her own shell collection.

SUPPLIES & EQUIPMENT

Baby formula and disposable diapers are available in all pharmacies; supermarkets also sell disposable diapers. The cost of diapers in Italy is similar to that in other countries, but American brands such as Pampers and Huggies cost slightly more than in the United States. COOP, a reliable local brand, runs about €13 for 50 diapers, while Pampers cost about €9 for 20 and Huggies go for about €11 for 34.

Italian formula (both in premixed and powder forms) generally contains more vitamins than its American counterparts; Plasmon is a good brand. Italian bottles are identical to American ones, but it is difficult to find no-spill cups for toddlers; it's best to bring a couple along with you.

COMPUTERS ON THE ROAD

Getting online in Venice isn't difficult; Internet points and Internet cafés, sometimes open 24 hours a day, are becoming more and more common. Prices and deals vary—franchise operators may charge more initially, but you'll be able to carry unused time to Florence or Rome. Some hotels have Internet access in the lobby; others have in-room modem lines, but as with phones, using the hotel's line is relatively expensive. Always check modem rates before plugging in. You may need an adapter for your computer for the European-style plugs. As always, if you are traveling with a laptop, carry a spare battery and an adapter. Never plug your computer into any socket before asking about surge protection. IBM sells a pea-size modem tester that plugs into a telephone jack to check if the line is safe to use.

🛈 Internet Cafés **Internet Cafe net house** ✉ Campo Santo Stefano, San Marco 2967/2958 ☎ 041/2771190 ⌚ 24 hours. **Planet Internet** ✉ 5 minutes from train station on Strada Nova, Cannaregio 1519 ☎ 041/5244188 ⌚ 9 AM–midnight.

CONSUMER PROTECTION

Most stores in Italy do not allow customers to return or exchange merchandise, even if there is a minor flaw in the product. Clothing stores are particularly inflexible.

Whether you're shopping for gifts or purchasing travel services, pay with a major credit card whenever possible, so you can cancel payment or get reimbursed if there's a problem (and you can provide documentation). If you're buying a package or tour, always consider travel insurance that includes default coverage (⇨ Insurance).

CUSTOMS & DUTIES

When shopping abroad, keep receipts for all purchases. Upon reentering the country, be ready to show customs officials what you've bought. Pack purchases together in an easily accessible place. If you think a duty is incorrect, appeal the assessment. If you object to the way your clearance was handled, note the inspector's badge num-

ber. In either case, first ask to see a supervisor. If the problem isn't resolved, write to the appropriate authorities, beginning with the port director at your point of entry.

IN AUSTRALIA

Australian residents who are 18 or older may bring home A$400 worth of souvenirs and gifts (including jewelry), 250 cigarettes or 250 grams of cigars or other tobacco products, and 1,125 ml of alcohol (including wine, beer, and spirits). Residents under 18 may bring back A$200 worth of goods. Members of the same family traveling together may pool their allowances. Prohibited items include meat products. Seeds, plants, and fruits need to be declared upon arrival.

🛈 **Australian Customs Service** ⌂ Regional Director, Box 8, Sydney, NSW 2001 ☎ 02/9213-2000 or 1300/363263, 02/9364-7222 or 1800/020-504 quarantine-inquiry line 📠 02/9213-4043 ⊕ www.customs.gov.au.

IN CANADA

Canadian residents who have been out of Canada for at least seven days may bring in C$750 worth of goods duty-free. If you've been away fewer than seven days but more than 48 hours, the duty-free allowance drops to C$200. If your trip lasts 24 to 48 hours, the allowance is C$50. You may not pool allowances with family members. Goods claimed under the C$750 exemption may follow you by mail; those claimed under the lesser exemptions must accompany you. Alcohol and tobacco products may be included in the seven-day and 48-hour exemptions but not in the 24-hour exemption. If you meet the age requirements of the province or territory through which you reenter Canada, you may bring in, duty-free, 1.5 liters of wine *or* 1.14 liters (40 imperial ounces) of liquor *or* 24 12-ounce cans or bottles of beer or ale. Also, if you meet the local age requirement for tobacco products, you may bring in, duty-free, 200 cigarettes and 50 cigars. Check ahead of time with the Canada Customs and Revenue Agency or the Department of Agriculture for policies regarding meat products, seeds, plants, and fruits.

You may send an unlimited number of gifts (only one gift per recipient, however) worth up to C$60 each duty-free to Canada. Label the package UNSOLICITED GIFT—VALUE UNDER $60. Alcohol and tobacco are excluded.

🛃 **Canada Customs and Revenue Agency** ✉ 2265 St. Laurent Blvd., Ottawa, Ontario K1G 4K3 ☎ 800/461-9999 in Canada, 204/983-3500, 506/636-5064 ⊕ www.ccra.gc.ca.

IN ITALY

Of goods obtained anywhere outside the EU, the allowances are (1) 200 cigarettes or 100 cigarillos (under 3 grams) or 50 cigars or 250 grams of tobacco; (2) 2 liters of still table wine or 1 liter of spirits over 22% volume; and (3) 50 milliliters of perfume and 250 milliliters of toilet water.

Of goods obtained (duty and tax paid) within another EU country, the allowances are (1) 800 cigarettes or 400 cigarillos (under 3 grams) or 200 cigars or 1 kilogram of tobacco; (2) 90 liters of still table wine or 10 liters of spirits over 22% volume or 20 liters of spirits under 22% volume or 110 liters of beer.

There is no quarantine period in Italy, so if you want to travel with Fido or Tiger, it's possible. Contact your nearest Italian consulate to find out what paperwork is needed for entry into Italy with a pet; generally, it is a certificate noting that the animal is healthy and up-to-date on its vaccinations. Keep in mind, however, that the United States has some stringent laws about reentry: pets must be free of all disease, especially those communicable to humans, and they must be vaccinated against rabies at least 30 days before returning. This means that if you are in Italy for a short-term stay, you must find a veterinarian or have your pet vaccinated before departure. (This law does not apply to puppies less than three months old.) Pets should arrive at the point of entry with a statement, in English, attesting to this fact.

🛃 **Dogana Sezione Viaggiatori** ✉ Customs, Aeroporto Leonardo da Vinci, Fiumicino 00054 Rome ☎ 06/65954343. **Ministero delle Finanze, Direzione Centrale dei Servizi Doganali, Divisione I** ✉ Via Carucci 71, 00143 Rome, Italy ☎ 06/50242117.

IN NEW ZEALAND

All homeward-bound residents may bring back NZ$700 worth of souvenirs and gifts; passengers may not pool their allowances, and children can claim only the concession on goods intended for their own use. For those 17 or older, the duty-free allowance also includes 4.5 liters of wine or beer; one 1,125-ml bottle of spirits; and either 200 cigarettes, 250 grams of tobacco, 50 cigars, *or* a combination of the three up to 250 grams. Meat products, seeds, plants, and fruits must be declared upon arrival to the Agricultural Services Department.

🛃 **New Zealand Customs** ✉ Head office: The Customhouse, 17–21 Whitmore St., Box 2218, Wellington ☎ 09/300-5399 or 0800/428-786 ⊕ www.customs.govt.nz.

IN THE U.K.

If you are a U.K. resident and your journey was wholly within the European Union, you probably won't have to pass through customs when you return to the United Kingdom. If you plan to bring back large quantities of alcohol or tobacco, check EU limits beforehand. In most cases, if you bring back more than 200 cigars, 3,200 cigarettes, 400 cigarillos, 10 liters of spirits, 110 liters of beer, 20 liters of fortified wine, and/or 90 liters of wine, you have to declare the goods upon return. Prohibited items include unpasteurized milk, regardless of country of origin.

🛃 **HM Customs and Excise** ✉ Portcullis House, 21 Cowbridge Rd. E, Cardiff CF11 9SS ☎ 0845/010-9000 or 0208/929-0152 advice service, 0208/929-6731 or 0208/910-3602 complaints ⊕ www.hmce.gov.uk.

IN THE U.S.

U.S. residents who have been out of the country for at least 48 hours may bring home, for personal use, $800 worth of foreign goods duty-free, as long as they haven't used the $800 allowance or any part of it in the past 30 days. This exemption may include 1 liter of alcohol (for travelers 21 and older), 200 cigarettes, and 100 non-Cuban cigars. Family members from the same household who are traveling together may pool their $800 personal exemptions. For fewer than 48 hours, the duty-free allowance drops to $200, which may include 50 cigarettes, 10 non-Cuban cigars, and 150 ml of alcohol (or 150 ml of perfume containing alcohol). The $200 allowance cannot be combined with other individuals' exemptions, and if you exceed it, the full value of all the goods will be taxed. Antiques, which U.S. Customs and Border Protection define as objects more than 100 years old, enter duty-free, as do original works of art done entirely by hand, including paintings, drawings, and sculptures. This doesn't apply to folk art or handicrafts, which are in general dutiable.

You may also send packages home duty-free, with a limit of one parcel per addressee per day (except alcohol or tobacco products or perfume worth more than $5). You can mail up to $200 worth of goods for personal use; label the package PERSONAL USE and attach a list of its contents and their retail value. If the package contains your used personal belongings, mark it AMERICAN GOODS RETURNED to avoid paying duties. You may send up to $100 worth of goods as a gift; mark the package UNSOLICITED GIFT. Mailed items do not affect your duty-free allowance on your return.

To avoid paying duty on foreign-made high-ticket items you already own and will take on your trip, register them with Customs before you leave the country. Consider filing a Certificate of Registration for laptops, cameras, watches, and other digital devices identified with serial numbers or other permanent markings; you can keep the certificate for other trips. Otherwise, bring a sales receipt or insurance form to show that you owned the item before you left the United States.

For more about duties, restricted items, and other information about international travel, check out U.S. Customs and Border Protection's online brochure, *Know Before You Go.*

U.S. Customs and Border Protection ⊠ For inquiries and equipment registration, 1300 Pennsylvania Ave. NW, Washington, DC 20229 ⊕ www.cbp. gov ☎ 877/287-8667, 202/354-1000 ⊠ For complaints, Customer Satisfaction Unit, 1300 Pennsylvania Ave. NW, Room 5.2C, Washington, DC 20229.

DISABILITIES & ACCESSIBILITY

Italy has only recently begun to provide facilities such as ramps, telephones, and restrooms for people with disabilities; such things are still the exception, not the rule. In Venice, bridges, historic buildings that cannot be modernized, and traveling by boat complicate matters for people with mobility problems. Don't rely on tourist maps that indicate lifts on certain bridges around town; these rarely if ever work. Kiosks in the airport, train station, and parking areas that book hotels, can only dispense information member hotels provide; there is no set criteria for designating one's own hotel "accessible." *Informahandicap* has a Web site with helpful information for wheelchair users, and questions you e-mail to them in English will be answered.

Contact the nearest Italian consulate about bringing a Seeing Eye dog into Italy; this requires an import license, a current certificate detailing the dog's inoculations, and a letter from your veterinarian certifying the dog's health.

Local Resources **Informahandicap** ⊠ Viale Giuseppe Garibaldi 155, 30174 Mestre ☎ 041/5341700 ⊟ 041/5342257 ⊕ www.comune.venezia.it/handicap.

WHERE TO STAY

If you have mobility problems, ask for the lowest floor on which accessible services are offered. If you have a hearing impairment, check whether the hotel has devices to alert you visually to the ring of the telephone, a knock at the door, and a fire/emergency alarm. Some hotels provide these devices without charge. Discuss your needs with hotel personnel if this equipment isn't available, so that a staff member can personally alert you in the event of an emergency.

If you're bringing a guide dog, get authorization ahead of time and write down the name of the person with whom you spoke.

The Italian Government Travel Office (ENIT; ⇨ Visitor Information) can give you a list of hotels that provide access and addresses of Italian associations for travelers with disabilities.

Because Italian lodgings are often in buildings that are several hundred years old, many are not equipped with elevators. Many of them have steps at the entrance. When booking a hotel, inquire about entranceways: ramps are still rare.

In Venice, choose a hotel that has access to a Line 1 or Line 82 vaporetto landing without having to cross a bridge. Newer and newly restored buildings are more likely to meet the latest legal specifications. Some of the better choices in Venice include San Zulian and Ca' Pisani.

RESERVATIONS

When discussing accessibility with an operator or reservations agent, ask hard questions. Are there any stairs, inside *or* out? Are there grab bars next to the toilet *and* in the shower/tub? How large is the elevator? How wide is the door to the room? To the bathroom? To the shower? If you reserve through a toll-free number, consider also calling the hotel's local number to confirm the information from the central reservations office. Get confirmation in writing when you can.

SIGHTS & ATTRACTIONS

Most major historic buildings and museums are accessible without having to cross a bridge if you plan ahead and you use the correct vaporetto stop. Palazzo Ducale, Museo Correr, the Campanile di San Marco, Ca' Rezzonico, Palazzo Grassi, Ca' d'Oro, and Scuola di San Rocco have either elevators or stair-climbing machines that accommodate wheelchairs. Gallerie dell'Accademia has one such machine, but visitors must still overcome a few steps connecting exhibit rooms. Most churches, including the Basilica di San Marco, have at least a few steps at their entrances.

TRANSPORTATION

From the airport, the yellow ACTV bus 5 is ramped for chair loading or you can use a land taxi. Once in Venice, vaporetto Lines 1, 82, and LN (for Laguna Nord) have plenty of deck space and easy cabin entry, however, unless you can navigate a few steps aboard Lines 41, 51, and 61, you'll be forced to ride outdoors, or if the boat is very crowded, you won't even be allowed to board. Boarding water taxis is not easy. Floating docks are rare, and even when the boat can mechanically raise its deck level with the dock, waves can make the transfer exciting, to say the least. Private boats with a driver plus an assistant are available; they arrive equipped to lift and carry disabled passengers safely and comfortably. This service is best arranged by contacting a local tour operator experienced in such transfers who can also help you find rental wheelchairs, crutches, and other mobility aids.

Venice Santa Lucia station is an end-of-the-line train terminal, which means that you won't have to climb down stairs to walk underneath platforms. Though there are plenty of steps at the front door, these are easily bypassed by a ramped exit to your left as you leave the platform. Trenitalia, the Italian rail system, tries hard to accommodate travelers with mobility problems and, at least in Venice and 15 other major cities, they do quite well. If notified ahead of time, porters will meet arriving or departing passengers with a cart that lifts wheelchairs to the level of the train car. Visit its Web site to find out what services might make your trip easier. **Kele Teo** ⊠ Ponte dei Bareteri, San Marco 4930 between San Marco and Rialto ☎ 041/5208722 🖶 041/5208913 ⊕ www.keleteo.com. **Trenitalia** ☎ 041/785570, 041/785913, 8488-88088 (local call anywhere in Italy) 🖶 Fax 041-785167 ⊕ www.trenitalia.it.

Complaints Aviation Consumer Protection Division (⇨ Air Travel) for airline-related problems. **Departmental Office of Civil Rights** ⊠ For general inquiries, U.S. Department of Transportation, S-30, 400 7th St. SW, Room 10215, Washington, DC 20590 ☎ 202/366-4648 🖶 202/366-9371 ⊕ www.dot.gov/ost/docr/index.htm. **Disability Rights Section** ⊠ NYAV, U.S. Department of Justice, Civil Rights Division, 950 Pennsylvania Ave. NW, Washington, DC 20530 ☎ ADA information line 202/514-0301, 800/514-0301, 202/514-0383 TTY, 800/514-0383 TTY ⊕ www.ada.gov. **U.S. Department of Transportation Hotline** ☎ For disability-related air-travel problems, 800/778-4838 or 800/455-9880 TTY.

TRAVEL AGENCIES

In the United States, the Americans with Disabilities Act requires that travel firms serve the needs of all travelers. Some agencies specialize in working with people with disabilities.

Travelers with Mobility Problems Access Adventures/B. Roberts Travel ☒ 206 Chestnut Ridge Rd., Scottsville, NY 14624 ☎ 585/889-9096 ⊕ www.brobertstravel.com ⌫ dltravel@prodigy. net, run by a former physical-rehabilitation counselor. **CareVacations** ☒ No. 5, 5110-50 Ave., Leduc, Alberta, Canada, T9E 6V4 ☎ 780/986-6404 or 877/ 478-7827 🖷 780/986-8332 ⊕ www.carevacations. com, for group tours and cruise vacations. **Flying Wheels Travel** ☒ 143 W. Bridge St., Box 382, Owatonna, MN 55060 ☎ 507/451-5005 🖷 507/451-1685 ⊕ www.flyingwheelstravel.com.

Travelers with Developmental Disabilities Sprout ☒ 893 Amsterdam Ave., New York, NY 10025 ☎ 212/222-9575 or 888/222-9575 🖷 212/222-9768 ⊕ www.gosprout.org.

DISCOUNTS & DEALS

Be a smart shopper and compare all your options before making decisions. A plane ticket bought with a promotional coupon from travel clubs, coupon books, and direct-mail offers or purchased on the Internet may not be cheaper than the least expensive fare from a discount ticket agency. And always keep in mind that what you get is just as important as what you save.

DISCOUNT RESERVATIONS

To save money, look into discount reservations services with Web sites and toll-free numbers, which use their buying power to get a better price on hotels, airline tickets (⇨ Air Travel), even car rentals. When booking a room, always call the hotel's local toll-free number (if one is available) rather than the central reservations number—you'll often get a better price. Always ask about special packages or corporate rates.

When shopping for the best deal on hotels and car rentals, look for guaranteed exchange rates, which protect you against a falling dollar. With your rate locked in, you won't pay more, even if the price goes up in the local currency.

Hotel Rooms Accommodations Express ☎ 800/444-7666 or 800/277-1064 ⊕ www. accommodationsexpress.com. **Hotels.com**

☎ 800/246-8357 ⊕ www.hotels.com. **Steigenberger Reservation Service** ☎ 800/223-5652 ⊕ www.srs-worldhotels.com. **Turbotrip.com** ☎ 800/473-7829 ⊕ www.turbotrip.com.

PACKAGE DEALS

Don't confuse packages and guided tours. When you buy a package you travel on your own, just as though you had planned the trip yourself. Fly/drive packages, which combine airfare and car rental, are often a good deal. In cities ask the local visitor's bureau about hotel and local transportation packages that include tickets to major museum exhibits or other special events. If you buy a rail/drive pass you may save on train tickets and car rentals. All Eurailpass holders get a discount on Eurostar fares through the Channel Tunnel and often receive reduced rates for buses, hotels, ferries, sightseeing cruises, and car rentals.

EATING & DRINKING

The restaurants we list are the cream of the crop in each price category. Properties indicated by a ✕⊡ are lodging establishments whose restaurant warrants a special trip. For further information about dining in Venice, see *Know-How* in Chapter 2.

CATEGORY	COST
$$$$	over €22
$$$	€17–€22
$$	€12–€17
$	€7–€12
¢	under €7

Prices are for a second course (secondo piatto) *and are given in euros.*

A few pointers on Italian dining etiquette: menus are posted outside most restaurants (in English in tourist areas); if not, you might step inside and ask to take a look at the menu, but don't ask for a table unless you intend to stay. Italians take their food as it is listed on the menu, seldom making special requests such as "dressing on the side" or "hold the olive oil." If you have special dietary needs, though, make them known, and they can usually be accommodated. Although mineral water makes its way to almost every table, you can always order a carafe of tap water (acqua di rubinetto or acqua semplice) instead, but keep in mind that such water is highly chlorinated. Also, doing this will mark you distinctly as a tourist.

Spaghetti should be eaten with a fork rolled against the side of the dish, although a little help from a spoon will not horrify the locals the way cutting spaghetti into little pieces might. Wiping your bowl clean with a (small) piece of bread is fine in less formal eateries. Order your espresso (Italians almost never drink a cappuccino after breakfast) after dessert, not with it. When you are ready for it, ask for the check (il conto): unless it's well past closing time, no waiter will put a bill on your table without your having asked first. Don't ask for a doggy bag.

MEALS & SPECIALTIES

What's the difference between a *ristorante* and a *trattoria*? Can you order food at an *enoteca*? Can you go to a restaurant just for a snack, or order just a salad at a pizzeria? The following definitions should help.

Not too long ago, restaurants tended to be more elegant and expensive than *trattorie* and *osterie*, which served more traditional, home-style fare in an atmosphere to match. But the distinction has blurred considerably, and an osteria in the center of town might be far fancier (and pricier) than a ristorante across the street. An enoteca menu is often limited to a selection of cheese, cured meats, pickles, salads, and desserts, but if there is a kitchen, you'll also find vegetable soups, pasta, meat, and fish preparations. Venetian *bacari* are something between an old-style osteria and a wine bar: here it's possible to grab a fast snack (*cichetto*) at the counter swallowed down with a glass of wine (*ombra*), or, sometimes, to sit down for a fast meal. Most pizzerias don't offer just pizza, and although the other dishes on the menu are supposed to be starters, there's no harm in skipping the pizza. The typical pizzeria fare includes *affettati misti* (selection of cured meat), simple salads, and various kinds of *bruschetta* and *crostino* (similar to bruschetta, but baked). Pizzerias generally have fresh fruit, ice cream, and simple desserts.

Throughout the region, the handiest and least expensive way to grab a quick snack between sights is to hit a *bar, caffè,* or *pizza al taglio.* Most bars have a selection of *panini* (sandwiches), *toast,* (grilled sandwiches), and *tramezzini* (untoasted sandwich triangles). In cities, you may also find prepared salad, cold pasta dishes, and yogurt around lunchtime. Most bars have beer and a variety of alcohol, but few, except in Venice, sell wine by the glass. A caffè is like a bar but usually with more tables to sit down. Many caffès have limited restaurant licenses that allow them to serve hot pasta dishes, but choose carefully as some simply dispense microwaved portions. Pizza as well is often reheated. If you place your order at the counter, ask if you can sit down: some places, especially in Venice, charge extra for table service. In a self-service bar and caffè, it's good manners to clean up your table before you leave. Note that in some places you must pay before you place the order and be ready to show your *scontrino* (receipt) when you move to the counter. Few shops that sell *pizza al taglio* (by the slice) have places to sit down. Some pizzerias sell 1/8 of a large pizza as a slice, whereas in others, you'll pay by weight—just point out which kind you want and indicate how big a piece.

ELECTRICITY

To use electric-powered equipment purchased in the U.S. or Canada, bring a converter and adapter. The electrical current in Italy is 220 volts, 50 cycles alternating current (AC); wall outlets take Continental-type plugs, with two or three round prongs.

If your appliances are dual-voltage, you'll need only an adapter. Don't use 110-volt outlets marked FOR SHAVERS ONLY for high-wattage appliances such as blow-dryers. Most laptops operate equally well on 110 and 220 volts and so require only an adapter.

EMERGENCIES

No matter where you are in Italy, **dial 113 for all emergencies,** or find someone, such as a concierge, to call for you, as not all 113 operators speak English. The Italian word to use to draw people's attention in an emergency is *aiuto* (meaning "help," pronounced ah-*you*-toh). *Pronto soccorso* means "first aid" and will get you an ambulance (*ambulanza*). If you just need a doctor, ask for *un medico*. (Most hotels will be able to refer you to an English-speaking doctor.) Don't forget to ask the doctor for *una ricevuta* (receipt) to show to your insurance company for reimbursement. Other useful emergency words in Italian words are *al fuoco* ("fire," pronounced ahl fuh-*woe*-co), and *Al ladro* ("Follow the thief," pronounced ahl *lah*-droh).

Italy has a national police force (*carabinieri*) as well as local police (*polizia*, also known as *questura*). Both are armed and have the power to investigate crimes and make arrests. Always report the loss of your passport to either the carabinieri or the police (in addition to your consulate or embassy). *Polizia Municipale,* usually referred to as *vigili,* are the local police to call if you're involved in a minor traffic accident. They also hand out parking tickets and clamp cars, so before you even consider parking the Italian way, at least be able to spot the uniforms of these men and women who wear white in summer and black in winter.

Historic Venice has one hospital, SS. Giovanni e Paolo, in the Campo of the same name (vaporetto 41/42/51/52 stop Fondamente Nuove), which is used for emergencies and equipped with a decent emergency room. One can never count on finding an English speaker in the middle of the night. Serious problems are generally sent to Mestre where the hospital is better equipped and staffed.

🚩 Emergency Services **Carabinieri** (militarized police) 🕿 112. **Fire** 🕿 115. **Italian Automobile Club** 🕿 116. **Medical emergency and ambulance** 🕿 118. **Police** 🕿 113. **Vigili (Polizia Municipale)** 🕿 041/2748111 Venice, 049/8205111 Padua, 045/8077111 Verona, 0444/221111 Vicenza, 040/366111 Trieste, 0422/6581 Treviso, 0432/271111 Udine.

🚩 Hospitals **SS. Giovanni e Paolo** ✉ Campo SS. Giovanni e Paolo, Castello 🕿 041/5294111.

ENGLISH-LANGUAGE MEDIA

Cafoscarina, close to Università Ca' Foscari, has a large selection of English literature, mainly classics. Emiliana and Studium stock books about Venice and Italian food with a few fiction paperbacks. The Venice Pavilion, off Piazza San Marco near the Giardini Reali, has a good selection of books and novels featuring the city. For books about Venice's maritime culture, lagoon, and environment, try Maredicarta. A number of hotels around the city offer their guests the *Herald Tribune* or *USA Today*. Newsstands are likely to carry the Tribune but your best bet for the U.K. *Guardian, Times,* or *Financial Times* is the stall beside the San Marco post office (behind Museo Correr) or the one in Campo SS. Apostoli, between Rialto and Ca' d'Oro.

🛒 Bookstores **Cafoscarina** ✉ Campiello Squellini, 3259 Dorsoduro 🕿 041/5229602. **Emiliana** ✉ Calle Goldoni, 4487 San Marco, between Piazza San Marco and Campo San Luca 🕿 041/5220793. **Maredicarta** ✉ Fondamenta dei Tolentini, Santa Croce 222, across from train station 🕿 041/716304. **Studium** ✉ Calle de la Canonica, 337/c San Marco, off Piazzetta dei Leoncini 🕿 041/5222382. **Venice Pavilion** ✉ 2 San Marco 🕿 041/5225150.

ETIQUETTE & BEHAVIOR

Most churches require knees and shoulders be covered and many forbid cameras of any kind. A dress code is actively enforced at Basilica di San Marco and the Chorus group of churches, so it's wise to carry a sweater, or scarf, to wrap around your shoulders before entering a church. Do not enter a church with food, and do not drink from your water bottle while inside. Do not go in if a service is in progress. And if you have a cellular phone, turn it off before entering.

Italians who are friends greet each other with a kiss, first on the left cheek, and then on the right. When you meet a new person, shake hands.

Residents and shopkeepers are plagued by visitors who don't respect right-of-way courtesy in the narrow streets and on bridges (keep to the right). When strolling two or three abreast in a tiny calle, be aware of the local who may need to get by.

Posted around Piazza San Marco are signs detailing what the city considers polite comportment. Regardless of how hot the weather might be, shirtless men or women in the historic city, including on the Grand Canal, can be fined €40. Lying down in streets or squares is prohibited, as is sitting around your picnic lunch, unless you happen to be in one of the city's parks. Swimming or even dipping feet into canals is not permitted.

VAPORETTO ETIQUETTE
The vaporetto rules forbid men with tank tops, and riders must remove backpacks. When boarding the vaporetto, wait in the entry area instead of blocking the boarding ramp. Once aboard, move away from the entrance and don't block aisles with luggage. A significant number of Venice's residents are elderly—be considerate about yielding seats.

GAY & LESBIAN TRAVEL
Same-sex couples won't raise any eyebrows in Venice, but public displays of affection are rare. Clubs and bars in Venice and the Veneto are usually mixed rather than exclusively gay or lesbian.

Local Contacts Archigay Help Line ☎ 041/5384151, Mon. 7 PM-9 PM and Thurs. 9 PM-11 PM. **Casa de Uscoli** ☎ 349/7941393 ⊕ www.casadeuscoli.com. **Venice à la Carte** ⊕ www.tourvenice.org.

Gay- & Lesbian-Friendly Travel Agencies
Different Roads Travel ✉ 1017 N. LaCienega Blvd., Suite 308, West Hollywood, CA 90069 ☎ 310/289-6000 or 800/429-8747 (Ext. 14 for both) 🖷 310/855-0323 ✎ lgernert@tzell.com. **Kennedy Travel** ✉ 130 W. 42nd St., Suite 401, New York, NY 10036 ☎ 800/237-7433 or 212/840-8659 🖷 212/730-2269 ⊕ www.kennedytravel.com. **Now, Voyager** ✉ 4406 18th St., San Francisco, CA 94114 ☎ 415/626-1169 or 800/255-6951 🖷 415/626-8626 ⊕ www.nowvoyager.com. **Skylink Travel and Tour/Flying Dutchmen Travel** ✉ 1455 N. Dutton Ave., Suite A, Santa Rosa, CA 95401 ☎ 707/546-9888 or 800/225-5759 🖷 707/636-0951; serving lesbian travelers.

HEALTH
Though Italians are mineral water addicts, the *rubinetto* (tap water) in and around Venice is not bad. It may be a bit overchlorinated for some and certainly contains its share of calcium, but it won't hurt anyone unless they happen to be staying in a home that still has old lead pipes.

OVER-THE-COUNTER REMEDIES
It's always best to travel with your own tried and true medicines. The regulations regarding what medicines require a prescription are not likely to be exactly the same in Italy as in your home country—all the more reason to bring what you need with you. Aspirin (*l'aspirina*) can be purchased at any pharmacy, but Tylenol and Advil are unavailable.

PESTS & OTHER HAZARDS
Mosquitoes can be a problem in Venice. In many hotel rooms you'll find a *fornelletto antizanzare*, an electrical device that uses mosquito-repellent tablets. Insert a fresh tablet in the metal slot and plug the fornelletto in the wall (ideally in the vicinity of an open window): it should warm up after one minute. Leave at least one window open while the fornelletto is on and wash your hands carefully after touching the tablets. One tablet is good for one night.

HIKING & WALKING
The Dolomites have an extensive network of trails with many huts and hostels along the way. CAI, Club Alpino Italiano's Web site, is in Italian only and though your calls won't be answered in English, they promise to respond to faxes. Local tourist-information offices can also be helpful.

Hiking Organization CAI ✉ Via Petrella 19, 201124 Milan ☎ 02/2057231 🖷 02/205723201 ⊕ www.cai.it.

HOLIDAYS
National holidays include New Year's Day (January 1); Epiphany (January 6); Easter Sunday and Monday; Liberation Day (April 25); St. Mark's Day in Venice (April 25); Labor Day or May Day (May 1); Festa della Repubblica (June 2), Assumption of Mary, also known as Ferragosto (August 15); All Saints' Day (November 1); Immaculate Conception (December 8); Christmas Day and Boxing Day (December 25 and 26).

The feast days of patron saints are observed locally. Many businesses and shops may be closed in Venice on November 21 (Madonna della Salute).

INSURANCE

The most useful travel-insurance plan is a comprehensive policy that includes coverage for trip cancellation and interruption, default, trip delay, and medical expenses (with a waiver for preexisting conditions).

Without insurance you'll lose all or most of your money if you cancel your trip, regardless of the reason. Default insurance covers you if your tour operator, airline, or cruise line goes out of business. Trip-delay covers expenses that arise because of bad weather or mechanical delays. Study the fine print when comparing policies.

If you're traveling internationally, a key component of travel insurance is coverage for medical bills incurred if you get sick on the road. Such expenses aren't generally covered by Medicare or private policies. U.K. residents can buy a travel-insurance policy valid for most vacations taken during the year in which it's purchased (but check preexisting-condition coverage). British and Australian citizens need extra medical coverage when traveling overseas.

Always buy travel policies directly from the insurance company; if you buy them from a cruise line, airline, or tour operator that goes out of business you probably won't be covered for the agency or operator's default, a major risk. Before making any purchase, review your existing health and home-owner's policies to find what they cover away from home.

🗂 Travel Insurers In the U.S.: **Access America** ✉ 2805 N. Parham Rd., Richmond, VA 23294 ☎ 800/284-8300 🖷 804/673-1469 or 800/346-9265 ⊕ www.accessamerica.com. **Travel Guard International** ✉ 1145 Clark St., Stevens Point, WI 54481 ☎ 800/826-1300 or 715/345-1041 🖷 800/955-8785 or 715/345-1990 ⊕ www.travelguard.com. 🗂 In the U.K.: **Association of British Insurers** ✉ 51 Gresham St., London EC2V 7HQ ☎ 020/7600-3333 🖷 020/7696-8999 ⊕ www.abi.org.uk. In Canada: **RBC Insurance** ✉ 6880 Financial Dr., Mississauga, Ontario L5N 7Y5 ☎ 800/387-4357 or 905/816-2559 🖷 888/298-6458 ⊕ www.rbcinsurance.com. In Australia: **Insurance Council of Australia** ✉ Level 3, 56 Pitt St. Sydney, NSW 2000 ☎ 02/9253-5100 🖷 02/9253-5111 ⊕ www.ica.

com.au. In New Zealand: **Insurance Council of New Zealand** ✉ Level 7, 111-115 Customhouse Quay, Box 474, Wellington ☎ 04/472-5230 🖷 04/473-3011 ⊕ www.icnz.org.nz.

LANGUAGE

In Venice, language is not a big problem. You can always find someone who speaks at least a little English. Remember that the Italian language is pronounced exactly as it is written. (Many Italians try to speak English the same way, enunciating every syllable, with disconcerting results.) You may run into a language barrier in the countryside, but a phrase book and close attention to the Italians' astonishing use of pantomime and expressive gestures will go a long way. Try to master a few phrases for daily use, and familiarize yourself with the terms you'll need to decipher signs and museum labels.

More than a dialect, locally spoken *veneziano* is a real language with a rich history. All the Republic's official documents, all commercial transactions, and even many diplomatic missions to foreign states were written or conducted in the Venetian language. Unless you know some Italian, you may not realize how much of what you hear on the street is actually local language. If you listen closely, especially to the boatmen, or people in Castello or Cannaregio, you might notice a difference in tone, less enunciation, or the sound of a hard "g" or "z," normally not heard in Italian. Venetians also tend to drop consonants, so perhaps that's how an old Venetian greeting *sciavo* (literally "slave"), pronounced without the "v," became the Italian word *ciao*, used for both "hi" and "see you."

LANGUAGES FOR TRAVELERS

A phrase book and language-tape set can help get you started. *Fodor's Italian for Travelers* (available at bookstores everywhere) is excellent.

LODGING

The lodgings we list in this guide are the cream of the crop in each price category. We always list the facilities that are available—but we don't specify whether they cost extra: when pricing accommodations, always ask what's included and what costs extra.

Properties are assigned price categories based on the range between their least and most expensive standard double room at high season (excluding holidays). Properties marked ✕⊡ are lodging establishments whose restaurants warrant a special trip. Hotels with the designation **BP** (for Breakfast Plan) at the end of their listing include breakfast in their rate; offerings can vary from coffee and a roll to an elaborate buffet. Those designated **EP** (European Plan) have no meals included; **MAP** (Modified American Plan) means you get breakfast and dinner; **FAP** (Full American Plan) includes all meals.

CATEGORY	VENICE	ELSEWHERE
$$$$	over €300	over €210
$$$	€225–€300	€160–€210
$$	€150–€225	€110–€160
$	€75–€150	€60–€110
¢	under €75	under €60

Prices are for two people in a standard double room in high season, including tax and service and are given in euros.

APARTMENT RENTALS
If you want a home base that's roomy enough for a family and comes with cooking facilities, consider a furnished rental. These can save you money, especially if you're traveling with a group. Home-exchange directories sometimes list rentals as well as exchanges.

🛈 International Agents **At Home Abroad** ⌕ 163 3rd Ave., No. 319, New York, NY 10003 ☎ 212/421-9165 🖷 212/533-0095 ⊕ www.athomeabroadinc.com.**Drawbridge to Europe** ✉ 98 Granite St., Ashland, OR 97520 ☎ 541/482-7778 or 888/268-1148 🖷 541/482-7779 ⊕ www.drawbridgetoeurope.com. **Hideaways International** ✉ 767 Islington St., Portsmouth, NH 03801 ☎ 603/430-4433 or 800/843-4433 🖷 603/430-4444 ⊕ www.hideaways.com, annual membership $185. **Hometours International** ✉ 1108 Scottie La., Knoxville, TN 37919 ☎ 865/690-8484 or 866/367-4668 ✎ hometours@aol.com ⊕ thor.he.net/~hometour/. **Interhome** ✉ 1990 N.E. 163rd St., Suite 110, North Miami Beach, FL 33162 ☎ 305/940-2299 or 800/882-6864 🖷 305/940-2911 ⊕ www.interhome.us. **Solemar** ✉ 1990 N.E. 163rd St., Suite 110, North Miami Beach, FL 33162 ☎ 305/940-2299 or 800/882-6864 🖷 305/940-

2911 ⊕ www.solemar.us. **Vacation Home Rentals Worldwide** ✉ 235 Kensington Ave., Norwood, NJ 07648 ☎ 201/767-9393 or 800/633-3284 🖷 201/767-5510 ⊕ www.vhrww.com. **Villanet** ✉ 1251 N.W. 116th St., Seattle, WA 98177 ☎ 206/417-3444 or 800/964-1891 🖷 206/417-1832 ⊕ www.rentavilla.com. **Villas and Apartments Abroad** ✉ 183 Madison Ave., Suite 201, New York, NY 10016 ☎ 212/213-6435 or 800/433-3020 🖷 212/213-8252 ⊕ www.vaanyc.com.**Villas International** ✉ 4340 Redwood Hwy., Suite D309, San Rafael, CA 94903 ☎ 415/499-9490 or 800/221-2260 🖷 415/499-9491 ⊕ www.villasintl.com. 🛈 Italy-Only Agencies **Cuendet USA** ✉ 165 Chestnut St., Allendale, NJ 07041 ☎ 201/327-2333 ✉ **Suzanne T. Pidduck**, c/o Rentals in Italy, 1742 Calle Corva, Camarillo, CA 93010 ☎ 800/726-6702. **Vacanze in Italia** ✉ 22 Railroad St., Great Barrington, MA 01230 🖷 413/528-6610 or 800/533-5405.

FARM HOLIDAYS & AGRITOURISM
Staying on working farms or vineyards, often in old stone farmhouses that accommodate a number of guests, has become more and more popular. Contact local tourist offices or consult *Agriturism* (www.agriturismo.com) for more than 1,600 farms in Italy. Although it's in Italian, the publication has photos and descriptions that make it a useful resource.
🛈 Agencies **Italy Farm Holidays** ✉ 547 Martling Ave., Tarrytown, NY 10591 ☎ 914/631-7880 🖷 914/631-8831 ⊕ www.italyfarmholidays.com.

HOME EXCHANGES
If you would like to exchange your home for someone else's, join a home-exchange organization, which will send you its updated listings of available exchanges for a year and will include your own listing in at least one of them. It's up to you to make specific arrangements.
🛈 Exchange Clubs **HomeLink USA** ✉ 2937 NW 9th Terrace, Wilton Manors, FL 33311 ☎ 954/566-2687 or 800/638-3841 🖷 954/566-2783 ⊕ www.homelink.org; $75 yearly for a listing and online access; $45 additional to receive directories. **Intervac U.S.** ✉ 30 Corte San Fernando, Tiburon, CA 94920 ☎ 800/756-4663 🖷 415/435-7440 ⊕ www.intervacus.com; $128 yearly for a listing, online access, and a catalog; $68 without catalog.

HOSTELS
No matter what your age, you can save on lodging costs by staying at hostels. Hostels

in Italy are found both in remote towns and large cities. They range from the bare-bones dormitory-style rooms (no linens provided) to comfortable accommodations resembling bed-and-breakfasts. Many offer rooms for couples or families. When booking, inquire about the noise level—some hostels with a young clientele are lax in enforcing evening quiet hours.

In some 4,500 locations in more than 70 countries around the world, Hostelling International (HI), the umbrella group for a number of national youth-hostel associations, offers single-sex, dorm-style beds and, at many hostels, rooms for couples and family accommodations. Membership in any HI national hostel association, open to travelers of all ages, allows you to stay in HI-affiliated hostels at member rates; one-year membership is about $28 for adults (C$35 for a two-year minimum membership in Canada, £15 in the U.K., A$52 in Australia, and NZ$40 in New Zealand); hostels charge about $10–$30 per night. Members have priority if the hostel is full; they're also eligible for discounts around the world, even on rail and bus travel in some countries.

🏠 Local Hostels **Foresteria Valdese** ✉ 5170 Castello, off Campo Santa Maria Formosa, 30122 ☎ 041/5286797 🖷 041/2416238 ⊕ chiesavaldese. org/venezia. **Istituto Canossiano** ✉ Ponte Piccolo 428, Giudecca, 30133 ☎ 041/5222157, women only; no bookings, show up in the morning. **Ostello di Venezia** ✉ Fondamenta delle Zitelle 86, Giudecca, 30133 ☎ 041/5238211 🖷 041/5235689 ⊕ www. hostelbooking.com.

🏠 Organizations **Hostelling International–USA** ✉ 8401 Colesville Rd., Suite 600, Silver Spring, MD 20910 ☎ 301/495-1240 🖷 301/495-6697 ⊕ www. hiusa.org. **Hostelling International–Canada** ✉ 205 Catherine St., Suite 400, Ottawa, Ontario K2P 1C3 ☎ 613/237-7884 or 800/663-5777 🖷 613/ 237-7868 ⊕ www.hihostels.ca. **YHA England and Wales** ✉ Trevelyan House, Dimple Rd., Matlock, Derbyshire DE4 3YH, U.K. ☎ 0870/870-8808, 0870/ 770-8868, 0162/959-2600 🖷 0870/770-6127 ⊕ www.yha.org.uk. **YHA Australia** ✉ 422 Kent St., Sydney, NSW 2001 ☎ 02/9261-1111 🖷 02/9261-1969 ⊕ www.yha.com.au. **YHA New Zealand** ✉ Level 1, Moorhouse City, 166 Moorhouse Ave., Box 436, Christchurch ☎ 03/379-9970 or 0800/278-299 🖷 03/365-4476 ⊕ www.yha.org.nz.

HOTELS

Italian hotels are classified from five-star (deluxe) to one-star (very basic hotels and small inns). Stars are assigned according to standards set by regional boards (there are 20 in Italy), but rates are set by each hotel. During slack periods, or when a hotel is not full, you can often negotiate a discounted rate. In the major cities, room rates are on a par with other European capitals: deluxe and four-star rates can be quite extravagant. In these categories, ask for one of the better rooms, since less desirable rooms—and there usually are some—don't give you what you're paying for. Except in deluxe and some four-star hotels, rooms may be very small by U.S standards.

A lovely canal view may come at a price—noise. For a city without cars, diesel boats and vaporetto landings can become unnervingly noisy. Also beware of booking a room directly opening onto a campo or busy calle, especially during Carnevale season.

In all hotels there is a rate card inside the door of your room, or inside the closet door; it tells you exactly what you will pay for that particular room (rates in the same hotel may vary according to the location and type of room). On this card, breakfast and any other optionals must be listed separately. Any discrepancy between the basic room rate and that charged on your bill is cause for complaint to the manager and to the local tourist office.

Although, by law, breakfast is supposed to be optional, most hotels quote room rates including breakfast. When you book a room, specifically ask whether the rate includes breakfast (*colazione*). You are under no obligation to take breakfast at your hotel, but in practice most hotels expect you to do so. The trick is to "offer" guests "complimentary" breakfast and have its cost built into the rate. However, it is encouraging to note that many of the hotels we recommend are offering generous buffet breakfasts instead of simple, even skimpy "Continental breakfasts." Remember, if the latter is the case, you can eat for less at the nearest coffee bar.

Hotels that we list as ($$) and ($)—moderate to inexpensively priced accommodations—may charge extra for optional air-conditioning. In older hotels the quality of the rooms may be very uneven; if you don't like the room you're given, request another. This applies to noise, too. Front rooms may be larger and have a view, but they also may have a lot of street noise. If you're a light sleeper, request a quiet room when making reservations. Rooms in lodgings listed in this guide have a shower and/or bath, unless noted otherwise. Remember to specify whether you care to have a bath or shower, since not all rooms, especially in lodgings outside major cities, have both.

You can save considerably on hotel rooms in Venice during low season, especially November through March (except during Carnevale and from December 22 to January 6, both periods considered high season). In July and August, prices are slightly lower than in the spring and autumn months.

Associazione Veneziana Albergatori, an association of hotel keepers, operates a booking service by phone, fax, and at booths serving entry points around Venice. There's a kiosk inside Santa Lucia train station (open 8 AM–9 PM), one at Marco Polo airport (open 8 AM–10 PM), and one kiosk in each of the two Piazzale Roma parking garages (open 9 AM–10 PM). This service is free, but you'll have to pay a deposit (€11–€47 per person; Visa and MasterCard accepted), which will be deducted from your hotel bill. Alternatively, Venezia Sì offers free reservations over the phone Monday–Saturday 9–7.

🚩 Reserving a Room **AVA hotel-reservation service booths** ⊠ Piazzale Roma ☎ 041/5231397 and 041/5228640 ⊠ Santa Lucia train station ☎ 041/715288 and 041/715016 ⊠ Marco Polo airport ☎ 041/5415133. **Venezia Sì** ☎ 800/843006 in Italy [toll-free, Mon.–Sat. 9 AM–7 PM], 0039/0415222264 from abroad 🖷 0039/0415221242.

🚩 Toll-Free Numbers **Best Western** ☎ 800/528-1234 ⊕ www.bestwestern.com. **Choice** ☎ 800/424-6423 ⊕ www.choicehotels.com. **Comfort Inn** ☎ 800/424-6423 ⊕ www.choicehotels.com. **Hilton** ☎ 800/445-8667 ⊕ www.hilton.com. **Holiday Inn**

☎ 800/465-4329 ⊕ www.sixcontinentshotels.com. **Jolly** ☎ 800/247-1277 in New York state, 800/221-2626 elsewhere in U.S., 800/237-0319 in Canada, 800/017703 in Italy. **Quality Inn** ☎ 800/424-6423 ⊕ www.choicehotels.com. **Radisson** ☎ 800/333-3333 ⊕ www.radisson.com. **Ramada** ☎ 800/228-2828, 800/854-7854 international reservations ⊕ www.ramada.com or www.ramadahotels.com. **Sheraton** ☎ 800/325-3535 ⊕ www.starwood.com/sheraton. **Westin Hotels & Resorts** ☎ 800/228-3000 ⊕ www.starwood.com/westin.

MAIL & SHIPPING
The Italian mail system isn't the world's fastest and it can take up to 15 days for mail to or from the United States and Canada, and a week to or from the United Kingdom (or even within Italy). Though Posta Prioritaria and Postacelere are faster, they rarely meet their "guarantee" of delivery within 24 hours in Italy and 3–5 days abroad.

Venice's main post office is open Monday–Saturday 8:30–6:30.
🚩 Post Office **Venice main post office** ⊠ Fondaco dei Tedeschi, near Rialto Bridge ☎ 041/5289257, 160 countrywide postal information.

OVERNIGHT SERVICES
Overnight mail is generally available during the week in all major cities and at popular resorts. Service is reliable; a Federal Express letter to the United States costs about €30, to the United Kingdom, €51, and to Australia and New Zealand, €33. Overnight delivery usually means 24–36 hours.

If your hotel can't assist you, try an Internet café, many of which also offer overnight mail services using major carriers at reasonable rates.
🚩 Major Services **DHL** ☎ 199-199-345 ⊕ www.dhl.it. **Federal Express** ☎ 800/123800 ⊕ www.fedex.com. **SDA** ☎ 800/016027 ⊕ www.sda.it.

POSTAL RATES
Airmail letters and postcards sent *ordinaria* to the United States and Canada cost €0.65 for up to 20 grams, €1 for 21 to 50 grams, and €1.30 for 51 to 100 grams. Always stick the blue airmail tag on your mail, or write AIRMAIL in big, clear letters

beside the address. Mail sent *ordinaria* to Italy, the United Kingdom, and other EU countries costs €0.45 for the first 20 grams.

For faster service, use priority delivery *Posta Prioritaria* (for small letters and packages), which guarantees delivery within Italy in three to five business days and abroad in five to six working days. The more expensive express delivery *Postacelere* (for larger letters and packages) guarantees one-day delivery to most places in Italy and three- to five-day delivery abroad.

Mail sent as Posta Prioritaria to the United States and Canada costs €0.80 for up to 20 grams, €1.50 for 21 to 50 grams, and €1.80 for 51 to 100 grams; to Italy, the United Kingdom, and other EU countries it costs €0.62. Mail sent as Postacelere to the United States and Canada costs €35.05 for up to 500 grams. If you're shipping to the United Kingdom or elsewhere in Europe, the cost is €28.15.

Other package services to check are Quick Pack Europe, for delivery within Europe; and EMS ExpressMail Service, a global three- to five-day service for letters and packages that can be less expensive than Postacelere.

RECEIVING MAIL

Correspondence can be addressed to you care of the Italian post office. Letters should be addressed to your name, "c/o Ufficio Postale Centrale," followed by "Fermo Posta" on the next line, and "30124 Venice" on the next. You can collect it at the central post office by showing your passport or photo-bearing ID and paying a small fee. American Express also has a general-delivery service. There's no charge for cardholders, holders of American Express traveler's checks, or anyone who booked a vacation with American Express.

SHIPPING PARCELS

You can ship parcels via air or surface. Air takes about two weeks, and surface anywhere up to three months. If you have purchased antiques, ceramics, or other objects, inquire to see if the vendor will do the shipping for you; in most cases, this is a possibility.

MONEY MATTERS

Italy's prices are in line with those in the rest of Europe, with costs in the main cities comparable to those in other major capitals, such as Paris and London. Venice is the most expensive city in Italy, and is therefore one of Europe's priciest tourist destinations. Efforts are being made to hold the line on hotel and restaurant prices that have become inordinately high by U.S. standards. Depending on season and occupancy, you may be able to obtain unadvertised lower rates in hotels; always inquire.

In Venice, an inexpensive hotel room for two, including breakfast, is about €90 in low season, nearly twice as much during spring and fall, and can go even higher during Carnevale. An inexpensive restaurant dinner for two is €30, with a simple pasta dish on the menu running about €10 and ½-liter carafe of house wine €4. A *bacaro* (wine bar) lunch is €15, including a glass of good wine. A Coca-Cola (standing) at a caffè is €2, a cup of coffee €1, and a pint of beer from a pub or pizzeria (at the table) €5.

Prices throughout this guide are given for adults. Substantially reduced fees are almost always available for children, students, and senior citizens. For information on taxes, *see* Taxes.

ATMS

An ATM (*bancomat* in Italian) is the easiest way to get euros in Italy. They are fairly common in large cities and small towns, as well as in airports and train stations. They are not common in places like grocery stores. Be sure to memorize your PIN number, as ATM keypads in Italy don't always display letters.

CREDIT CARDS

All over Italy, Visa and MasterCard are preferred to American Express, but in tourist areas American Express is usually accepted. While increasingly common, not all establishments and stores take credit cards, and some require a minimum expenditure. If you want to pay with a card in a small hotel, store, or restaurant, it's a good idea to make your intentions known early on.

Throughout this guide, the following abbreviations are used: **AE**, American Express; **DC**, Diners Club; **MC**, Master-Card; and **V**, Visa.

🔳 Reporting Lost Cards **American Express** ☎ 800/874 333 international collect. **Diners Club** ☎ 702/797–5532 collect. **MasterCard** ☎ 800/ 870866 toll-free within Italy. **Visa** ☎ 800/877232 toll-free within Italy.

CURRENCY

The euro is the main unit of currency in Italy, as well as in 11 other European countries. Under the euro system there are 100 *centesimi* (cents) to the euro. There are coins valued at 1, 2, 5, 10, 20, and 50 cents, as well as 1 and 2 euros. There are seven notes: 5, 10, 20, 50, 100, 200, and 500 euros.

CURRENCY EXCHANGE

At this writing, the exchange rate was about 0.85 euros to the U.S. dollar; 0.74 euros to the Canadian dollar; 1.48 euros to the pound sterling; 0.64 euros to the Australian dollar; and 0.61 euros to the New Zealand dollar.

For the most favorable rates, change money through banks. Although ATM transaction fees may be higher abroad than at home, ATM rates are excellent because they're based on wholesale rates offered only by major banks. You won't do as well at exchange booths in airports or rail and bus stations, in hotels, in restaurants, or in stores. To avoid lines at airport exchange booths, get a bit of local currency before you leave home.

🔳 Exchange Services **International Currency Express** ✉ 427 N. Camden Dr., Suite F, Beverly Hills, CA 90210 ☎ 888/278–6628 orders 🖷 310/278–6410 🌐 www.foreignmoney.com. **Travel Ex Currency Services** ☎ 800/287–7362 orders and retail locations 🌐 www.travelex.com.

TRAVELER'S CHECKS

Do you need traveler's checks? It depends on where you're headed. If you're going to rural areas and small towns, go with cash; traveler's checks are best used in cities.

Lost or stolen checks can usually be replaced within 24 hours. To ensure a speedy refund, buy your own traveler's checks—don't let someone else pay for them: irregularities like this can cause delays. The person who bought the checks should make the call to request a refund. Make sure to get traveler's checks in euros, not U.S. dollars.

PACKING

The weather is milder in the Veneto region than in the north and central United States or Great Britain. In summer, generally stick with light clothing, but keep in mind that, after dark, a light sweater can come in handy, especially at higher altitudes. An umbrella can spare you a sudden drenching from the all too common summer afternoon thundershowers (and it's handy in winter as well). Do not underestimate the humid cold of Venetian winters; a waterproof coat is a must, and it should be well-lined. A hat, scarf, gloves and comfortable, watertight shoes or boots will make walking tours more enjoyable. Some museums and most churches lack central heating, but elsewhere you should be able to escape the cold indoors.

Venetians may be less fashion-conscious than Romans, Florentines, and Milanese, but Italians in general dress exceptionally well. You won't see Venetians wearing shorts and tennis shoes around town. Men aren't required to wear ties or jackets anywhere, except in some of the grander hotel dining rooms and top-level restaurants, but they are expected to look reasonably sharp—and they do. Italian women usually wear skirts even in winter, and if pants are worn, they're generally the dressy sort. Formal wear has become the exception rather than the rule at the opera, though people in expensive seats usually do dress up.

For sightseeing, pack a pair of binoculars; they will help you get a good look at painted ceilings and domes. If you stay in budget hotels, take your own soap; many such hotels do not provide it, or give guests only one tiny bar per room.

The benefit of packing light is especially is compounded when you visit Venice. Getting around can be difficult even when un-encumbered, and can become a nightmare when toting large bags. The wheeled variety help, except when crossing bridges and when flooded streets force you to lift them onto raised walkways. Porters are notoriously hard to find even at the train station, and crosstown porterage is expensive. When riding the vaporetto, if you're bag exceeds 50 cm (28 in), you can be forced to buy an extra ticket for the bag.

In your carry-on luggage, pack an extra pair of eyeglasses or contact lenses and enough of any medication you take to last a few days longer than the entire trip. You may also ask your doctor to write a spare prescription using the drug's generic name, as brand names may vary from country to country. In luggage to be checked, never pack prescription drugs, valuables, or un-developed film. And don't forget to carry with you the addresses of offices that handle refunds of lost traveler's checks. Check *Fodor's How to Pack* (available at on-line retailers and bookstores everywhere) for more tips.

To avoid customs and security delays, carry medications in their original packaging. Don't pack any sharp objects in your carry-on luggage, including knives of any size or material, scissors, and corkscrews, or anything else that might arouse suspicion.

To avoid having your checked luggage chosen for hand inspection, don't cram bags full. The U.S. Transportation Security Administration suggests packing shoes on top and placing personal items you don't want touched in clear plastic bags.

CHECKING LUGGAGE

You're allowed to carry aboard one bag and one personal article, such as a purse or a laptop computer. Make sure what you carry on fits under your seat or in the overhead bin. Get to the gate early, so you can board as soon as possible, before the overhead bins fill up.

Baggage allowances vary by carrier, destination, and ticket class. On international flights, you're usually allowed to check two bags weighing up to 70 pounds (32 kilograms) each, although a few airlines allow checked bags of up to 88 pounds (40 kilograms) in first class. Some international carriers don't allow more than 66 pounds (30 kilograms) per bag in business class and 44 pounds (20 kilograms) in economy. If you're flying to or through the United Kingdom, your luggage cannot exceed 70 pounds (32 kilograms) per bag. On domestic flights, the limit is usually 50 to 70 pounds (23 to 32 kilograms) per bag. In general, carry-on bags shouldn't exceed 40 pounds (18 kilograms). Most airlines won't accept bags that weigh more than 100 pounds (45 kilograms) on domestic or international flights. Expect to pay a fee for baggage that exceeds weight limits. Check baggage restrictions with your carrier before you pack.

Airline liability for baggage is limited to $2,500 per person on flights within the United States. On international flights it amounts to $9.07 per pound or $20 per kilogram for checked baggage (roughly $640 per 70-pound bag), with a maximum of $634.90 per piece, and $400 per passenger for unchecked baggage. You can buy additional coverage at check-in for about $10 per $1,000 of coverage, but it often excludes a rather extensive list of items, shown on your airline ticket.

Before departure, itemize your bags' contents and their worth, and label the bags with your name, address, and phone number. (If you use your home address, cover it so potential thieves can't see it readily.) Include a label inside each bag and pack a copy of your itinerary. At check-in, make sure each bag is correctly tagged with the destination airport's three-letter code. Because some checked bags will be opened for hand inspection, the U.S. Transportation Security Administration recommends that you leave luggage unlocked or use the plastic locks offered at check-in. TSA screeners place an inspection notice inside searched bags, which are re-sealed with a special lock.

If your bag has been searched and contents are missing or damaged, file a claim with the TSA Consumer Response Center as soon as possible. If your bags arrive damaged or fail to arrive at all, file a written report with the airline before leaving the airport.

⚑ Complaints U.S. Transportation Security – Administration Contact Center ☎ 866/289–9673 ⊕ www.tsa.gov.

PASSPORTS & VISAS

When traveling internationally, carry your passport even if you don't need one (it's always the best form of ID) and make two photocopies of the data page (one for someone at home and another for you, carried separately from your passport). If you lose your passport, promptly call the nearest embassy or consulate and the local police.

U.S. passport applications for children under age 14 require consent from both parents or legal guardians; both parents must appear together to sign the application. If only one parent appears, he or she must submit a written statement from the other parent authorizing passport issuance for the child. A parent with sole authority must present evidence of it when applying; acceptable documentation includes the child's certified birth certificate listing only the applying parent, a court order specifically permitting this parent's travel with the child, or a death certificate for the nonapplying parent. Application forms and instructions are available on the Web site of the U.S. State Department's Bureau of Consular Affairs (⊕ travel.state.gov).

ENTERING ITALY

Citizens of Australia, Canada, New Zealand, and the United States need only a valid passport to enter Italy for stays of up to 90 days. Citizens of the United Kingdom need only a valid passport to enter Italy for an unlimited stay.

PASSPORT OFFICES

The best time to apply for a passport or to renew is in fall and winter. Before any trip, check your passport's expiration date, and, if necessary, renew it as soon as possible.

⚑ Australian Citizens Passports Australia Australian Department of Foreign Affairs and Trade ☎ 131–232 ⊕ www.passports.gov.au.

⚑ Canadian Citizens Passport Office ✉ to mail in applications: 70 Cremazie St., Gatineau, Québec J8Y

3P2 ☎ 819/994–3500 or 800/567–6868 ⊕ www.ppt.gc.ca.

⚑ New Zealand Citizens New Zealand Passports Office ☎ 0800/22–5050 or 04/474–8100 ⊕ www.passports.govt.nz.

⚑ U.K. Citizens U.K. Passport Service ☎ 0870/521–0410 ⊕ www.passport.gov.uk.

⚑ U.S. Citizens National Passport Information Center ☎ 877/487–2778, 888/874–7793 TDD/TTY ⊕ travel.state.gov.

RESTROOMS

Public restrooms aren't common in Italy, but Venice does have pay toilets scattered throughout the city, including on the Lido and the other islands. They're well posted and strategically located along the main tourist routes: at Piazzale Roma; near Rialto Bridge (both sides); on Strada Nova, near Ponte delle Guglie; near Accademia Bridge vaporetto landing; and next to the tourist information office at the Giardinetti Reali, close to Piazza San Marco. The charge is €.50 and nearly all are accessible to wheelchairs. While private businesses rarely permit passersby to use their toilets, most bars will allow you if you ask politely, or alternatively, buy a little something—a mineral water or espresso—in exchange for their kindness. Standards of cleanliness and comfort vary greatly. While hotels, department stores like La Rinascente and Coin, and restaurants, including McDonald's, tend to have the cleanest restrooms, those in pubs and bars rank among the worst. It is always best to carry your own tissue. You'll find well-kept pay toilets (for €.50–€1) in airports, major train stations, and in most museums. There are also bathrooms at highway rest stops and gas stations where a small tip (€.25–€.50) to the cleaning person is standard practice. Churches, post offices, public beaches, or subway stations rarely have public facilities.

SAFETY

Day or night, violent crime is extremely rare in Venice, but this is a city ripe for crimes of opportunity. Expert thieves couldn't find a better place to work than where vacationing spenders are too busy ogling to be aware of stealthy pickpockets. Concentrating in busy streets and squares, jam-packed vaporetti, and chaotic train stations, these pros, generally working in teams, can stall traffic, jostle a person, and pass colleagues the wallet too fast for anyone's reflexes to respond. Protect yourself *before* going out. A money belt or a pouch hung around the neck works as long as strings or bulges are not visible, otherwise these too have disappeared. Slinging bags or cameras across your body bandolier-style, and even covering them with your coat are not bad ideas, but are not guarantees. Nothing protects better than awareness.

WOMEN IN ITALY

The difficulties encountered by women traveling alone in Italy are often overstated. Younger women have to put up with much male attention, but it is rarely dangerous. Ignoring whistling and questions is the best way to get rid of unwanted attention.

SENIOR-CITIZEN TRAVEL

EU citizens over 60 are entitled to free admission to state museums, as well as to many other museums—always ask at the ticket office. Older travelers may be eligible for special fares on Alitalia.

To qualify for age-related discounts, mention your senior-citizen status up front when booking hotel reservations (not when checking out) and before you're seated in restaurants (not when paying the bill). Be sure to have identification on hand. When renting a car, ask about promotional car-rental discounts, which can be cheaper than senior-citizen rates.

F Educational Programs **Elderhostel** ⊠ 11 Ave. de Lafayette, Boston, MA 02111-1746 ☎ 877/426–8056, 978/323–4141 international callers, 877/426–2167 TTY ᕍ 877/426–2166 ⊕ www.elderhostel.org. **Interhostel** ⊠ University of New Hampshire, 6 Garrison Ave., Durham, NH 03824 ☎ 603/862–1147 or 800/733–9753 ᕍ 603/862–1113 ⊕ www.learn.unh.edu.

SIGHTSEEING TOURS

BOAT TOURS

Boat tours to the islands of Murano, Burano, and Torcello, organized by Serenissima Motoscafi and Consorzio San Marco, leave from various docks around Piazza San Marco daily. These 3½-hour trips cost €18 (Serenissima Motoscafi) or €40 (Consorzio San Marco) and can be annoyingly commercial, often emphasizing glass-factory showrooms and pressuring you to buy at prices even higher than normal. Trips depart at 9:30 and 2:30 April–October, at 2:30 November–March.

More than a dozen major travel agents in Venice have grouped together to provide frequent, good-quality tours of the city. Serenaded gondola trips, with or without dinner (€73, €35), can be purchased at any of their offices or at American Express. Nightly tours leave at 7:30 and 8:30 April–September, at 7:30 only in October, and at 3:30 November–March.

F **American Express** ⊠ Salizada San Moisè, San Marco 1471 ☎ 041/5200844 ᕍ 041/5229937. **Consorzio San Marco** ☎ 041/2406712. **Serenissima Motoscafi** ☎ 041/5224281.

EXCURSION TOURS

American Express and other agencies offer several excursions in the Veneto region of the Venetian Arc. A boat trip to Padua along the Brenta River makes stops at three Palladian villas, and you return to Venice by bus. The tours run three times a week (Tuesday, Thursday, and Saturday) from March to October and cost €62 per person (€86 with lunch); bookings need to be made a few days in advance.

Bassani offers excursions as well as personalized travel through the Veneto and other Italian cities.

F **American Express** ⊠ Salizada San Moisè, San Marco 1471 ☎ 041/5200844 ᕍ 041/5229937. **Avventure Bellissime** ⊠ San Marco 2442/A ☎ 041/5208616 ᕍ 041/2960282 ⊕ www.tours-italy.com. **Bassani** ⊠ San Basilio, Santa Marta, Fab. 17 ☎ 041/5203644 ᕍ 041/5204009 ⊕ www.bassani.it

WALKING TOURS

More than a dozen major travel agents offer a two-hour walking tour of the San Marco area (€28), which ends with a glassblowing demonstration daily (no Sunday tour in winter). From April to October there's also an afternoon walking tour that ends with a gondola ride (€37). Venice-scapes, an Italo-American cultural association, offers several themed itineraries focusing on history and culture as well as tourist sights. Their three- to seven-hour tours are private, and groups are small (generally six to eight people). Reservations are recommended during busy seasons, and prices start at €200 for two people. Walks Inside Venice also does several themed tours for small groups starting at €65 per hour and lasting up to three hours.

Alba Travel ⊠ Calle del Magazin, San Marco 4538 ☎ 041/5210123 🖷 041/5200781 ⊕ www.albatravel.it. **Oltrex Viaggi** ⊠ Castello 4192 ☎ 041/5242840 🖷 041/5221986 ⊕ www.oltrex.it. **Venicescapes** ⊠ Campo San Provolo, Castello 4954 ☎🖷 041/5206361 ⊕ www.venicescapes.org. **Walks Inside Venice** ☎🖷 041/5202434 ⊕ www.walksinsidevenice.com.

SMOKING

In 2005, smoking was banned in many public places, including bars and restaurants. Although Italians are for the most part unrepentant smokers, they are begrudgingly obeying the law. Always check to see if there's a VIETATO FUMARE (no smoking) sign before lighting up. All Italian trains have no-smoking cars (ask for one when making reservations), and Eurostar trains are smoke-free.

STUDENTS

The Rolling Venice pass, costing €3 and valid throughout a calendar year, buys visitors ages 14–29 discounts on 72-hour vaporetto passes and at assorted hotels, restaurants, and shops, as well as admission to many museums. To purchase a card you need to show your passport at Vela ticket offices (major vaporetto stops), at the Assessorato alla Gioventù (weekdays 9:30–1, plus Tuesday and Thursday afternoons 3–5), or at the Associazione Italiana Alberghi per la Gioventù (Monday through Saturday 8–2).

Rolling Venice ☎ 041/2714747 ⊕ www.comune.venezia.it/rol2/. **Assessorato alla Gioventù** ⊠ Corte Contarina, San Marco 1529, behind Piazza San Marco post office ☎ 041/2747651. **Associazione Italiana Alberghi per la Gioventù** ⊠ Calle Castelforte, San Polo 3101, near San Rocco ☎ 041/5204414. **Centro Turistico Studentesco** (CTS) ⊠ opposite Ca' Foscari University, Dorsoduro 3252 Venezia ☎ 041/5205660 ⊕ www.cts.it.

TAXES

VALUE-ADDED TAX

The V.A.T. is 20% on clothing, wine, and luxury goods. On consumer goods it's already included in the amount shown on the price tag, whereas on services it may not be. If your purchases total more than €155 at a store displaying a EURO TAX FREE sign, present your passport and request a "Tax Free Shopping Check."

When making a purchase, ask for a V.A.T. refund form and find out whether the merchant gives refunds—not all stores do, nor are they required to. Have the form stamped like any customs form by customs officials when you leave the country or, if you're visiting several European Union countries, when you leave the EU. Be ready to show customs officials what you've bought (pack purchases together, in your carry-on luggage); budget extra time for this. After you're through passport control, take the form to a refund-service counter for an on-the-spot refund (which is usually the quickest and easiest option), or mail it to the address on the form (or the envelope with it) after you arrive home.

A service processes refunds for most shops. You receive the total refund stated on the form. Global Refund is a Europe-wide service with 210,000 affiliated stores and more than 700 refund counters—located at major airports and border crossings. Its refund form is called a Tax Free Check. The service issues refunds in the form of cash, check, or credit-card adjustment. If you don't have time to wait at the refund counter, you can mail in the form to an office in Europe or Canada instead.

V.A.T. Refunds Global Refund Canada ✉ Box 2020, Station Main, Brampton, Ontario L6T 3S3 ☎ 800/993-4313 🖷 905/791-9078 ⊕ www.globalrefund.com.

TAXIS

The only land taxi service is to and from the airport. Taxi stands are located in Piazzale Roma, and they also line up at the vaporetto landing as people arrive in Lido.

Taxi Companies Radio (land) Taxi ☎ 041/936222.

TELEPHONES

CALLS WITHIN ITALY

Italy's telephone system is quite reliable. Two basic facts to remember: telephone numbers do not have a standard number of digits (they can range anywhere from four to seven) and the entire area code must be included even when calling a number in the same city.

Cell phones are widely used by Italians, and as a result there isn't an abundance of public pay phones. If you need to make a lot of calls, consider renting or even buying a cell phone. Renting one costs about €20 per week plus the cost of a calling card, and a €100 deposit is normal. Buying a basic phone runs between €80 and €125.

Public pay phones may take coins, but more often require a *carta telefonica* (phone card) purchased at newsstands and tobacco shops. There are national cards and international cards, so make sure to specify which you want.

AREA & COUNTRY CODES

The country code for Italy is 39. Area codes (*prefissi*) for major cities in the Veneto region are as follows: Venice, 041; Verona, 045; Treviso, 0422; Padua, 049; Belluno, 0437; Vicenza, 0444; Rovigo, 0425. Note that in Italy, all calls, including local ones, must be preceded by the appropriate regional area code, zero included. Calls from abroad must be preceded by 39 and the regional area code, zero included. For example, a call from New York to Venice would be dialed as 011 + 39 + 041 + local phone number; from Venice to another number in Venice, dial 041 + local phone number; from Rome to Venice, 041 + local phone number. Country codes are 1 for the United States and Canada, 61 for Australia, 64 for New Zealand, and 44 for the United Kingdom.

CELL PHONES

In Italy, you're rarely beyond earshot of ringing *telefonini* ("little phones" or "cell phones"), which have become a national compulsion and are left on in restaurants, theaters, museums, trains, and buses. The three major service companies are Tim, Omnitel, and Wind. Each company has a series of prefixes (328, 338, 345), which never begin with a "0." For example, from New York, you dial an Italian cell phone with: 011 + 39 + 338 + personal phone number; in Italy, dial 338 + personal number. Receiving calls on Italian cell phones is free, unless the phone is outside of Italy and using another phone carrier for "roaming."

DIRECTORY & OPERATOR ASSISTANCE

For general information in English, dial 4176. To place international telephone calls via operator-assisted service, dial 170 or long-distance access numbers (⇨ Long-Distance Services, *below*).

INTERNATIONAL CALLS

Since hotels charge exorbitant rates for long-distance and international calls, it's best to call from public phones using telephone cards. You can make collect calls from any phone by dialing 170, which will get you an English-speaking operator. Rates to the United States are lowest all day Sunday and 10 PM–8 AM the rest of the week.

LOCAL & LONG-DISTANCE CALLS

For all calls within Italy, whether local or long-distance, dial the area code followed by the number. Rates for long-distance calls vary according to the time of day; it's cheaper to call before 9 AM and after 7 or 8 PM.

LONG-DISTANCE SERVICES

AT&T, MCI, and Sprint access codes make calling long-distance relatively convenient, but you may find the local access number blocked in many hotel rooms. First ask the hotel operator to connect you. If the hotel operator balks, ask for an international operator, or dial the international operator yourself. One way to improve your odds of getting connected to your long-distance carrier is to travel with more than one company's calling card (a hotel may block Sprint, for example, but not MCI). If all else fails, call from a pay phone. If you are travelling for a longer period of time, consider renting a cell-phone from a local company.

☑ Access Codes AT&T Direct ☎ 800/172-444. **MCI WorldPhone** ☎ 800/172-401/404. **Sprint International Access** ☎ 800/172-405.

PHONE CARDS

Prepaid *carte telefoniche* (phone cards) are available throughout Italy. Cards in different denominations are sold at post offices, newsstands, tobacco shops, and bars. For local or national cards, tear off the corner of the card and insert it in the slot. When you dial, its value appears in the window. After you hang up, the card is returned. International calling cards are different; you must call a toll-free number and dial a code number on the back of the card. The best card to use when calling North America or Europe is the €5 or €10 Europa card, which gives you a local number to dial and 180 minutes and 360 minutes of calling time.

TIME

Venice is 6 hours ahead of New York, 1 hour ahead of London, 10 hours behind Sydney, and 12 hours behind Auckland. Italy keeps time using the 24-hour (or "military") method, which means that after 12 noon you continue counting the hours forward: 1 PM is 13:00, 2 PM is 14:00, and so on.

TIPPING

Among Italian travelers, tipping until recently was considered the exception rather than the rule; however, the influx of foreigners in Venice has raised expectations among service industry workers. The following guidelines, which apply to Venice, could be reduced in smaller cities and towns. In an osteria or trattoria, unless the menu states that service is included, a service charge of about 12% may appear as a separate item on your bill. Either way, it's customary to leave an additional 5% to 10% tip, depending on the quality of service and the number of servers involved. Higher-priced restaurants rarely charge for service, relying on diners' generosity to compensate their staff. Tip checkroom attendants €.50 per person, restroom attendants €.20–€.30 (more in expensive hotels and restaurants). When seated at a bar, tip about 10% of the bar bill.

Italians tip taxi drivers only under exceptional circumstances but in Venice, where boat drivers are often expected to hoist heavy bags on and off the boat, €5–€10 is reasonable per couple. Railway and airport porters charge a fixed rate per bag but if porters are very helpful, tip an additional €1 per person. On sightseeing tours, tip guides about €1–€2 per person for a half-day group tour, more if they are very good. In museums and other places of interest where admission is free, helpful assistants should be tipped €1.

In Venice, though the hotel *portiere* (concierge) usually receives compensation from restaurants and taxis booked on your behalf, he still expects to be tipped, based on service you received, €10–€20. For two people in a double room in a moderately priced hotel, leave the chambermaid about €1–€2 per day and tip a minimum of €1 for valet or room service. Double those amounts in an expensive hotel. In expensive hotels, tip doormen €1 for calling a cab and a minimum of €2 for carrying bags to the check-in desk, bellhops €3–€4 for carrying your bags to the room.

TOURS & PACKAGES

Because everything is prearranged on a prepackaged tour or independent vacation, you spend less time planning—and often get it all at a good price.

BOOKING WITH AN AGENT

Travel agents are excellent resources. But it's a good idea to collect brochures from several agencies, as some agents' suggestions may be influenced by relationships with tour and package firms that reward them for volume sales. If you have a special interest, find an agent with expertise in that area. The American Society of Travel Agents (ASTA) has a database of specialists worldwide; you can log on to the group's Web site to find one near you.

Make sure your travel agent knows the accommodations and other services of the place being recommended. Ask about the hotel's location, room size, beds, and whether it has a pool, room service, or programs for children, if you care about these. Has your agent been there in person or sent others whom you can contact?

Do some homework on your own, too: local tourism boards can provide information about lesser-known and small-niche operators, some of which may sell only direct.

BUYER BEWARE

Each year consumers are stranded or lose their money when tour operators—even large ones with excellent reputations—go out of business. So check out the operator. Ask several travel agents about its reputation, and try to book with a company that has a consumer-protection program. (Look for information in the company's brochure.) In the United States, members of the United States Tour Operators Association are required to set aside funds (up to $1 million) to help eligible customers cover payments and travel arrangements in the event that the company defaults. It's also a good idea to choose a company that participates in the American Society of Travel Agents' Tour Operator Program; ASTA will act as mediator in any disputes between you and your tour operator.

Remember that the more your package or tour includes, the better you can predict the ultimate cost of your vacation. Make sure you know exactly what is covered, and beware of hidden costs. Are taxes, tips, and transfers included? Entertainment and excursions? These can add up.

🗐 Tour-Operator Recommendations **American Society of Travel Agents** (⇨ Travel Agencies). **CrossSphere–The Global Association for Packaged Travel** ⊠ 546 E. Main St., Lexington, KY 40508 ☎ 859/226-4444 or 800/682-8886 🖷 859/226-4414 ⊕ www.CrossSphere.com. **United States Tour Operators Association (USTOA)** ⊠ 275 Madison Ave., Suite 2014, New York, NY 10016 ☎ 212/599-6599 🖷 212/599-6744 ⊕ www.ustoa.com.

TRAIN TRAVEL

In Italy, traveling by train is simple and efficient. Service between major cities is frequent, and trains usually arrive on schedule. You can either purchase your tickets in advance (all major credit cards are accepted online at ⊕ www.raileurope.com) or after you arrive at any train station or travel agency. If you are considering using a Eurail Pass or any of its

variations you must buy the pass before leaving your home country, as they are not sold in Italy.

You must validate your ticket before boarding the train by punching it at a yellow box located in the waiting area of smaller train stations or at the end of the track in larger stations. Always purchase tickets before boarding the train, as you can no longer purchase one from a conductor. Fines are steep for pasengers without tickets.

The fastest trains on *Trenitalia,* the Italian State Railways, are the Eurostar trains that run between major cities. You will be assigned a specific seat in a specific coach. To avoid having to squeeze through narrow aisles, board only at your designated coach (the number on your ticket matches the one on near the door of each coach). The next-fastest trains are the *Intercity* (IC) trains. Reservations, required for some IC trains, are always advisable. *Diretto* and *Interregionale* trains make more stops and are a little slower. *Regionale* and *locale* trains are the slowest; many serve commuters. There are refreshments on all long-distance trains, purchased from a mobile cart or a dining car.

Traveling by night is a good deal, as you do not pay extra for a bed. More comfortable trains run on the longer routes (Sicily–Rome, Sicily–Milan, Sicily–Venice, Rome–Turin, Lecce–Milan); ask for the good-value T3, Intercity Notte, and Carrozza Comfort. The Vagone Letto Excelsior has private bathrooms, coffee machines, microwave ovens, refrigerators, and a suite with a double bed and TV.

Some cities—Milan, Turin, Genoa, Naples, Florence and Rome included—have more than one train station, so be sure you get off at the right place. Except for Pisa and Rome, none of the major cities have trains that go directly to the airports, but there are commuter bus lines connecting train stations and airports.

Train strikes of various kinds are also common, so it's a good idea to make sure your train is running.
🗐 Train Information **Trenitalia** ☎ 892021 in Italy ⊕ www.trenitalia.com.

CLASSES

Most Italian trains have first and second classes. On local trains a first-class fare gets you little more than a clean doily on your headrest, but on long-distance trains you get wider seats, more legroom, and better ventilation and lighting. At peak travel times, a first-class fare is worth the price as the coaches are less crowded. In Italian, *prima classe* is first class; second is *seconda classe*.

CUTTING COSTS

To save money, look into rail passes. But be aware that if you don't plan to cover many miles, you may come out ahead by buying individual tickets. If Italy is your only destination, consider an Italian Flexi Rail Card Saver. Over the course of a month you can travel on four days ($239 first class, $191 second class) or eight days ($260 first class, $206 second class). These tickets are sold only outside Italy. They are cheaper if you travel in a group or are under 26.

Once in Italy, travelers over 60 can buy a *Carta d'Argento* (Silver Card). For €30 you get a 15% discount on first- and second-class tickets. Travelers under 26 can get the same deal with a *Cartaverde* (Green Card). Those under 26 can also get discount fares under the Billet International Jeune (BIJ) and Euro Domino Junior plans. *Comitive Ordinarie* (Ordinary Group Travel) entitle parties of at least six people to a 20% discount on most tickets.

Italy is one of 17 countries that accept Eurailpass, which allows unlimited first-class travel. If you plan to rack up the miles, get a standard pass. Passes are available for 15 days ($588), 21 days ($762), one month ($946), two months ($1,338), and three months ($1,654). You also get free or discounted fares on some ferry lines. The Eurail Selectpass allows for travel in three to five contiguous countries. Five days of first-class travel in three countries is $370; four countries $414; five countries $446.

In addition to standard Eurailpasses, ask about special plans. Among these are the Eurail Youthpass (for those under 26), the Eurail Flexipass (which allows a certain number of travel days within a set period), the Eurail Saver Flexipass (which give a discount for two or more people traveling together), and the EurailDrive Pass (which combines travel by train and rental car). All Eurailpasses must be purchased before you leave home. Order them on the Rail Europe Web site.

Remember that you need to reserve seats even if you are using a rail pass.

🚄 **Information & Passes** CIT Rail ✉ 15 W. 44th St., New York, NY 10036 ☎ 800/248-7245. **DER Tours** ☎ 800/782-2424 🖷 800/282-7474. **Rail Europe** ✉ 44 S. Broadway, White Plains, NY 10601 ☎ 800/438-7245 or 877/257-2887 ⊕ www.raileurope.com.

PAYING

You can pay for your train tickets in cash or with a major credit card such as American Express, Diners Club, MasterCard, and Visa.

RESERVATIONS

Trains can be very crowded, so it's always a good idea to make a reservation. You can reserve seats up to two months in advance at the train station or at a travel agent. Simply holding a train ticket does not guarantee a seat. In summer it's fairly common to see people standing for part of the journey.

TRAVEL AGENCIES

A good travel agent puts your needs first. Look for an agency that has been in business at least five years, emphasizes customer service, and has someone on staff who specializes in your destination. In addition, make sure the agency belongs to a professional trade organization. The American Society of Travel Agents (ASTA)—the largest and most influential in the field with more than 10,000 members in some 140 countries—maintains and enforces a strict code of ethics and will step in to help mediate any agent-client disputes involving ASTA members if necessary. ASTA also maintains a Web site that includes a directory of agents. (If a travel agency is also acting as your tour operator, *see* Buyer Beware *in* Tours and Packages.)

🚄 **Agents in Venice** Albatravel ✉ Calle dei Fabbri, San Marco 4538 ☎ 041/5210123 🖷 041/5200781.

American Express ✉ Salizzada San Moisè, San Marco 1471 ☎ 041/5200844 🖷 041/5229937. **Gran Canal** ✉ Ponte del Ovo, near the Rialto Bridge, San Marco 4759 ☎ 041/2712111 🖷 041/5223380. **Kele Teo** ✉ Ponte dei Bareteri, San Marco 4930 between San Marco and Rialto ☎ 041/5208722 🖷 041/5208913.
🛈 Local Agent Referrals **American Society of Travel Agents** (ASTA) ✉ 1101 King St., Suite 200, Alexandria, VA 22314 ☎ 703/739-2782 or 800/965-2782 24-hr hotline 🖷 703/684-8319 ⊕ www. astanet.com and www.travelsense.org. **Association of British Travel Agents** ✉ 68-71 Newman St., London W1T 3AH ☎ 020/7637-2444 🖷 020/7637-0713 ⊕ www.abta.com. **Association of Canadian Travel Agencies** ✉ 130 Albert St., Suite 1705, Ottawa, Ontario K1P 5G4 ☎ 613/237-3657 🖷 613/237-7052 ⊕ www.acta.ca. **Australian Federation of Travel Agents** ✉ Level 3, 309 Pitt St., Sydney, NSW 2000 ☎ 02/9264-3299 or 1300/363-416 🖷 02/9264-1085 ⊕ www.afta.com.au. **Travel Agents' Association of New Zealand** ✉ Level 5, Tourism and Travel House, 79 Boulcott St., Box 1888, Wellington 6001 ☎ 04/499-0104 🖷 04/499-0786 ⊕ www.taanz.org.nz.

VISITOR INFORMATION
Learn more about foreign destinations by checking government-issued travel advisories and country information. For a broader picture, consider information from more than one country.
🛈 At Home **Italian Government Tourist Board** (ENIT) ⊕ www.italiantourism.com ✉ 630 5th Ave., New York, NY 10111 ☎ 212/245-4822 🖷 212/586-9249 ✉ 401 N. Michigan Ave., Chicago, IL 60611 ☎ 312/644-0990 🖷 312/644-3019 ✉ 12400 Wilshire Blvd., Suite 550, Los Angeles, CA 90025 ☎ 310/820-0098 🖷 310/820-6357 ✉ 1 Pl. Ville Marie, Suite 1914, Montréal, Québec H3B 3M9 ☎ 514/866-7667 🖷 514/392-1429 ✉ 1 Princes St., London W1R 8AY ☎ 020/7408-1254 🖷 020/7493-6695.
🛈 Local Tourist Offices **Venice Tourist Offices** ⊕ www.turismovenezia.it ✉ Train Station, Cannaregio ☎ 041/5298727 ✉ Procuratie Nuove, San Marco 71/f, near Museo Correr ☎ 041/5298740 ✉ Venice Pavilion, San Marco, near Giardini Reali ☎ 041/5225150 ✉ Garage Comunale, Piazzale

Roma ☎ 041/2411499 ✉ S. Maria Elisabetta 6/a, Lido ⊕ Summer only ☎ 041/5265721.

Marostica ✉ Piazza Castello 1, 36063 ☎ 0424/72127 ⊕ www.marosticascacchi.it. **Padua** ✉ Stazione Ferroviaria, 35100 ☎ 049/8752077 ⊕ www.turismopadova.it. **Treviso** ✉ Piazzetta Monte di Pietà 8, 31100 ☎ 0422/547632 ⊕ www. provincia.treviso.it. **Trieste** ✉ Piazza dell'Unità Italia 4/b, 34100 ☎ 040/3478312 ✉ Via San Nicola 20, between train station and Piazza Unità ☎ 040/67961 ⊕ www.triestetourism.it. **Udine** ✉ Piazza Primo Maggio 7, 33100 ☎ 0432/295972 ⊕ www. turismo.fvg.it. **Verona** ✉ Piazza Brà, 37100 ☎ 045/8068680 ✉ Stazione FS ☎ 045/8000861 ⊕ www. tourism.verona.it. **Vicenza** ✉ Piazza Matteotti 12, 36100 ☎ 0444/320854 ⊕ www.vicenzae.org.
🛈 Government Advisories **U.S. Department of State** ✉ Bureau of Consular Affairs, Overseas Citizens Services Office, 2201 C St. NW, Washington, DC 20520 ☎ 202/647-5225, 888/407-4747 or 317/472-2328 for interactive hotline ⊕ www.travel.state.gov. **Consular Affairs Bureau of Canada** ☎ 800/267-6788 or 613/944-6788 ⊕ www.voyage.gc.ca. **U.K. Foreign and Commonwealth Office** ✉ Travel Advice Unit, Consular Directorate, Old Admiralty Building, London SW1A 2PA ☎ 0870/606-0290 or 020/7008-1500 ⊕ www.fco.gov.uk/travel. **Australian Department of Foreign Affairs and Trade** ☎ 300/139-281 travel advisories, 02/6261-1299 Consular Travel Advice ⊕ www.smartraveller.gov.au or www.dfat. gov.au. **New Zealand Ministry of Foreign Affairs and Trade** ☎ 04/439-8000 ⊕ www.mft.govt.nz.

WEB SITES
Do check out the World Wide Web when planning your trip. You'll find everything from weather forecasts to virtual tours of famous cities. Be sure to visit Fodors.com (⊕ www.fodors.com), a complete travel-planning site. You can research prices and book plane tickets, hotel rooms, rental cars, vacation packages, and more. In addition, you can post your pressing questions in the Travel Talk section. Other planning tools include a currency converter and weather reports, and there are loads of links to travel resources.

Exploring Venice

WORD OF MOUTH

"There's no way to adequately describe the uniqueness, the beauty, and the charm of Venice. It's like the Gand Canyon. It doesn't matter how many pictures you've seen, until you've come face to face with her, you can't begin to imagine her splendor."

—dcd

"Going through a city that has no cars, wandering over the many bridges and small canals, is thrilling. The sights are lovely, but the entire city is the important sight. You can *easily* avoid the tourist crowds by just walking away from the main tourist centers. And Venice at night is probably one of the most romantic places on earth."

—progol

Updated by
Pamela Santini

IT IS CALLED LA SERENISSIMA, or "the most serene," a reference to the monstrous power, majesty, and wisdom of this city that was for centuries the unrivaled leader in trade between Europe and the Orient and the staunch bulwark of Christendom against the tides of Turkish expansion. "The most serene" also refers to the way in which those visiting have looked upon Venice, a miraculous city imperturbably floating on its calm blue lagoon.

Built entirely on water by men who dared defy the sea, Venice is like no other place in the world. No matter how many times you have seen it in movies or TV commercials, the real thing is more dreamlike than you could ever imagine. Its most famous buildings, the Basilica di San Marco and the Palazzo Ducale, seem hardly Italian: delightfully idiosyncratic, they're exotic mixes of Byzantine, Gothic, and Renaissance styles. Shimmering sunlight and silvery mist soften every perspective here, making it easy to understand how the city became renowned in the Renaissance for its artists' rendering of color. It's a place full of secrets, inexpressibly romantic, and at times given over entirely to pleasure.

Getting Oriented & Getting Around

What you've heard is true: there really are no cars in Venice. You get around primarily on foot, but with occasional trips by boat on the famous canals that lace through the city.

The first step in understanding the lay of the land is to know that central Venice is divided into six *sestieri* (neighborhoods): **San Marco, Castello, Dorsoduro, Cannaregio, San Polo,** and **Santa Croce.** The districts were mandated by the government in 1170; what was at first a rather arbitrary dissection of the city now seems almost as natural a feature of Venice as its hundreds of man-made islands and canals. Over the course of time, each neighborhood developed its own distinctive atmosphere and layout. (*See* "What's Where" at the front of this book for descriptions of their distinguishing characteristics.)

Venetians have unique terms for the geographical features of their unique city. Here, a street is a **calle,** unless it runs alongside a canal, in which case it becomes **riva** or **fondamenta.** A street with shops can be a **ruga,** and if it's called **salizzada** that means it was among the first to be cobbled or paved. A small canal is a **rio** (**rii** plural), and a **rio terà** is a street created when a canal has been filled in. San Marco is the only square called a piazza in Venice—all the rest are called **campo, campiello,** or **corte** (field, little field, or yard), harking back to a time when they were used to grow vegetables and raise poultry.

Unlike other towns in Italy, Venice rarely has streets and squares dedicated to places or great figures in Italian history. Many streets retain names from establishments that once stood nearby, such as Calle del Cafetier (named for a coffee shop) or Ponte Tette (Bridge of Breasts, named for a nearby brothel). Others were named for saints or noble families, such as Corner, Morosini, and Tron. No one is certain what prompted such names as Ponte delle Maravegie (Bridge of the Wonders) or Ponte della Donna Onesta (Bridge of the Honest Woman); Ponte dei Pugni (Bridge of Fists), crossing Canale San Barnaba, earned its name for the ritual fistfights it once hosted, and you can still see on it the footprints that marked the fighters' starting corners.

Traveling by Boat

These are your basic boat-going options:

Vaporetto. Water buses run up and down the Grand Canal, around the city, and out to the surrounding islands. They're Venice's primary means of public transportation.

Gondola. Traveling by gondola is a romantic, pricey joyride (rather than a way to get from one place to another). You pay by the hour. Be sure to agree on the fare before boarding, and ask to be taken down smaller side canals.

Traghetto. There are only three bridges across the Grand Canal. *Traghetti* are gondola-like ferries (rowed by gondoliers in training) that fill in the gaps, going from one bank to the other in eight spots. They can save a lot of walking, and they're a cheap (€.50), quick taste of the gondola experience.

Water taxi. A more accurate name might be "water limousine"—sky-high fares make taxis an indulgent way to get around.

For all the details, see "Boat & Ferry Travel" in the Smart Travel Tips section at the front of the book.

Traveling by Foot

Finding your way around Venice on foot presents some unusual problems: the city's layout has few straight lines; house numbering seems nonsensical; and the sestieri all duplicate each other's street names.

To minimize confusion, yellow signs are posted on many busy corners pointing toward the major landmarks—San Marco, Rialto, Accademia, etc.—though you can't count on finding such markers once you've gotten into the quieter residential neighborhoods. Place-names are neatly hand-painted at nearly every square and bridge, but they don't always agree with maps, and they may look nothing like names you've seen in other Italian towns.

Addresses don't clarify things. Because street names repeat from one sestiere to another, the address system was "simplified" in 1841, when houses were numbered by sestiere rather than street. Except for churches, which go only by their saint's name, all Venetian addresses consist of the name of the sestiere and a number. The hitch is that the numbers don't run sequentially, so San Marco 3672 and 3673 might be several narrow, winding streets away from one another. When getting directions, be sure to ask for the nearest campo, bridge, or calle.

Although the smaller canals are often spanned by several bridges, the Grand Canal can only be crossed on foot at three points: **Ponte degli Scalzi,** near the train station (Ferrovia); **Ponte di Rialto,** at the Rialto; and **Ponte dell'Accademia,** between Campo Santo Stefano and the Gallerie dell'Accademia. If you find yourself on the wrong bank with no bridge in

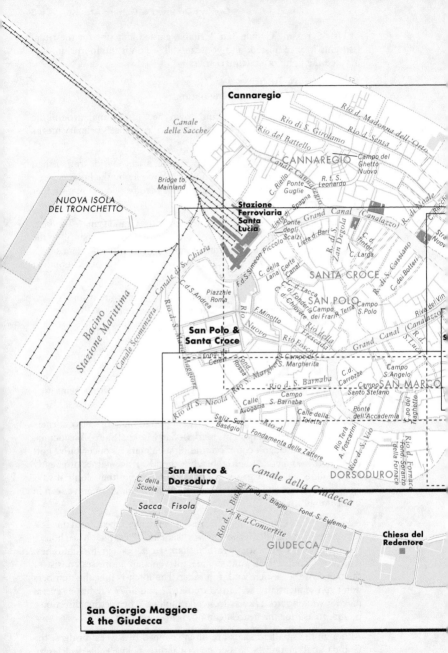

Cannaregio

Canale delle Sacche

Rio d. Madonna dell'Orta

Rio di S. Girolamo

Rio d. Sensa

Rio del Battello

Campo del Ghetto Nuovo

CANNAREGIO

Canale Cannaregio

R. t. S. Leonardo

R. d. Rocchi

C. Riello

Ponte Guglie

Bridge to Mainland

Stazione Ferroviaria Santa Lucia

Lista di Spagna

Grand Canal (Canalazzo)

R. di Noale

Strada Nuova

NUOVA ISOLA DEL TRONCHETTO

Ponte degli Scalzi

Ponte Piccolo

Lista d. Bari

R. di Zan Degola

C. d. Tintor

C. Larga

R. di S. Cassiano

F. d. S. Simeon Piccolo

C. della Lana

Corte

SANTA CROCE

C. dei Botteri

Canale di S. Chiara

C. d. S. Andrea

Piazzale Roma

CC. d'Lacca

C. d. Fonderia

Campo d' Chiovere

SAN POLO

Campo dei Frari

Terra

Campo S.Polo

Riva del Vin

Bacino Stazione Marittima

Canale Scomenzera

Rio d. S. Andrea

F. Minotto

Rio Nuovo

Rio della Frescada

Grand Canal (Canalazzo)

R. d. S. Luca

San Polo & Santa Croce

Rio Fosca

Fond. dei Cereri

Fond. Rosso

Rio S. Margher.

Campo di S. Margherita

C. d. Carrozze

Campo S.Angelo

Rio d. S. Barnaba

Campo S. Stefano

SAN MARCO

Rio di S. Nicolò

Calle Avogaria

Campo S. Barnaba

Calle della Toletta

Ponte dell'Accademia

Saliz. San Baségio

Rio d.

Fondamenta delle Zattere

Rio Terà A. Foscarini

Rio d. S. Vio

Rio d. Fornace

Fond. Soranzo della Fornace

San Marco & Dorsoduro

C. della Scuola

DORSODURO

Sacca Fisola

Rio d. S. Biagio

Fond. S. Biagio

R.d.Convertite

Canale della Giudecca

Fond. S. Eufemia

Chiesa del Redentore

GIUDECCA

San Giorgio Maggiore & the Giudecca

Laguna Veneta

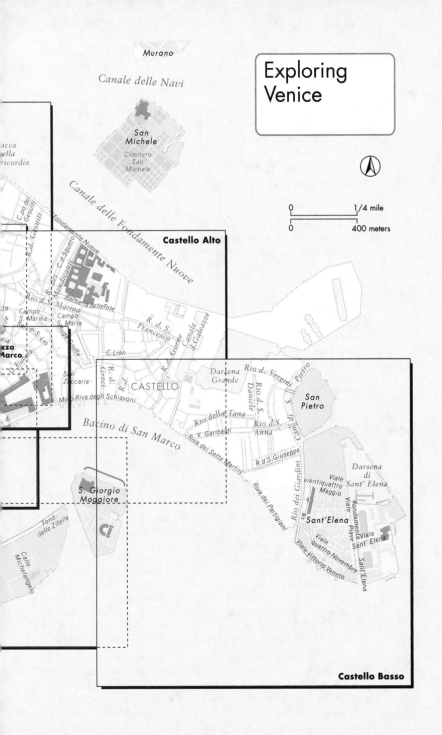

Murano

Canale delle Navi

San
Michele

Cimitero
San
Michele

Exploring
Venice

0   1/4 mile

0   400 meters

Canale delle Fondamente Nuove

Castello Alto

acca
ella
ricordia

C.po dei
Gesuiti

R. d. Gatami

Fondamente Nuove

R. di S. C.d.Squero Nuove

Mendicanti

Barbaria delle Tole

Rio d. S. Marina

Campo
S. Marina

Campo
S. Maria

R. d. Ruga Giuffa

to
S. Marina

ria
S. di S. Lio

za
Marco

C. Fiubera

R. d. S.
Francesco

R. d. Gorne

Canale
d. Galeazze

C. Lion

San
Zaccaria

R. d.
Greci

CASTELLO

R. d.
Greci

Darsena
Grande

Rio della Tana

V. Garibaldi

Rio d. S.
Daniele

Rio d. Vergini

S. Pietro

San
Pietro

Moro Riva degli Schiavoni

Bacino di San Marco

Rio d. S.
Anna

Riva dei Sette Martiri

R. d. S. Giuseppe

S. Giorgio
Maggiore

Riva dei Partigiani

Rio dei Giardini

Viale
vientiquattro
Maggio

Viale
Sant' Elena

Darsena
di
Sant' Elena

Fond.
delle Zitelle

Sant'Elena

Viale
quattro Novembre

Fondamenta
Piave

Viale
Sant' Elena

Calle
Michelangelo

Viale Vittorio Veneto

Sant'Elena

Castello Basso

sight, look for a traghetto—they exist precisely because of the shortage of bridges.

Planning Your Time

A great introduction to Venice is a ride on **vaporetto Line 1** from the train station all the way down the Grand Canal. If you've just stepped off the train and have luggage in tow, you'll need to weigh the merits of taking this trip right away versus getting settled at your hotel first. (Crucial factors: your mood, the bulk of your bags, and your hotel's location.)

Seeing **Piazza San Marco** and the sights bordering it can easily fill a day, but if you're going to be around awhile, consider holding off on your visit there—the crowds can be overwhelming, especially when you're fresh off the boat. A good alternative is to start your first day at the church of **Santa Maria Gloriosa dei Frari** and the **Scuola Grande di San Rocco** in the San Polo sestiere. Then wander through the neighboring Dorsoduro sestiere, choosing between visits to **Ca' Rezzonico**, the **Gallerie dell'Accademia**, the **Peggy Guggenheim Collection**, and **Santa Maria della Salute**— all A-list attractions. End the afternoon with a gelato-fueled stroll along the **Zattere** boardwalk. Then tackle San Marco on day two.

In succeeding days, these sights should be top priorities: the **Rialto fish and produce markets; Ca' d'Oro** and the **Jewish Ghetto** in Cannaregio; **Santa Maria dei Miracoli** and **Santi Giovanni e Paolo** in Castello; and, across the water from Piazza San Marco, **San Giorgio Maggiore**. (In Venice, there's a spectacular church for every day of the week, and then some.) A day on the outer islands of **Murano, Burano**, and **Torcello** is good for a change of pace.

Saving Money with Sight Passes

In 1997 a group of parish priests founded a nonprofit organization to raise money for maintenance and protection of fifteen of Venice's finest churches—Santa Maria del Giglio, Santo Stefano, Santa Maria Formosa, Santa Maria dei Miracoli, Santa Maria Gloriosa dei Frari, San Polo, San Giacomo dell'Orio, San Stae, Sant'Alvise, Madonna dell'Orto, San Pietro di Castello, SS. Redentore, San Sebastiano, Gesuati, and San Giovanni Elemosinario. Known as the **Chorus Churches** (☎ 041/2750462 ⊕ www.chorusvenezia.org), they're open to visitors all day except Sunday mornings. There's usually someone to provide information and a free leaflet (available in English), and postcards and booklets are on sale. Single church entry costs €2.50, or you can buy a €9 Chorus pass that allows you one admission to each church and is good for a year. The pass includes use of audio guides except in Basilica dei Frari, where guides cost €1.60. The artwork in Chorus churches is labeled, and the staff can show you where to switch on special lighting for certain paintings.

Eleven museums currently make up Venice's **Musei Civici** (☎ 041/2715911 ⊕ www.museiciviciveneziani.it), and a Museum Pass for €15.50 (valid three months) lets you make one visit to each museum. For access to only the Piazza San Marco group—Palazzo Ducale, Museo Correr, Museo Archeologico, and Biblioteca Marciana—you can purchase a Mu-

VENICE THROUGH THE AGES

VENICE WAS FOUNDED in the 5th century when the Veneti, inhabitants of the mainland region roughly corresponding to today's Veneto, fled their homes to escape invading Lombards. The unlikely city, built atop wooden posts driven into the marshes, would evolve into a great maritime republic. Its fortunes grew as a result of its active role in the Crusades, beginning in 1095 and culminating in the Venetian-led sacking of Constantinople in 1204. The defeat of rival Genoa in the Battle of Chioggia (1380) established Venice as the dominant sea power in Europe.

As early as the 7th century, Venice was governed by a participatory democracy, featuring a ruler, the doge, who was elected to a lifetime term. Beginning in the 12th century, the doge's power was increasingly subsumed by a growing number of councils, commissions, and magistrates. In 1268 a complicated procedure for the doge's election was established to prevent nepotism, but by this point power rested foremost with the Great Council, which at times numbered as many as 2,000 members. Though originally an elected body, the Great Council from 1297 onward was an aristocratic stronghold, with members inheriting seats from their noble ancestors. Laws were passed by the Senate, a group of 200 elected from the Great Council, and executive powers belonged to the College, a committee of 25 leaders. In 1310, the Council of Ten was formed to protect state security. When circumstances abroad or at home endangered the republic's democracy, the doge could expedite decision making and guarantee greater secrecy by consulting only the Council of Ten. In order to avoid too great a concentration of power, these ten served only one year and had to belong to different families.

Venice reached the height of its power in the 15th and 16th centuries, during which time its domain extended inland to include all of the Veneto region and part of Lombardy. But beginning in the 16th century, the tide turned. The Ottoman Empire blocked Venice's Mediterranean trade routes, and newly emerging sea powers such as Britain and the Netherlands ended Venice's monopoly by opening oceanic trading routes. The republic underwent a long, slow decline. When Napoléon arrived in 1797, he took the city without a fight, eventually delivering it to the Austrians, who ruled until 1848. In that tumultuous year throughout Europe, the Venetians rebelled, an act that would ultimately lead to their joining the Italian republic in 1866.

Early in its history, Venice brought in Byzantine artists to decorate its churches with brilliant mosaics, still glittering today. In the 13th through 15th centuries the influence of Gothic architecture produced the characteristic type of palace in the Florid Gothic style, with the finely wrought facades for which the town is famous. Renaissance sensibilities arrived in Venice comparatively late. Early Venetian Renaissance artists—Carpaccio, Giorgione, and the Bellini brothers, Giovanni and Gentile—were active in the late 15th and early 16th centuries. Along with the stars of the next generation— Veronese, Titian, and Tintoretto—they played a decisive role in the development of Western art, and their work still covers walls and ceilings all over the city.

Like its steadily dwindling fortunes, Venice's art and culture underwent a prolonged decline, leaving only the splendid monuments to recall a fabled past, with the 18th-century paintings of Canaletto and frescoes of Giambattista Tiepolo striking a glorious swan song.

seum Card for €11. An €8 ticket buys entry to all three "museums of 18th-century culture"—Ca' Rezzonico, Palazzo Mocenigo, and Casa Goldoni. A €6 ticket will allow you to visit both the Burano Lace Museum and the Murano Glass Museum.

CRUISING THE GRAND CANAL

There's no better introduction to Venice than a trip down the Grand Canal, or as Venetians refer to it, Canalazzo. Without a doubt one of the world's great "avenues," Venice's main thoroughfare competes with Piazza San Marco for the honor of being the city's most famous landmark. For 4 km (2½ mi) it winds its way in a backward "S," past 12th- to 18th-century palaces built by the city's richest families. A handful still belong to the descendants of those who built them, but many have been converted to other uses. A dozen museums, several five-star hotels, a few modest inns, government and city offices, courts, university departments, a post office, a casino, and even a TV station, are housed in Renaissance studios and baroque ballrooms, hiding behind those Byzantine and Gothic facades.

There is a definite theatrical quality to the Grand Canal, something particularly noticeable as you pass in a vaporetto or a gondola; it's as if each facade had been designed to steal your attention from its rival across the way. The most romantic way to see the canal is from a gondola. Take a ride from Rialto to San Marco an hour or so before sunset, or at daybreak when dreamlike scenery will be there just for you. The next best thing—at a fraction of the cost—is to take in the view from vaporetto Line 1. Although you can board at any of the 16 stops along the canal, it makes sense to begin your voyage from Piazzale Roma or the train station (Ferrovia) and take the full 45-minute ride to San Marco or San Zaccaria. Lean back in your seat, take in the view, and marvel at the history steeped in the grand past of this Grand Canal. Below is a description of what you'll see. For more detailed information about the major sights, see the neighborhood tours that follow.

Don't leave Venice until you have seen it by night from the water—but bring a warm scarf in winter and mosquito repellent in summer. Once off the vaporetto, keep in mind that traghetti at many points along the Grand Canal will ferry you from one bank to the other for just €.50.

Numbers in the text correspond to numbers on the Grand Canal map.

Timing

From Piazzale Roma to San Zaccaria, vaporetto Line 1 takes about 45 minutes; service runs between 5 AM and midnight, with departures every 10 minutes during the day, and every 20 minutes early in the morning and after 9:30 PM. There is *servizio notturno* (night service) from midnight to 5 AM, with "N" boats running between Piazzale Roma and San Zaccaria every 40 minutes (to and from Rialto every 20 minutes). A trip down the Grand Canal by gondola takes about an hour and a half. Never let a gondolier help you climb down into his gondola without having discussed the duration and cost of the ride.

THE WORLD'S MOST ELEGANT TAXI

MORE THAN WINGED LIONS or *Carnevale masks*, gondolas have become the symbol of Venice, re-created en masse as plastic toys, snow globes, and virtually every other tchotchke known to man. But if you look beyond the kitsch, you'll find an austerely beautiful and elegantly designed boat that has evolved over centuries to meet Venice's unique needs.

The gondola is among the most enduring of numerous flat-bottomed craft that were developed to navigate the lagoon's shallow waters. The first written reference to a gondola dates to the 11th century, and images of the boats appear in Venetian art as early as the 1300s. At the height of their popularity in the 17th century, more than 5,000 gondolas were active on Venice's waterways. (Their number has now dwindled to around 500.) They were made slim to maneuver the narrowest canals and topped with felzi, small cabins that allowed a city full of Casanovas to travel incognito.

The republic's fall in 1797 and the subsequent economic decline triggered experiments in gondola construction that would allow the boats to be handled by one gondolier rather than two. Boat-builder Domenico Tramontin perfected the design in the late 1800s, creating an ingenious asymmetrical hull that keeps the gondola traveling in a straight line even though it's being rowed by a single oar. This would be the last genetic modification to one of the world's loveliest dinosaurs—for within fifty years, the gondola would be driven to the brink of extinction by engine-driven boats, most notably the vaporetto, Venice's water bus.

Gondolas are made and repaired in a workshop called a squero. Starting with well-seasoned wood, boatbuilders can construct a gondola body in about a month, but embellishments, carved and gilded, can take much longer. The finishing touch is the ferro, the ornament that adorns the bow. According to common wisdom, the ferro's graceful "S" curve is meant to mimic the bends of the Grand Canal, its six prongs represent Venice's six sestieri, and its rounded top echoes the shape of the doge's hat. This explanation was most likely invented by gondoliers in the early 20th century to impress their passengers, but it's ingenious enough to have endured for 100 years and become part of gondola lore.

The most conspicuous squero of the few that remain is at San Trovaso, just down the small canal near the Zattere boat landing. Not far from there is the squero **Domenico Tramontin and Sons** (⊠ Dorsoduro 1542, Fondamente Ognissanti, near Giustinian Hospital ☎ 041/5237762 ⊕ www.tramontingondole.it), where Domenico's great-grandson Roberto and grandson Nedis continue to practice the family trade. Tours with a translator can be arranged by contacting Roberto via fax or through the Web site. North Carolinian Thom Price came to Venice with a fellowship to study gondola making and never went back. At his **Squero Canaletto** (☎ 041/2413963 ⊕ www.squero.com) he not only builds boats but also conducts weeklong workshops on gondola construction and Venetian rowing.

The shapely forcola (oarlock) used in Venetian-style rowing is itself a work of refined engineering. To see forcole being made, visit the shop of **Saverio Pastor** (⊠ Fondamenta Soranzo, Dorsoduro 341 ☎ 041/5225699 ⊕ www.forcole.com), open weekdays 8–6. While there you can buy a forcola for yourself; architects I. M. Pei and Frank Gehry are among those who have taken one home.

From Piazzale Roma to Rialto

If you arrive in Venice by train or car, you'll immediately encounter this first tract of the Grand Canal, which flows between the sestieri of Cannaregio and Santa Croce. Highlights include the baroque San Stae church, Venice's fabulous casino, and the sensational Ca' d'Oro.

Vaporetto Line 1 starts at Piazzale Roma, the beginning of the Grand Canal, and its first stop is the train station or **Ferrovia ❶** (officially called "Stazione Ferroviaria Santa Lucia"). Piazzale Roma and Ferrovia are among the city's more modern areas, but more classically Venetian architecture isn't far off. Near the Ferrovia stop is the baroque **Chiesa degli Scalzi ❷**, named after the order of barefoot friars who founded it. The church was partially rebuilt after being struck by an Austrian bomb in World War I that destroyed two Tiepolo ceiling frescoes. Venice's last, rather inept doge, Ludovico Manin, was aptly buried here on the edge of town. The first of the Grand Canal's three bridges, **Ponte degli Scalzi ❸**, is also its newest, built in the 1930s.

Opposite the landing of Riva di Biasio, a plaque on the wall near the church of **San Geremia ❹** is a memorial to the Church of Santa Lucia, which was demolished to make room for the train station. The reliquary of the patron saint of eyesight (according to Catholics, Lucia tore her eyes out after being complemented on their beauty by one of her pagan jailers) was moved to San Geremia. The imposing palace half-hidden behind the bell tower is the famous **Palazzo Labia ❺** (⇨ Cannaregio, *below*), with magnificent frescoes by Tiepolo. A left turn into the Canale di Cannaregio would bring you to the north side of the lagoon facing the town of Mestre and the industrial complex of Marghera.

The uncompleted facade of the church of **San Marcuola ❻**, lets you see what's behind the marble decorations of similar 18th-century churches. On the other riva, flanked by two *torricelle* (side wings in the shape of small towers) and a triangular *merlatura* (crenellation), is the **Fondaco dei Turchi ❼**. It was once the largest palazzo on the Grand Canal and has a checkered history of occupants and restorations (⇨ San Polo and Santa Croce, *below*). Next comes the plain brick **Depositi del Megio ❽**, a 15th-century millet granary; a lion marks it as Serenissima property. Next door is obelisqued **Ca' Belloni-Battagia ❾** designed by Baldassare Longhena after the Belloni family bought itself into aristocracy. It's somewhat overshadowed by **Palazzo Vendramin-Calergi ❿** on the other bank. Charismatic Doge Leonardo Loredan led Venice to victory against the League of Cambrai, which was formed in 1508 by the pope, the Holy Roman Emperor, and the kings of France and Spain with the intention of destroying the republic. He commissioned this Renaissance gem from Mauro Codussi (1440–1504) in the 1480s, at a time when the late-Gothic style was still fashionable. German composer Wagner died here in 1883 soon after the success of his *Parsifal*. A banner with gilded lettering heralds this as the home of Venice's casino.

White and whimsically baroque, the church of **San Stae ⓫** welcomes visitors with a host of marble saints. Another example of the baroque awaits farther down the bank at **Ca' Pesaro ⓬**. Today it's home to a gallery of contemporary paintings and a collection of Asian art, but it was once home to the man who declared war against Napoléon (⇨ San Polo and Santa Croce, *below*). One block and two rii ahead stands a tall, balconied palace named for a queen, **Ca' Corner della Regina** ⓭. In 1468, 13-year-old Caterina Cornaro, the "daughter of the republic," was married to the king of Cyprus in a foreign policy maneuver by the Serenissima. Although her descendents demolished the queen's birthplace in the 1720s to build this Ca' Corner, the old name stuck. In the 1970s, it became a library and *cineteca* (film archive) for the Biennale. The archive has since been moved to the mainland to allow for the palace to be restored.

The **Ca' d'Oro** ⓮, or "Golden House," takes its name from the gilding that once accentuated the marble carvings of its facade. One of the most striking palazzos on the Canal, it holds a good collection of antiquities and paintings (⇨ Cannaregio, *below*). Opposite is one of the oldest outdoor food markets in Europe. The loggia-like, neo-Gothic **Pescheria** ⓯ marks the spot where fish from the lagoon and the Dalmatian coast have been sold for the last 1,000 years. Fruit and vegetable stalls fill the spacious fondamenta, and cheese shops and butchers pack the buildings in the background. Next is the porticoed edifice built by Sansovino in 1555 to house the republic's equivalent of a stock exchange and chamber of commerce. Today it contains Venice's Tribunal and Court of Justice. Opposite, the 13th-century Byzantine **Ca' da Mosto** ⓰, with its water porch, looks like it could use a face-lift, but in the 18th century it was the fashionable Leon Bianco hotel. The canal narrows and boat traffic increases as you approach Rialto, a commercial hub with a concentration of souvenir booths and inexpensive retail stores. On the left, just before your boat passes under the bridge, is the central post office, once frescoed with alluring female figures by Giorgione and Titian. It was apt decoration for what was then the busiest trading center of the republic—the **Fondaco dei Tedeschi** ⓱—where merchants from Germany, Austria, Bohemia, and Hungary kept warehouses, shops, and sleeping quarters. The curiously angled **Ca' dei Camerlenghi** ⓲ stands opposite. Built in 1525 to accommodate the powerful State Treasury, it had a jail for tax evaders on the ground floor. The **Rialto Bridge** ⓳, arched high to allow galleys to pass beneath, dates from the late 16th century (⇨ San Polo & Santa Croce, *below*). As the vaporetto pulls over to stop on the left, it passes Sansovino's **Ca' Dolfin-Manin** ⓴, designed in the 1560s. The home of Venice's last doge is today occupied by the Banca d'Italia.

From Rialto to the Ponte dell'Accademia

Heading toward more noble quarters, the Grand Canal continues its loop through the southern part of town, encircling sestiere San Marco. Mansions of the many families that gave the republic its doges line the San Polo and Dorsoduro side, vying with homes on the San Marco side for the passersby's glance. Wavering reflections on the canal's jade green water seem to echo the question of the wicked witch in *Snow White*: Who's the fairest one of all? . . .

Rialto is the only point along the Grand Canal where buildings do not have principle entrances on the water, a consequence of the two long

The Grand Canal

and spacious *rive* (streets), which were once used for unloading two vital staples: coal and wine. On your left along Riva del Carbon stand **Ca' Loredan** ㉑ and **Ca' Farsetti** ㉒, 13th-century Byzantine works that today make up Venice's city hall. On Riva del Vin, just past the San Silvestro landing, is the 12th–13th-century facade of **Palazzo Barzizza** ㉓, an elegant example of Veneto-Byzantine architecture that managed to survive a complete renovation of the building in the 17th century. Across the water is the sternly Renaissance **Ca' Grimani** ㉔, an intimidating presence that seems the appropriate location for today's Court of Appeals. Just past a canal, the white-and-red-striped Casetta Tron (small house) is sandwiched between the 15th-century **Ca' Corner-Contarini dei Cavalli** ㉕, named for the horses on its coat of arms, and massive **Ca' Martinengo** ㉖. This was the residence of Conte Volpi, who modernized the city during the first half of the 20th century. Venice has him to thank for innovations such as electricity, the nearby industrial zone in Porto Marghera, the foundation of Mestre, the chain of five-star CIGA hotels, and the now-famous Biennale film festival.

Cruising into the landing at Sant'Angelo, the vaporetto passes close to **Ca' Corner-Spinelli** ㉗ built by Mauro Codussi. It became a prototype for other Grand Canal buildings; Codussi himself copied its windows when building Palazzo Vendramin-Calergi. The building opposite, **Palazzo Barbarigo della Terrazza** ㉘, home of the German Institute, has an expansive terrace with an unsurpassed view of the canal. Standing grandly next door, dressed in a salmon color that seems to change with the time of day, is elegant **Palazzo Pisani Moretta** ㉙, with twin water entrances where modern-day revelers arrive for candlelit dinner parties. On the other bank, four-storied **Ca' Garzoni** ㉚, part of the Università di Venezia Ca' Foscari, is beside the San Tomà traghetto, which has operated since 1354. As the vaporetto stops on the right at San Tomà, you can look across at **Ca' Mocenigo** ㉛, where a plaque notes that Lord Byron lived there (1818–1819), but neglects to mention that he shared the apartment with two monkeys, a bear, two parrots, and a fox, and had 14 servants, a butler, and a gondolier at his service. The boat makes a sharp turn, and on the right passes one of the city's tallest Gothic palaces, **Ca' Foscari** ㉜. Built for 15th-century Doge Francesco Foscari—under whose reign the republic reached its greatest size—it's been a part of Venice's university since the 1870s. Positioned at one of the busiest junctures along the Grand Canal, this palace has suffered severe foundation damage from relentless waves. Renovation work, which started in 1996, was completed in 2005 and has returned the palazzo to its former splendor. Richard Wagner lived next door in **Ca' Giustinian** ㉝ while he was working on *Tristan and Isolde*.

The vaporetto passes **Ca' Rezzonico** ㉞ so closely that you get to look inside one of the most fabulous entrances along the canal. The architect Longhena began work on the palace in 1649, but it wasn't completed until almost a century later. Today it houses the Museo del Settecento Veneziano (⇨ San Marco & Dorsoduro, *below*). Opposite stands the Grand Canal's youngest mansion, **Palazzo Grassi** ㉟, commissioned in 1749 by a Bolognese tycoon from architect Giorgio Massari—who also completed Ca' Rezzonico after Longhena's death. Just beyond Grassi and Campo San Samuele, the first house past the garden was once Titian's studio. It's followed by **Palazzo Falier** ㊱, instantly recognizable by its twin loggias (windowed porches). It's said to have been the home of Doge Martin Falier, who was beheaded for treason in 1355.

Ahead, **Accademia Bridge** ㊲, like the Eiffel Tower, with which it shares a certain structural grace, was never intended to be permanent. Built in 1933 as a quick alternative to a rusting iron bridge built by the Austrians, it was so well liked by Venetians that a perfect replica with steel bracing was created in 1986. Among the scores of religious institutions suppressed by Napoléon were the church, convent, and scuola of Santa Maria della Carità. As the vaporetto stops at the bridge, on your right you'll see the **Gallerie dell'Accademia** ㊳ (⇨ San Marco & Dorsoduro, *below*), which grew out of the Accademia di Belle Arti (founded in 1750 with Tiepolo as director), installed in the former church buildings in 1807. Its original collection of paintings quickly grew with works collected from other suppressed churches and confraternities.

From the Ponte dell'Accademia to San Zaccaria

You're only three stops from the end of the the Grand Canal, but this last tract is like a rich dessert after a delicious meal: a baroque creation resembling a wedding cake topped with meringue and whipped cream marks the end of what Charles VIII's ambassador to Venice called the *"plus belle rue en tout le monde"* (the most beautiful street in all the world).

Lovely **Ca' Franchetti** ㊴, with a central balcony made in the style of Palazzo Ducale's loggia, dates from the late Gothic period, but its gardens are no older than the cedar tree that stands at their center—until the late 19th century, this was a *squero* (workshop) where gondolas were made and repaired. **Ca' Barbaro** ㊵ next door was the residence of the illustrious family who rebuilt the church of Santa Maria del Giglio (⇨ San Marco & Dorsoduro, *below*). In more recent times it hosted guests such as Monet, Henry James, and Cole Porter (who later lived aboard a boat in Giudecca Canal). Farther along on the left bank, a garden, vibrant with flowers in summer, surrounds **Casetta Rossa** ㊶ (small red house) as if it were the centerpiece of its bouquet. Across the canal, bright 19th-century mosaics on **Ca' Barbarigo** ㊷ give you some idea how the frescoed facades of many Venetian palaces must have looked in their heyday. A few doors down are the lush gardens growing within the walls of the unfinished **Palazzo Venier dei Leoni** ㊸. A scale model of the palace in the Museo Correr gives some credit to the theory that Venier's construction was somehow sabotaged by the family living in Sansovino's **Ca' Grande** ㊹ across the canal, who didn't want the new house obstructing their view of the lagoon. In 1951 Venier was bought by American heiress and art collector Peggy Guggenheim, who kept her private gondola parked at the door and left her ever-present dogs standing guard in place of roaring lions (⇨ Peggy Guggenheim Collection *in* San Marco & Dorsoduro, *below*).

Lovely, leaning **Ca' Dario** ㊺ is more notable for its colorful marble facade than for its structural engineering. However tilted Dario might be, it has outlasted its many owners, who seem plagued by misfortune, including Italian industrialist Raul Gardini, whose 1992 suicide followed charges of corruption and his unsuccessful bid for the America's Cup. Ca' Dario has been on the real estate market for some time. Past the landing of Santa Maria del Giglio stands the 15th-century **Ca' Pisani-Gritti** ㊻, best known as the Gritti Palace Hotel. On the other bank, narrow **Palazzo Salviati** ㊼, with its 20th-century mosaic facade, was among the last glass factories to operate within the Venice city center. As you approach the cupola of **Santa Maria della Salute** ㊽ (⇨ San Marco & Dorsoduro, *below*), save a glance or two for the picturesque Rio di San Gregorio, and what's left of the namesake Gothic abbey, now privately owned.

Leaving **Punta della Dogana** ㊾ and its Palla della Fortuna (golden ball, topped by a weather vane depicting Fortune) shining against the sky, the vaporetto stops on the left at the famous Harry's Bar, near **Giardinetti Reali** ㊿, planted by Napoléon after he tore down the republic's grain warehouse. The Grand Canal has officially ended, but stay on board one more stop (to San Zaccaria) for the greatest view of all: **Piazzetta San Marco** ㊶, **Basilica di San Marco** ㊷, and **Palazzo Ducale** ㊸ (⇨ Piazza San Marco, *below*). This sight moved Thomas Mann to claim that arriving in Venice over the bridge from the mainland (he had taken the train) was like entering the house of a beautiful woman through the service entrance.

PIAZZA SAN MARCO

One of the world's most evocative squares, Piazza San Marco (St. Mark's Square) is the heart of Venice, a vast open space bordered by an orderly procession of arcades marching toward the fairy-tale cupolas and marble lacework of the Basilica di San Marco. Perpetually packed by day with people and fluttering pigeons, it can be magical at night, especially in winter, when mists swirl around the lampposts and the Campanile.

If you face the basilica from in front of the Correr Museum, you'll notice that rather than being a strict rectangle, this square opens wider at the basilica end, creating the illusion that it's even larger than it is. On your left, the long, arcaded building is the Procuratie Vecchie, built in the early 16th century as offices and residences for the powerful procurators (magistrates) of San Marco. On your right is the Procuratie Nuove, built half a century later in a more grandiose classical style. It was originally planned by Venice's great Renaissance architect, Sansovino, to carry on the look of his Libreria Sansoviniana (Sansovinian Library), but he died before construction on the Nuove had begun. Vincenzo Scamozzi (circa 1552–1616), a neoclassicist pupil of Andrea Palladio (1508–80), completed the design and construction. Still later, the Procuratie Nuove was modified by architect Baldassare Longhena (1598–1682), one of Venice's baroque masters.

When Napoléon (1769–1821) entered Venice with his troops in 1797, he called Piazza San Marco "the world's most beautiful drawing room"— and promptly gave orders to redecorate it. His architects demolished a 16th-century church with a Sansovino facade in order to build the Ala

Napoleonica (Napoleonic Wing), or Fabbrica Nuova (New Building), which linked the two 16th-century procuratie and effectively enclosed the piazza.

Piazzetta San Marco, the "little square" leading from Piazza San Marco to the waters of Bacino San Marco (St. Mark's Basin), is a *molo* (landing) that was once the grand entryway to the republic. It's distinguished by two columns towering above the waterfront. One is topped by the winged lion, a traditional emblem of St. Mark that became the symbol of Venice itself; the other supports St. Theodore, the city's first patron, along with his dragon. Between these columns the republic traditionally executed convicts.

It takes a full day to take in everything on the piazza thoroughly, so if time is limited you'll have to prioritize. Plan on 1½ hours for the Basilica and its Pala d'Oro, Galleria, and Museo Marciano. You'll want at least two hours to appreciate the Palazzo Ducale. Do take time to enjoy the piazza itself from a café table, or on a clear day, from atop the Campanile.

Numbers in the margin correspond to the numbers on the Piazza San Marco map.

The Main Attractions

❸ **Basilica di San Marco.** An opulent synthesis of Byzantine and Romanesque
FodorśChoice styles, this church, Venice's gem, is laid out in a Greek-cross (four arms
★ of equal length) floor plan and topped with five plump domes. The basilica did not actually become the cathedral of Venice until 1807, but its role as the Chiesa Ducale (doge's private chapel) gave it immense power and wealth. The original church was built in 828 to house the body of St. Mark the Evangelist. His remains were stolen from Alexandria by two agents of the doge and, so the story goes, hidden in a barrel beneath layers of pickled pork to sneak them past Muslim guards. The escapade is depicted in the 13th-century mosaic above the front entrance door to the farthest left. This semicircular arch is the earliest mosaic on the heavily decorated facade; look closely and you'll see an image of the basilica as it appeared at that time.

A 976 fire destroyed most of the original church; rebuilding began in 1063 and it reopened in 1094. Over the centuries it stood as a symbol of Venetian wealth and power, endowed with all the riches the republic's admirals and merchants could carry off from the Orient, becoming so opulent it earned the nickname Chiesa d'Oro (Golden Church). The four bronze horses that prance and snort over the entrance are copies of sculptures that victorious Venetians took from Constantinople in 1204 (the originals are in the Museo Marciano). Look for a medallion of red porphyry set in the porch floor, just inside the central doorway. It marks the spot where in 1177 a great political coup by Doge Sebastiano Ziani brought reconciliation between Barbarossa, the Holy Roman Emperor, and Pope Alexander III. The basilica's dim light, the *matroneum* (women's galleries) high above the naves, the *iconostasis* (altar screen), and the single massive Byzantine chandelier all seem to wed Christianity with the Orient, giving San Marco its exotic blend of majesty and mystery.

The basilica is famous for its 43,055 square feet of stunning mosaics, made possible by an innovative roof made of brick vaulting rather than wood. Many of the original windows were filled in to make room for even more artwork. Only between 11:30 AM and 12:30 PM, when the interior is fully illuminated, do these mosaics come alive—their tiny gold tiles are nothing short of magical. The earliest mosaics are from the 11th and 12th centuries and the last were added in the early 1700s. One of the most recent is the *Last Judgment* on the arch between the porch and the nave, said to be based on drawings by Tintoretto (1518–94). Inside the main entrance, turn right on the porch to see the Book of Genesis depicted on the ceiling. Ahead, **Cappella Zen** (Zen Chapel)—named for a local cardinal, not a form of Buddhism—shows St. Mark's life in 13th-century mosaics. Cappella Zen, like the basilica's **Battistero** (Baptistery), and underground **Crypt** is open only to scholars.

Two chapels in the left transept are worth a special look: the **Cappella della Madonna di Nicopeia** (Chapel of the Madonna of Nicopeia) takes its name from a precious icon that many consider Venice's most powerful protector. In the nearby **Cappella della Madonna dei Mascoli** (Chapel of Madonna of the Males), the life of the Virgin Mary is depicted in fine

15th-century mosaics, possibly based on drawings by Jacopo Bellini (circa 1400–70), and his son-in-law, Andrea Mantegna.

In the **Santuario** (Sanctuary), the main altar is built over the tomb of St. Mark, its green marble canopy lifted high on carved alabaster columns. Even more impressive is the extraordinary **Pala d'Oro**, a dazzling gilded silver screen encrusted with 1,927 precious gems and 255 enameled panels. Originally commissioned in Constantinople by Doge Pietro Orseolo I in the 10th century, it was continually enlarged and embellished over the next four hundred years by master craftsmen and wealthy merchants. The bronze door leading from the sanctuary back into the sacristy is another Sansovino work. In the top left corner the artist included a self-portrait and, above that, a picture of his friend and fellow artist Titian (circa 1485–1576). The **Tesoro** (Treasury), entered from the right transept, contains many treasures carried home from Constantinople and other conquests.

From the atrium, climb the steep stairway to the **Galleria** and the **Museo Marciano.** From here you get the best possible overview of the basilica's interior, and you can step outdoors for a sweeping panorama of Piazza San Marco and the Piazzetta dei Leoncini. The highlight of the museum is a close-up look at the original four gilded bronze horses that once pranced upon the outer gallery. They were probably cast in Rome and taken to Constantinople. When Napoléon conquered Venice in 1797, he took them back to Paris with him. They were returned after the fall of the French Empire, but came home "blind": their big ruby eyes had been sold.

Be warned: guards at the entrance to the basilica turn away anyone wearing shorts, short skirts, tank tops, and other attire considered inappropriate (no bare shoulders or knees). If you want to take a free guided tour in English during summer months (with less certainty in winter, as the guides are volunteers), look for groups forming on the porch inside the main door. You might also arrange a free tour by appointment. ⊠ *Piazza San Marco* ☎ *041/5225205 Basilica, 041/5225697 tours* ✉ *Basilica free, Tesoro €2; Santuario and Pala d'Oro €1.50, Galleria and Museo Marciano €3* ☉ *Mon.–Sat. 9:30–5, Sun. 2–4; last entry ½ hr before closing* Ⓥ *Vallaresso/San Zaccaria.*

★ ⊙ ❹ **Campanile.** Venice's famous brick bell tower (325 feet tall, plus the angel) had been standing nearly 1,000 years when in 1902, practically without warning, it collapsed, taking with it Jacopo Sansovino's 16th-century marble loggia at the base. The crushed loggia was promptly restored and the new tower, rebuilt to the old plan, reopened in 1912. In the 15th century, clerics found guilty of immoral behavior were suspended in wooden cages from the tower. Some were forced to subsist on bread and water for as long as a year, while others were left to starve. The stunning view from the tower on a clear day includes the Lido, the lagoon, and the mainland as far as the Alps but, strangely enough, none of the myriad canals that snake through the city. ⊠ *Piazza San Marco* ☎ *041/5224064* ✉ *€6* ☉ *Apr.–Sept., 9:30–5:30; Oct.–Mar., 9:30–4:30; last entry ½ hr before closing* Ⓥ *Vallaresso/San Zaccaria.*

CloseUp

TO LIVE LIKE A DOGE

IT WASN'T EASY BEING THE DOGE. *Called the Serenissimo ("Most Serene"), Venice's head of state led a life that was anything but.*

In the 1,100 years of the republic (697–1797), 121 men were elected to lifetime terms as doge through a convoluted process: first, 41 electors, all from noble families, were chosen through drawings and secret votes. Sequestered in the Palazzo Ducale, they deliberated until at least 25 agreed on the selection, a process that took anywhere from a few hours to several months. When a new doge was chosen, cannons sounded from boats in the harbor and the city's bells rang. On Coronation Day, 80 arsenal workers carried the doge through Piazza San Marco, where throngs cheered while pocketing silver coins he tossed to them.

Severe measures were taken to ensure the doge didn't abuse his office. He wasn't allowed to send notes (not even to his wife). He couldn't accept gifts other than flowers and rosewater. He wasn't allowed to go to theaters and cafés, where he might plot against democracy. And he had to pay his own office bills, though he couldn't engage in money-making activities.

The doge was expected to lead the Venetian fleet into battle; bad health and old age didn't excuse him from the duty. The blind, 90-year-old Enrico Dandolo proudly laid siege to Constantinople in 1203 and 1204, making off with the four horses that now adorn the Basilica. Even the resting place of the doge was dictated by protocol: for much of the history of the republic, doges were mummified and put on display in the Chiesa dei Santi Giovanni e Paolo. But Venetian embalmers weren't as skilled as those of ancient Egypt. After several centuries of unpleasant odors, "symbolic" mummies replaced the real ones, which were interred in family chapels.

❷ **Palazzo Ducale** (Doge's Palace). Rising above the Piazzetta San Marco, this Gothic-Renaissance fantasia of pink-and-white marble is a majestic expression of the prosperity and power attained during Venice's most glorious period. Some architectural purists contend that the building is top-heavy, with dense upper floors resting awkwardly upon the graceful ground-floor colonnade, but it's hard to imagine the Piazza with any other design. Always much more than a residence, this Palazzo was White House, Senate, torture chamber, and prison rolled into one.

Fodor'sChoice
★

Though a fortress for the doge existed on this spot in the early 9th century, the building you see today began in the 12th century, and like the basilica next door, was continually remodeled over the centuries. You can exit through the ornately Gothic **Porta della Carta** (Gate of the Paper), where official decrees were traditionally posted, but the main visitor entrance is under the portico facing the water. It opens onto an immense courtyard with the city's only two bronze *pozzi* (wellheads). Ahead is the **Scala dei Giganti** (Stairway of the Giants), guarded by huge statues of Mars and Neptune by Sansovino. Being an ordinary mortal, you won't get to climb these stairs, but if you walk along the arcade to reach the central interior staircase, you'll be dazzled by the sumptuously gilded

Scala d'Oro (Golden Staircase), also designed by Sansovino. Although it may seem odd that the government's main council rooms and reception halls would be so far upstairs, imagine how this extraordinary climb must have impressed and even intimidated foreign emissaries.

The rooms are no less impressive than the climb. Even though goldsmiths at that time could hammer one gram of gold into one square yard of gold leaf, there's still been an amazing amount of gold lavished on the palace ceilings—those that aren't covered with works by Venice's greatest artists. In the **Anticollegio**, a waiting room outside the Collegio's chamber, you can see Tintoretto's *Bacchus and Ariadne Crowned by Venus* and Veronese's (1528–88) *Rape of Europa*. Veronese also painted the ceiling of the adjacent **Sala del Collegio** (College Chamber). The ceiling of the **Sala del Senato** (Senate Chamber) features *Triumph of Venice* by Tintoretto, magnificent in its own right but dwarfed by his masterpiece *Paradise* in the **Sala del Maggiore Consiglio** (Great Council Hall). A vast work commissioned for a vast hall, this dark, dynamic mural is the world's largest oil painting (23 by 75 feet). The room's carved and gilded ceiling is breathtaking, even dizzying, as you wheel around searching for the best vantage point from which to admire Veronese's majestic *Apotheosis of Venice* filling one of the center panels. Around the upper part of the walls, study the frieze of portraits of the first 76 doges and you'll notice one picture is missing near the left corner of the wall opposite *Paradise*. A black painted curtain marks the place where Doge Marin Falier's portrait should be. A Latin inscription bluntly explains that Falier was beheaded for treason in 1355, when, at age 71 and less than a year into his reign, he was accused of plotting to establish an autocracy.

A narrow canal separates the Palace's east side from the cramped, gloomy cell blocks of the so-called **Prigioni Nuove** (New Prisons). High above the water arches the enclosed marble **Ponte dei Sospiri** (Bridge of Sighs), which earned its name from the sighs of those being led to prison or execution. Look out its windows and you'll see the last earthly view many of these prisoners had. During the Romantic era of the 19th century, the bridge's melancholy history made it a tourist must-see, and the sight still backs up pedestrian traffic as visitors crowd to take pictures.

The palazzo's **"secret itinerary"** guided tour takes you to the doge's private apartments, through hidden passageways to the torture chambers, where prisoners were "interrogated," and into the rooftop *piombi* prison, named for the building's leaded roofing. Giacomo Casanova (1725–98), Venetian-born writer and libertine, was imprisoned here in 1755, having offended someone in power. (He was officially charged with being a Freemason). He and an accomplice made a daring escape 15 months later and Casanova fled to France, where he continued his career of intrigue and scandal. They were the only prisoners ever to escape, and their guard was imprisoned for 10 years. 🎫 *€15 "Secret Itinerary" tour* ⊗ *English tours daily 9:55 and 11:55, reservations advisable.* ⊠ *Piazzetta San Marco* 🕾 *041/5209070* 🎫 *€11 Piazza San Marco museums, €15.50 Musei Civici pass* ⊗ *Apr.–Oct., daily 9–7; Nov.–Mar., daily 9–5; last tickets sold 1 hr before closing* Ⓥ *Vallaresso/ San Zaccaria.*

need a break?

Coffee, which for centuries had been a popular drink throughout countries to the East, may have first arrived in Europe aboard Venetian cargo ships. Merchants were regularly importing beans in the early 1600s, and coffee shops opened in Venice, Paris, and Vienna shortly thereafter. Since **Caffè Florian** (☎ 041/5205641), located in the Procuratie Nuove, brewed its first cup, it has served the likes of Casanova, Dickens, and Proust. It's Venice's oldest café, continuously open since 1720 (though you'll find it closed on Wednesday in winter). Counter seating is less expensive than taking a table, especially when there's live music. In the Procuratie Vecchie, **Caffè Quadri** (☎ 041/5289299), exudes almost as much history as Florian across the way and is similarly pricey. It was shunned by 19th-century Venetians when the occupying Austrians made it their gathering place. During slow season, it closes Monday.

Also Worth Seeing

5 Biblioteca Marciana (Marciana Library). There's a wondrous collection of centuries-old books and illuminated manuscripts at this library, located across the Piazzetta from Palazzo Ducale in two buildings designed by Renaissance architect Sansovino, **Libreria Sansoviniana** and the adjacent **Zecca**. Unfortunately, the books can only be viewed by written request and are primarily the domain of scholars. But the **Gilded Hall** in the Sansoviniana is worth visiting for the works of Veronese, Tintoretto, and Titian that decorate its walls. You reach the Gilded Hall, which often hosts special exhibits relating to Venetian history, through Museo Correr. ⊠ *Piazza San Marco, enter through Museo Correr* ☎ *041/2405211* 🎫 *€11 Piazza San Marco museums, €15.50 Musei Civici pass* ☉ *Apr.–Oct., daily 9–7; Nov.–Mar., daily 9–6; last tickets sold 1 hr before closing* Ⓥ *Vallaresso/San Zaccaria.*

1 Chiostro di Sant'Apollonia. Behind the Basilica and over a bridge, a short fondamenta leads right toward the unassuming entrance of the **Museo Diocesano** (upstairs), housed in a former Benedictine monastery. Its peacefully shady 12th-century cloister has been modified over the centuries, but it remains the only surviving example of a Romanesque cloister in Venice. The brick pavement is original, and the many inscriptions and fragments on display (some from the 9th century) are all that remain of the first Basilica di San Marco. The museum contains an array of sacred vestments, reliquaries, crucifixes, ex-votos, and paintings from various Venetian churches. ⊠ *Ponte della Canonica, Castello 4312* ☎ *041/5229166* 🎫 *Free (donations welcomed)* ☉ *Mon.–Sat. 10:30–12:30; ring bell* Ⓥ *Vallaresso/San Zaccaria.*

6 Museo Archeologico. This museum was first conceived in 1523, when Cardinal Domenico Grimani, a noted humanist, left his collection of original Greek (5th–1st centuries BC) and Roman (mostly from the imperial era) marbles to the republic. Highlights include the statue of Kore (420 BC), an Attic original known as Abbondanza Grimani; the 1st-century BC Ara Grimani, an elaborate Hellenistic altar stone with a bacchanalian scene; a tiny but refined 1st-century BC crystal woman's head, which some say depicts Cleopatra; and a remarkable gallery of Roman

WADING THROUGH THE ACQUA ALTA

YOU HAVE TO WALK *almost everywhere in Venice, and where you can't walk, you go by water. Occasionally you walk in water, when normally higher fall and spring tides are exacerbated by falling barometers and southeasterly winds. The result is acqua alta—flooding in the lowest parts of town, especially Piazza San Marco, which lasts a few hours, until the tide recedes.*

Venetians handle the high waters with aplomb, donning waders and erecting temporary walkways, but they're well aware of the damage caused by the flooding and the threat it poses to their city. Work has begun on the Moses Project, an elborate, enormously expensive network of flood gates that would close off the lagoon when high tides threaten, but it's a controversial response to an emotionally charged problem.

busts. Don't miss the small collection of Egyptian and Assiro-Babylonian relics, including two mummies and a brick bearing the name of King Nebuchadnezzar. ⊠ *Piazza San Marco, enter through Museo Correr* ☎ *041/5225978* ✆ *€11 Piazza San Marco museums; €15.50 Musei Civici pass. Contact the museum for information about free guided tours in English* ☉ *Apr.–Oct., daily 9–7; Nov.–Mar., daily 9–5; last tickets sold 1 hr before closing* Ⓥ *Vallaresso/San Zaccaria.*

★ ❼ **Museo Correr.** Exhibits in this museum of Venetian art and history range from the absurdly high-soled shoes worn by 16th-century Venetian ladies (who walked with the aid of servants) to old master paintings. Visit Correr after you've seen a bit of the town as it looks today—so much the better to appreciate La Serenissima's glorious past. From the first 1830 donation by Teodoro Correr, the museum has become so richly endowed that many of its treasures are warehoused and rotated into exhibits as time and space permit. Don't miss the huge, intricate *Grande Pianta Prospettica* in which Jacopo de' Barbari (circa 1440–1515) details in carved wood every inch of 16th-century Venice, including the old version of the Rialto Bridge and the neighborhood that once stood in the Giardini della Biennale before Napoléon demolished it. Whole rooms are devoted to Admiral Francesco Morosini (doge from 1688 to 1694), to intriguing objects and garments used by the doges through the ages, and even to antique games. In the second floor **Quadreria** (Picture Gallery), Room 36 is entirely given over to the talented Bellini family of Renaissance painters, Jacopo and his sons, Giovanni (1430–1516) and the lesser known Gentile (1429–1507). Room 30 houses a small but evocative Pietà by Cosmè Tura (1430–95). In Room 38 is Carpaccio's (circa 1465–1525) *Two Venetian Ladies,* formerly referred to as *The Courtesans.* Experts are still debating whether this painting is an extension of a larger Carpaccio work. If the *Hunt in the Valley* (J. P. Getty Museum, Malibu) depicts another part of the same scene, these two ladies may in fact be waiting for the return of their gentlemen hunters. ✉ *Piazza San Marco, Ala Napoleonica* ☎ *041/2405211* 🎫 *€11 Piazza San Marco museums; €15.50 Musei Civici pass* ⊘ *Apr.–Oct., daily 9–7; Nov.–Mar., daily 9–5; last tickets sold 1 hr before closing* Ⓥ *Vallaresso/San Zaccaria.*

❽ Torre dell'Orologio. Erected between 1496 and 1499, the Clock Tower has an enameled timepiece and animated Moorish figures that strike the hour. On Epiphany (January 6) and during Ascension Week (40 days after Easter), an angel and three wise men go in and out of the doors and bow to the Virgin Mary. The complicated clock mechanism also indicates the phase of the moon and the path of the sun across the signs of the zodiac. If the tower's inscription is true—HORAS NON NUMERO NISI SERENAS ("I only count happy hours")—then perhaps happy times may again come to Venice if they ever manage to fix the clock; it's been under restoration since 1999 and completion has been set for 2006. You can however visit the famous three wise men on the ground floor of Palazzo Ducale where parts of the clock are on display. ✉ *Northern side of Piazza San Marco.*

SAN MARCO & DORSODURO

The sestiere of San Marco stretches from the Rialto Bridge to Piazza San Marco, and is the part of town generally considered the most fashionable—meaning it has the most expensive hotels, restaurants, and shops. San Marco's fairly straight main drag runs between Campo San Bartolomeo, at the foot of the Rialto Bridge, and Campo Santo Stefano, at the foot of Accademia Bridge. Both squares are popular meeting places, with monuments and bars where Venetians break for an espresso and the inevitable *telefonino* (cell phone) chat while waiting for friends. Between this last campo and Calle Larga XXII Marzo are the Teatro La Fenice and the gloomy network of alleys where the film *Death in Venice* was shot.

South of San Marco, the long, narrow Dorsoduro sestiere may owe its name, which translates literally as "hardback," to the solid clay foundation of the area. Its eastern end, Punta della Dogana, was for centuries the Serenissima's customs office. Its western section of Santa Marta, formerly a poor fishermen's neighborhood, is now part of the Port of Venice's busy passenger terminal. Spread between the southern stretch of the Grand Canal and the broader, deeper Giudecca Canal, this part of the city is prone to great changes in color and weather; extremely blue and warm under the sun, it becomes creamy white and icy when the fog rolls in, hazy gray under a summer storm, and tinged with fiery orange at sunrise or sunset.

Except perhaps for Lido beach, there's no sunnier spot in Venice than Fondamenta delle Zattere. It's the city's gigantic public terrace, with bustling bars and gelaterie. It's the place to stroll, read in the open air, go for a run, or play hooky from sightseeing. The call of the seagulls or the whistle of the boats on their way to port recalls days gone by. This vaguely intellectual and cosmopolitan part of town is home to the Università degli Studi di Venezia and the Accademia di Belle Arti. At the border of the small sestiere of Santa Croce is a prestigious institute of architecture, frequented by students from all over Europe. Campo Santa Margherita, the largest square in Dorsoduro, is lively from early morning fish market to late-night cafés.

It takes a full day to see the sights here—probably more if you want to do them justice. The Gallerie dell'Accademia, Venice's main art museum, demands the most time; a few hours will allow you to see a good sampling of the collection, though with the help of the audio guide you can zip through the highlights in about an hour. Give yourself at least 1½ hours for the Peggy Guggenheim Collection—although the gardens, gift shop, café, and air-conditioning might tempt you to linger even longer. Ca' Rezzonico also deserves a couple of hours. The churches and Scuola dei Carmini are not large, and unless something grabs your attention, a half hour should be enough for each one.

Numbers in the margin correspond to the numbers on the San Marco & Dorsoduro map.

The Main Attractions

⑬ Ca' Rezzonico. English critic John Ruskin (1819–1900) may have called this "the silliest palace" on the Grand Canal, but today a visit to its **Museo del Settecento Veneziano** (Museum of 18th-Century Venice) provides a fascinating peek into the lives of Venetian nobles and commoners of a bygone era. The palace was given a 17th-century baroque design by Longhena, but wasn't completed until nearly 100 years later by Giorgio Massari (1686–1766). It was acquired by the city in 1935. Its frescoes, gilded salons, and marble fixtures show how elegance held on in Venice despite the city's declining fortunes. Bought and sold frequently over the centuries, Ca' Rezzonico once belonged to English poet Robert Browning's son. During a visit Browning caught a cold and died here. His epitaph-like quip, "Open my heart and you will see graven inside of it Italy," is still visible on the facade. The mansion is loaded with sumptuous brocade, fine furniture, and chandeliers of Murano glass. Concerts, often held in the elegant ballroom, call to mind parties from a bygone era, and a lovely alcoved bedroom might have welcomed Casanova and his intrigues. The carefully reconstructed **Farmacia ai Do San Marchi** (Pharmacy at the Two St. Marks), with its jars full of powders and potions, gives a sense of how 18th-century people dealt with health and medicine. A worthwhile art gallery includes genre pictures by Pietro Longhi (1702–85) showing life in the parlors and kitchens behind the Grand Canal's facades. Donations have added nearly 300 works to the collection, most from various schools of Venetian painting. Alongside more somber pieces by Tintoretto and Bonifacio, Sebastiano Ricci's (1659–1734) *Venus with Sartyr and Cupid,* and Gaspare Diziani's (1689–1767) *Pan and the Sleeping Nymph* seem lighthearted, even magical. Several portraits by Rosalba Carriera (1675–1757), one of Venice's few female painters, deserve attention, as do cityscapes by Francesco Guardi (1712–93), a great painter whose misfortune was being a contemporary of the more popular Canaletto. ⊠ *Fondamenta Rezzonico, Dorsoduro 3136* ☎ *041/2410100* ⌑ *€6.50; €8 Museums of 18th-Century Culture pass; €15.50 Musei Civici pass* ☉ *Apr.–Oct., Wed.–Mon. 10–6; Nov.–Mar., Wed.–Mon. 10–5; last entry 1 hr before closing* Ⅴ *Ca' Rezzonico.*

FodorśChoice ★

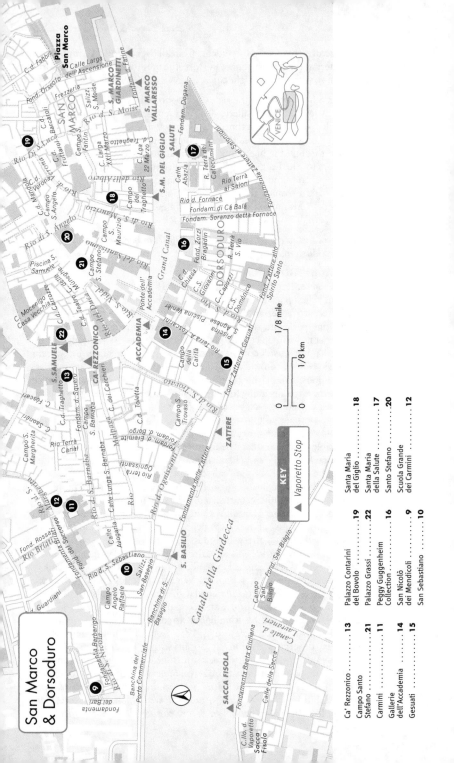

San Marco & Dorsoduro

KEY

▲ Vaporetto Stop

⑭ Gallerie dell'Accademia (Accademia Galleries). Napoléon founded these

Fodor's Choice galleries in 1807 on the site of a religious complex he'd suppressed, and

★ what he initiated amounts to the world's most extraordinary collection of Venetian art. Many works come from churches, convents, and scuole that either were suppressed by the French leader or were judged unsuitable places to house such treasures.

Byzantium was an early influence on the art of Venice, as evidenced by the gold, enamel colors, and unreal narrative structure that became part of Venetian Gothic style, which is on display in Room 1 of the galleries. In the 14th-century polyptychs by Paolo Veneziano (circa 1290–1360) and Lorenzo Veneziano (active 1356–72)—no relation—you see the distinct influence of the Byzantine Church. Further into Room 1 are works by masters of the 15th-century Gothic style, Jacobello del Fiore (circa 1370–1439) and Antonio Vivarini (circa 1415–1476/84).

Room 2 demonstrates a second characteristic central to Venetian painting, rich color. The emphasis on color can be attributed to the city itself: light reflected off the lagoon often seems to blur contours and melt colors together. While Italian Renaissance painters elsewhere concentrated on perfect drawing, balanced arrangement, and perspective, their colleagues in Venice became masters of color, using it to bring figures together and give unity to their works.

Jacopo Bellini (circa 1400–1470), father of artist sons Giovanni and Gentile, is also considered the father of the Venetian Renaissance. Apprenticing in Perugia under Gentile da Fabriano, Jacopo practiced perspective drawing and sketching from life, and he would carry these techniques home to Venice. Study his harmonious *Madonna and Child with Saints*; comparing this to Room 2's other large altarpieces—Cima da Conegliano's touching *Madonna of the Orange Tree,* or Carpaccio's narrative *Ten Thousand Martyrs of Mt. Ararat*—shows how Venice's early Renaissance masters built on Jacopo's foundation.

Works by Bellini's son Giovanni (circa 1430–1516) draw your eye not with their subject matter but with their mellowness and richness of color. Rooms 4 and 5 are full of his Madonnas, many painted for shrines in private homes. Though the subject is the same, they're far from repetitive; note the contrast between the young Madonna with baby hanging beside the grieving, elderly Madonna whose son has just died—you'll see the colors of dawn and dusk in Venice.

Color was often more important than content for Giorgione (circa 1478–1510); his enigmatic *Tempest* (Room 5), which has intrigued centuries of viewers and critics, depicts a storm approaching as a nude woman nurses her child and a soldier looks on. According to 20th-century art historian E. H. Gombrich, "Though the figures are not particularly carefully drawn, and the composition is somewhat artless, the picture is clearly blended into a whole simply by the light and air that permeates it all . . . ; for the first time, it seems, the landscape is not just a background. . . ." Giorgione broke away from the tradition of painting only beautiful figures; in his *Old Woman,* the subject holds in her right hand a piece of paper reading *col tempo* (with time), reminding viewers that everyone must age. Next door in Room 7, Lorenzo Lotto's *Young Man in his Study*, with his intense expression of melancholy, is one of the most compelling portraits in the Galleries.

In the 16th century, only Michelangelo was more famous than Titian (circa 1487–1576). Giorgione's heir and the official painter of the Venetian republic, he was the guest of royal courts throughout Europe; though he traveled south to paint a portrait for Pope Paul III, he refused to remain in Rome. His *Presentation of the Virgin* (Room 24) is the only work in the collection that was originally created for the building in which it hangs. He was finishing *Pietà* (Room 10) for his tomb in Chiesa dei Frari when he died of the plague in 1576. Over this masterpiece's shadowy background you can see how Titian applied glowing colors with his hands, often his tools of choice. You can also see a self-portrait of the artist as an old man—he's pictured to the viewer's right of Jesus.

Tintoretto and Veronese, two more Venetian Renaissance giants, are featured in Room 10. The first of Jacopo Tintoretto's (1518–1594) four scenes from the *Life of San Marco* shows the saint dreaming of Venice. Tintoretto was often at odds with critics, who described his work as crude and carelessly executed; he strove to show emotion and felt the incomparable beauty of Titian's works rendered them more pleasing than moving. Perhaps the artist believed a careful "finish" impeded the drama of his painting. Paolo Veronese (1528–1588), on the other hand, wanted his work to be attractive and pleasing. *Feast in the House of Levi* shows the Venetian high Renaissance in all its richness and glamour. Commissioned as a *Last Supper* by Dominican friars, this painting was rejected and the artist was reported to the Inquisition, which took issue with the painting's jesters, dogs, and German (therefore Protestant) soldiers. Veronese cleverly avoided the charges of profanity by changing the painting's title to the *Feast in the House of Levi,* representing a bawdy but nonetheless biblical event.

Rooms 20 and 21 feature series of canvases by Gentile Bellini (1429–1507) and Vittore Carpaccio, masters of Renaissance narrative painting. These renderings of Venetian life are exceptional sources of historical information, detailing everything from shoe and hair styles to boat design. Bellini's *Procession of the Relic of the Cross* (circa 1496), painted for the Scuola Grande di San Giovanni Evangelista, serves as a snapshot of Piazza San Marco, circa 1496—it's fascinating to see how things have changed, and how they've stayed the same. Carpaccio's *Miracle of the True Cross at Rialto* (also known as *Healing of a Lunatic*), shows the old wooden bridge at Rialto, which opened to let large boats pass. If the people depicted in the paintings are particularly realistic, it's because they were often painted from life. Monks and nobles of the 15th century frequently sat for the artist; note Caterina Cornaro, Queen of Cyprus, at the lower left of the *Recovery of the Relic from the Canal of San Lorenzo,* and the red-haired Patriarca di Grado witnessing the *Miracle at Rialto.*

In the 1700s, fresco and stucco became popular art forms, exemplified by Giambattista Tiepolo (1696–1770). Sections of a Tiepolo fresco, salvaged from Chiesa dei Scalzi after a World War I bombing, hang in Room 11. Another trend of the 1700s was landscape painting; travelers wanted souvenirs of their trips to Venice, and a new school of painters rose to the occasion. Two of the greatest had their destinies written in their names: Antonio Canal (1697–1768), called Canaletto, which literally translates as "Small Canal," and Francesco Guardi (1712–1793) whose surname means "You Look." Their styles couldn't have been more different. Canaletto, whose work is on display in Room 17, became official landscape painter of the republic and was courted throughout Europe for his remarkable verisimilitude and precise Flemish details. Guardi (Room 15) left your eye to imagine that which he didn't reveal in paint; in *Island of San Giorgio,* his gondoliers consist of a few deftly placed patches of color. So popular was Canaletto that little of his work remained in Venice; so precise was his work that modern researchers are tracing rising tides by studying buildings in his paintings. In the adjacent room hang portraits by Rosalba Carriera (1675–1758), one of Venice's best known female artists. She imported colors from Paris, where soft shades, like powdered skin, had become fashionable. The aging artist went mad, which you may be able to sense in her self-portrait.

Though not essential, prebooking your tickets to the Gallerie allows you to bypass the line during busy seasons and costs only an additional €1. Booking is necessary to see the **Quadreria,** a narrow exhibition room where additional works by Venetian masters cover every inch of the walls. It's open for limited, irregular hours (another reason to call ahead); a free map identifies the art and artists, and the bookshop sells an English-language booklet with additional information. In the main Gallerie, a €4 audio guide saves reading but adds little to each room's excellent English annotation; audio/video guides (€6) are more exhaustive and ease navigating. ⊠ *Campo della Carità, near Accademia Bridge, Dorsoduro 1050* ☎ *041/5222247, 041/5200345 reservations* ⊕ *www.gallerieaccademia.org* ✆ *€6.50; €11 also includes Ca' d'Oro and Oriental* ☉ *Tues.–Sun. 8:15–7, Mon. 8:15–2* Ⓥ *Accademia.*

> **need a break?** If ice cream is the food of gods, then heaven's as close as the Zattere, where generations of Venetians have chosen **Gelateria Nico** (⊠ Dorsoduro 922 ☎ 041/5225293). Grab a chocolaty *gianduiotto,* their famous nutty slab of chocolate ice cream floating on a cloud of whipped cream, and relax on the biggest, most welcoming deck in town.

★ ⓰ **Peggy Guggenheim Collection.** Extremely rich, provocative, and extravagant, Peggy Guggenheim (1898–1979)—wife of Max Ernst and niece of Solomon Guggenheim, founder of the New York museum bearing their name—was among the 20th century's greatest collectors of modern art. On display in Palazzo Venier dei Leoni, her residence for 30 years, are works representing the most important artistic movements from the early 20th century through the postwar period: Cubism (Picasso and Braque); Futurism (Balla, Severini, and Boccioni); metaphysical painting (*The Red Tower* by De Chirico); abstract painting (Kandinsky); and a large group of Surrealist masterpieces, including Magritte's *Empire* *of Light,* Max Ernst's outstanding large Dada canvases *The Kiss, The Attirement of the Bride,* and *The Anti-Pope* (he gave the last two to Guggenheim as a wedding present), and Miró's *Dutch Interior II* and *Seated Woman II.* The modernist generation of painters is represented by Rothko, Motherwell, Pollock, and Bacon. A room is dedicated to the lively little pictures made by the heiress's daughter Pegeen, who disappeared under mysterious circumstances. Scattered around the two beautiful gardens of the villa are sculptures ranging from Giacometti's ethereal bronze figures to a giant phallus pointing out to the Grand Canal. (Beverages, snacks, and light meals are served in the gardens.) In a tiny family cemetery, several tombstones indicate the resting place of Guggenheim herself and her beloved dogs. Don't miss the gift shop, with large black-and-white pictures (not for sale) of the young heiress living her dazzling life, and an array of thematic gifts such as mugs and neckties designed by architect Frank Lloyd Wright, Mondrianesque umbrellas, and Modigliani pins. ⊠ *Calle San Cristoforo, Dorsoduro 701* ☎ *041/ 2405411* ⊕ *www.guggenheim-venice.it* 🖾 *€10* ☉ *Wed.–Mon. 10–6; last entry 15 mins before closing* Ⓥ *Accademia.*

★ ⑰ **Santa Maria della Salute.** The view of "La Salute," as Venetians affectionately call it, from the Riva degli Schiavoni at sunset or from the Accademia Bridge under the moonlight is simply unforgettable. Early birds should also go for a walk to the Piazzetta at the break of dawn to see the lines of the temple's dome slowly emerge from the morning mist. The architect Baldassare Longhena was only 32 years old when, together with 10 colleagues, he participated in the design competition to build a great shrine in Venice dedicated to the Virgin Mary in gratitude for liberation from a terrible plague that from 1630 to 1631 killed 47,000 people in Venice alone. Presenting his project, Longhena spoke of it as an "unprecedented work which had never been even imagined in total or in part by other churches in this city." His plan for a classically inspired white octagonal temple covered by a colossal cupola, with a Palladian-style facade and bizarre baroque decorations, effortlessly conquered the avant-garde judges of the competition.

The grandiose temple is made of *marmorino* (brick covered with marble dust) and Istrian stone, an inexpensive material used in Venice for framing windows and lining steps on bridges. Building it was no easy task: about 100,000 trunks of oak were used to reinforce the muddy terrain. The luminous interior features six chapels with one altar each and a beautiful polychrome marble floor. Look for Titian's *Pentecost* across the aisle to the left. Since it was brought from Crete by Francesco Morosini in 1672, the Byzantine icon above the main altar has been venerated as the Madonna della Salute (of Health). (A small-scale silver replica still hangs in many Venetian bedrooms.) To its side is a remarkable sculpture group showing Venice on bended knee, asking the Virgin for protection from the plague, represented as a fleeing old woman. The **Sacrestia Maggiore** contains a wealth of art, including five works by Titian, the best of which are the *Five Saints* altarpiece; a large *Nozze di Canaan* by Tintoretto; and a precious 15th-century *paliotto* (tapestry), made from a drawing in the style of Mantegna (1431–1506) and Bellini on wool, silk, and silver thread that represents the Pentecost against a naturalistic background. A traditional thanksgiving pilgrimage during November's Festa della Madonna della Salute is one of the most evocative Venetian festivals. ⊠ *Punta della Dogana, Dorsoduro* ☎ *041/2743928* 🖾 *Church free, sacristy €1.50* ☼ *Daily 9–noon and 3–5:30* Ⓥ *Salute.*

Also Worth Seeing

㉑ **Campo Santo Stefano.** Although Venetians steadfastly refer to this campo by its old saint designation, on maps and walls it bears the name of Francesco Morosini (1618–92). Morosini came from a family that had already given the republic four doges; he became captain of a galley at age 23 and supreme commander of the Venetian navy at 39. Fondly remembered by Venetians as their last great sea hero, he made his mark on the world when in 1687 a cannon under his command fired a direct hit that practically obliterated the Parthenon in Athens, which the Turks had been using as a powder magazine. Elected doge while he was taking the Peloponnese, Morosini returned home to a 125-foot-tall triumphant arch that spanned Piazzetta San Marco. Wine flowed through two enormous fountains, and the republic placed his bronze bust inside Palazzo Ducale, an honor previously granted only posthumously.

Santo Stefano's doesn't have a statue of Morosini, but there is one of Nicolò Tommaseo (1802–74), an important figure in the rebellion against Austria in 1848. **Ca' Morosini** (at No. 2802–3) was sold after the last heir died in 1884, and the city acquired the family's records and personal effects, which are now in Museo Correr. To the right, **Palazzo Pisani,** once the largest private home in Venice, has been a conservatory of music since 1897 and is closed to the public. A very busy crossroad, this campo is a favorite meeting point for Venetians and visitors. During Carnevale and Christmas it hosts popular outdoor fairs. Ⓥ *Accademia.*

⑪ **Carmini.** This rather simple Gothic red-brick basilica has two remarkable altarpieces: a *Nativity* by Cima da Conegliano (circa 1459–1517), and *Sts. Nicholas, John the Baptist, and Lucy,* by Lorenzo Lotto (circa 1480–1556). The church is named after Santa Maria del Carmelo, who was left for several centuries without even a painting in her honor, until her followers finally managed to build the scuola nearby., ⊠ *Campo dei Carmini, Dorsoduro* ☎ *041/5226553* 🖾 *Free* ☼ *Daily 8–noon and 2:30–7* Ⓥ *Ca' Rezzonico.*

⑮ **Gesuati.** As soon as the Dominicans took over the church of Santa Maria della Visitazione from the suppressed order of Gesuati laymen, Giorgio Massari was commissioned to build this church in its place. Venice's favorite architect of the day, Massari had a populist attitude, saying, "An architect who doesn't want to starve must by necessity adapt himself to see and think according to classical norms and models." Inside, Gesuati is a triumph of 18th-century baroque. Images of saints in Dominican attire are rendered by Giambiattista Piazzetta (1683–1754), Sebastiano Ricci (1659–1734), and Giambattista Tiepolo, whose works here include the splendid ceiling. Sadly, only during holidays dedicated to the Virgin does the church display Stefano di Sant'Agnese's beautiful 15th-century *Madonna delle Grazie.* ⊠ *Zattere, Dorsoduro* ☎ *041/*

2750462 Chorus ✉ *€2.50; €9 Chorus pass* ⊙ *Mon.–Sat. 10–5, Sun. 1–5.* Ⓥ *Zattere.*

🔆 **⑲ Palazzo Contarini del Bovolo.** Easy to miss despite its vicinity to Piazza San Marco, this Renaissance-Gothic palace is accessible only through a narrow backstreet that connects Campo Manin with Calle dei Fuseri. Built around 1500 by the renowned Contarini family, it was closed for decades in the late 20th century, until structural reinforcement made its striking six-floor spiral staircase (*bovolo* means "snail" in Venetian dialect) climbable again. From the rooftop you can try to identify all of the bell towers you've seen around town. ✉ *Corte del Bovolo, San Marco 4299* ☎ *041/924933* ✉ *€3.50* ⊙ *Apr.–Oct., daily 10–6; Nov.–Mar. weekends 10–4* Ⓥ *Rialto.*

㉒ Palazzo Grassi. Having bought their way into Venetian aristocracy in 1718, the Bolognese Grassi family became the new kids on the Grand Canal block thirty years later, when architect Giorgio Massari began work on their neoclassical palazzo; it was to be the canal's last grand addition. Fiat, Italy's leading automaker, acquired the palazzo in 1985 and restored it as a venue for temporary art exhibits. Shows in the past have featured artists Picasso, Modigliani, and Balthus, and historical subjects such as the Phoenicians and Etruscans. After the death of Gianni Agnelli and Fiat's decision to sell Palazzo Grassi, the fate of the palazzo has become a mystery. With any luck, Palazzo Grassi will some day return to its former glory, offering exquisite art exhibitions. ✉ *Campo San Samuele, San Marco 3231* Ⓥ *San Samuele.*

★ **❾ San Nicolò dei Mendicoli.** Padovans fleeing the Lombard invasion in the 7th century chose this scrap of an island called *Mendigola* to found their church. A humble fishing village grew up around it and became the west end haunt of the Nicolotti, one of the town's two historic "gangs." A community unto itself, it had its its own lion atop a column (wingless but still there), its own flag, and even a leader dubbed the Doge of the Nicolotti. The current 12th-century church of San Nicolò has had enough renovations to document changing fashions of church architecture. The bell tower has survived since the 12th century but only just—it took a stray shell during the German withdrawal in World War II. The facade and its 13th-century windows were rediscovered only when 18th-century restoration shucked the bad remodeling that had covered them over interim centuries. The Gothic-style porch was a popular 15th-century feature among Venetian churches, built to shelter the *pinzocchere* (female beggars). The interior, brilliantly restored after Venice's 1966 flood by the Venice in Peril Fund, is covered with paintings by Veronese's pupils, including Alvise Dal Friso (1554–1608). Also worth seeing is Palma il Giovane's (1544–1628) *Resurrection.* ✉ *Campo San Nicolò dei Mendicoli, Dorsoduro* ☎ *041/2750382* ✉ *Free* ⊙ *Daily 10–noon and 4–6* Ⓥ *San Basilio.*

★ **❿ San Sebastiano.** The treasure this dull facade conceals is an example of what you could miss hidden behind Venice's many masks. This jewel holds an extraordinary collection by Paolo Caliari, better known as Veronese (1528–1588), who in his early twenties came to Venice from his hometown of Verona (hence the nickname). The first frescoes he painted in San Sebastiano launched an intense and celebrated career for this grand-scale decorator, famous for glowing colors. A contemporary of Tintoretto, Veronese lived in the salizzada nearby and took great pride in embellishing this, his parish church. He began in the period 1555–56 with Old Testament scenes in the Sacristy and episodes from the Book of Esther in the coffered ceiling. He progressed to the upper part of the nave, choir, organ doors, and frontispiece. Between 1562–70, he created *Madonna in Glory with St. Sebastian, Saints Mark and Marcellino Led to their Martyrdom,* and the *Martyrdom of St. Sebastian.* The artist, not surprisingly, was buried here; beneath his bust near the organ. ⊠ *Campo San Sebastiano, Dorsoduro* ☎ *041/2750462 Chorus* ☜ *€2.50; €9 Chorus pass* ☉ *Mon.–Sat. 10–5; Sun. 1–5.* Ⅴ *San Basilio.*

⑱ Santa Maria del Giglio. This white, airy church is one of the most remarkable examples of Venetian baroque. If you step back and look up at the facade's upper-left corner, the angel seems about to take flight. Santa Maria del Giglio is often referred to as Santa Maria Zobenigo, after the family that built the original 9th-century church, but this present building is dedicated to the the painting *Virgin with the Lily,* which hangs inside. In the iconography of the Annunciation, the angel offers Mary a white lily, a symbol of purity and inside you will see a painting showing this scene. Virgin and lilies aside, this church seems more like one large monument to the five Barbaro brothers, who financed its reconstruction. Along with their statues decorating the facade, are the maps of Zara, Candia, Padua, Rome, Corfu, and Spalato, the cities where Antonio Barbaro spent his life in service to the republic. The interior has more the feeling of an art gallery than a place of worship, as the walls and ceiling are packed with paintings of all sizes and shapes, including a good stations-of-the-cross series by various artists. Ask the doorkeeper to light the area behind the main altar to better appreciate Tintoretto's *Four Evangelists,* and the moving *Annunciation* by Salviati (died 1575). The cozy Cappella Molin is full of exquisite gold and silver reliquaries containing everything from fragments of bones to fingernails. Newly encased in its protective frame is the only work by Rubens in Venice, *Madonna and Child with Young St. John.* The **Sacristy,** open only 10–11:30, contains several lesser-known works. ⊠ *Campo Santa Maria del Giglio, San Marco* ☎ *041/2750462 Chorus* ☜ *€2.50; €9 Chorus pass* ☉ *Mon.–Sat. 10–5, Sun. 1–5* Ⅴ *S. Maria del Giglio.*

⑳ Santo Stefano. The third-largest convent building in Venice after the Frari and San Zanipolo, the church of Santo Stefano was founded by Augustinian hermits in the 13th century. Perhaps there was something wrong from the very beginning—the church had to be entirely rebuilt in the 14th century, and the story goes that it was reconsecrated six times because of bloodstains that appeared on the ceiling. The church's entrance portal by Bartolomeo Bon is striking, and tall interior pillars make this an excellent example of florid Gothic style. Here you appreciate the Venetian ingenuity in lightening structures that otherwise would have sunk into their muddy foundations: in place of the typically heavy roofs that bore down on static walls, the master shipbuilders of the lagoon envisioned and created a wooden roof shaped like a ship's keel. Three paintings by Tintoretto are on display in the sacristy, and Doge Francesco Morosini (died 1694), the city's most celebrated admiral, is buried beneath a huge marble slab in the main aisle. ⊠ *Campo Santo Stefano, San Marco* ☎ *041/2750462 Chorus* ⬚ *€2.50; €9 Chorus pass* ☉ *Mon.–Sat. 10–5, Sun. 1–5* Ⓥ *Accademia.*

★ ⑫ **Scuola Grande dei Carmini.** By the time Longhena completed this scuola in the 1670s, the brotherhood of Santa Maria del Carmelo had grown to 75,000 members, making it the largest fraternal order of the period. It was also one of the wealthiest, so little expense was spared in the decorating, which includes stuccoed ceilings, carved ebony paneling, and choice paintings. The real show, however, began in 1739 when the **Sala Capitolare** was entrusted to Tiepolo. Many consider the nine canvases that adorn the vault to be his best work. Using vivid techniques, Tiepolo was able to transform some rather unpromising religious themes into flamboyant displays of color and movement. Mirrors in the rooms may make it easier for ceiling-viewers' necks. ⊠ *Campo dei Carmini, Dorsoduro 2617* ☎ *041/5289420* ⬚ *€5* ☉ *Nov.–Mar., daily 9–4; Apr.–Oct., Mon.–Sat. 9–6, Sun. 9–4* Ⓥ *Ca' Rezzonico.*

SAN POLO & SANTA CROCE

The smallest of Venice's six sestieri, San Polo and Santa Croce were named after their main churches, though the Chiesa di Santa Croce was demolished in 1810. The city's most famous bridge, the Ponte di Rialto, which unites sestiere San Marco (east) with San Polo (west), takes its name from *Rivoaltus,* the high ground on which it was built. Shops abound here; on the San Marco side of the bridge they sell everything that's hip, on the San Polo side everything edible. Chiesa di San Giacometto, where you see the first fruit vendors as you come off the bridge on the San Polo side, was probably built in the 11th and 12th centuries, about the time the surrounding market came into being. Public announcements were traditionally read in the church's campo; its 24-hour clock, though lovely, has rarely worked. If you want to take part in the food shopping, come early to beat the crowds and bear in mind that a *metà kilo* is about a pound and an *etto* is a few ounces.

The sestiere has some other important sites, such as Santa Maria Gloriosa dei Frari and the Scuola Grande di San Rocco, as well as some worthwhile but lesser-known churches. There's a lot to see, so if you do any shopping, or even pop in at a few churches along the way, you'll need at least a half day. West of the main thoroughfare that takes you from the Ponte di Rialto to Santa Maria Gloriosa dei Frari is San Giacomo dell'Orio campo and church, a peaceful place for a drink, a rest, and a chance to glimpse daily life. Not far from the campo is the whimsically baroque church of San Stae and Ca' Pesaro, the site of both the Museum of Modern Art and the Oriental Museum. You'll want at least two hours to see both collections at Ca' Pesaro.

Numbers in the margin correspond to the numbers on the San Polo & Santa Croce map.

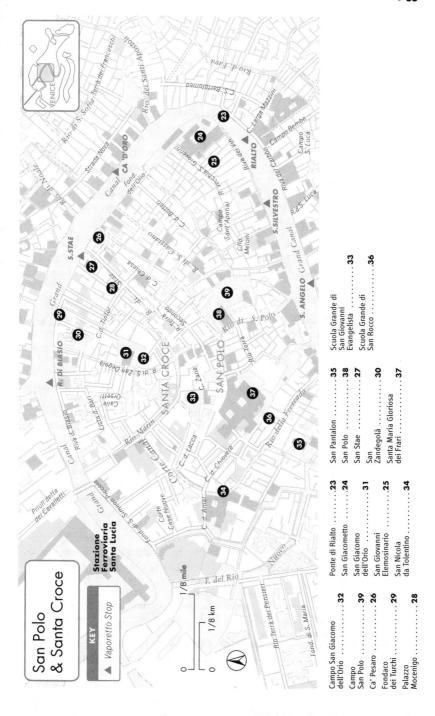

San Polo & Santa Croce

KEY

▲ Vaporetto Stop

Stazione
Ferroviaria
Santa Lucia

0 — 1/8 km
0 — 1/8 mile

The Main Attractions

㉓ **Ponte di Rialto** (Rialto Bridge). It is rather startling to consider that
Fodor'sChoice Venice, which by the end of the 12th century had already produced its
★ first version of Palazzo Ducale and most of Basilica di San Marco,
didn't build a permanent stone bridge across the Grand Canal until the
late 1500s. It was not as if there hadn't been a need: earlier there had
been an inconvenient toll bridge, replaced in the 13th century by a rick-
ety wooden bridge (which collapsed twice). In the 15th century a larger
bridge was built, this time with shops and an open central corridor, but
a century later it had deteriorated so badly that the republic finally gave
up on wood. The competition to design the Grand Canal's first stone
bridge attracted the best architects, including Michelangelo, Palladio,
and Sansovino, but the job went to the appropriately named Antonio
da Ponte. His pragmatic design featured shop space and was high
enough for galleys to pass beneath; it kept decoration and cost to a minimum at a time when the republic's coffers were low due to continual
wars against the Turks and the opening of oceanic trade routes. A single arcade, more than 91 feet in length, supports two rows of shops selling jewelry, leather, lace tablecloths, and souvenirs, with windows that
open onto the central passage. Along the railing you'll find one of the
city's most famous views: the Grand Canal vibrant with gondola and
motorboat traffic. Ⓥ *Rialto.*

㊲ **Santa Maria Gloriosa dei Frari.** St. Francis was still alive when a group
Fodor'sChoice of friars from his order arrived in Venice in 1222. They remained with-
★ out a fixed residence for about 30 years, until the Doge Tiepolo gave
them an abandoned abbey on a vast tract of land in the San Polo sestiere. The Friars replaced the abbey's old church with a newer building
which served them until the huge Gothic temple you see today was completed in the 1400s, culminating a century of work. Known locally as
I Frari, it's believed to have been designed by architect and Franciscan
friar Scipione Bon, also known as Beato Pacifico, whose portrait is in
the right transept beneath his funeral monument.

Abstinence and poverty were fundamental tenets of the Franciscan
order, an austerity that echoes from plain russet-color walls. (Look
closely and you'll find them painted in a faux-brick pattern.) Save for
its richly carved choir stalls, the church was always known for its relative absence of artwork, but paradoxically, I Frari does contain a few
of the most sumptuously brilliant paintings in any Venetian church, including the magnificent Titian altarpieces, which are among the most
dazzling works this prolific artist produced. Visit the sacristy first, to
see Giovanni Bellini's 1488 triptych *Madonna and Child with Saints* in
all its mellow luminosity, painted for precisely that spot. Contrast this
with the heroic energy of Titian's large *Assumption* over the main
altar—painted little more than 30 years later—to appreciate the rapid
development of Venetian Renaissance painting. This work caused a
sensation when unveiled in 1518 and was immediately acclaimed for
its winning combination of Venetian color—especially the glowing
reds—and classical Roman figure style. It was said that this piece raised
Venetian painting to the level of art being produced for the pope. Many

believe Titian made an even greater artistic stride in his subsequent painting, the *Madonna di Ca' Pesaro* (in left nave). It took almost 10 years to complete and was created for nobleman Jacopo Pesaro in gratitude for victory over the Turks. Looking at the Madonna, modeled after the artist's wife who died soon afterward in childbirth, it's hard to appreciate the radical break from convention she represented, but it was unheard of in Titian's time to move the Virgin out of picture center and portray the surrounding saints as active participants in the scene.

The church lost some of its asceticism when a number of grandiose 19th-century mausoleums were added. Especially conspicuous is the pyramid-shaped tomb of sculptor Antonio Canova (1757–1822), with its sleepy lion (perhaps hinting at Venice's captivity under the Austrians). Opposite this is an equally ponderous monument to Titian, a man so revered that Venetians exhumed his body from a communal grave used for plague victims. Conclude your visit with a look at the arrestingly realistic wooden sculpture *St. John the Baptist,* which Donatello made for the Florentine community in 1438. ☒ *Campo dei Frari, San Polo* ☏ *041/2728618, 041/2750462 Chorus* 🔊 *€2.50; €9 Chorus pass* ☉ *Mon.–Sat. 9–6, Sun. 1–6.* Ⓥ *San Tomà.*

> **need a break?**
>
> On a narrow passage between Frari and San Rocco, **Gelateria Millevoglie** (a Thousand Desires; ☏ 041/5244667) has pizza slices, calzones, and gelato so popular it backs up traffic. It's closed in December and January, but the rest of the year it's open 10 AM to midnight, seven days a week.

★ ㉟ **Scuola Grande di San Rocco.** The Brotherhood of San Rocco grew up around a French-born medical student who renounced career and wealth to make a pilgrimage to Italy. He dedicated himself to helping plague sufferers and in the process became infected. Legend says that he hid in a forest, and each day a dog brought him bread until he healed miraculously. Upon return to France, he was not recognized by his family and died in prison at age 32, but he'd already planted a seed in Italy and a sect dedicated to San Rocco was recognized by the republic in 1478. The cult of St. Rocco, invoked against the plagues that decimated Europe, was particularly strong in Venice, and after the grave epidemic of 1576, the saint was made co-patron of the city. Generous donations to the brotherhood led to the construction of a church and one of the most sumptuous scuole in the city.

Apart from being a great example of Venetian Renaissance architecture, the Scuola Grande di San Rocco is famous for a series of more than 60 paintings by Tintoretto that some have referred to as Venice's Sistine Chapel. More mystical and devout than his contemporaries, Tintoretto sought pathos and emotional tension rather than refined brushstrokes. He carried Titian's love of motion and unusual composition to highly dramatic ends: his wall-size *Crucifixion* left even tough-skinned critic Ruskin speechless. The story goes that in 1564 Tintoretto won the competition to decorate the Albergo of the scuola by submitting a finished work—*St. Rocco in Glory* at the center of the ceiling—instead of a sketch. He offered the painting for free "not to win, but to honor St. Rocco" and spent the next 23 years on the cycle of paintings. Start from the Albergo on the first floor, which also houses two intense works on easels attributed to Giorgione and Titian. Then return to the large adjoining hall, where Tintoretto worked from 1576 to 1588, after the scuola agreed to pay him an annual pension for life. On the ceiling are episodes from the Old Testament; the three larger, central subjects are *Moses Striking Water from the Rock to Quench the People's Thirst*; *The Brazen Serpent* (serpent wrapped around a staff); and *The Fall of Manna*. These represent humanity's three bodily sufferings—thirst, disease, and hunger—which San Rocco and later his brotherhood worked to eliminate. The walls feature New Testament scenes and some conspicuous wood carvings by 17th-century sculptor Francesco Pianta. The mildly satirical, bizarre figures are allegories of the sentiments, such as Fury (the winged youth with the blindfold, flask of wine, and cannon); of activities like Espionage (the man wrapped in a large scarf); and of the arts—symbolized by a bad-tempered Tintoretto, with a bunch of brushes. The eight canvases on the ground floor, conceived when Tintoretto was in his sixties, show his innovative use of light and shadow, which play a key role in the economy of his masterpiece *Flight into Egypt*. The Old and New Testament works were restored in the 1970s, making all the more evident Tintoretto's inventive use of light. ⊠ *Campo di San Rocco, San Polo 3052* ☎ *041/5234864* ⊠ *€5.50* ☉ *Nov. 3–Mar. 27, daily 10–4; Mar. 28–Nov. 2, daily 9–5:30; last entrance ½ hr before closing* Ⓥ *San Tomà.*

> **need a break?**

A popular student hangout, **Café Noir** (⊠ Calle Crosera, Dorsoduro 3805 ☎ 041/710925) is a good place to sit down for a coffee or have a sandwich. The scene really comes to life in the evenings when music and regulars begin spilling out into the street. It's one of the few places in town open until 2 AM but it's closed Sunday. **Pasticceria Tonolo** (⊠ Dorsoduro 3764 ☎ 041/5237209) has been fattening Venetians since 1886. Tonolo truly is a Venetian landmark, almost as much as Piazza San Marco. During Carnevale, it's still the best place in town for *fritelle,* fried doughnuts (traditional raisin or cream-filled); during acqua alta, the staff dons rubber boots and keeps working. The cakes, pastries and coffee make it a favorite among Venetians of all ages and when they are invited over for dinner, rest assured that a tray of Tonolo's treats will be in hand. The place is closed on Monday, and there's no seating anytime. If you're in the mood for a good glass of wine, **Vinus Venezia** (⊠ Dorsoduro 3961) is just around the corner. This restyled wine bar, *bacaro* in Venetian dialect, serves Veneto wines as well as the standard Chianti and light snacks the locals call *cichetti.*

Also Worth Seeing

㉜ Campo San Giacomo dell'Orio. Perhaps it is fitting that the name of this campo and its church is derived not from some torturous saintly martyrdom, but from the *orio* (laurel tree) that once provided the area shade. Trees today give the pleasantly odd-shaped campo character, and when you add a few benches and a fountain (with drinking bowl for

VENICE'S SCUOLA DAYS

AN INSTITUTION you'll inevitably encounter from Venice's glory days is the scuola (plural scuole). These weren't schools, as the word today translates, but rather an important network of institutions established by different social groups—tradesmen, parishioners, enclaves of foreigners, followers of a particular saint.

One of the main purposes of the scuole was to conduct charitable work. The tradesmen's and servants' scuole formed social security nets for elderly and disabled members. Wealthier scuole assisted orphans or provided dowries so poor girls could marry. By 1500, there were more than 200 major and minor scuole in Venice, some of which contributed substantially to arts and crafts guilds. The republic encouraged their existence—the scuole kept strict records of the names and professions of contributors to the brotherhood, which helped when it came time to collect taxes.

dogs), it becomes a welcoming place for meeting friends, having picnics, and watching neighborhood kids at play. Several streets lead into it at odd angles, and the church sits nicely among the houses rather than towering above them. On the south side of the campo you can cross over the Ponte dell'Anatomia, into secluded Corte dell'Anatomia. Early scientists and students were reputed to hide here when authorities raided their anatomy classes. Although an anatomy theater was officially established here in 1507—some 87 years before the more famous Università di Padua theater opened—itinerant anatomical experiments were taking place in Venice as early as 1368.

39 Campo San Polo. Not long ago this campo, second in size only to San Marco, was a throbbing center of activity, hosting shows, bull races, fairs, military parades, and packed markets. Today the activity has dissipated, and children zooming around on bikes and scooters, their voices echoing off surrounding palaces, make San Polo feel even more cavernous. The campo only really comes alive on summer nights, when it hosts the city's outdoor cinema. A stone's throw from the Grand Canal, this neighborhood was settled by some of the richest families of the city. The early 15th-century Palazzo Soranzo (at No. 2170–1) was entirely decorated with frescoes by Giorgione; the baroque building at No. 1957 took the place of the Gothic mansion of the Bernardo family, covered with frescoes by Salviati. The facade of the Renaissance **Palazzo Corner Mocenigo,** facing the canal, is best seen by looking right from Ponte San Polo on the way to the Frari. If you leave the campo through the Sottoportico dei Cavalli (No. 1957), cross the bridge, take a left, and then cross another bridge and take another left, you'll reach the 17th-century **Palazzo Albrizzi,** occasionally open to the public for temporary exhibits. ⓥ *San Tomà.*

26 Ca' Pesaro. Designed by Baldassare Longhena in grand baroque style, this impressive mansion was completed in 1710, nearly thirty years after both its commissioner and architect had died. After trading hands several times, the palace was turned over to the city on the condition that it be used to exhibit the works of young Venetian artists. Initially, the **Galleria Internazionale d'Arte Moderna** (Gallery of Modern Art) fulfilled this condition by exhibiting paintings and sculpture from the Biennale, an international art event that, with few interruptions, has taken place in Venice every two years since 1895. Years of acquisitions and donations have turned it into one of Italy's most varied collections of modern art, with works by such artists as Klimt, Kandinsky, Matisse, and Miró. Reopened in 2002 after several years of restoration, the building is well lit and the works are well presented. Ca' Pesaro's upper floors house the **Museo d'Arte Orientale**, (Oriental Art Museum), an assortment of art, garments, armor, and musical instruments from China and Japan. Poor lighting and labeling detract from otherwise interesting exhibits, but the view across neighborhood rooftops is lovely. ⊠ *San Stae, Santa Croce 2076* ☎ *041/5240695 Galleria, 041/5241173 Museo Orientale* ⊙ *Apr.–Oct., Tues.–Sun. 10–6; Nov.–Mar., Tues.–Sun. 10–5* 🖃 *€5.50 includes both museums; €15.50 Musei Civici pass; €11 includes only Museo Orientale, Ca' d'Oro, Accademia* Ⓥ *San Stae.*

㉙ **Fondaco dei Turchi.** Built in 1225 by an immigrant from Pesaro, this palace was so beautiful that in 1381 it was bought by the republic. They loaned it to the Duke of Ferrara, from whom it was periodically confiscated in conflicts, and at the same time used it as a hotel for visiting emissaries. Ownership passed through a number of families, until in 1621 it was leased to Turkish merchants, who used it as a warehouse and residence, even installing a mosque and bathhouse.

From the Grand Canal, Fondaco dei Turchi is striking, with its pink and white marble facade and crenellated top. It was the original 19th-century home of Museo Correr but now contains the city's **Museo di Storia Naturale** (Museum of Natural History). It has collections of flora and fauna native to the lagoon and the skeletons of two prehistoric reptiles. Although some parts of the building are still closed for renovation, the museum has recently reopened the dinosaur exhibit and has temporary exhibitions as well. ⊠ *Salizzada del Fontego dei Turchi, Santa Croce 1730* ☎ *041/2750206* 🖃 *Free* ⊙ *Weekdays 9–1; weekends 10–4.*

㉘ **Palazzo Mocenigo.** So well preserved it looks like a movie set, this palazzo gives a sense of how wealthy families lived in the last years of the republic. Bequeathed to the city in 1945 by the last surviving Mocenigo heir, the home is richly decorated with polished floors, fabric-covered walls, and glass chandeliers from Murano. The *portego* (entry hall), typical of Venetian palazzos, occupies about one-third of the total floor space; once used for receptions and balls, it now occasionally hosts classical concerts. Sparsely furnished, it's lined with portraits of the seven Mocenigo family doges and other notables. Doors on both sides of the portego open onto bedrooms and salons, where visitors were received with a cup of hot chocolate in the early morning hours after nights typically spent at parties or seated at gambling tables. Furniture and paintings are all original and constitute a permanent exhibit. The mannequins' clothing, lace, fabrics, and accessories on display come from the **Cen-**

ter for the History of Textiles and Costumes (housed in a wing of the palace) which organizes 15th- to 18th-century thematic exhibits. ⊠ *Salizzada San Stae, Santa Croce 1992* ☎ *041/721798* ✆ *€4; €8 Museums of 18th-Century Culture pass; €15.50 Musei Civici pass* ☉ *Daily 10–4* Ⓥ *San Stae.*

㉔ San Giacometto. Legend says a church was founded here in the 5th century by some of the lagoon's earliest refugees, but this building was probably constructed in the 11th and 12th centuries, the same time as the neighboring market. Doges traditionally paid visits here every Good Friday. Across from the church's front door is a squat marble pedestal where public announcements were read. Beneath the steps to the pedestal stands what people have long referred to as the Rialto *gobbo* (hunchback); the figure is now thought to represent a working man, symbolically bent from the weight of the steps. The conspicuous 24-hour clock has had a horrible reputation for timekeeping since it was installed—it hasn't worked for years. Behind the church is a cross-shaped inscription that entreats merchants to be honest in law, exact in weights and measures, and faithful in contracts. The church is rarely open except for evening concerts. ⊠ *Rialto Market* Ⓥ *Rialto.*

㉛ San Giacomo dell'Orio. Founded according to legend in the 9th century on an island still populated by wolves, the church as it presently stands was built in 1225. Its short, unmatched Byzantine columns survived renovation during the Renaissance, and the church never lost the feel of an ancient pagan temple sheltering beneath its 15th-century ship's keel roof. A religious sense is restored in the sanctuary with large marble crosses surrounded by a bevy of small medieval Madonnas. Above the main altar is one of the few works by Lorenzo Lotto that remained in Venice, *Madonna with Child and Saints* (1546). The sacristies contain several works by Palma il Giovane (circa 1544–1628). ⊠ *Campo San Giacomo dell'Orio, Santa Croce* ☎ *041/2750462 Chorus* ✆ *€2.50; €9 Chorus pass* ☉ *Mon.–Sat. 10–5, Sun. 1–5.* Ⓥ *San Stae.*

㉕ San Giovanni Elemosinario. Intimately bound to Rialto Market, this church has storefronts for a facade and the altars built by market guilds—poultry sellers, messengers, and fodder merchants. During San Giovanni Elemosinario's restoration, workers found frescoes by Pordenone (1484–1539) that had been painted over centuries earlier (as well as the bones of 80 unidentified people). Look for Titian's *St. John the Almsgiver* and Pordenone's *Saints Catherine, Sebastian and Roch,* which were returned after 30 years by Gallerie dell'Accademia, a rarity for Italian museums. ⊠ *Ruga Vecchia S. Giovanni, Rialto* ☎ *041/2750462 Chorus* ✆ *€2.50, €9 Chorus pass* ☉ *Mon.–Sat. 10–5, Sun. 1–5* Ⓥ *San Silvestro or Rialto.*

㉞ San Nicola da Tolentino. When San Gaetano da Thiene arrived in Venice in 1528 with a handful of monks and even less cash, he was given a small oratory. Years of contributions allowed the monks to hire Vincenzo Scamozzi (1552–1616), whose projects included Piazza San Marco's Procuratie Nuove, to work on their church from 1591 to 1602. The Corinthian portico with very tall columns was added in the early 18th century and gives character to an otherwise plain building. Also giving it character is the cannonball lodged in the facade, an Austrian souvenir of the siege of 1849. There's so much scrollwork inside that it's hard to tell where stucco ends and similar painted work begins. Most of the artwork is by lesser-known painters. Worth noting are *Charity of St. Lawrence* by Bernardo Strozzi (1581–1644) near the third chapel in the left transept, and *St. Jerome Visited by an Angel* by Giovanni Lys (circa 1597–1630) in the right transept. The interior is too dark to be seen after sundown. ⊠ *Fondamenta Tolentino, Santa Croce* ☎ *041/5222160* ⊙ *Daily 8–noon and 4–6:30* Ⓥ *Piazzale Roma.*

㉟ San Pantalon. Say the name Pantalon in Venice and most people think of a theater character popular in traditional commedia dell'arte—a greedy old merchant with a hooked nose, a cantankerous personality, and a weakness for *le belle putte* (pretty girls), who love to tease him. This church is named for a very different sort of character, a poor doctor martyred by Roman Emperor Diocletian. Do not come here without a supply of €.50 pieces for the coin-operated lights; this is one of the least illuminated churches in town, and it's open only in the late afternoon.

Put some coins in the slot in the right nave marked *illuminazione soffitto* (ceiling illumination), and out of the darkness emerges the *Martyrdom of St. Pantaleo,* Gian Antonio Fumiani's (circa 1643–1710) colossal (4,750-square-foot) masterpiece. It's actually made up of 40 separate canvases joined together to look like a large fresco. This technique was not unheard of, but the enormity of the work demanded tremendous mastery of perspective, and consumed the last 24 years of the little-known artist's life. Legend says he fell to his death while applying finishing touches. The **Cappellina del Sacro Chiodo** (Little Chapel of the Holy Nail) holds a splendid *Coronation of the Virgin* by Antonio Vivarini; the custodian sells a book that can help sort out who's who in the picture's dense world of Gothic symbolism. There are also four small works by Paolo Veneziano: *Madonna with Child, Annunciation, Sleeping Virgin,* and *Presentation to the Temple.* Often overlooked in this chapel is a beautiful gilded alabaster carving of the Virgin and Child, dating from the late 1300s by an unknown artist. One of the last works by Veronese, *St. Pantalon Healing a Child,* is in the second chapel to the right. ⊠ *Campo San Pantalon, Santa Croce* ☎ *041/5235893* ⊠ *Free* ⊙ *Daily 8–10 and 4–6* Ⓥ *San Tomà.*

㊳ San Polo. Founded in the 9th century, the church of San Polo underwent a major reconstruction in the late Gothic period and a neoclassical makeover in the early 1800s. Extensive restoration in the 1930s brought back the wonderful wooden ship's keel roof, as well as the earlier Byzantine window on the facade. The artwork inside is not particularly engaging, as the 19th-century alterations were so costly that the friars had to sell the best paintings in order to pay the bills. Though Giambattista Tiepolo is represented here, his work is outdone by 16 works by his son Giandomenico (1727–1804), including the *Stations of the Cross* in the oratory to the left of the entrance. The younger Tiepolo also created a series of remarkably expressive and theatrical paintings of the saints.

Look for the altarpieces by Tintoretto and Veronese, which managed to escape auction. San Polo's sturdy bell tower has remained unchanged through the centuries—don't miss the two lions guarding it, playing with a detached human head. ⊠ *Campo San Polo* ☎ *041/2750462 Chorus* 🖼 *€2.50; €9 Chorus pass* ⊙ *Mon.–Sat. 10–5, Sun. 1–5* Ⓥ *San Tomà.*

🕗 **San Stae.** The most renowned sculptors of the time decorated the facade here, paid with a legacy left by Doge Alvise Mocenigo II, who's buried in the center aisle. San Stae's painting collection is small, but it has one of the best assortments of works by Venice's early-18th-century masters, from Giambattista Tiepolo, Gregorio Lazzarini, and Sebastiano Ricci to the lesser known Giovanni Pellegrini, Giambattista Piazzetta, and Giambattista Pittoni. ⊠ *Campo San Stae, Santa Croce* ☎ *041/2750462 Chorus* 🖼 *€2.50; €9 Chorus pass* ⊙ *Mon.–Sat. 9–5, Sun. 1–5* Ⓥ *San Stae.*

🕗 **San Zandegolà.** Founded in 1007, this frequently overlooked little church is among the lagoon's oldest. It was dedicated to San Giovanni Decollato (St. John the Beheaded), and many still refer to it by that name. In keeping with the Romanesque style, the church exterior is very simple, but there's great detail inside, with Greek marble columns and remnants of the frescoes that once covered walls and ceiling. For about a century, starting in 1818, the church was closed for worship and used as a warehouse. Restoration initiated in the 1940s revealed many Byzantine frescoes, and as recently as 1993 workmen moving a marble altarpiece for restoration stumbled upon a Gothic fresco of St. Michael the Archangel believed to date back to about 1380. ⊠ *Campo di San Zandegolà, Santa Croce* 🖼 *Free* ⊙ *Mon.–Sat. 10–noon* Ⓥ *Riva de Biasio.*

🕗 **Scuola Grande di San Giovanni Evangelista.** Starting from Campo San Stin, two turns bring you to a rather magical Lombardesque marble wall; the great intimidating eagle perched on top signals the sacred territory of the apostle St. John. Founded in 1349 by the powerful brotherhood of St. John the Evangelist, the Scuola Grande was closed by Napoléon and then bought from the Austrian government in 1857 by the Guild of Arti Edificatorie (Guild of Building Arts), which still runs the place. Its lovely facade and front yard are captivating examples of Lombardesque-Renaissance style, and since 1998 the Guild—for the first time in its long history—has opened its doors to the public (for very limited hours, by appointment only).

The layout inside suits the standard requirements of any Venetian scuola, whose primary function was to host crowds of petitioners as well as the wealthier members of the fraternal order. The plain, spacious entry hall was meant to welcome the needy. It now contains architectural fragments and sculptures from around town, which were dumped here "for storage" after the suppression of the brotherhood in the 1800s. Note a rare 14th-century sculpture of the beloved *Madonna della Misericordia,* with the faithful gathered beneath her ample mantle; and the Gothic capitals with the pastoral symbol of St. John in Ephesus inserted between the portraits of different praying brothers to signify the intercession of the Apostle. The double flight of stairs, skillfully designed by Codussi, takes care of the narrow space with a simple perspective trick, in which the steps incrementally increase in height, creating the illusion of depth. The engravings on the marble threshold representing the tools of the guild were added in the 20th century.

The richer scuole would typically commission the decoration of their main meeting hall, called the **Sala del Capitolo,** from the best available artists. But here, Tintoretto painted only some of the episodes from the *Life of St. John* that cover the walls. Although Tiepolo had discussed redoing the ceiling with the famous architect Massari, the painter left for Spain (where he ultimately died) and the job was eventually given to a group of minor artists. The addition of several extra rooms, most notably the Albergo (sort of a deluxe hostel for pilgrims) and a small chapel, added to the efficiency and prestige of the larger scuole. Here the chapel is dedicated to the relics of the Holy Cross. The carved pole to the left of the altar was used to carry these relics across town, as you can see in Carpaccio and Gentile Bellini's *Miracles of the Holy Cross* series now hanging in Gallerie dell'Accademia. The scuola's scale model shows where these paintings originally hung. In the 14th-century painting *Madonna with Child and Saints Peter, John the Baptist, and John,* the most significant work the scuola retained, you'll immediately recognize the headless St. John. When you step outside, note the stone marker set about waist high into the corner of the courtyard showing the level water reached in the city's 1966 flood. ⊠ *Campiello della Scuola, San Polo 2454* ☎ *041/718234* 🖅 *Free (donation welcomed)* ☉ *Most weekday mornings; call ahead* Ⓥ *Ferrovia.*

CANNAREGIO

Cannaregio's main drag, which is also the longest street in Venice, winds its way parallel to the Grand Canal. Lined with fruit and vegetable stalls near Ponte delle Guglie, quiet shops, gelaterias, and bakeries, the Strada Nova (literally, "New Street," as it was opened in 1871) serves as a pedestrian expressway from the train station to Ca' d'Oro. A number of nightspots, including Venice's only disco, have cropped up along this paved ribbon, which, although bereft of sights itself, is a convenient point of reference while exploring Cannaregio. Seen from above, this part of town seems like a wide field plowed by several long, straight canals that are linked by intersecting straight streets—not typical of Venice, where the shape of the islands usually defines the shape of the canals. But these canals were cut through a vast bed of reeds (hence the name Cannaregio, which means "Reed Place"), and not even the Venetians could overlook such an opportunity to make long, straight thoroughfares. The daylight reflected off the bright-green canals, wooden boats painted vivid red or blue, and the big sky visible from the fondamente make this a particularly luminous area of town. It's no surprise, perhaps, that Titian and Tintoretto had houses nearby.

Though Cannaregio has noble palaces built along the Grand Canal, the northern part of the sestiere was, and still is, a typical working-class neighborhood, where many *bacari* (wine bars) fill up with old card players every afternoon. The Jewish Ghetto, with its rooftop synagogues, and several striking churches are architectural highlights, while Ca' d'Oro's Galleria Franchetti and the Tiepolo Ballroom in Palazzo Labia add color to your visit.

Numbers in the margin correspond to the numbers on the Cannaregio map.

The Main Attractions

⑮ Ca' d'Oro. This exquisite Venetian Gothic palace was once literally a "Golden House," when its marble traceries and ornaments were embellished with pure gold. Created in 1434 by the enamored patrician Marino Contarini for his wife, Ca' d'Oro became a love offering a second time when a 19th-century Russian prince gave it to Maria Taglioni, a celebrated classical dancer who collected palaces along the Grand Canal. The last proprietor, perhaps more taken with Venice than with any of his lovers, left Ca' d'Oro to the city, after having had it carefully restored and filled with antiquities, sculptures, and paintings that today make up the **Galleria Franchetti.** Besides Mantegna's celebrated *St. Sebastian* and other first-rate Venetian works, the Galleria Franchetti contains the type of fresco that once adorned the exteriors of Venetian buildings (commissioned by those who could not afford a marble facade). One such detached fresco displayed here was made by a young Titian for the (now grayish-white) facade of the Fondaco dei Tedeschi, now the main post office. ⊠ *Calle Ca' d'Oro, Cannaregio 3933* ☎ *041/5238790* €5; *€11 includes Accademia and Museo Orientale* ☉ *Tues.–Sun. 8:15–7:15, Mon. 8:15–2; last entry ½ hr before closing* Ⓥ *Ca' d'Oro.*

★ **㊷ Jewish Ghetto.** The neighborhood that gave the world the word "ghetto" is today a quiet warren of backstreets that is still home to Jewish institutions, a kosher restaurant, a rabbinical school, and several synagogues. Jews may have come to Venice as early as the 11th century, but the first synagogues weren't built, nor was a cemetery founded, until the Ashkenazim, or Eastern European Jews, arrived in the late 1300s. Over the centuries, Jews would be alternately welcomed and expelled. In return for the right to live and work in Venice, protection in case of war, and religious freedom, the Jews paid increasingly heavier taxes and were forced to lend money at low interest. Throughout the Middle Ages, Rialto's commercial district, as vividly recounted in Shakespeare's *The Merchant of Venice,* depended on Jewish merchants and moneylenders for trade and to help cover ever-increasing war expenses.

Relentless local opposition forced the Senate in 1516 to confine Jews to the periphery of town. An island in Cannaregio was selected, then named for its foundry (*geto* in Venetian), which produced cannons. Gates at the entrance to the neighborhood were locked at night, and boats patrolled the surrounding canals. The first settlers were Central Europeans, whose German accents changed "geto" into "ghetto." They were allowed only to lend money, operate government-controlled pawnshops, trade in textiles, and practice medicine. Jewish doctors were highly respected for their skills and could leave the ghetto at any hour when on duty. Men were required to wear yellow circles stitched on their coats, and women had to wear yellow scarves. Jews were nevertheless safe, and in

*Fodor's*Choice
★

the 16th century the community grew considerably with refugees from the Near East, southern and central Italy, Spain, and Portugal. The Ashkenazim built their two synagogues, **Schola Grande Todesca** (1528) and **Schola Canton** (1531), on the top floors of adjacent houses. The Levantine Jews were wealthy enough to purchase land on the island across the rio and in 1541 built sumptuous **Schola Levantina,** currently used for worship in winter. A third atticlike synagogue was built by the poor Italian Jews in 1575, its tentative dome barely visible from the campo below. Finally, in 1589, the ghetto became refuge for Sephardic Jews fleeing from Spain. Their **Schola Spagnola** stands just across from Schola Levantina in the Campiello delle Scuole and is used for summer services.

In the early 17th century about 5,000 Jews lived in the ghetto. It had been allowed to expand twice, but still had the city's densest population and consequently ended up with the city's highest buildings (nine stories); notice the slanting apartment blocks on Campo del Ghetto Nuovo. Although the gates were pulled down after Napoléon's 1797 arrival, Jews realized freedom only in the late 19th century with the founding of the Italian state. On the eve of World War II there were about 1,500 Jews left in the ghetto: 247 were deported by the Nazis. Eight returned.

The area has Europe's highest density of ancient synagogues, and visiting them is a unique cross-cultural experience. Though each is marked by the tastes of its individual builders, Venetian influence is clearly evident. Women's galleries resemble theater galleries typical of the times, and some were decorated by artisans who were simultaneously working in local churches. Tours in Italian and English leave hourly from the **Museo Ebraico.** The small but well-arranged museum highlights centuries of Jewish culture with splendid silver Hanukkah lamps and torahs and handwritten, beautifully decorated wedding contracts in Hebrew. You might complete your tour of Jewish Venice with a visit to the **Antico Cimitero Ebraico** (⊠ Ancient Jewish Cemetery, Via Cipro ☎ 041/ 715359 ⛄ €8.50 ⊘ Tour Apr.–Oct., Sun. 2:30; call for arrangements Ⓥ Lido–S.M.E.) on the Lido, full of fascinating old tombstones half-hidden by ivy and grass. The cemetery was in use until the end of the 18th century, and the earliest grave dates to 1389. *Museo Ebraico ⊠ Campo del Ghetto Nuovo, Cannaregio 2902/b ☎ 041/715359 ⊕ www.museoebraico.it ⛄ €3 museum only; €8.50 museum, synagogues ⊘ June–Sept., Sun.–Fri. 10–7, last hourly tour 5:30; Oct.–May, Sun.–Fri. 10–5:30, last hourly tour 4:30 Ⓥ San Marcuola or Guglie.*

need a break? You'll find authentic Venetian refreshment where Calle del Cristo (San Marcuola) crosses Strada Nova. **Enoteca Do Colonne** (☎ 041/ 5240453) stocks dozens of Veneto wines and an array of cichetti that will dazzle eyes and taste buds. They're closed Saturday, but open all winter, when you shouldn't miss the chance to try *musetto,* a Venetian specialty sausage.

★ ㊹ **Madonna dell'Orto.** From a campo elegantly parqueted in red brick and white Istrian stone rises an Oriental-style campanile complete with its own cupola. There, captured between earth and sky are the 12 Apostles, hovering upon the facade of this 14th-century church. Though squatly Romanesque and sporting a later pre-Renaissance doorway, Madonna dell'Orto remains one of the most typical Gothic churches in Venice. Built near a busy shipping area that served merchants and pilgrims sailing the often treacherous northern lagoon, it was suitably dedicated to St. Christopher, patron saint of travelers and boatmen. But after a statue that had been in a nearby *orto* (garden) became renowned as a miracle worker, St. Christopher was displaced by the Madonna dell'Orto as the church's namesake. The statue is believed to be the work of Giovanni di Santi, and though years outdoors took their toll on its soft white stone, the faces of mother and child, now displayed inside the **Cappella di San Mauro,** are still captivating.

Tintoretto lived nearby, and this, his parish church, contains some of his most powerful work. Lining the chancel are two huge (45 feet by 20 feet) canvases, *Adoration of the Golden Calf* and *Last Judgment.* In the latter, a dramatic scene of heavenly justice, there hardly seems enough space to contain the flurry of activity. As the holy ascend, converging with the celestial court, the damned are violently swept downward by a wildly gushing river, which uproots trees and piles sinners along the shore to await Charon's boat, sailing in from the flames in the lower right. In glowing contrast to this awesome spectacle is Tintoretto's *Presentation at the Temple* and the simple chapel where Tintoretto and his children, Marietta and Domenico, are buried. Several paintings by Domenico also hang in the church, though the son's work pales alongside that of his famous father. Of a totally different texture and scope than Tintoretto's paintings is the fresh and luminous masterpiece by Cima da Conegliano, *St. John the Baptist and Saints,* which seems to be a concentrated effort to represent peace, both within the soul and in the surrounding world. Finally, the first chapel to the left displays a photographic reproduction of a precious *Madonna with Child* by Giovanni Bellini. The original was stolen one night in March 1993. ⊠ *Campo della Madonna dell'Orto, Cannaregio* 🕾 *041/2750462 Chorus* 🖾 *€2.50; €9 Chorus pass* ۞ *Mon.–Sat. 10–5, Sun. 1–5* Ⓥ *Orto.*

Also Worth Seeing

㊻ Gesuiti. Extravagantly baroque, this 18th-century church completely abandoned classical Renaissance straight lines in favor of flowing, twisting forms. Its interior walls resemble brocade drapery, and only touching will convince skeptics that rather than paint, the green-and-white walls are actually inlaid marble. Over the first altar on the left, the *Martyrdom of St. Lawrence* is a dramatic example of Titian's feeling for light and movement. ⊠ *Campo dei Gesuiti, Cannaregio* 🕾 *041/5286579* ۞ *Daily 10–noon and 4–6* Ⓥ *Fondamente Nuove.*

㊶ Palazzo Labia. Once among Venice's showiest 18th-century families, the Labias bought their way into the city's aristocracy. At their palace, boasting facades on two canals and a campo, they were famous for serving meals on golden plates and then throwing them out of the window to the cry of: *"L'abia o no l'abia, sarò sempre Labia"* ("With or without it, I'll always be a Labia")—although it seems that a net strung across the bottom of the canal recovered the plates in time for the next dinner party. Today the palace is the Venetian headquarters of RAI, the Italian national radio and television network. It's hard to imagine a modern broadcasting company set among such baroque splendor, but in Italy it somehow makes sense. The gorgeous **Tiepolo Ballroom,** which after the decline of the Labias was turned into a school and then a laundry room, exhibits the final flowering of Venetian painting: Giambattista Tiepolo's frescoes of *Anthony and Cleopatra,* dressed like noble Venetians of the time, teeming with dwarfs, Barbary pirates, and toy dogs. Note that at this writing the palazzo was closed for restoration, with no reopening date set. ⊠ *Campo San Geremia, Cannaregio 275* 🕾 *041/781111* ۞ *Closed for restoration* Ⓥ *Ferrovia.*

㊵ San Giobbe. Like San Pietro di Castello, Sant'Elena, and San Francesco della Vigna, San Giobbe once marked the city limits, yet even in this peripheral church you'll find the remains of a doge. Cristoforo Moro had San Giobbe built for the poor residents of a nearby hospice, testimony to just how far the Venetian republic went to protect even its humblest citizens. Begun in Gothic style (note the brick bell tower, the well, and what survives of the cloister) and finished by Pietro Lombardo in the early 1470s, this church is Venice's first example of Renaissance church architecture. A triptych by Antonio Vivarini in the **Sanctuary** is especially worth seeing as is the **Cappella Martini,** with its blue and yellow majolica decorations. Jacopo Bellini's *Madonna with Saints* (better known as the *Pala di San Giobbe*) and Carpaccio's *Presentation to the Temple* once hung here, and though efforts were begun in the late 1990s to reclaim them from Gallerie dell'Accademia, they've so far proved futile. They have however revived a long-standing controversy in Italy about the display of artistic masterpieces out of the context for which they were created. In their absence, the best Renaissance picture here is a nativity scene by Gian Girolamo Savoldo (circa 1485–1548). ⊠ *Campo di San Giobbe (near Tre Archi bridge), Cannaregio* ☎ *041/5241889* 🎫 *Free* ⊙ *Weekdays 10–noon and 3:30–6; Sat. 3:30–6; Sun. 8–noon.*

⊕ Sant'Alvise. Founded by young patrician Antonia Venier in the late 14th century after St. Louis, the bishop of Toulouse, had appeared to her in a dream, the church of Sant'Alvise takes its name from the Venetian dialect version of the saint's name. Three canvases depicting Christ's passion, which Giambattista Tiepolo originally created as a triptych, now hang here separated. The *Ascent to Calvary* in the chancel looks all the more painfully tragic because of its veritable parade of spectators. To the right, the pathos continues with *Crowning with Thorns* and the *Flagellation.* The ceiling's trompe l'oeil, a late-1600s work attributed to Pietro Antonio Torri and Pietro Ricchi, is striking for its use of color and perspective—it seems to break right through the roof. In the back, supported by pillars, is the nuns' *barco* (choir stall), which connected directly to the convent. Below the barco are eight tempera paintings with biblical scenes that Ruskin enthusiastically identified as "baby Carpaccios." However, it turns out Carpaccio truly was little more than an infant at the time they were created; they've now been attributed to Lazzaro Bastiani (active 1449–1512), and the so-called Carpaccio signature identified as a 19th-century forgery. ⊠ *Campo Sant'Alvise, Cannaregio* ☎ *041/ 2750462 Chorus* 🎫 *€2.50; €9 Chorus pass* ⊙ *Mon.–Sat. 10–5, Sun. 1–5* Ⓥ *Sant'Alvise.*

CASTELLO ALTO

Castello, Venice's largest sestiere, includes all of the land from east of Piazza San Marco to the city's easternmost tip. Its name probably comes from a fortress that once stood on one of the eastern islands. Venetians divide the sestiere into Castello Basso (low), the southernmost area following Riva dei Sette Martiri to Sant'Elena, and Alto (high), which runs along the northern shore of Fondamente Nove, with its eastern edge at Arsenale and its western along Piazza San Marco. Roughly speaking, the low-numbered addresses are in Castello Basso and higher numbers in Castello Alto.

Not every well-off Venetian family could afford to build a palazzo on the Grand Canal. Many that couldn't instead settled in Castello Alto, taking advantage of its proximity to the Rialto and San Marco, and built the noble palazzos that today distinguish this neighborhood from the fishermen's enclave in the adjacent streets of Castello Basso.

Castello Alto isn't lacking in colorful history. In the early 15th century, large Greek and Dalmatian communities moved into the area along the Riva degli Schiavoni, where many of them sold dried fish and meat; the Confraternity of San Marco, based in what is now the hospital on Campo Santi Giovanni e Paolo, was patronized by Venetian high society in the 16th to 18th centuries; and nearby Campo Santa Maria Formosa served as a popular open-air theater for shows of various kinds (some including livestock among the cast members), until Napoléon conquered the republic. When 12th-century Doge Michiel's diplomatic trip to Byzantium resulted in nothing but a plague (which had already decimated his crew and proceeded to infect the city), the general assembly turned against him and the public called for blood. Michiel fled for the safe haven of Castello Alto's San Zaccaria Church but was killed before he could get there. His assassin, though acting out the will of the people, was executed nonetheless, and orders were given to raze not only the killer's home, where he hid after the crime, but the entire neighborhood along Calle delle Rasse. This 1172 edict prevented any permanent construction in the area until 1948; you can't help but notice one part of the Danieli Hotel is too modern to blend in with the surroundings.

There is a lot to see here. San Giorgio dei Greci and Carpaccio's paintings at the Scuola di San Giorgio degli Schiavoni are worth a long look. San Francesco della Vigna, with its comforting cloister, is a 30-minute stop. Santi Giovanni e Paolo and San Zaccaria are both closed during lunch hours, but Santa Maria dei Miracoli and Santa Maria Formosa are open, as is Querini-Stampalia, which has a café on the premises.

Numbers in the margin correspond to numbers on the Castello Alto map.

The Main Attractions

⑰ Santa Maria dei Miracoli. Tiny, yet perfectly proportioned, this early Renaissance gem has a marble-sheathed exterior and inside is decorated with exquisite marble reliefs. Architect Pietro Lombardo (circa 1435–1515) seems to have compressed Miracoli into its confined space and then made it look bigger through various optical illusions: the varied color of the marble exterior creates the effect of greater distance; extra pilasters make the building's canal side looks longer than it is; offsetting the arcade windows makes the arches appear deeper. From Ponte dei Miracoli you can appreciate how the church actually hangs out over a rio.

FodorsChoice
★

The church was built in the 1480s to house Nicolò di Pietro's 1408 painting of the Virgin Mary, *I Miracoli* (look for it on the high altar), which is said to perform miracles. At one time it was Venice's most important shrine to the Virgin Mary, celebrating more than 40 masses daily. The church's only other paintings are on the coffered ceiling, but if you're here when afternoon sun filters through the large round window, the marble decoration seems to come alive with soft pink shades. The immaculate flight of stairs leading to the altar's holy icon is a favored Venetian wedding stage. On the parapet are four small, detailed sculptures by Tullio Lombardo (1455–1532), among them *Saint Francis* and *Santa Chiara,* both known for their devotion to the Madonna. ⊠ *Campo Santa*

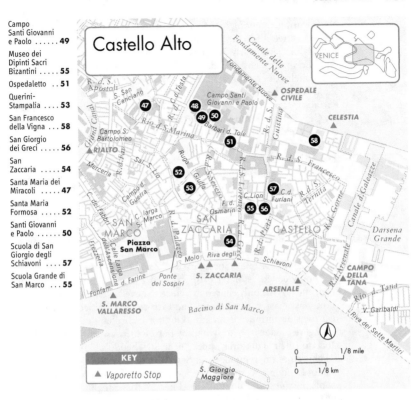

Castello Alto

KEY
▲ Vaporetto Stop

Maria Nova, Cannaregio ☎ *041/2750462 Chorus* ✉ *€2.50; €9 Chorus pass* ⊙ *Mon.–Sat. 10–5, Sun. 1–5* Ⓥ *Rialto.*

**need a
break?**

Grab an outdoor table at **Bar ai Miracoli** (✉ Campo Santa Maria Nova ☎ 041/5231515) and gaze across the canal at Maria dei Miracoli, Lombardo's miracle in marble. To satisfy your sweet tooth, head for Campo Santa Marina, the next square over, and the family-owned and -operated **Didovich Pastry Shop** (☎ 041/5230017). They make extraordinary cream-filled pastry and tasty *pizzette*, the small pizzas with spinach and ricotta cheese or tomato and anchovies. There is limited seating inside, but in the warmer months you can sit at one of the tables on the square.

★ ❺❸ **Querini-Stampalia.** Home to the venerable Querini family for centuries, this Renaissance palace now contains a library and a fine collection of Venetian art. Highlights include Giovanni Bellini's *Presentation in the Temple,* and Sebastiano Ricci's triptych *Dawn, Afternoon, and Evening.* Portraits of newlywed Francesco Querini and Paola Priuli were left unfinished by the death of Palma Il Vecchio in 1528 (note the groom's hand and the bride's dress). The home's original 18th-century furniture and stuccowork are a fitting background for Pietro Longhi's period portraits.

Not mentioned among artist stars, Gabriele Bella (1730–99) captured Venetian street life in a style more resembling that of a photojournalist than painter; his nearly 70 works displayed here tell stories beyond the republic's pomp and parades. Museum admission on Friday and Saturday includes evening concerts performed on antique instruments at 5 and 8:30. The library is open only for research. ⊠ *Campo Santa Maria Formosa, Castello 5252* ☎ *041/2711411* ⊕ *www.querinistampalia.it* 🔁 *€6* ☉ *Tues.–Thurs. and Sun. 10–6; Fri. and Sat. 10 AM–10 PM* Ⓥ *San Zaccaria.*

need a break? | **Barbarigo Caffetteria** (⊠ Campo Santa Maria Formosa ☎ 041/ 5289758), inside Querini-Stampalia, is a small restaurant/café where you can continue to admire the art as you sip coffee or grab a bite to eat. Drinks, specialty pastries, and full lunches are available every day except Monday.

★ ⑤⓪ **Santi Giovanni e Paolo.** While Franciscan friars were laboring away on Santa Maria Gloriosa dei Frari in San Polo, the Dominicans were similarly busy in Castello. Some say San Zanipolo, as the church here is commonly called, is better proportioned and more luminous than the Frari, and it is the only church in Venice to have benefited from the work of the glass masters of Murano. The 15th-century stained glass window near the side entrance is breathtaking for its brilliant colors and beautiful figures, made from drawings by Bartolomeo Vivarini and Gerolamo Mocetto (their signatures appear near St. Theodore). The second official church of the republic after San Marco, this is the Venetian equivalent of London's Westminster Abbey, with a great number of important people, including 25 doges, buried here. Artistic highlights include an outstanding polyptych by Giovanni Bellini (right nave, second altar), Alvise Vivarini's *Christ Carrying the Cross* (sacristy), and Lorenzo Lotto's *Charity of St. Antonino* (right transept). Don't miss the *Cappella del Rosario* (Rosary Chapel), off the left transept. It was built in the 16th century to commemorate the 1571 victory of Lepanto in western Greece, when Venice led a combined European fleet to defeat the Turkish navy. The chapel was devastated by a fire in 1867 and restored in the early years of the 20th century with works from other churches, among them the sumptuous Veronese ceiling paintings.

However quick your visit, be sure to see the tomb Pietro Mocenigo, to the right of the main entrance, a monument built by the ubiquitous Pietro Lombardo and his sons. Also worth seeking out is the sepulchre of Doge Michele Morosini, in the choir, which was described by Ruskin as "the richest monument of the Gothic period in Venice." Oddities include a foot of St. Catherine of Siena and an urn containing the skin of commander Marcantonio Bragadin, tortured and flayed alive by the Turks during the siege of Cyprus in 1571. ⊠ *Campo Santi Giovanni e Paolo, Castello* ☎ *041/5235913* 🔁 *€ 2.50* ☉ *Daily 7–7* Ⓥ *Fondamente Nuove or Rialto.*

★ ⑤⑦ **Scuola di San Giorgio degli Schiavoni.** Founded in 1451 by the Dalmatian community, which still owns it today, this scuola served as a social and cultural headquarters for migrants who crossed the Adriatic Sea from what is now Croatia. The small scuola is lavishly decorated, yet somehow unpretentious and harmoniously balanced. Not well known outside Venice, where he spent all his life, Vittore Carpaccio painted devotional *teleri* (large narrative canvases of legendary and religious scenes) against a background of Venetian architecture. He combined observation with fantasy, a sense of warm color with a sense of humor (don't miss the body parts in the dragon's lair). In Scuola di San Giorgio, Carpaccio concentrated on three saints especially venerated in Dalmatia: St. George, St. Tryphone, and St. Jerome. The two paintings to the left and the one opposite the entrance tell the story of St. George, who was passing through Selene (in Libya) when he found a beautiful virgin princess had been offered as a sacrifice to a dragon. The exuberant *St. George Charging the Dragon* is a contrast to the more somber baptism of the king and queen—St. George wouldn't slay the dragon until the royals became Christians. In the central painting, the saint stands triumphantly over his adversary, while the king and queen, with their newly freed princess, look on. The fourth painting shows the child St. Tryphone freeing the emperor's daughter from the devil. Paintings five and six are called, respectively, the *Agony in the Garden* and the *Calling of St. Matthew.* The remaining three teleri are dedicated to St. Jerome, who in the seventh painting is about to take a thorn out of the lion's paw while monks flee in terror. The *Funeral of St. Jerome* and the *Vision of St. Augustine* follow. This last work—especially vivid in detail—is the faithful representation of the "office" of a 15th-century humanist. Augustine is writing a letter to his dear friend Jerome, when the latter appears and delivers the news that he'd died and gone to heaven.

The adjoining small room displays old garments and other objects used by the brotherhood. The first floor features many portraits of brothers and sisters. Try to visit in the morning, as the fraternal order sometimes closes the church in the afternoon for its own use. ✉ *Calle dei Furlani, Castello 3259/a* ☎ *041/5228828* ✉ *€3* ☉ *Apr.–Oct., Tues.–Sat. 9:30–12:30 and 3:30–6:30, Sun. 9:30–12:30; Nov.–Mar., Tues.–Sat. 10–12:30 and 3–6, Sun. 10–12:30* Ⓥ *San Zaccaria.*

Also Worth Seeing

49 Campo Santi Giovanni e Paolo. This large, attractive square is the site of three city landmarks: the imposing namesake Gothic church; the Scuola Grande di San Marco, with one of the loveliest Renaissance facades in Italy; and the only equestrian monument ever erected by La Serenissima. The rider, Bartolomeo Colleoni, served Venice well as a *condottiere*, or mercenary commander—the Venetians preferred to pay others to fight for them on land. When he died in 1475, he left his fortune to the city on the condition that a statue be erected in his honor "in the piazza before San Marco." The republic's shrewd administrators coveted Colleoni's ducats but had no intention of honoring anyone, no matter how valorous, with a statue in Piazza San Marco. So they collected the loot, commissioned a statue by Florentine sculptor Andrea del Verrocchio (1435–88), and put it up before the Scuola Grande di San Marco, which, before becoming part of the city hospital, was headquarters of a powerful fraternal order.

CloseUp

ODES TO VENICE

SINCE THE EARLY 19TH CENTURY, *Venice has been a stop on every sensitive scribe's Grand Tour, and the result has been a centuries-long serenade sung by some of English literature's greats. Lord Byron, for one, was so enchanted that he moved to Venice in 1817. Charles Dickens seems to have fallen head over heels for the city; in an 1844 letter he wrote, "The gorgeous and wonderful reality of Venice is beyond the fancy of the wildest dreamer; it is a thing you would shed tears to see."*

Among the other literary giants entranced by Venice were Edith Wharton, George Eliot, Henry James, and Marcel Proust— who came on a visit with his mother and refused to leave. Mark Twain arrived in 1867 but failed to be seduced. In Innocents Abroad *he dismissed the fabled gondola and gondolier as "the one an inky, rusty old canoe with a sable hearse-body clapped on to the middle of it, and the other a mangy, barefooted gutter-*

snipe." In the 20th century, such varied talents as Ernest Hemingway, Erica Jong, and Ezra Pound all adored the place.

Venice's literati have for the most part been tourists like the rest of us, inspired by the traveler's Venice that you can see every day. Pound was moved by nothing greater than the play of light on an evening gondola ride: "The prows rose silver on silver, taking light in the darkness."

If you find that words fail you, you won't be alone. Dickens wrote to a friend, "With your foot upon its stones, its pictures before you, and its history in your mind, it is something past all writing or speaking of—almost past all thinking of." On the other hand, Shakespeare set two plays in Venice without setting foot here—proof that for some, the Venice of the imagination is inspiration enough.

---

need a break? Baking and catering since 1879, the **Rosa Salva** family has their lagoon headquarters in Campo Santi Giovanni e Paolo (☎ 041/ 5227949). Stop in for pastries and coffee or homemade gelato.

⑤⑤ Museo dei Dipinti Sacri Bizantini (Museum of Sacred Byzantine Painting). Housed in the former hospital of Baldassare Longhena's Scuola di San Nicola dei Greci, this rich post-Byzantine collection is one of a kind in Europe. Though at first glance the icons may seem identical in color and style, careful inspection reveals a variety of subjects. Elegantly gilded Madonnas date back to the 14th century. Several Last Judgment scenes elaborately detail the poor sinners' fates. Other Biblical scenes include Theodore Poulakis's whimsical 17th-century depiction of Noah's shipmates arriving for their cruise. ⊠ *Scuola di San Nicola dei Greci (near Ponte dei Greci), Castello 3412* ☎ *041/5226581* 🎫 *€4* 🕘 *Daily 9–4:30* Ⓥ *San Zaccaria.*

⑤① Ospedaletto. This 16th-century "little hospital" (as the name translates) was one of four church foundling homes, each of which had an orchestra and choir of orphans. Entering through the church of **Santa Maria dei Derelitti** (St. Mary of the Destitute), you'll see a large gallery built for the young musicians. The orphanage is now a home for the elderly, but its beautiful 18th-century **Sala della Musica** (Music Room), the only one of its kind to survive, has been carefully restored. On the far wall, Jacopo Guarana's (1720–1808) fresco depicts Apollo, god of music, surrounded by the orphan musicians and their conductor, Pasquale Anfossi. ✉ 6691 Castello, Calle Barbaria delle Tole, Castello ☎ 041/924933 ✉ €2 ⊙ Thurs.–Sat. 3:30–6:30; for other days and times, call for reservations Ⓥ Fondamente Nuove.

❺❻ **San Giorgio dei Greci.** With the fall of the Byzantine Empire in 1453, Venice's Greek Orthodox community grew considerably with refugees fleeing the Turks. La Serenissima allowed them to found a fraternal order and a scuola, and a papal bull entitled them to build a church in the 16th century to celebrate their own rites. Over the centuries, the scuola became the richest and most important center of Greek Orthodoxy in the Western world, before losing its property when Napoléon conquered Venice. The interior of the church of San Giorgio is luminously gold, its walls covered by intense icons and mosaics. These are mostly the work of little-known 17th-century artists from Crete, whose figurative style has been passed down to the workshops of the monks of Mt. Athos. Among the images of saints, madonnas, and prophets, it is the extremely rich yet subtle iconostasis with a large *Annunciation* mosaic that draws your attention. The second focal point of this jewel box of a church is the stunning ceiling fresco by 16th-century artist Giovanni di Cipro, representing a tidy *Last Judgment* with Christ the Pantocrator at the center surrounded by scenes of *Preparation of the Throne* (first ring), *Apostles and Angels* (second ring), and *Prophets* (third and largest ring). ✉ Ponte dei Greci, Castello 3412 ☎ 041/5226581 ✉ Free ⊙ Wed.–Mon. 9–12:30 and 2–4:30 Ⓥ San Zaccaria.

★ ❺❹ **San Zaccaria.** When 12th-century doge Giustiniano Partecipazio paid a visit to Constantinople as a gesture of submission, Emperor Leo V was so pleased by the visit that he presented Venice with the remains of St. Zachary, father of St. John the Baptist. Leo went even further when he sent along a group of masons, decorators, *scalpellini* (stonecutters), and mosaic artists to build a church dedicated to the saint. The adjacent Benedictine convent quickly became the richest—and least chaste—in the city. This was the convent where girls whose families couldn't afford marriage dowries ended up, by misfortune rather than choice or devotion. San Zaccaria always enjoyed the protection of the doge, who attended Easter Mass here every year. The tilted square bell tower dates from the 13th century.

The striking Renaissance facade, with central and upper portions representing some of Codussi's best work, is only the last chapter in the long story of the building, which features a coronet of four chapels instead of the apse—a Gothic layout typical of the great northern European cathedrals but unusual for Italy. Where the apse of the original church once was there's now a crypt, with tombs of eight of the earliest doges. Be sure to bring with you a pocket full of €.50 coins, which you'll need to turn on the lighting for the major artwork. Giovanni Bellini's celebrated altarpiece is easily recognizable in the left nave. It portrays one of the artist's best Madonnas, this time in the company of an angel playing an ancient viola and four very silent saints. Ask the custodian to show you to the **Cappella di Sant'Atanasio,** also called Cappella del Coro, to see a copy of the magnificent choir stalls that once belonged to the church of Sant'Elena in Castello Basso. The five gilded chairs on the right were used by the doge and his entourage during his annual visit. The **Cappella di San Tarasio** displays frescoes by Tuscan Renaissance artists Andrea del Castagno (1423–57) and Francesco da Faenza (circa 1400–1451). The three outstanding Gothic polyptychs attributed to Antonio Vivarini earned it the nickname "Golden Chapel." From here, you might want to descend to the spooky crypt, as long as the tide is low and it's not flooded. ⊠ *Campo San Zaccaria, 4693 Castello* ☏ *041/5221257* ⌨ *Church free, chapels and crypt €1* ☉ *Mon.–Sat. 10–noon and 4–6, Sun. 4–6* Ⓥ *San Zaccaria.*

㊾ Santa Maria Formosa. Directed by his vision of a beautiful Madonna, 7th-century St. Magno followed a small white cloud and built a church where it settled. Gracefully white, the marble building you see on the same spot today dates from 1492, when Mauro Codussi grafted it onto the 11th-century foundations of the church that had replaced Magno's original. The interior is an architectural blend of Renaissance decoration and Codussi's Byzantine cupola, barrel vaults, and narrow-columned screens. Of interest are two fine paintings: Bartolomeo 's *Madonna of the Mercy,* sheltering a group of petitioners under her cloak, and Palma Il Vecchio's *Santa Barbara,* the patron saint of gunpowder. Outside, the surrounding square bustles with sidewalk cafés and a produce market on weekday mornings. ⊠ *Campo Santa Maria Formosa, Castello* ☏ *041/5234645, 041/2750462 Chorus* ⌨ *€2.50; €9 Chorus pass* ☉ *Mon.–Sat. 10–5, Sun. 1–5* Ⓥ *Rialto.*

㊺ Scuola Grande di San Marco. Where else but in Venice will you find a city's main public hospital with a Lombardo marble facade? The building started out as a scuola in 1260 and became one of the city's six *scuole grandi* (a term applied to Venice's most wealthy confraternities, which took on the responsibility of caring for some of the city's poorest residents). Fire destroyed a substantial part of it in 1485, and though much of the remainder is closed to the public, it's worth a look behind the striking facade at the ballroomlike main entry. Also in the scuola is the **Medical Museum**—not for the young or squeamish, but adults, especially those in the medical professions, are likely to find the displays entertaining and enlightening. Itinerant anatomical experimenting was going on in Venice as early as 1368, some 100 years before Venice founded a reputable anatomical theater and more than 200 years before the famous Università di Padua theater opened. The elaborately illustrated books on display perfectly depict not only complex anatomy, but also some of the clandestine, backwoods operating theaters. There's a collection of tools of the trade that, lacking specific labeling, often seem less therapeutic than torturous. To find the museum, walk through the main hospital entrance, past the front desk, through the lobby, and go up the stairway on the right-hand side. (You can also ask the doorman for directions.) ⊠ *Campo San Giovanni e Paolo, Castello* ☏ *041/5294323* ⌨ *Free* ☉ *Weekdays 8:30–2.*

Off the Beaten Path

★ ⑤⑧ **San Francesco della Vigna** (St. Francis of the Vineyard). Legend says this is where an angel awakened St. Mark the Evangelist with the famous words, "Pax tibi Marce Evangelista meus" (Peace to you Mark, my Evangelist), which became the motto of the Venetian republic. The land was given in 1253 to the Franciscans, who kept the vineyard but replaced the ancient church with a new one dedicated to St. Francis. Nearly three centuries later the Franciscan church was enlarged and rebuilt by Sansovino in 1534. Be sure to come here with a pocket full of coins—you'll need them to illuminate the surprising artwork inside. Antonio Vivarini's (circa 1415–84) triptych of Saints Girolamo, Bernardino da Siena, and Ludovico hangs to your right as you enter the main door. Giovanni Bellini's *Madonna with Saints* is down some steps to the left, inside the Cappella Santa. The glittering gold *Madonna Adoring the Child* by Antonio da Negroponte, near the church's side door, is an inspiring work that invites contemplation. Painted in the second half of the 15th century, this masterpiece marks the transition from Gothic style, of which it preserves a certain formal rigidity, to the Renaissance style revealed in its elaborately detailed decoration and naturalistic subjects. Two pretty cloisters open out from the left nave, their pavement constructed entirely of tombstones of patricians, admirals, and cardinals, testimony to San Francesco della Vigna's former popularity among noble Venetians. ✉ *Campo di San Francesco della Vigna, Castello* ☎ *041/5206102* 🎫 *Free* ☉ *Daily 8–12:30 and 3–6:30* Ⓥ *Celestia.*

CASTELLO BASSO

Until about 100 years ago, the neighborhood of Castello Basso was occupied by fishermen, lace artisans, pearl stringers, and shipbuilders who worked at the Arsenale. Nobles never chose this area for their palaces, nor have today's designer boutiques and souvenir shops chosen to infiltrate. Castello Basso is a chance to see Venice unmasked, with its laundry hanging across narrow streets and its butchers and bakers going about their business. Early in the evening, the neighborhood around Via Garibaldi, the city's widest street, is a vision of Venetians conducting their daily lives: kids too young to ride scooters or play tag are pushed in carriages, men prop up one bar or another, and elderly ladies hold forth on park benches.

The large eastern quarter, known as Sant'Elena, was once an island hermitage. As its church grew, so too did the island by repeatedly building then backfilling new, more distant bulwarks. It was further enlarged by the Austrians in the 19th century to create a parade ground for staging military exercises. Continuing military tradition, this is now home to the Italian Navy's Morosini Naval Military School. It's also the home of Venice's soccer team, which has bounced into and out of the Italian League's first division so often that even fans have trouble keeping track. The football stands look more like temporary scaffolding than anything that should be trusted to support 10,000 fans. Plans for a new facility near Mestre on the mainland have blossomed and subsequently wilted.

The presence of trees and the relative scarcity of bridges and canals makes a visit to Sant'Elena seem almost like a walk on the mainland. During Austrian occupation, its open spaces became a favorite Sunday retreat for Venetians who didn't happen to have country villas. The 1920s Fascist government enlarged the islands by building upon refuse dumps and turned it into working-class, residential housing. You'll notice how relatively modern some of the buildings look and how the streets, instead of being calle, are called *viali,* as in other Italian towns. A small monument amid a breezy pine grove recalls a disaster that struck the area on a warm September afternoon in 1970, when the sky blackened suddenly and a tornado uprooted trees, tore off roofs, and capsized a vaporetto, killing 89 passengers.

Numbers in the margin correspond to the numbers on the Castello Basso map.

The Main Attractions

★ ☝ 62   **Arsenale.** The immense Arsenale dockyard was founded, according to tradition, by Doge Falier in 1104 and was built up considerably throughout the 16th century. For a republic founded on sea power, having a huge, state-of-the-art shipyard was of paramount importance, and this one was legendary for its size and efficiency. Galleys 200 feet long were built here, capable of carrying 300 tons of ginger, pepper, silk, and silver. Until the middle of the 16th century, when slaves began to be used in the galleys, the crew was made up of men who volunteered in exchange for an opportunity to amass pounds of precious merchandise from ports all around the Eastern Mediterranean, to be resold if they survived the perils of the trip. With 16,000 "Arsenalotti" on the payroll, a perfectly armed warship could be built in just 12 hours; 100 ships were built in 60 days in 1597 for the battle against the Turks at Cyprus. After that war, the old Venetian word *arzanà* (from the Arabic *darsina'a,* meaning workshop) was adopted by another 14 languages. Dante visited the shipyards several times, and the half-naked bodies of the workers, armed with pitches and boiling tar, inspired his vision of the seventh plane of Hell for his *Inferno.*

The impressive Renaissance **gateway** (1460) is guarded by four lions, war booty of Francesco Morosini, who took the Peloponnese from the Turks in 1687. The 10-foot-tall lion to the left has had a 2,000-year career standing sentinel, beginning in a harbor near Athens. Experts say its mysterious inscription is Scandinavian runic "graffiti" left by one of the Viking mercenaries hired by the Byzantine emperor to suppress 11th-century revolts in Piraeus. If you look at the winged lion above the doorway, you'll notice that the Gospel at his paws is open but lacks the customary *Pax* inscription; praying for peace perhaps seemed inappropriate above a factory that manufactured weapons.

Modernization under the Austrians and the Kingdom of Italy enabled the Arsenale to make several World War I battleships, and though these marked the end of its shipbuilding career, the shipyard still has active dry docks that haul out and service sizable ships. Some buildings inside have been restored and are used by the Italian Navy, but there are many more in urgent need of care. The debate over what to do with this massive, historically important site is ongoing. The Arsenale isn't regularly open to the public, but it's open for the Biennale and for Venice's festival of traditional boats, held every May. If you're here during those times, don't miss the chance for a look inside. ⊠ *Campo dell'Arsenale, Castello* Ⓥ *Arsenale.*

need a break?

Castello's **Via Garibaldi** is the bazaar of bars, cafés, and osterie. The farther from the water you get the less touristy these become, and with choices on both sides of this, Venice's widest street, you can pick between sunny and shady to fit your whim.

Ⓒ ❻ **Museo Storico Navale** (Museum of Naval History). A 12-foot replica of the doge's ceremonial boat, the *Bucintoro*, and Peggy Guggenheim's private gondola, complete with *felze*, the romantic cabin popular in Casanova's time, are among the highlights of this museum. Models, parts from galleys, old and modern naval weapons, fishermen's ex-votos, and even a few real boats round out the collection. Maps and scale models of the Arsenale will help you appreciate this "town within the town." The museum also houses a large seashell collection, donated to the city by Venetian-born fashion designer Roberta da Camerino. ⊠ *Campo San Biagio, Castello* ☎ *041/5200276* 🎟 *€1.55* ⊘ *Weekdays 8:45–1:30; Sat. 8:45–1* Ⓥ *Arsenale.*

Also Worth Seeing

❺❾ **Chiesa della Pietà.** Unwanted babies were left on the steps of this religious institute, founded by a Franciscan friar in 1346. The girls were immediately taken in at the adjoining orphanage, which provided the children with a musical education. The church flourished during the years of the Venetian republic, when it was traditionally visited by the doge on Palm Sunday, protected by the pope, and supported by generous benefactors. The quality of the performances here reached Continental fame—the in-house conductor was none other than Antonio Vivaldi (1675–1745), who wrote some of his best compositions here for the hospice. The original church was rebuilt in the 15th century, and again after the death of the great musician. Today, with its ceiling frescoes by Tiepolo, it is an elegant example of a Venetian sacred site, and more like a small theater than a church. In an adjoining room to the left of the entrance is a tiny collection of baroque instruments, including the violin played by Vivaldi. Often closed during the day, the Pietà hosts baroque concerts, usually with Venetian composers such as Vivaldi, Galuppi, and Marcello on the program. Some are performed in 17th-century costume. ⊠ *Riva degli Schiavoni, Castello* ☎ *041/5222171* 🎟 *Free* ⊘ *June–Oct., weekdays 10–noon and 4–6, weekends 10–noon and 4–5:30* Ⓥ *San Zaccaria.*

❻⓪ **San Giovanni in Bragora.** This humble redbrick church is said to have been one of the lagoon's first churches—it's so old that no one is sure what the word *bragora* means. At the beginning of the 8th century, St. Magno, the same bishop whose vision of a beautiful Madonna led to the building of Santa Maria Formosa, wanted to dedicate a church to

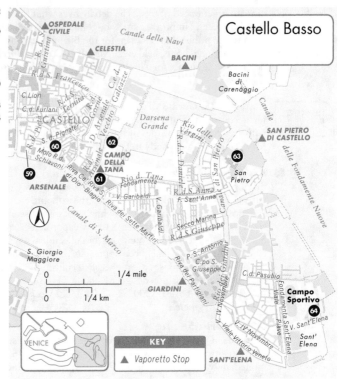

St. John the Baptist, but the relics in the second chapel to the right are those of St. John the Almsgiver. After undergoing two restorations, the church was completely redone in a light Gothic style in 1475. You'll find works by two sons of Antonio Vivarini. *Madonna with Child* in the left nave is by Alvise (circa 1445–1503), but it's his *Christ Risen,* right of the main altar, that shows the freedom and movement that would lead him to become a leader in the late-15th-century Veneto school of painting. His brother Bartolomeo's (1432-99) *Madonna with Child and Saints* is clearly Gothic by comparison. Contrast these works with Cima da Conegliano's (circa 1459–1517) altarpiece *Baptism of Christ.* This luminous scene is realistic not only in its gaunt St. John administering sacrament, but in the beautifully rendered Veneto countryside. Be sure to bring €.50 coins for lighting the paintings. ⊠ *Campo Bandiera e Moro, Castello* ☎ *041/5205906* ✆ *Free* ⌚ *Mon.–Sat. 9–11 and 3:30–6, Sun. 9:30–11* Ⓥ *Arsenale.*

Off the Beaten Path

㊹ San Pietro di Castello. A 7th-century church dedicated to Byzantine saints Sergio and Bacchus was replaced two centuries later with a new church honoring St. Peter the Apostle. Palladio redesigned the facade at the end of the 16th century and added its stark campanile, the first in Venice built from marblelike Istrian stone rather than brick. It stands out against the picturesque, workaday slips along the Canale di San Pietro and the peaceful Renaissance cloister, which for years was a sort of squatters colony. Veneti lived on this island long before Venice was officially founded as a city, but now it's a sleepy, almost forgotten place, with little to suggest that for more than 1,000 years this church was Venice's cathedral—until the Basilica di San Marco replaced it in 1807. The interior has some minor 17th-century art and San Pietro's ancient *cattedra* (throne) in the right nave. According to legend, this marble seat, inscribed with verses from the Koran, was used by Peter at Antioch. ⊠ *Campo San Pietro, Castello* ☏ *041/2750462 Chorus* ⌑ *€2.50; €9 Chorus pass* ⊙ *Mon.–Sat. 10–5, Sun. 1–5* Ⓥ *San Pietro di Castello or Giardini.*

64 **Sant'Elena.** Hermit monks in the ninth century built the first chapel on what was then a scrap of land flanked by mud flats. The church here today was a 13th-century creation built to receive pilgrims bound for the Holy Land and was aptly dedicated to Emperor Constantine's mother, Sant'Elena, who legend says, chose this island herself as a final resting place—it seems the Venetian galley transporting Sant'Elena's reliquary from Constantinople mysteriously ran aground near the island. Monks from Mt. Olive in Tuscany rebuilt the church and added its Renaissance doorway with Commander Vittore Cappello kneeling before St. Helen in Antonio Rizzo's sculptural group. The interior, touching in its simplicity, has faded frescoes with floral and angelic motifs awaiting restoration. There are ceiling nets strung to protect worshippers from loose debris; they make it hard to appreciate three medallions on the cross vault representing San Marco, San Benedetto, and San Nicola da Bari, patron saint of navigators. Sant'Elena wasn't nearly as stark before Napoléon closed the church and spirited away 60 carved wooden choir stalls, for which the church was renowned, and much of the other artwork as well. He might have taken the saint herself if someone hadn't stashed her in nearby San Pietro di Castello. You can see her now in the chapel to the right of the front door.

Work on Sant'Elena's foundation revealed a history few had even guessed when a number of *forni* (ovens) were uncovered. It seems the monks were in business baking bread for sea voyages and cooking for crews anchored nearby. Historians believe Sant'Elena was used to offload precious cargo, often as not pilfered, during Serenissima naval excursions. The land around the church grew considerably in the last century due to the deposit of the city's refuse as landfill, which makes the foundation for the nearby naval school and soccer stadium. The church's 1950s cement bell tower, though not a great match for the rest of the structure, has become a fixture in the skyline for so long it's unlikely to disappear anytime soon—at least not like a former one did. Though old drawings show a bell tower, it vanished without a trace, never to be seen nor written about after the 1700s. ⊠ *Sant'Elena, Castello* ☏ *041/5205144* ⌑ *Free* ⊙ *Mon.–Sat. 5–7, Sun. 9–noon* Ⓥ *Sant'Elena.*

need a break?
A short calle inland from Sant'Elena's park is **Osteria Sant'Elena** (⊠ Campo Stringare ☎ 041/5208419), where with the peace and quiet of this grassy square, you'll swear you've found an oasis in Venice. Another option in the area is **Vincent Bar** (⊠ Viale IV Novembre 36 ☎ 041/5204493). Sit outside with the locals and have a drink or enjoy the homemade gelato.

SAN GIORGIO MAGGIORE & THE GIUDECCA

Beckoning travelers across St. Mark's Basin, sparkling white through the mist, is the island of San Giorgio Maggiore, separated by a small channel from the Giudecca. A tall brick campanile on that distant bank perfectly complements the Campanile of San Marco. Beneath it looms the stately dome of one of Venice's greatest churches, San Giorgio Maggiore. The island of Giudecca, a crescent cupped around the southern shore of Venice, has a history shrouded in mystery, but today it's about as down-to-earth as you can get and one of the city's few remaining neighborhoods that feel truly Venetian.

A half day should give you enough time to enjoy the sights. Allow at least an hour to visit each of the churches and another hour or two to visit the Giudecca neighborhood.

Numbers in the margin correspond to the numbers on the San Giorgio Maggiore & the Giudecca map.

The Main Attractions

★ ⑥⑤ **San Giorgio Maggiore.** There's been a church on this island since the late 8th century, with a Benedictine monastery added in the 10th century. The present neoclassical church of red brick and white marble was begun in 1566 by Palladio, and it displays his architectural hallmarks of geometric harmony and affinity for classical antiquity. Inside, it's refreshingly airy and simply decorated. *The Last Supper* and *The Gathering of Manna,* two of Tintoretto's later works, line the chancel. Right of the entrance hangs *Adoration of the Shepherds* by Jacopo Bassano (1517–92); his portrayal of country life and use of earth-tone colors show the influence of his upbringing in the foothills of Bassano del Grappa. Ask the monks to see Carpaccio's *George and Dragon*; it hangs in a private room, but they're happy to escort you if they have time. Take the elevator to the top of the campanile for some of the finest views in town. ⊠ *Isola di San Giorgio* ☎ *041/5227827* ⌚ *Church free; €3 campanile* ☉ *Daily 8–12:30 and 2–6:30* Ⓥ *San Giorgio.*

⑥⑥ **Santissimo Redentore.** After a 16th-century plague claimed 50,000 people, one-third of the city's population, Andrea Palladio was asked to design a commemorative church. Giudecca's Capucin friars offered land and their services, provided the building was in keeping with the simplicity of their hermitage. Consecrated in 1592, Palladio's creation is dominated by a dome and a pair of slim, almost minaretlike bell towers. Its simple, stately facade leads to a bright, airy interior, perfectly proportioned like San Giorgio Maggiore and in distinct contrast to the dusky Byzantine mystery of the Basilica di San Marco.

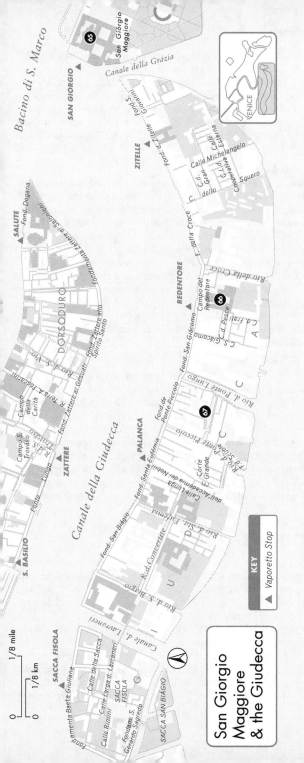

Bacino di S. Marco

SAN GIORGIO

ZITELLE

REDENTORE

PALANCA

S. BASILIO

SALUTE

ZATTERE

DORSODURO

Canale della Giudecca

SACCA FISOLA

San Giorgio
Maggiore
& the Giudecca

KEY

▲ Vaporetto Stop

VENICE

0   1/8 mile
0   1/8 km

For hundreds of years, on the third weekend in July the doge would make a pilgrimage here to give thanks to the Redeemer for ending a 16th-century plague. The event has become the Festa del Redentore, a favorite Venetian festival featuring boats, fireworks, and outdoor feasting. It's the one time of year you can walk to Giudecca—across a temporary pontoon bridge connecting Redentore with the Zattere. ⊠ *Fondamenta San Giacomo, Giudecca* ☎ *041/5231415, 041/2750462 Chorus* ✉ *€2.50; €9 Chorus pass* ☉ *Mon.–Sat. 10–5, Sun. 1–5* Ⓥ *Redentore.*

Also Worth Seeing

⑥⑦ The Giudecca. Seeing Venice from the Giudecca is a bit like seeing the earth from the moon. On a clear day you can take in the city's full panorama, from the Giardini della Biennale to your right (east) to the fuming factories of Marghera industrial complex on the mainland to your left. The island is delightfully mysterious in light fog, but rain or northerly *bora* winds can turn an otherwise perfect walk into cold misery. Few tourists venture beyond the main fondamenta, and few Venetians bother coming to Giudecca at all, unless it's to visit Sacca Fisola's Friday market or the public swimming pool. The original name for the island was *Spinalunga* (long spine), and how it came to be called Giudecca is something of a mystery. It may derive from a possible 14th-century Jewish settlement, or it may be the result of 9th-century nobles being condemned to *giudicato* (exile) here.

Giudecca became a pleasure garden for wealthy Venetians during the republic's long and luxurious decline. Through much of the 20th century it was largely working-class, but of late it has become increasingly gentrified. The island is the site of the exclusive Cipriani hotel, but also the International Youth Hostel and a women's prison. Here and there the ruins of an industrial past—watchmaking, beer brewing, textiles, and a granary—all dating from the 19th century, are being resurrected into housing. Mulino Stucky, an 1895 neo-Gothic flour mill, abandoned for years, is being slowly transformed into a hotel and condominiums overlooking the city's port. Other renovated properties are offering special terms to help make it affordable for Venetians to remain in their city of birth.

ISLANDS OF THE LAGOON

The perfect vacation from your Venetian vacation is an escape to Murano, Burano, and Torcello, the islands of the northern lagoon. Torcello offers greenery, breathing space, and picnicking opportunities, as long as you remember to pack a lunch. Burano is a toy town of houses painted in a riot of color—blue, yellow, pink, ocher, and dark red. Visitors still love to shop here for "Venetian" lace, despite the fact that these days it's almost all machine made in Asia. Just as Murano is renowned for its glass, Murano tours, even those organized by top hotels, are notorious for high-pressure sales. Vaporetto connections aren't difficult, and for the price of a boat ticket you'll buy your freedom and more time to explore. The Murano "guides" herding new arrivals follow a rotation so that factories take turns giving tours, but you can avoid the hustle by just walking away.

From April through October, San Zaccaria is connected to Murano by Line 5, an express boat stopping at Navagero, Faro, and Colonna before returning to San Zaccaria; the trip takes about 30 minutes. Local Line 41 takes about 45 minutes to get from San Zaccaria to Murano; it doesn't go to Burano or Torcello, but does stop at San Michele. From Fondamente Nuove boats leave every 10 minutes. Line LN (for Lagoon North) goes from Fondamente Nuove direct to Murano, Burano, and Torcello; the full trip takes 45 minutes each way. Hitting all the sights on all the islands takes a full day. If you limit yourself to Murano and San Michele, a half day will suffice. If you enjoy riding boats, try an alternate route back; continue on Line 12 another 30 minutes to Punta Sabbione on the mainland, where Line 6/14 connects directly to San Marco.

Numbers in the margin correspond to the numbers on the Islands of the Lagoon map.

The Main Attractions

★ ⑦ **Burano.** Colorfully painted houses line the canals of this quiet fishing village where centuries ago lace making rescued a faltering economy. As you walk the 100 yards from the dock to Piazza Galuppi, the main square, you pass stall after stall of lace vendors. These good-natured ladies won't press you with a hard sell, but don't expect precise product information or great bargains. Remember that real handmade Burano lace is very rare and costs €1,000 to €2,000 for a 10-inch doily. What you see in the stalls is almost certainly made elsewhere.

Museo del Merletto (Lace Museum) lets you marvel at the intricacies of Burano's lace making. Try to imagine the hours it took to produce the articles on display and you'll understand why genuine handmade lace commands the price it does. The museum is also a skills center— more a sewing circle than a school—so on weekdays you'll often find women continuing the centuries-old tradition that made the island famous throughout Europe. They sometimes have authentic pieces for sale privately. ⊠ *Piazza Galuppi 187* ☎ *041/730034* ⊠ *€4, €6 with Museo Vetrario, €15.50 Musei Civici pass* ◷ *Apr.–Oct., Wed.–Mon. 10–5; Nov.–Mar., Wed.–Mon. 10–4* Ⓥ *Burano.*

☾ ⑦ **Murano.** As in Venice, bridges here link a number of small islands, dotted with houses that once were workmen's cottages. The republic, concerned about fire hazard in the 13th century, moved its glassworks to Murano, and today you can visit the factories and watch glass being made. Many of them line the Fondamenta dei Vetrai, the canal-side walkway leading from the Colonna vaporetto landing. Before you reach Murano's Grand Canal (250 yards from the landing) you'll pass the **Chiesa di San Pietro Martire.** Reconstructed in the 16th century, it houses Giovanni Bellini's *Madonna and Child* and Veronese's *St. Jerome.* ⊠ *Fondamenta dei Vetrai* ☎ *041/739704* ◷ *Mon.–Sat. 9–12:30 and 2–5* Ⓥ *Colonna.*

The collection at **Museo Vetrario** (Glass Museum) ranges from price-less antiques to only slightly less expensive modern pieces. You'll see au-thentic Venetian styles and patterns, including the famous Barovier wedding cup (1470–80). ⊠ *Fondamenta Giustinian 8* ☎ *041/739586* ⛴ *€4, €6 with Museo del Merletto, €15.50 entry to all Musei Civici, including Palazzo Ducale* ⊙ *Apr.–Oct., Thurs.–Tues. 10–5; Nov.–Mar., Thurs.–Tues. 10–4; last tickets sold ½ hr before closing* Ⓥ *Museo.*

Basilica dei Santi Maria e Donato, just past the glass museum, is among the first churches founded by the lagoon's original inhabitants. The elab-orate mosaic pavement includes the date 1140; its ship's keel roof and Veneto-Byzantine columns add to the air of an ancient temple. ⊠ *Fondamenta Giustinian* ☎ *041/739056* ⛴ *Free* ⊙ *Daily 8–noon and 4–7* Ⓥ *Museo.*

Also Worth Seeing

⑱ The Lido. Separating the lagoon from the sea, this long sandbar of an is-land was once a garden plot providing vegetables to Venice. Only its southern end, Malamocco, which was the republic's 8th-century ad-ministrative center, was inhabited, the rest being cultivated. But from the 1850s through World War II, the Lido became a fashionable sea re-sort, and its name was subsequently borrowed by many seaside resorts throughout the world. This was where Austrian Archduke Maximilian built his summer residence, where Thomas Mann wrote *Death in Venice,* and where Iran's former Shah Reza Pahlavi came to water-ski. The Lido's popularity peaked in the late 1930s, following the launch of the Biennale film festival, the building of one of Italy's first airports (now used only for private traffic), and the opening of the casino (now closed). Some of the glamour and architecture of those days remains in the Moorish-looking Grand Hotel Excelsior and on the quiet streets branch-ing from Gran Viale Santa Maria Elisabetta, adorned with many art deco villas. Today, the Lido is where locals keep holiday houses and crowds of commuters from Venice and the mainland spend a good portion of their summer. The water looks murky because of the fine sand, celebrated by Byron and Shelley, but it's actually quite clean. Small waves make for relatively safe swimming, even for children. The best way to explore the Lido is by renting a bicycle, alternating sightseeing with sunbathing. Ⓥ *S. M. Elisabetta Lido, Lines 1, 6/14, 51, 61, and in summer 82.*

⑳ San Michele. This cypress-lined island is home to the pretty Renaissance church of **San Michele in Isola**—and to some of Venice's most illustri-ous deceased. The church was designed by Codussi; the graves include poet Ezra Pound (1885–1972), impresario and art critic Sergey Diaghilev (1872–1929), and composer Igor Stravinsky (1882–1971). Surrounded by the living sounds of Venice lagoon, this would seem the perfect final resting place. However, these days newcomers are exhumed after 10 years and transferred to a less grandiose location. ☎ *041/7292811* ⛴ *Free* ⊙ *Apr.–Sept., daily 7:30–6; Oct.–Mar., daily 7:30–4* Ⓥ *San Michele.*

Off the Beaten Path

⑲ San Lazzaro Degli Armeni. When a leprosy epidemic hit Venice in 1185, those infected were confined to a hospital on this island in the lagoon, which was subsequently dedicated to San Lazzaro (St. Lazarus), the

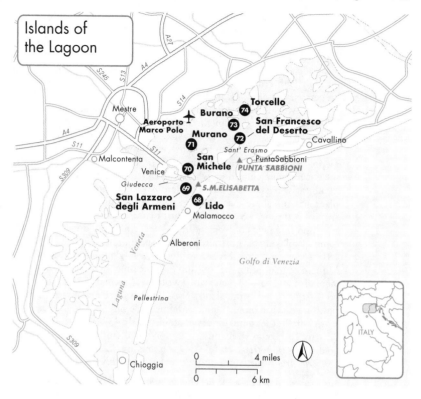

Islands of
the Lagoon

Mestre

Aeroporto
Marco Polo

Burano 74

San Francesco
del Deserto

Murano 73

71   Sant' Erasmo   Cavallino

San
Michele 72 PuntaSabbioni

70   PUNTA SABBIONI

Malcontenta

Venice

Giudecca 69 S.M.ELISABETTA

San Lazzaro
degli Armeni 68 Lido

Malamocco

Alberoni

Golfo di Venezia

Veneta

Laguna

Pellestrina

ITALY

Chioggia

0   4 miles

0   6 km

leper of biblical fame. San Lazzaro later served as a shelter for beggars.
In 1717 Doge Giovanni Corner II gave the island to Peter of Manug, better known as Father Mekhitar ("the Consoler"), an Armenian priest who
had founded an order of monks in Morea, today's Peloponnese. (Armenia
had been the first country in the world to adopt Christianity as its state
religion, though it did not recognize the pope's authority.) Following the
Turkish invasion of Greece, Mekhitar fled to Venice, where a small but
wealthy Armenian community had thrived since the 13th century. On
San Lazzaro he built the monastery that still stands today, more than tripled
the size of the island with landfill, and established what was then the world's
largest center of Armenian culture outside of Armenia.

Only 15 minutes from the San Zaccaria vaporetto stop, San Lazzaro feels
a world apart from the touristy hubbub of San Marco. Its 322,920
square feet are covered with trees, orchards, and gardens impeccably kept
by a community of some 20 Mekhitarist priests and seminarians. Apart
from the monastery, San Lazzaro houses a flock of sheep, a church, a
picture gallery, a museum, two libraries, and a collection of precious
manuscripts.

The daily afternoon tour—led by guides fluent in several languages, including English—begins with a brief lesson on Armenian history beneath

the turquoise ceiling of the 14th-century **church.** It was partially rebuilt by Mekhitar, and today features rococo decorations and Austrian stained glass. In the refectory is an 18th-century *Last Supper* inspired by Leonardo da Vinci's masterpiece. Mekhitar's staircase leads to the **picture gallery,** with about 100 paintings by Armenian artists from the 18th through 19th centuries, and to Mekhitar's room, which still contains his personal possessions. With nearly 200,000 volumes, the main library holds the world's richest collection of Armenian writing, some of which belonged to the founder himself. Unlike other Venetian monasteries, which Napoléon destroyed, this one was spared because the French conqueror believed it to be more of a learning center than a religious institution. Tiepolo's *Peace and Justice* painting is on the ceiling as you enter the eclectic **museum collection,** where you can appreciate the encyclopedic Mekhitarist passion for culture. Here Armenian pottery, swords, and silver artwork share space with an Egyptian mummy, an Indian wood-and-ivory throne, a Sanskrit Buddhist manuscript, Chinese ivory carvings, and fragments of Roman urns. A few steps lead down to **Byron's room,** displaying his portrait. The poet spent months here in 1816 and 1817 recovering from his separation from England and Anne Isabelle Milbanke. To appease the soul and pass the time, Byron studied the Armenian language—he even helped write an Armenian-English grammar book (still printed by the island's press), which you'll find in the gift shop, right next to the monks' famous homemade *marmellata di rose* (rose jam). Finally, the **round library** contains nearly 4,000 mostly Armenian 8th- to 18th-century manuscripts, some brilliantly illuminated with gold. ☎ *041/5260104* ⌂ *€6* ⊙ *One tour daily, 3:25–5* Ⓥ *Line 20 from San Zaccaria (near Pensione Wildner) at 3:10 only.*

⓻ San Francesco del Deserto. Legend says St. Francis of Assisi visited the lagoon in 1220 with his follower Illuminato on their way back from a preaching tour of Palestine. They'd thought about settling on Torcello, but found it too rich for their tastes. Instead, they rowed to this tiny deserted island, then known as Due Vigne ("Two Vineyards"). When Francis planted his pilgrim's stick into the ground, it miraculously grew into a pine tree and birds came to sing for him. Reaching Assisi, he sent some friars to the island, who in 1228 built the first church. Today the island is a floating grove of cypress trees, with a peaceful monastery and cloisters—it's about as far from Venice's bustle as you can get. You'll learn more about Franciscan lore while being shepherded around by one of the 10 resident friars. ☎ *041/5286863* ⊕ *www.isola-sanfrancescodeldeserto.it* ✉ *Donation welcomed; water taxi from Burano landing to San Francesco del Deserto, €25–30 round-trip* ⊙ *Tues.–Sun. 9–11 and 3–5* Ⓥ *Burano.*

★ ⓼ Torcello. In their flight from barbarians 1,500 years ago, the first Venetians landed here, prospering even after many left to found the city of Venice. As malaria took its toll and the island's wool manufacturing was priced out of the market, Torcello became a ghost town. In the 16th century there were 10 churches and 20,000 inhabitants; today you'll be lucky to see one of the island's 16 permanent residents.

Santa Maria Assunta was built in the 11th century, and Torcello's wealth at the time is evident in the church's high-quality Byzantine mosaics. The massive *Last Judgment* shows sinners writhing in pain, while opposite, above the altar, the Madonna looks calmly down from her field of gold. Ask to see the inscription dated 639 and a sample of mosaic pavement from the original church. The adjacent **Santa Fosca** church, added when the body of the saint arrived in 1011, is still used for religious services. It's worth making the climb up the adjacent **Campanile** for an incomparable view of the lagoon wetlands. ⊠ *Torcello* ☎ *041/ 730119* 🖾 *Santa Maria Assunta €3; campanile €3* ⊗ *Mar.–Oct., daily 10:30–6; Nov.–Feb., daily 10–5* Ⓥ *Torcello.*

Where to Eat

2

Updated by
Jeff Booth

THE CATCHWORD IN VENICE, at both fancy restaurants and holes-in-the-wall, is fish, often at its tastiest when it looks like nothing you've seen before. How do you learn first-hand about the catch of the day? An early morning visit to the Rialto's *pescheria* (fish market) is more instructive than any book.

There's no getting around the fact that Venice has more than its share of overpriced, mediocre eateries that prey on tourists. Avoid places with cajoling waiters standing outside, and beware of restaurants that don't display their prices. At the other end of the spectrum, showy *menu turistico* (tourist menu) boards make offerings clear in a dozen languages, but for the same 15–20 euros you'd spend at such places you could do better at a *bacaro* (the local version of a wine bar) making a meal of *cichetti* (savory snacks).

Dining options in Venice range from the ultra-high end, where jackets and ties are required, to the super-casual, where the clientele (almost all of them tourists) won't notice if you're wearing shorts. Some of Venice's swankiest restaurants—the ones that usually have only male waiters wearing white jackets and bow ties—trade on longstanding reputations and might seem a little stuffy and faded. The food at such places tends toward interpretations of international cuisine and, though often expertly prepared, can seem as old-fashioned as the waiters who serve it. On the other hand, mid-range restaurants are often more willing to break from tradition, incorporating ingredients such as ginger and wasabi in their creations.

Budget-conscious travelers, and those simply looking for a good meal in unpretentious surroundings, might want to stick to trattorias and *bacari*. Trattorias often serve less highfalutin versions of classic Venetian dishes at substantially reduced prices; bacari offer lighter fare, usually eaten at the bar (though sometimes tables are available), and wine lists that offer lots of choices by the glass.

Although pizzerias are not hard to find, Venice is not much of a pizza town—standards aren't what they are elsewhere in Italy, and local laws impede the use of wood-burning ovens. Beware of the gooey, soggy pizza at bar-pizzerias, which is commonly precooked and reheated. *Tramezzini,* the triangular white-bread sandwiches served in bars all over Italy, however, are particularly good in Venice. Many bars here still make their own mayonnaise, and few skimp on the fillings.

Tiramisu lovers will have ample opportunity to sample this creamy concoction made from ladyfingers soaked in espresso and covered with sweetened mascarpone cheese. It was invented here in the Veneto. In addition to sorbets and *semifreddi* (frozen ice cream and cake desserts), other sweets that frequently appear on Venetian menus are almond cakes and strudels, as well as dry cookies served with sweet white wine. Ice cream is sold at every corner but, with a few notable exceptions, rarely rises above mediocrity.

Burano

$$–$$$ ✕ **Al Gatto Nero da Ruggero.** Even cats know that this restaurant dedicated to one of their own offers the best fish on Burano. The "Black Cat," with its vivid blue facade, stands out among the low, brightly colored buildings animating the picturesque Fondamenta della Giudecca. All pastas and desserts are made in-house; the flavors come alive in chef/owner Ruggero's spaghetti *alla scogliera*, which teems with treats from the sea. The *fritto misto* (fish fry) is outstanding for its lightness and variety of fish. ⊠ *Fondamenta della Giudecca 88, Burano* ☎ *041/730120* ▤ *AE, DC, MC, V* ۩ *Closed Mon. and 3 wks in Nov.* Ⓥ *Burano.*

Cannaregio

$$$$ ✕ **Al Bacco.** Located not far from the Ghetto, this ancient osteria caters to young locals and those tourists who make the effort to seek it out. Among the classic Venetian dishes, sample the *sarde sotto sale* (salted sardines) or the old favorite *bigoli in salsa* (rough-shaped spaghetti in an anchovy sauce). For alfresco dining, the charming garden has a few tables. ⊠ *Fondamenta Capuzine, Cannaregio 3054* ☎ *041/717493* ▤ *AE, DC, MC, V* ۩ *Closed Mon. No lunch* Ⓥ *San Marcuola.*

$$–$$$$ ✕ **Fiaschetteria Toscana.** Contrary to what the name suggests, there's nothing Tuscan about this restaurant's menu. It was formerly a Tuscan wine and oil storehouse, and it's worth a visit for its cheerful and courteous service, fine *cucina* (cooking), and noteworthy cellar. The owners, Albino and Mariuccia Busatto, make their presence felt as they walk among the well-appointed tables, opening special bottles of wine and discussing the menu. Highlights include a light *tagliolini neri al ragù di astice* (thin spaghetti served with squid ink and mixed with a delicate lobster sauce), and zabaglione. ⊠ *Campo San Giovanni Crisostomo, Cannaregio 5719* ☎ *041/5285281* ▤ *AE, DC, MC, V* ۩ *Closed Tues. and 4 wks July–Aug. No lunch Mon.* Ⓥ *Rialto.*

★ **$$$** ✕ **A la Vecia Cavana.** Since they took over in 2004, the owners have focused on presenting a highly refined menu. The young, talented kitchen staff creates winning Italian and Venetian dishes such as *filetti di pesce a cottura differenziata* (fish fillet, cooked on one side and quickly seared on the other), tender baby cuttlefish, and, among desserts, *gelato al basilico* (basil ice cream). The 18th-century *cavana* (boathouse) maintains its original low columns, arches, and brick walls, but has been decorated with contemporary flair. ⊠ *Rio Terà SS. Apostoli, Cannaregio 4624* ☎ *041/5287106* ▤ *AE, DC, MC, V* ۩ *Closed Mon., 2 wks in Jan., and Aug.* Ⓥ *Rialto/Ca' d'Oro.*

$$–$$$ ✕ **Antica Mola.** You'll find a warm welcome at this family-run trattoria. Whether you choose the terrace overlooking the canal or the shaded garden in back, owners Antonietta and Franco will entertain you with their lively presence. The cooking is reliably good, homey fare with the accent on seafood—spaghetti *coi caparozzoli* (with carpet-shell clams) is a favorite. ⊠ *Fondamenta dei Ormesini, Cannaregio 2800* ☎ *041/717492* ▤ *AE, DC, MC, V* ۩ *Closed Aug.* Ⓥ *San Marcuola.*

2

The logistics of restaurant meals in Italy are different from those in the United States (and many other places). When you sit down in a *ristorante,* trattoria, or *osteria,* you're expected to order two courses at a minimum, such as a *primo* (first course) and a *secondo* (second course), or an antipasto (starter) followed by a primo or secondo. A secondo isn't a "main course" that can serve as a full meal.

The handiest places for a snack between sights are bars, cafés, and the quintessentially Venetian bacari. Bars are places for a quick coffee and a *panino* (sandwich, often warmed on a griddle) or *tramezzino* (sandwich on untoasted white bread, usually with a mayonnaise-based filling). A café (*caffè* in Italian) is like a bar but usually with more seating. If you place your order at the counter, ask if you can sit down: some places charge considerably more for table service. Often you'll pay a cashier first, then give your *scontrino* (receipt) to the person at the counter who fills your order.

Mealtimes & Closures
Breakfast (*la colazione*) is usually served from 7 to 10:30, lunch (*il pranzo*) from 12:30 to 2, dinner (*la cena*) from 7:30 to 10. Many bacari open as early as 8 AM, but they do not serve typical breakfast items or coffee; some Venetians partake of cichetti for their morning meal.

Reservations & Dress
Reservations are always a good idea in restaurants, especially on weekends. We mention them in reviews only when they are essential or not accepted. We mention dress only when men are required to wear a jacket or a jacket and tie. Keep in mind that Italian men never wear shorts or running shoes in a restaurant or bacaro, no matter how humble. The same "rules" apply to ladies' casual shorts, running shoes, and plastic sandals. Shorts are acceptable in pizzerias and cafés.

Prices & Tipping
All prices include tax. Prices include service *(servizio)* unless indicated otherwise on the menu. It's customary to leave a small tip (from a euro to 10% of the bill) in appreciation of good service. Tips are always given in cash. Most restaurants have a "cover" charge, usually listed on the menu as *"pane e coperto."* It should be modest (€1–€2.50 per person) except at the most expensive restaurants. Some instead charge for bread, which should be brought to you (and paid for) only if you order it. When in doubt, ask about the policy upon ordering. The price of fish dishes is often given by weight (before cooking); the price on the menu will be for 100 grams; a typical fish portion will come to 350 grams. Keep some cash on hand, because many osterie, bacari, and pizzerias don't take credit cards.

WHAT IT COSTS				
	$$$$	$$$	$$	$	¢
AT DINNER	over €22	€17–€22	€12–€17	€7–€12	under €7

Price for a second course (secondo piatto).

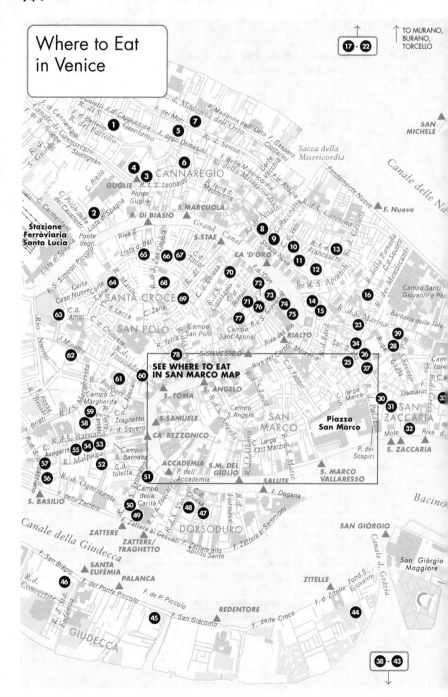

Where to Eat
in Venice

TO MURANO,
BURANO,
TORCELLO

17 - 22

SAN
MICHELE

SEE WHERE TO EAT
IN SAN MARCO MAP

0

O,

0   1/8 mile

0   1/8 km

Cimitero
San
Michele

Navi

OSPEDALE
CIVILE

ti
Paolo

CELESTIA

BACINI

ampo
.orenzo
C.Lion   C.d.
Furlani

R.d.S. Francesco

R.d.S. Termit

CASTELLO

Darsena
Grande

R.d. Vergin

R.d.S. Danilte

D. Arsenale C.e d. Galeazze

R. d. Pret   D. Arsenal Vecchio

S. d. Pignater

d. Schiavoni

Riva Ca.

CAMPO
DELLA
TANA

ARSENALE

Riva S.
di Dio.   Biagio

F. della Tana

R. della Tana

V. Garibaldi

R. d.S.Anna

F. Sant'Anne

Viale Garibaldi

Riva dei Sette Martiri

no di S. Marco

Secco
Marina

R.d.S.Gius

Paludo S
Antónic
C.po S.
Giusepp

GIARDINI

Riva dei Partigiani

io
e

Bacino d.
S. Giórgio

KEY

ℹ️ *Tourist*
Information

▲ *Vaporetto*
Stop

$$-$$$ ✕ **Osteria al Bomba.** Locals (mostly middle-aged men) flock to this bacaro/trattoria to have a glass of wine and a plate of pasta while bantering with the genial proprietors, Marco and Giacomo. Take a seat at the long communal table if you can, as it's more pleasurable to enjoy the food while sitting down. Among the offerings are saor three ways—the *gamberetti* (small shrimp) in saor might even be better than the classic version made with sardines. The grilled vegetables provide a fine counterpoint to delicacies from the sea. ✉ *Calle dell'Oca, off Campo Santa Sofia, Cannaregio* ☎ *041/241146* ▭ *MC, V* Ⓥ *Ca' d'Oro.*

★ **$$** ✕ **Vini da Gigio.** A friendly, family-run trattoria on the quayside of a canal just off the Strada Nova, da Gigio is very popular with Venetians and visiting Italians, who appreciate the affable service, the well-prepared pasta, fish, and meat dishes, the imaginative and varied wine cellar, and the high-quality draft wine. It's good for a simple lunch at tables in the barroom. ✉ *Fondamenta de la Chiesa, Cannaregio 3628/a* ☎ *041/ 5285140* ▭ *DC, MC, V* ☾ *Closed Mon., Tues., 2 wks in Jan., and 3 wks in Aug.* Ⓥ *Ca' d'Oro.*

$-$$ ✕ **Anice Stellato.** Hidden away on one of the most romantic fondamente of Cannaregio, this family-run bacaro/trattoria is the place to stop for fairly priced, great-tasting food in a part of town that doesn't teem with restaurants. The space has plenty of character: narrow columns rise from the colorful mosaiclike floor, dividing the room into cozy booths. Traditional Venetian fare is enriched with such offerings as *carpacci di pesce* (thin slices of raw tuna, swordfish, or salmon dressed with olive oil and fragrant herbs), tagliatelle with king prawns and zucchini flowers, and several tasty fish stews. Meat dishes are also served, including a tender beef fillet stewed in Barolo wine with potatoes. ✉ *Fondamenta de la Sensa, Cannaregio 3272* ☎ *041/720744* ▭ *AE, DC, MC, V* ☾ *Closed Mon., Tues., and Aug.* Ⓥ *S. Alvise.*

$-$$ ✕ **Da Bepi.** This neighborhood hangout teems with regulars who clearly appreciate the home-style cooking. At peak times you might have to wait a few minutes before receiving any attention, but you'll be consoled by the inviting aromas wafting through the busy dining room. All dishes are fresh and well prepared: try the *tortelli con spinaci, patate, e ricotta* (ravioli filled with spinach, potato, and ricotta cheese) or, for a break from the usual Venetian fare, the *spiedini di pollo* (chicken on skewers). ✉ *Salizzada del Pistor, off Campo Santi Apostoli, Cannaregio 4550* ☎ *041/ 5285031* ▭ *MC, V* ☾ *Closed Thurs. and 2 wks in July* Ⓥ *Ca' d'Oro.*

$-$$ ✕ **Gam-Gam.** At the edge of the Jewish Ghetto near Ponte delle Guglie is one of the very few kosher restaurants in Italy, with a name that in Hebrew means "more-more" and recalls the Italian word *gnam-gnam* ("yum-yum"). The informal dining room is narrow and pink. The Orthodox staff is helpful in explaining the blend of Israeli and other Middle Eastern dishes highlighting the menu, which include falafel with tahini sauce and couscous prepared several different ways. Vegetarians might create their own salad from the salad bar or try the *piatto di melanzane* (eggplant plate). ✉ *Sottoportico del Ghetto Vecchio, Cannaregio 1122* ☎ *041/715284* ▭ *No credit cards* ☾ *Closed Sat. and 1st week in Feb. No dinner Fri.* Ⓥ *San Marcuola.*

★ **$** ✕ **Bentigodi da Andrea.** *Bentigodi* is Venetian for "you'll enjoy yourself," and such a jaunty name is well suited to this trendy osteria, decorated with fishing-boat lamps and old-fashioned prints on whitewashed walls. The menu includes tartare of tuna and swordfish, steamed orata with green apple and lemon, *masorini con alici e capperi* (duck with anchovies and capers), and game in winter. Good homemade desserts include cakes made with pumpkin and almond or chocolate and walnut, a rich bread pudding, and simple *panna cotta* served with fresh fruit. ⊠ *Calesele, Cannaregio 1423* ☎ *041/716269* ▤ *No credit cards* ⊘ *Closed Sun., Mon., and 3 wks in Jan.* Ⓥ *San Marcuola.*

$ ✕ **Da Alberto.** An amicable trattoria that doubles as a bacaro, Alberto is always packed with locals. The faux-antique decor makes the place look old, but missing is the characteristic bacaro odor that comes from years of serving wine. However, what you cannot smell, you see: heaping barrels and demijohns full of white tocai and red raboso. Vegetarians will appreciate the range of nonmeat dishes on the menu. Pasta is made to order, and fish can be better here than in most of the city center's pricier restaurants. ⊠ *Calle Giacinto Gallina, Cannaregio 5401* ☎ *041/5238153* ▤ *MC, V* ⊘ *Closed Sun., 1st wk in Feb., and 3 wks July–Aug.* Ⓥ *Ca' d'Oro.*

$ ✕ **Trattoria Ca' d'Oro (Alla Vedova).** This warm trattoria not far from the

Fodor's Choice Ca' d'Oro (commonly referred to by its nickname, alla Vedova) was

★ opened as a bacaro by the owner's great-grandparents. A Venetian terrazzo floor, old marble counter, and rustic furnishings lend a pleasant authenticity that's matched by the food and service. Cichetti include tender *seppie roste* (grilled cuttlefish), *polpette* (meatballs), and *baccalà mantecato* (cod spread). The house winter pasta is the *pastisso de radicio rosso* (lasagna with sausage, radicchio, and béchamel sauce). In spring the chef switches to pastisso *de asparagi* (with asparagus). ⊠ *Calle del Pistor, Cannaregio 3912* ☎ *041/5285324* ▤ *No credit cards* ⊘ *Closed Thurs. No lunch Sun.* Ⓥ *Ca' d'Oro.*

¢ ✕ **Tiziano.** They serve inexpensive salad plates and daily pasta specials at this modest restaurant, but you should concentrate instead on the staggering array of tramezzini that line the display cases. It's a handy place for a quick detour and snack at very modest prices. Vegetarians will delight in Tiziano's version of the classic Italian toasted sandwich, in this case with cheese, eggplant slices, and roasted zucchini. ⊠ *Salizzada San Giovanni Crisostomo, Cannaregio 5747* ☎ *041/5235544* ▤ *No credit cards* Ⓥ *Rialto.*

Castello

$$$$ ✕ **Al Covo.** This small, charming osteria changes its menu according to the day's bounty—mostly local seafood caught just hours before and specialties from other European waters. Cesare Benelli and his American wife, Diane, insist on only the freshest ingredients. Specialties include the *zuppa di pesce* (fish soup) and the fish of the day (grilled, baked, or steamed). Desserts are homemade, and the wine list is extensive. Lunch and dinner have the same fixed-price menu options (€59 or €78, with several filling courses). The friendly, down-home atmosphere combined with the refined menu sets Al Covo apart. ⊠ *Campiello della Pescaria, Castello 3968* ☎ *041/5223812* ▤ *MC, V* ⊘ *Closed Wed., Thurs., 1 wk in Aug., and Jan.* Ⓥ *Arsenale.*

$$$$ ✕ **Do Leoni.** The Two Lions, in the Hotel Londra Palace, is a sumptuous candlelit setting in which to sample Venetian and other Italian cuisine. The kitchen turns out creative dishes, such as millet soup with bacon; the seven-course tasting menu utilizes ingredients not commonly found in Italian kitchens, including vanilla and ginger. The summer terrace occupies a good portion of the Riva. ⊠ *Riva degli Schiavoni, Castello 4171* ☎ *041/5200533* ⌕ *Reservations essential* ▭ *AE, DC, MC, V* Ⓥ *San Zaccaria.*

$$$–$$$$ ✕ **Alle Testiere.** A strong local following can make it tough to get one of
Fodor'sChoice   the 22 seats at this tiny trattoria near Campo Santa Maria Formosa. With
★   its decidedly unglamorous ceiling fans, the place feels as informal as a bistro (or a saloon); the food, however, is much more sophisticated. Chef Bruno Gavagnin's dishes stand out for lightness and balance: try the *gnocchetti con moscardini* (little gnocchi with tender baby octopus) or the linguine with *coda di rospo* (monkfish), or inquire about the carpaccio of the day. The well-assembled wine list is particularly strong on local whites. ⊠ *Calle del Mondo Novo, Castello 5801* ☎ *041/5227220* ⌕ *Reservations essential* ▭ *MC, V* ⊗ *Closed Sun., Mon., 3 wks Jan.–Feb., 4 wks July–Aug.* Ⓥ *Rialto/San Zaccaria.*

★ **$$–$$$** ✕ **Corte Sconta.** You're close to seafood heaven at this firm favorite on the Venetian dining scene. Simple wooden tables are arranged around an open courtyard with outdoor seating in summer. You could make a meal of the seafood antipasti alone, but you'd miss out on such delights as spaghetti *neri alle capesante e zucchine* (cuttlefish-ink pasta with scallops and zucchini) and *vongole veraci spadellate allo zenzero* (clams sauteed in ginger). The house dessert is a warm zabaglione with Venetian cookies, and the house pour is a smooth, still prosecco, backed up by a good range of bottled wines. ⊠ *Calle del Pestrin, Castello 3886* ☎ *041/5227024* ⌕ *Reservations essential* ▭ *MC, V* ⊗ *Closed Sun., Mon., 4 wks Jan.–Feb., 4 wks July–Aug.* Ⓥ *Arsenale.*

$–$$$ ✕ **Da Bruno.** A country *taverna* (tavern) in the center of Venice, this popular restaurant grills its meat over an open fire. First, though, don't overlook the cichetti at the counter, such as the paper-thin prosciutto wrapped around *grissini* (thin bread sticks). For main courses, take your pick from such Italian specialties as fillet of beef with pepper sauce or veal with wild mushrooms. Fish fans may gravitate toward the scampi, calamari, or squid with polenta. ⊠ *Calle del Paradiso, Castello 5731* ☎ *041/ 5221480* ▭ *AE, DC, MC, V* Ⓥ *San Marco or Rialto.*

$$ ✕ **Al Mascaron.** The convivial, crowded Al Mascaron, with its paper tablecloths and informal atmosphere, is always filled with Venetians who drop in to gossip, drink, play cards, and eat cichetti at the bar. You can bet on delicious fish, pastas, risottos, and seafood salads. Locals complain that the prices have become somewhat inflated, but grudgingly admit that the food is good. ⊠ *Calle Lunga Santa Maria Formosa, Castello 5225* ☎ *041/5225995* ▭ *No credit cards* ⊗ *Closed Sun. and mid-Dec.–mid-Jan.* Ⓥ *Rialto or San Marco.*

$–$$ ✕ **Dai Tosi.** Finding a restaurant in Castello Basso can be difficult; this neighborhood trattoria is the only fairly priced place near San Pietro di Castello. The red, hand-painted sign above the window reflects the homey interior and also the cheerfulness of service: *tosi* refers to the "young lads" on the waitstaff, as opposed to the grumpy, aging career waiters you might encounter elsewhere. The lunch menu offers the usual array

NAVIGATING THE VENETIAN MENU

THE SEAFOOD PILED HIGH at the Rialto pescheria (fish market) comes from local waters and carries names peculiar to Venice. Inevitably, much of it finds its way to Venetian tables: moeche (soft-shell crabs) are caught at molting time (spring and fall) and fried in an egg-and-Parmesan batter. Seppie in tecia (tender baby cuttlefish) turn deep black after being stewed in their ink and a dash of tomato sauce and are customarily served with golden yellow polenta.

A vast array of tasty shellfish, including caparozzoli (carpet-shell clams), garusoli (snail-like mollusks), and peoci (mussels), are tossed with pasta, stirred into risotto or soups, or simply boiled and dressed with olive oil, lemon juice, and parsley. Capesante (sea scallops) are usually baked, either plain or with bread crumbs, Parmesan, and parsley. Crustaceans include gamberetti (shrimp), scampi (king prawns), schie (tiny gray shrimp), granseola (spider crab), and canocie (mantis shrimp). One very traditional preparation for fish, found on just about every bacaro, osteria, and restaurant menu, is sarde in saor, or just saor (boned sardines fried in olive oil, then marinated in a sauce of sautéed onion, vinegar, raisins, and pine nuts).

Less strictly Venetian but nevertheless often found on menus throughout the city are dishes featuring fish from the Mediterranean such as branzino (sea bass, also called spigola), orata (gilthead), sogliola (sole), rombo (turbot), and dentice (sea bream). Common preparations include ai ferri (grilled), al forno (baked, usually with potatoes), al sale (baked under a sea-salt crust), and a filetti (as fillets).

A Venetian specialty savored all over Italy is fegato alla veneziana (thin slices of calf's liver quickly sautéed and dressed with onion, then briefly stewed in olive oil and butter and sprinkled with parsley). Adventurous diners should try bisatto all'ara, a local variety of fleshy eel with a thin skin cooked on a bed of bay leaves. Bisatto can also be deep-fried or stewed.

Although pasta with seafood sauce is generally well prepared, other pasta dishes are better elsewhere in Italy. Venice is justifiably proud of its rice dishes, including risottos and a springtime specialty called risi e bisi made with arborio rice and baby peas. The fertile, salty soil of the larger islands of the lagoon is legendary for the quality of the vegetables that grow from it. Now just a few stalls at the Rialto market sell locally grown crops, but produce from the regions surrounding Venice is itself of high quality.

Spring treats are the fat white asparagus from Bassano and artichokes, either called castraure (baby artichokes sautéed with olive oil, parsley, and garlic) or fondi (hearts of globe artichokes, simmered in olive oil, parsley, and garlic). From mid-December to early March, red radicchio di Treviso (from Treviso) comes to market and is best grilled or used as a base for risotto. Fall brings small, brown wild mushrooms called chiodini and zucca barucca, a bumpy squash often baked, used in soups, or stuffed into ravioli. In the cooler months, keep an eye out for pasta e fasioi, a thick bean soup enriched with fresh pasta.

Tiramisu is the most popular dessert in town, but no matter how many times you try it it's always a bit different, as each restaurant follows its own tiramisu creed. Just to mention a few of the possible variations, sweet liqueur can be added to the coffee, whipped cream or crème anglaise stirred in the basic mascarpone and egg-yolk filling, or bits of bitter chocolate scattered on top instead of cocoa.

of Venetian primi at lower-than-usual prices. Monday through Thursday, only pizza is served in the evening; on Friday, Saturday, and Sunday nights the daily lunch restaurant menu is available as well. ⊠ *Seco Marina, Castello 738* ☎ *041/5237102* ⊟ *MC, V* ☺ *Closed Wed. and 2–3 wks in Aug.* Ⓥ *Giardini.*

$ ✕ **Da Remigio.** Locals almost always fill this place, especially on the weekend (you'll need to book ahead), and it's easy to see why: the food is good, the service prompt, and the atmosphere lively. The *canocchio bollite* (boiled, then chilled, shredded mantis shrimp) is a perfect starter, particularly when paired with an effervescent local white wine. Though the second courses are strong on fish, Da Remigio also turns out respectable nonfish dishes such as the spaghetti *con porcini* (with mushrooms) and grilled meats. ⊠ *Salizzada dei Greci, Castello 3416* ☎ *041/5230089* ⟍ *Reservations essential* ⊟ *AE, DC, MC, V* ☺ *Closed Tues., 2 wks July–Aug., and 4 wks Dec.–Jan. No dinner Mon.* Ⓥ *Arsenale.*

$ ✕ **Osteria al Portego.** At this bacaro, located on a calle where bacari have thrived for centuries, the emphasis is more on food than on wine. Regulars swear by the gelatinous *nervetti* (veal cartilage) served with beans. (It's an acquired taste.) Equally good, though less unusual, are the deep-fried crab claws, *folpetti* (baby octopus), and hard-boiled eggs with pickles and anchovies. A big pot of risotto is made once or twice a day and served on the spot. ⊠ *Calle della Malvasia, Castello 6015* ☎ *041/5229038* ⊟ *No credit cards* ☺ *June–Sept., closed weekends; Oct.–May, closed Sun., no dinner Sat.; closed over Christmas, 2 wks in June, and 2 wks in Aug.* Ⓥ *Rialto.*

$ ✕ **Rivetta.** A reasonably priced trattoria among sandwich shops and tourist traps, Rivetta is a safe bet for a bite to eat near Piazza San Marco. Crowded and narrow, it's redeemed by fast service and a solid selection at the counter: try *insalata di mare* (seafood salad) and *un bianco* (a glass of house white wine). If you take a seat, consider the *pasticcio* (fish lasagna) pasta special. If you have recently taken a gondola ride, there's a fair chance you will run into your gondolier—the ultimate stamp of value and quality. Those who park at the nearby Ponte della Canonica, San Zaccaria, and Bacino di San Marco are regulars here. ⊠ *Ponte San Provolo, Castello 4625* ☎ *041/5287302* ⊟ *MC, V* ☺ *Closed Mon. and three wks in July–Aug.* Ⓥ *San Zaccaria.*

Dorsoduro

$$$–$$$$ ✕ **Ai Gondolieri.** If you're tired of fish, this is the place to go, as meat dishes from the mainland are menu mainstays. Despite the tourist-trap name and proximity to the Guggenheim Museum, it's a favorite with Venetians looking to splurge. Feast on *filetto di maiale con castraure* (pork fillet with baby artichokes), duck breast with apple and sweet onion, or more traditional dishes from the Veneto hills such as horse meat and game, gnocchi, and polenta. The wine list is above average in quality and variety. ⊠ *Fondamenta dell'Ospedaletto, Dorsoduro 366* ☎ *041/5286396* ⊟ *AE, DC, MC, V* ☺ *No lunch July–Aug.* Ⓥ *Accademia.*

$$–$$$$ ✕ **Locanda Montin.** Peggy Guggenheim used to take famous painters—including Jackson Pollock and Mark Rothko—to this archetypal Venetian inn not far from her Palazzo Venier dei Leoni. The walls are still

covered with modern art, but it's far from the haute bohemian hangout it used to be (except for when the Biennale crowd takes over). Outside, you can dine under an elongated arbor on such specialties as rigatoni *ai quattro formaggi* (with four cheeses), spaghetti Adriatica (with fish sauce), and antipasto Montin (seafood antipasto). ☒ *Fondamenta Eremite, Dorsoduro 1147* ☎ *041/5227151* ▭ *MC, V* ⊗ *Closed Wed., Jan. to Carnevale, and Tues.–Wed. in July and Aug.* Ⓥ *Accademia.*

$$–$$$
Fodor'sChoice
★
✕ **Avogaria.** In terms of both food and architecture, ultra-fashionable Avogaria lends modern flavor to the Venice restaurant scene. The clean, elegant design of the dining room and garden leaves no doubt that you're in the Venice of the present, not the past. The cuisine is Pugliese (from the region in the heel of Italy's boot); highlights among the primi include orecchiette with turnip tops, and zucchini *involtini* (roll-ups) made with fresh stracciatella cheese. Pugliese cooking, like Venetian, reveres fresh seafood, and you can taste this sensibility in the slow-cooked, sesame-encrusted tuna steak. ☒ *Calle Avogaria, Dorsoduro 1629* ☎ *041/ 2960491* ▭ *AE, DC, MC, V* ⊗ *Closed Tues.*

$$–$$$ ✕ **Cantinone Storico.** On a quiet, romantic canal near the Accademia, this comfortable trattoria with alfresco tables serves well-prepared specialties such as risotto *terra mare* (with seafood, vegetables, and porcini mushrooms) and tagliolini alla granseola (available only with advance notice). The place draws mostly tourists, but it's hard to beat for location and reasonable prices. The house stocks a good selection of wines. ☒ *Fondamenta di Ca' Bragadin, Dorsoduro 660/1* ☎ *041/5239577* ▭ *AE, MC, V* ⊗ *Closed Sun., Nov., and Jan.* Ⓥ *Accademia.*

★ **$$** ✕ **La Bitta.** The decor is more discreet, the dining hours longer, and the service friendlier and more efficient here than in many of Venice's small restaurants—and the creative nonfish menu is a temptation at every course. You can start with a light salad of Treviso radicchio and crispy bacon, followed by smoked-beef carpaccio or *gnocchetti ubriachi al Montasio* (small marinated gnocchi with Montasio cheese). Then choose from secondi such as lamb chops with thyme, *anatra in pevarada* (duck in a pepper sauce), or Irish Angus fillet steak. Secondi are served with vegetables, which helps keep down the price. The restaurant is open for dinner only, from 6:30 to 11. ☒ *Calle Lunga San Barnaba, Dorsoduro 2753/A* ☎ *041/5230531* ▭ *No credit cards* ⊗ *No lunch. Closed Sun.* Ⓥ *Ca' Rezzonico.*

★ **$$** ✕ **L'Incontro.** This trattoria between San Barnaba and Campo Santa Margherita has a faithful clientele of Venetians and visitors, attracted by flavorful Sardinian food, sociable service, and reasonable prices. Starters include Sardinian sausages, but you might skip to the delicious traditional primi, such as *culingiones* (large ravioli filled with pecorino, saffron, and orange peel). The selection of secondi is heavy on herb-crusted meat dishes such as *coniglio al mirto* (rabbit baked on a bed of myrtle sprigs) and the *costine d'agnello con rosmarino e mentuccia* (baby lamb ribs with rosemary and wild mint). ☒ *Rio Terrà Canal, Dorsoduro 3062/ a* ☎ *041/5222404* ▭ *AE, DC, MC, V* ⊗ *Closed Mon., Jan., and 2 wks in Aug. No lunch Tues.* Ⓥ *Ca' Rezzonico.*

$–$$ ✕ **Pizzeria al Profeta.** Though Pizzeria al Profeta offers more than 100 types of pizza, its real strength is massive portions of roast and grilled meats and, on occasion, fresh fish. Two or three people can split the baked pie filled with Angus beef, porcini mushrooms, and radicchio. For a wonderfully medieval feeling, sit at a wooden table in the spacious, simple garden and use both hands to tear into a large leg of lamb. Sharing one of the ample dishes can make for a great value. ⊠ *Calle Lunga San Barnaba, Dorsoduro 2671* ☎ *041/5237466* ▭ *MC, V.*

$–$$ ✕ **Taverna San Trovaso.** A wide choice of Venetian dishes served in robust portions, economical fixed-price menus, pizzas, and house wine by the glass or pitcher keep this two-floor, no-nonsense tavern abuzz with young Venetians and budget-conscious visitors in the know. It's always packed, and table turnover is fast. Not far from the Gallerie dell'Accademia, this is a good place to slip into while sightseeing in Dorsoduro. ⊠ *Fondamenta Priuli, Dorsoduro 1016* ☎ *041/5203703* ▭ *AE, MC, V* ◷ *Closed Mon. and 1 wk Dec.–Jan.* Ⓥ *Zattere.*

$ ✕ **Ai 4 Feri.** The paper tablecloths and cozy, laid-back ambience are all part of this small restaurant's charm. The all-seafood menu varies according to what's fresh that day; imaginative combinations of ingredients in the primi—herring and sweet peppers, salmon and radicchio, giant shrimp and broccoli (with pumpkin gnocchi)—are the norm. A meal here followed by after-dinner drinks at Campo Santa Margherita, a five-minute walk away, makes for a lovely evening. The kitchen closes early on weekdays. ⊠ *Calle Lunga San Barnaba, Dorsoduro 2754/a* ☎ *041/5206978* ▭ *No credit cards* ◷ *Closed Sun. and June* Ⓥ *San Basilio or Ca' Rezzonico.*

¢–$ ✕ **Alla Dona Onesta.** The virtue of the "Honest Woman" is still maintained by the owners of this small, neat trattoria perched along the rio. Through the glass door you'll see a well-kept old structure with no frills— the style is dark-brown wooden chairs and white tablecloths. The menu posted outside offers a reasonable choice of staple Italian pasta dishes, fish, and meat. Few tourists stop here, and the little English you'll hear is likely to be a conversation among professors from the nearby Università Ca' Foscari, who are lunchtime regulars. ⊠ *Ponte de la Dona Onesta, Dorsoduro 3922* ☎ *041/710586* ▭ *AE, DC, MC, V* Ⓥ *Accademia.*

Giudecca

★ $$$$ ✕ **Cipriani.** A cut above most Italian restaurants in ambience, service, and view, the Cipriani is an expensive, world-class experience worth having once. In white-peach season (July to early September), start with the famous blossom-scented Bellini. The cuisine is rooted in Venetian tradition, prepared with a star chef's hand, and matched with a superb wine list. Sole fillets instead of whole sardines are used for the saor; deep-fried prawns, coated in semolina flour, stay wonderfully crisp. Desserts are spectacular: a decadent tiramisu is served in a bitter-chocolate shell topped by a gondola. ⊠ *Fondamenta San Giovanni 10, Giudecca* ☎ *041/5207744* ⚲ *Reservations essential* ▭ *AE, DC, MC, V* ◷ *Closed mid-Nov.–mid-Mar.* Ⓥ *Zitelle.*

★ $–$$ ✕ **Altanella.** This Giudecca institution facing a large canal is the right place to taste some of the strange-looking fish sold at the stalls in the

Rialto's pescheria. The Altanella is a favorite among locals, although a trilingual menu makes it clear that visitors find their way here as well. Start with a salad of folpetti, followed by a creamy risotto or gnocchi with a seppie (cuttlefish) sauce. Secondi include grilled or deep-fried fish, or seppie *in umido* (in a stew with its black ink and a dash of tomato sauce), served with polenta. Wine is not this rustic place's strong suit. ⊠ *Calle delle Erbe 268, Giudecca* ☎ *041/5227780* ⊟ *No credit cards* ☉ *Closed Mon., Tues., most of Aug., and last 3 wks in Jan.* Ⓥ *Redentore or Palanca.*

Lido

$$–$$$ ✕ **Trattoria Favorita.** This neighborhood eatery has been in the same family's hands since the 1920s and offers you the choice between a wood-beamed dining room and a vine-covered garden. Seafood is the specialty, always fresh and lovingly prepared; you won't go wrong ordering the tagliolini with shrimp and zucchini or the divine gnocchi con granseola. ⊠ *Via Francesco Duodo 33, Lido* ☎ *041/5261626* ⌂ *Reservations essential* ⊟ *AE, DC, MC, V* ☉ *Closed Mon. and Jan.–mid-Feb. No lunch Tues.* Ⓥ *Lido.*

$$ ✕ **Al Vecio Cantier.** The wild scenery, with intersecting canals and reeds, contributes to the appeal of one of the liveliest places on the Lido, always filled to the gills during the film festival. There's efficient cichetti service, but the restaurant deserves a longer visit for a relaxing meal in the best Venetian tradition: try whipped baccalà with polenta, or tagliolini *con gamberetti e carciofi* (with shrimp and artichokes) in spring. Homemade desserts include lemon and almond tarts, or you can dip cookies in a glass of *vino passito,* a dessert wine. Outside dining is in a pretty garden. ⊠ *Via della Droma 76, Lido* ☎ *041/5268130* ⊟ *AE, DC, MC, V* ☉ *Closed Mon. No lunch Tues., Nov., or Jan.* Ⓥ *Lido.*

$–$$ ✕ **Le Garzette.** A small, family-run trattoria inside the agriturismo of the same name, Le Garzette serves very fresh fish, homegrown vegetables, and home-raised poultry, including duck. Meals are available to those not rooming here only at Friday dinner and lunch and dinner on weekends. You won't find anything new on the menu, but everything tastes genuine, and the staff won't look down on you if you are wearing shorts. ⊠ *Lungomare Alberoni 32, Lido* ☎ *041/731078* ⌂ *Reservations essential* ⊟ *No credit cards* ☉ *Closed Dec.–Feb. and Mon.–Thurs. No lunch Fri.* Ⓥ *Lido.*

$ ✕ **Bar Trento.** This neat, old-style osteria 10 minutes from Piazzale Santa Maria Elisabetta has a soft spot for meat and innards (one of the owners was a *bechèr,* or butcher). Lunch is the only meal served, but *ombre* (the Venetian term for a glass of wine) and *cichetti* (tapas-like snacks) are available from 8 to 8. Many of the tasty snacks are made from organ meats (and thus not for squeamish eaters), but there are more familiar options as well, including baccalà *alla vicentina* (stewed with onion, milk, and Parmesan); pasta with seafood; and several seasonal risottos. As a secondo, fish can be cooked any way you want. ⊠ *Via Sandro Gallo 82, Lido* ☎ *041/5265960* ⊟ *No credit cards* ☉ *Closed Sun. No dinner except during Biennale* Ⓥ *Lido.*

Murano

$$–$$$$ ✕ **Valmarana.** The most upscale restaurant on Murano is housed in a palace on the *fondamenta* (street) across from the Museo Vetrario. Stuccoed walls and glass chandeliers complement well-appointed tables, and although the menu contains no surprises, the cuisine is more refined than at other places here. Try the baked sea scallops, the crab with fresh herbs, or the rich risotto *alla pescatora,* containing all kinds of fish. In warm weather, reserve a table in the back garden or on the terrace overlooking the canal. ⊠ *Fondamenta Navagero 31, Murano* ☎ *041/739313* ▤ *AE, DC, MC, V* ☉ *Closed 3 wks in Jan. No dinner* Ⓥ *Navagero.*

$–$$ ✕ **Ai Frati.** A walk along the Fondamenta dei Vetrai brings you to the large iron bridge spanning Murano's Grand Canal; down to the left, hanging over the Canale degli Angeli, is the attractive terrace of Ai Frati. As elsewhere in Venice, the key word here is fish, prepared any way you want. The risottos are nicely done. If you want to taste a famous dish from Murano and you're lucky enough to be here in November, ask when you book for the *bisatto sull'ara,* a local variety of fleshy eel traditionally cooked on a bed of bay leaves. ⊠ *Fondamenta Sebastiano Venier 4, Murano* ☎ *041/736694* ▤ *V* ☉ *Closed Thurs. and Feb. No dinner* Ⓥ *Venier.*

$–$$ ✕ **Antica Trattoria.** This lunch-only trattoria can be easily spotted by the bright red walls close to the Grand Canal on the island of Murano. For company you'll probably find local glass workers with a *caffè corretto con grappa* (espresso with grappa liqueur) in front of them. If it's more solid nourishment you're after, go for the freshly grilled fish or the seppie in tecia, served in the rear garden. ⊠ *Riva Longa 20, Murano* ☎ *041/739610* ▤ *AE, DC, MC, V* ☉ *Closed Sat. and Feb. No dinner* Ⓥ *Murano.*

$–$$ ✕ **Busa alla Torre da Lele.** A pretty square with olive trees and a well sets the stage for Da Lele, a favorite of the Muranese. On the ground floor of a dark-red building with a loggia, the restaurant stretches out on the campo, where you eat in the shade of large umbrellas. Check the blackboard for such daily specials as antipasto Busa, with granseola and garusoli; *bavette alla busara* (flat spaghetti with a hot spicy shrimp and tomato sauce); and baked rombo or branzino with potato. Homemade cookies are served with *fragolino,* a sweet, sparkling wine redolent of strawberries. ⊠ *Campo Santo Stefano 3, Murano* ☎ *041/739662* ▤ *AE, DC, MC, V* ☉ *No dinner* Ⓥ *Faro.*

San Marco

$$$$ ✕ **Al Graspo de Ua.** Opened in the 19th century as a small osteria, the "Bunch of Grapes" became the meeting place of artists and movie stars back in the 1960s. Today, it serves a faithful clientele of wealthy Italians. The decor is a miscellanea of plants, sculpture, candlelight, and paintings set against brick and white-stucco walls. The owner, Lucio Zanon, speaks fluent English and will introduce you to a wide-ranging menu of fresh pasta, seasonal risotto, and meat and seafood. A treat in late spring is the thick white asparagus from Bassano, which, with a couple of fried eggs, is eaten as a main course. Desserts are all homemade.

⊠ *Calle dei Bombaseri, San Marco 5094* ☎ *041/5223647* ▭ *AE, DC, MC, V* ⊘ *Closed Mon. and 1 wk in Jan.* Ⓥ *Rialto.*

$$$$ ✕ **Antico Martini.** If you're after old-world Venetian elegance, this is your place. Born in 1792 as a café for the artists, intellectuals, singers, and conductors loitering around the opera house La Fenice, Antico Martini has changed management only twice, and since 1921 the Baldi family have maintained it as a bastion of traditional starched-collar dining. Intimate candlelit tables, antique oil paintings, and a patrician air complement classic Venetian fare, sometimes given an innovative twist. Salmon rolls filled with caviar and sour cream might be followed by homemade tagliatelle with prawn and arugula or angelfish with black peppercorns. ⊠ *Calle del Cafetier, off Campo San Fantin, San Marco 1983* ☎ *041/5224121* ⚞ *Reservations essential* 🏛 *Jacket required* ▭ *AE, DC, MC, V* ⊘ *Closed Tues. No lunch Wed.* Ⓥ *San Marco or Santa Maria del Giglio.*

★ **$$$$** ✕ **Antico Pignolo.** The "Old Pine Nut" occupies a former spice shop dating from the 1200s; adventurous types might want to arrive by boat, as the place has its own private landing. If you're in town in warm weather, book a table in the exquisite garden, where white flowers match the table settings. Top-notch staff, also clad in white, serve creative interpretations of Venetian classics. The *crostino di polenta con baccalà mantecato* (creamy salt cod served on polenta) may be the definitive version. The carefully culled wine list alone is worth the trip. ⊠ *Calle degli Specchieri, San Marco 451* ☎ *041/5228123* ▭ *AE, DC, MC, V* Ⓥ *San Marco.*

$$$$ ✕ **Da Arturo.** This tiny eatery on the Calle degli Assassini has the distinction in Venice of *not* serving seafood. Instead you can choose from salads and fresh vegetable dishes; tasty, tender meat courses in generous portions, including the subtly pungent *braciola alla veneziana* (pork chop schnitzel with vinegar); and an authentic creamy homemade tiramisu to finish. Noncarnivores make their way here as well, as the *antipasti* and *primi* offerings are more than hospitable. ⊠ *Calle degli Assassini, San Marco 3656* ☎ *041/5286974* ▭ *No credit cards* ⊘ *Closed Sun., 10 days after Carnevale, and 4 wks in Aug.* Ⓥ *San Marco or Rialto.*

$$$$ ✕ **Da Ivo.** An enclave of Tuscan cuisine two minutes from Piazza San Marco, this is a cozy, relaxing—and very expensive—spot, with paintings and copper pots hanging on white walls and candlelight at dinner. Start with the un-Tuscan tagliolini *alla bottarga* (with roe). The reputation of the restaurant has been built on its famous *bistecche fiorentine* (two-pound Chianina beef steaks grilled over olive-wood charcoal), but game and fish are also reliable standards. ⊠ *Ramo dei Fuseri, San Marco 1809* ☎ *041/5285004* ⚞ *Reservations essential* ▭ *AE, DC, MC, V* ⊘ *Closed Sun. (except during Sept. and Oct.), and Jan.* Ⓥ *San Marco.*

$$$$ ✕ **Grand Canal.** The elegant restaurant of the Hotel Monaco & Grand Canal is a favorite with Venetians, who enjoy eating on the lovely canalside terrace in summer and in the cozy dining room in winter. All the pasta is made fresh daily on the premises, and the smoked and marinated salmon are also prepared here. The chef's traditional Venetian cuisine is topflight; you'll marvel at savory dishes such as *scampi alla Buséra* (shrimp in a cognac sauce). ⊠ *Hotel Monaco & Grand Canal,*

Where to Eat in San Marco

Al Graspo de Ua **12**
Antico Martini **6**
Antico Pignolo **19**
Caffè Paolin **1**
Canova **16**
Da Arturo **4**
Da Ivo **9**

Dal Col **13**
Enoteca al Volto **10**
Grand Canal **15**
Harry's Bar **17**
La Caravella **8**
Le Café **2**
Marchini **3**

Quadri **18**
Rosa Salva **11, 14**
Taverna la Fenice **5**
Vino Vino **7**

1/8 mile
1/8 km

VENICE

Calle Vallaresso, San Marco 1325 ☎ *041/5200211* ⊟ *AE, DC, MC, V* Ⓥ *San Marco.*

$$$$ ✗ **Harry's Bar.** The humble door of this famed watering hole leads to the legendary Venetian hangout of such notables as Hemingway, Maugham, and Onassis. Such company doesn't come cheap, but Harry's is still known for the driest martinis and the most heavenly Bellinis in town, as well as decent, though overpriced, *cucina veneta.* The decor is boring beige-on-beige, but the view upstairs—looking out on spectacular Chiesa di Santa Maria della Salute—competes with the finest Canaletto *vedute* (scenic paintings). Remember, you come to Harry's for the phenomenal atmosphere, not for the less-than-phenomenal food. ⊠ *Calle Vallaresso, San Marco 1323* ☎ *041/5285777* ⌚ *Reservations essential* ⊟ *AE, DC, MC, V* Ⓥ *San Marco.*

$$$$ ✗ **La Caravella.** It's been a Venetian classic for the past forty years, and even though the decor, made to suggest the interior of a seagoing vessel, might evoke a theme restaurant, there's nothing gimmicky about the cuisine. The seasonal menu offers such treats as *ravioli con scampi, zafferano, e noce* (ravioli with shrimp, saffron, and walnuts), and variations on Ventian standards such as *bigola con anatra* (a thick pasta with a fragrant duck sauce). The pretty garden courtyard is open from May through September. ⊠ *Saturnia Internazionale, Calle Larga XXII Marzo, San Marco 2397* ☎ *041/5208901* ⌚ *Reservations essential* ⊟ *AE, DC, MC, V* Ⓥ *Santa Maria del Giglio.*

$$$$ ✗ **Quadri.** In the 19th century, princes, dukes, and countesses dined here, and you'll feel like one when you walk into the gilded salons of Venice's most beautiful restaurant. The decor is stunning—Quadri's second-floor aerie gives you a pigeon's-eye view of Piazza San Marco—and the cuisine is classic Venetian, with lots of fish. (Truffles are a major draw in the fall.) Come September, when the Biennale is in session, the sequins-and-sunglasses set takes over. ⊠ *Piazza San Marco, San Marco 120–124* ☎ *041/5289299* ⌚ *Reservations essential* ⊟ *AE, DC, MC, V* ⊘ *Closed Mon. Nov.–Apr. except during Christmas and Carnevale* Ⓥ *San Marco.*

$$$$ ✗ **Taverna la Fenice.** The lovely (and bilingual) Odette Zora presides over this Old Venetian restaurant steps away from La Fenice. Though the velvet-laden interior may feel somewhat dated, the menu is up-to-the-minute. The *carpaccio di branzino di mare* (thinly sliced raw sea bass) benefits from the judicious addition of ginger and, yes, wasabi. Avocado and asparagus adorn the *insalata di granchio* (crab salad). The wine list, particularly strong on wines from the Veneto, is well thought out. When it's warm, you can dine alfresco. ⊠ *Campo San Fantin, San Marco 1939* ☎ *041/5223856* ⊟ *AE, DC, MC, V* ⊘ *Closed Mon.* Ⓥ *San Marco.*

$$$–$$$$ ✗ **Canova.** The restaurant of the Hotel Luna Baglioni is on the pricey side, but the excellent service, tasteful surroundings, and inventive dishes all make for one of the most reliably good dining experiences close to Piazza San Marco. Fresh, nicely presented dishes might include a warm salad of scallops and cannellini beans in a lemon rosemary sauce, or veal medallions with champagne vinegar, capers, and herbs. ⊠ *Luna Baglioni, San Marco 1243* ☎ *041/5289840* ⊟ *AE, DC, MC, V* Ⓥ *San Marco.*

¢–$ ✗ **Vino Vino.** The annex of the extremely expensive Antico Martini restaurant is an informal wine bar where you can sample wines by the glass from an impressive list. You can also partake of a light lunch or dinner buffet style. Typical offerings include pastas of the day, vegetables, and a couple of meat dishes. Service is friendly and patient: given its location, it attracts crowds who come for a quick bite to eat before heading off to another museum. If you're traveling with children, consider stopping here. ⊠ *Calle delle Veste, near Campo San Fantin, San Marco 2007/a* ☎ *041/2417680* ⚑ *Reservations not accepted* ⊟ *No credit cards* ⊘ *Closed Tues.* Ⓥ *San Marco or Santa Maria del Giglio.*

¢ ✕ **Enoteca al Volto.** Just steps away from the Rialto Bridge, this bar has been around since 1936; the fine cichetti and primi have a lot to do with its staying power. Two small, dark rooms with wooden tables and chairs provide the backdrop to enjoy simple fare. The place prides itself on its considerable wine list of both Italian and foreign wines; if you stick to the panini and a cichetto or two, you'll eat very well for very little. If you opt for one of the primi of the day, the price category goes up a notch. ⊠ *Calle Cavalli, San Marco 4081* ☎ *041/5228945* ⊟ *No credit cards* ⊘ *Closed Sun.* Ⓥ *Rialto.*

San Polo

$$$$ ✕ **Osteria da Fiore.** Tucked away on a little calle off the top of Campo
Fodor'sChoice San Polo, Da Fiore is a favorite among high-end diners for its superbly
★ prepared Venetian cuisine and refined yet relaxed atmosphere. A superlative seafood lunch or dinner here might include delicate hors d'oeuvres of moeche, scallops, and tiny octopus, followed by a succulent risotto or tagliolini *con scampi e radicchio* (with shrimp and radicchio), and a perfectly cooked main course of rombo or *tagliata di tonno* (tuna steak). Jackets aren't mandatory, but men may feel out of place wearing anything more casual. ⊠ *Calle del Scaleter, San Polo 2202* ☎ *041/721308* ⚑ *Reservations essential* ⊟ *AE, DC, MC, V* ⊘ *Closed Sun., Mon., Aug., and Dec. 25–Jan. 20* Ⓥ *San Tomà.*

$$–$$$$ ✕ **Poste Vecie.** A tiny wooden bridge connects this historic osteria with the Rialto pescheria. In the 16th century, Poste Vecie (Old Post Office) served as a base for Venetian couriers, who stopped here to sort the mail between a glass of wine and a bowl of risotto. The place went upscale, but the large fireplaces are still here, along with the wooden ceiling, hand-painted plates, and some bizarre frescoes depicting allegories of vices (gluttony has been left out). Besides the usual Venetian specialties, you'll find the more rare *bisatto in umido* (stewed eel with polenta) and moeche in springtime. An inner garden opens up in warm weather. ⊠ *Pescheria, San Polo 1608* ☎ *041/721822* ⊟ *AE, DC, MC, V* ⊘ *Closed Tues.* Ⓥ *Rialto.*

$$–$$$ ✕ **Da Ignazio.** Conveniently located on the route from Campo San Polo to the Frari, this pleasant family restaurant serves good, honest Venetian cuisine. The house specialty is a generous portion of creamy white polenta topped by shelled scampi, in the fall served with porcini. Poorly prepared elsewhere in town, the *capesante gratinate* (scallop gratin) here is made with just enough bread crumbs to make it nice and crusty on top. Desserts—standards such as crème caramel—are homemade and light. The garden is a charming spot to dine in fair weather. ⊠ *Calle*

WITH CHILDREN?

DINING IN VENICE can present some obstacles if you're traveling with children. Most notable is the fish factor: the notorious non-favorite with kids dominates Venetian menus. Most—though not all—restaurants will have other offerings; if fish is going to be a problem, it's a good idea to check what alternatives are available before booking or taking your seat.

Generally, children will feel welcome at casual establishments such as trattorias, but only very well-behaved children should go to higher-end restaurants; indeed, it's rare to see Italian children in them. Some restaurants and trattorias will have high chairs or cushions for children to sit on, but you won't find a children's menu. Instead, ask the waiter for a mezza porzione (half portion) or porzione da bambino (child's portion) of any dish. Though spaghetti and meatballs isn't found on menus, other pasta dishes such as spaghetti al pomodoro (with tomato

sauce) may prove to be suitable substitutions. Italian children are fond of pasta in bianca (with butter) and con olio e parmigiano (with olive oil and Parmesan); even if they're not on the menu, most chefs will be happy to prepare them. Many restaurants serve prosciutto e melone (cured ham and melon, available in season) and insalata caprese (mozzarella, tomatoes, and basil), both of which can be attractive alternatives for a child confronted with calf's liver and cuttlefish.

Venetian pizza is a last resort, or nearly so; though most of it is forgettable at best, the familiar wedge of dough and cheese may be the closest thing to comfort food a young diner will find. That is, unless you count McDonald's, which has found its way to La Serenissima, to the chagrin of many natives and visitors alike. The most central location is near the Rialto bridge.

---

dei Saoneri, San Polo 2749 ☎ 041/5234852 ▤ AE, DC, MC, V ♥ Closed Sat., 2 wks over Christmas, and 1st 3 wks in Aug. Ⓥ San Tomà.

$ ✕ **Osteria al Garanghelo.** Superior quality, competitive prices, and great ambience mean this place is often packed with Venetians, especially for lunch and an after-work ombra and cichetti. The location is a few steps from the Rialto market, and chef Renato puts the fresh ingredients to good use. He prefers cooking many dishes al vapore (steamed). The spicy fagioli al uciletto (literally beans, bird-style) has an unusual name and Tuscan origins, and is a perfect companion to a plate of fresh pasta. Don't confuse this centrally located restaurant with one of the same name on Via Garibaldi. ✉ Calle dei Boteri, San Polo 1570 ☎ 041/721721 ▤ MC, V ♥ Closed Sun.

Santa Croce

$$–$$$ ✕ **Ribò.** Signor Martini loves thoroughbreds, so when he took over this spot he renamed it after the champion European horse Ribot. His kitchen puts out purebred Venetian cuisine—food that's fanciful but not fancy. Several homemade pasta dishes are always on the menu, and the fish rolls with eggplant, when available, are worth a medal. The pleasant interior garden is a rarity for Venetian restaurants. ✉ Fondamenta

Minotto, Santa Croce 158 ☏ 041/5242486 ▭ AE, DC, MC, V ⊗ Closed 10 days in Jan. and 2 wks in Aug. Ⓥ Stazione.

$$–$$$ ✕ **Vecio Fritolin.** Until not so long ago, fish was fried and sold "to go" throughout Venice just as in London, except that it was paired with polenta rather than chips. A sign advertising fish to go still hangs outside the "Old Fry Shop," but nowadays you can only dine in. A second sign, announcing cichetti available to go, still holds true. At this tidy bacaro *con cucina* (with kitchen) you can have a traditional meal featuring such dishes as *bigoli in salsa* (thick spaghetti with anchovy sauce), baked fish with herbs, and non-Venetian lamb chops. ✉ *Calle della Regina, Santa Croce 2262* ☏ *041/5222881* ▭ *AE, DC, MC, V* ⊗ *Closed Mon.* Ⓥ *San Stae.*

$$ ✕ **Antica Besseta.** Tucked away in a quiet corner of Santa Croce, with a few tables under an ivy shelter, the Antica Besseta dates from the 18th century, and it retains some of its old feel. The menu focuses on vegetables and fish, according to what's at the market: spaghetti with caparozzoli or cuttlefish ink, schie with polenta, and plenty of grilled fish. ✉ *Salizzada de Ca' Zusto, Santa Croce 1395* ☏ *041/5240428* ▭ *AE, MC, V* ⊗ *Closed Mon. and Tues. No lunch Wed.* Ⓥ *Rive di Biasio.*

$$ ✕ **La Zucca.** The place feels as much like a typical vegetarian restaurant as you could expect to find in Venice, what with its simple place settings and exposed wood walls. Though the menu does have superb meat dishes such as the *sfilacci di cavallo con radicchio trevigiano* (smoked horse meat with radicchio), more attention is paid to dishes from the garden: try the *sedano rapa gratina al pecorino* (celery root gratin with pecorino cheese) or the *finocchi piccanti con olive* (fennel in a spicy tomato-olive sauce). Friendly service in a number of languages is the norm. ✉ *Calle del Tintor, Santa Croce 1762* ☏ *041/5241570* ▭ *AE, DC, MC, V* ⊗ *Closed Sun., 1 wk in Aug., and over Christmas* Ⓥ *S. Stae.*

$ ✕ **Bancogiro.** Come to this casual spot for a change from standard Venetian food. Yes, fish is on the menu, but offerings such as *mousse di gamberoni con salsa di avocado* (shrimp mousse with an avocado sauce) and Sicilian-style *sarde incinte* (stuffed, or "pregnant," sardines) are far from typical fare. The wine list and the cheese plate are both divine. The location is in the heart of the Rialto market in a 15th-century loggia, with tables upstairs in a carefully restored room with a partial view of the Grand Canal; when it's warm, you can sit outdoors and get the full canal view. ✉ *Campo San Giacometto 122 (under the porch), Santa Croce* ☏ *041/ 5232061* ▭ *No credit cards* ⊗ *Closed Mon. No dinner Sun.* Ⓥ *Rialto.*

FodorśChoice
★

$ ✕ **Do Spade.** A rough Venetian floor and the motto *Vinum bonum fortificat cor hominis* (good wine fortifies the man's heart) are tip-offs to the character of this classic bacaro that was once the haunt of Casanova. The plump host, Giorgio Lanza, is the town's unofficial authority on little sandwiches. He coined the term *paperini* for his own creations— cichetti served on bruschetta—and after tasting one you'll happily add the word to your Venetian vocabulary. At mealtimes, the bacaro doubles as a trattoria; stick to more traditional dishes such as *salsicce* (sausage) di secole, bean soup, baccalà, and cuttlefish. ✉ *Calle Do Spade, San Polo 860* ☏ *No phone* ▭ *No credit cards* ⊗ *Closed Sun., 2 wks in Aug., and 10 days in Jan.* Ⓥ *Rialto.*

¢–$ ✕ **Ae Oche.** There's nothing Venetian about this saloonlike pizzeria with shelves of imported stouts and Americana signage on the walls. Seventy-nine pizza combinations include the Campagnola, lavishly topped with a mix of tomato, mozzarella, mushroom, Brie, and *speck* (smoked prosciutto). Purists can stick to the *margherita,* with tomato, mozzarella, and basil. A selection of 16 salads plus a few pasta dishes make the Oche an ideal stop for a light meal between sights. ⊠ *Calle delle Oche, Santa Croce 1552/a–b* ☎ *041/5241161* ▭ *MC, V* Ⓥ *San Stae.*

★ ¢–$ ✕ **Al Prosecco.** Locals stream into this place, order the "spritz bitter" (a combination of white wine, Campari, and seltzer water), and continue on their way. Or they linger over a glass of one of the numerous wines on offer, perhaps also tucking into a tasty panino, such as the *porchetta romane verdure* (roasted pig, Roman style, with greens). Proprietors Davide and Stefano preside over a young and friendly staff who reel off the day's specials with ease. There are a few tables in the enticing back room, and when the weather's warm, you can eat outside on a beautiful campo. ⊠ *Campo S. Giacomo da l'Orlo, Santa Croce 1503* ☎ *041/5240222* ▭ *No credit cards* ⊘ *Closed Sun.* Ⓥ *San Stae.*

Torcello

$$$$ ✕ **Locanda Cipriani.** Owned by a nephew of Arrigo Cipriani–the founder of Harry's Bar—this inn profits from its idyllic location on the island of Torcello. Hemingway, who loved the silence of the lagoon, came here often to eat, drink, and brood under the green veranda. The food is not exceptional, especially considering the high-end prices, but dining here is more about getting lost in Venetian magic. The menu features pastas, *vitello tonnato* (chilled poached veal in a tuna and caper sauce), baked orata with potatoes, and lots of other seafood. A vaporetto service runs until 11:30 PM, and then upon request; service is sporadic. ⊠ *Piazza Santa Fosca 29, Torcello* ☎ *041/730150* ◁ *Reservations essential* ▭ *AE, DC, MC, V* ⊘ *Closed Tues. and early Jan.–early Feb.* Ⓥ *Torcello.*

Bacari (Wine Bars)

While the list below covers some of the best of Venice's bacari, it's by no means exhaustive. Venetians themselves don't know how many bacari thrive in their hometown, and often the perfect one is the one you happen upon when hunger strikes.

¢ ✕ **Aciugheta.** Though the "tiny anchovy" (as the name translates) doubles as a pizzeria, stick to the tasty cichetti offered at the bar, like the eponymous anchovy mini-pizzas. The selection of wines by the glass changes daily, but there are always the ubiquitous local whites on hand, as well as some Tuscan and Piedmontese choices thrown in for good measure. Don't miss the *tonno con polenta* (tuna with polenta) if it's offered. ⊠ *Campo SS. Filippo e Giacomo, Castello 4357* ☎ *041/5224292* ▭ *MC, V* Ⓥ *San Zaccaria.*

¢ ✕ **Cantina Do Mori.** This *bacaro* par excellence—cramped but warm
Fodor'sChoice and cozy under hanging antique copper pots—has been catering to the
★ workers of the Rialto market since the 15th century. In addition to young,
local whites and reds, the well-stocked cellar offers about 600 more-re-
fined labels, many available by the glass. Between sips you can munch
on crunchy grissini draped with prosciutto or a few well-stuffed, tiny
tramezzini, appropriately called *francobolli* (postage stamps). Don't
leave without tasting the delicious baccalà mantecato. ⊠ *Calle dei Do
Mori, San Polo 429* ☎ *041/5225401* ⊟ *No credit cards* ⊗ *Closed
Sun., 3 wks in Aug., and 1 wk in Jan.* Ⓥ *Rialto.*

¢ ✕ **Cantinone già Schiave.** This beautiful 19th-century bacaro opposite the
Fodor'sChoice *squero* (gondola repair shop) of San Trovaso has original furnishings and
★ one of the best wine cellars in town—the walls are covered floor to ceiling by bottles for purchase. Cichetti here are the most inventive in
Venice—try the crostini-style layers of bread, smoked swordfish, and sliv-
ers of raw zucchini, or pungent slices of parmeggiano, fig, and toast. They
also have a creamy version of baccalà mantecato spiced with herbs.
There are nearly a dozen open bottles of wine for experimenting at the
bar. ⊠ *Fondamenta Nani, Dorsoduro 992* ☎ *041/5230034* ⊟ *No credit
cards* ⊗ *Closed Sun. after 2 PM and 2 wks in Aug.* Ⓥ *Zattere.*

¢ ✕ **Da Dante Alle Alpi.** A little oasis thriving in the deserted lands of
Castello, this bacaro has the usual fish cichetti, including folpetti *consi*
(with olive oil, parsley, and boiled potatoes). Locals flock here to play
the gambling machines and to savor Dante's divine *calamari fritti* (fried
squid). Plan to arrive around lunchtime, when succulent fish dishes
start emerging from the kitchen. ⊠ *Corte Nova, near the Scuola di San
Giorgio degli Schiavoni, Castello 2877* ☎ *041/5285163* ⊟ *No credit
cards* ⊗ *Closed Sun.* Ⓥ *San Zaccaria.*

¢ ✕ **Da Pinto.** At the heart of the Rialto market and with tables outside,
Da Pinto starts serving cichetti by 10:30 in the morning to curious visitors, fish vendors, and clerks of the nearby Tribunale (Court of Justice).
It's a functional spot for a quick bite; the cichetti at the bar are better
than the bland primi served at the tables. ⊠ *Campo delle Becarie, San
Polo 367* ☎ *041/5224599* ⊟ *AE, DC, MC, V* ⊗ *Closed Mon. and 2
wks in Nov.* Ⓥ *San Marco.*

¢ ✕ **Enoteca la Mascareta.** An offspring of the popular casual restaurant
Fodor'sChoice Al Mascaron, the Mascareta offers refined cichetti and a selection of
★ cured pork and cheeses, washed down with quality ombre such as
Chardonnay Friuliano. The place doesn't open until 6 PM, but doesn't
close until past midnight. ⊠ *Calle Lunga Santa Maria Formosa, Castello
5183* ☎ *041/5230744* ⊟ *MC, V* ⊗ *Closed Wed., Thurs. and over
Christmas. No lunch* Ⓥ *Rialto or San Marco.*

¢ ✕ **Minibar da Lele.** A three-minute stroll from Piazzale Roma, Lele's 6-
by-10-foot place is a blessing for hungry commuters on their way to work.
Not strictly a bacaro, it offers equally good food and wine. Try the freshly
made, enormous tramezzini and tiny panini filled with vegetables and
cured pork. ⊠ *Campo dei Tolentini, Santa Croce 183* ☎ *No phone* ⊟ *No
credit cards* ⊗ *Closed weekends* Ⓥ *Stazione.*

¢ ✕ **Osteria da Toni.** This unpretentious bar-bacaro sits on the western edge
of the Zattere promenade, near a pretty, breezy side canal. It caters mainly

STOPPING IN AT A BACARO

HUSBAND AND WIFE *Lino and Sandra Gastaldi run the bacaro (wine bar) Cantinone Già Schiavi, on Fondamenta Nani, across from the squero (gondola workshop), in Dorsoduro. Following the bacaro tradition, they serve cicchetti—distinctly Venetian snacks—with their wine. Lino pours and handles distribution, while Sandra makes exquisite panini and crostini, for which she's received international acclaim. The couple works seven days a week, with assistance from three of their four sons.*

All in the Family
"We have been here since 1949," Lino explains. "My father took the business over from the Schiavi family—we kept the name. Soon I'll retire and my sons will take over. It's always been a family-run business, and I hope it stays that way. Over the years our business has continued to grow, and we have a wide range of customers—the regulars who come in every day at the same time, university students who stop in for a bite before class, as well as an increasing number of foreign visitors."

Cicchetti and Ombre
"I love bacari and fight to keep the tradition alive," Sandra says. "There aren't many left in Venice that still follow the tradition of cicchetti and ombre, which has been around for over 500 years. Il cicchetto was the typical break taken by Venetians at about 10 o'clock in the morning. In past centuries, workers would stop and have a sandwich or piece of cheese with a small glass of wine in the shade of the bell tower in Piazza San Marco. The term ombra, which means shade or shadow in Italian, is the name for a glass of wine in Venetian dialect. Nowadays people come in throughout the day—it's busiest at lunchtime and early in the evening.

"Some typical Venetian cicchetti are baccalà mantecato, whipped codfish served on bread, chunks of mortadella or salted pork meat with peppers, hard-boiled eggs served with onion, folpeti—tiny octopus—and polpette, which are deep-fried meatballs. I've added my own recipes as well because I love creating new cicchetti—like my tuna and leek spread or crostini with cheese and figs."

The Bacaro State of Mind
Sandra surveys Cantinone and declares, "This is bacaro." Her husband and sons hustle at the counter; behind them, the wall is lined with wine bottles. Customers sip, snack, and chat, creating a pleasant buzz. "People come to socialize. That's the real bacaro—you come in, have a ciccheto, and talk. It's like you're part of the family."

Despite the sociable atmosphere, bacari aren't meant for lingering—they're places to stop for a quick bite, taken standing at the counter. "Many visitors don't understand this, and they come in and go all the way to our storage room at the back looking for a table, or sit outside on the steps of the San Trovaso bridge. This is a definite bacaro faux pas."

But as the population of native Venetians declines, such bacaro traditions are slowly eroding. Few places meet Sandra's high standards. "The only traditional bacaro is Do Mori, near the Rialto market. It's run by the Schiavi family who used to own Cantinone. The bacaro there dates back to the 15th century."

to workers from the harbor over the bridge, with a raw and real atmosphere full of dialect, rounds-on-the-house, and jokes from the young owners Matteo and Silvano. The classic cichetti are available, and lunch features a good-value set menu, with dishes such as pasta with shrimp and zucchini. ⊠ *Fondamenta San Basilio, Dorsoduro 1642* ☎ *041/5238272* ☰ *No credit cards* ⊙ *Closed Mon. and 3 wks Aug.–Sept.* Ⓥ *Zattere.*

Pasticcerie (Pastry Shops)

Venetians have always loved pastry, not so much as dessert at the end of a meal, but rather as something that could go well with a glass of sweet wine or a cup of hot milk. Traditional cookies are sold in *pasticcerie* (pastry shops) throughout town, either by weight or by the piece, and often come in attractive gift packages. Search for *zaeleti* (cookies made with yellow corn flour and raisins), *buranelli* (S-shape cookies from Burano, which also come in heavy, fat rings), and *baicoli* (crunchy cookies made with yeast). Many bakeries also sell pastry by the portion: from apple strudel to *crostate* (jam tarts) and *torta di mandorle* (almond cake)—just point out what you want. After Christmas and through Carnevale, a great deal of frying takes place behind the counter to prepare the tons of pastries annually devoured by Venetians and tourists alike in the weeks preceding Lent: specialties are *frittole* (doughnuts with pine nuts, raisins, and candied orange peel, rolled in sugar), best eaten warm; the ribbonlike *galani* (crunchy, fried pastries sprinkled with confectioners' sugar); and walnut-shape *castagnole* (fried pastry dumplings rolled in sugar).

Dal Col. This is a good spot near Piazza San Marco for coffee and pastry on the run, with bar (coffee and beverage) service at the counter. ⊠ *Calle dei Fabbri, San Marco 1035* ☎ *041/5205529* ☰ *AE, MC, V* ⊙ *Closed Aug. 5–20* Ⓥ *San Marco.*

Dal Mas. Crisp croissants, pastries such as *kranz* (a braided pastry filled with almond paste and raisins) and strudel from the Friuli region, and bar service make this a great place for breakfast. ⊠ *Lista di Spagna, Cannaregio 150/a* ☎ *041/715101* ☰ *MC, V* ⊙ *Closed Tues.* Ⓥ *Stazione.*

Didovich. Here you'll find all the usual amenities of a pasticceria, and also some sublime vegetable tortes. ⊠ *Campo di Santa Marina, Castello 5909* ☎ *041/5230017* ☰ *No credit cards* ⊙ *Closed Sun. June–Sept.; closed Sun. afternoon Oct.–May* Ⓥ *Rialto.*

Giovanni Volpe. This is the only place in town that all year round still bakes traditional Venetian-Jewish pastry and delicious *pane azimo* (matzo bread), although the days of operation give away that the shop is not kosher. ⊠ *Calle del Ghetto Vecchio, Cannaregio 1143* ☎ *041/ 715178* ☰ *No credit cards* ⊙ *Closed Sun.* Ⓥ *San Marcuola.*

Harry's Dolci. With tables outside in warm weather and an elegant room inside, Harry's makes for a perfect break while exploring the Giudecca, or you can fill your bag to go. ⊠ *Fondamenta San Biagio 773, Giudecca* ☎ *041/5208337* ☰ *AE, MC, V* ⊙ *Closed Tues. and Nov.–Mar.* Ⓥ *Santa Eufemia.*

Maggion. It's worth the trip to the Lido even in bad weather for celebrated, custom-made fruit tarts (to be ordered one day ahead; no bar service). ✉ *Via Dardanelli 46, Lido* ☎ *041/5260836* ▤ *No credit cards* ☉ *Closed Mon. and Tues.* Ⓥ *Lido.*

Marchini. The best-known and most expensive pasticceria in town has a fantastic display of tarts and gifts (no bar service at the main shop, though there is at another branch in Castello). ✉ *Spadaria, San Marco 676* ☎ *041/5229109* ▤ *AE, MC, V* Ⓥ *San Marco.*

Rizzardini. This is the tiniest and prettiest pastry shop in Venice, with a counter dating from the late 18th century. Frittole and *pastine di riso* (pastry with a creamy rice filling) are especially good. ✉ *Calle Fibuera, San Marco 951* ☎ *041/5223835* ▤ *No credit cards* ☉ *Closed Tues.* Ⓥ *San Marco.*

Rosa Salva. There are several branches to this venerable pasticceria in town; the headquarters is a small shop on Calle Fiubera in San Marco with a wide selection of pastry and savory snacks as well as bar service at the counter. ✉ *Calle Fiubera, San Marco 951* ☎ *041/5210544* ✉ *Campo San Luca, San Marco 4589* ▤ *AE, DC, MC, V* ☎ *041/ 5225385* ☉ *Closed Sun.* Ⓥ *Rialto.*

Tonolo. Students from the nearby Università di Ca' Foscari crowd the counter at Tonolo, which makes for a nice break while visiting the Frari district. ✉ *Calle San Pantalon, Dorsoduro 3764* ☎ *041/5237209* ▤ *No credit cards* ☉ *Closed Mon., Aug.* Ⓥ *San Tomà.*

Vio. Besides the usual selection of small pastries and drinks, here you can get a piece of *crostata di marroni* (chestnut tart) or a bag of spicy cookies made with chili. ✉ *Fondamenta Rio Marin, Santa Croce 784* ☎ *041/718523* ▤ *No credit cards* ☉ *Closed Wed.* Ⓥ *Stazione.*

Gelaterie (Ice Cream Shops)

According to Venetians, Marco Polo imported from China a dessert called *panna in ghiaccio* (literally, "cream in ice"), a brick of frozen cream between wafers. There's no documentation to support the claim, but the myth lives on. Several local *gelaterie* (gelato shops) sell panna in ghiaccio, the supposed "ancestor" of gelato, but you'll have to ask around for it, because it's almost never kept on display. On a hot summer day, nothing is better than a cup of fruit-flavored gelato to restore your energy: light and refreshing, it will help you go that extra mile before you call it a day. Most gelaterie are open nonstop from mid-morning to late evening; some keep longer business hours in the summer.

Boutique del Gelato. Good value and a long list of flavors have won this gelateria a dedicated following. ✉ *Salizzada San Lio, Castello 5727* ☎ *041/5223283* ☉ *Closed Jan.* Ⓥ *Rialto.*

Caffè Paolin. The morning sun draws crowds of all ages and nationalities to take a seat on busy Campo Santo Stefano and enjoy a little cup at this favorite bar-gelateria. A scoop of *limone* (lemon) gelato is particularly refreshing on a hot summer day. ✉ *Campo Santo Stefano, San*

Marco 3464 🕾 *041/5220710* ⊘ *Closed Sat.* Ⓥ *San Samuele or Sant' Angelo.*

Da Titta. On the Lido, strategically located on the main drag between the vaporetto stop and the most central beaches, Titta is one of the oldest gelaterie in Venice. Get your receipt at the *cassa* (register) for a cone to go, or enjoy one of the special combinations while lolling in a swinging chair under the trees that line the Gran Viale. There's also bar service. ✉ *Gran Viale Santa Maria Elisabetta 61, Lido* 🕾 *041/5260359* ⊘ *Closed Nov.–early Mar.* Ⓥ *Venice Lido.*

Gelateria Ca' d'Oro. Here you'll find the usual array of flavors, plus panna in ghiaccio and some chocolate-covered specialties in the freezer to the side of the counter. ✉ *Strada Nova, near Campo Santi Apostoli, Cannaregio 4273/b* 🕾 *041/5228982* Ⓥ *Ca' d'Oro.*

Gelateria Il Doge. This popular take-out gelateria, just off Campo Santa Margherita, offers a good selection of flavors, from a few low-calorie options to the extra-rich *strabon* (Venetian for "more than good," which in this case means made with cocoa, espresso, and chocolate-covered almonds), as well as granitas in summer. It's open late most of the year. ✉ *Campo Santa Margherita, Dorsoduro 3058/a* 🕾 *041/5234607* ⊘ *Closed Nov.–Feb.*

Le Café. On Campo Santo Stefano across from Paolin, Le Café has see-and-be-seen tables outside year-round. It also has bar service and afternoon tea and offers a variety of hot chocolate drinks and desserts. ✉ *Campo Santo Stefano, San Marco 2797* 🕾 *041/5237201* Ⓥ *San Samuele or Sant' Angelo.*

Nico. With an enviable terrace on the Zattere, Nico is the city's gelateria with a view. The house specialty is the *gianduiotto,* a brick of dark chocolate ice cream flung into a tall glass filled with freshly whipped cream. There's also bar service. ✉ *Zattere, Dorsoduro 922* 🕾 *041/5225293* ⊘ *Closed Thurs., Dec. 21–Jan. 8* Ⓥ *Zattere.*

Where to Stay

3

Updated by
Cristina
Gregorin

VENETIAN MAGIC CAN STILL LINGER when you retire for the night, whether you're staying in a grand hotel or budget find. Many Venetian hotel rooms are swathed in brocades and glitter with Murano chandeliers, and even in the less grand *pensioni* you stand a chance of finding antiques, Oriental carpets, and a canal view. No satellite TV to keep you company? Just open the window and listen to the gondoliers' serenades or watch the ebb and flow of city life in the campo below.

There are hotels in Venice catering to all tastes and price ranges. Deluxe and upscale hotels are often filled with antiques and art collections and retain much of the feel of the past, with coffered ceilings, frescoes, stucco, and fireplaces in the best rooms. Renovations are usually made as discreetly as possible, paying respect to Gothic and Renaissance structures. With a few exceptions, there's a widespread dislike for modern design among Venetian hoteliers, and even the moderately priced establishments usually opt for 18th-century Venetian style. This means curvaceous, carved furnishings and wallpaper in soft colors—pale yellow and green are big favorites—with gilded or flowery decorations.

Before choosing a hotel, decide in advance what's important to you and don't be reluctant to ask detailed questions. The staff members at most Venetian hotels will be able to converse with you in English. Space is at a premium, and even exclusive hotels have some small, dowdy, Cinderella-type rooms. Rooms tend to be different even on the same floor: windows with canal views and windows looking onto bleak alleyways are both common. If you're not happy with the room you've been given, ask to be moved.

Although the city has no cars, it does have boats plying the canals and pedestrians chattering in the streets, even late at night, so request a quiet room if noise bothers you—but be aware that you could be sacrificing a view for the quiet. During the summer months, don't leave your room lights on *and* your window wide open at night: mosquitoes can descend en masse.

Cannaregio

$$$$ 🏨 **Grand Hotel dei Dogi.** Dei Dogi, housed in an old Venetian palace that once served as the French embassy, offers easy access to the northern lagoon, a private garden, lounges with tall Renaissance-style windows, and majestic Murano chandeliers. Well-appointed rooms featuring red Venetian floors, Oriental carpets, and antique-looking furnishings are all here at two-thirds the price of comparable Venetian hotels. The quiet and romantic beauty of the surroundings makes the (relative) splurge worthwhile. ✉ *Fondamenta Madonna dell'Orto, Cannaregio 3500, 30121* ☎ *041/2208111* 🖨 *041/722278* ⊕ *www.boscolohotels.com* 🛏 *58 rooms, 11 suites* ⚒ *Restaurant, cable TV, bar, in-room data ports, dry cleaning, laundry service, concierge, meeting room, Internet, some pets allowed, no-smoking rooms* 🖃 *AE, DC, MC, V* ⦿*❘ BP* Ⓥ *Madonna dell'Orto.*

$$$–$$$$ 🏨 **Giorgione.** Tucked away in a little-visited part of town not far from Rialto Bridge, the Giorgione is a dignified cross between old and new.

3

It is *essential* to know how to get to your hotel when you arrive. Unless you take a (very expensive) water taxi that deposits you at your hotel's door, you may find yourself wandering down side streets—luggage in hand—with relapses of déjà vu. Although in Venice you can't go terribly wrong in terms of "good" areas to stay, each neighborhood offers different advantages. The area in and around San Marco is always the most crowded and often more expensive: even two- and three-star hotels cost more here than in other parts of town. If you want to stay in less-trafficked surroundings, consider the usually quieter hotels in Dorsoduro and Cannaregio (though hotels near the train station in Cannaregio have their own noise issues). A stay in the Lido in shoulder season offers serenity, but it also includes about a half-hour boat ride to San Marco. The Lido in the summer is crowded with beachgoers.

Facilities Most hotels occupy old buildings, and preservation laws prohibit elevators in some, so ask ahead if an elevator is essential. In the ¢–$$ price categories, hotels may not have lounge areas, and some rooms may be cramped. Bathrooms are on the small side (tubs are considered a luxury) but are usually well equipped. Carpeted floors are rare. Air-conditioning can be a blessing in summer; a few of the budget hotels make do with fans. If you're pestered by mosquitoes, ask at your hotel's desk for a Vape, an antimosquito device.

Reservations You should book your room far in advance. Planning your trip four to five months ahead will give you much greater freedom of room choice. Double-booking is not uncommon, so ask for a written confirmation of your reservation with a description of any special requirements (tub or shower, first or top floor, and so on). Many hotels accept reservations online; the Web site ⊕ www.veniceinfo.it offers information (with photographs) about most hotels in town. If you don't have reservations when you arrive, try **Venezia Sì** (☎ 800/843006 toll-free in Italy daily 9–7, 0039/0415222264 from abroad), which offers a free reservation service by phone. It's the public relations arm of AVA (Venetian Hoteliers Association) and has booths where you can make same-day reservations at **Piazzale Roma** (☎ 041/5231397 ☉ Daily 9 AM–10 PM), **Santa Lucia train station** (☎ 041/715288 or 041/715016 ☉ Daily 8 AM–9 PM), and **Marco Polo Airport** (☎ 041/5415133 ☉ Daily 9 AM–10 PM).

Prices You can find hotels in all price ranges in Venice, but in general prices run higher here than elsewhere in Italy for the same quality of facilities. You can save off-season—November through March, excluding Christmas and Carnevale.

WHAT IT COSTS In euros					
	$$$$	$$$	$$	$	¢
FOR 2 PEOPLE	over €300	€225–€300	€150–€225	€75–€150	under €75

Prices are for two people in a standard double room in high season.

A 15th-century palace and a modern building with many common areas are set around a private garden with a lily pond. Guest rooms feature golden brocades on the walls, carpeted floors, and unusual furnishings in a Venetian-Chinese style: red lacquered headboards decorated with Oriental motifs, rounded chests of drawers, and nightstands. Some split-level rooms come with the lovely bonus of a small, private balcony. ⊠ *Calle dei Proverbi, near Campo Santi Apostoli, 4587 Cannaregio, 30121* 🕾 *041/5225810* 🖷 *041/5239092* ⊕ *www.hotelgiorgione.com* ⤶ *56 rooms* ৬ *In-room safes, minibars, cable TV, billiards, bar, Internet, no-smoking floor* ⊟ *AE, DC, MC, V* ⃥ᴼ *BP* Ⓥ *Ca' d'Oro.*

★ **$$$–$$$$** ⊞ **Hotel Antico Doge.** If you're looking for a small, intimate hotel in a quiet yet central location, look no farther. This delightful palazzo was once home to Doge Marino Falier. It has been completely modernized in elegant Venetian style, with a wealth of textiles and some fine original furnishings. Some rooms have *baldacchini* (canopied beds) and views; all have fabric walls and hardwood floors. On a small canal and only minutes away from San Marco and the Rialto Bridge, this is an oasis of tranquillity. An ample buffet breakfast is served in a room with a frescoed ceiling and a Murano chandelier. ⊠ *Campo SS. Apostoli, Cannaregio 5643, 30131* 🕾 *041/2411570* 🖷 *041/2443660* ⊕ *www. anticodoge.com* ⤶ *20 rooms, 1 suite* ৬ *In-room safes, minibars, cable TV, in-room data ports, bar* ⊟ *AE, DC, MC, V* ⃥ᴼ *BP* Ⓥ *Ca' D'oro.*

$$$ ⊞ **Abbazia.** The only Venetian abbey turned into a hotel, the Abbazia is not recognizable as such from the outside. The guest rooms are in the former convent—a low, white stucco structure with no exposed brick or Gothic windows. Numerous details survive from the building's religious past: tiny wooden pulpits hang on the walls, and holy-water bowls await around many corners. Brass chandeliers befit the austerity of the place, as does the cream-white and beige decor of the rooms (considerably larger than monks' cells), although some touches of gaudy colors are found in the tapestries and couches. ⊠ *Calle Priuli dei Cavaletti, 68 Cannaregio, 30121* 🕾 *041/717333* 🖷 *041/717949* ⊕ *www.abbaziahotel.com* ⤶ *49 rooms* ৬ *In-room safes, minibars, cable TV, in-room data ports, some pets allowed, no-smoking rooms* ⊟ *AE, DC, MC, V* ⃥ᴼ *BP* Ⓥ *Stazione Ferrovia.*

★ **$$** ⊞ **Ca' Gottardi.** Ca' Gottardi is one of a new generation of small hotels that dusts off traditional Venetian style and mixes in some contemporary design. The entrance, on the second floor of a Renaissance palace, is done in white marble and glass, making a graceful contrast to the Murano chandeliers and wall brocades of the guest rooms. Bathrooms are large and modern, and a rich breakfast is served in a salon that's pleasantly full of light. Location is another plus: it's just off the Grand Canal, near the Ca' d'Oro and across the canal from the Rialto markets. ⊠ *Strada Nova, Cannaregio 2283, 30121* 🕾 *041/2759333* 🖷 *041/ 2759421* ⊕ *www.cagottardi.com* ⤶ *10 rooms, 1 suite* ৬ *Minibars, in-room data ports, cable TV, bar, babysitting* ⊟ *DC, MC, V* ⃥ᴼ *BP* Ⓥ *Ca' d'Oro.*

$$ ⊞ **Hesperia.** A quiet, friendly hotel housed in a two-floor building (no elevator) just across from the Jewish Ghetto, the Hesperia is within walking distance to the train station but also safely removed from the noise and commercial clutter. Half the rooms offer a beautiful view of the wide (and clean) Cannaregio Canal. The decor doesn't lend much atmosphere, with basic furniture, spare tapestry in pastel shades, and humble, black-and-white versions of Venetian floors, but the space is less cramped than in comparable hotels. Its not-so-central location makes it a possibility when the rest of town is booked solid. ✉ *Calle Riello, Cannaregio 459, 30121* ☎ *041/715251* 🖷 *041/715112* 🌐 *www.hotelhesperia.com* *15 rooms, 13 with bath* *In-room safes, minibars, cable TV, bar, Internet, some pets allowed* 💳 *AE, DC, MC, V* 🍽 *BP* Ⓥ *Stazione Ferrovia.*

$ **Bernardi Semenzato.** This is a particularly inviting little place just off Strada Nova and near the gondola ferry to the Rialto market. Some rooms have exposed ceiling beams, and some have rooftop or garden views. Practical pluses include in-room coffee- and tea-making facilities. All rooms are very basic, but those in the nearby *dipendenza* (annex) are larger, with newer amenities. ✉ *Calle dell'Oca, Cannaregio 4366, 30121* ☎ *041/5211052* 🖷 *041/5222424* 🌐 *www.hotelbernardi.com* *24 rooms, 20 with bath* *In-room safes, cable TV, Internet, some pets allowed, no-smoking rooms* 💳 *AE, DC, MC, V* ⏲ *Closed Jan.* 🍽 *BP* Ⓥ *Ca' d'Oro.*

$ **Ca' San Marcuola.** Opened in 2002 in a busy area of shops, trattorias, and wine bars frequented by Venetians and tourists alike, this family-owned hotel stands out for its relaxed and familiar atmosphere. The comfortable rooms, all full of light and with spacious bathrooms, are furnished in a quiet Venetian mode with delicate pastel colors. An elevator that provides access to all floors and a very convenient location close to a waterbus stop on the Grand Canal make this a good choice for those with limited mobility. ✉ *Campo San Marcuola, Cannaregio 1763, 30121* ☎ *041/716048* 🖷 *041/2759217* 🌐 *www.casanmarcuola.com* *14 rooms* *In-room safes, minibars, in-room data ports, cable TV, bar, Internet, concierge* 💳 *AE, DC, MC, V* ⏲ *Closed 4 wks Dec.–Jan.* 🍽 *BP* Ⓥ *San Marcuola.*

$ **Minerva e Nettuno.** This friendly, family-run place located near the train station is popular with backpackers and Italian families. It offers spotless rooms with solid wood furniture. The *vippino* (VIP) treatment for €13 extra entitles you to a soft bathrobe, a copy of a booklet with literary extracts about Venice, and lunch or dinner at I Quattro Rusteghi, located in the heart of the Jewish Ghetto. ✉ *Lista di Spagna, Cannaregio 230, 30121* ☎ *041/715968* 🖷 *041/5242139* 🌐 *www.minervaenettuno.it* *27 rooms, 11 with bath* *In-room data ports, some pets allowed, some cable TV* 💳 *AE, DC, MC, V* 🍽 *BP* Ⓥ *Stazione Ferrovia.*

$ **Rossi.** Most guests stay here for the reasonable price and the convenient, if not central, location not far from the train station. Rooms are comfortable and clean, with tile floors and dark, solid wood furniture. Some face an adjacent private garden that houses a colony of songbirds, others the dead-end street below. Skip the house breakfast and instead take advantage of the hotel's vicinity to Cannaregio's best pastry shop, Dal Mas. ✉ *Calle de le Procuratie, off Lista di Spagna, Cannaregio 262, 30121* ☎ *041/715164* 🖷 *041/717784* 🌐 *www.hotelrossi.net* *14 rooms, 10 with bath* 💳 *MC, V* 🍽 *BP* Ⓥ *Stazione Ferrovia.*

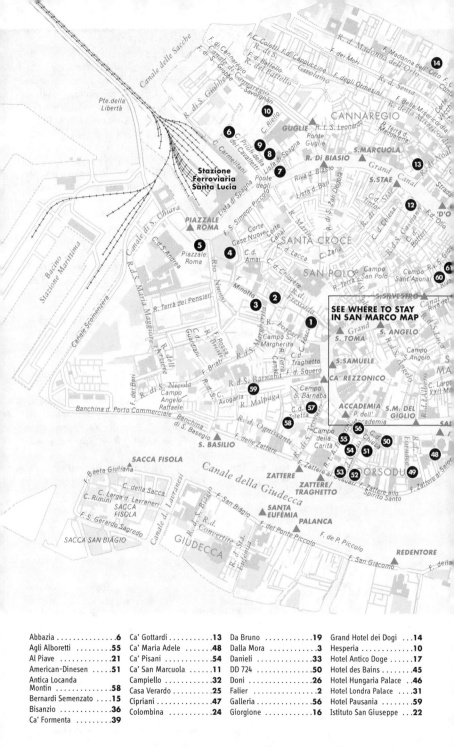

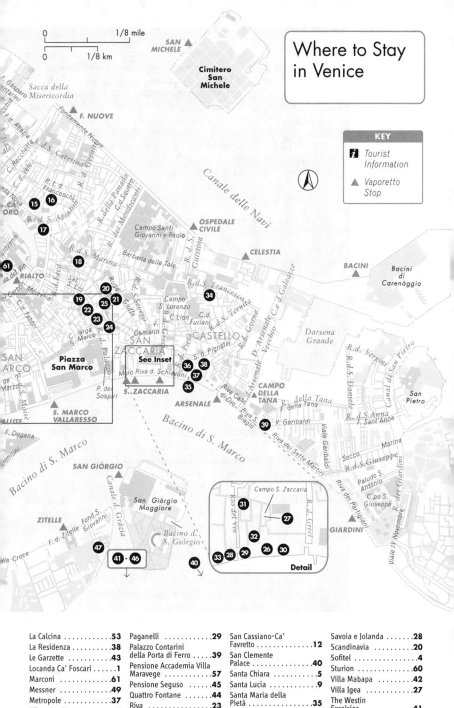

Where to Stay in Venice

$ ▦ **Santa Lucia.** Set in a narrow alleyway just off the Lista di Spagna—steps from the train station and a stone's throw from a vaporetto stop—this small and plain hotel makes a quiet oasis in the midst of the hustle and bustle. The best feature is the surprisingly spacious garden, where you can picnic (there's a fountain for washing fruit) or take breakfast. Rooms (some without private bathroom) are simply furnished but benefit from facing the garden. ⊠ *Calle della Misericordia, Cannaregio 358, 30121* ☎ *041/715180* 🖷 *041/710610* ⊕ *www.hotelslucia.com* 🛏 *15 rooms, 9 with bath* ⚿ *Some pets allowed, cable TV, bar* ⊟ *AE, DC, MC, V* ☺ *Closed Dec. 15–Feb. 5* ⦿❘ *BP* Ⓥ *Stazione Ferrovia.*

Castello

$$$$ ▦ **Bisanzio.** Managed by the Busetti family since 1969, this fine hotel is in a restored 16th-century building, right by the church of La Pietà, where Vivaldi was choirmaster and violin master. The peaceful rooms are decorated in Venetian antique style. Generous buffet breakfasts are served in a bright and airy salon, and a lounge opens onto an old courtyard, close to a private mooring for gondolas and other boats. Better rooms have private balconies. ⊠ *Calle della Pietà, Castello 3651, 30122* ☎ *041/5203100* 🖷 *041/5204114* ⊕ *www.bisanzio.com* 🛏 *40 rooms* ⚿ *In-room data ports, some in-room safes, minibars, cable TV, bar, babysitting, dry cleaning, laundry service, concierge, some pets allowed, no-smoking rooms* ⊟ *AE, DC, MC, V* ⦿❘ *BP* Ⓥ *San Zaccaria.*

$$$$ ▦ **Colombina.** What in the 16th century was a private palazzo is now
FodorsChoice   an intimate and romantic inn. Minutes away from the bustle of San Marco,
★   Colombina is on a quiet side canal. Many of the rooms, all with deep bathtubs and most with dramatic Murano chandeliers, face this canal; at night, all you can hear is the lapping of the water. There's an ample breakfast buffet, which you can supplement with extras (such as scrambled eggs) à la carte for an additional charge. The stellar staff provides the perfect complement to this enchanting spot. ⊠ *Calle del Remedio, Castello 4416, 30122* ☎ *041/2770525* 🖷 *041/2776044* ⊕ *www. hotelcolombina.com* 🛏 *33 rooms, 3 suites* ⚿ *In-room data ports, in-room safes, minibars, cable TV with movies, dock, bar, babysitting, dry cleaning, some pets allowed* ⊟ *AE, DC, MC, V* ⦿❘ *BP* Ⓥ *San Marco.*

$$$$ ▦ **Danieli.** You'll feel like a doge in Venice's largest luxury hotel, a complex of newer buildings and a 14th-century palazzo. Sumptuous Venetian decor prevails from the moment you set foot in the soaring atrium with its sweeping staircase. Long favored by world leaders and movie stars, Danieli is predictably expensive and very elegant. The rooftop terrace restaurant has a heavenly view but unexceptional food. May through October, you have access to the pool, tennis courts, and beach of the Hotel Excelsior on the Lido via a private (free) launch running on the hour. ⊠ *Riva degli Schiavoni, Castello 4196, 30122* ☎ *041/ 5226480, 041/2961222 reservations in English* 🖷 *041/5200208* ⊕ *www. starwoodhotels.com/danieli* 🛏 *221 rooms, 12 suites* ⚿ *Restaurant, room service, in-room safes, minibars, cable TV, in-room data ports, bar, babysitting, dry cleaning, laundry service, concierge, Internet, business services, meeting rooms, some pets allowed, no-smoking rooms* ⊟ *AE, DC, MC, V* ⦿❘ *EP* Ⓥ *San Zaccaria.*

$$$$ ⊞ **Hotel Londra Palace.** A wall of windows overlooking the lagoon and the island of San Giorgio makes this the hotel of choice for soaking up that extraordinary lagoon view—sweeping all the way from the Salute to the Lido. The downstairs restaurant is all glass, light, and water views, and 34 rooms offer the same spectacle. The view must have been pleasing to Tchaikovsky, who wrote his 4th Symphony here in 1877. Neoclassical public rooms, with splashes of blue-and-green glass suggesting the sea, play nicely off guest rooms, which have fine fabric, damask drapes, Biedermeier furniture, and Venetian glass. The staff is top-notch, as are the restaurant and bar. ⊠ *Riva degli Schiavoni, Castello 4171, 30122* ☎ *041/5200533* 🖷 *041/5225032* ⊕ *www.hotelondra.it* ⇩ *36 rooms, 17 suites* ⚐ *Restaurant, room service, in-room fax, in-room safes, minibars, cable TV, in-room data ports, piano bar, wine bar, babysitting, dry cleaning, laundry service, concierge, Internet, business services, meeting room* ⊟ *AE, DC, MC, V* ⎮◯⎮ *BP* Ⓥ *San Zaccaria.*

$$$$ ⊞ **Metropole.** Eccentrics, eclectics, and fans of Antonio Vivaldi (who taught music here) love the Metropole, a labyrinth of unusual spaces furnished with antiques and jammed with cabinets displaying some very unusual collections indeed. The owner, a lifelong collector of odd objects, displays enough antiques to fill a dealer's shop—some of which furnish the beautifully appointed rooms. The best rooms here are up in the roof— two with spacious roof-top terraces—but only 6 of the standard double rooms offer lagoon views. ⊠ *Riva degli Schiavoni, Castello 4149, 30122* ☎ *041/5205044* 🖷 *041/5223679* ⊕ *www.hotelmetropole.com* ⇩ *43 rooms, 26 suites* ⚐ *Restaurant, room service, in-room safes, minibars, cable TV, in-room data ports, bar, babysitting, dry cleaning, laundry service, concierge, meeting room, some pets allowed* ⊟ *AE, DC, MC, V* ⎮◯⎮ *BP* Ⓥ *San Zaccaria.*

$$$$ ⊞ **Palazzo Contarini della Porta di Ferro.** Formerly the residence of the Contarinis, one of the most powerful families of Venice, this late-14th-century palace has been a hotel since 2001. The building's aristocratic past shows in the elegant inner courtyard with a majestic marble staircase. All differently furnished, the spacious, light-filled rooms have high wood-beamed ceilings, while the apartments include a kitchen, dining room, and open mezzanine. The large Torcello Suite also has a wooden roof terrace from which you can take in a spectacular view of the city. On the *piano nobile* (main floor) is a large, well-appointed hall overlooking the garden; private dinners, meetings, and small conferences are sometimes held here. In sunny weather breakfast is served in the small garden. The hotel has an elevator and a private dock for boats. ⊠ *Salizada S. Giustina, Castello 2926, 30122* ☎ *041/2770991* 🖷 *041/2777021* ⊕ *www. palazzocontarini.com* ⇩ *6 rooms, 11 apartments* ⚐ *In-room safes, minibars, cable TV, in-room data ports, room service, babysitting, dry cleaning, Internet, concierge, some pets allowed* ⊟ *AE, MC, V* ⎮◯⎮ *BP.*

$$$$ ⊞ **Santa Marina.** In the small neighborhood campo that's home to this hotel, five minutes from the Rialto Bridge, you will probably see more Venetians than tourists passing by. Immaculate rooms are outfitted with pastel colors and lacquered Venetian-style furniture. There are no sitting areas, but in summer a cheerful veranda is set up on the square and breakfast is served behind rows of pink geraniums by the kind and helpful staff. ✉ *Campo Santa Marina, Castello 6068, 30122* ☎ *041/5239202* 📠 *041/5200907* ⊕ *www.hotelsantamarina.it* 🛏 *41 rooms, 2 suites* ♨ *In-room safes, minibars, in-room data ports, cable TV, laundry service, concierge, some pets allowed, no-smoking rooms* ▭ *AE, DC, MC, V* ¶ *BP* Ⅴ *Rialto.*

★ **$$$–$$$$** ⊞ **Savoia e Jolanda.** Here you'll get the best deal from among the high-end hotels along the San Marco Basin waterfront. Fifteen of the guest rooms open directly onto the lagoon panorama, and all are decorated with tapestries, fine fabric curtains, and Murano glass chandeliers; they have high ceilings—some are coffered—and many get a great deal of light. There's a copious buffet breakfast, and the restaurant stays open all day. ✉ *Riva degli Schiavoni, Castello 4187, 30122* ☎ *041/5206644* 📠 *041/5207494* ⊕ *www.hotelsavoiajolanda.com* 🛏 *36 rooms, 15 suites* ♨ *Restaurant, room service, in-room safes, some in-room hot tubs, minibars, cable TV, in-room data ports, bar, babysitting, dry cleaning, laundry service, concierge, Internet, some pets allowed, no-smoking rooms* ▭ *AE, DC, MC, V* ¶ *BP* Ⅴ *San Zaccaria.*

$$$ ⊞ **Da Bruno.** A fairly priced hotel in a very central location, Da Bruno is just a five-minute walk from Piazza San Marco and the Rialto. Rooms are simple and well maintained, done up in Venetian style with chairs and bed stands in carved wood, mirrors set in glass frames, and glass chandeliers. You can sip hot and cold drinks on the *terrazzino* (terrace) upstairs in perfect quiet—it's so tiny it holds just one table (first come, first served). If you find it picturesque to watch the flow of pedestrians from your window, ask for a room with a view of the Salizzada. There are two floors but no elevator. ✉ *Salizzada San Lio, Castello 5726/a, 30122* ☎ *041/5230452* 📠 *041/5221157* ⊕ *www.hoteldabruno.it* 🛏 *32 rooms* ♨ *In-room safes, cable TV, bar, some pets allowed, no-smoking rooms* ▭ *AE, MC, V* ¶ *BP* Ⅴ *Rialto.*

$$–$$$ ⊞ **Ca' Formenta.** You're in residential rather than tourist Venice here, but the front rooms still have a wonderful lagoon view. Dating from the 15th century, the simple building underwent a complete makeover before opening in 2003 as a hotel with high-quality services, an elevator, and a canal-side entrance for guests arriving by water taxi. The 15-minute stroll along the waterfront between Piazzo San Marco and this friendly gem of a hotel is through a genuinely "local" part of the city, with plenty of cafés and restaurants. One of the rear rooms has direct access to a pleasant rooftop terrace with tables. ✉ *Via Garibaldi, Castello 1650, 30122* ☎ *041/5285494* 📠 *041/5204633* ⊕ *www.hotelcaformenta.it* 🛏 *14 rooms* ♨ *In-room safes, minibars, cable TV, in-room data ports, laundry service* ▭ *AE, DC, MC, V* ¶ *BP* Ⅴ *Arsenale or Giardini.*

$$–$$$ ⊞ **Casa Verardo.** Close to the Campo Santa Maria Formosa and just a few minutes from San Marco, this hotel is one of the best bargains in the district. Rooms, three of which have canal views (two others look onto a small courtyard), are spotless and have a predominantly antique tone. ✉ *Calle della Sacrestia, Castello 4765, 30122* ☎ *041/5286127* 📠 *041/5232765* ⊕ *www.casaverardo.it* 🛏 *15 rooms, 4 suites* ♨ *In-room safes, minibars, cable TV, babysitting, some pets allowed, no-smoking rooms* ▭ *AE, MC, V* ¶ *BP* Ⅴ *San Zaccaria.*

$$–$$$ 🏠 **Paganelli.** Right between the Danieli and Londra Palace hotels, this pleasant, unpretentious, family-run pensione has the same deluxe views as its pricey neighbors. It's an enchanting small hotel, decorated in the Venetian style. A quieter annex in Campo San Zaccaria is a former convent, where some rooms preserve the original coffered ceilings. ⊠ *Riva degli Schiavoni, Castello 4687, 30122* 🕾 *041/5224324* 🖷 *041/5239267* ⊕ *www.hotelpaganelli.com* ♻ *Cable TV, in-room data ports, bar, babysitting* 🖃 *AE, MC, V* ⫶◯⫶ *BP* Ⓥ *San Zaccaria.*

$$ 🏠 **Al Piave.** This is a stylish little hotel with reasonable rates, set on a busy street but not too noisy inside. Rooms are a bit cramped but tastefully furnished, though with no views to speak of. It's a good choice if you're traveling with children, as they have family suites—two connecting rooms—that can sleep up to five people. ⊠ *Ruga Giuffa, Campo Santa Maria Formosa, Castello 4838–40, 30132* 🕾 *041/5285174* 🖷 *041/5238512* ⊕ *www.hotelalpiave.com* ⤺ *25 rooms* ♻ *Cable TV in some rooms, minibars, some pets allowed* 🖃 *AE, DC, MC, V* ⫶◯⫶ *BP* Ⓥ *San Zaccaria or Rialto.*

$$ 🏠 **Campiello.** The good location, old-fashioned appointments, and modest prices are the best reasons to come to this hotel. Marble floors and gracious furnishings add a certain luster to the public rooms, and guest rooms are functional if unexceptional. There is a bar but no restaurant, though plenty of dining choices exist in the neighborhood. ⊠ *Calle del Vin, Castello 4647, 30122* 🕾 *041/5205764* 🖷 *041/5205798* ⊕ *www.hcampiello.it* ⤺ *15 rooms* ♻ *In-room safes, cable TV, bar, Internet, no-smoking rooms* 🖃 *AE, DC, MC, V* ⊙ *Closed 2 wks in Jan.* ⫶◯⫶ *BP* Ⓥ *San Zaccaria.*

$$ 🏠 **La Residenza.** The word *residenza* in Italian suggests a good deal of aristocratic elegance, and this hotel, with more the feeling of a private mansion than a hotel, does not disappoint. The grand hall on the *piano nobile* (main floor) of this 15th-century building looks almost disproportionately opulent. Well-preserved 18th-century stuccowork adorns the ceilings and walls, along with precious oil paintings. Oriental carpets partially hide the beautiful Venetian terrazzo floor. The rooms are spacious, some with views over the campo in front. ⊠ *Campo Bandiera e Moro, Castello 3608, 30122* 🕾 *041/5285315* 🖷 *041/5238859* ⊕ *www.venicelaresidenza.com* ⤺ *14 rooms* ♻ *In-room safes, minibars, lounge; no smoking* 🖃 *MC, V* ⫶◯⫶ *BP* Ⓥ *Arsenale.*

$$ 🏠 **Scandinavia.** Central but off the main tourist arteries, the Scandinavia is housed in a building dating from the 11th century. Despite the name, the rooms are done in Venetian style, with brocade tapestry and Murano chandeliers. The top suite has a covered veranda with a view of the nearby church. ⊠ *Campo Santa Maria Formosa, Castello 5240, 30122* 🕾 *041/5223507* 🖷 *041/5235232* ⊕ *www.scandinaviahotel.com* ⤺ *33 rooms, 1 suite* ♻ *Cable TV, babysitting, dry cleaning, laundry service, some pets allowed, no-smoking rooms; no a/c in some rooms* 🖃 *AE, MC, V* ⫶◯⫶ *BP* Ⓥ *San Zaccaria or Rialto.*

★ $$ 🏠 **Villa Igea.** The villa offers all the intimacy of a private home (albeit a somewhat large one), which is what it was in the 19th century. It looks on to the church and square of San Zaccaria and, despite its rather central location, is an oasis of tranquility. Rooms are decorated in light pastels; some of them have tiny private balconies, and one has its own terrace. Six rooms have extra beds, making them particularly well-suited for families. ⊠ *Campo San Zaccaria, Castello 4684, 30122* ☎ *041/2410956* 🖶 *041/5206859* ⊕ *www.hotelvillaigea.it* ↵ *27 rooms* ⚲ *Room service, in-room safes, minibars, cable TV, dry cleaning, laundry service, some pets allowed* ☰ *AE, DC, MC, V* ⅊ *BP* Ⓥ *San Zaccaria.*

$$ 🏨 **Wildner.** The lagoon views here so impressed Henry James that he wrote the Wildner up in the preface to his *Portrait of a Lady.* The rooms are spread over four floors (no elevator), half with a view of San Giorgio and half looking out onto the quiet Campo San Zaccaria. The simple, no-nonsense decor features parquet floors and solid, dark furniture matched by brown leather headboards. Light, white curtains and creamy bedspreads further enhance the Wildner's understated ambience. ⊠ *Riva degli Schiavoni, Castello 4161, 30122* ☎ *041/5227463* 🖶 *041/2414640* ⊕ *www.veneziahotels.com* ↵ *16 rooms* ⚲ *In-room safes, cable TV, bar, restaurant, Wi-Fi, Internet, babysitting, dry cleaning, laundry service, some pets allowed* ☰ *AE, DC, MC, V* ⅊ *BP* Ⓥ *San Zaccaria.*

$ 🏨 **Doni.** This former palace occupies a prime position on a canal a couple of stone's throws from Piazza San Marco. The rooms at the front look out onto gondolas through ogee windows. It's a family-run place with wooden floors, solid if uninspiring furniture, and old-fashioned wallpaper to match, although some rooms have frescoed ceilings and chandeliers. ⊠ *Calle del Vin, Castello 4656, 30122* ☎ *041/5224267, 041/5206682 in Jan.* ⊕ *www.albergodoni.it* ↵ *13 rooms, 4 with bath* ⚲ *Fans, babysitting, some pets allowed, no-smoking rooms; no a/c, no room phones, no room TVs* ☰ *MC, V* ⊘ *Some years closed Jan.* ⅊ *BP* Ⓥ *San Zaccaria.*

$ 🏨 **Riva.** This small hotel, close to San Marco, is at the junction of three canals much used by all manner of Venetian watercraft. Although they are endlessly fascinating to watch, here you take the good with the bad—the passing gondolier at sunset travels the same waters as the buzzing water taxi at dawn. Rooms differ in size, and climbing up to the fourth floor (no elevator) wins you a better view. The decor is typical of Venetian hotels—a mix of Murano chandeliers, 18th-century-style furniture, exposed ceiling beams, and beds lacquered in pastel shades. ⊠ *Ponte dell'Angelo, Castello 5310, 30122* ☎ *041/5227034* 🖶 *041/5285551* ↵ *12 rooms, 10 with bath* ⚲ *No a/c in some rooms, no room TVs* ☰ *No credit cards* ⊘ *Closed mid-Nov.–Carnevale (except 2 wks at Christmas)* ⅊ *BP* Ⓥ *Vallaresso or San Zaccaria.*

$ 🏨 **Santa Maria della Pietà.** There's more space—both public and private—in this *casa per ferie* (vacation house) than in many four-star hotels in Venice. It occupies two historic palaces that opened as a hotel in 1999. Completely restored with Venetian terrazzo floors throughout, it has big windows and a huge rooftop terrace with coffee shop, bar, and unobstructed lagoon views. It's well situated—just 100 yards from the main waterfront and about 10 minutes' walk from Piazza San Marco—meaning you'll have to book early to stay here. The spartan rooms have only beds and wardrobes, but the shared bathrooms are plentiful, spacious, and scrupulously clean. Some family rooms with up to six beds are available. ⊠ *Calle della Pietà, Castello 3701, 30122* ☎ *041/2443639* 📠 *041/ 2411561* 🛏 *15 rooms* 🔥 *Coffee shop, bar, lounge; no room phones, no room TVs* ▤ *No credit cards* ⑩ *BP* Ⓥ *San Zaccaria/Arsenale.*

¢ 🏨 **Istituto San Giuseppe.** This religious institution, in an excellent loca-
Fodor'sChoice tion north of Piazza San Marco, is one of several lodgings in Venice run
★ by nuns. Rooms are spartan in decor but spotless and very quiet, overlooking the inner cloister. Book well ahead, as the unbeatable prices draw
crowds, mostly Italians in the know. Curfew is at 11 (10:30 in the winter), and no breakfast is served. You'll need patience to deal with the
language barrier if making reservations over the phone, but your virtue
is rewarded with a remarkable deal. ⊠ *Ponte della Guerra, Castello 5402,
30122* ☎ *041/5225352* 📠 *041/5224891* 🛏 *12 rooms* 🔥 *Fans; no a/c,
no room phones, no room TVs* ▤ *No credit cards* ⑩ *EP* Ⓥ *San Marco.*

Dorsoduro

$$$$ 🏨 **Ca' Pisani.** Here's a breath of fresh air: a Venetian hotel with no brocades and chandeliers to be found. Instead there's a tasteful mix of modern design and well-chosen antique pieces. The entrance hall has marble
floors and an interesting play of colors and lights; the rooms contain
original art deco pieces from the 1930s and '40s (every bed is different). The wine bar La Rivista serves light meals all day, and upstairs are
a Turkish bath and a wooden rooftop terrace where you can take the
sun. ⊠ *Rio Terà Antonio Foscarini, Dorsoduro 979/a, 30123* ☎ *041/
2401411* 📠 *041/2771061* ⊕ *www.capisanihotel.it* 🛏 *25 rooms, 4
suites* 🔥 *Restaurant, room service, in-room safes, minibars, cable TV
with movies, in-room data ports, Turkish bath, wine bar, dry cleaning,
laundry service, concierge, Internet, some pets allowed* ▤ *AE, DC,
MC, V* ⑩ *BP* Ⓥ *Accademia.*

★ $$$–$$$$ 🏨 **American–Dinesen.** This quiet, family-run hotel has a yellow stucco
facade typical of Venetian houses. A hall decorated with reproduction
antiques and Oriental rugs leads to a breakfast room reminiscent of a
theater foyer, with red velvet chairs and gilt wall lamps. Rooms are spa-
cious and tastefully furnished in sage-green and delicate pink fabrics,
with lacquered Venetian-style furniture throughout. Some front rooms
have terraces with canal views. Note that the four-story building has no
elevator. ⊠ *San Vio, Dorsoduro 628, 30123* ☎ *041/5204733* 📠 *041/
5204048* ⊕ *www.hotelamerican.com* 🛏 *28 rooms, 2 suites* 🔥 *In-room
safes, minibars, cable TV, in-room data ports, babysitting, Internet, no-
smoking rooms* ▤ *AE, MC, V* ⑩ *BP* Ⓥ *Accademia/Salute.*

$$$–$$$$ 🏨 **Ca' Maria Adele.** Venice's most elegant small hotel is a mix of classic
Fodor'sChoice style—terrazzo floors, dramatic Murano chandeliers, antique furnish-
★ ings—and touches of modern design, found in the African-wood reception
area and breakfast room. Five "concept rooms" take on themes from
Venetian history; the Doge's Room is draped in deep red brocades,
while the Oriental Room is inspired by the travels of Marco Polo. Ca'
Maria Adele's location is a quiet spot near the church of Santa Maria
della Salute. ⊠ *Campo Santa Maria della Salute, Dorsoduro 111, 30123*
☎ *041/5203078* 📠 *041/5289013* ⊕ *www.camariaadele.it* 🛏 *12 rooms,
2 suites* 🔥 *Bar, room service, cable TV, in-room data ports, in-room safes,*

minibars, babysitting, laundry service, dry cleaning, some pets allowed ▤ *AE, DC, MC, V* ⦿| *BP* Ⓥ *Salute.*

$$$-$$$$ ⊡ **DD 724.** This small design hotel, with modern furnishings and origi-nal works of contemporary art, makes no concessions to the traditional Venetian fondness for rich ornamentation. But modern doesn't mean stark: soft lighting and a cream-and-brown color scheme create a warm, comfortable environment. You can sense the attention to detail everywhere—including the spacious bathrooms, which are decorated with mosaics. ✉ *Next to Guggenheim Collection, Dorsoduro 724, 30123* ☎ *041/2770262* 🖷 *041/2960633* ⊕ *www.dd724.it* ⇆ *7 rooms* ♦ *In-room safes, in-room data ports, cable TV, minibars, Wi-Fi, Internet, dry cleaning, babysitting, some pets allowed* ▤ *AE, DC, MC, V* ⦿| *BP* Ⓥ *Accademia.*

$$-$$$ ⊡ **Hotel Pausania.** From the moment you ascend the grand staircase ris-ing above the fountain of this 14th-century palazzo, you sense the combination of good taste and modern comforts that characterize Hotel Pausania. Light-colored rooms are spacious, with comfortable furniture and carpets strewn with rugs. Some rooms face the small canal (which can be noisy early in the morning) in front of the hotel, while others look out over the large garden courtyard. ✉ *Fondamenta Gher-ardini, Dorsoduro 2824, 30123* ☎ *041/5222083* 🖷 *041/5222989* ⊕ *www.hotelpausania.it* ⇆ *26 rooms* ♦ *Minibars, cable TV, Internet, bar, babysitting, dry cleaning, some pets allowed* ▤ *AE, MC, V* ⦿| *BP* Ⓥ *Ca' Rezzonico.*

$$-$$$ ⊡ **Pensione Accademia Villa Maravege.** A secret garden awaits just be-
Fodor's Choice yond an iron gate, complete with a mini Palladian-style villa, flower beds, ★ stone cupids, and verdant trees—all rarities in Venice. Aptly nicknamed "Villa of the Wonders," this patrician retreat once served as the Rus-sian embassy and was the residence of Katharine Hepburn in the movie *Summertime*. Conservative rooms are outfitted with Venetian-style an-tiques and fine tapestry. The location is on a promontory where two side canals converge with the Grand Canal, which can be seen from the gar-den. Book well in advance. ✉ *Fondamenta Bollani, Dorsoduro 1058, 30123* ☎ *041/5210188* 🖷 *041/5239152* ⊕ *www.pensioneaccademia. it* ⇆ *27 rooms* ♦ *In-room safes, minibars, cable TV, bar, babysitting, dry cleaning, laundry service* ▤ *AE, DC, MC, V* ⦿| *BP* Ⓥ *Accademia.*

$$ ⊡ **Agli Alboretti.** The Alboretti is one of the many hotels clustered at the foot of the Ponte dell'Accademia. It has unpretentious, rather small rooms with plenty of light. The nautical decor, with original pieces taken from old ships' cabins, goes well with the cries of seagulls living along the nearby Giudecca Canal. In warm weather, breakfast is served in an inner courtyard under a rose bower, and a small terrace with potted plants is open. ✉ *Rio Terrà Foscarini, Dorsoduro 884, 30123* ☎ *041/5230058* 🖷 *041/5210158* ⊕ *www.aglialboretti.com* ⇆ *20 rooms* ♦ *Restau-rant, cable TV, bar, dry cleaning, laundry service, concierge, some pets allowed* ▤ *AE, MC, V* ⦿| *BP* Ⓥ *Accademia.*

$$ ⊡ **Pensione Seguso.** This venerable establishment, run by the third gen-eration of the Seguso family and housed in a modern building with good views of the Giudecca Canal, is the most authentic pensione in Venice. The option of half-board adds character to your stay, with meals served in a dining room adorned with heirloom silver plate and old wall lamps.

Rooms are spare—no TV, minibars, and some without private bathrooms—but they're decorated with attractive wooden furniture that will charm the flea-market lovers. Persian rugs, leather couches, and darkwood paneling set the tone for the intimate reading salon. ⊠ *Zattere, Dorsoduro 779, 30123* ☎ *041/5286858, 041/5222472 when closed* 🖷 *041/5222340* 🛏 *36 rooms, 16 with bath* 🖒 *Restaurant, bar, some pets allowed; no a/c* ⊟ *AE, DC, MC, V* ❖◎❘ *MAP* ⊘ *Closed Dec. and Feb.* Ⓥ *Zattere or Accademia.*

★ **\$-\$\$** 🖵 **Galleria.** For atmosphere and location, this hotel is the gem of its price range, but the secret is out, and you will probably need to book months ahead for the sensational view of the Grand Canal and the Accademia Bridge. Rooms differ in size (some are small even by local standards) and decorated in classic Venetian style, with a few whimsical touches such as huge cane armchairs, faux liberty-style lamps, and brocades on the walls. There's no breakfast room, but a small Italian-style *colazione* (breakfast) of croissants and hot drinks is brought to your room. The Galleria is a few steps away from the Accademia vaporetto landing. ⊠ *Accademia Bridge, Dorsoduro 878/a, 30123* ☎ *041/5232489* 🖷 *041/5204172* ⊕ *www.hotelgalleria.it* 🛏 *9 rooms, 7 with bath* 🖒 *Fans; no a/c* ⊟ *AE, MC, V* ◎❘ *BP* Ⓥ *Accademia.*

★ **\$-\$\$** 🖵 **La Calcina.** The Calcina sits in an enviable position along the sunny Zattere, with front rooms offering views across the wide Giudecca Canal. You can sunbathe on the *altana* (wooden roof terrace) or have afternoon tea in one of the reading corners of the lounge, which has flickering candlelight and barely perceptible classical music. A stone staircase (there's no elevator) leads to the rooms upstairs, which have parquet floors, original art deco furniture and lamps, and firm beds. Besides full meals at lunch and dinner, the Piscina bar and restaurant serves drinks and freshly made snacks all day in the elegant dining room and on the wooden waterside terrace out front. ⊠ *Zattere, Dorsoduro 780, 30123* ☎ *041/5206466* 🖷 *041/5227045* ⊕ *www.lacalcina.com* 🛏 *27 rooms, 26 with bath, 5 suites* 🖒 *Restaurant, in-room safes, cable TV* ⊟ *AE, DC, MC, V* ◎❘ *BP* Ⓥ *Zattere.*

\$ 🖵 **Antica Locanda Montin.** Only a streetlamp hanging above the entrance marks this waterway inn, which, in spite of its low-key looks, won the hearts of John Ruskin, Peggy Guggenheim, and Italian poet Gabriele d'Annunzio. Rooms have worn decor, inexpensive furniture, and good contemporary paintings left by the many artists who have stayed here in years past. Though a romantic view of the canal or the pretty internal garden and a durable reputation as a den for artists and literati keep the Locanda full all year long, the bargain rates are its primary appeal. ⊠ *Fondamenta delle Romite, Dorsoduro 1147, 30123* ☎ *041/5227151* 🖷 *041/5200255* ⊕ *www.locandamontin.com* 🛏 *12 rooms, 6 with bath* 🖒 *Restaurant, fans, bar, concierge, Internet, some pets allowed; no a/c in some rooms, no room TVs* ⊟ *AE, DC, MC, V* ◎❘ *BP* Ⓥ *Accademia or Zattere.*

\$ 🖵 **Locanda Ca' Foscari.** Although an unprepossessing choice, this is a homey and relaxed pensione on the border of Dorsoduro and San Polo. The English-speaking owner will proudly show you to your small but surprisingly well-decorated room. Booking ahead may ensure you get one of the few rooms with a pleasant view. ⊠ *Calle della Frescada, Dorso-duro 3887/b, 30123* ☎ *041/710401, 041/5211365 when closed* 🖷 *041/710817* ⊕ *www.locandacafoscari.com* 🖘 *11 rooms, 5 with bath* ♨ *Babysitting; no a/c, no room phones, no room TVs* ▭ *MC, V* ⊘ *Closed Dec.–mid. Jan.* ❙⊙❙ *BP* Ⓥ *San Tomà.*

★ $ 🏨 **Messner.** Located in a modest, two-story palace on a luminous fondamenta, this is a budget hotel that fulfills your highest expectations. Several rooms, the best featuring Gothic-style balconies, face the clean and sunny *rio* (canal) below. All rooms have sturdy wooden furniture, white curtains, and blue carpeting. You can opt for the half-board plan for just €13 more per day. An annex has 23 less-expensive rooms without a view. ⊠ *Fondamenta Ca' Balà, Dorsoduro 216, 30123* ☎ *041/5227443* 🖷 *041/5227266* ⊕ *www.hotelmessner.it* 🖘 *34 rooms, 6 suites* ♨ *Dining room, in-room safes, cable TV in some rooms, some in-room data ports, bar, Internet, some pets allowed, no-smoking rooms; no a/c in some rooms, no TV in some rooms* ▭ *AE, DC, MC, V* ⊘ *Closed Dec.–Jan. (except 1 wk at Christmas)* ❙⊙❙ *BP* Ⓥ *Salute.*

Giudecca

$$$$ 🏨 **Cipriani.** It's impossible to feel stressed in this oasis of stunning rooms and suites, some with garden patios. The hotel launch whisks you to Giudecca from San Marco and back at any hour; those dining at the exceptional Ristorante Harry Cipriani can use it as well. For rooms, the restored 17th-century-style Palazzo Vendramin is the premium choice, with views across to Piazza San Marco, but the main hotel and Palazzetto, a modern annex facing the Canale della Giudecca, also offer extraordinary luxury. Prices are sky-high even by Venetian standards, but this is the only place in town with such extensive facilities and services, from an Olympic-size pool and tennis courts to cooking courses, fitness programs, and even a vineyard. ⊠ *Giudecca 10, 30133* ☎ *041/5207744* 🖷 *041/5207745* ⊕ *www.hotelcipriani.it* 🖘 *54 rooms, 50 suites* ♨ *4 restaurants, room service, in-room safes, minibars, cable TV, Wi-Fi, Internet, tennis court, saltwater pool, health club, spa, bar, babysitting, dry cleaning, laundry service, concierge, Internet, meeting room* ▭ *AE, DC, MC, V* ⊘ *Main hotel closed Nov.–Mar.; Palazzo Vendramin and Palazzetto closed 4 wks in Jan.–Feb.* ❙⊙❙ *BP* Ⓥ *Zitelle.*

Lagoon

$$$$ 🏨 **San Clemente Palace.** If you prefer wide-open spaces to the intimacy of Venice, this is your hotel. It occupies an entire island, about 15 minutes from Piazza San Marco by (free) shuttle launch, with acres of parkland, a swimming pool, tennis courts, wellness center, and three restaurants. The 19th-century buildings are on the site of a 12th-century monastery, of which only the chapel remains. They form a large quadrangle and contain spacious, modern rooms. The view back to Venice with the Dolomites behind on a clear day is stunning. You get all the five-star comforts: there are even three holes of golf. ⊠ *Isola di San Clemente 1, San Marco, 30124* ☎ *041/2445001* 🖷 *041/2445800* ⊕ *www.sanclemente.thi.it* 🖘 *107 rooms, 96 suites* ♨ *3 restaurants, cof-*

WITH CHILDREN?

AN EXTRA BED or a crib for children can usually be added in Venetian hotel rooms, but it rarely comes free of charge—expect to pay between 20% and 40% extra. Some hotels in Venice allow children under a certain age to stay in their parents' room at no extra cost, but others charge for them as extra adults; be sure to find out the cutoff age for children's discounts. Good family choices include Al Piave, Sturion, Villa Igea, and Sofitel.

While a pool is a blessing—for adults as well as kids—in the heat of summer, it comes at a cost: Venice's only hotels with pools are the high-end Cipriani and San Clemente Palace, both located on outer islands. Hotels on the Lido provide beach access, but they put you a fair distance (about a half-hour boat ride) from the heart of the city. The Hotel Des Bains is right on the water and has a parklike area for children.

fee shop, in-room safes, minibars, cable TV, in-room data ports, 3-hole golf course, 2 tennis courts, pool, exercise equipment, health club, hair salon, spa, bar, shop, laundry service, convention center, meeting rooms, some pets allowed, no-smoking rooms ⊟ *AE, DC, MC, V* ⦿ *BP.*

Lido

$$$$ ⊞ **Hotel des Bains.** This is a classic spot to soak up some of the atmosphere in Venice's Lido district. Thomas Mann wrote his haunting novella *Death in Venice* here, and it appeared in the book's film adaptation. The art deco tone has survived pretty much intact, making this a favorite stopover for the beautiful people during the Biennale. Rooms are sumptuously furnished, overlooking either the garden or the sea, and the facilities, including the beach, are superb. A minibus links the hotel with the nearby Excelsior, from which shuttle boats cross to San Marco every 30 minutes. ⊠ *Lungomare Marconi 17, Lido, 30126* ☎ *041/5265921, 041/2961222 for reservations in English* 🖷 *041/5260113* ⊕ *www.sheraton.com/desbains* ⇱ *172 rooms, 19 suites* 🛇 *In-room safes, minibars, cable TV, in-room data ports, babysitting, dry cleaning, laundry service, concierge, Internet, Wi-Fi, some pets allowed, 2 restaurants, snack bars, 2 tennis courts, pool, wading pool, gym, sauna, beach* ⊟*AE, DC, MC, V* ⊗ *Closed mid-Nov.–mid-Mar.* ⦿*BP* Ⓥ *Venice Lido.*

$$$$ ⊞ **The Westin Excelsior.** The Excelsior's imposing, Moorish-style building with its green cupolas and inner courtyard comes complete with potted lemon trees and fountains; the feel is decidedly southern Mediterranean. No longer a haunt of the noble and famous of the dolce vita days (except during the Biennale), the hotel nonetheless offers the same panache, luxury, and space as ever. Rooms are tastefully modern, done in bright colors, and face either the inner garden or the beach below. A shuttle boat between the hotel and San Zaccaria runs every half hour. ⊠ *Lungomare Marconi 41, Lido, 30126* ☎ *041/5260201* 🖷 *041/*

5267276 ⊕ *www.westin.com/excelsiorvenicelido* ⬗ 197 rooms, 19 suites ⏶ 3 restaurants, in-room data ports, in-room safes, minibars, cable TV with movies, 6 tennis courts, pool, wading pool, hair salon, beach, windsurfing, waterskiing, 3 bars, babysitting, dry cleaning, laundry service, concierge, meeting rooms, business services, Wi-Fi, gym, parking (fee), some pets allowed ⊟ AE, DC, MC, V ⊘ Closed mid-Nov.–mid-Mar. ⍊◯⍊ BP ▣ Venice Lido.

$$–$$$$ ⊞ **Quattro Fontane.** This fine hotel in a well-maintained mansion run by Danish sisters Bente and Pia Bevilacqua offers the serenity of the Lido in a location that's a 15-minute walk and 20-minute boat ride from Piazza San Marco. Well-decorated rooms with period furniture and tasteful tapestries overlook the lush surrounding garden of mature trees and shrubs, with clearings for dining tables in summer. Common areas contain an odd collection of masons' aprons, pipes, ex-votos, masks from Jakarta, Roman seals, and seashells. A huge fireplace adds warmth and character in the colder months. After a full day you can relax in the library, stocked with books in many languages. ⊠ *Via Quattro Fontane 16, Lido, 30126* ☎ *041/5260227* 🖷 *041/5260726* ⊕ *www.quattrofontane.com* ⬗ 54 rooms, 4 apartments ⏶ Restaurant, in-room safes, minibars, cable TV, Internet, tennis court, bar, library, babysitting, dry cleaning, laundry service, meeting room, some pets allowed ⊟ AE, DC, MC, V ⊘ Closed Nov.–Mar. ⍊◯⍊ BP ▣ Lido.

$$$ ⊞ **Hotel Hungaria Palace.** Art Nouveau lovers, and those simply in search of a non-Venetian hotel in Venice, should consider a stay at this one-of-a-kind place. It was built in 1905, and its fanciful facade and colorful majolica tiles are a glamorous throwback to a bygone age. Simply furnished public rooms have some of the hotel's original furniture; the curvaceous bar is also original. Most rooms, some with furniture dating to the turn of the 20th century, have deep, tiled bathtubs, and prints and photographs of Venice adorning the walls. ⊠ *Gran Viale S.M. Elisabetta 28, Lido, 30126* ☎ *041/2420060* 🖷 *041/5264111* ⊕ *www.hungaria.it* ⬗ 78 rooms, 4 suites ⏶ In-room data ports, minibars, cable TV, Wi-Fi, restaurant, bar, room service, bicycles, babysitting, playground, dry cleaning, laundry service, meeting room, free parking, some pets allowed ⊟ AE, DC, MC, V ⍊◯⍊ BP.

$$–$$$ ⊞ **Villa Mabapa.** Built as a private house in the 1930s and subsequently converted into a hotel, this lodging is still run by the original owners and preserves its air of a family home. A rustic atmosphere prevails, and the shady garden is a good spot for an alfresco dinner of classic Venetian dishes. The name (in case you're wondering) is a combination of *mamma, bambini,* and *papa.* ⊠ *Riviera San Nicolò 16, Lido, 30126* ☎ *041/5260590* 🖷 *041/5269441* ⊕ *www.villamabapa.it* ⬗ 70 rooms ⏶ Restaurant, in-room safes, minibar, cable TV, Wi-Fi, Internet, bar, babysitting, dry cleaning, laundry service, free parking, meeting room, some pets allowed ⊟ AE, DC, MC, V ⍊◯⍊ BP ▣ Venice Lido.

$ ⊞ **Le Garzette.** As the only *agriturismo* (working farm with guest accommodations) available in Venice, this place is a bit of an oddity, situated at the greener end of the island about a half hour from San Marco. The quiet guest rooms, some of which have balconies facing the sea, are furnished with 19th-century antiques. The restaurant—which is open to nonguests on weekends—takes its ingredients directly from the surrounding orchards and gardens. Bicycles are available free, and the beach is literally steps away. With so few rooms available, you'd do well to book early. A one-week stay is mandatory in July and August. ⊠ *Lungomare Alberoni 32, Lido, 30010* ☎ *041/731078* 🖷 *041/2428798* ⊕ *www.legarzette.on.to* 🖚 *5 rooms* ♿ *Restaurant, Internet, bicycles, some pets allowed* ⊟*No credit cards* ⊙ *Closed 2 wks at Christmas* ⏝|*BP* Ⓥ *Venice Lido.*

San Marco

$$$$ 🏨 **Concordia.** Half of the rooms in this attractive, well-run hotel catch a side view of the Basilica di San Marco, as does the spacious breakfast room–bar, where light meals and snacks are served all day. Rooms are decorated with brocade tapestry and have cream, aqua, or peach color schemes. The romantic *mansarda* (rooftop room) has a panoramic view over the Piazza San Marco. The management offers good deals at offpeak times, so check when booking. ⊠ *Calle Larga San Marco, San Marco 367, 30124* ☎ *041/5206866* 🖷 *041/5206775* ⊕ *www.hotelconcordia. com* 🖚 *55 rooms, 3 suites* ♿ *Room service, in-room safes, minibars, cable TV, some in-room hot tubs, restaurant, bar, Wi-Fi, babysitting, dry cleaning, laundry service, meeting room, some pets allowed* ⊟ *AE, DC, MC, V* ⏝| *BP* Ⓥ *Vallaresso or San Zaccaria.*

$$$$ 🏨 **Gritti Palace.** Queen Elizabeth, Greta Garbo, and Winston Churchill all made this their Venetian address. The feeling of being in an aristocratic private home pervades this legendary hotel replete with fresh flowers, fine antiques, sumptuous appointments, and old-style service. The dining terrace on the Grand Canal is at its best in the evening, when the boat traffic dies down. May through October you have access to the pool, tennis courts, and beach of the Hotel Excelsior on the Lido via a private (free) launch. ⊠ *Campo Santa Maria del Giglio, San Marco 2467, 30124* ☎ *041/794611* 🖷 *041/5200942* ⊕ *www. starwoodhotels.com/grittipalace* 🖚 *84 rooms, 6 suites* ♿ *Restaurant, room service, in-room safes, minibars, cable TV with movies, in-room data ports, bar, babysitting, dry cleaning, laundry service, concierge, Internet, Wi-Fi, business services, meeting rooms, some pets allowed, nosmoking rooms* ⊟ *AE, DC, MC, V* ⏝| *BP* Ⓥ *Giglio.*

$$$$ 🏨 **Il Palazzo at the Bauer.** Il Palazzo, under the same management as the larger Bauer Hotel, is an all-out luxury experience. Bevilacqua and Rubelli fabrics cover the walls, and though no two rooms are decorated the same, they have in common high ceilings, Murano glass, marble bathrooms, and damask drapes. Many also have sweeping views. Breakfast is served on Venice's highest terrace, appropriately named il Settimo Cielo (Seventh Heaven). The outdoor hot tub, also on the seventh floor, offers views of La Serenissima that won't quit. ⊠ *Campo San Moisè, San Marco 1413/d, 30124* ☎ *041/5207022* 🖷 *041/5207557* ⊕ *www. ilpalazzovenezia.com* 🖚 *36 rooms, 40 suites* ♿ *Restaurant, room service, in-room fax, in-room safes, some in-room hot tubs, minibars, cable TV with movies, in-room data ports, golf privileges, health club, outdoor hot tub, massage, sauna, Turkish bath, dock, bar, babysitting,*

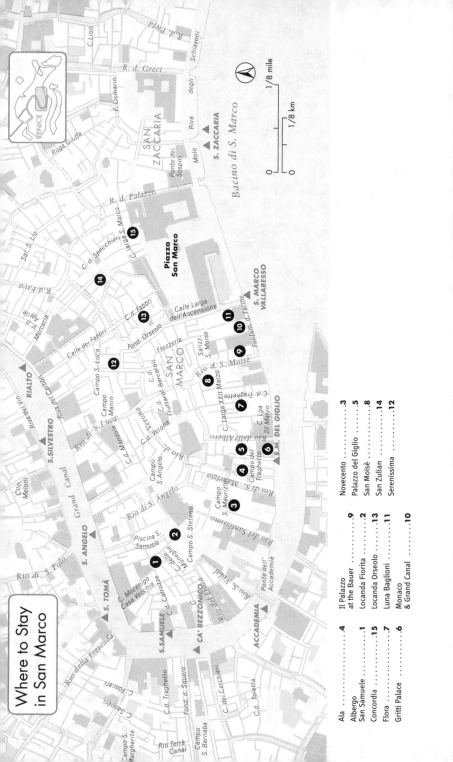

Where to Stay in San Marco

Ala **4**
Albergo San Samuele **1**
Concordia **15**
Flora **7**
Gritti Palace **6**

Il Palazzo at the Bauer **9**
Locanda Fiorita **2**
Locanda Orseolo **13**
Luna Baglioni **11**
Monaco & Grand Canal **10**

Novecento **3**
Palazzo del Giglio **5**
San Moisè **8**
San Zulian **14**
Serenissima **12**

dry cleaning, laundry service, concierge, Internet, Wi-Fi, some pets allowed, no-smoking rooms ▭ *AE, DC, MC, V* 🍴 *EP* Ⓥ *Vallaresso.*

$$$$ **Luna Baglioni.** Two minutes from San Marco, this handsome hotel has elegant rooms, several with a view of the Grand Canal. Breakfast is served in a salon fit for a king, adorned with frescoes by the school of Tiepolo, 18th-century furniture, and Venetian floors. Most suites are lavish affairs, with fireplaces, jetted tubs, and terraces. Restaurant Canova offers modern Venetian cuisine. ✉ *Calle Vallaresso, San Marco 1243, 30124* ☎ *041/5289840* 📠 *041/5287160* 🌐 *www.baglionihotels.com* *107 rooms, 11 suites* *Restaurant, room service, in-room data ports, in-room safes, in-room hot tubs, minibars, cable TV, dock, bar, piano bar, babysitting, dry cleaning, laundry facilities, concierge, Internet, some pets allowed, no-smoking rooms* ▭ *AE, DC, MC, V* 🍴 *BP* Ⓥ *Vallaresso.*

$$$$ **San Moisè.** The closest you can get to staying in an 18th-century Venetian house, the San Moisè deserves special mention for its warm decor and choice location. Rooms are decorated with Oriental rugs, glass chandeliers, rich tapestries, and handsome furniture. Some have a view of the rio, and others face a small inner courtyard, home to a lush wisteria tree. The dimensions of some rooms are irregular, but the result never feels awkward. There is no elevator, but you won't have to climb higher than the second floor. ✉ *Piscina San Moisè, San Marco 2058, 30124* ☎ *041/5203755* 📠 *041/5210670* 🌐 *www.sanmoise.it* *27 rooms* *Minibars, in-room safes, cable TV, bar, babysitting, dry cleaning, laundry service, some pets allowed* ▭ *AE, DC, MC, V* 🍴 *BP* Ⓥ *Vallaresso.*

$$$–$$$$ **Ala.** The Ala is in the "aristocratic" part of town, between Piazza San Marco and Campo Santo Stefano, a few steps from the Santa Maria del Giglio vaporetto and traghetto stop. The owner's collection of armor is displayed in the hall and sitting rooms, where daily English-language newspapers are at your disposal. Some rooms are large, with coffered ceilings and old-style furnishings; others are smaller with more modern decor. Most come with a view of either the campo below or the side canal. ✉ *Campo Santa Maria del Giglio, San Marco 2494, 30124* ☎ *041/5208333* 📠 *041/5206390* 🌐 *www.hotelala.it* *85 rooms* *In-room safes, in-room data ports, minibars, cable TV with movies, Internet, babysitting, dry cleaning, laundry service, meeting room* ▭ *AE, DC, MC, V* 🍴 *BP* Ⓥ *Santa Maria del Giglio.*

★ **$$–$$$$** **Monaco & Grand Canal.** This landmark canal-side hotel is a blend of Venetian elegance and contemporary design. The centerpiece of the restored original section is the convivial waterfront restaurant; many guest rooms share the same panoramic lagoon views. A big, bright reception area, created by roofing an inner courtyard with glass, leads to the newer rear section, which was once the Sala del Ridotto, a luxurious gambling house. It's almost worth staying here just to spend time in the sumptuous lounge with adjoining bar. Rooms in both sections are in modern Italian style, with spacious bathrooms in a warm, beige marble. ✉ *Calle Vallaresso, San Marco 1332, 30124* ☎ *041/5200211* 📠 *041/5200501* 🌐 *www.hotelmonaco.it* *87 rooms, 12 suites* *Restaurant, room service, in-room safes, minibars, cable TV, in-room data ports, dock, bar, piano bar, babysitting, dry cleaning, laundry service, concierge, meeting rooms, some pets allowed, no-smoking rooms* ▭ *AE, DC, MC, V* 🍴 *BP* Ⓥ *Vallaresso.*

$$$ ▥ **Flora.** The Flora is distinguished by its pretty courtyard and many sitting rooms. It's in a quiet but central spot near San Moisè and Piazza San Marco. Rooms have Venetian period decor and are a bit dark; a few are small, with tiny bathrooms. Ask for a room with a view of the courtyard or the garden. Some rooms were completely renovated in 2004. ⊠ *Calle Bergamaschi, off Calle Larga XXII Marzo, San Marco 2283/a, 30124* ☎ *041/5205844* 🖷 *041/5228217* ⊕ *www. hotelflora.it* ⤳ *44 rooms* ♨ *In-room safes, cable TV, in-room data ports, bar, babysitting, dry cleaning, laundry service, Internet* ▤ *AE, DC, MC, V* ⫙*⧜ BP* Ⓥ *Vallaresso.*

$$$ ▥ **Locanda Orseolo.** This small hotel just behind Piazza San Marco has a friendly staff and comfortable, well-appointed rooms. Classic Venetian design is given a Carnevale theme, with each room dedicated to a traditional mask. The friendly atmosphere pervades at breakfast, where it's not common to get engrossed in conversation with the other guests. ⊠ *Corte Zorzi (off Campo San Gallo), San Marco 1083, 30124* ☎ *041/ 5204827* 🖷 *041/5235586* ⊕ *www.locandaorseolo.com* ⤳ *12 rooms* ♨ *In-room safes, minibars, cable TV, in-room data ports, Internet, babysitting, dry cleaning, some pets allowed* ▤ *AE, DC, MC, V* ⫙*⧜ BP* Ⓥ *Vallaresso.*

★ $$$ ▥ **San Zulian.** A minimalist entrance hall leads to rooms that are a refined variation on the Venetian theme, with lacquered 18th-century-style furniture and parquet floors. Room 304 is on two levels and has its own delightful covered veranda. Two ground-floor rooms have bathrooms equipped for people with disabilities. The handy location near San Marco and the Rialto and the top-notch staff make a stay here eminently enjoyable. ⊠ *Campo della Guerra, San Marco 534/535, 30124* ☎ *041/ 5225872 or 041/5226598* 🖷 *041/5232265* ⊕ *www.hotelsanzulian. com* ⤳ *25 rooms* ♨ *In-room safes, minibars, cable TV, some pets allowed* ▤ *AE, DC, MC, V* ⫙*⧜ BP* Ⓥ *Vallaresso/San Zaccaria.*

$$–$$$ ▥ **Novecento.** In a quiet street just a 10-minute walk from Piazza San **Fodor'sChoice** Marco you'll find this small family-run hotel. Inspired by the style of **★** Mariano Fortuny, the early-1900s artist and fashion designer, the intimate rooms are a surprisingly elegant mélange of exotic, multiethnic furnishings. The Mediterranean, Indian, and Venetian fabrics, silverware, chandeliers, and furniture create a sensual turn-of-the-20th-century atmosphere. In fine weather breakfast is served in the inner courtyard. ⊠ *Calle del Dose (Campo San Maurizio), San Marco 2683/84, 30124* ☎ *041/2413765* 🖷 *041/5212145* ⊕ *www.novecento.biz* ⤳ *9 rooms* ♨ *In-room safes, minibars, cable TV, in-room data ports, bar, dry cleaning, laundry service, Internet, Wi-Fi* ▤ *AE, DC, MC, V* ⫙*⧜ BP* Ⓥ *Santa Maria del Giglio.*

$$ ▥ **Palazzo del Giglio.** A block of orange stucco houses overlooking Campo Santa Maria del Giglio make up this hotel and short-term residence. The modern decor doesn't have much charm, and the rooms lack views and are rather overpriced in high season. The real appeal lies in the apartments, which have hotel service, house two to six people, and offer views of the campo below. The larger units are outfitted with two bedrooms, two bathrooms, a spacious common area, and a fully equipped kitchen. It's essential to reserve months ahead. Fortunately, there's no minimum stay. ⊠ *Campo Santa Maria del Giglio, San Marco 2462, 30124* ☎ *041/2719111* 🖷 *041/5205158* ⊕ *www.hotelgiglio.com* ⤴ *24 rooms, 19 apartments* ⚵ *Room service, in-room safes, in-room data ports, minibars, cable TV, babysitting, dry cleaning, laundry service,* ⊟ *AE, DC, MC, V* ¶◎¶ *BP* Ⅴ *Santa Maria del Giglio.*

$$ 🎞 **Serenissima.** Run with pride by the amiable Dal Borgo family since 1960, the Serenissima offers quiet rooms in the heart of town at reasonable prices. An effort to create some warmth has been made in the common areas, but the waxed wooden floors, Oriental rugs, and dark-burgundy leather couches don't lend too much to the atmosphere. A similar style characterizes the guest rooms, which, within their category, stand out for good maintenance and comfort. The busy Calle Goldoni below does not really count as a view, so your best bets are the quieter rooms at the back, all facing an inner courtyard. ⊠ *Calle Goldoni, San Marco 4486, 30124* ☎ *041/5200011* 🖷 *041/5223292* ⊕ *www.hotelserenissima. it* ⤴ *38 rooms* ⚵ *In-room data ports, cable TV, Internet, some pets allowed* ⊟ *AE, MC, V* ¶◎¶ *BP* Ⅴ *Rialto or Calle Vallaresso.*

$ 🎞 **Albergo San Samuele.** Near the Grand Canal and Palazzo Grassi, this friendly hotel has clean, sunny rooms in surprisingly good shape for the price. Five of the bathrooms, with white and gray-blue tiles, are relatively new, and the walls are painted in crisp, pleasant shades of pale pink or blue. Curtains and bedspreads are made from antique-looking fabrics, and although the furniture is of the boxy modern kind, the owners are gradually adding more interesting-looking pieces. ⊠ *Salizzada San Samuele, San Marco 3358, 30124* ☎☎ *041/5228045* ⊕ *www. albergosansamuele.it* ⤴ *10 rooms, 7 with bath* ⚵ *Fans, some pets allowed; no a/c, no room TVs* ⊟ *No credit cards* ¶◎¶ *BP* Ⅴ *San Samuele or Sant'Angelo.*

$ 🎞 **Locanda Fiorita.** This small hotel is tucked away in a sunny little square near the Ponte dell'Accademia. The entrance is through a vine-covered porch, a section of which belongs to the best guest room. Beamed ceilings give some character to otherwise bland but practical furnishings. ⊠ *Campiello Novo o dei Morti, San Marco 3457/a, 30124* ☎ *041/5234754* 🖷 *041/5228043* ⊕ *www.locandafiorita.com* ⤴ *18 rooms, 14 with bath* ⚵ *Cable TV, babysitting, Internet* ⊟ *AE, MC, V* ¶◎¶ *BP* Ⅴ *Accademia.*

San Polo

$$$$ 🎞 **Marconi.** With its location next to the Rialto Bridge in the Riva del Vin area—once renowned for its taverns—it's no surprise to learn that the Marconi was itself an *osteria* until its conversion in the 1930s into an elegant hotel. Rooms are furnished in antique style but equipped with up-to-date facilities. Two of the guest rooms have outstanding views overlooking the Grand Canal, but they're on the small side. The bustling produce market is steps away. ⊠ *Rialto, Riva del Vin, San Polo 729, 30125* ☎ *041/5222068* 🖷 *041/5229700* ⊕ *www.hotelmarconi.it* ⤴ *26 rooms* ⚵ *Room service, cable TV, in-room safes, minibars, bar, babysitting, dry cleaning, laundry service, Wi-Fi, Internet, some pets allowed* ⊟ *AE, DC, MC, V* ¶◎¶ *BP* Ⅴ *Rialto.*

$$$ ⊞ **Sturion.** At the end of the 13th century this building housed foreign merchants selling their wares at the Rialto, and the painter Vittore Carpaccio depicted it in his 1494 *Miracle of the Cross* (on view at the Accademia). Now it's decorated in 18th-century Venetian style and run with care by a Venetian family. Rooms (two with views of the Grand Canal) are done in red-and-gold brocade; there's also a small but inviting breakfast room. Two rooms comfortably sleep four, making them good choices for families. All rooms have coffee- and tea-making facilities, an uncommon feature for Italy. Be warned that the stairs are steep, the hotel is on the fourth and fifth floors, and there's no elevator. ⊠ *Calle del Sturion, San Polo 679, 30125* ☎ *041/5236243* 🖷 *041/5228378* ⊕ *www.locandasturion.com* ⇗ *11 rooms* ⌂ *In-room safes, minibars, Internet, some pets allowed* ⊟ *MC, V* ⊧◯⊨ *BP* ☑ *San Silvestro or Rialto.*

Santa Croce

$$$$ ⊞ **Sofitel.** Housed inside a new, well-maintained pink palazzo just 300 yards from Piazzale Roma and with access to all main vaporetto lines, the Sofitel is the luxury hotel of choice for travelers with children, as kids under 12 stay free in their parents' bedroom. You'll find an efficient staff and modern comforts, including soft carpets, noise insulation, and spacious bathrooms with tubs and windows. The decor mixes wooden furniture, large mirrors, glass chandeliers, and pastel-shade walls. ⊠ *Giardini Papadopoli, Santa Croce 245, 30135* ☎ *041/710400* 🖷 *041/710394* ⊕ *www.sofitel.com* ⇗ *92 rooms, 5 suites* ⌂ *Restaurant, room service, in-room data ports, in-room safes, minibars, cable TV with movies, dock, bar, babysitting, concierge, meeting room, some pets allowed, no-smoking floor* ⊟ *AE, DC, MC, V* ⊧◯⊨ *BP* ☑ *Piazzale Roma.*

★ $$$$ ⊞ **San Cassiano-Ca' Favretto.** This Renaissance-era red-stucco and stone building was home to the families of several aristocratic families before being purchased by the Venetian painter Giacomo Favretto (1849–87). The spacious portego preserves the original 20-foot beamed ceiling, from which hang two huge Murano chandeliers fit for a royal ballroom; old tapestries arranged high on the walls add glamour and a medieval feel. All rooms are furnished with either genuine antiques or well-made replicas. Nearly every window frames a great view; those facing the Grand Canal open on the lacy facade of the Ca' d'Oro, which at sunset picks up magic shades of pink. ⊠ *Calle della Rosa, Santa Croce 2232, 30135* ☎ *041/5241768* 🖷 *041/721033* ⊕ *www.sancassiano.it* ⇗ *35 rooms* ⌂ *In-room safes, minibars, cable TV, bar, babysitting* ⊟ *AE, DC, MC, V* ⊧◯⊨ *BP* ☑ *S. Stae.*

$$ ⊞ **Falier.** The name Falier (recalling a former doge) is a bit misleading for this simple, decidedly undogelike hotel. In fact, if it weren't for the red-and-white checked floor of the portego, the decor wouldn't be at all Venetian. Terra-cotta floors and basic wood furniture recall a budget mountain chalet; in most rooms the feeling is enhanced by rustic wooden ceilings and short curtains. Bathrooms are on the small side and have showers only. Views are not great, and the first floor is rather dark. The exception is room 41, with a lovely little terrace set amid the neigh-

boring roofs. ⊠ *Salizzada San Pantalon, Santa Croce 130, 30135* ☎ *041/710882* 🖷 *041/5206554* ⊕ *www.hotelfalier.com* ⟿ *19 rooms* ♿ *Cable TV, bar, babysitting, Internet, some pets allowed* ⊟ *AE, DC, MC, V* ⊺⊙⊺ *BP* Ⓥ *Piazzale Roma.*

$$ 🏠 **Santa Chiara.** You can drive your car to the entrance of the Santa Chiara and yet still find yourself staying in a room overlooking the Grand Canal. The hotel was built where the convent and church of Santa Croce once stood; a surviving wall is incorporated into the present-day structure. Wood-beam ceilings and red-and-white-checked floors give character to the common areas. Rooms are bright and well appointed and generally larger than average within this price category. The most coveted room is the attic, with a private terrace and panoramic view. Twelve rooms in the nearby annex are wheelchair accessible. ⊠ *Piazzale Roma, Santa Croce 548, 30135* ☎ *041/5206955* 🖷 *041/5228799* ⊕ *www. hotelsantachiara.it* ⟿ *40 rooms* ♿ *In-room safes, minibars, cable TV, bar, dry cleaning, laundry service, Internet, free parking* ⊟ *AE, DC, MC, V* ⊺⊙⊺ *BP* Ⓥ *Piazzale Roma.*

★ **$** 🏠 **Dalla Mora.** On a quiet calle beyond the main flow of traffic, this hotel occupies two simple, well-maintained houses, both with views. The cheerful, tiny entry hall leads upstairs to a terrace lined with potted geraniums, the perfect place to catch the breeze on summer evenings. Rooms are all quite spacious, with basic wooden furniture and tile floors. The annex across the calle has rooms without private bathrooms and others with only showers and sinks. The excellent price and good views make this an attractive place to stay if you're on a budget. ⊠ *Off Salizzada San Pantalon, Santa Croce 42, 30135* ☎ *041/710703* 🖷 *041/723006* ⊕ *www.hoteldallamora.it* ⟿ *14 rooms, 6 with bath* ♿ *Internet, some pets allowed; no a/c, no room TVs* ⊟ *DC, V* ⊺⊙⊺ *BP* Ⓥ *Piazzale Roma.*

Nightlife & the Arts

4

Updated by
Jeff Booth

YOUR FIRST IMPRESSION may well be that Venice doesn't have a nightlife. As the last rays of daylight slip away, so too do most signs of a bustling town. Boat traffic drops to the occasional vaporetto, shutters roll down, and signs go dark. Even though *bacari* (wine bars) would seem to be natural after-hours gathering spots, most close around 9 PM. Yet sprinkled judiciously around the city's residential-looking calli and campi, you'll stumble upon *locali* (nightspots) that stay open until 1 or 2 AM. Some even offer live music, though rarely past midnight—a city ordinance prohibits too much wildness except during Carnevale. Though there are no suitable venues for rock shows, Piazza San Marco has hosted some less rambunctious concerts on summer evenings. Except for a couple of lounge bars with dancing, nightlife tends to be student oriented.

Venice is a stop for major traveling art exhibits, from Mayan to contemporary. From mid-June to early November in odd-numbered years, the Biennale dell'Arte attracts several hundred contemporary artists from around the world. Classical music buffs can rely on a rich season of concerts, opera, chamber music, and some ballet. Smaller venues and churches offer lower-priced, occasionally free performances, often highlighting Venetian composers. Though the city has no English-language theater, during Carnevale foreign companies act in their mother tongue. All films screened at the Venice Film Festival are shown in the original language, with subtitles in English, Italian, or both. During winter months, the movie theater Giorgione Movie d'essai screens English-language films on Tuesday nights.

A Guest in Venice, a monthly bilingual booklet, free at hotels, is probably your most accessible, up-to-date guide to Venice happenings. It also includes information about pharmacies, vaporetto and bus lines, and the main trains and flights. You can visit their Web site, ⊕www.aguestinvenice. com, for a preview of musical, artistic, and sporting events. *Venezia News,* available at newsstands, has similar information but also includes in-depth articles about noteworthy events; listings are bilingual, but most articles are in Italian. The tourist office publishes *Leo* and *Bussola,* bimonthly brochures in Italian and English listing events and updated museum hours. *Venezia da Vivere* is a bilingual guide that comes out seasonally listing night spots and live music. Venice information Web sites give you a chance to scan the cultural horizon before you arrive; try ⊕www. ombra.net (which has a fantastic map function to find any address in Venice), ⊕ www.veniceonline.it, and ⊕ www.venicebanana.com. Italian speakers can find useful information at ⊕ www.comune.venezia.it and ⊕ www.veneziacultura.it. Last but not least, don't ignore the posters you see everywhere in the streets; they're often as current as you can get.

THE ARTS

Art has been a way of life in Venice for so many centuries that it seems you need only inhale to enjoy it. While the Biennale is a whirlwind of contemporary arts, Carnevale masks and costumes let revelers dance with history. Costumed musicians will entice you to performances in the finest churches and palaces, but don't ignore the opera wafting from the gondolas or the conservatory students practicing with open windows.

Art Exhibitions

★ Venice's major site for temporary exhibits is **Palazzo Grassi** (✉ Campo San Samuele, San Marco 3231 ☎ 041/5231680 ⊕ www.palazzograssi. it Ⓥ San Samuele), a stately 18th-century palace on the Grand Canal that hosts art and cultural shows of international importance, ranging from contemporary painting to Etruscan finds. Banners flying on the Island of San Giorgio Maggiore herald an exhibit by the **Cini Foundation** (☎ 041/ 5289900 ⊕ www.cini.it), which occasionally hosts artistic and cultural shows. If you're near Campo Santa Margherita, visit **Fondazione Bevilacqua La Masa** (✉ Rio San Barnaba, Dorsoduro 2826 ☎ 041/5207797 Ⓥ Ca' Rezzonico), which often exhibits contemporary artists.

From time to time, museums such as Palazzo Ducale, Ca' Rezzonico, Museo Correr, Querini-Stampalia, Galleria di Palazzo Cini, and the Peggy Guggenheim Collection host temporary exhibits. There's usually no extra charge to visit such shows. Exhibits are advertised with banners, on city walls, and at museum entrances. Publications such as *A Guest in Venice, Leo,* and *Venezia News* also list these events.

Concerts

The band Pink Floyd made rock history with a 1989 concert staged aboard a pontoon floating near Piazza San Marco. Fans made such a mess of the piazza and loud music stirred up such antipathy that the show was destined to become the city's first and last rock happening. Nearby Mestre, Padua, Verona, Trieste, and Treviso sometimes host artists on their European tours. Though the Biennale Musica and some clubs in Venice do spotlight contemporary music, the vast majority of the city's concerts are classical.

Local publications have up-to-date information, as do **Tourist Offices** (⇨ Smart Travel Tips, *Visitor Information*). **Vela** (✉ Calle dei Fuseri, San Marco 1810 ☎ 041/2424 ✉ Piazzale Roma), which handles vaporetto and bus ticket sales, sells tickets for some musical events. It has sales kiosks at key vaporetto landings.

If you hear something you like and want to take a recording home with you, stop by **Vivaldi** (✉ Fontego dei Tedeschi 5537, opposite Rialto Post Office ☎ 041/5221343), a shop that specializes in Venetian classical music of all kinds and handles tickets for some concerts. Open Monday through Saturday 10:30–7:30 and Sunday 11–7, it's a good source of information about the musical events in town.

Classical

Many of Venice's myriad orchestras perform "greatest hits" programs marketed toward tourists, complete with musicians and ticket vendors in period costume. Groups may have a semi-permanent venue, such as a church or *scuola,* but these change frequently. In addition to the commercial groups, other professional orchestras perform less regularly, usually in museums or palazzi. Churches, scuole, palazzi, and museums sometimes sponsor concerts of their own, especially around the holidays, often featuring touring musicians. During summer months, costumed

THE BIENNALE, AN ARTS FEAST

A VENICE INSTITUTION, the Biennale (as the name suggests) started as an art festival held every two years, but during the century-plus of its existence it's outgrown the name, becoming one of the world's major interdisciplinary art expositions. "Biennale" now refers to the group that coordinates festivals of art, film, music, dance, theater, and architecture. For information on all events, contact **La Biennale di Venezia** (✉ Ca' Giustinian, San Marco 1364/a ☎ 041/5218711 🖷 041/5227539 🌐 www.labiennale.org).

The **Biennale dell'Arte** was originated in 1894 and, except for World War interruptions, has taken place every two years since. In 1910 Klimt and Renoir had their own exhibition rooms, while Picasso was removed from the Spanish salon over concern his paintings were too shocking. Picasso's work was finally shown in 1948, the same year Peggy Guggenheim brought her collection to Venice at the Biennale's invitation.

The Biennale dell'Arte currently takes place from mid-June to early November in odd-numbered years. The Giardini della Biennale, located in the Castello sestiere, was developed specifically for the event. In this parklike setting overlooking the lagoon, 30 countries have permanent pavilions to exhibit works by their native artists. In the neighboring Arsenale's Corderie, a long, beautiful building otherwise off-limits to visitors, works by artists from smaller nations, as well as some more avant-garde installations, are shown. Numerous palaces, warehouses, and churches all over town also hold exhibits, often allowing you to visit buildings not normally open to the public.

The **Biennale del Cinema** (also known as the Mostra Internazionale del Cinema, or Venice Film Festival) was first held in 1932 and soon turned into an annual event.

Films are shown in several theaters at the **Palazzo del Cinema** (✉ Lungomare Guglielmo Marconi 90, Lido ☎ 041/2726511 Ⓥ Lido Casinò or S.M. Elizabetta), a low, boxy structure that's closed most of the year but comes to life in August with fresh paint, bright lights, movie stars, and thousands of fans. Ten days of 9 AM to 2 AM screenings include films vying for awards as well as retrospectives and debuts of mainstream releases. Films are shown in their original language, with subtitles in Italian and English. Advance tickets are recommended for the most eagerly awaited films (the tourist office has details). The night after films play the Palazzo del Cinema, they're shown at Campo San Polo's open-air cinema and at the Giorgione Movie d'essai. San Polo screens the winner of the Leone d'Oro (Golden Lion) prize the night following the awards ceremony.

Since its launch in 1930, the **Biennale Musica** has attracted world-famous composers and performers. Igor Stravinsky premiered his Rake's Progress during the 1951 festival, and four years later it was George Gershwin's turn with Porgy and Bess. The annual event stretches over several months, with performances in some of the city's smaller venues.

Scheduling is similar for the newest addition to the cultural family, **Biennale Danza,** as well as the **Biennale Teatro,** both of which stage some performances in the city's campi. The Theatro Verde, an outdoor amphitheater on the island of San Giorgio, was restored for Biennale use, and can't beat the Venetian lagoon as a backdrop. The least established of the Biennale events, the **Biennale of Architecture,** began in 1980 but has yet to develop a regular schedule.

musicians sometimes play aboard a specially built boat with the audience riding along nearby in 10 to 12 gondolas; suffice it to say, sound quality varies, but acoustics are not this activity's draw.

L'Offerta Musicale, the city's main chamber orchestra, is one of the best classical groups giving concerts, often in Museo Ca' Rezzonico's lovely ballroom. The young, talented musicians perform works by a variety of composers rather than focusing on Vivaldi, as other local groups are apt to do. Call for information about performances. ☎ *041/5241143.*

Gruppo Accademia di San Rocco plays baroque music on original 17th- and 18th-century instruments throughout the summer on Sunday at beautiful **Scuola Grande di San Rocco,** where concertgoers can enjoy more than 60 works by Tintoretto. The musicians are members of the Interpreti Veneziani group. ⊠ *Campo San Rocco, San Polo 3054* ☎ *041/ 5234864 venue, 041/962999 booking* ⊕ *www.musicinvenice.com* 🎫 *€22* Ⓥ *San Tomà.*

Interpreti Veneziani string ensemble performs most evenings except Sunday at **Chiesa di San Vidal.** Their repertoire frequently includes Vivaldi's *Four Seasons.* ⊠ *Campo Santo Stefano, San Marco 2862/b* ☎ *041/2770561* ⊕ *www.interpretiveneziani.com* 🎫 *€22* Ⓥ *Accademia.*

Musici Veneziani perform in 18th-century costume year-round at the **Scuola Grande di San Teodoro.** Vivaldi will be there, as always, and twice a week they're joined by a soprano and baritone for a bit of opera. ⊠ *Campo San Salvador (near Rialto), San Marco 4811* ☎ *041/5210294 booking* ⊕ *www.musicaemusicasrl.com* 🎫 *€21–€31* Ⓥ *Rialto.*

Museo Querini-Stampalia stays open late Friday and Saturday evenings to host *musica antica,* concerts featuring centuries-old music played on antique instruments. Your museum ticket includes the concert, and Florian Art e Caffè on the premises has food and drink available. ⊠ *Campo Santa Maria Formosa, Castello 5252* ☎ *041/2711411* 🎫 *€6.*

Cini Foundation, located on the island of San Giorgio, often has concerts, which are generally free. It's well worth attending, even if only to visit the lovely Benedictine monastery, which is normally closed to the public. ⊠ *Isola di San Giorgio* ☎ *041/5289900* ⊕ *www.cini.it.*

Contemporary

Contemporary music options are at their richest during Biennale Musica (⇨ *see Biennale close-up box*), when concerts are held throughout Venice and advertised on billboards in all major campi. **Vortice—Associazione Culturale** hosts modern, ethnic, and avant-garde concerts and dance at **Teatro Fondamente Nuove.** ⊠ *Near Chiesa dei Gesuiti, Cannaregio 5013* ☎ *041/713913 office, 041/5224498 venue* ⊕ *vortice. provincia.venezia.it.*

Festivals

Festa della Madonna della Salute

This thanksgiving festival celebrates not a harvest, but survival. Every November 21, Venetians make pilgrimage to the church of Madonna della Salute, where they light candles to thank the Virgin Mary for liberating the city from the plague of 1630–31 and to pray for health in the year to come. It was while the plague was raging that the church was commissioned, but before the saint could intervene nearly one third of the city's 145,000 inhabitants were dead. To make the pilgrims' progress more expedient, a temporary bridge is erected across the Grand Canal between Campo Santa Maria del Giglio (near the Gritti Palace hotel) and the sestiere of Dorsoduro. The weather is usually cold and foggy, and the winter season is traditionally ushered in with a traditional stew called *castradina*. Outside the church is a carnival-like atmosphere, with *frittelle* (fritters), *palloncini* (balloons on strings), clowns, and votive candles.

Festa della Sensa

The oldest Venetian festival, the Festival of the Ascension, was initiated by Doge Pietro Orseolo II in the year 1000, after he led the Venetian fleet to victory over the Slavic pirates (who had invaded the Istrian-Dalmatian coast) on Ascension Day. Originally the Ascension was a very simple ceremony in which the doge led a procession of boats to the entrance of the port of San Nicolò di Lido to meet the religious leader of the period, the bishop of San Pietro di Castello, who blessed the waters as a sign of peace and gratitude.

In 1177, with the famous "Peace of Venice" between Emperor Frederick Barbarossa and Pope Alexander III, the festival was transformed into the so-called "wedding with the sea." The story goes that following the occupation of Rome by Barbarossa's troops, Alexander III escaped to Venice disguised as a pilgrim, and after having passed the first night in the open air on the Sottoportego della Madonna near the Church of Sant' Aponal (now marked by a wooden plaque), he found work in the kitchens of the Convento della Carità (today home of the Gallerie dell' Accademia). Some time later, Alexander III was recognized by a Roman high prelate who was visiting the monastery. When the doge Sebastiano Ziani heard of this, he immediately began peace talks with the emperor. But Barbarossa did not want to make peace, so the doge armed a strong fleet and with the blessing of Alexander III set off from Piazzetta di San Marco to attack the imperial ships in the Istrian waters. The Venetians won and captured Barbarossa's son, thereby forcing the emperor to negotiate. In gratitude the pope gave a gold ring to the doge, with which he could remarry Venice with the sea every year.

In Republican times, the Ascension began with a series of performances and celebrations that went on for 15 days and culminated with a large fair in Piazza San Marco. Today the Ascension is held on the Sunday following Ascension Day, the Thursday that falls 40 days after Easter, and begins at about 9 AM with a procession of ships led by the mayor, who tosses a ring into the water and pronounces the ritual phrase *"In segno di eterno dominio, noi, Doge di Venezia, ti sposiamo o mare!"* (As a symbol of our eternal dominion, we wed you, o sea!). Masses in the Chiesa di San Nicolò and boat races follow later in the afternoon. In the Sala del Maggior Consiglio in Palazzo Ducale, you can see several objects that are part of the ceremony, such as the thick candle, the umbrella, the gilded throne, and the eight white, red, blue, and yellow banners. The Museo Storico Navale has an 18-foot-long scale model of the gilded boat used by the doge.

Festa del Redentore

On the third Sunday of July, crowds of pilgrims cross the Canale della Giudecca by means of a pontoon bridge, which is traditionally built every year to commemorate the doge's annual visit to Palladio's Chiesa del Redentore to offer thanks to the Redeemer for the end of a 16th-century plague. Over the course of the Saturday before, neighbors mark off picnic turf with tables and chairs along the fondamenta on Giudecca and Zattere, and even off in Sant'Elena park. As evening falls, thousands take to the streets and tables, and thousands more take to the water. Boats decorated with colored lanterns, well-provisioned with wine, watermelon, and snacks, jockey for position to watch the grand event. Around midnight, from a barge floating in the Bacino di San Marco, Venice kicks off a fireworks display right over the top of the boat fleet, moored so densely across the bacino that you could almost walk from San Marco and San Giorgio. Hotels overlooking the bacino organize terrace dinners and parties (reserve well ahead), and many tourist boats host evening excursions. Anywhere along Piazza San Marco, Riva degli Schiavoni, or Giardini you'll find good viewing, or try Zattere, as close to Punta Dogana as you can get. Anywhere along the Giudecca is good, but the Zitelle end is the most popular. The show is not held in the rain, but no one can recall the last time it rained for Festa del Redentore. After the fireworks you can join the young folks staying out all night and greeting sunrise on the Lido beach, or rest up and make the procession to mass Sunday morning.

Festa di San Marco

The festival honoring the Evangelist who for 1,000 years protected his city is somewhat eclipsed by the fact that April 25 is also Italian Liberation Day, a national holiday. On St. Mark's Day men traditionally buy *boccoli* (red roses) for ladies in their lives (wives, mothers, sisters, cousins, friends)—the longer the stem the deeper the token of love. Legend tells of a soldier enamored of the doge's daughter who was mortally wounded in a far-off battle. As it spilled, his blood was transformed into red roses, which he entrusted his companion to bring to the girl. The story doesn't say if the flowers arrived on the saint's day, but by tradition Venetians celebrate the miracle on this date.

Opera and Ballet

Teatro La Fenice, located between Piazza San Marco and Campo San Stefano, is one of Italy's oldest opera houses and a shrine for opera lovers. It has witnessed many memorable operatic premieres, including, in 1853, the dismal first-night flop of Verdi's *La Traviata*. It has also witnessed its share of disasters. The most recent was a terrible fire, deliberately set in January 1996, followed by delays in reconstruction. However, in keeping with its name (which translates as The Phoenix, coined when it was built over the ashes of its predecessor in 1792), La Fenice rose again, luxuriously restored and reopened to great fanfare

UNFETTERED FETING AT CARNEVALE

WHAT MARDI GRAS IS to New Orleans and Carnaval to Rio, Carnevale is to Venice. For the 12 days leading up to quaresima (Lent), the city is given over to feasting and celebration, with more than half a million people attending masquerade balls, historical processions, concerts, plays, street performances, fashion shows, and all other manner of revelry.

The first record of Carnevale dates back to 1097, but it was in the 18th century that Venice earned its international reputation as the "city of Carnevale." During that era the partying began after Epiphany (January 6) and transformed the city for over a month into one ongoing, decadent masquerade. After the Republic's fall in 1797, the tradition of Carnevale was abandoned.

Festivities were revived in the 1970s, when locals began taking to the calli and campi for impromptu celebrations as a way to beat the winter doldrums. It wasn't long before events became more elaborate, emulating their 18th-century predecessors (with encouragement from the tourism industry). The trademark feature of present-day Carnevale is the commedia dell'arte mask, worn by would-be Casanovas (and their would-be conquests), often dressed in lavish costumes.

Many of Carnevale's costume balls are open to the public—but they come with a high price tag, and the most popular of them need to be booked in advance. Balls cost roughly €350–€450 per person, dinner included, and though you can rent a standard costume for €200–€400 (not including shoes or mask), the most elaborate attire can cost much more. (See "Costumes & Accessories" in the Shopping chapter for resources.) Some of the more noteworthy events:

Ballo del Doge (☎ 041/5233851 🖷 041/5287543 ⊕ www.ballodeldoge. com) is held at Palazzo Pisani-Moretta the last Saturday of Carnevale.

Ballo dei Sospiri (☎ 041/2411607 🖷 041/52335558 ⊕ www. venicemasquerade.com) moves to a different palazzo every year, such as Ca' Zenobio or Contarini.

Ballo Tiepolo (☎ 041/524668 🖷 041/722285 ⊕ www.meetingeurope.com) also takes place in the Tiepolo-frescoed ballroom of Pisani-Moretta.

Count Emile Targhetta d'Audiffret (✉ Cannaregio 6293, 30121 ☎ 041/5230242)—a Venice resident who embraces the spirit of Carnevale with utter abandon—opens his palazzo on the Fondamente Nuove for evenings of masquerade, dancing, and follies; write for information.

You don't have to blow the bank on a masquerade ball in order to take part in Carnevale—many people go simply for the exuberant street life. Be aware, though, that the crowds are enormous, and ball or no ball, prices for everything absolutely skyrocket.

Carnevale events and schedules change from year to year. If you want to attend, first check out these resources:

A Guest in Venice (⊕ www.aguestinvenice. com) gives free advertising to public and private events, and as a result it's one of the most complete Carnevale guides.

Consorzio Comitato per il Carnevale di Venezia (☎ 041/717065, 041/2510811 during Carnevale ⊕ www.meetingeurope. com) is one of the primary event organizers. The **Tourist Office** (☎ 041/5298711 ⊕ www.turismovenezia.it) has detailed information about daily events.

in 2004. Visit www.teatrolafenice.it for a calendar of performances and to buy tickets. You can also purchase tickets by faxing **La Fenice** (🖷 041/786580), calling the **Vela Call Center** (☎ 041/2424 🕓 8 AM–8 PM), going to the one of the **Vela sales offices** (✉ Piazzale Roma, Ferrovia, or in Calle dei Fuseri), or going to the theater box office an hour before showtime.

An alternate location to La Fenice for symphony, opera, and ballet performances is **Teatro Malibran** (✉ Campo San Giovanni Crisostomo, Cannaregio 5873 Ⓥ Rialto). When built by the powerful Grimani family in 1677, it was one of Europe's most famous opera houses. It was converted into a movie theater in 1927 and reopened for performances in 2001 after lengthy restoration.

Theater

Though most theatrical performances are in Italian or in the local Venetian dialect, they can still be entertaining, especially if the production is a classic play you're already familiar with. Venetian Carlo Goldoni (1707–93), a leading figure in Venice's Commedia dell'Arte, wrote many works based on simple stories that should be easy to follow even if you don't understand the language.Venice's **Teatro Carlo Goldoni** (✉ near Rialto, San Marco 4650b ☎ 041/2402011 ⊕ www.teatrogoldonive.it) produces many plays by Goldoni, as well as works by other playwrights.

NIGHTLIFE

Nightspots in and around Venice can be difficult to categorize. Pubs, of the English or Irish variety, with beer on tap and occasional live music, are easy enough to identify but are especially popular with local and traveling youth. When you're looking to dance, things get murkier: lounge-type piano bars generally have small dance floors, while dance clubs often serve snacks and even late-night meals. Bars and cafés are even harder to classify, as availability of snacks, meals, beverages, and music varies with the time of day and the season. Many also decorate their walls with works by local artists, whose paintings are for sale.

Bars

Al Chioschetto is among Venice's "nonbars," consisting only of a kiosk set up to serve some outdoor tables. Located on the Zattere, it's popular in nice weather for late-night *panini* (sandwiches) or a sunny breakfast. Live funk, reggae, jazz, or soul is on tap once a week in summer, usually Friday or Saturday. ✉ *Near Ponte Lungo, Dorsoduro 1406/a* ☎ *338/1174077* Ⓥ *Zattere.*

Bácaro Jazz has hot jazz on the sound system and hot meals until 2 AM. It also has a very interactive owner and staff, so you're not likely to feel lonely even if you arrive alone. ✉ *In front of Rialto Post Office* ☎ *041/5285249* Ⓥ *Rialto.*

Comfortably warm **Bagolo,** with its contemporary Murano glass sconces that are never too bright, welcomes clientele of all ages and all lifestyles. It's open daily except Monday from 7 AM until midnight or later. ⊠ *Campo San Giacomo dell'Orio, Santa Croce 1584* ☎ *041/717584* Ⓥ *San Stae.*

Caffè Blue is a very popular bar for students from nearby Ca' Foscari, with a top-shelf whiskey selection, absinthe for the adventurous, and free Internet for patrons. Sandwiches are available from noon until 2 AM. There are frequent art openings and occasional live music performances. ⊠ *Calle dei Preti, near San Pantalon, Dorsoduro 3778* ☎ *041/710227* Ⓥ *San Tomà.*

Codroma is one of the few bacari that often stays open late, but its hours are utterly unpredictable. Sometimes there's live jazz, but the biggest attraction is the after-hours drinks, served Monday through Saturday. This Venetian institution was founded in the early 1900s by the bearded cook whose picture is near the window. ⊠ *Ponte del Soccorso, near Carmini Church, Dorsoduro 2540* ☎ *041/5246789* Ⓥ *San Basilio.*

★ **Il Caffè,** commonly called "Bar Rosso" for its bright-red exterior, hosts occasional summer jazz concerts and has far more tables outside than in. A favorite with students, it's famous for strong *spritz,* the preferred Venetian aperitif, of white wine, Campari or Aperol, soda water, and a twist of lemon. ⊠ *Campo Santa Margherita, Dorsoduro 2963* ☎ *041/5287998* Ⓥ *Ca' Rezzonico.*

Modern, hip, and complemented by a nice garden, **Orange** anchors the south end of Campo Santa Margherita, the liveliest campo in Venice. You can have *piadine* sandwiches and drinks while watching soccer games on a massive screen inside, or sit at the tables in the campo. ⊠ *Campo Santa Margherita, Dorsoduro 3054/a* ☎ *041/5234740* Ⓥ *Ca' Rezzonico.*

Paradiso Perduto (Paradise Lost) has been catering to night owls since the '70s with drinks, wine, and slightly overpriced fish dishes. It also serves up live music on weekends, mainly jazz and ethnic music. With closely placed tables, this huge room is full of conviviality. It's open Thursday through Monday. ⊠ *Fondamenta della Misericordia, Cannaregio 2540* ☎ *041/720581* Ⓥ *San Marcuola.*

Nothing special by day, **Torino@notte** is a lively nightspot, often spilling out into the campo in summer. Cocktails, served until 2 AM, include the popular *cubino* (rum and Coke). Snacks are available until 7 PM. ⊠ *Campo San Luca, San Marco 459* ☎ *041/5223914* Ⓥ *Rialto.*

Zanzibar is a kiosk bar that's very popular on warm summer evenings, especially Fridays, when there's live music. The fare is limited to sandwiches and ice cream, but the location along the canal near Chiesa di Santa Maria Formosa makes it a pleasant place to sip a drink. ⊠ *Campo Santa Maria Formosa, Castello 5840* ☎ *347/1460107* Ⓥ *San Zaccaria.*

Casinos

The city-run gambling casino in splendid **Palazzo Vendramin-Calergi** is a classic scene of well-dressed high rollers playing French roulette, Caribbean poker, chemin de fer, 30–40, and slots. You must be 18 to enter and men must wear jackets. ⊠ *Cannaregio 2040* ☎ *041/5297111* 📠 *€10 entry includes €10 in chips* ⊙ *Slots 2:45 PM–2:30 AM; tables 3:30 PM–2:30 AM* Ⓥ *San Marcuola.*

Mestre's **Ca' Noghera** casino, near the airport, has slots, blackjack, craps, poker, and roulette. The minimum age is 18, and there's no dress code. ⊠ *Via Triestina 222, Tessera, Mestre* ☎ *041/5297111* 📠 *€10 entry includes €10 in chips* ⊙ *Slots 11 AM–3:30 AM; tables 3:30 PM–3:30 AM.*

Dance Clubs

With only one good disco in the historic center, Venice's club scene is rather skimpy. Dedicated dancers are often willing to face long and dangerous drives to reach the celebrated seaside clubs in Rimini and Riccione, south of Venice. On the mainland around Venice, clubs come and go frequently, and their opening hours are often seasonal and unpredictable. The discos listed here are well established, but it's still a good idea to call ahead. If you go to Mestre or Jesolo, you can plan your night so your return to Venice coincides with sunrise over the lagoon, but make sure you check public transportation details before you leave town.

Metallic walls, red leather couches, and theme nights at **Casanova** attract a young and often wild clientele. By day they serve up meals and Internet access; by night, it's disco and football matches on a large-screen TV. ⊠ *Lista di Spagna, Cannaregio 158/a* ☎ *041/2750199* 📠 *Fri. and Sat., €10 includes 1 drink; other nights free* Ⓥ *Ferrovia.*

Dancing and clubbing is hard to find on the Venetian islands, so your best bets are on terra firma. **Magic Bus** (⊠ Via delle Industrie 118, Second Industrial Zone, Marcon ☎ 041/5952151) is an alternative rock club with pop-art walls and zebra-striped floors that showcases new and established European acts every weekend.

Cult favorites such as Jimi Hendrix and the Cure are daily fare at **Sound Garden Rock Café**, a club favored by the youth of Venice. On weekends cutting-edge local bands often play, and they give away an electric guitar, so you can join in the music. Along with dancing, you can play pool and other games, and stroll the beach, just 20 yards away. From Piazzale Roma it's about an hour by **ATVO bus** (☎ 041/5205530), or from San Marco take the **motonave** (☎ 041/2714747 or 899/909090) to Punta Sabbione, where you pick up a bus; this trip also takes about an hour, and boats stop running at midnight or 1 AM. ⊠ *Piazza Mazzini, Jesolo Lido* ☎ *338/8752823* 📠 *€8 includes 1 drink* ⊙ *Closed Oct.–Dec.*

Late Night

Campo Santa Margherita, where you'll find Il Caffè, Orange, Imagina, and Margaret Duchamp, is one of the livelier gathering places in town after dark.

Midnight Snacks

Venice may be a sleepy city, but there are a number of places where you can answer the call of late-night hunger.

Karaoke on weekends and six specialty brews on tap set **Brasserie Vecchia Bruxelles** apart from other late-night eateries. There's no cover charge for table seating or live music; you can get pizza and light entrées until midnight and sandwiches until 2 AM. ⊠ *Near San Pantalon, Santa Croce 81* ☎ *041/710636.*

★ One of the newest and hippest bars for the late-night, chilled-out crowd, **Centrale** (⊠ Piscina Frezzeria, San Marco 1659/B ☎ 041/2960664) is in a former movie theater, and the clientele looks more Hollywood than Venice. Excellent mojitos and other mixed drinks, black leather couches, and dim lighting set the lounge mood, and the DJs keep the beats cool.

★ **Gelateria il Doge** has over 30 flavors of gelato and several lighter varieties of milk-free sorbet. Try their decadently rich chocolate or the unique *strabon* (Venetian for extra good) made with vanilla, chocolate, and almond brittle. In summer you'll also find refreshing granita that isn't pumped out of a machine. Il Doge stays open until 2 AM. ⊠ *Campo Santa Margherita, Dorsoduro 3058/a* ☎ *041/5234607* ☉ *Closed Nov.–Feb.*

Tables along a canal and a great atmosphere for catching Italian football matches make **Gibo Bar** a dependable address all year round. Board games and an Internet corner don't encourage fast turnover, but if tables are full you can sit Venetian style on the canal wall while dining on *cicheti* and sandwiches, served from lunchtime to late at night. ⊠ *Ponte della Donna Onesta, San Polo 2925* ☎ *041/5229969* ☉ *Closed Sun.* Ⓥ *San Tomà.*

Festooned with sombreros, **Iguana** is a bustling nightspot with live music once a week and a wide selection of Mexican beers and tequilas. It's open until 2 AM, and the more-Italian-than-Mexican kitchen stays open until midnight. ⊠ *Fondamenta della Misericordia, Cannaregio 2515* ☎ *041/713561* ☉ *Closed Mon.* Ⓥ *San Marcuola.*

Artsy and upscale **Imagina** keeps well-dressed hipsters happy for aperitifs and again near midnight, when DJs often spin in the back-room art gallery. ⊠ *Campo Santa Margherita, Dorsoduro 3126* ☎ *041/2410625* Ⓥ *Ca' Rezzonico.*

The French-sounding name **Margaret Duchamp** befits this café-brasserie with an artfully minimalist decor. Warm sandwiches and light salads take the place of cicheti, but you won't pay more for the "designer touch." It's open till 2 AM. ⊠ *Campo Santa Margherita, Dorsoduro 3019* ☎ *041/5286255* Ⓥ *Ca' Rezzonico.*

Moscacieka is a wine bar with bruschetta (toasted bread with toppings), grilled sandwiches, and salads. The name means "Blind Fly" (it also translates as "Blindman's Bluff"), and the ceiling features huge, blue Styrofoam flies. You'll find a matching blue Murano-glass bar and a dozen wooden tables. Though there's no live music, the location is handy, and it's open until midnight. ⊠ *Calle dei Fabbri, San Marco 4717* ☎ *041/ 5208085* ☺ *Closed Sun.* Ⓥ *Rialto.*

The hole-in-the-wall **Pizza al Volo** sells whole pies and slices to go until 1 or 1:30 AM in all the classic styles: *margarita* (tomato and mozzarella), *ai funghi* (with mushrooms), and *al prosciutto* (with ham). ⊠ *Campo Santa Margherita, Dorsoduro 2944/a* ☎ *041/5225430* Ⓥ *Ca' Rezzonico.*

Nightcaps

During Carnevale, many ordinary bars, which close around dinnertime the rest of the year, stay open around the clock.

If you can manage to turn your back on the San Marco's piazza and basilica, you'll enjoy the incredible view of San Giorgio and the Giudecca from the waterside tables of **Bar Al Todaro.** There's no inside seating, but it's a good place for sunny cocktails or midnight moonlit snacks. ⊠ *Piazzetta San Marco 3* ☎ *041/5285165* ☺ *Closed winter* Ⓥ *Vallaresso.*

★ **Caffè Florian** opened up in 1720 as Venezia Trionfante (Triumphant Venice) but was soon renamed after its founder, Floriano Francesconi. The café started as a fashionable spot for a hot chocolate, but during the Austrian domination of Venice it became the favorite meeting place of Italian patriots and intellectuals who boycotted the rival Caffè Quadri across the piazza because of its Austrian military clientele. Stucco, mirrors, wooden carvings, and intimate booths date back to 1859, but the historical atmosphere comes at a price: though an espresso at the bar costs €2, sitting doubles that price, and live music will double it again. Afternoon tea can end up costing as much as a meal, but they do take credit cards, and it's certainly less painful than textbooks for absorbing world history. ⊠ *Piazza San Marco 56, Procuratie Nuove* ☎ *041/ 5205641* Ⓥ *Vallaresso.*

Caffè Quadri may be less glamorous and less intimate than the Florian across the piazza, but it too opened in the 18th century, making it equally historic (and pricey). This café has had its fair share of famous regulars, including Stendhal and Balzac. It's open late for starlit music on summer nights. ⊠ *Piazza San Marco 120, Procuratie Vecchie* ☎ *041/ 5289299* Ⓥ *Vallaresso.*

No Venice watering hole is more famous for a nightcap or an aperitif than **Harry's Bar,** once a favorite haunt of Ernest Hemingway. With a loan from an American named Harry Pickering in the 1930s, Giuseppe Cipriani turned an old rope factory into a cozy, wood-paneled bar, and today, his son Arrigo runs the place. If you'd like to follow in Hemingway's footsteps, ante up for a Bellini, the trademark blend of white peach juice and sparkling prosecco—it's a treat you shouldn't miss during summer peach season, even though you will pay for the privilege. ⊠ *Calle Vallaresso, San Marco 1323* ☎ *041/5285777* Ⓥ *Vallaresso.*

Piano Bars

Just outside Piazza San Marco (near Museo Correr), Hotel Luna Baglioni's **Caffè Baglioni** is perfect for an intimate chat in the cold winter months. There's live piano music from 6 until midnight Thursday,

Friday, and Saturday. ⊠ *Calle Larga de l'Ascension, San Marco 1243* ☎ *041/5289840* Ⓥ *Vallaresso.*

Attached to the fashionable restaurant of the same name, **Martini Scala Club** is the only place in town where you'll find full meals served until 2 AM. The dance floor is big enough and the lights are low enough in this elegant piano bar to dance away your Venice nights from 10 PM until 3:30 AM. ⊠ *Campo San Fantin, San Marco 1980* ☎ *041/5224121* ۞ *Closed Tues. and July–Aug.* Ⓥ *Santa Maria del Giglio.*

Pubs

Thirsty sailors can find night moorage at **Capo Horn Pub,** a roomy watering hole on two floors, decked out like an old ship, with wooden benches, ropes, and brass lamps. Thirty different beers, twenty aged whiskies, and an assortment of wine should slake the thirst of even the briniest deckhand. It opens at 10 AM weekdays, 5 PM Saturday, and the galley whips up tasty salads, sandwiches, and pasta until 1:30 AM every night. You have to be alert to find the place—there's no sign out front. ⊠ *San Pantalon, Dorsoduro 3740* ☎ *041/5242177* Ⓥ *San Tomà.*

Devil's Forest Pub, not far from Rialto Bridge, is one of the more popular Irish pubs in town, and one of the best decorated—right down to its proper red phone booth. There are plenty of board games and Irish beers on tap, and they serve up some tasty pasta at lunch. ⊠ *Calle dei Stagneri 5185, off Campo San Bartolomeo* ☎ *041/5200623* Ⓥ *Rialto.*

Fiddler's Elbow, a typical Irish pub (of the Italian variety), serves plenty of Guinness and gab from 5 PM to 1 AM. There are four Irish brews, plus cider, on tap, as well as sports on TV and occasional live music, either Irish or rock. ⊠ *Corte dei Pali, off Strada Nova, Cannaregio 3847* ☎ *041/5239930* Ⓥ *Ca' d'Oro.*

The popular Italo-Irish pub **Innishark,** located midway between San Marco and Rialto, is known for its variety of international brews. It's open until 1:30 AM. ⊠ *Calle Mondo Novo, near San Lio, Castello 5787* ☎ *051/5235300* ۞ *Closed Mon.* Ⓥ *Rialto.*

Olandese Volante (The Flying Dutchman) is decorated to look like an old ship, but the tables outside in the pretty campo are even more scenic. The central location makes this a convenient late-night stop for a simple bite and a beer. ⊠ *Campo San Lio, Castello 5658* ☎ *041/5289349* Ⓥ *Rialto.*

Senso Unico is a popular neighborhood hangout, decorated in wood and brick with a couple of tables that have a great view of the canal. There are four brews on tap and plenty of wine and sandwich choices from 10 AM to 1 AM. ⊠ *Past Campo San Vio, before the Guggenheim, Dorsoduro 684* ☎ *348/3720847* ۞ *Closed Mon.* Ⓥ *Accademia.*

Sports & the Outdoors

5

WORD OF MOUTH

"I ran every morning around 5 AM. Watching the city come awake—the gondoliers cleaning their gondolas, the docent unlocking St Mark's— being alone in places that are crowded later, feeling like Venice is for your eyes alone—it's enchanting."

—ssachida

"I was there for the Regata Storica. . . . I found my place on the quay across from the train station, with my legs dangling over the Grand Canal. It took almost an hour for the boats to reach the station, so I got quite a tan. It was enjoyable and worth seeing, but not something to build a trip around (even though that's what I did)."

—Dick Patterson

Updated by
Jeff Booth

WITH ALL THE BRIDGES TO CROSS and streets to walk, getting from place to place in their carless world is the principal exercise for most Venetians—and it serves them well, to judge from the level of fitness you see, especially among the older residents. You'll find recreational facilities here, but as is the case with so many aspects of life in Venice, you have to put conventional expectations aside and accept the city on its own terms. A jog in La Serenissima, though not obstacle-free, will certainly be memorable.

Beaches

 The **Lido's** 12 km (8 mi) of beaches have very fine sand (unlike many other Italian beaches), which makes for wonderful barefoot walks but which also turns the water murky—a shame, since this part of the Adriatic is much less polluted than other Italian waters. Unless there's a storm, Lido rarely sees breaking waves, and the water is so shallow you have to walk out at least 100 feet before you can swim. It makes these beaches ideal for toddlers and young children, who can safely play in the water and hunt for the few surviving crabs. The best times to visit the Lido beaches are in June and September, when you can enjoy long walks, play *racchettoni* (a paddle game), and swim without human obstacles. April through May and October are great for walks, but it's too cold to swim. July and August are, predictably, the busiest months of the year.

Most beaches are within 2 km (1 mi) of the vaporetto landing. A straight bus ride or 15-minute walk down Gran Viale takes you to the sea. There's a narrow stretch of free beach close to where Gran Viale meets the sea, but aside from that you have to travel north to San Nicolò or, for a bit more space, to the south end of the island at Alberoni to find *spiagge libere* (free beaches). These have no amenities, so you have to come prepared with food, water, and sunscreen. Technically, the law says "private beaches" can't throw you out as long as you're in the water or on the first couple of yards of sand; you aren't likely to get hassled as long as you don't call attention to yourself. Although nonguests aren't permitted to use private beach facilities, including bathrooms, in practice many locals discreetly use them anyway.

Privately run beaches have such facilities as hot showers, shady porches, *capanne* (cabanas), mini-bungalows with eating areas, bars serving drinks and snacks, and even surfing—the Internet variety. They are almost all exclusively open May through mid-September. The rest of the year the buildings are deserted and the beaches wide open. Just left of where Gran Viale meets the sea are **Lungomare G. D'Azzunzio** (☎ 041/5260236, 041/5261346 in winter), which, along with the neighboring **San Nicolò,** is operated by Venezia Spiagge. They rent *camerini* (private dressing rooms where you can lock your valuables) for daily rates between €16 and €23 (prices highest in July). *Ombrelloni* (umbrellas) cost €10–€15 per day, and *sdraii* or *lettini* (chaise longues) cost €5–€9. Often less crowded than larger beaches, **Sorriso** (✉ Lungomare Marconi, 150 yards past Excelsior ☎ 041/5261066, 041/5260729 in winter) has good prices, with lettini as low as €4 and camerini for €16. It's a good base for exploring the rockier Murazzi coastline nearby, where water can be less murky.

Just right of where Gran Viale meets the sea is **Bagni Des Bains** (☎ 041/ 2716808). On the left as you enter are a few of the old straw-roofed bungalows that survived the flood of 1966. Des Bains beach and hotel featured prominently in Luchino Visconti's haunting film *Death in Venice*. The Oriental-looking dome of the Westin Excelsior towers over the Lido's most famous beach, the **Bagni Excelsior** (✉ Lungomare Marconi ☎ 041/2716808). From the 1930s, when the Venice Film Festival began right here at the Excelsior, this beach has been a favorite of movie stars and their wealthy companions. At **Consorzio** (also known as CAPLI; ✉ Lungomare Marconi ☎ 041/5260356), you can rent a well-furnished hut for €55–€140 (maximum eight people). They also rent small private changing rooms where you can lock your clothes for €30 (for two to three people) and then lie out on the sand. At most private beaches you can rent a *pedalò* (paddleboat) or *moscone* (wooden pontoon) by the hour: these are the best ways to get a good tan under the breeze or to go for a swim away from the crowds.

Biking

FodorśChoice   Bikes are popular on the long, flat island of **Lido,** and though there are
★   no official bike lanes, cars are accustomed to sharing the road. Single or tandem bikes are available for rent, as well as quadricycles with canopy roofs that make it easy for families with small children to get around. Note that helmets are not mandatory in Venice, and they aren't available for rent. As soon as you leave the Lido vaporetto stop, you'll find **Gardin** (✉ behind the Panorama Hotel ☎ 041/2760005), which has the island's best prices for bike rentals: €2.60 per hour or €8 per day. March through October it's open daily 9–1 and 2–7:30; November through February it's closed Sunday; hours other days are somewhat erratic and depend on the weather, but are usually 9:30–1 and 4–7. **Bruno Lazzari** (✉ Gran Viale 21/b ☎ 041/5268019), two minutes from the vaporetto, rents bikes March through October, daily 8–8, and November through February, Monday–Saturday 8:30–1 and 2:30–7. Prices are €3 an hour or €9 a day. **Giorgio Barbieri** (✉ Gran Viale 79A ☎ 041/5261490) rents and repairs bikes. The location is at the intersection of Gran Viale and Via Zara, a five-minute walk from the vaporetto landing. Hours are March through October, daily 8:30–8; bikes rent for €3 an hour or €9 a day.

The Lido is too narrow to get lost—even without a map. Don't miss riding down Via Lepanto. It runs along a canal at the island's center and is lined with shade trees and lovely art deco villas. For a full, adventurous day you can take your bike on the ferry to Pellestrina, an equally long sandbar beach, minus the crowds, located to the south of the Lido, or even visit Chioggia, a canal-laced city of fishermen beyond Pellestrina on the mainland.

Boating

For those sailing into Venice, slip space for boats up to 45 feet is available at **Diporto Velico** (✉ Sant'Elena ☎ 041/5231927). Although you can't reserve a slip, it doesn't hurt to call a few hours ahead. Boats pay by length and type (motorboats cost more), from €13 to €55, plus €3 per person per day. Directly opposite Piazza San Marco, **Compagnia della Vela** (⊠ San Giorgio Maggiore ☎ 041/5200884 ⊕ www.compvela. com) is one of the world's most beautiful marinas. Docking fees range from €32 to €120 (maximum 48 feet), and you can book a day ahead.

If you've fallen in love with the lagoon, **Mare di Carta** (⊠ Fondamenta dei Tolentini, Santa Croce 222, across from train station ☎ 041/716304 ⊕ www.maredicarta.com) can help you get out and enjoy the water. In this full-service nautical store you'll find up-to-the-minute information about rentals and cruises, as well as books and charts to help you explore safely. Those planning to explore on their own need to be aware that some rules of the road are unique to Venice. Keep in mind that the lagoon has vast, unmarked shallow areas, and that weather changes can be unpredictable and abrupt—*trombe d'aria* (waterspouts) are not uncommon.

No license is required, but a good map and some tips from Venetians on right-of-way rules in the labyrinthine canals are needed to rent a boat. At €20 per hour or €130 per day including fuel, **Brussa** (⊠ near Ponte delle Guglie, Cannaregio 331 ☎ 041/715787 ⊙ weekdays 7–5:30, Sat. 7–noon, and Sun. by arrangement) rents small skiffs with 15hp motors for a maximum of six people. **Noleggi Oscar** (⊠ near Scuola di San Giorgio degli Schiavoni, Castello 3255 ☎ 041/739767, 335/259435 mobile) rents skiffs for six to eight people with 10hp outboards at €20 per hour or €150 for a full day (not including fuel). **Vela Club Venezia** (☎ 041/5352088 ⊕ www.velaclubvenezia.it) in Mestre rents sailboats by day or week starting at €140 per day. Pietro Tosi's **Big Game Sport Fishing** (⊠ Campo Stringari 13, Sant'Elena ☎ 335/6276725 ☎ 041/5239042 ⊕ www.biggamesportfishing.it) organizes expeditions that have landed record-size tuna and shark.

Fitness Centers

There are a few modern fitness centers around town open to short-term visitors. Most exercise classes are conducted in Italian.

Fitness Point (⊠ near Campo Santa Maria Formosa, Calle del Pestrin, Castello 6141 ☎ 041/5209246), open weekdays 8 AM–10 PM, Saturday 8–3, Sunday 9:30–12:30, has daily aerobic and step classes. One visit costs €10, and passes for one month are €58.

Palestra Club Delfino (⊠ Zattere, Dorsoduro 788/a ☎ 041/5232763 ⊕ www.palestraclubdelfino.com) has personal trainers by appointment, intensive wellness weeks, cardio machines, and classes. One visit costs €13, and you can buy a week's admission for €44. It's open September through June, weekdays 9 AM–10 PM and Saturday 9–noon; July and August, weekdays 9 AM–9:30 PM.

Wellness Center (⊠ Calle della Pietà, 3697 Castello, off Riva degli Schiavoni ☎ 041/5231944) has English-speaking trainers by appointment, a sauna, and a tanning center in a 2,000-square-foot space on two floors. One entry costs €16, and a three-day pass is €40. It's open weekdays 9–9, Saturday 9–1.

A DAY AT THE RACES

VENICE'S MOST DISTINCTIVE spectator sports, fittingly enough, take place on the water. The city conducts annual rowing races that are a combination of athletic contests and centuries-old traditions.

Regata delle Befane

On January 6, Bucintoro Rowing Club celebrates the Epiphany with the first rowing race of the year. The Regata delle Befane features the club's senior members, each dressed in tattered clothes like a Befana—a mythical old woman with hooked nose, warts, and a scarf over her gray hair, who, in Santa-like fashion, brings candy to good kids and charcoal (black sugar lumps) to bad ones. At the finish line under the Rialto Bridge, Bucintoro club members dispense (to good and bad alike) hot cocoa, mulled wine, candy, and cookies called galani.

La Vogalonga

A cannon fires, oars are hoisted high in the air, and a cry of "Viva San Marco!" echoes across Bacino San Marco. Then the oars drop in the water and the Vogalonga (long row), a 30-km (19-mi) lagoon race from San Marco through Burano, Murano, and Cannaregio, gets underway.

The event takes place on a Sunday in May and is open to any oar-powered boat. It began in 1975 as a way to spark more interest in Voga alla Veneta, Venetian-style stand-up rowing, and to protest moto ondoso, the destructive wave action created by motorboats. Participation has risen from 500 boats in the first year to nearly 2,000, with rowers from around the world.

The Vogalonga begins at 9 AM, and the finish line closes at 2 PM. For a view of the start, you can't beat the campanile of either San Marco or San Giorgio, but Piazzetta San Marco isn't a bad option as well. Around noon rowers start returning through narrow Canal de Cannaregio, where you can get a close-up look at the different boats.

Entrants pay a registration fee of €12 and show up with their own boat. All rowers must be over 16. Information, including directions for registration, is available from **Comitato Organizzatore Vogalonga** (✉ Rosa Salva, San Marco 951 ☎ 041/5210544 📠 041/5200771 🌐 www.vogalonga.it).

Regata Storica

On the first Sunday in September all of Venice turns out for the Regata Storica, the Olympics of Venetian-style rowing.

The day kicks off with a procession of historic boats, with crews and passengers in Renaissance costumes, followed by four races through the Grand Canal. The first is for teen pairs, the second for women pairs in mascarete (short, wide boats). Caorline (heavy transport boats) are then raced by teams of six men, followed by the main event, the season championship of the gondolini (two-oared, gondola-like boats).

The top four crews in each event receive cash prizes and coveted flags: blue for fourth, green for third, white for second, and the prized Bandiera Rossa, or red flag, for first place. The races vary in length, but the longest, the two men's events, start at the entrance to the Grand Canal, round a mark at Piazzale Roma, and finish at Ca' Foscari.

A window overlooking the Grand Canal provides the best view in town, but Riva del Vin or Riva del Carbon near the Rialto Bridge aren't bad, nor are Campiello San Vio, or Campo San Samuele.

Golf

The 18-hole course of the **Lido Golf Club** (✉ Strada Vecchia 1, Alberoni, Lido ☎ 041/731015) isn't exceptional, but it fulfills the basic needs of golf addicts. Greens fees are €55–€70; you can rent clubs for €15 and pullcarts for €6. The course is closed Monday.

Serious golfers will find it well worth the seven-mile taxi ride to **Ca' Della Nave** (✉ Piazza della Vittoria 14, Mestre ☎ 041/5401555 🖷 041/5401926). Wednesday through Monday you can play this beautiful 18-hole, par-72 course for €40–€50 or the executive 9-hole course for €15. Rental clubs are available for €15 and carts for €25.

Horseback Riding

The iron rings on some buildings around town were once used to tie up horses. These days, you'll only find horses on the Lido. **Circolo Ippico Veneziano** (✉ Ca' Bianca, Lido ☎ 041/5265162 🖷 041/5268091) rents horses for use in its riding arena and on nearby trails. It can also refer you to other clubs around the Veneto region. It's closed Sunday afternoon and Monday.

Rowing

All kinds of rowing are popular here, but the lagoon's quintessential sport is **Voga alla Veneta,** the gondolier-style, stand-up rowing used in many types of traditional boats. You can arrange lessons from one of Venice's more than thirty *remiere* or *canottieri* (rowing clubs), as long as you don't insist that the instructor speak English.

FodorśChoice ★

The easiest place for beginning rowers to get their sealegs is the calmest part of the lagoon; **Giudecca** (✉ Fondamente del Ponte Lungo, Giudecca 259 ☎ 041/5287409) offers five lessons for €40 or eight for €60. Venice's oldest rowing club, **Bucintoro** (✉ Zattere, Dorsoduro 15 ☎ 041/5205630), has a package of eight lessons for €90, or you can become a nonresident member for €170 and receive lessons for free. **Querini** (✉ Fondamente Nuove, Castello 6576 ☎ 041/5222039), in the north lagoon, gives eight lessons for €80.

Running

Jogging through Venice can certainly combine exercise with your sightseeing, but be ready to slalom around the nonrunners, and look out for slippery pavement and steps. Northern exposure makes **Fondamente Nuove,** near Campo Santi Giovanni e Paolo, one of the cooler places to jog in summer. It's enough off the beaten track that you can enjoy a long uninterrupted stretch. You can return to the center on Calle Racchetta and Strada Nova or take Via Barbaria delle Tole and Campo Santa Maria Formosa in the opposite direction. **Zattere** promenade is definitely scenic, but unless you're out very early in the day, there are likely to be lots of people to dodge. A pleasant, central route is along **Riva degli Schiavoni** starting from Hotel Danieli and heading east to Sant'Elena. Because the starting point is near Piazza San Marco, it may be packed during peak hours. You can return by way of San Pietro di Castello and Via Garibaldi, which are much less crowded. A good place for distance trainers is the long, flat **Lido,** where drivers are surprisingly polite to bikers and pedestrians. Beaches have compact sand near the water, but from June through September you'll find them too crowded for running between 9 AM and 7 PM. From San Zaccaria, Line 6 gets you to Lido in 10 minutes, and a 10-minute run down Gran Viale S. M. Elisabetta will have you on the beach.

The last Sunday in October is usually the date for the world-class **Venice Marathon** (⊠ In Italy: Venicemarathon, Via Torino 133, 30172 Mestre ☎ 041/5321871 🖳 041/5227744 ⊕ www.venicemarathon.it ✉ In US: Marathon Tours & Travel, 261 Main St., Boston, MA 02129 ☎ 800/444–4097 🖳 617/242–7686). The course, covering the standard 42 km (26 mi), begins in the mainland town of Strà near Padua, follows the Brenta River to Mestre, and crosses Ponte della Libertà into historic Venice. It continues along the Zattere, through Dorsoduro, then crosses a floating bridge, erected just for the event, to Piazza San Marco, and reaches the finish line at Sant'Elena. The field is limited to 6,500 runners. Fees are lower with early registration.

Su e Zo per i Ponti (Up and Down the Bridges; ⊕ www.tgseurogroup.it/suezo), held on a Sunday in March or April, is a family fun run, more popular with local children and joggers-for-a-day than with elite athletes. It begins around 9 AM in Piazza San Marco, where you can register right before the start. Various itineraries let you choose runs from 5 km (3 mi) to 10 km (6 mi) in length, and all participants receive a souvenir medal.

Swimming

The first public swimming pool in Venice opened only in 1986. It was not too long ago that most children learned to swim in the canals, with their waist securely tied to a rope held by a teacher standing on top of a bridge. Until boat traffic got too heavy after World War II, daily swimming races from Piazzetta di San Marco to the Lido were part of Venetian summers.

Venice's two public pools are open some hours for *nuoto libero* (open swim); both close entirely in July and August. Entry costs €5 per visit, and a €30 monthly pass allows swimming two mornings a week. Though neither facility has lockers, receptionists will usually keep valuables for you. With eight lanes and a glass wall overlooking the lagoon, 26-meter **Piscina Comunale** (⊠ Island of Sacca Fisola, Giudecca ☎ 041/5285430 Ⓥ Sacca Fisola), is by far the better of the two public pools. Four-lane, 25-meter **Sant'Alvise** (⊠ Cannaregio 3161 ☎ 041/713567 Ⓥ Sant'Alvise) is located near the Sant'Alvise church in a building that was once the community laundry. **Club Ca' del Moro** (⊠ Via F. Parri 6, Lido ☎ 041/770965) has an outdoor pool (no lanes) open May through September (€15.50 per day).

Tennis

The Lido is the place for tennis players. **Lido Tennis Club** (✉ Via Sandro Gallo 163 ☎ 041/5260954) has courts available for €14 to €28 per hour. **Club Ca' del Moro** (✉ Via F. Parri 6 ☎ 041/770965) has indoor tennis courts for €14 to €25 per hour and outdoor courts for €8 to €14 per hour. (Rates vary according to the number of players.)

Soccer

After more than 30 years in the minor leagues, Venice's soccer team, **Venezia,** was promoted to Serie A (First Division) in 1998, to the jubilation of its fans. Their joy was short-lived, for since then Venezia has been down- and upgraded repeatedly. The team's tired-looking stadium, located on Sant'Elena island at the east end of the Castello sestiere, does little to boost morale; built in 1913 and neglected for decades along with its hapless team, it now ranks as one of the worst facilities in Italy. Plans for a new stadium near Mestre on the mainland blossomed and subsequently wilted. The lengthy Italian soccer season runs from early fall to late spring, with matches usually played in the early afternoon on Sunday; if you want to sit among the local green-and-black-clad fans, reserve ahead through your hotel, or buy tickets through **Vela** (✉ Piazzale Roma, next to the vaporetto stop ☎ 041/2424 ☉ Mon.–Sat. 7:30–7). For further information about professional soccer in Venice, contact **Venezia Calcio** (✉ Via Alfredo Ceccherini 19, 30175 Mestre ☎ 041/2380711 ⊕ www.veneziacalcio.it).

Shopping

6

WORD OF MOUTH

"I walked the length and breadth of Venice, and I found that as one got farther away from San Marco the shopping choices seemed more affordable, more interesting, and less touristy."
—elaine

"We quickly learned if you find something you like somewhere buy it, as you may never find the place again."
—wanderer

Updated by
Pamela Santini **BRING AN EXTRA SUITCASE** for all your newfound treasures, because
Venice is a paradise for shoppers of all varieties. There's no better place
for gifts and souvenirs, from kitschy to one-of-a-kind. The hunting
ground is vast, and while warrens in the city center are devoted to high
fashion, glass artwork, and antiques, quieter parts of town are home to
a number of artisans' shops, where paper is glued, pressed, and shaped
into masks, and gilded cherubs are born from the hands of wood-
carvers.

Alluring shops abound. You'll find countless vendors of trademark
Venetian wares such as glass and lace; the authenticity of some goods
can be suspect, but they're often pleasing to the eye regardless of their
heritage. For more sophisticated tastes (and deeper pockets), there are
jewelers, antiques dealers, and high-fashion boutiques on a par with those
in Italy's larger cities but often maintaining a uniquely Venetian flair.
It's always a good idea to mark the location of a shop that interests you
on your map; otherwise you may not be able to find it again in the maze
of tiny streets.

Store Hours
Regular store hours are usually 9–12:30 and 3:30 or 4–7:30 PM; some
stores are closed on Saturday afternoon or Monday morning. Food shops
are open 8–1 and 5–7:30, and are closed all day Sunday and on Wednesday afternoon. However, many tourist-oriented shops are open all day,
every day. Some shops close for both a summer and a winter vacation.

Tax Refunds
If you make a major purchase, take advantage of tax-free shopping with
the value-added tax (V.A.T., or IVA in Italian) refund. On clothing and
luxury-goods purchases totaling more than €155 made at a single store,
non-EU residents are entitled to get back the roughly 20% tax included
in the purchase price. (For details, see "Taxes" in the Smart Travel Tips
section at the front of this book.)

Department Stores
You wouldn't expect to find a department store sandwiched between
Venice's canals and alleyways, but the upscale chain **Coin** (✉ Salizzada
San Crisostomo, near Campo San Bartolomio ☎ 041/5203581 Ⓥ Rialto) has managed to settle into one of Venice's largest storefronts, from
which it sells clothing, leather goods, and housewares. Coin has a second location called **Coin Beauty** (✉ San Marco 4546, Campo San Luca
☎ 041/5238444 Ⓥ Rialto or Sant'Angelo) that sells only perfume and
lingerie.

Markets
The itinerant flea markets operating on the mainland periodically include Venice in their tours, but the majority of markets left in town trade
in food. The morning open-air **Rialto Fruit and Vegetable Market,** on the
Santa Croce side of the Rialto Bridge (open Monday through Saturday,
roughly 8–1), has been in business since the 11th century. It offers animated local color and gorgeous produce that's tantalizing to browse

through even if you have no plans to buy. The same holds true for the adjacent **Rialto Fish Market,** or *pescheria*, where you're almost certain to find species you've never seen before. It's in operation Tuesday through Saturday, roughly 8–1.

Smaller but still lively food markets are located on Via Garibaldi, near the Giardini della Biennale, and on Strada Nova, not far from the train station (both open mornings, Monday through Saturday). Every Tuesday morning there's a big open-air market on the Lido where you can find housewares and clothing as well as fruit and vegetables. The same is true Friday on the island of Sacca Fisola, at the west end of the Giudecca.

Shopping Districts

Piazza San Marco
The rule here is simple: the closer you are to Piazza San Marco, the higher the prices. The serious jewelry and glasswork in the windows of the shops of the Procuratie Vecchie and Nuove make for a pleasant browse, and during the summer your stroll will be accompanied by the music from the bands that set up in front of Caffè Quadri and Florian. Under the arcades you'll also find an art gallery, a few old-fashioned shops selling kitschy souvenirs, and an assortment of lace, linen blouses, and silk ties and scarves.

Mercerie
The network of streets between the tower clock in Piazza San Marco and Campo San Salvador near Rialto is called the Mercerie. For centuries this was where Venetians came to shop—the word *merceria* comes from *merce* (goods). Only a few of the more refined, locally operated shops survive—the rest are spread out along other streets in the center of town—and a run of anonymous clothing stores and souvenir boutiques has taken their place. On Campo San Zulian is Cartier, which is always worth a look.

One of the three Gucci shops in town is on Merceria dell'Orologio, but its flagship store, which rivals sister shops in Florence and Milan, is on Calle XXII Marzo. For a sweet treat, try Marchini, Venice's most famous chocolate shop, on Calle Spadaria, just parallel to Merceria dell'Orologio. Duca d'Aosta, on Merceria del Capitello, has designer labels for both men and women. Up ahead on Campo San Salvador is a La Perla boutique, with lingerie so elegant it could be mistaken for evening wear, and Fratelli Rossetti, carrying high-quality leather for your feet.

Campo San Bartolomeo & Rialto
Other good shopping areas surround Campi San Salvador and San Bartolomeo. The department store Coin is just past the central post office and down Ponte dell'Olio. The Rialto district is the mecca for buyers of traditional, inexpensive souvenirs: *pantofole del gondoliere,* velvety slippers with rubber soles that resemble the traditional gondoliers' shoes; 18th-century-style wooden trays and coasters that look better after a little wear; and glass "candies," which make a nice, inexpensive (if inedible) gift. Clothing and shoe shops are concentrated between the Rialto

Bridge and San Polo, along Ruga Vecchia San Giovanni and Ruga Ra-
vano, and around Campo Sant'Aponal.

West of Piazza San Marco

The area of San Marco sestiere west of the piazza has a concentration
of boutiques, jewelry shops, antiques dealers, and the most important
art galleries in the city, including Bugno.

Specialty Shops

Antiques & Art Dealers

You probably won't ship home a 19th-century bed from Venice, and
even a relatively common item like an art deco chest of drawers is more
easily found in Rome, Florence, or Naples. But if you have a taste for
odd accessories from another age, Victorian silver plate, prints, or
portable antiques with a *je ne sais quoi* to fill an empty corner, you might
just find what you weren't even looking for.

Antichità Pietro Scarpa, next to the Gallerie dell'Accademia, sells old master paintings—originals, not copies—with accordingly rarified prices.
If your budget doesn't accommodate such an indulgence, you can always fantasize about having one in your next life. ⊠ *Campo della Carità, Dorsoduro 1023/a* ☎ *041/5239700* Ⓥ *Accademia.*

Antiquus, a cozy shop from another era, sells a bit of everything, from
old master paintings to jewelry. Among the hottest items are the lovely
earrings and brooches in the shape of Moors' heads. ⊠ *Calle delle Botteghe, San Marco 3131* ☎ *041/5206395* Ⓥ *San Samuele.*

Claudia Canestrelli is a tasteful shop with a limited choice of antiques,
small paintings, and plenty of interesting-looking bric-a-brac, including silver ex-votos and period souvenirs such as brass ashtrays in the
shape of lions' heads. ⊠ *Campiello Barbaro, near the Peggy Guggenheim Collection, Dorsoduro 364/a* ☎ *041/5227072 or 340/5776089*
Ⓥ *Accademia or Salute.*

Kleine Galerie is a good address for antique books and prints, majolica,
and other ceramics. ⊠ *Calle delle Botteghe, San Marco 2972* ☎ *041/
5222177* Ⓥ *San Samuele.*

Luisa Semenzato offers a good selection of furniture, a few paintings by
minor masters, and European ceramics, as well as a miscellanea of more
affordable objets d'art. ⊠ *Mercerie San Zulian, San Marco 732* ☎ *041/
5231412* Ⓥ *San Marco.*

Art Galleries

Art galleries have become a burgeoning business in Venice. After centuries of commercial slumber, the city seems on its way to finally catching up with the world's contemporary art scene.

Bac Art Studio was founded in 1977 by Paolo Baruffaldi and Cadore,
two etchers with a soft spot for angels, views of Venice and the lagoon,
flowers, cats, and insects. The gallery also hosts exhibits of other local
artists. Prices start around €10 for a 2-inch x 1-inch etching. ⊠ *Fon-*

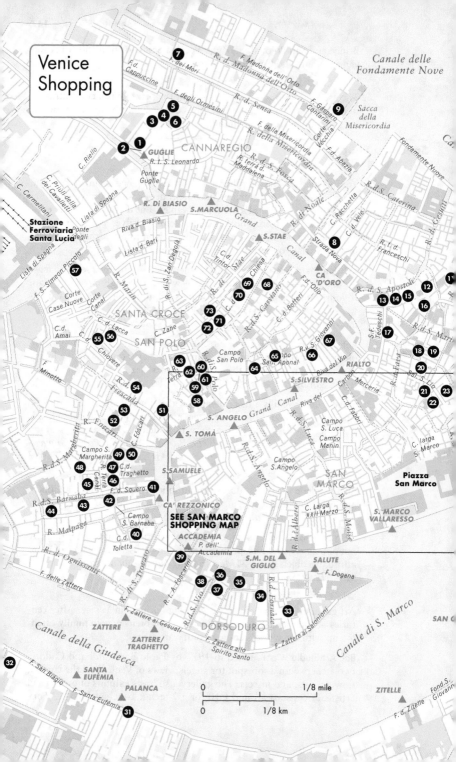

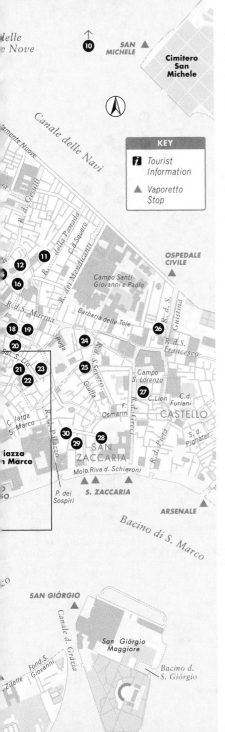

damenta Venier, near the Gallerie dell'Accademia, Dorsoduro 862
☎ *041/5228171* ⊕ *www.bacart.com* Ⓥ *Accademia.*

Bugno, a retailer of contemporary art, puts together windows representative
of the whole gallery—most notably, Missagia's fruit and apples on tex-
tured backgrounds made of pasted newspaper and cardboard, and De-
marchi's sexy wooden sculptures. ⊠ *Campo San Fantin, San Marco 1996/
d* ☎ *041/5229315* Ⓥ *Sant'Angelo.*

Contini shows only 20th-century artists, including such household names
as Picasso, Chagall, Magritte, and Giacometti. It's also Italy's only
dealer for Botero, Navarro Vires, Zoran Music, and the marble and bronze
sculptures by Mitorag. ⊠ *Campo Santo Stefano, San Marco 2765*
☎ *041/5207525 or 041/5204942* Ⓥ *Accademia.*

Galleria del Leone is run by Pierre Higonnet, a French art dealer specializing
in contemporary etching, sculpture, and works on paper. Artists represented include Joan FitzGerald, Mauro Corda, and Serge d'Urach.
⊠ *Fondamenta Sant'Eufemia, Giudecca 597* ☎ *041/5288001 or 339/
6886954* ⊕ *www.galleriadelleone.com* Ⓥ *Palanca/ Giudecca.*

Gallery Holly Snapp focuses on the works by the eclectic English-born
artist Geoffrey Humphries, including paintings, drawings, and etchings
ranging from landscapes to portraits; he also produces watercolors of
Venetian vistas. ⊠ *Calle delle Botteghe, San Marco 3133* ☎ *041/
5210030 or 041/2960824* Ⓥ *San Samuele.*

At **Le Sculture di Livio de Marchi,** Signor De Marchi's swift hands turn
wood into outstanding full-scale sculptures that perfectly reproduce everyday objects such as hats, laundry hung out to dry, telephones, jackets, books, fruit, lace—even underwear. Prices start at about €80 but
can reach four figures. The shop is closed weekends. ⊠ *Salizzada San
Samuele, near Palazzo Grassi, San Marco 3157/a* ☎ *041/5285694*
⊕ *www.liviodemarchi.com* Ⓥ *San Samuele.*

Melori & Rosenberg shows young Italian artists on their way up, including
Luigi Rocca (hyper-realist scenes of modern life), Francesco Mancini (views
of Venice and impressionistic nudes), and Michele Giorgio Riva (still
lifes). ⊠ *Campo del Ghetto Nuovo, Cannaregio 2919* ☎ *041/2750039*
⊕ *www.melori-rosenberg.com* Ⓥ *San Marcuola.*

Ravagnan has been the exclusive dealer since 1967 of some of the most
famous living artists on the Italian scene, including Venetian surrealist
Ludovico de Luigi and metaphysical painter Andrea Vizzini. Glass sculptures by Primo Formenti and collages by Piero Princip are also available here. ⊠ *Procuratie Nuove, Piazza San Marco 50/a* ☎ *041/5203021*
⊕ *www.ravagnangallery.com* Ⓥ *San Marco.*

Scriba, run by a delightful husband-and-wife team, sells exclusive Ital-
ian-made crafts, along with maps, fine prints, and paintings by Italian
and international artists. ⊠ *Campo dei Frari, San Polo 3030* ☎☎ *041/
5236728* ⊕ *www.scriba-net.com* Ⓥ *San Tomà.*

Ceramics

With so much attention concentrated on Venetian glass, it's not surprising that the city has never been known for its pottery. You can find replicas of 19th-century chocolate cups, usually cream-white and delicately gilded (not for daily use); pottery from Bassano, typically decorated with reliefs of fruit and vegetables; and some modern, handmade plates and mugs.

Angela Greco, a must for lovers of antique ceramics, has affordable items such as replicas of 19th-century Venetian chocolate cups. ⊠ *Campo Santa Maria del Giglio, San Marco 2433* ☎ *041/5234573* Ⓥ *Santa Maria del Giglio.*

★ **Fustat** is the workshop and showroom of Cinzia Cingolani, who creates exquisite handmade pottery. Her keen sense of color and unique forms make each piece a work of art. Raku demonstrations and ceramics courses are also offered. ⊠ *Campo Santa Margherita, Dorsoduro 2904* ☎ *041/5238504* Ⓥ *Ca' Rezzonico.*

Margherita Rossetto creates faience-style majolica on a white background, with figures of animals, flowers, and fruit designed in oxidized copper. ⊠ *Sotoportego della Siora Bettina, off Campo San Cassiano, Santa Croce 2345* ☎ *041/723120* Ⓥ *S. Stae or Rialto.*

Rigattieri sells pottery from Bassano, ranging from white plates with a lace border to serving bowls in the shapes of hens and geese to platters with asparagus in relief. They also have lanterns in blown glass that will give a Venetian touch to your garden or porch, as well as other objects in porcelain and silver. ⊠ *Calle dei Frati, between Campo Santo Stefano and Campo Sant'Angelo, San Marco 3532* ☎ *041/5231081* Ⓥ *Sant'Angelo.*

Clothing

Venetian streets are lined with so many designer stores and tiny, pricey boutiques that you may wonder how Venetians can afford to keep themselves clothed. (The truth is that most head to the mainland for the bulk of their shopping.) The best prices are to be had during the semi-annual sale periods, January 7 until mid-February and July to early September.

Agnona has incredibly warm cashmere and wool knitwear and winter coats—all in soft natural colors (creamy white and various shades of beige). If you're undecided what to buy the guy or gal who has everything, consider one of the luscious scarves. ⊠ *Calle Vallaresso, San Marco 1316* ☎ *041/5205733* ⊕ *www.agnona.com* Ⓥ *San Marco.*

Armani, in a rather grand space, delivers its superlative signature style and service—women's silk shirts are especially striking for quality, design, and price. Those waiting for the dressing rooms can rest on comfortable couches. ⊠ *Calle Goldoni, San Marco 4412* ☎ *041/5234758* Ⓥ *San Marco.*

Camiceria San Marco is the town's top custom shirtmaker, with a fine assortment of blouses and shirts. Only the finest fabrics are used (they can also be bought by the meter). Elegant pajamas, gowns, and ladies' dresses complete the scene. ⊠ *Calle Vallaresso, San Marco 1340* ☎ *041/5221432* Ⓥ *San Marco.*

Emporio Armani flaunts the famous stylist's casual line, with his eagle symbol emblazoned on just about everything. ⊠ *Calle dei Fabbri, San Marco 989* ☎ *041/5237808* Ⓥ *Rialto or San Marco.*

Fiorella Mancini Gallery is your best bet for original creations and the craziest looks in town. ⊠ *Campo Santo Stefano, San Marco 2806* ☎ *041/5209228* Ⓥ *Accademia or San Samuele.*

Kirikù is the place for trendy children's wear. Fashion lines include all the lastest names for boys and girls, from infants to early teens. The clothing is so spectacular, you may wish you were still a kid. ⊠ *Calle de la Madoneta, San Polo 1465* ☎ *041/2960619* Ⓥ *San Silvestro.*

La Coupole, with three shops a stone's throw from one another, offers an excellent selection of name-brand *alta moda* (high fashion) for men, women, and children. ⊠ *Calle Larga XXII Marzo, San Marco 2366* ☎ *041/5224243* ⊠ *Calle Larga XXII Marzo, San Marco 2414* ☎ *041/ 2960555* ⊠ *Calle Larga XXII Marzo, San Marco 2254* ☎ *041/5231273* Ⓥ *San Marco.*

Venice's **Prada** is one of the largest Prada stores in Italy. Suit up in clean-cut, modern-looking articles made out of high-tech materials, leather, or natural fibers. ⊠ *Campo San Moisè, San Marco 1469* ☎ *041/ 5283966* Ⓥ *San Marco.*

Florentine native **Roberto Cavalli** has a Venetian boutique as well; rock stars and rock-star wannabes need look no further. ⊠ *Calle Vallaresso, San Marco 1314* ☎ *041/5205733* Ⓥ *San Marco.*

Trussardi sells the clothing, shoes, and bags of its namesake Italian designer. ⊠ *Spadaria, San Marco 695* ☎ *041/5285757* Ⓥ *San Marco.*

MEN'S FASHIONS **Al Duca d'Aosta** stocks such classics as Burberry and Ralph Lauren. ⊠ *Merceria del Capitello, San Marco 4946* ☎ *041/5220733* Ⓥ *Rialto or San Marco.*

Ceriello is the only place in town selling Brioni suits. ⊠ *Campo SS. Filippo e Giacomo, San Marco 4275* ☎ *041/5222062* Ⓥ *San Zaccaria.*

Élite is the source for not-so-casual Italian outdoor wear as well as the quintessentially English Aquascutum coats that so many Italians favor. Silk ties and cashmere scarves complete the English country look. ⊠ *Calle Larga San Marco, San Marco 284* ☎ *041/5230145* Ⓥ *San Marco.*

La Bottega is the place to go if you like the comfort and style of leading Italian classic designers Cerruti and Ermenegildo Zegna. ⊠ *Merceria dell'Orologio, San Marco 223* ☎ *041/5225608* Ⓥ *Rialto or San Marco.*

Otello has a great selection of brightly colored waistcoats and bow ties—not for the conservative dresser. ⊠ *Calle delle Acque, San Marco 4989* ☎ *041/5223142* Ⓥ *Rialto.*

WOMEN'S FASHIONS **Al Duca d'Aosta,** no longer the Venetian bulwark of classy Italian fashion, now offers a selection of international prêt-à-porter on its two floors: Jil Sander, Rebecca Moses, Donna Karan, and Ralph Lauren. ⊠ *Merceria del Capitello, San Marco 4922* ☎ *041/5204079* Ⓥ *Rialto or San Marco.*

Arras sells exclusive scarves as well as a few blouses and jackets, all hand-woven in wool or silk. It also occasionally organizes weaving workshops. ⊠*Campiello Squellini, Dorsoduro 3234* ☎*041/5226460* Ⓥ*Ca' Rezzonico.*

Fodor'sChoice **Barbieri** has scarves and shawls for women in a myriad of colors as well ★ as textures, and you can also pick up fine men's ties while you're here. They've been successfully plying their wares since 1945. ⊠ *Ponte dei Greci, Castello 3403* ☎ *041/5228177* Ⓥ *San Zaccaria.*

Caberlotto has cornered the market on fabulous fur coats and hats. They sell interesting wool blazers—ideal for off-season walks about town—and pashmina shawls by Rosenda Arcioni Meer to wrap around your neck. They also have a complete line of luxurious cashmere clothing. ⊠ *Larga Mazzini, San Marco 5114* ☎ *041/5229242* Ⓥ *Rialto.*

Godi Fiorenza atelier is home to the creations of the Fiorenza sisters. Patrizia's designs in silk chiffon appear more sculpted than sewn—they're highly tailored pieces that both conceal and expose. Samatha is a jewelry designer and silversmith whose unique pieces compliment any outfit. ⊠ *Rio Terà San Paternian, San Marco 4261* ☎ *041/2410866* ⊕ *www.veneziart.com* Ⓥ *Rialto.*

Gucci sells shoes, bags, accessories, and clothes at three different locations in Venice. ⊠ *Calle Larga XXII Marzo, San Marco 2102* ☎ *041/2413968* ⊠ *Calle Valleresso, San Marco 1317* ☎ *041/5207484* ⊠ *Merceria dell'Orologio, San Marco 258* ☎ *041/5229119* Ⓥ *San Marco.*

Hermès offers its famous French foulards and accessories. ⊠ *Procuratie Vecchie, San Marco 127* ☎ *041/5210117* Ⓥ *San Marco.*

★ **Hibiscus** is an explosion of colors and textures. The clothing here is ethnic-chic and definitely original. Accessories are eye-catching as well. ⊠ *Calle dell'Olio, near the Rialto Market, San Polo 1060* ☎ *041/5208989* Ⓥ *Rialto.*

La Perla specializes in extremely elegant lingerie that's comfortable, too. ⊠ *Campo San Salvador, San Marco 4828* ☎ *041/5226459* Ⓥ *Rialto.*

Le Ragazze di Cima carries the best Italian brands of lingerie, from glossy silk to cotton lace. ⊠ *Strada Nova, near Ponte San Felice, Cannaregio 3683* ☎ *041/5234988* Ⓥ *Ca' d'Oro.*

Malo is recognized as one of Italy's highest-quality producers of cashmere garments. Its styles are tasteful and refined, designed and made to be worn for many years. ⊠ *Calle de le Ostreghe, San Marco 2359* ☎ *041/5232162* Ⓥ *San Marco or Santa Maria del Giglio.*

Missoni sells scarves and clothing made of wool, linen, or cotton, all rigorously knitted and dramatically colorful. ⊠ *Calle Vallaresso, San Marco 1312* ☎ *041/5205733* Ⓥ *San Marco.*

Valentino only sells clothing signed by the famous eponymous Roman designer. ⊠ *Salizzada San Moisè, San Marco 1473* ☎ *041/5205733* Ⓥ *San Marco.*

Valeria Bellinaso designs expensive, attractive straw hats, perfect for a romantic spring gondola ride. The store also features shawls full of character and foldable silk bags that are light as a feather yet large enough to pack for the weekend. ⊠ *Campo Sant'Aponal, San Polo 1226* ☎ *041/5223351* Ⓥ *San Silvestro.*

Zazù clothing and accessories have a definite Eastern feel. Owner Federica Zamboni is also a jewelry expert; ask to see her collection of antique Indian necklaces and earrings. ⊠ *Calle dei Saoneri, San Polo 2750* ☎ *041/715426* Ⓥ *San Tomà.*

Costumes & Accessories
Atelier Pietro Longhi rents and sells costumes inspired by 18th- and 19th-century models, with masks (for sale only) to match. Large sizes are available for both sexes. ⊠ *Rio Terrà dei Frari, San Polo 2604/b* ☎ *041/714478* Ⓥ *San Tomà.*

Flavia is a good address for historical costumes, either made-to-order or for rent; you can also rent tuxedos all year round. When you walk into the shop, ask for either Adriano or Susan, both of whom speak flawless English, to take you to the atelier nearby. ⊠ *Near Campo San Lio, Castello 6010* ☎ *041/2413200 or 041/5287429* Ⓥ *Rialto.*

Laboratorio Arte & Costume is the place if you are making your own costume and need some professional sartorial assistance. Monica Daniele will fix your problem as quickly as her sewing machine will go. In the meantime you can take a look at the assorted hats, bags, and vintage clothing. ⊠ *Calle del Scaleter, near Campo San Polo, San Polo 2235* ☎ *041/5246242* Ⓥ *San Tomà.*

At **Laboratorio Parrucche Carlotta,** wig maker Carlotta Carisi believes that at Carnevale details count, and her sensational creations are the ideal way to top off an elegant costume. The quality comes at a price (€230–€500), and credit cards are not accepted. ⊠ *Campo Widman, Cannaregio 5415* ☎ *041/5207571* Ⓥ *Ca' d'Oro.*

Nicolao Atelier is the largest costume-rental showroom in town, with nearly 7,000 choices ranging from the historical to the fantastic, including thematic costumes ideal for group masquerades. At the **tailor's workshop** (⊠ Calle del Bagatin, near Campo SS. Apostoli, Cannaregio 5565 Ⓥ Ca' d'Oro) you can see the costumes being made (by appointment only). ⊠ *Calle del Magazin, near Campo SS. Apostoli, Cannaregio 5590/a* ☎ *041/5209749* Ⓥ *Ca d'Oro.*

At **Venetia** the colorful, fanciful display window of 18th-century Venetian outfits often makes passersby stop to admire the mannequins. Less-glamorous medieval-style garments, masks, and accessories are kept behind the curtains inside. ⊠ *Frezzeria, San Marco 1286* ☎ *041/5224426* Ⓥ *San Marco.*

English-Language Books
Venice, unlike Rome or Florence, does not have an English-language bookstore. However, some places carry small selections of books in English. For newspapers and magazines in English, the best-stocked newsstands are in San Marco near the Museo Correr or at the foot of the Accademia bridge.

Ca' Foscarina, the bookstore of Università di Venezia Ca' Foscari, has a reasonable selection of books in English. Shelves teem with literature and history, but there's also a handful of travel books, as well as the latest best sellers. ⊠ *Campiello Squellini, Dorsoduro 3259* ☎ *041/ 5229602* Ⓥ *Ca' Rezzonico.*

Fantoni specializes in coffee-table books on art, architecture, photography, and design, mostly in Italian, but the beautiful illustrations speak for themselves. You'll find books in English on Venice and Italian food. ⊠ *Off Campo San Luca, San Marco 4119* ☎ *041/5220700* Ⓥ *Rialto or Sant'Angelo.*

Libreria Mondadori, Venice's answer to Barnes & Noble, is the biggest bookstore in town, with three floors of reading material. There is a large selection of English-language titles. ⊠ *Salizada San Mois, San Marco 1345* ☎ *041/5222193* ⊕ *www.libreriamondadorivenezia.it* Ⓥ *San Marco.*

Libreria San Pantalon sells children's books (some in English), small arts and crafts, and books on music and opera (in Italian). ⊠ *Crosera, also known as Calle Lunga San Pantalon, Dorsoduro 3950* ☎ *041/5224436* Ⓥ *San Tomà.*

Studium is a good stop for books in English, especially guidebooks and books on Venetian culture and food. It's also particularly strong on English-language fiction with Italian, mostly Venetian, settings and themes; in addition, it has a small but worthy collection of recent hardcover fiction. ⊠ *Calle della Canonica, San Marco 337/C* ☎ *041/5222382* Ⓥ *San Marco.*

Gifts

At **Angelo Dalla Venezia,** Signor Angelo crafts objects in wood including "eggs" for mending socks and knitwear. He also has hard-to-find wooden bobbins for lace making. ⊠ *Calle del Scaleter, off Campo San Polo, San Polo 2204* ☎ *041/721659* Ⓥ *San Tomà.*

Antichità Santomanco della Toffola sells Russian and English silver work, paintings, period glass and jewelry, and bric-a-brac. ⊠ *Ramo Secondo Corte Contarina, San Marco 1567* ☎ *041/5236643* Ⓥ *San Marco.*

Fusetti Diego Baruch has all manner of handmade Jewish handicrafts, including copies of antique menorahs, in glass, bronze, gold, silver, and mosaic. It's closed Saturday. ⊠ *Ghetto Vecchio, Cannaregio 1218* ☎ *041/720092* ⊕ *www.shalomvenice.com* Ⓥ *Ferrovia Santa Lucia.*

The workshop of **Giro Vago** produces trendy, up-to-the-minute handmade copper jewelry and leather bags. It's almost always open, but sometimes the owner is out of town at markets and fairs, so it's a good idea to call ahead. ⊠ *Ponte dei Miracoli, near the Chiesa dei Miracoli, Cannaregio 6019* ☎ *041/5225217* Ⓥ *Ca' d'Oro.*

Giuliana Longo is a hat shop that's been around since 1901; it has a special corner dedicated to accessories for antique cars. You could also use the leather goggles and helmets for skiing. ⊠ *Calle del Lovo, San Marco 4813* ☎ *041/5226454* Ⓥ *San Marco.*

Il Baule Blu specializes in *orsi artistici,* teddy bears to collect and treat with great care. All are painstakingly handmade and have articulated paws and glass eyes; when squeezed on their tummy, they can either grumble or play a carillon tune. Some are stark naked; others are dressed in old baby garments trimmed with lace and ribbons. They come in many sizes and colors. ⊠ *Calle Prima, off Campo San Tomà, San Polo 2916/ a* ☎ *041/719448* Ⓥ *San Tomà.*

La Stamperia del Ghetto sells black-and-white prints of the old Ghetto. It's closed Saturday. ⊠ *Calle del Ghetto Vecchio, Cannaregio 1185/a* ☎ *041/2750200* Ⓥ *San Marcuolo or Ponte delle Guglie.*

Madera combines traditional and contemporary design to create a mix of most interesting objects, including dishware, carved wooden bowls, jewelry, and ceramic pieces. They're the work of craftswoman and architect Francesca Meratti and a team of local and international artisans. ⊠ *Campo San Barnaba, Dorsoduro 2762* ☎ *041/5224181* ⊕ *www. maderavenezia.it* Ⓥ *Ca'Rezzonico.*

Perle Veneziane, two minutes from Piazza San Marco, fits the bill when you've got last-minute gifts to buy. There's an assortment of necklaces, faux-period Venetian glass jewelry, and loose modern beads, along with *murrine* (pour tops for olive oil bottles), and an assortment of other glass curios. ⊠ *Ponte della Canonica, San Marco 4308* ☎ *041/5289059* Ⓥ *San Marco.*

Signor Blum makes solid, large-piece jigsaw puzzles (painted or in natural wood colors) depicting animals, views of Venice, and trompe l'oeil scenes. Ideal toys for toddlers, the puzzles also look nice hanging on a wall. ⊠ *Fondamenta Gherardini, off Campo San Barnaba, Dorsoduro 2840* ☎ *041/5226367* ⊕ *www.signorblum.com* Ⓥ *Ca' Rezzonico.*

Glass

Glass, most of it made in Murano, is Venice's trademark product: you can't avoid encountering a mind-boggling variety of it in shop windows, often in kitschy displays. Take your time and be selective. If you want to make an investment, the important producers to remember are Barovier, Pauly, Poli, Seguso, Toso, and Venini. Freelance designers create pieces for more than just a single glasshouse: look for signatures and certificates of authentication. Bear in mind that the value of any piece— signature and shape apart—is also based on the number of colors, the presence of gold, and, in the case of goblets, the thinness of the glass. Prices are about the same all over, but be warned that some shops sell glass made in Taiwan. All shops will arrange for shipping.

Al Campanil specializes in replicas of antique Murano pieces and jewelry made with tiny glass Venetian beads. The jewelry designer here, Sabina, is a teacher at the International School of Glass on Murano. ⊠ *Calle Lunga Santa Maria Formosa, Castello 5184* ☎ *041/5235734* Ⓥ *Rialto.*

Antichità displays attractive period objects made with the tiniest Murano glass beads "woven" on linen threads, as well as more modern creations, such as stunning flowers and necklaces in the shape of snakes. The antique and the modern are hard to tell apart, as they are crafted with the same antique beads. You can also purchase small quantities of antique beads for making your own jewelry. ✉ *Calle della Toletta, Dorsoduro 1195* ☎ *041/5223159* Ⓥ *Accademia.*

Do Maghi means "two magicians," but in fact there's only one at work here, Hans Peter Neidhardt, who despite his name is a native Venetian and has been making glass since 1982. Though he's clearly cognizant of the Murano tradition, he injects humor and whimsy into his creations, from his goldfish in bowls to single long-stemmed red roses. ✉*Calle Dolfin, Cannaregio 5621* ☎ *041/5208535* ⊕ *www.evercom.it* Ⓥ *Ca' d'Oro.*

Domus has a selection of smaller objects and jewelry from the best glassworks. ✉ *Fondamenta dei Vetrai 82, Murano* ☎*041/739215* Ⓥ *Murano.*

Genninger Studio is the retail outlet for Leslie Ann Genninger, an American from Ohio who was the first woman to enter the male-dominated world of Murano master bead makers. She established her own line of jewelry, called Murano Class Act, in 1994 using period glass beads, and when she could no longer find antique beads she started designing her own. ✉ *Calle del Traghetto, off Campo San Barnaba, Dorsoduro 2793/a* ☎ *041/5225565* Ⓥ *Accademia.*

Gianfranco Penzo decorates Jewish ritual vessels in glass and makes commemorative plates. He takes special orders. ✉ *Campo del Ghetto Nuovo, Cannaregio 2895* ☎ *No phone* Ⓥ *Ferrovia Santa Lucia.*

L'Isola has chic, contemporary glassware signed by Carlo Moretti. ✉ *Campo San Moisè, San Marco 1468* ☎ *041/5231973* Ⓥ *San Marco.*

★ **Ma.Re** sells Salviati glass, as well as blown and solid glass. It also sells one-of-a-kind objects by leading glass artists. ✉ *Via XXII Marzo, San Marco 2088* ☎ *041/5231191* ☎ *041/5285745* ⊕ *www.mareglass.com* Ⓥ *San Marco.*

★ **Marina and Susanna Sent** have had their glass jewelry featured in *Vogue.* Vases and design pieces are also exceptional. ✉ *Campo San Vio, Dorsoduro 669* ☎ *041/5208136* Ⓥ *Accademia.*

Marina Barovier's Gallery has an excellent selection of collectible contemporary glass. She's the exclusive Venice dealer of famous glass artists such as Lino Tagliapietra, Dale Chihuly, and Ettore Sottsass. ✉ *Calle delle Botteghe, off Campo Santo Stefano, San Marco 3216* ☎ *041/5236748* ☎ *041/2447042* ⊕ *www.barovier.it* Ⓥ *San Samuele.*

Paropàmiso sells stunning Venetian glass beads and jewelry from all over the world. ✉ *Frezzeria, San Marco 1701* ☎ *041/5227120* Ⓥ *San Marco.*

Pauly has a large showroom in Piazza San Marco, with a wide array of glassware and chandeliers as well as glassblowing demonstrations. ✉ *Ala Napoleonica, San Marco 73–77* ☎ *041/5209899* ⊕ *www. paulyglassfactory.com* Ⓥ *San Marco.*

Tre Erre is a reliable and respected firm for both traditional and contemporary glass designs. ☒ *Piazza San Marco 79/b* ☎ *041/5201715* ⓥ *San Marco.*

Venini has been an institution since the 1930s, attracting some of the foremost names in glass design. ☒ *Piazzetta dei Leoncini, San Marco 314* ☎ *041/5224045* ⊕ *www.venini.it* ⓥ *San Marco.*

Gold, Wood & Metalwork

Venice's passion for glittering golden objects, which began with the decoration in the Basilica di San Marco and later spread into the finest noble homes, kept specialized gold artisans (called *doradori*) busy throughout the city's history. They still produce lovely cabinets, shelves, wall lamps, lanterns, candleholders, banisters, headboards, frames, and the like by applying gold leaf to wrought iron and carved wood. Numerous skilled silversmiths still cater to the faithful; in their workshops you'll find silver devotional icons of the Madonna della Salute and of the Madonna Nicopeia, traditionally hung in Venetian bedrooms. Most foundries have long since closed their doors, but you can still find top-quality brass pieces at Valese Fonditore.

Cornici Trevisanello has wonderful handcrafted frames, made of gold-leafed wood and inset with antique glass beads, mosaic tesserae, and small ceramic tiles. Either Byzantine or rich Renaissance in appearance, the more elaborate pieces are at their best when used to frame an old mirror. ☒ *Fondamenta Bragadin, off Campo San Vio* ☎ *041/5207779* ⓥ *Accademia.*

E. Pandian e Figli creates artisanal silver work, most notably icons of venerated Venetian Madonnas. ☒ *Campo Santa Maria Mater Domini, Santa Croce 2171* ☎ *041/5241398* ⓥ *S. Stae.*

Gilberto Penzo is the gondola expert in Venice. He creates scale models of gondolas and lagoon boats and real gondola *forcole* (oarlocks) in his *laboratorio* (workshop) nearby. (If the retail shop is closed, a sign posted on the door will explain how to find Signor Penzo.) When he's not busy sawing and sanding, Mr. Penzo writes historical and technical books about gondola building. Here you'll also find gondola model kits, a great gift for the boatbuilder in your life. ☒ *Calle Seconda dei Saoneri, San Polo 2681* ☎ *041/719372* ⊕ *www.veniceboats.com* ⓥ *San Tomà.*

Giora is a workshop and showroom for lamp shades, handmade ornaments, and gilded mirrors. ☒ *Campo Santa Maria Nova, Cannaregio 6043/b* ☎ *041/5286098* ⓥ *Rialto.*

Fodor'sChoice **Il Milione** has a small but refined collection of handmade Fortuny-style
★ lamps made with painted silk fabric. Prices are slightly better than Venetia Studium, and patterns are more original. ☒ *Campo Santa Marina, Castello 6025* ☎ *041/2410722* ⊕ *www.ilmilionevenezia.com* ⓥ *Rialto.*

Jonathan Ceolin makes traditional wrought-iron chandeliers, wall lamps, and Venetian lanterns, either plain black or gilded (like in the old days), in his tiny workshop near Campo Santa Maria Formosa. ☒ *Ponte Marcello off Campo Santa Marina, Castello 6106* ☎ *041/5200609* ⓥ *Rialto.*

Fodor'sChoice ★ **Le Forcole di Saverio Pastor** sells the sculpted walnut-wood oarlocks *(forcole)* used by Venetian rowers. Though their purpose is utilitarian, forcole are beautiful, custom-made objects that make for uniquely Venetian gifts or souvenirs. Saverio Pastor is one of the few remaining oar and *forcola* makers left in Venice. Bookmarks, postcards, and a small selection of books on Venetian boat works are also on sale. ⊠ *Fondamenta Soranzo, Dorsoduro 341* ☎ *041/5225699* ⊕ *www.forcole.com* Ⓥ *Salute.*

Luca Sumiti carries on the work of his father, Maurizio; this is a great place for traditional wrought-iron chandeliers and lamps. They come unadorned, gilded, or tastefully enameled in bright colors. Here you'll also find conspicuous, 5-foot-tall wooden sculptures of *mori veneziani* (Venetian Moors). ⊠ *Calle delle Bande, Castello 5274* ☎ *041/5205621* Ⓥ *Rialto or San Marco.*

At **Studio d'Arte Artù,** Tobia Morra practices wood and stone restoration. He also sells painted tables and chairs. ⊠ *Barbaria delle Tole, near Campo dei Santi Giovanni e Paolo, Castello 6656* ☎ *041/2777838* 🖷 *041/2777783* Ⓥ *Fondamenta Nove.*

Valese Fonditore has been creating works in brass, bronze, copper, and pewter since 1913. The various metals are cast into artistic handles, menorahs, Carnevale masks, and real gondola decorations (which make great paperweights, bookends, or shelf pieces). The coups de grâce are the brass chandeliers, exactly like those that hang in the Oval Office in the White House. The foundry is open every day, but things only get interesting when they pour. Call to arrange a visit. ⊠ *shop: Calle Fiubera, San Marco 793* ☎ *041/5227282* Ⓥ *San Marco* ⊠ *foundry: Cannaregio 3535, near Madonna dell'Orto* ☎ *041/720234* Ⓥ *San Marcuola.*

Jewelry

Venetians have always liked gold, and the city is packed with top-of-the-line jewelry stores, as well as more modest shops found outside the San Marco area, most notably around the Rialto district. One of the most typical pieces of inexpensive jewelry that you can buy is a *murrina*, a thin, round slice of colored glass (imagine a bunch of colored spaghetti firmly held together and sliced) encircled with gold and sold as pendants or earrings. The Museo del Vetro at Murano does a good job of explaining how they're made.

Bastianello has classic jewelry as well as pieces made with semiprecious stones. ⊠ *Via Due Aprile, off Campo San Bartolomio, San Marco 5042* ☎ *041/5226751* Ⓥ *Rialto.*

Bulgari is one of the best-known Italian jewelry designers. ⊠ *Calle Larga XXII Marzo, San Marco 2282* ☎ *041/2410553* ⊕ *www.bulgari. com* Ⓥ *San Marco.*

Cartier has watches and jewelry by the famous designer. ⊠ *Campo San Zulian, San Marco 606* ☎ *041/5222071* Ⓥ *San Marco.*

Elena carries pieces designed by world-famous firms such as Buccellati and Omega. ⊠ *Merceria dell'Orologio, San Marco 214-216* ☎ *041/ 5226540* Ⓥ *San Marco.*

Gualti makes creative jewelry in colored resin that looks as fragile as glass but is as strong and soft as rubber. Earrings take the shape of mysterious sea creatures—sea anemones or jellyfish—brooches look like fall leaves, and necklaces are reminiscent of Queen Elizabeth's ruffled collars. Silk shoes can be custom "garnished" with jewelry. ⊠ *Rio Terà Canal, near Campo Santa Margherita, Dorsoduro 3111* ☏ *041/5201731* ⊕ *www.gualti.it* Ⓥ *Ca' Rezzonico.*

Laberintho is a tiny *bottega* near Campo San Polo run by a team of young goldsmiths and jewelry designers specializing in inlaid stones. The work on display in their shop is exceptional, and they also create customized pieces. ⊠ *Calle del Scaleter, San Polo 2236* ☏ *041/710017* ⊕ *www. laberintho.it* Ⓥ *San Stae or San Tomà.*

★ At **Laboratorio Orafo Guido Carbonich,** Guido Carbonich's interest in Byzantine and Oriental art comes out in his unique jewels, made from silver, coral, and precious and semiprecious stones. Huge rings (meant for men more than for women), sensual serpentine bracelets, and earrings in the shape of Moors' heads are his strong points. For unique yet affordable bracelets and rings, this is *the* place. ⊠ *Ponte delle Guglie, Cannaregio 1297* ☏ *041/720461.*

Missiaglia is a landmark in Piazza San Marco, selling fabulous jewelry and a few silver accessories. ⊠ *Procuratie Vecchie, San Marco 125* ☏ *041/5224464* Ⓥ *San Marco.*

Nardi sells exquisite *moretti*—earrings and brooches in the shape of Moors' heads—studded with diamonds, rubies, or emeralds. ⊠ *Under Procuratie Nuove, San Marco 69* ☏ *041/5225733* ⊕ *www.nardi-venezia. com* Ⓥ *San Marco.*

Pomellato is a leading Italian designer, with shops also in Rome and Milan. ⊠ *Calle Seconda dell'Ascensione, San Marco 1298* ☏ *041/5201048* Ⓥ *San Marco.*

Salvadori specializes in watches but also has sparkling diamonds and other precious stones set in its own designs. ⊠ *Merceria San Salvador, San Marco 5022* ☏ *041/5230609* ⊕ *www.salvadori-venezia.com* Ⓥ *Rialto.*

Leather Goods

In Venice you'll find a good assortment of leather goods, especially shoes and ladies' bags. All shoe shops listed below are for both men and women. Unless stated otherwise, these shops tend to carry upmarket designer articles. For less fancy items, explore the areas of Rialto and Campo San Polo.

Bottega Veneta is a prestigious Italian chain selling bags typically made with intertwined strips of leather, plus smooth bags and elegant low-heeled shoes (for women only). ⊠ *Calle Vallaresso, San Marco 1337* ☏ *041/5228489* Ⓥ *San Marco.*

Daniela Ghezzo Segalin Venezia makes custom shoes, following in the footsteps of the shop's founder, Rolando Segalin. The team of artisans here can give life to your wildest shoe fantasy (see the gondola and cat-paw creations in the window) as well as make the most classic designs. ✉ *Calle dei Fuseri, San Marco 4365* ☎ *041/5222115* Ⓥ *San Marco.*

Emporium has traveling bags and suitcases by Alviero Martini, typically decorated with maps in light colors, and Trussardi accessories. ✉ *Spadaria, San Marco 670* ☎ *041/5235911* Ⓥ *San Marco.*

Fanny, run by a family of market stall sellers, combines good value, friendly service, and cheerful design. Leather and suede bags come in many different colors and sizes and can be embroidered; soft leather gloves are warm but not bulky. ✉ *Calle dei Saoneri, San Polo 2723* ☎ *041/ 5228266* Ⓥ *San Tomà.*

Fendi carries bags, shoes, and leather and fur winter clothing designed by the Fendi sisters. ✉ *Salizzada San Moisè, San Marco 1474* ☎ *041/ 2778528* Ⓥ *San Marco.*

Francis Model is a tiny workshop specializing in handmade leather bags in all shapes and sizes. The craftsmanship is exceptional; Bottega Veneta look-alikes at half the price. ✉ *Ruga Rialto, San Polo 773/a* ☎ *041/ 5212889* Ⓥ *San Silvestro.*

Fratelli Rossetti has bags, boots, leather jackets, and shoes of the Rossetti brothers—for once, the selection here is better than in the Rome shop. ✉ *Campo San Salvador, San Marco 4800* ☎ *041/5230571* Ⓥ *San Marco.*

Fodor'sChoice ★ Cobbler-designer **Giovanna Zanella Caeghera** creates whimsical contemporary footwear in a variety styles and colors. She was a student of the famous Venetian master cobbler Rolando Segalin. ✉ *Calle Carminati, Castello 5641* ☎ *041/5235500* Ⓥ *Rialto.*

Glamour is a tiny neighborhood shop with a sign proudly stating CHAUSSURE DE TENDENCE (trendy shoes). Vic Matiè and Silvia Vera are designers on the rise, who make attractive, reasonably priced footwear. ✉ *Ponte delle Guglie, Cannaregio 1298* ☎ *041/716246* Ⓥ *San Marcuola.*

Kalimala should not be missed if you are looking for soft leather bags, a perfect match for almost any outfit, or very pretty, inexpensive copper jewelry. ✉ *Salizzada San Lio, near Campo Santa Maria Formosa, Castello 5387* ☎ *041/5283596* ⊕ *www.kalimala.it* Ⓥ *Rialto.*

La Parigina is a Venetian institution, with five large windows in two neighboring shops. You'll find the house collection here, plus a dozen lesser-known designers such as Piero Guidi, Alexander Nicolette, and Testoni. ✉ *Merceria San Zulian, San Marco 727* ☎ *041/5226743* ✉ *Merceria San Zulian, San Marco 733* ☎ *041/523155* Ⓥ *San Marco.*

Louis Vuitton, the famous French maker of travel bags and boxes, has marvelous window displays. ✉ *Calle Larga dell'Ascensione, San Marco 1255* ☎ *041/5224500* Ⓥ *San Marco.*

★ The evening shoes at **Macri** are so glamorous and over-the-top that you might feel compelled to buy a pair and then create an occasion to wear them. René Caovilla's shoes are meant for showing off, not walking around town (especially in Venice). These high-heeled works of art are

VENETIAN MASKS REVEALED

IN THE TIME OF THE REPUBLIC, the mask trade was vibrant—Venetians wore masks all year to go about town incognito. Napoléon suppressed their use, a by-product of his effort to end Carnevale, and when Carnevale was revived in the late 1970s, mask making returned as well. Though many workshops use centuries-old techniques, none have been in business for more than 30 years.

A landmark date in the history of Venetian masks is 1436, when the mascareri (mask makers) founded their guild, but masks were popular well before then. Laws regulating their use appeared as early as 1268, intended to prevent wearers from carrying weapons and masked men disguised as women from entering convents to seduce nuns.

In the 18th century, masks started being used by actors playing the traditional roles of the commedia dell'arte. Inexpensive papier-mâché versions of these masks can be found everywhere. The character Arlecchino has the round face and surprised expression, Pantalone is the one with the curved nose and long mustache, and Pulcinella has the protruding nose.

The least expensive mask is the white Bauta, smooth and plain with a short, pointed nose intended to disguise the wearer's voice; in the 18th century it was commonly accompanied by a black three-cornered hat and a black cloak. The pretty Gnaga, which resembles a cat's face, was used by gay men to "meow" proposals to good-looking boys. The basic Moretta is a black oval with eyeholes. The Medico della Peste (the Plague Doctor) has a beaklike nose and glasses; during the plague of 1630 and 1631, doctors wore masks with herbs inside the nose intended to filter infected air and glasses to protect the eyes.

studded with sparkling bits of multicolored leather and crystal and decorated with feathers, flowers, and butterflies. Prices start at €350. ⊠ *Calle dell'Ascensione, San Marco 1296* ☎ *041/5231221* Ⓥ *San Marco.*

Mariani is one of Venice's best shoe shops, with very affordable prices. ⊠ *Calle del Teatro, off Campo San Luca, San Marco 4775* ☎ *041/ 5222967* Ⓥ *Rialto or Sant'Angelo.*

Masks

The boom in Venetian mask shops started only in the early 1980s, due to the resurrection of the Carnevale tradition. Since that time the mask business has grown so large that, while in the past it was enough to say visitors rarely left Venice without a piece of glass, now you must add "or a mask of some sort."

Scores of mask shops cluster around famous sights. You'll encounter countless sizes, colors, designs, and materials. Prices go up dramatically for leather and gilded masks, and you might come across expensive *pezzi da collezione* (collectors' items)—unique pieces whose casts are destroyed. In general, you'll get better deals direct from producers, so make a point to visit several of the largest workshops.

Ca' Macana, a large workshop offering lots of gilded creations, both traditional and new, is a must-see. ⊠ *Calle delle Botteghe, off Campo San Barnaba, Dorsoduro 3172* ☎ *041/2776142* ⊕ *www.camacana.com* Ⓥ *San Tomà.*

Il Canovaccio is a treasure trove of papier-mâché objects, panels, and masks designed for the theater stage. Mask-making classes are offered by appointment. ⊠ *Calle delle Bande, Castello 5369* ☎ *041/5210393* Ⓥ *Rialto or San Marco.*

FodorśChoice **Mondo Novo** is the "new world" of master craftsman Guerrino Lovato.
★ His masks have appeared in films by Stanley Kubrick, Kenneth Branagh, and Franco Zeffirelli. You can also admire his work in the recently restored Fenice opera house, where he designed the papier-mâché ceiling figures. ⊠ *Rio Terrà Canal, off Campo Santa Margherita, Dorsoduro 3063* ☎ *041/5287344* Ⓥ *Ca' Rezzonico.*

Family-owned and operated **Scheggi di Arlecchino** has windows full of the usual assortment of masks. What makes the shop distinctive are its masks inspired by the works of famous painters, including Picasso, Klimt, and de Chirico, to name but a few. ⊠ *Calle Longa Santa Maria Formosa, Castello 6185* ☎ *041/5225789* Ⓥ *Rialto.*

Tragicomica has a good selection, and it's a useful resource for information about Carnevale parties. It also turns out a limited number of Carnevale costumes and hats made from hand-printed cotton fabric. ⊠ *Calle dei Nomboli, off Campo San Tomà, San Polo 2800* ☎ *041/721102* ⊕ *www. tragicomica.it* Ⓥ *San Tomà.*

Paper Goods
Twenty years ago there was only one *legatoria* (bookbindery) in town. Nowadays you find dozens of them, usually next door to a mask shop. Hand-printed paper and ornate leather-bound diaries marked with St. Mark's lion are hot souvenirs, and the young folks who run these shops come out with new ideas all the time, the latest invention being a glass pen to dip into colored ink (with a matching ink bottle, of course)—a necessary desk accessory to go along with your handmade writing paper, wax, and seals.

Antica Legatoria Piazzesi, the oldest bookbindery in Venice, used to make wonderful hand-printed paper using carved wood *stampi* (plates for a press), which the artisans carefully filled with colored inks. The stampi are on exhibit in the shop, and the last of this gorgeous paper is slowly being sold off. Due to the high production costs, this kind of paper is now only made to order. Although Piazzesi is a charming little place of great historical value, you'll probably find a more attractive selection in the newer shops. ⊠ *Campo della Feltrina, near Campo Santa Maria del Giglio, San Marco 2511* ☎ *041/5221202* Ⓥ *Santa Maria del Giglio.*

Cartavenezia stands out in the showy panorama of Venetian bookbindery shops. From handmade writing paper to cards and paper objects, everything is white here, so you'll be kindly asked to wear gloves while browsing. ⊠ *Off Campo Santa Maria Mater Domini, Santa Croce 2125* ☎ *041/5241283* Ⓥ *San Stae.*

A WELL-WOVEN TRADITION

THE CRAFT OF WEAVING brocades, damasks, and velvets is still very much alive in Venice, with top manufacturers catering to royal courts, theaters, and the movie industry. At the time of the tourist boom in the 1980s, the descendants of underpaid embroiderers opened up fine lace and handicraft boutiques. Prices range from €120 per meter for old-style fabrics woven on power looms to €1,500 per meter for handmade silk velvets of unparalleled softness and beauty.

On the lower end of the price range are striking lampases, brocades, and damasks, which come in different floral and striped patterns as well as solid colors. Sometimes the fabrics are hand dyed after they've been woven to obtain mellow watercolor effects. It's always worth inquiring about sales for discontinued designs—you might want to give a Venetian look to your favorite reading chair.

Although most of the lace sold in town is machine made in China or Taiwan, you can still find something that more closely resembles the real thing in the best shops. Surprisingly, period lace (made between 1900 and 1940) is easier to find and less expensive than contemporary lace, even though the former is a finer product, made ad ago (with the needle), while the latter is made with thicker threads or a fusello (with the bobbin).

At the Museo del Merletto (Lace-Making Museum) in Burano you get an idea of how lace once looked. Despite the reopening of the Scuola del Merletto (Lace-Making School), lace makers no longer sell their creations in shops, but older ones might accept jobs on commission. The best way to contact them is to ask around in Burano (they object to having their names advertised), but consider that a 10-inch doily takes about 400 hours to make, and the price will show it.

Ebrû is a Turkish word meaning "cloudy" and refers to the technique of decorating paper with motifs that imitate veins of marble. Alberto Valese uses this method to decorate not only paper, but silk ties and paperweights as well. ⊠ *Campo Santo Stefano, San Marco 3471* ☎ *041/5238830* ⊕ *www.albertovalese-ebru.com* Ⓥ *Accademia.*

Il Pavone, whose name aptly translates as "The Peacock," offers a great selection of *coda di pavone,* a kind of paper with colors and patterns resembling peacock feathers. Little prints with grapes, cherubs, and more peacocks make inexpensive gifts. The artisans here are particularly proud of their hand-painted paper. ⊠ *Fondamenta Venier, Dorsoduro 721* ☎ *041/5234517* Ⓥ *Zattere.*

La Ricerca is the biggest bookbindery in town. Here you'll find marbled paper, writing paper, bookmarks, leather-bound diaries, notepads, photo albums, colored prints of Venice that can function as postcards, and even a medieval writing kit, complete with personalized wax seal. ⊠ *Ponte delle Ostreghe, near Campo Santa Maria del Giglio, San Marco 2431* ☎ *041/5212606* Ⓥ *Santa Maria del Giglio.*

Legatoria Polliero has the usual array of beautiful leather-bound blank books, desk accessories, and picture frames, at some of Venice's most reasonable prices. ⊠ *Campo dei Frari, San Polo 2995* ☎ *041/5285130* Ⓥ *San Tomà.*

Precious Fabrics, Lace & Linen

Annelie has some lace baby clothing and a small selection of night-gowns and towels. ⊠ *Calle Lunga San Barnaba, Dorsoduro 2748* ☎ *041/5203277* Ⓥ *San Tomà or Accademia.*

★ **Bevilacqua** has kept the weaving tradition alive in Venice since 1875, using 18th-century hand looms for its most precious creations. Its repertoire of 3,500 different patterns and designs yields a ready-to-sell selection of hundreds of brocades, Gobelins, damasks, velvets, taffetas, and satins. In the little shop near Piazza San Marco you'll also find tapestry, cushions, and braiding. Fabrics made by this prestigious firm have been used to decorate the Vatican, the Royal Palace of Stockholm, and the White House. ⊠ *Campo di Santa Maria del Giglio, San Marco 2520* ☎ *041/2410662* Ⓥ *Santa Maria del Giglio* ⊠ *Fondamenta della Canonica, San Marco 337/b* ☎ *041/5287581* ⊕ *www.luigi-bevilacqua.com* Ⓥ *San Marco* ⊠ *Factory: Campiello della Comare, Santa Croce 1320* ☎ *041/721576* ۞ *Visits by appointment only* Ⓥ *Riva di Biasio.*

★ **Capricci e Vanità,** a small shop near the Church of San Pantalon, is where owner and lace-lover Signora Giovanna Gamba sells her wonderful authentic Burano lace. She specializes in tablecloths and lingerie made on the bobbin as well as more rare and precious pieces made with a needle in the extralight Burano stitch. ⊠ *Calle San Pantalon, Dorsoduro 3744* ☎ *041/5231504* Ⓥ *San Tomà.*

Fortuny Tessuti Artistici is the original Fortuny textile factory, now converted into a showroom. Prices are over-the-top at €150 a meter, but it's worth a trip to see the extraordinary colors and textures of their hand-printed silks and velvets. ⊠ *Fondamenta San Biagio, Giudecca 805* ☎ *041/5224078* Ⓥ *Palanca.*

Frette sells high-quality sheets and bath towels—lace and embroidery are machine made, but the general effect is nonetheless luxurious and elegant. ⊠ *Calle Larga XXII Marzo, San Marco 2070/a* ☎ *041/5224914* Ⓥ *San Marco.*

G. Scarpa is an old-fashioned shop with no dressing room: you'll have to make do in a tiny corner behind a folding screen. Its top-of-the-line silk lace shirts, from €40 to €50, are well worth the trouble, as are the lace cooking aprons. ⊠ *Campo San Zaccaria, Castello 4683* ☎ *041/5287883* Ⓥ *San Zaccaria.*

You need to ring the bell to be admitted inside **Gaggio,** one of Venice's most prestigious fabric shops. Bedcovers, cushions, tapestry, and the like are available, plus a line of delightful small bags made in silk velvet with dark wooden frames. The colors of the fabric are never garish—they tend toward mellow autumn tones. ⊠ *Calle delle Botteghe, near Campo Santo Stefano, San Marco 3451* ☎ *041/5228574* ☏ *041/5228958* ⊕ *www.gaggio.it* Ⓥ *San Marco.*

Il Merletto, reached from Piazza San Marco by way of a private bridge, seems to make a point of putting on display just the low end of what's

BEAUTY BENEATH YOUR FEET

FLOORING MADE FROM cement and marble dust is another traditional Venetian craft. The tiny showroom of **Benito Turco** is one of the last surviving places where this centuries-old art is kept alive; it's worth seeking out for the dozens of different samples on display.

Turco started making terrazzi alla veneziana (Venetian floors) when still in primary school. One wall of his showroom is covered with samples of many different colors. The technique for making them all is basically the same: multicolored pebbles or marble particles are scattered onto a bed of cement dyed with colored marble dust; the floor is pressed flat and left to dry, then polished and waxed. Prices are not as high as you might expect, and the logistics of getting a floor shipped are difficult but not impossible. For most visitors, though, this is a place to witness a uniquely Venetian craft. ⊠ Calle della Lacca, San Polo 2458 ☎ 041/5240999 Ⓥ San Tomà.

---

sold upstairs. To see the difference, ask for the authentic, handmade lace kept in the drawers behind the counter. This is the place to arrange lace-making demonstrations in Venice. ⊠ *Sotoportego del Cavalletto, under the Procuratie Vecchie, Piazza San Marco 95–96* ☎ *041/5208406* Ⓥ *San Marco.*

Jesurum is Venice's top name for lace and embroidered linen. Here you'll find an assortment of dreamy gowns and nightshirts, sheets, bedcovers, and towels ready to buy, or you can order yours custom-made. ⊠ *Fondamenta della Sensa, Cannaregio 3219* ☎ *041/5242540* ⊕ *www.jesurum.it* Ⓥ *Sant'Alvise.*

La Bottega di Cenerentola, or "Cinderella's Workshop," creates unique handmade lamp shades out of silk, old lace, and real parchment, embroidered and decorated with gold braids and cotton or silk trim. The pieces on display are a perfect match for country- and antique-style furniture. The owner, Lidiana Vallongo, will be happy to discuss special orders. ⊠ *Calle dei Saoneri, San Polo 2718/a* ☎ *041/5232006* ⊕ *www.cenerentola.net* Ⓥ *San Tomà.*

La Fenice Atelier sells attractive lace nightdresses and handwoven bath towels at affordable prices. ⊠ *Calle dei Frati, down the bridge on Campo Sant'Angelo, San Marco 3537* ☎ *041/5230578* Ⓥ *Sant'Angelo.*

Lorenzo Rubelli offers the same sumptuous brocades, damasks, and cut velvets used by the world's most prestigious decorators. ⊠ *Campiello del Teatro, San Marco 3877* ☎ *041/5236110* Ⓥ *Sant'Angelo.*

Pina Bonzio offers the usual array of inexpensive lace souvenirs, from handkerchiefs and baggy blouses to lovely bookmarks; the draw is that, despite the proximity to Piazza San Marco, the prices can't be beat. ⊠ *Merceria dell'Orologio, San Marco 298* ☎ *041/5226791* Ⓥ *San Marco.*

Trois is one of those humble little shops often overlooked by passersby. It stocks original "Tessuti Artistici Fortuny," the handwoven and hand-dyed fabrics "invented" by Mariano Fortuny, which are great for curtains, bedspreads, cushions, and more. The stunningly vibrant colors of these fabrics are all obtained from natural pigments. ⊠ *Campo San Maurizio, San Marco 2666* ☎ *041/5222905* Ⓥ *San Marco.*

FodorśChoice ★ **Venetia Studium** creates exclusive velvet fabrics in a splendid array of colors and turns them into scarves, bags, stoles, and pillows of various sizes. They also make the famous pleated Fortuny dress and Fortuny lamps. ⊠ *Calle Larga XXII Marzo, San Marco 2403* ☎ *041/5229281* ⊠ *Merceria San Zulian, San Marco 723* ☎ *041/5229859* Ⓥ *San Marco.*

Southern Veneto

Padua, Verona, Vicenza, Lake Garda

7

WORD OF MOUTH

"To me, Padua, even more than Venice, is evocative of the 'old' Italy. In the old city (città vecchia) are many wonderful places. The maze of tiny streets is just the thing for wandering around and getting lost."

—Wayne

"Verona and Vicenza are both stunningly beautiful cities that we liked very much. Vicenza is smaller and seems to have more green space. It's also less touristy. Verona gives you the 'Romeo and Juliet' thing. Although I personally didn't find any one attraction in Verona that impressive, the city as a whole stole my heart."

—Jocelyn P

Updated by
Robin
Goldstein

IN THE TERRITORY STRETCHING WEST TO VERONA and south as far as Rovigo, the winged lion of St. Mark, emblem of Venice, is very much in evidence, emblazoned on palazzos and standing atop lofty columns. It's a symbol of the strong influence Venice has had over the region: the architecture, art, and way of life all bask in the reflected splendor of La Serenissima, and much of the pleasure of exploring this area comes from discovering the individual variations on the Venetian theme, conferring special charm on the towns you visit.

Long before Venice came to dominate, Ezzelino III da Romano (1194–1259), a larger-than-life scourge who was excommunicated by Pope Innocent IV and even had a crusade launched against him, laid claim to as much land as he could. He seized the cities of Verona, Padua, Este, Montagnana, and Monselice and their surrounding territory. After his fall, powerful families such as the Carrara in Padua and the della Scala (Scaligeri) from Verona vied with each other during the 14th century to annex these towns.

When not destroying each other, the noble families of the region bestowed on their progeny a rich legacy of architectural and artistic jewels, infusing the area with an opulence that is today the hallmark of Padua, Vicenza, and Verona. This trio of cities, though sharing the Venetian influence, has a diverse and multifaceted appeal, their individual characters well defined long before Venice arrived on the scene. Padua had established itself as a city-state during the 12th century. Its university, founded in 1222, counted Galileo among its teachers and drew the poets Dante and Petrarch into its orbit. In the 14th century, the cultural flowering found its most sublime expression in the frescoes of Giotto, a landmark in the history of art, and later in the painters and sculptors of the Renaissance, most notably Donatello and Mantegna.

Vicenza lays claim to a scion who was to have a predominant influence on the course of Western architecture, Andrea di Pietro della Gondola—better known as Palladio, whose mark can be seen in practically every capitol in the United States. Not only did Palladio create new buildings, he grafted his classically inspired designs on the existing Gothic palazzos; his spirit prevails also in numerous villas in the surrounding countryside. In Verona, on the other hand, there's no escaping a much earlier epoch, for this was once a city of ancient Rome, and its awe-inspiring arena is the third largest in Italy. Here "circuses" still astound audiences, though the spectacles have moved on from the gladiatorial to the operatic, in the form of large-scale productions complete with animals. Among the performances, there is an annual Shakespeare Festival—one more reminder that this is the home of that most fabled of love stories, *Romeo and Juliet*.

In the hinterland, redbrick castles and fortifications with fishtail or square crenellations bear testimony to the struggles of the medieval warring families. A better example would be hard to find than walled Montagnana—a town that changed hands 13 times in the course of its history—or Monselice, with its beautifully restored castle. Once Venice had established its presence in the region, a time of relative peace en-

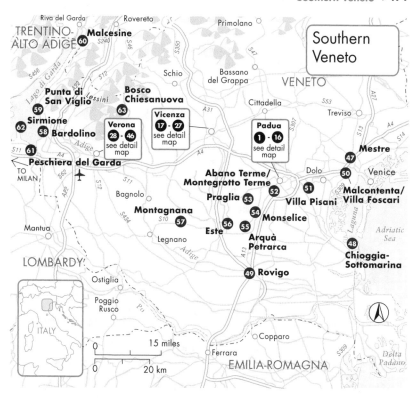

sued, exquisitely marked by the blooming of Venetian palazzos and the works of master artists. The three Ts—Titian, Tintoretto, and Tiepolo—have all contributed to the impressive heritage of the zone. These sophisticated traces of art contrast with the simpler delights of the Euganean Hills, south of Padua, where the unspoiled medieval village of Arquà Petrarca seems to exist in a separate dimension, unruffled by time's encroachments. A similar sense of peace reigns in and around Lake Garda, about which the German poet Goethe wrote, "I could have reached Verona by nightfall, but only a few steps away was this spectacular exhibition of nature, this stupendous panorama known as Lake Garda, and I simply could not tear myself away." Similar sentiments have been echoed by throngs of newcomers, who have added the joys of windsurfing and other lake sports to the delights of walking and taking in grand mountain scenery.

When Venetians took vacations, they made sure they did it in style, their retreats designed by the best architects and decorated by the best painters of the day. Palladio was first choice for the job, and his work is nobly illustrated by the superlative Villa La Rotonda, near Vicenza, and at Villa Foscari, near Venice. For two centuries, villas in the style of the master sprouted up in prime locations, such as along the Brenta Canal. Many of these are now in private hands, but some open to the public. For requirements of the flesh, Abano Terme and Montegrotto Terme provide an excuse for pampering the body and rolling in mud, while the bustling fishing port of Chioggia is *the* place to savor fish.

Exploring Southern Veneto

Lake Garda and the trio of prominent towns—Padua, Verona, and Vicenza—are easily and quickly reached from Venice by the A4 autostrada and the parallel S11 running west as far as Milan. Public transport is frequent and fast, with regular services from Verona, the jumping-off point for buses and trains to Peschiera and buses to Sirmione, both on Lake Garda's southern shore. The S249 hugs the lake's eastern shore and leads to Garda and Malcesine.

About the Restaurants & Hotels

In the main cities of the Veneto region, restaurants are generally moderately priced. In smaller towns and in the countryside you can find some real bargains.

The area around Venice has been playing host to visitors for centuries, and the result is a range of comfortable accommodations at every price. As with dining, common sense should tell you that the slightly out-of-the-way small hotel will cost you less than its counterpart in a bigger town, especially when trade fairs are underway (a common occurrence). Expect to pay more as you approach Venice, since many of the mainland towns absorb the overflow when Venice becomes crowded, at Carnevale time and throughout the summer. However, at no time do prices approach those in Venice proper. Padua, in fact, can be used in dire circumstances as a base for day trips to Venice. Touristy Sirmione is an expensive place all around, and prices in the Lake Garda area as much as double during high season.

Verona has a free hotel booking service through **Cooperativa Albergatori Veronesi** (⊠ Via Patuzzi 5, 37100 ☎ 045/8009844 ⊟ 045/8009372). Vicenza's **Consorzio di Promozione Turistica** (⊠ Via Fermi 34, 36100 ☎ 0444/964380) can provide information about hotel and restaurant discounts.

WHAT IT COSTS In euros				
$$$$	**$$$**	**$$**	**$**	**¢**
RESTAURANTS over €22	€17–€22	€12–€17	€7–€12	under €7
HOTELS over €210	€160–€210	€110–€160	€60–€110	under €60

Restaurant prices are for a second course (secondo piatto). Hotel prices are for two people in a standard double room in high season, including tax and service.

When to Go

To get the most out of your stay, consider coming in May, June, July, or September, when weather conditions are most comfortable and opera and theater are performed outdoors. Spring, the season of blossom, is always enchanting, and Lake Garda is especially enticing during the summer months, when there's always a cooling breeze blowing from the mountains and the water is comfortably warm. Summer also sees crowds, however, and you won't be alone in such places as Verona and Sirmione during this period.

You'll have more elbow room during winter, but the sights will have shorter opening hours, and hotels are often closed in November and February. This is also the season for fog, and you'll certainly find snow on the higher ground. Visitors in February or March, however, will encounter Carnevale shenanigans—Carnevale is not only the preserve of Venice—and you could find yourself sitting next to bearded nuns on the train, being served cappuccino by a long-tailed cat in the local bar, or smiling at a clown dining with a mouse at the next table.

PADUA

Bustling with bicycles and lined with frescoes, Padua has long been one of the major cultural centers in northern Italy. It's home to the peninsula's—and the world's—second-oldest university, founded in 1222, which attracted the likes of Dante (1265–1321), Petrarch (1304–74), and Galileo Galilei (1564–1642), thus earning the city the sobriquet *La Dotta* (The Learned). Padua's Basilica di Sant'Antonio, begun not long after the university in 1234, is dedicated to St. Anthony, the patron saint of lost and found objects, and attracts grateful pilgrims in droves, especially on his feast day, June 13. Three great artists—Giotto (1266–1337), Donatello (circa 1386–1466), and Mantegna (1431–1506)—left great works here, with Giotto's Scrovegni chapel one of the best-known, and most meticulously preserved, works of art in the country.

Today, cycle-happy students still rule the roost, flavoring every aspect of local culture. Don't be surprised if you spot a *laurea* (graduation) ceremony marked by laurel leaves, mocking lullabies, and X-rated caricatures.

Exploring Padua

The train station lies a few minutes' walk north of the main thoroughfare, Corso del Popolo, the bus station a few minutes east. The *corso* leads south through the walls into the heart of the city and the oval square, Prato della Valle, changing its name as it goes to Corso Garibaldi and, where it meets the university, to Via VIII Febbraio. The core of the city spreads north and west from here and includes the central squares of Piazza delle Frutte and Piazza delle Erbe. To the south, the Basilica di Sant'Antonio (Il Santo) and the Prato della Valle are within easy walking distance.

If you arrive by car, leave your vehicle in one of the parking lots on the outskirts or at your hotel, as much of the center is given over to pedestrians. Coming to Padua by autostrada, exit at Padova Est; there's a parking area in Via Tommaseo. Coming from Padova Ovest or Sud, park in Prato della Valle. Buses 3, 8, 10, and 12 go to the center. If you're staying in a central hotel, expect to pay to park.

The **Padova Card,** which costs €15, is valid for 48 hours—or the whole weekend if you get it on Friday—and gets you into most of Padua's sights. If you're going to do the circuit, it represents a significant cost savings; the Scrovegni Chapel alone normally costs €12, but with the Padova Card, you need only pay a €1 reservation fee. It's available from the tourist office or any of the sights it covers.

The Main Attractions

★ ⓫ **Basilica di Sant'Antonio.** Thousands of worshippers throng to Il Santo, a cluster of Byzantine domes and slender, minaretlike towers that gives this huge basilica an Asian-inspired style reminiscent of San Marco in Venice. The interior is sumptuous, too, with marble reliefs by Tullio Lombardo (1455–1532), the greatest in a talented family of marble carvers who decorated many churches in the area, among them Venice's Santa Maria dei Miracoli.

The artistic highlights here, however, bear Donatello's name; the 15th-century Florentine master did the remarkable series of bronze reliefs illustrating the life of St. Anthony—whose feast day, June 13, draws pilgrims from all over Europe—as well as the bronze statues of the Madonna, the saints on the high altar, and the bronze crucifix. The **Cappella del Santo** was built to house the green marble tomb of the saint and is now the object of votive offerings. Reconstructed in the 16th century, it shows Italian High Renaissance at its best. The **Cappella del Tesoro** (☉ Daily 8–noon and 2:30–7) holds the not-so-pristine tongue of the saint in a 15th-century reliquary.

In front of the church is Donatello's powerful statue of the *condottiere* (mercenary general) Erasmo da Narni, known by the nickname Gattamelata. It was cast in bronze—a monumental technical achievement in 1453—and had an enormous influence on the development of Italian Renaissance sculpture. There are multimedia presentations about the life of St. Anthony and the construction of the church from 9–12:30 and 2:30–6. ✉ *Piazza del Santo* ☎ *049/8789722* ⊕ *www.santantonio.org* ☉ *Daily 6:30 AM–7 PM.*

❶ **Cappella degli Scrovegni** (Scrovegni Chapel). Padua's greatest artistic treasure is probably the second-most-famous chapel in Italy, surpassed only by the Vatican's Sistine. It was erected in the 13th century by a wealthy Paduan, Enrico Scrovegno, to atone for the usury of his deceased father, Reginaldo, as chronicled in Dante's *Inferno*. (The fresco above the door, which depicts the dedication of the chapel, shows Enrico dressed in violet, the color of penitence.)

FodorśChoice
★

Scrovegno called on Giotto to decorate the interior, a task that occupied the great artist and his helpers from 1303 to 1305. They created a magnificent fresco cycle, arranged in typical medieval comic-strip fashion, illustrating the lives of Mary and Christ, allegorical forms of the seven deadly sins and the seven virtues, and the Last Judgment. The realism in these frescoes—which include the first blue skies in Western painting—was revolutionary. Today, in glorious restoration, Giotto's starry firmament glows in splashes of brilliant color.

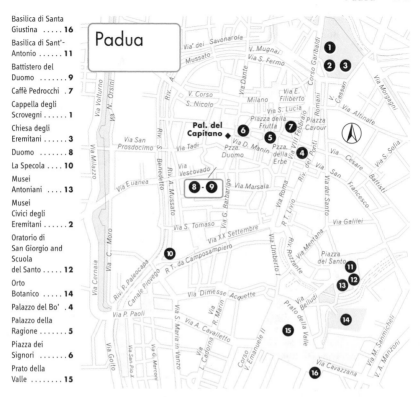

You get a sense of the esteem the frescoes are held in by the regimented way you go about seeing them. You're required to make a reservation, which you can book by phone or on the Web, ideally at least a couple of days in advance. (If you haven't planned ahead, you can usually make a reservation on the spot, but you might have to wait awhile to get in.) In order to preserve the art, doors are opened only once every 15 minutes. Twenty-five visitors at a time spend 15 minutes in an acclimatization room before being allowed in a for 15-minute chapel visit. You can see fresco details as part of a virtual tour at Museo Civico Eremitani. ⊠ *Piazza Eremitani 8* ☎ *49/2010020 for reservations* ⊕ *www.cappelladegliscrovegni.it* ⊑ *€12 including Musei Civici, or €1 with Padova Card* ⊙ *Daily 9 AM–10 PM.*

★ **2 Musei Civici degli Eremitani** (Civic Museum). The museum is housed in what used to be the monastery of the church and divided into three parts. The ground floor houses the **archaeological section** containing Etruscan, Roman, Egyptian, Greek, and early Christian objects. The **Pinacoteca** (art gallery) upstairs displays the work of Veneto masters from the 14th through 19th centuries and some Flemish and Dutch painters. Notable are the Giotto Crucifix, which was once in the Scrovegni chapel, the *Heavenly Host in Battle* by Guariento (1338–1368 or 1379), and the *Portrait of a Young Senator* by Bellini (1432–1516). The corridors are hung with 19th- and 20th-century prints and paintings, and the **Museo Bottacin** holds an important collection of more than 50,000 coins and medals. ⊠ *Piazza Eremitani 10* ☎ *049/8204551* 🖾 *Church free; museum €10, €12 with Scrovegni chapel, or Padova Card* ⊙ *Daily 9–7.*

❺ Palazzo della Ragione. Also known as Il Salone, this spectacular, arcaded
Fodor'sChoice palace, which divides the Piazza delle Frutte and Piazza delle Erbe, is
★ the most memorable architectural image of the city. It was built in the Middle Ages as the seat of Padua's parliament. Today its street-level arcades shelter shops and cafés. The **Salone** on the upper level is, at 85 feet high, one of the largest and most architecturally pleasing halls in Italy, covered by a wooden roof and frescoed with religious and astrological subjects. Inside, pride of place is taken by an enormous wooden horse, a replica of the bronze steed in Donatello's equestrian statue of Gattamelata and originally built for a tournament held in the Piazza dei Signori in 1446. In the northeast corner is the Railing Stone, where debtors had to sit three times repeating *"Cedo bonis"* (I give up all worldly goods) before leaving the city. ⊠ *Piazza della Ragione, enter from Via VIII Febbraio* ☎ *049/8205006* 🖾 *€8 or Padova Card* ⊙ *Tues.–Sun. 9–7.*

Also Worth Seeing

⑯ Basilica di Santa Giustina. Two red marble griffins flank the steps of the unclad brick facade of this church, whose eight cupolas are reminiscent of Sant'Antonio's basilica. Inside are finely carved and inlaid 15th-century choir stalls and a colossal altarpiece, *The Martyrdom of St. Justina*, by Veronese (1528–88). Among the monuments are the sarcophagus that once contained the body of St. Luke, and in the Chapel of St. Luke, the resting place of Elena Piscopia, the first woman to receive a university degree. ⊠ *Prato della Valle* ☎ *049/8220411* ⊙ *Weekdays 7:30–noon and 3:30–8, Sun. 7:30–12:40 and 3:45–8.*

❾ Battistero del Duomo. The often overlooked 12th-century baptistry contains mid-1370s frescoes depicting scenes from the Book of Genesis. They're the greatest work of Giusto de' Menabuoi, who further developed Giotto's style of depicting human figures naturally, using perspective and realistic lighting. The building is a refreshingly cool retreat from the city. ⊠ *Piazza del Duomo* ☎ *049/656914* 🖾 *€2.50 or Padova Card* ⊙ *Daily 10–6.*

❼ Caffè Pedrocchi. This neoclassical building was designed by Giuseppe Jappelli (1753–1852) in 1831 for Antonio Pedrocchi, called by Stendhal "the best caterer in Italy." Take the outside staircase up one flight to the *piano nobile* (first floor) for a delightful series of rooms decorated in a melee of antique styles—Etruscan, Roman, Egyptian, Renaissance—not to mention themed rooms such as the Rossini Room and the Herculaneum Room. The downstairs is a coffee shop and informal restaurant with periodic art exhibits. ⊠ *Piazzetta Pedrocchi* ☎ *049/8205007* 🖾 *€3 or Padova Card* ⊙ *Daily 9:30–12:30 and 3:30–6.*

❸ Chiesa degli Eremitani. The 13th-century church contains some fragments of frescoes—most were destroyed by the Allied bombing of 1944—by Andrea Mantegna, the brilliant locally born artist. In the vestibule is a bronze copy of a *Pietà* by Antonio Canova (1757–1822).

✉ *Piazza Eremitani 10* ☎ *049/8756410* 💷 *Free* 🕙 *Mon.–Sat. 8:15–6:15, Sun. 10–1 and 4:15–7.*

8 Duomo. Padua's cathedral was designed by a pupil of Michelangelo. The 17th- to 18th-century interior contains many paintings dating from the same era, as well as some 14th-century pieces in the sacristy such as *Virgin and Child* and *Life of St. Sebastian,* both by Nicolò Semitecolo (1353–70). ✉ *Piazza del Duomo* ☎ *049/662814* 🕙 *Mon.–Sat. 7:30–noon and 3:30–7:30, Sun. 8–1 and 3:30–8:30.*

13 Musei Antoniani. To mark the 800th anniversary of the birth of St. Anthony in 1195, new galleries were opened in 1995 on the first floor of the church cloister building, with 300 exhibits relating to the image of the saint and of the basilica. ✉ *Piazza del Santo* ☎ *049/8225656* 💷 *€2.50* 🕙 *Daily 9–1 and 2:30–6:30.*

12 Oratorio di San Giorgio and Scuola del Santo. The San Giorgio Oratory and adjoining gallery are next to the Basilica di Sant'Antonio. The Romanesque oratory served as a prison in Napoleonic times. It displays frescoes dating from 1384 by two pupils of Giotto, Altichiero di Zevio and Jacopo Avanzo, that illustrate the lives of St. George, Catherine of Alexandria, and St. Lucy. The scuola, up a pretty stairway on the first floor, came into being after the canonization of St. Anthony in 1231; the present building was completed in 1504. The walls of the upper part are lined with frescoes, four of which are attributed to Titian. They depict the life and work of St. Anthony, including the saint reattaching the foot of a young man and bringing back to life a child who had fallen into a cauldron of boiling water. ✉ *Piazza del Santo* ☎ *049/8755235* ⊕ *www.arciconfraternitasantantonio.org* 💷 *€2* 🕙 *Apr.–Sept., daily 9–12:30 and 2:30–7; Oct.–Mar., daily 9–12:30 and 2:30–5.*

14 Orto Botanico. The botanic garden was founded in 1545 by order of the Venetian Republic to supply the university with medicinal plants, and is one of the few Renaissance gardens to retain its original layout. The so-called Palm of St. Peter, planted in 1585, still stands, protected in its private little greenhouse. It was admired by Goethe (1749–1832) on his travels through Italy in 1786. Take time to wander through interesting hothouses, beds of plants that were first introduced to Italy in this garden, and the arboretum. ✉ *Via Orto Botanico 15, a few steps south of the basilica* ☎ *049/8272119* ⊕ *www.ortobotanico.unipd.it* 💷 *€4 or Padova Card* 🕙 *Apr.–Oct., daily 9–1 and 3–6; Nov.–Mar., Mon.–Sat. 9–1.*

4 Palazzo del Bo'. The 16th-century palace (with an18th-century facade) is the main building of the **Università di Padova,** founded in 1222. The palace is named after the Osteria del Bo' (*bo'* is Italian for "ox"), an inn that once stood on the site. The exquisite and perfectly proportioned anatomy theater was built in 1594. William Harvey (1578–1657), famous for his theory of the circulation of the blood, took a degree here in 1602, at the same time as Galileo was teaching. Galileo's *cattedra* (lectern) is still on display. In the courtyard there's a statue of Elena Lucrezia Cornaro Piscopia (1646–84), who, in 1678, was the first woman in the world to be confirmed with a university degree. If you're superstitious, don't jump over the chain in this courtyard, as, according to students, it will bring you bad luck. ⊠ *Via VIII Febbraio* ☎ *049/ 8273044* 🖾 *€3* ⊘ *Guided visits only, Mon., Wed., and Fri. 3:15, 4:15, and 5:15; Tues., Thurs., and Sat. 9:15 AM, 10:15 AM, and 11:15 AM.*

❻ **Piazza dei Signori.** The large, sequestered square exhibits examples of 15th- and 16th-century buildings. On the west side the **Palazzo del Capitanio** sports an impressive **Torre dell'Orologio,** which has a fine astronomical clock dating from 1344.

⓯ **Prato della Valle.** Laid out in 1775, this immense space with a central oval park is surrounded by a canal along which stand 78 statues of local worthies. It hosts a general market on Saturday and an antiques market on the third Sunday of the month.

Off the Beaten Path

❿ **La Specola.** At this small astronomical museum, open only on weekends for guided tours, you can see instruments used by Galileo himself, as well as more up-to-date tools for observing the heavens. ⊠ *Vicolo dell'Osservatorio 5* ☎ *049/8293469* ⊕ *www.pd.astro.it/museo-laspecola* 🖾 *€7. Tickets must be purchased in advance from S. Michele Oratory (50 yards from La Specola) Tues.–Fri. 10 AM–1 PM, weekends 3–6 PM* ⊘ *Guided visits only, Oct.–Apr., Sat. at 11 and 4, Sun. at 4; May–Sept., Sat. at 11 and 6, Sun. at 6.*

Where to Stay & Eat

★ **$$$$** ✕ **Antico Brolo.** Housed in a 16th-century building not far from central Piazza dei Signori, charming Antico Brolo is one of the best restaurants in town. The outdoor area has a simpler menu, while the indoor restaurant is more elaborate. Pastas are uniformly excellent; seasonal specialties are prepared with flair and might include starters like tiny flans with wild mushrooms and herbs or fresh pasta dressed with zucchini flowers. The wine list doesn't disappoint. ⊠ *Corso Milano 22* ☎ *049/ 664555* ⊕ *www.anticobrolo.it* 🖃 *AE, DC, MC, V* ⊘ *No lunch Mon.*

$$$ ✕ **La Vecchia Enoteca.** The ceiling is mirrored, the shelves are filled with books and wine, the silver service on which your meal arrives once belonged to a shipping line, and the flower displays are extravagant. In this luxurious ambience enjoy *branzino in crosta di patate* (sea bass with a potato crust) or beef with rosemary and balsamic vinegar, followed by a homemade dessert such as *crema catalana* (cream caramel). Reservations are advised. ⊠ *Via Santi Martino e Solferino 32* ☎ *049/8752856* 🖃 *MC, V* ⊘ *Closed Sun. and 1st 3 wks in Aug. No lunch Mon.*

$$ ✕ **Bastioni del Moro.** The genial owner devises his own recipes according to season, with vegetarians and calorie watchers in mind, although carnivores are well cared for, too. Gnocchi, eggplant, artichokes, and pumpkin all appear on the menu in different guises. For starters, you could try *tagliolini gratinati con prosciutto* (thin ribbons of egg noodles with prosciutto) or *gnocchi con capesante e porcini* (gnocchi with scallops and porcini mushrooms). The garden is put to good use in summer. Reservations are recommended. ⊠ *Via Pilade Bronzetti 18* ☎ *049/ 8710006* ⊕ *www.bastionidelmoro.it* 🖃 *AE, DC, MC, V* ⊘ *Closed Sun. and 2 wks in Aug.*

ON THE MENU

SEAFOOD IS THE SPECIALTY *along the coast, naturally—there's almost an embarrassment of choices. Both saltwater fish (sea bass, gilthead, sardines, eel) and freshwater (carp, trout, tench) are abundant, as are crustaceans. Inland, you'll encounter delicate and creamy risotto, radicchio di Treviso, and asparagus, all of which can accompany hearty grilled meat. (Don't be surprised to find horse meat on the menu and shops devoted to its sale.)*

Jewish influence has made its mark in such dishes as risi e bisi (rice and peas), sarde in saor (fried sardines marinated in vinegar, onions, pine nuts, and raisins), and bigoli in salsa (thick, rough spaghetti in anchovy sauce). Montagnana is famous for its deliciously sweet prosciutto and schizoto, an unleavened bread. Polenta, a creamy cornmeal concoction, is a staple throughout the area, served with thick, rich sauces or grilled as an accompaniment to meat.

The Veneto produces more D.O.C. (Denominazione di Origine Controllata) wines than any other region in Italy. The country's main trade wine fair, Vinitaly, takes place in Verona in April. The southern shores of Lake Garda and the gentle Euganean Hills provide optimum conditions for growing wine grapes. Amarone, the region's crowning achievement, is a robust and powerful red wine with an alcohol content as high as 16%. Valpolicella and Bardolino are other notable appellations. Ripasso is made by adding the lees (dried grape skins) from Amarone to Valpolicella, striking a balance between the powerful Amarone and the more mild Valpolicella. And in recent years, blends that rival Amarone have come into vogue. The best of the whites are Soave; sweet, sparkling prosecco; pinot bianco (pinot blanc); and tocai (though the best of this variety comes from Friuli).

$-$$ ✕ **Gigi Bar.** Simple and unpretentious: yellow walls and tablecloths brighten this inexpensive restaurant with a high-ceilinged second-floor seating area. The central kitchen is behind a counter low enough for the convivial owner-chef Ferrucio to see and supervise the equally friendly dining-room staff. The terrific and popular fish soup is one of the affordable seafood dishes that keep locals lining up. There are also tasty steaks, salads, vegetable plates, and pizzas with surprisingly light crust. ⊠ *Via Verdi 18/20* ☎ *049/8760028* ⊟ *DC, MC, V* ⊗ *Closed Tues. and 2 wks in July.*

★ **¢-$** ✕ **L'Anfora.** Sometimes you stumble across an osteria so full of local character that you wonder why every meal can't be this atmospheric, this representative of local cuisine, this effortlessly delicious. L'Anfora, in Padua's old center, with dark wooden walls and typically brusque service, is that kind of local gem. Skip the fried appetizers, which can get soggy as they sit, and start with some cheese: a nearly perfect piece of mozzarella *di bufala campana* (water-buffalo mozzarella from the Campania region) or, even better, an impossibly creamy *burrata*. After that, you might move on to tagliatelle with fresh seasonal mushrooms, or perhaps a plate of simply grilled artichokes and potatoes. The place is packed

at lunchtime, so expect a wait. ⊠ *Via Soncin 13* ☎ *049/656629* ▤ *AE,
V* ⊗ *Closed Sun. except in Dec.; closed 1 wk in Aug.*

¢ ✕ **Hostaria Ai Do Archi.** Frequented by a weathered older crowd, this is
nothing more—or less—than a Paduan version of the *bacari* (wine bars)
that are so typical of the Veneto. You can either sit or stand as you sip
wine, sample local snacks, and chat with your neighbor. It's a true experience. ⊠ *Via Nazario Sauro 23* ☎ *049/652335* ▤ *No credit cards*
⊗ *Closed Tues. No lunch.*

$$$ ▦ **Donatello.** Directly opposite the Basilica di Sant'Antonio, the Donatello
has rooms with a view of the square and church, though the back rooms
are quieter. The entrance hall is all mirrors, marble, and chandeliers, and
gives direct access to the separately managed bar and restaurant out front
and to the basement garage. ⊠ *Via del Santo 102, 35123* ☎ *049/
8750634* 🖷 *049/8750829* ⊕ *www.hoteldonatello.net* ⤳ *45 rooms*
⌂ *In-room safes, minibars, bar, parking (fee), some pets allowed* ▤ *AE,
DC, MC, V* ⊗ *Closed Dec. 15–Jan. 15* ℈ *EP.*

$$$ ▦ **Grand' Italia.** The art nouveau decorative detail on the outside of this
superbly converted palace continues inside to the dramatic, sweeping
stairway and curvy reception desk—both in sculpted marble. High ceilings, wooden floors, and elegant furnishings make the chic, modern rooms
both spacious and inviting. Right across the road from the train station,
this is an ideal base for visiting Venice. ⊠ *Corso del Popolo 81, 35131*
☎ *049/8761111* 🖷 *049/8750850* ⊕ *www.hotelgranditalia.it* ⤳ *61
rooms* ⌂ *In-room data ports, in-room safes, minibars, bar, meeting rooms,
parking (fee), some pets allowed* ℈ *BP.*

$$$ ▦ **Methis.** The strikingly modern Methis takes its name from the Greek
word for style and spirit. Four floors of minimalist guest rooms are de-
signed to reflect the elements: gentle earth tones, fiery red, watery cool
blue, and airy white (in the top-floor suites). Rooms have Japanese-style
tubs, and four are equipped for guests with disabilities. The lobby bath-
room is worth a visit just to wash your hands in the fountain. ⊠ *Riv-
iera Paleocapa 70, 35141* ☎ *049/8725555* 🖷 *049/8725135* ⊕ *www.
methishotel.com* ⤳ *52 rooms, 7 suites* ⌂ *In-room safes, minibars,
cable TV with movies and video games, in-room data ports, gym, bar,
Internet, meeting room, free parking, no-smoking floor* ▤ *AE, DC, MC,
V* ℈ *BP.*

$$$ ▦ **Plaza.** There aren't many hotels near downtown Padua, and this is
one of the few comfortable options. Even if the design of the hotel seems
trapped in a 1960s modernist fantasy, that's not necessarily a bad thing;
the giant globes that illuminate the sidewalk out front add an element
of fantasy to an otherwise nondescript block of apartments and office
buildings. Rooms are spacious, modern, and comfortable, and you're only
a five-minute walk from the middle of things. ⊠ *Corso Milano 40,
35139* ☎ *049/656822* 🖷 *049/661117* ⊕ *www.plazapadova.it* ⤳ *130
rooms, 9 suites, 7 apartments* ⌂ *Restaurant, bar, Internet, in-room safes,
minibars, gym, meeting rooms, parking (fee)* ▤ *AE, DC, MC, V* ℈ *BP.*

★ $$–$$$ ▦ **Majestic Toscanelli.** The elegant entrance, with potted evergreens flank-
ing the steps, sets the tone in this stylish, central hotel close to the Piazza della Frutta. It's easily the best-located hotel in the city, but the rooms
and service by themselves justify a stay here. Plants feature strongly in
the breakfast room as well, and the charming bedrooms are furnished

in different styles from 19th-century mahogany and brass to French Empire. ⊠ *Via dell'Arco 2, 35122* ☎ *049/663244* 🖷 *049/8760025* ⊕ *www. toscanelli.com* 🖘 *26 rooms, 6 suites* ♤ *In-room data ports, some inroom safes, minibars, bar, meeting room, parking (fee), some pets allowed, no-smoking floor* ⊟ *AE, DC, MC, V* ⊧⊙⊧ *BP.*

$ 🖽 **Al Fagiano.** Close to the Basilica di Sant'Antonio and the river, this modest hostelry has basic facilities (some rooms have showers but no tubs), an amiable staff, and a calm atmosphere. Some rooms have views of the church's spires and cupolas. ⊠ *Via Locatelli 45, 35100* ☎ *049/ 8750073* 🖷 *049/8753396* ⊕ *www.alfagiano.it* 🖘 *30 rooms* ♤ *Restaurant, bar, some pets allowed* ⊟ *AE, DC, MC, V* ⊧⊙⊧ *EP.*

¢–$ 🖽 **Casa del Pellegrino.** Facing the Basilica di Sant'Antonio, this rather austere hotel has something of a monastic air, with simple, fairly spartan rooms arranged hospital-fashion off long, polished corridors. Rooms in the newer annex, 100 yards behind the main hotel, are more luxurious (and quieter), and offer more amenities, including air-conditioning. A cavernous restaurant downstairs serves cheap, simple fare. Breakfast is not included in the price. ⊠ *Via Cesarotti 21, 35123* ☎ *049/8239711* 🖷 *049/8239780* ⊕ *www.casadelpellegrino.com* 🖘 *133 rooms, 115 with bath* ♤ *Restaurant, bar, parking (fee); no a/c in some rooms* ⊟ *AE, MC, V* ⊙ *Closed last week Dec.–Jan.* ⊧⊙⊧ *EP.*

Nightlife & the Arts

The Arts

The **Auditorium Pollini** (⊠ Via Carlo Cassan 15 ☎ 049/8759880) puts on classical recitals and concerts from October to April. Ticket prices vary according to show. The **Teatro Verdi** (⊠ Via dei Livello 32 ☎ 049/ 8770213 ⊕ www.teatrostabileveneto.it) has a top-quality program of classical and modern theater year-round.

Nightlife

BARS One of Padua's greatest traditions is the outdoor en masse consuming, most nights in decent weather, of aperitifs: *spritz* (a mix of Aperol or Campari, soda water, and wine), *prosecco,* and nonsparkling wines are the most common drinks. It all happens in the Piazza delle Erbe and Piazza delle Frutte—several bars around the two piazzas provide drinks in plastic cups to masses of people who take them outside to consume while standing. The ritual, practiced religiously by students most of all, begins at 6 PM or so, and can be accompanied by a snack from one of the outdoor seafood vendors. On weekends the open-air revelry continues into the wee hours, transitioning from a lively cocktail hour to a wine-soaked bash.

Kolar (⊠ Via dell'Arco 37 ☎ 049/8762385) is decoupaged floor to ceiling with recycled newspapers. This bar serves beverages, appetizers, and a lively mix of rock and jazz Tuesday through Sunday from 5 PM until 2 AM. **Limbo** (⊠ Via San Fermo 44 ☎ 049/656882), closed on Monday and Tuesday, is a restaurant-pizzeria that stays open late, with live music and a disco downstairs. **Victoria** (⊠ Via Savonarola 149 ☎ 049/ 8721530) is a *birreria* (bar serving primarily beer) that occasionally has live rock music; it's closed on Monday.

CAFÉS **Caffè Margherita** (✉ Piazza delle Frutte 44 ☎ 049/8760107) is the perfect place to watch the busy piazza and admire the nearby Palazzo della Ragione. It's closed on Sunday.

The ever-popular **Caffè Pedrocchi** (✉ Piazzetta Pedrocchi ☎ 049/8781231), in a monumental 19th-century neoclassical coffeehouse, looks like a cross between a museum and a stage set, with rooms ranging in color from red to white to green. You can indulge in a full-scale lunch or just sip a cappuccino here. In days gone by it was a haunt for the city's intellectuals, who hung out all hours of the day and night. It's closed on Monday during the summer only.

Shopping

Markets

You could be forgiven for spending more time on the ground floor of Padua's **Palazzo della Ragione** (✉ Piazza della Ragione) than in the gallery upstairs: it is the city's mouthwatering permanent food market, with shops offering choice salami and cured meats, fresh local cheeses, wine, coffee, and tea. A fruit and vegetable market is held from 8 to 2, every morning except Sunday, in the **Piazza delle Erbe.** In the nearby **Piazza delle Frutte,** a general market, selling mainly clothing and trinkets, is held weekday mornings and all day Saturday. Padua's Saturday market in **Prato della Valle** has a wide range of goods. An antiques market is held the third Sunday of every month with some 220 stalls—you're sure to find a bargain, but it's more likely to be '50s or '60s bric-a-brac than a genuine antique.

Specialty Stores

CLOTHING There's no lack of fashion boutiques in Padua's center. You'll find many in the **Galleria Ezzelino** just off the Piazza delle Erbe. Close to the same piazza is **Paolo Prata** (✉ Via Santi Martino e Solferino 42 ☎ 049/ 665508), specializing in women's clothes.

FOOD & WINE Heaven awaits your sweet tooth at **Dolciaria** (✉ Via Santi Martino e Solferino 35 ☎ 049/663463), a specialist at fulfilling chocoholic dreams with candy, biscuits, and gifts from all over the world. **R. Vignato** (✉ Via Roma 64 ☎ 049/8751320) is well known for its cheese, salami, olive oil, honey, and wine. It sells potato chips by the scoop, too.

VICENZA

Vicenza bears the distinctive signature of the 16th-century architect Andrea Palladio (1508–80), whose name is the root of the style referred to as "Palladian." He gracefully incorporated elements of classical architecture—columns, porticoes, and domes—into a style that reflected the Renaissance celebration of order and harmony. His elegant villas and palaces were influential in propagating classical architecture in Europe, especially Britain, and later in America—most notably at Thomas Jefferson's Monticello.

In the mid-16th century, Palladio was given the opportunity to rebuild much of Vicenza, which had suffered great damage during the bloody wars waged against Venice by the League of Cambrai, an alliance of the papacy, France, the Holy Roman Empire, and several neighboring city-states. He imposed upon the city a number of his grand Roman-style buildings—rather an overstatement, considering the town's status. With the basilica, begun in 1549 in the very heart of Vicenza, Palladio ensured his reputation and embarked on a series of lordly buildings, all of which adhere to the same rigorous classicism. Today Vicenza—one of Europe's biggest producers of gold jewelry and home to a diversity of light industry—is among the richest cities in Italy. This is readily apparent in the mod style of dress, the elegance of the shops, and the large number of late-model BMWs and Mercedes.

Exploring Vicenza

Vicenza can easily be covered in a day or less. The broad main street, Corso Palladio, cuts through the historical center, leading east from Piazza del Castello to Piazza Matteotti. Palladio's buildings share this street with Venetian Gothic and baroque palaces, banks, offices, and elegant boutiques. The main square, Piazza dei Signori, lies to the south of the corso; from there it's an easy walk to the Teatro Olimpico. Make sure you save some time to visit the Villa La Rotonda, just south of the city.

The Main Attractions

㉒ The Basilica. At the heart of Vicenza, Palladio's **Palazzo della Ragione** is commonly known as the Basilica, though it was built to serve as a courthouse and public meeting hall. Palladio made his name by successfully modernizing the medieval building, grafting a graceful two-story exterior loggia onto the existing structure. The **Torre di Piazza,** the slender tower at the corner of the basilica, was built in the 12th century and is all that remains of the original building. The opening hours of the hall change during the frequent exhibitions. ⊠ *Piazza dei Signori* ☎ *0444/ 323681* ☜ *€1* ☉ *Tues.–Sun. 9–1 and 3–7.*

㉒ Contrà Porti. A fine cluster of Palladio's buildings occupies this short street. The architect contributed a wing to **Palazzo Thiene,** at No. 47, which was started in 1484 and incorporates another Renaissance palace (1489) by Lorenzo da Bologna. At Contrà Porti 21, the **Palazzo Porto Festa** (1552) was begun but not finished by Palladio. With its mullioned windows, the strikingly Gothic **Palazzo Porto Breganze,** on the corner with Contrà Riale, is not Palladio's work, but his **Palazzo Barbaran da Porto** (1570), beyond, is the home of the International Center of Palladian Architectural Studies (CISA). On Via Fogazzaro, **Palazzo Valmarana Braga** (1566) is a perfect example of Palladio's ability to integrate his buildings with the surroundings. All these buildings can be admired from the outside.

★ ㉑ Palazzo Chiericati. This exquisite and unmistakably Palladian palace houses the **Museo Civico,** with a representative collection of Venetian paintings including Tiepolo (1696–1770) and Tintoretto (1519–94). Also noteworthy are the stucco relief *Madonna and Child* by Sansovino (1486–1570) and, in the Flemish room, another *Madonna and Child* attributed to Brueghel the Elder (circa 1520–69) and *Three Ages of Man*

by Van Dyck (1599–1641). ⊠ *Piazza Matteotti* ☎ *0444/321348* 🎫 *€8, includes admission to Teatro Olimpico and Museo Naturalistico e Archeologico* ☉ *Sept.–June, Tues.–Sun. 9–5; July and Aug., Tues.–Sun. 9–6.*

⑱ Santa Corona. Begun in 1261 to house a thorn from Christ's crown, a gift from Louis IX of France, this church is said to possess the oldest Gothic interior in the Veneto. In addition to the Holy Thorn, which is kept in a gold reliquary and displayed only on Good Friday, it also holds an exceptionally fine *Baptism of Christ* (1500) by Giovanni Bellini (1430–1516) over the altar on the left, just in front of the transept, and an equally fine *Adoration of the Magi* by Paolo Veronese (1528–88). The high altar is a splendid example of 18th-century craftsmanship in inlaid marble and mother-of-pearl. The church was the original burial place of Palladio until his remains were transferred in the 19th century to the cemetery of Santa Lucia. The cloisters are now home to the **Museo Naturalistico-Archeologico,** containing remains of a Roman theater excavated in the 19th century and a natural history and geology section upstairs. ⊠ *Contrà Santa Corona 4* ☎ *Church 0444/ 321924, museum 0444/320440* 🎫 *Museum €8, includes Teatro Olimpico and Palazzo Chiericati* ☉ *Church Mon. 4–6, Tues.–Fri. 8:30–noon and 3–6, weekends 3–5. Museum Sept.–June, Tues.–Sun. 9–5; July and Aug., Tues.–Sun. 9–6.*

★ **⑰ Teatro Olimpico.** This is Palladio's last, and perhaps most exciting work. It was completed in 1584 by Vincenzo Scamozzi (1552–1616), who was also responsible for the permanent set. Based closely on the model of the ancient Roman theater, it nonetheless represents an important development in theater and stage design and is noteworthy for its acoustics and the cunningly devised false perspective of a classical street in the permanent backdrop. The anterooms are all frescoed with important figures in Venetian history. ⊠ *Piazza Matteotti* ☎ *0444/222800* ⊠ *€8, includes admission to Palazzo Chiericati and Museo Naturalistico e Archeologico* ☉ *Sept.–June, Tues.–Sun. 9–5, July and Aug., Tues.–Sun. 9–7.*

⑳ Villa La Rotonda. This is the most famous Palladian villa of all. In truth
Fodor'sChoice   it can hardly be called a villa, since the architect was inspired by an-
★   cient Roman temples. Take the time to admire it from all sides, and you'll see that it was in turn inspiration not just for Monticello but for nearly every state capitol in the United States. The interior is typical of Palladio's grand style, with a distinctive use of negative space. It is a 20- to 30-minute walk from the center of Vicenza, along a pleasant route well away from the busy traffic. Go through the Palladio triumphal arch where Viale Margherita meets Viale Risorgimento and climb the steps. Turn left into Via Bastian, which becomes Via dei Nani and leads to the Villa ai Nani. A pedestrian path (Via Valmarana) then winds down to Villa La Rotonda. Or take Bus 8 from Viale Roma and ask the driver to let you off at La Rotonda. Note that the interior is open only on Wednesday, from April through October. ⊠ *Via della Rotonda 29* ☎ *0444/ 321793* ⊠ *Villa €10, grounds €5* ☉ *Villa mid-Mar.–Oct., Wed. 10–noon and 3–6. Grounds mid-Mar.–Oct., Tues.–Sun. 10–noon and 3–6; Nov.–mid-Mar., Tues.–Sun. 10–noon and 2–5.*

Also Worth Seeing

㉔ Casa Pigafetta. This ornate, red marble house was built shortly before the birth of the sailor after whom it is named. Antonio Pigafetta (1491–1534) was a crew member of Magellan's when the latter circumnavigated the globe in 1519. ⊠ *Contrà Pigafetta.*

㉕ Duomo. Vicenza's Gothic cathedral is notable for a gleaming altarpiece by the 14th-century Venetian painter Lorenzo Veneziano (1356–72). The marble high altar could be an early work of Palladio as it comes from the workshop of Pedemuro, where he was employed as a novice. The cathedral itself was partly destroyed in World War II, but nearly all the damaged areas have been restored. The Romanesque bell tower stands apart from it. ⊠ *Piazza del Duomo* ⊕ *www.vicenza.chiesacattolica.it* ☉ *Mon.–Sat. 10:30–noon and 3:30–7.*

㉓ Loggia del Capitaniato. Opposite the Basilica in Piazza dei Signori, this building was commissioned for the commander of the city and designed by Palladio, but never completed. The reliefs on the facade celebrate the defeat of the Turks at Lepanto in 1571. ⊠ *Piazza dei Signori.*

⑲ Santo Stefano. This small church is worth tracking down for the fine painting contained within, the *Madonna and Child with Sts. George and Lucy* by Palma Vecchio (1480–1528), who was to influence Veronese's paint-

186 < Southern Veneto

ings. Note the extremely brief hours that it's open. ⊠ *Contrà Santo Stefano* ☎ *0444/524168* ⊘ *Mon.–Sat. 8:30–9:45 and 5–6:30, Sun. 8:30–9:45.*

㉖ Villa Valmarana ai Nani. A short walk from Villa La Rotonda, this 18th-century country house is decorated with a series of marvelous frescoes by Giambattista Tiepolo. These are fantastic visions of a mythological world, including one of his most stunning works, the *Sacrifice of Iphegenia*. The neighboring Foresteria, or guest house, holds more frescoes depicting vignettes of 18th-century Veneto life at its most charming, executed by Tiepolo's son, Giandomenico (1727–1804). In case you're wondering, *nani* means "dwarves": story has it that the villa was protected by the dwarf servants of a girl who used to live here. The dwarves were subsequently turned to stone, and you can see their statues all along the garden wall. ⊠ *Via dei Nani 2/8* ☎ *0444/544546* ⬚ €6 ⊘ *Mar.–Oct., Wed., Thurs., and weekends 10–noon and 3–6, Tues. and Fri. 10–noon.*

Where to Stay & Eat

$$ ✕ **Antico Ristorante agli Schioppi.** Veneto country-style decor matches simple yet imaginative cuisine in this family-run restaurant established in 1897. Begin with the Parma ham served with eggplant mousse and Parmesan. The *baccalà* (salt cod) is a must, as are the *petto d'anitra all'uva moscata e indivia* (duck breast with muscat grapes and endive) and *coniglio alle olive nere* (rabbit with black olives). Desserts include ever-so-light fruit mousse and a pear cake with red wine sauce. ⊠ *Contrà del Castello 26* ☎ *0444/543701* ⬚ *AE, DC, MC, V* ⊘ *Closed Sun., last week of July–mid-Aug., and Jan. 1–6. No dinner Sat.*

$–$$ ✕ **Dai Nodari.** Seven restaurant veterans—with a shared passion for good food and hard work—opened this exciting restaurant in January 2005. They must also share a flare for the dramatic: a silent film shows in the bar and Dante's Inferno plays in the men's room. Appetizers include tuna marinated in orange, and interesting cheeses such as *bastardo del drappa* (aged 60 days). Move on to fish or steak, or try rabbit roasted with juniper berries. There are also several pasta and salad choices. ⊠ *Contrà do Rode 20* ☎ *0444/544085* ⬚ *AE, DC, MC, V.*

$ ✕ **Il Cursore.** The front section of this cozy, 19th-century osteria is given over mainly to bar service, offering local wines and typical savory snacks like *cotechino* (boiled sausage) and *soppressa* (premium salami). There are some cramped tables against the wall, but the back rooms are better for a sit-down meal of local classics such as *bigoli* (thick, whole wheat spaghetti) with duck, spaghetti with salt cod and, in spring, *risi e bisi* (rice with peas). Desserts include the ubiquitous tiramisu and fruit tarts. ⊠ *Stradella Pozzetto 10* ☎ *0444/323504* ⬚ *V* ⊘ *Closed Tues. and last week July–Aug. 15. No lunch Sun.*

¢ ✕ **Righetti.** After staking out seats, line up (and be ready to jockey for position) at the self-service food counters here. There's a daily pasta, a risotto, and a hearty soup such as *orzo e fagioli* (barley and bean) on the menu. Vegetables, salads, and baccalà are standards; at dinner meats are grilled to order. Once you have your meal on your tray, help yourself to bread, wine, and water. Sharing tables is the norm. After you've finished, tell the cashier what you had and he'll total your (very reasonable) bill. Low prices and simple, enjoyable food have generated a loyal following. ⊠ *Piazza Duomo 3* ☎ *0444/543135* ▤ *No credit cards* ⊘ *Closed weekends.*

$$$–$$$$ ▥ **Campo Marzio.** This elegant hotel sits right in front of the city walls and is a five-minute walk from the railway station. The more expensive rooms are furnished in a variety of styles; choose from Asian, neoclassical, and floral themes. Many bathrooms have whirlpool baths. A special perk is the availability of bicycles at no extra charge. ⊠ *Viale Roma 21, 36100* ☎ *0444/545700* 🖷 *0444/320495* ⊕ *www.hotelcampomarzio. com* ➴ *35 rooms* ᴧ *Restaurant, bicycles, bar, free parking, some pets allowed* ▤ *AE, DC, MC, V* ᵢ○ᵢ *BP.*

$$ ▥ **Giardini.** You're in good company here: the other sides of the central piazza on which the hotel stands are flanked by Palladio's Teatro Olimpico and Palazzo Chiericati, while the town center itself is just a few steps away. Rooms have a modern Italian style, with sleek, mid-tone wood floors and multicolor bedspreads; two rooms are equipped for guests with disabilities. ⊠ *Viale Giruioli 10, 36100* ☎ *0444/326458* 🖷 *0444/326458* ⊕ *www.hotelgiardini.com* ➴ *17 rooms* ᴧ *In-room safes, minibars, cable TV, bar, meeting room, free parking* ▤ *AE, DC, MC, V* ⊘ *Closed Dec. 23–Jan. 2 and 3 wks in Aug.* ᵢ○ᵢ *BP.*

$ ▥ **Due Mori.** In the heart of Vicenza off Piazza dei Signori, this is allegedly the first hotel in town, dating from 1883, and is a favorite with regular visitors. It's light and airy, with tall ceilings and pale walls, yet at the same time cozy, with substantial wood beds. The rooms are individually furnished with antiques and wood detail in the bathrooms. ⊠ *Contrà Do Rode 26, 36100* ☎ *0444/321886* 🖷 *0444/326127* ⊕ *www.hotelduemori.com* ➴ *30 rooms, 27 with bath* ᴧ *Bar, some pets allowed, free parking; no a/c, no room TVs* ▤ *AE, MC, V* ⊘ *Closed last 2 wks in July* ᵢ○ᵢ *BP.*

Nightlife & the Arts

The Arts

MUSIC & THEATER The monthly *Informa Città*, available from the tourist office, will give you details of all events, including walking trips. Contact the tourist office for details of **Concerti in Ville,** a series of concerts held in nearby villas during June and July. Vicenza's **Teatro Olimpico** (☎ 0444/222800, 0444/ 222801 box office ⊕ www.comune.vicenza.it) hosts a jazz festival in May, classical music concerts in June, and classical drama performances in September. Even if your Italian is dismal, it's particularly thrilling to see a performance in Palladio's magnificent theater.

Nightlife

BAR **Rebar** (⊠ Via Zugliano 43 ☎ 0444/500151) has live rock, jazz, and funk on Friday nights.

Shopping

Markets

A daily fruit-and-vegetable market is held in **Piazza delle Erbe,** behind the basilica. A general market is held Thursday in **Piazza dei Signori.**

Shopping Districts

Shops center on the main Corso Palladio, Contrà Cavour, and Piazza dei Signori.

Specialty Shops

JEWELRY Vicenza is one of Italy's leading centers for the production and sale of jewelry. For gold, silver, jewelry, and watches at factory prices, visit **Cash & Gold** (⊠ Viale della Scienza 14 ☎ 0444/965947), a complex of more than 100 traders. Buses 20 and 21 from the train station will get you there. **Fiera di Vicenza** (⊠ Via dell'Oreficeria ☎ 0444/969111) holds a series of trade fairs selling mainly jewelry, pictures, ceramics, and coins. Most shows are open to the general public.

MEN'S CLOTHING For seriously elegant Italian men's fashion, step into **Pal Zileri** (⊠ Corso Palladio 33 ☎ 0444/540768).

PASTICCERIE If you see a procession of people carrying beribboned packages across the Piazza dei Signori, you can bet they're coming from one of two great pastry shops. In addition to its wonderful old-fashioned look and great pastries, **Pasticceria Sorarù** (⊠ Piazzetta Palladio 17 ☎ 0444/320915) is famous for its hot chocolate. **La Meneghina** (⊠ Corso Cavour 18 ☎ 0444/323305), also with a delectable, quaint appeal, doubles as a wine bar.

VERONA

On the banks of the fast-flowing Adige River, enchanting Verona lays claim to classical and medieval monuments, a picturesque town center where bright geraniums bloom in window boxes, and a romantic reputation, thanks to its immortalization as the setting of Shakespeare's *Romeo and Juliet*. It is one of Italy's most alluring cities, despite extensive industrialization and urban development in its newer sections. There's an opulence in the air and in the shops that line the red Verona marble pavements with their enticing and elegant wares. Inevitably, with its lively Venetian feel and proximity to Lake Garda, it attracts hordes of tourists, especially Germans and Austrians; tourism peaks during summer's renowned season of open-air opera in the Arena and spring's Vinitaly, one of the world's most important wine expos, where for five days you can sample the work of more than 3,000 wineries from dozens of countries. (Book months in advance for hotels at fair time, usually the second week in April.)

Verona grew to power and prosperity within the Roman Empire as a result of its key commercial and military position in northern Italy. After the fall of the Empire, the city continued to flourish under the guidance of Barbarian kings such as Theodoric, Alboin, Pepin, and Berenger I, reaching its cultural and artistic peak in the 13th and 14th centuries under the della Scala (Scaligeri) dynasty. You'll see the *scala,* or ladder, emblem all over town. In 1404 Verona traded its independence for security and placed itself under the control of Venice; the winged lion of St. Mark, symbol of Venetian rule, is another symbol often seen throughout the historical center. Verona remained under Venetian protection until

1797, when Napoléon invaded. In 1814 the entire Veneto region was won by the Austrians; it was finally united with the rest of Italy in 1866.

Exploring Verona

With its small streets, secret courtyards, elegant boutiques, and comely air, Verona is an extremely walkable city. Note that the Duomo and churches in Verona enforce a strict dress code: no tank tops, sleeveless shirts, shorts, or short skirts. You might want to consider buying the €5 combined ticket that allows admittance to most churches in town, including the Duomo, San Zeno, and Sant'Anastasia. Alternately, buy a VeronaCard for one or three days (€8 or €12), which gains you admission to most of the city's major museums and churches as well as access to public transportation. You can get a VeronaCard at the participating museums, monuments, and churches, but not at the tourist office. Cars are not allowed in the historic city center from 7:30 to 10 in the morning and 1:30 to 4:30 in the afternoon. Numerous parking areas are found beyond the center, and one-hour disk parking (⇨ Parking *in* Smart Travel Tips) is permitted on the nearby streets.

The Main Attractions

③⓿ ⟳ Arena di Verona. Only the Colosseum and the arena in Capua can outdo **Fodor'sChoice** this ancient amphitheater in size. Just four arches remain of the arena's **★** outer arcade, but the main structure is so complete that it takes little imagination to picture it as the site of the cruel deaths of countless gladiators, wild beasts, and Christians. Today it hosts, among other events, Verona's summer opera, famous for spectacular productions before audiences of up to 16,000. (*See* Opera *below.*) ⊠ *Arena di Verona, Piazza Brà 5* ☎ *045/8003204* ⊕ *www.arena.it* ☞ *€5 or VeronaCard; €1 1st Sun. of month* ⊙ *Mon. 1:30–7:15, Tues.–Sun. 8:30–7:15, on performance days 8–3:30; last entry 45 mins before closing.*

㉙ Castelvecchio (Old Castle). This crenellated, russet brick building with massive walls, towers, turrets, and a vast courtyard was built for Cangrande II della Scala in 1354. It presides over a street lined with attractive old buildings and palaces of the nobility. Inside, the **Museo di Castelvecchio** gives you a good look at the castle's vaulted halls and some treasures of 15th- to 18th-century Venetian and Veronese painting and sculpture. Look out for the precious, 14th-century Via Trezza jewels, Cangrande's belt and sword in Room VIII, and the original painted walls of Room XI. In the courtyard Cangrande I stands imposingly on a pedestal. Behind the castle is the Ponte Scaligero, a public walkway spanning the River Adige. ⊠ *Corso Castelvecchio 2* ☎ *045/594734* ☞ *€4 or VeronaCard; free 1st Sun. of month* ⊙ *Mon 1:30–7:30, Tues.–Sun. 8:30–7:30; last entry 45 mins before closing.*

㊶ Duomo. The ornate red-and-white-striped Romanesque Duomo is an amalgamation of religious buildings, the earliest dating back to 380; it's ornately Romanesque but also shows Venetian and even Byzantine influences. The church has a grand organ and a wealth of decorative architectural detail, especially around each chapel. The first chapel on the left holds an *Assumption* (1535) by Titian. Fine reliefs on the 12th-

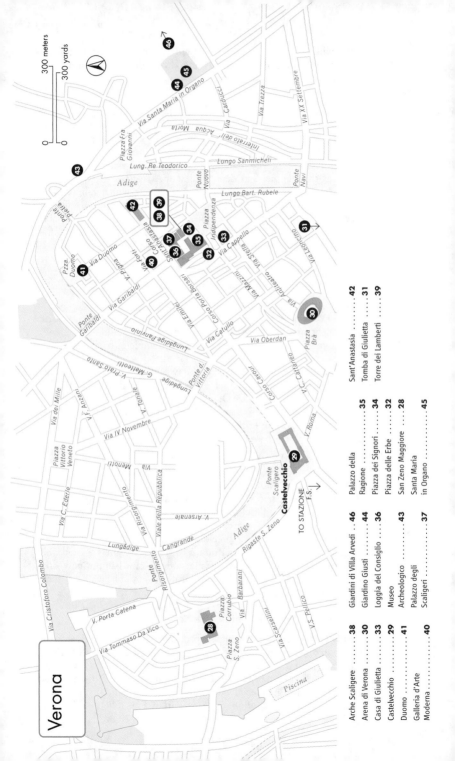

Verona

century south porch depict *Jonah and the Whale,* and on the west porch are statues of *Roland* and *Oliver,* paladins of Charlemagne. Unlike in most Italian cities, this Duomo is tucked away in one of the quieter parts of town. ✉ *Piazza Duomo* ☎ *045/592813* 🎫 *€2.50, € 5 for combined churches ticket, or VeronaCard* ⊗ *Nov.–Feb., Tues.–Sat. 10–4, Sun. 1–5; Mar.–Oct., Mon.–Sat. 10–5:30, Sun. 1:30–5:30.*

㉞ Piazza dei Signori. Verona's most impressive piazza, the center of things for more than 1,000 years, is today lorded over by a pensive statue of Dante, often as not with a pigeon on his head. His back is toward the Loggia del Consiglio and his left hand points toward the Palazzo degli Scaligeri. He faces Palazzo del Capitanio (to his left) and Palazzo della Ragione (to his right). All these buildings are closed to the public except those on government business.

★ **㉜ Piazza delle Erbe.** A Roman forum once bustled on this site, and until recently it was the location of the daily fruit-and-vegetable market. Many of the stalls have now gone, though there are still plenty of trinkets, postcards, snacks, and so forth for sale. The surrounding frescoed town houses, the fountains, and the buzz of people and vendors all combine to make this one of northern Italy's most charming city piazzas.

㉘ San Zeno Maggiore. Possibly Italy's finest Romanesque church, San Zeno stands between two medieval bell towers and has a 12th-century portal. The 13th-century rose window represents the wheel of fortune. Of special note are the 11th- and 12th-century bronze doors depicting biblical scenes and episodes from the life of San Zeno, Verona's patron saint, and Mantegna's *Madonna and Saints* triptych over the main altar. Look for the statue *San Zeno Laughing* to the left of the main altar— the unknown artist, or perhaps the saint himself, must have had a sense of humor. Zeno is buried in the crypt, and a peaceful cloister lies off the left nave. ✉ *Piazza San Zeno* ☎ *045/8006120* 🎫 *€2.50, €5 for combined churches ticket, or VeronaCard* ⊗ *Nov.–Feb., Tues.–Sat. 10–4, Sun. 1–5; Mar.–Oct., Mon.–Sat. 8:30–6, Sun. 1–6.*

Fodor'sChoice
★

㊷ Sant'Anastasia. Verona's largest church, completed in 1481, is a fine example of Gothic brickwork. The Gothic interior contains numerous frescoes; the most outstanding are the richly decorative and glowing *St. George and the Princess* by Pisanello (1377–1455) above the Pellegrini Chapel and one by Altichiero (1320–95) in the sacristy. As you come in, look for the *gobbi* (hunchbacks), with holes in their pants, supporting the holy water stoup. ✉ *Piazza Sant'Anastasia* ☎ *045/592813* ⊕ *www. chieseverona.it* 🎫 *€2.50, €5 for combined churches ticket, or VeronaCard* ⊗ *Nov.–Feb., Tues.–Sat. 10–4, Sun. 1–5; Mar.–Oct., Mon.–Sat. 9–6, Sun. 1–6.*

Also Worth Seeing

㊳ Arche Scaligere. The impressive marbled Gothic monuments of the Scaligeri family tombs are set in the grounds of the church of Santa Maria Antica. Cangrande I ("Big Dog") looks down from atop his pinnacled tomb—this statue is a copy of the original that stands in the Castelvecchio. Mastino II ("Mastiff") is buried to the left of the church close to Cansignorio ("Top Dog"). Look for the ladder motif on the wrought-iron grille surrounding the tombs. ⊠ *Via Arche Scaligere* 🎫 *€4* ⊙ *Visible at all times from the outside; inside open for walks among the tombs, Mon. 1:30–7:30, Tues.–Sun. 8:30–7:30; last entry 30 mins before closing.*

③③ Casa di Giulietta (Juliet's House). The balcony in the small courtyard will help to bring Shakespeare's play to life, even if it was built in the 20th century. Historians now believe that Romeo and Juliet had no real-life counterparts, but this hasn't discouraged anyone from imagining that they did. After all, historians are not as renowned for their storytelling as Shakespeare is. You can see the balcony without paying to enter. ⊠ *Via Cappello 23* 🕾 *045/8034303* 🎫 *€4* ⊙ *Mon. 1:30–7:30, Tues.–Sun. 8:30–7:30; last entry 45 mins before closing.*

④⓪ Galleria d'Arte Moderna (Gallery of Modern Art). The handsome **Palazzo Forti** was the 13th-century home of Ezzelino III and once provided lodgings for Napoléon. It's now a gallery hosting art exhibitions of works by major contemporary artists. ⊠ *Via Forti 1, entrance on Vicolo Volto Due Mori 4* 🕾 *045/8001903* ⊕ *www.palazzoforti.it* 🎫 *€5* ⊙ *Tues.–Sun. 10–6.*

④④ Giardino Giusti. In 1570 Agostino Giusti designed these formal gardens on the hillside behind his villa. Though the toothy mask halfway up the hill no longer breathes flames, little has changed in Giusti's maze, statues, fountains, and stalactite grotto. And though Verona might no longer be recognizable to Johann Wolfgang von Goethe (1749–1832), you can still enjoy the terrace views that inspired the German poet and dramatist to record his impressions. ⊠ *Via Giardino Giusti 2* 🕾 *045/ 8034029* 🎫 *€5* ⊙ *Apr.–Sept., daily 9–8; Oct.–Mar., daily 9–7.*

③⑥ Loggia del Consiglio. This graceful structure was built in the 12th century to house city council meetings and still serves as the seat of the provincial government. Over the door is the inscription bearing testimony to Verona's loyalty to Venice and Venice's love for Verona, *Pro summa fide summa amor MDXCII* ("Greatest love for the greatest loyalty 1592"). ⊠ *Piazza dei Signori.*

④③ Museo Archeologico. An old monastery above the **Teatro Romano** houses fine Greek, Roman, and Etruscan artifacts. The theater, built in the same era as the Arena di Verona and now restored, is still used for dramatic productions and a jazz festival. ⊠ *Regaste del Redentore 2* 🕾 *045/ 8000360* 🎫 *€3 or VeronaCard; free 1st Sun. of month* ⊙ *Mon. 1:30–7:30, Tues.–Sun. 8:30–7:30; last entry 45 mins before closing. Open shorter hours during theater season.*

③⑦ Palazzo degli Scaligeri. This was the medieval stronghold from which the della Scalas ruled Verona with an iron fist. Admire it from the outside; it's not open to the public. ⊠ *Piazza dei Signori.*

③⑤ Palazzo della Ragione. An elegant, pink marble staircase leads up from the *mercato vecchio* (old market) courtyard to the magistrates' chambers in the 12th-century palace also known as the Palazzo del Comune. The building is undergoing renovation and will be turned into a conference center. ⊠ *Piazza dei Signori.*

AMARONE WINE COUNTRY

TOURING WINERIES *in the lush landscape that produces world-class Amarone and Valpolicella wines can be a good way to see, and taste, southern Veneto. You need call ahead for an appointment—but the rewards are many. Your hotel or the local tourist office should be able to help with arrangements. Here are two good choices near Verona:*

Allegrini, *one of the top producers in the region, is also one of the friendliest; at their Fumane estate, less than a half-hour's drive from downtown Verona, you can tour the facility and watch a video of their story, which goes back to 1854. And, of course, you can taste their wines, including an award-winning Amarone Classico and a spectacular, full-bodied wine called La Poja, made from 100% corvina grapes. From Verona, follow the superstrada toward Sant'Ambrogio and San Pietro in Cariano, then head north on SP 33 to reach Fumane.* ✉ *Via Giare 7* ☎ *045/6832011* ⊕ *www.allegrini.it* ✉ *Free* ⏱ *By appointment.*

Masi, a major Amarone producer, doesn't offer tours, but the affiliated **Serègo Alighieri** *does. The Dante connection in the name is no coincidence. The poet lived several years in Castel dei Ronchi, in tiny Gargagnano, 20 km (12 mi) from Verona. The castle and estate, now an inn and convention center, still belong to a descendant of Dante. His Amarone, which is vinified, bottled, and aged by Masi, is delicious; only the bottle aging happens in Gargagnano. At the shop, you can also taste Masi's own wines, and buy older Amarone vintages. From Verona, take the superstrada toward Sant'Ambrogio and head west on SP 4.* ✉ *Gargagnano di Valpolicella* ☎ *045/7703622* ⊕ *www.seregoalighieri.it* ✉ *Tours €8; wines €.50–€2.50 per taste* ⏱ *Shop Mon.–Sat. 10–6; tours by appointment 3 days in advance.*

㊺ Santa Maria in Organo. The choir and sacristy of this medieval church are decorated with inlaid-wood masterpieces by the 15th-century monk Fra Giovanni. A series of panels depicts varied scenes—local buildings, an idealized Renaissance town, wildlife, and fruit—that radiate a love of life and reveal the artist's eye for detail. ✉ *Via Interrato dell'Acqua Morta* ☎ *045/591440* ⏱ *Apr.–Oct., daily 8:30–noon and 3–6; Nov.–Mar., daily 8:30–noon.*

㊳ Torre dei Lamberti. Standing 270 feet above Piazza dei Signori, this tower, which remains open as it undergoes restoration, was begun in the 12th century and finished in the 15th. Taking the elevator costs only slightly more than walking up the 368 steps for the panoramic view—but the burnt calories are priceless. ✉ *Piazza dei Signori* ☎ *045/8032726* ✉ *Elevator €3, stairs €2* ⏱ *Tues.–Sun. 8:30–7:30, Mon. 1:30–7:30.*

Off the Beaten Path

㊻ Giardini di Villa Arvedi. Formal gardens surround a 17th-century villa 8 km (5 mi) northeast of town. ✉ *Statale per Grezzana* ☎ *045/907045* ✉ *€6* ⏱ *By appointment only, minimum 8–10 people.*

㉛ Tomba di Giulietta. Romantic souls may want to see the pretty spot claimed to be Juliet's tomb, near the river just a few minutes walk from the Arena. Authentic or not, it is still popular with lovesick Italian teenagers, who leave notes for the tragic lover. A small museum of frescoes is inside. ⊠ *Via del Pontiere 35* ☎ *045/8000361* ⚏ *€3 or Verona-Card; free 1st Sun. of month* ⊗ *Mon. 1:30–7:30, Tues.–Sun. 8:30–7:30; last entry 45 mins before closing.*

Where to Stay & Eat

$$$$ ✕ **Arquade.** Master chef Bruno Barbieri and his team present nouvelle
Fodor'sChoice Italian cuisine that is a delight to both eye and palate at the Hotel Villa
★ del Quar's restaurant, which regularly ranks among the best in all of Italy. You can sit in the softly lit converted chapel, furnished with antiques, or out on the beautiful terrace amid the greenery. The creative menu works wonders with lobster, with scampi, and with local mushrooms and foie gras. Simpler dishes, such as a platter of steamed fish, meet with equal success. The sommelier will match your meal with treasures from his wine cellar. ⊠ *Via Quar 12, Pedemonte di San Pietro in Cariano, 5 km (3 mi) northwest of Verona* ☎ *045/6800681* ⚏ *045/ 6800604* ⊕ *www.hotelvilladelquar.it* ⚏ *Reservations essential* ⊟ *AE, DC, MC, V* ⊗ *Closed Jan.–Mar.14 and Mon. mid-Mar–Apr.*

★ **$$$$** ✕ **Il Desco.** *Cucina dell' anima* (food of the soul) is how Chef Elia Rizzo describes his cuisine, in which natural flavors are preserved through quick cooking and a limited number of ingredients per dish. He spares no expense in selecting those ingredients, and you pay accordingly. The results are standout dishes like *petto di faraona con purea di topinambur, salsa al ll'aceto balsamico e cioccolato* (breast of guinea fowl with Jerusalem artichoke puree and a chocolate and balsamic vinegar sauce). For a real splurge, order the tasting menu (€110), which includes appetizers, two first courses, two second courses, and dessert. Decor is elegant, if overstated, with fine tapestries, paintings, and an impressive 16th-century lacunar ceiling. ⊠ *Via Dietro San Sebastiano 7* ☎ *045/ 595358* ⚏ *Reservations essential* ⊟ *AE, DC, MC, V* ⊗ *Closed Sun. Closed Dec. 25–Jan. 8 and June 6–25. No dinner Mon. Jan.–June, Sept. and Oct.*

$$$–$$$$ ✕ **Dodici Apostoli.** Vaulted ceilings, frescoed walls, and a medieval ambience make this an exceptional place to enjoy classic regional dishes. Near Piazza delle Erbe, it stands on the foundations of a Roman temple. Specialties include gnocchi *di zucca e ricotta* (with squash and ricotta cheese) and *vitello alla Lessinia* (veal with mushrooms, cheese, and truffles). ⊠ *Vicolo Corticella San Marco 3* ☎ *045/596999* ⊕ *www.12apostoli.it* ⊟ *AE, DC, MC, V* ⊗ *Closed Mon. and Jan. 1–10 and June 15–30. No dinner Sun.*

$–$$ ✕ **Hostaria dall'Orso.** One of the small, friendly *osterie* (wine bars serving food) that line this quiet street, dall'Orso is particularly strong in the kitchen. The extremely traditional, lunch-only menu includes such classics as eggplant parmigiana and *vitello tonnato* (cold roast veal rolled with a tuna mayonnaise). The wine list is excellent, whether by the glass or the bottle; there are tables on the sidewalk; and the old men who hang out in the dining room just add to the atmosphere. ⊠ *Via Sottoriva 3/c* ☎ *045/597214* ⊟ *MC, V* ⊗ *Closed Sun. No dinner.*

★ **$**   ✕ **Antica Osteria al Duomo.** You'd think, from the name of the place, that this would be a tourist trap. Quite the contrary—this side-street eatery, lined with old wooden walls and ceilings and decked out with musical instruments, serves local food to a local crowd; they come to quaff wine (just €1–€3 per glass) and savor typically northern dishes like *canederli con speck, burro fuso, e rosmarino* (dumplings with bacon, melted butter, and rosemary) and *stracotto di cavallo con polenta* (horse meat with polenta). ⊠ *Via Duomo 7/a* ☎ *045/8004505* ▭ *AE, MC, V* ⊘ *Closed Thurs. Oct.–Mar., Sun. Apr.–Sept.*

$ ✕ **Osteria Sottoriva.** This hole-in-the-wall serves great, simple local *salumi* (cured meats) to go along with the Veneto wines. It's most popular at midday, when the local businesspeople and seniors flock in to gulp wine and munch on *pasta e fagioli* or lovingly prepared meatballs. There's no printed menu, so try to go with the flow and savor whatever's on offer that day. It's also a great place just to drink a glass of wine or beer. ⊠ *Via Sottoriva 9/a* ☎ *045/8014323* ▭ *No credit cards* ⊘ *Closed Wed.*

¢–**$**   ✕ **Du de Cope.** Il Desco's star chef decided to branch into pizza making, and the result is four-star wood-fire pizza at one-star prices. Toppings like buffalo mozzarella and Parmigiano Reggiano cheese cover the lightest crust that ever hovered on a plate. Notice how well modern drop lighting merges with old-fashioned, blue-and-white tile walls; place mats quilt the hardwood tables and burlap tapestries decorate the walls. ⊠ *Galleria Pellicciai 10* ☎ *045/595562* ▭ *AE, DC, MC, V* ⊘ *Closed Tues. No lunch Sun.*

★ ¢–**$**   ✕ **Osteria al Duca.** Folks jam this place at lunchtime, sharing tables, wine, and conversation in a building that legend claims to have been Romeo's birthplace. Beneath low-slung ceilings, generous portions of local specialties are served for a very reasonable fixed price along with a wine list that belies the simplicity of the surroundings. Try Gorgonzola served with polenta, vegetarian eggplant with mozzarella, or homemade *bigoli al torchio,* a thick spaghetti forced through a press. This may be some of the best food available for the price in town. ⊠ *Arche Scaligere 2* ☎ *045/594474* ▭ *MC, V* ⊘ *Closed Sun. and mid-Dec.–mid-Jan.*

★ ¢   ✕ **Osteria Montebaldo.** The Veronese flock here for lunch; it's hard to tell whether they're more attracted by the pleasant, bustling vibe; by the startlingly inexpensive prices; or by the light, delicious cuisine, which might include a well-executed *insalata di piovra* (octopus salad) or swordfish carpaccio carefully shaved onto a fresh green salad. The only difficulty might be the wait for a table, but things move fast, so don't fret. ⊠ *Via Rosa 12* ☎ *No phone* ▭ *No credit cards* ⊘ *Closed Sun.*

$$$$ ▭ **Gabbia d'Oro.** Set in a historic building off Piazza delle Erbe in the

Fodor's Choice   ancient heart of Verona, this hotel is a tasteful fantasia of romantic ornamentation, lavish trimmings, exquisite fabrics, and gorgeous period pieces. Rooms—each one different and more attractive than the last—have frescoes, beamed ceilings, pretty wallpaper, antique prints and furnishings, and canopy beds, some festooned with rosy-cheeked cherubs. You can relax outdoors in the medieval courtyard, in the leafy orangerie, or on the roof terrace. The breakfast spread (not included in the price during the summer opera season) is to die for. ⊠ *Corso Porta*

Borsari 4/a, 37121 ☎ *045/8003060* 📠 *045/590293* ⊕ *www.hotelgabbiadoro.it* 🛏 *8 rooms, 19 suites* ♨ *Restaurant, in-room safes, minibars, cable TV, bar, parking (fee), some pets allowed* ▭ *AE, DC, MC, V* ⍦ *BP.*

★ **$$$$** 🏨 **Villa del Quar.** This tranquil 16th-century villa, famous for its restaurant (Arquade above), is surrounded by gardens and vineyards in the Valpolicella country, 10 minutes by taxi from the city. Architect Leopoldo Montresor and his wife, Evelina, who live here with their children, converted part of the villa into a stylish and sophisticated hotel. No expense has been spared: all rooms have marble bathrooms (some with whirlpool baths) and European antiques, while an outdoor pool is set just a few feet away from the rolling fields. In keeping with the Relais & Chateaux philosophy, the service is familiar and impeccable. ⊠ *Via del Quar 12, 37020 Loc. Pedemonte, S. Pietro In Cariano, 5 km (3 mi) north of Verona* ☎ *045/6800681* 📠 *045/6800604* ⊕ *www.hotelvilladelquar.it* 🛏 *18 rooms, 10 suites* ♨ *Restaurant, pool, gym, massage, sauna, 2 bars, minibars, in-room safes, free parking, Internet, meeting room, some pets allowed* ▭ *AE, DC, MC, V* ⍦ *BP.*

$$ 🏨 **Hotel Europa.** The third generation of this innkeeping family, which has operated the Europa since 1956, welcomes you to a convenient downtown hotel. Expect hardwood floors and pastel *marmarino* (Venetian polished plaster) walls. Rooms are comfortable and up-to-date, and the breakfast room on the ground floor is exceptionally bright. ⊠ *Via Roma 8, 37121* ☎ *045/594744* 📠 *045/8001852* ⊕ *www.veronahoteleuropa.com* 🛏 *46 rooms* ♨ *In-room safes, minibars, cable TV, parking (fee), no-smoking rooms* ▭ *AE, DC, MC, V* ⍦ *BP.*

$$ 🏨 **Torcolo.** It doesn't look like much from the outside, but the Torcolo has several advantages: a warm welcome from the owners, Signoras Diana and Silvia, pleasant rooms decorated unfussily, and a central location on a peaceful street close to Piazza Brà and the Arena. Breakfast, which costs an extra €7–€12, is served outside on the terrace in front of the hotel in summer. ⊠ *Vicolo Listone 3, 37121* ☎ *045/8007512 or 045/8003871* 📠 *045/8004058* ⊕ *www.hoteltorcolo.it* 🛏 *19 rooms* ♨ *Bar, in-room safes, minibars, parking (fee), some pets allowed* ▭ *AE, MC, V* ⍦ *BP.*

★ **$** 🏨 **Armando.** Located in a largely residential area a few hundred yards southeast of the Arena, this bright, contemporary family hotel is a welcome respite from the busy city center just a few minutes' walk away. (Parking is easier here, too.) The rooms are decorated with light, modern furniture, and there are family rooms sleeping up to five. In the airy breakfast room downstairs, Signora Diana serves a hearty breakfast (not included in the price) of yogurt, fresh fruit, cheese, rolls and coffee, with melon and prosciutto in summer. ⊠ *Via Dietro Pallone 1, 37120* ☎ *045/8000206* 📠 *045/8036015* 🛏 *19 rooms* ♨ *Bar, free parking* ▭ *MC, V* ⊙ *Closed Dec. 24–31* ⍦ *BP.*

Nightlife & the Arts

The Arts

MUSIC & CONCERTS   The beautiful **Teatro Filarmonico** (⊠ Via dei Mutilati 4/k ☎ 045/8009108 ⊕ www.arena.it) puts on a varied program of traditional and experi-

LOVE & DEATH IN VERONA

*"While Verona by that name is known,
There shall no figure at such rate be set
As that of true and faithful Juliet."*
(Romeo and Juliet, Act V, Scene 3)

SO PROMISED LORD MONTAGUE to Lord Capulet, as they ended the ancient family feud that doomed Romeo and Juliet to their tragic end. By the looks of things, he's kept his vow. Romeo and Juliet are said to have made their ill-fated match in the 13th century, and Shakespeare's play dates to the 16th, but no matter—English literature's best-known lovesick teenagers are even today the first couple of Verona, and they've turned this somewhat staid northern town into a mecca for romantic pilgrims with a literary bent.

Italy was a favorite dramatis loca for Shakespeare, and he set plays all along the peninsula, from Messina (Much Ado About Nothing) to Venice (The Merchant of Venice). No other city, however, wears its Shakespearean legacy as much on its sleeve as "fair Verona."

In fact, the timeless story of doomed love was originally Verona's, not Shakespeare's—the tale of young lovers torn apart by feuding between the Montecchi (Montagues) and Cappellelli (Capulets) was first published in the 16th century by Veronese Luigi Da Porto, then popularized by retellings in French and English, one of which, Brooke's Romeus and Juliet: Being the Original of Shakespeare's Romeo and Juliet, *by Arthur Brooke,* is thought to have inspired Shakespeare's play.

Shakespeare's play, in turn, seems to have inspired Verona—or at least the tourists that flock there. Romeo and Juliet live on in the names of restaurants and hotels, and star-crossed-lover postcards and T-shirts are sold at every turn.

The city hosts a Shakespeare festival every summer, and guess what play takes center stage? (Hint: it's not Two Gentlemen of Verona.) Some Veronese romantics have formed a Juliet Club, dedicated to answering letters for Juliet they say arrive from all over the world. Each year, they sponsor a love-letter writing contest on Juliet's birthday, September 16. The City of Romeo and Juliet basks in its reputation for romance, attracting flocks of lovebirds every year.

Starry-eyed visitors can stroll down not one but two Lovers' Lanes (Via Amanti and Vicolo Amanti), gaze up at the balcony of Juliet's house (Via Cappello 23), and dab moist eyes at Juliet's marble tomb next to the Museo degli Affreschi on Via del Pontiere. The more literal minded will note that historians doubt Romeo and Juliet ever lived, much less loved, and that "Juliet's Balcony," built in the 20th century, is attached to a house that was not the Cappellellis' (although the Casa di Romeo, at Via Arche Scaligere, was indeed the Montecchi home). But what's in a name?

What are authentic are the remains of the more than 700 defense towers and fortresses dating from the 13th century, testament to the real family feuding that took many more lives than Romeo's poison and Juliet's dagger.

— *Valerie Hamilton*

mental concerts, opera, and ballet attracting international artists. A September classical music festival brings in outstanding orchestras from all over the world. In addition, many churches put on concerts throughout the year.

In the first week of June, **Verona Jazz** (✉ Via Regaste del Redentore 2 ☎ 045/8077500 ⊕ www.estateteatraleveronese.it) is held at the Teatro Romano, with added venues in the Arena and Teatro Nuovo. The city is awash in cultural events in July and August—the Arena doesn't have a monopoly on all the entertainment. From Thursday through Saturday in both the afternoon and evening throughout June and July, free concerts called **I Concerti Scaligeri** (☎ 045/8077500 for information) take place in Piazza dei Signori, Piazza Dante, and elsewhere in town. There's a wide range of national and international offerings, from Mozart to Gershwin, country to Indian ragas.

OPERA
Fodor'sChoice
★

Of all the venues for enjoying opera in the region, the best is probably the **Arena di Verona.** The season runs from July through August, and the audience is seated on stone terraces dating from the time when gladiators fought to the death, or in modern cushioned seats in the stalls. The opera stage is huge and best suited to grand, splashy productions such as *Aïda*—operas that demand huge choruses, enormous sets, lots of color and movement, and, sometimes, camels, horses, and/or elephants. But the experience is memorable and the music excellent no matter what is being performed. If you book a place on the cheaper terraces, be sure to take or rent a cushion—four hours on 2,000-year-old marble can be an ordeal. Sometimes, while sipping a drink in a café at **Piazza Brà,** you can overhear the opera. Tickets can be ordered by phone, online, or from the Arena box office. Tickets start at €22. *Fondazione Arena di Verona box office* ✉ *Via Dietro Anfiteatro 6B* ☎ *045/8005151* ⊕ *www.arena. it* ⊙ *Box office open weekdays 9–noon and 3:15–5:45, Sat. 9–noon. From June 21–Aug. 31, 10–9 on performance days and 10–5:45 on nonperformance days.*

THEATER

The Teatro Romano is the setting for annual summer events, including the **Summer Theater Festival** (✉ Via Regaste del Redentore 2 ☎ 045/8077201 ⊕ www.estateteatraleveronese.it), which highlights Shakespeare. The **Accanto a Shakespeare** (✉ Cortile di Giulietta, Via Cappello 23 ☎ 045/8006100 ⊕ www.teatrodiverona.it), at the Teatro Nuovo (✉ Piazza Viviani 10) is devoted exclusively to the Bard; tickets cost €10. For a week in late July and from the end of August through early September, strolling players from that same company perform multilingual scenes from Shakespeare's *Romeo and Juliet* at the Cortile di Giulietta, in the very place where the story is said to have unfolded.

Nightlife

DISCOS

Lounge with drink in hand on Kasbah cushions at **Cappa Café** (✉ Piazzetta Brà ☎ 045/8004516). You can also have a full meal while overlooking the River Adige and listening to jazz until 2 AM. **Alter Ego** (✉ Via Torricelle 9 ☎ 045/915130) packs in a twentysomething crowd with a vaguely alternative attitude. It's open weekends only from 9 PM to 4 AM. **Eolo** (✉ Via Provolo 24 ☎ 045/597858) attracts an even younger crowd.

WINE BAR **Enocibus** (⊠ Vicolo Pomodoro 3 ☎ 045/594010), one block off Piazza Brà, serves great wine and great food.

Shopping

Food & Wine

De Rossi (⊠ Corso Porta Borsari 3 ☎ 045/8002489) sells baked bread and cakes, pastries, and biscotti that are lusciously caloric. **Salumeria Albertini** (⊠ Corso S. Anastasia 41 ☎ 045/8031074) is Verona's oldest delicatessen: look for the prosciutto and salami hanging outside.

The famous international wine show **Vinitaly** (⊠ Fiera di Verona, Viale del Lavoro 8 ☎ 045/8298170 ⊕ www.vinitaly.com) takes place for five days in early April. It claims to make Verona the "world capital of quality wines" for the week, attracting more than 3,000 exhibitors from dozens of countries. The show costs €35 per day (€30 if purchased in advance) and runs daily 9–7.

Markets

On the third Saturday of every month an antiques and arts-and-crafts market is held in **Piazza San Zeno.** The city's main general market is held at the **Stadio** on Saturday from 8:30 AM–1 PM.

Specialty Stores

ANTIQUES The area around the Gothic church of Sant'Anastasia is full of antiques shops, most of them catering to serious collectors. (After a strenuous day of antiques hunting, it's pleasant to picnic on the Piazza dei Signori.) Try **La Bottega del Tempo** (⊠ Corso S. Anastasia 1 ☎ 045/8005999) for "portable" antiques: the shop specializes in watches and jewelry.

CLOTHING & Via Mazzini is full of the well-known names—Maxmara, Versace, and
ACCESSORIES Stefanel to name but a few. **Furla** (⊠ Via Mazzini 60 ☎ 045/8004760) displays distinctive bags, watches, umbrellas, and key rings. **Pollini** (⊠ Via Mazzini 64 ☎ 045/8032247) is nirvana for shoe collectors. **Prada** (⊠ Corso Porta Borsari ☎ 045/8013861) features Miuccia's postmodern designs.

ENGLISH- The **Bookshop** (⊠ Via Interrato dell'Acqua Morta 3/a ☎ 045/8007614)
LANGUAGE has a good range of English-language books and an English-speaking
BOOKS staff.

THE LAGOON & THE ADRIATIC

Crossing the lagoon from Venice over the Ponte della Libertà to the mainland, you'll be confronted with the sight of oil tankers and red-and-white-striped cranes. Nevertheless, it can make a less-hectic and less-expensive base for exploring the Veneto and Venice itself, which is a mere 10 minutes away by bus or train, and some attractive hotels and restaurants are worth seeking out. What's more, you'll have no parking problems here. Crossing the flat expanse of the lagoon from Venice in the other (southerly) direction brings you to Chioggia, scene of a decisive naval battle between the rival sea powers Venice and Genoa in 1379. Now a bustling fishing port, it's based on a grid alleyway system and has excellent fish restaurants. The long strip of beach at nearby Sottomarina makes it a popular vacation spot for Italians. Rovigo, an inland town due south of Padua on A16, is a working city that's not geared up for tourists, but it does have a good art gallery and its own fine Rotonda. The area between Rovigo and the sea, the Po delta, with its slow-moving rivers, fields, and marshes, offers opportunities for quiet walks, bird-watching, and contemplation.

Mestre

47 *9 km (5½ mi) northwest of Venice.*

Budget travelers sometimes stay at the low-priced accommodations here and make the 10-minute train commute into Venice each day. If you go that route, don't allot much time for Mestre itself; although the city has become the town where the "real Venetians" now live, having been forced out by high rents, it feels more like a bleakly industrial '70s-style suburb than a culture-infused outskirt. However, the small historic center still reveals a few remnants of the medieval defense system: the tower in the main square, Piazza Ferretto; the 14th-century **Scuola dei Battuti**, now a retirement home; and the **Torre dell'Orologio** in Piazzetta Mattei. This brick tower with typical dovetail battlements dates from 1100, but the clock was added in the 16th century. Via Palazzo, the main street, makes for a pleasant stroll, lined as it is with arcaded buildings from the 16th to the 20th century. Note that the train station is marked "Venezia Mestre."

Where to Stay & Eat

$ ✕ **La Pergola.** The rustic atmosphere in this convivial osteria, which has been in this location near the train station since the 1930s, is a welcome break from Mestre's brash modernity. You can take a break from the usual seafood of the Venice area here, too: the menu is strictly meat. The seasonal selection may include dishes such as *coniglio piccante con peperoni e maggiorana* (spicy rabbit with peppers and marjoram) and *sella di maialino da latte al forno* (roast saddle of suckling pig). ✉ *Via Fiume 42* ☎ *041/974932* 🍽 *MC, V* 🕐 *Closed Sun. No lunch Sat.*

$$ 🏨 **Cris.** Completely restored and modernized in 2002, the Cris is still an excellent value for a cheaper visit to Venice. This charming, green-shuttered building is on a quiet side-street just 200 yards from the train station and a 10-minute walk from Mestre city center. There is access for disabled guests, and the entire hotel is strictly no-smoking. ✉ *Via Montenero 3/A, 30171* ☎ *041/926773* 🖷 *041/937106* 🌐 *www.hotelcris. it* 🛏 *18 rooms, 1 without bath* ♿ *In-room data ports, bar, free parking; no TV in some rooms* 🍽 *MC, V* 🍴 *BP.*

$–$$ 🏨 **Vivit.** Many of the rooms here look directly out over one of the few historic parts of Mestre: its main piazza and medieval tower. This area and much of the rest of this busy city center are closed to traffic, so from here you can walk almost everywhere. The bar on the first floor has a cool terrace for relaxing away from the crowds and for enjoying an alfresco breakfast in summer. ✉ *Piazza Ferretto 73, 30174* ☎ *041/ 951385* 🖷 *041/958891* 🌐 *www.hotelvivit.com* 🛏 *33 rooms, 2 suites* ♿ *In-room data ports, in-room safes, minibars, bar, free parking* 🍽 *AE, DC, MC, V* 🍴 *EP.*

Chioggia & Sottomarina

48 *44 km (27 mi) south of Mestre, 35 km (22 mi) south of Venice.*

Only a thin strip of the lagoon separates Chioggia from Sottomarina, but they're as different as chalk from cheese. If you skip the outskirts of Chioggia (after Venice it's the largest settlement on the lagoon), you'll find a gridded series of *calli* (alleyways) and the busiest fishing port of the Venetian lagoon. Cross the Ponte Translagunare and you'll come to Sottomarina, with 9 km (5½ mi) of beach stretching to the river Brenta; it's a popular resort—though one not as spiffy as Venice's Lido. A regular public transport service (No. 11) involving two ferries and two buses leaves hourly from Chioggia for the Lido, offering both an enjoyable lagoon trip and a cheap visit to Venice. In summer a direct service is operated privately. Contact the **Chioggia tourist office** (✉ Lungomare Adriatico 101, 30019 Chioggia ☎ 041/401068) for details. Practically all the hotels are situated in Sottomarina; you'll find the good restaurants in Chioggia.

Topped by the ubiquitous symbol of Venice, St. Mark's lion (irreverently known as "the cat"), the **Vigo Column** marks the eastern end of wide Corso del Popolo, which runs the length of the town and along which you'll find the main monuments. It's impossible to get lost in this grid plan. Parallel to the Corso, the Canale Vena is spanned by eight bridges, the most picturesque of which is the **Ponte Vigo** at the eastern end, Chioggia's version of the Rialto. Take an hour or so to stroll along the main drag, or poke around the fish market (held Tuesday through Saturday) and the narrow alleys with gently flapping washing strung across their balconies.

Walking down the corso from the Vigo column, you'll pass the 18th-century church of **Sant'Andrea.** After going by Sant'Andrea, you'll soon arrive at the **Palazzo del Granaio** (1322), formerly the town granary and one of the few buildings to have survived the sea battle. A niche on the facade has a *Madonna and Child* by the sculptor Jacopo Sansovino (1486–1570). The **Chiesa della Santa Trinità** contains paintings by the schools of Tintoretto and Veronese. ✉ *Piazzetta XX Settembre* ⊙ *Open for Mass.*

The Romanesque bell tower predates the imposing but austere **Duomo** designed by Baldassare Longhena (1604–82). The interior holds some fine 18th-century paintings including work by Piazzetta (1683–1754) and Tiepolo (1696–1770). ✉ *Piazza del Duomo 77* ☎ *041/400496* ⊙ *Daily 7–noon and 4–6.*

Hotels stretch out along the **Lungomare Adriatico,** scene of a permanent *passeggiata* (stroll), even in winter. The beach is visible from the upstairs windows of hotels, but it's so encumbered with a barrier of buildings that you can't see it from the road. You'll have to pay to get on the beach unless you walk to the far west end, though many hotels will have their own strip for guests. You'll find the usual crop of discos, swimming pools, bars, entertainment, opportunities for horseback riding, sailing, boat trips, and a teeming nightlife with karaoke on the beach and outdoor films.

In summer, classical concerts are held in the town's churches and in the museum garden.

Where to Stay & Eat

$$ ✕ **El Gato.** Signor Silvano cooks the vegetables grown in his own garden and Signora Alba is an old hand at the *dolci* (desserts). It's a winning combination. Try a creamy risotto with shrimp and arugula, spaghetti with sardines and pine nuts, and the linguine *con molluschi* (with smoky-tasting shellfish). The brick arches and wooden ceiling give a rustic air to the proceedings. ⊠ *Campo Sant'Andrea 653* ☎ *041/401806* ⊕ *www.elgato.it* ⌂ *Reservations essential* ▭ *AE, DC, MC, V* ⊘ *Closed Mon. and late Jan.–mid-Feb. No lunch Tues.*

$–$$ ✕ **Ai Vaporetti.** This restaurant overlooks the lagoon and Ponte Lagunale: a perfect spot for a summer evening. Downstairs, the whole ceiling is covered by a canvas fishing boat's sail, and above the intimate alcoves is a mezzanine level with a wrought-iron balcony. The menu is restricted to fish cooked over a wood fire. You could go for the eels, or maybe the clams in tomato sauce. There's a good local wine list. ⊠ *Campo Traghetto 1256, Sottomarina Lido* ☎ *041/400841* ⊕ *www. aivaporetti.com* ⌂ *Reservations essential* ▭ *AE, DC, MC, V* ⊘ *Closed Tues. and 3 wks in Nov.*

$–$$ ✕ **Bella Venezia.** In summer you can eat in the courtyard amid the glory of the plants at this local mainstay, which has been in town across from the old fish market since the late 1800s. Try the *carpaccio di branzino e scampi* (raw sea bass and scampi). Chilled port or grappa is a refreshing treat. ⊠ *Calle Corona 51* ☎ *041/400500* ⊕ *www.ristorantebellavenezia. com* ⌂ *Reservations essential* ▭ *AE, DC, MC, V* ⊘ *Closed Thurs. and Jan. No dinner Wed. and Oct.–Feb.*

$$–$$$ 🏨 **Grande Italia.** An important waterside landmark in Chioggia since 1914, the Grande marks the beginning of town from the lagoon side. Facing directly onto the Ponte Vigo, its elegantly furnished rooms look out over the sea on one side or down the pedestrian-only corso on the other. Spacious, marble-lined bathrooms add a real sense of luxury to a hotel that is perfectly placed for visiting Venice: a one-hour ferry ride up the lagoon. The very renowned (and expensive) restaurant closes on Tuesday. ⊠ *Rione Sant'Andrea 597, 30015* ☎ *041/ 400515* 🖷 *041/400185* ⊕ *www.hotelgrandeitalia.com* ↴ *45 rooms, 8 suites* ⌂ *Restaurant, health club, bar, parking (fee)* ▭ *AE, DC, MC, V* ⦿ *BP.*

$$ 🏨 **Bristol.** Of the many hotels along the Lungomare, this Best Western is one of the most tasteful and spacious, with service that does not take itself too seriously. You'll find a sizeable swimming pool, an opulent restaurant, and piano accompaniment in the evenings. The €5 extra fee for a room with a water view is worth it. ⊠ *Lungomare Adriatico 46, 30019* ☎ *041/5540389* 🖷 *041/5541813* ⊕ *www.hotelbristol.net* ↴ *70 rooms* ⌂ *Restaurant, in-room safes, minibars, pool, beach, piano bar, children's programs (all ages), meeting rooms, free parking, some pets allowed* ▭ *AE, DC, MC, V* ⦿ *BP.*

Rovigo

49 *70 km (44 mi) southwest of Venice, 53 km (33 mi) southwest of Chioggia-Sottomarina.*

Between Chioggia and Rovigo the land is flat, given over to market gardening and agriculture. Rovigo itself is a fairly quiet, personable town that is noticeably less prosperous than its northern neighbors, reflected in generally lower prices, especially for accommodation. Join the farmers doing their town business in the wood-panelled **Caffè Borsa** (⊠ Piazza Garibaldi 2 ☎ 0425/21999) for an espresso and snack. It's closed Thursday. If you're in the center of the city, the first thing to catch your eye will most likely be the **Torre Dona,** one of the tallest towers in Italy, and the **Torre Mozza,** the one remaining tower of the castle built in 920 by the Bishop of Adria. Both appear to be rather alarmingly out of kilter. Like other towns and cities in the area, Rovigo submitted to the yoke of Venice, which controlled the town from 1482 until the end of the Republic.

The main **Piazza Vittorio Emanuele II** holds some fine palaces, including the **Palazzo Roncale** designed in 1555 by Sanmichele (1484–1559). Also in the main square is the **Accademia dei Concordi,** which was founded in 1580 and now houses the Pinacoteca (Art Gallery), with a fine, intimate collection of Veneto masters, including Bellini's *Madonna.* ⊠ *Piazza Vittorio Emanuele II 14* ☎ *0425/21654* ☜ *€2.50* ☉ *Sept.–June, weekdays 9:30–12:30 and 3:30–6:30, weekends 10–noon; July and Aug., Mon.–Sat. 10–1.*

An impressive dual row of pine trees leads up to the church of Santa Maria del Soccorso di Rovigo, better known as **La Rotonda.** Contrasting against the trees stands the white, Palladian-influenced octagonal structure, surrounded by a portico of Tuscan columns. It was designed by Francesco Zamberlan (1529–1606) in 1594, and the brick campanile was added in 1673 by Baldassare Longhena. The interior, both walls and dome, is entirely covered by 17th-century Veneto paintings. ⊠ *Piazza XX Settembre 37* ☎ *0425/24914* ☜ *Free* ☉ *Mon.–Sat. 8–noon and 3:30–7:30, Sun. 9–noon and 4–7.*

Where to Stay & Eat

$$ ✕ **Tavernetta Dante.** The comprehensive menu of Veneto specialties, including plenty of seafood, is complemented by an excellent choice of wines in this convivial, long-established restaurant. The main room is decorated in warm tones of pink plaster and brick; the other (no-smoking), in cool shades of green, gives onto a plant-filled terrace for outdoor summer dining. The menu changes frequently according to season, with dishes like radicchio and sausage risotto, *tagliata con rucola e grano* (beef steak with arugula and Parmesan), or a tempting mixed grilled seafood. ⊠ *Corso del Popolo 212* ☎ *0425/26386* ▭ *AE, MC, V* ☉ *Closed Sun. and Aug. 10–30.*

$ ▥ **Villa Regina Margherita.** The most attractive of Rovigo's hotels, this early-20th-century villa glows a welcoming pink and reflects an art nouveau style. Large comfortable armchairs, velvet upholstery, and potted palms give an air of luxury, and the restaurant is very highly regarded.

Book ahead, as rooms fill quickly. ⊠ *Viale Regina Margherita 6, 45100* ☎ *0425/361540* 🖷 *0425/31301* 🖵 *20 rooms, 2 suites* 🍴 *Restaurant, bar, free parking, some pets allowed* 🚭 *AE, DC, MC, V* ⦿❘ *BP.*

ALONG THE BRENTA

Once upon a time, the Brenta River was a constant source of trouble to the settlers of the area, as it was prone to flooding and caused the lagoon to silt up. Steps had been taken to regulate matters since the 11th century, but it was not until Venice took control of the area in 1405 that matters were really taken in hand. Diversions were created, banks strengthened, and the deposit of silt controlled. By the 16th century the land was safe enough for extensive farming and for wealthy Venetians to enjoy *villeggiatura*, a vacation from harried city life, by building princely residences on their country estates. The best architects, sculptors, and artists were summoned, and elegant symmetry and baroque sumptuousness remain the characteristic style. Some of the 100 or so villas built served as farmhouses, while others were just used for pleasure. A handful of these are now open to the public, often for only a couple of days a week, so check before arranging your itinerary. Two of the best villas, each reflecting the different basic designs of Palladio, are the Villa Pisani and the Villa Foscari.

Malcontenta & Villa Foscari

★ ➎ *8 km (5 mi) west of Venice.*

Malcontenta is the first village along the Brenta River from Venice. Legend has it that the name "Malcontenta" (unhappy) was derived from the wife of one of the Foscari brothers, the lady having been banished here for "inappropriate behavior," but the real explanation is likely to be more prosaic, as the name was already in use before the arrival of the Foscari. Built in 1560 by—who else—Palladio, **Villa Foscari** is not one of his long, low designs but one of his large cubes with portico and dome, its lawn running down to the river. Giovanni Batista Zelotti (1526–78) lent his hand in decorating the walls inside, covering them with allegorical and mythological figures in mock architectural effects. ⊠ *Malcontenta* ☎ *041/5470012* ⊕ *www.lamalcontenta.com* ✉ *€7* ☾ *May–Oct., Tues. and Sat. 9–noon.*

Villa Pisani

★ ☾ ➎ *37 km (23 mi) west of Malcontenta, 34 km (21 mi) west of Venice.*

Extensive grounds with rare trees, ornamental fountains, and garden follies surround this extraordinary 18th-century palace in Stra. It was one of the last of many stately residences constructed along the Brenta River from the 16th to 18th centuries by wealthy Venetians for their vacation and escape from the midsummer humidity. The trompe l'oeil frescoes by Giambattista Tiepolo on the ceiling of the ballroom alone are worth the visit. If you have youngsters in tow surfeited with old masters, explore the gorgeous **park** and the **maze** (open April through September only). ✉ *Stra* ☎ *049/502074* 🏛 *Villa, maze, and grounds €5; maze and grounds only, €2.50* 🕒 *Apr.–Sept., Tues.–Sun. 9–7; Oct.–Mar., Tues.–Sun. 9–4; last entry 1 hr before closing.*

Euganean Hills: Abano Terme & Montegrotto Terme

52 *12 km (7 mi) south of Padua, 49 km (30 mi) west of Venice.*

Rising abruptly out of the plain, the volcanic Euganean Hills are a pleasure to explore in any season, the gentle slopes strewn with chestnut trees, olive groves, and vineyards that encroach upon the road. The hills themselves enfold unspoiled villages, and at their feet you'll find abbeys and villas. Take time to wander along the paths marked for walkers, look for wild mushrooms, and enjoy the microclimates that produce Mediterranean and Alpine flowers, myrtle, and even prickly pears. In spring the blossom of almond and cherry trees turns the hills a frothy pink and white. For information about the regional park here contact the **Parco Regionale dei Colli Euganei** (✉ Via Rana Cà Mori 8, Este ☎ 0427/612010).

Fango (mud) draws people in droves to the two conjoined resorts of **Abano Terme** and **Montegrotto Terme.** There's no escaping the steam that rises from streets and gardens at every turn and is channeled into the collection of hotels and thermal clinics that make up one of Europe's foremost spa destinations. Water emanates from the Dolomites after a journey deep underground and resurfaces at a temperature of 87°F, full of salt, bromine, and iodine. Each hotel has its series of slimy mud basins and clients in dressing gowns submitting to mud massage, inhalations, or irrigations. If you're not interested in mud, or indulge in one of the nine five-star hotels here, you'll probably be happier staying in one of the small towns in the area.

Even if you're not staying in Abano or Montegrotto, you can schedule individual health and beauty treatments at a number of spa hotels operated by **GB Terme Hotels.** ✉ *Via Pietro d'Abano 1, Abano Terme* ☎ *049/8665100* 🖷 *049/8669779* ⊕ *www.gbhotels.it.*

You can also test the waters with a thermal swim at **Columbus Garden.** ✉ *Via Martiri D'Ungheria 22, Abano Terme* ☎ *049/8601555* 🏛 *Weekdays €8, weekends €9* 🕒 *July and Aug., daily 9 AM–11 PM; Sept.–June, weekdays 12:30–11, Sat. 9 AM–11 PM, Sun. 9 AM–10 PM.*

Montegrotto Terme's so-called **Butterfly Arc,** encompassing the Casa delle Farfalle (Butterfly House) and Bosco delle Fate (Fairies' Wood), is one of the world's best collections of live butterflies. You can watch more than 400 exotic species feed, court, and reproduce. The Bosco, which is said to be enchanted, is studded with statues of fairies and elves. This is hands down one of the best attractions in the region for kids. ✉ *Via degli Scavi 21 bis, Montegrotto Terme* ☎ *049/8910189* 🏛 *€7* 🕒 *Feb.–Mar. and Oct.–Nov., daily 9:30–12:30 and 2–4; Apr.–Sept., daily 9:30–12:30 and 2:30–5:30. Closed some days in Feb. and Nov.; call ahead.*

Where to Stay & Eat

★ **$$** ✕ **Aubergine.** Here's an unusual combination: a semiformal restaurant, a pizzeria, and minigolf course, all run by one family. The restaurant menu changes regularly to focus on seasonal specialties, creatively interpreted by the lady of the house who presides over the kitchen. Before dipping into the tempting selection of chocolate desserts, try the polenta with truffles (fall), chicken breast with ham and sage (summer), or spinach and cheese gnocchi (winter). A range of pizzas includes one, of course, with eggplant. ⊠ *Via Ghislandhi 5* ☎ *049/8669910* ▭ *AE, DC, MC, V* ⊗ *Closed Wed. and first 2 wks of Aug.*

$ ✕ **Al Bosco.** A 3-km (2-mi) drive out of Montegrotto in the Torreglia direction (signposted left) brings you to this hilltop setting near the woods. The restaurant's rustic decor features large copper pans and cowbells. Cooking is done *alla brace* (barbecued) in summer, and the accent is on meats such as *scottadito di agnello* (barbecued lamb chops) and *fiorentina* (char-grilled T-bone steak, priced according to weight). ⊠ *Via Cogolo 8, Parco dei Colli Euganei* ☎☎ *049/794317* ▭ *AE, MC, V* ⊗ *Closed Wed. and last 3 wks of Jan. No dinner Tues.*

$$$–$$$$ 🏨 **Bristol Buja Spa.** One of Abano's modern, first-class hotels, the Bristol Buja offers all the usual mud treatments, diet regimes, and exercise classes in outdoor pools. The indoor pool is covered by a colorful stained-glass roof. The bright, well-furnished, luxurious rooms all look out over the tree-studded front lawns. Most guests come for several days to subject themselves to all the treatments on half- or full-board arrangements, but single-night guests are also welcome. ⊠ *Via Monteortone 2, 35031 Abano Terme* ☎ *049/8669390* 🖷 *049/667910* ⊕ *www. jpmoser.com/bristolbuja.html* ⇴ *116 rooms* ⚫ *Restaurant, in-room safes, minibars, driving range, golf privileges, Internet, tennis courts, 3 pools, gym, health club, spa, bicycles, boccie, bar, meeting rooms, free parking, some pets allowed* ▭ *AE, DC, MC, V* ⊗ *Closed Nov. 21–Dec. 19* ⦿❘ *BP.*

Praglia

★ 🟢 *8 km (5 mi) west of Abano Terme, 12 km (7 mi) southwest of Padua.*

You can tour the evocative 15th-century halls and cloisters of this Benedictine monastery set at the foot of the Euganean Hills. The monastery was founded in the 11th century, but the present buildings date from the 15th and 16th centuries and consist of four cloisters, two refectories—one with a fine *Crucifixion* by Montagna—and the church with its Romanesque campanile containing paintings by Veneto masters. Known for book restoration, the monastery has a library of more than 100,000 books on its 16th-century shelves. The monks sell the wine and honey produced here. ⊠ *Loc. Bresseo di Teolo* ☎ *049/9999300* 🏷 *Free; donations appreciated* ⊗ *Guided tours only, every ½ hr., Apr.–Oct., Tues.–Sun. 3:30–5:30; Nov.–Mar., Tues.–Sun. 2:30–4:30.*

Monselice

54 *7 km (4½ mi) south of Montegrotto Terme, 61 km (38 mi) southwest of Venice.*

Rising out of the Paduan plain, Monselice's defensive walls skirt the base of the volcanic hill around which the town is ranged, making its lofty position unique in this part of the country. The foremost building of the town is the **Castello di Monselice,** or Ca' Marcello—a must to visit. Passing through the hands of Ezzelino III da Romano, who extended the original 12th-century building, and then to the Carrara and Marcello families, this castle has been lovingly and meticulously restored by Count Vittorio Cini, into whose care it came after World War I. As you enter the Salone d'Onore, you will immediately notice the wonderful chimney with its tiered arches on columns of majolica set against the red-and-white checkerboard walls. It's everything a medieval castle should be, both inside and out. ⊠ *Via del Santuario 24* ☎ *0429/72931* ▦ *€5.50* ☉ *Mar. 20–Nov., Tues.–Sun. 9–noon and 3–6; Dec.–Mar. 19, guided tours only, Tues.–Sun. every hr 2–5.*

The Via Santuario leads to the **Via Sette Chiese,** a private road that climbs up the hill to the **Villa Duodo,** summer residence of the Duodo family built in 1593 by Scamozzi. At the lower end of the street stands the Romanesque Gothic **Duomo Vecchio** (☎ 0429/72130) and six little pilgrimage churches, where those in need of forgiveness could stop and pray on their way to the seventh, San Giorgio. **San Giorgio** houses relics of some of the first Christian martyrs. These were transferred from the catacombs of Rome at the behest of the Duodo family and are displayed in glass cases. Among the relics are those of St. Valentine, and surely it's no surprise to hear that there's an annual pilgrimage here on February 14. San Giorgio is open on Sunday; contact the **tourist office** (⊠ Via del Santuario 6 ☎ 0429/783026) for opening hours at other times.

Where to Stay & Eat

$$–$$$ ✕ **La Torre.** You can't dine in Monselice's castle, but the next best thing is a meal within the medieval walls, right on the main square. The accent here is on seasonal ingredients, especially vegetables. If you're here in April you can sample the local white asparagus, but just as delightful are the *fior di zucca* (zucchini blossoms), which in summer, along with wild porcini, are picked as fillings for the homemade ravioli. You'll find truffles as well, but you'll be digging deep in your pocket for the tubers. ⊠ *Piazza Mazzini 14* ☎ *0429/73752* ⚏ *Reservations essential* ▤ *AE, DC, MC, V* ☉ *Closed Mon., Aug., and Dec. 24–Jan. 7. No dinner Sun.*

$$ ▦ **Hotel Ceffri.** Hidden away on its own leafy grounds, the Ceffri is only a few minutes from the Monselice autostrada exit, on the outskirts of town. The rooms are spacious and quiet, each with its own balcony. There's a pleasant garden next to the pool, a perfect place for sipping a long drink or a *thè freddo* (iced tea) in summer. The adjacent restaurant associated with the hotel, the Villa Corner, provides local and international dishes. To be recommended is the dessert *strudel con crema e pinoli* (strudel with cream and pine nuts). ⊠ *Via Orti 7/b, 35043*

☎ 0429/783111 🖶 0429/783100 ⊕ *www.ceffri.it* ⏎ *32 rooms, 12 suites* ⚐ *Restaurant, minibars, pool, piano bar, meeting rooms, free parking, no-smoking rooms* ⊟ *AE, DC, MC, V* ⏐⊙⏐ *BP.*

Nightlife & the Arts

FESTIVALS Monselice relives the Middle Ages with a festival on the first three Sundays of September. It culminates in the medieval festival **Giostra della Rocca** on the third Sunday, when musclemen perform feats of strength with millstones, archers strive for glory, and riders on horseback gallop around the town in the *quintana*. To add to it all, there's a market with vendors in medieval costume. For more information contact the tourist office. ⊠ *Via del Santuario 6* 🖶🖶 *0429/783026.*

Arquà Petrarca

⑤⑤ *22 km (14 mi) south of Padua, 9 km (5½ mi) northeast of Este.*

This village, tucked away in the Euganean Hills, is a little jewel. The narrow cobbled streets wind their way between carefully restored medieval houses and pretty gardens surrounded by the mellow green of the hills and vineyards. It's a good spot for lunch. The poet Francesco Petrarca (1304–74), more often referred to by his Anglicized name, Petrarch, spent the last four years of his life in this little haven: visit his house, **Casa di Petrarca**, and trace his life through the medieval frescoes on its walls (they were retouched in the 17th century). You can see his chair and desk here and visit his sarcophagus by the church in the center of the village. ⊠ *Via Valesella 4* ☎ *0429/718294* ☒ *€3* ⊙ *Mar.–Oct., Tues.–Sun. 9–noon and 3–6:30; Nov.–Feb., Tues.–Sun. 9–noon and 2:30–5.*

Where to Eat

$$–$$$ ✕ **La Montanella.** The oil used here is cold pressed from the century-old olive trees in the garden, which you can admire from the restaurant's veranda. The strictly local cuisine highlights homemade pasta, poultry, and game—including venison and boar. Only fresh, seasonal vegetables are used and in summer these will include delicacies like wild herbs and nettles. Try the orange blossom or quail risotto, or the *papero alla frutta* (duck with pear, grapes, or cherries), made to an original 17th-century recipe, complemented with a full-bodied merlot or cabernet from the Euganean hills. ⊠ *Via Costa 33* ☎ *0429/718200* ⊕ *www.montanella. it* ⊟ *AE, DC, MC, V* ⊙ *Closed Tues., Jan. 2–15, and Aug. 10–25. No dinner Mon.*

Nightlife & the Arts

The **Festa delle Giuggiole** (Jujube Festival) on the first and second weekends of October involves local food and wine tastings, buskers, and flag-waving performances. Call the **Comune di Arquà Petrarca** (☎ 0429/ 777100) for information.

Este

⑤⑥ *9 km (5½ mi) southwest of Monselice, 80 km (50 mi) southwest of Venice.*

Este was an important center of the Veneto before becoming Roman Ateste, retaining its prominent role under the rule of the Este family, later to become dukes of Ferrara. Power was then transferred to Venice. Dominating the town is the **Castello dei Carraresi,** now in ruins, although the gardens are open to the public. Abutting the walls, housed in a 16th-century palace, is the **Museo Nazionale Atestino,** where you can see the Veneto's best collection of pre-Roman and Roman artifacts, including some fine bronzes such as the 7th-century *Situla Benvenuti* and the *Dea di Caldevigo* dating from the 5th century. ⊠ *Via Guido Negri 2* 🕾 *0429/2085* 🖾 *€2* ⊙ *Open daily 9–8.*

The baroque **Duomo** is dedicated to Santa Thecla, who is represented in a large painting by Tiepolo. ⊠ *Piazza Santa Thecla 6* 🕾 *0429/2009* ⊙ *Apr.–Sept. 9:30–noon and 4–6; Oct.–Mar. 9:30–noon and 3–6.*

Where to Stay & Eat

$–$$ ✕ **Sapio.** Tucked up a little alley in the center of town, this is the place for wine lovers, for it's a well-stocked *enoteca* (wine shop/bar) as well as a restaurant. There's no set menu—the chef is inventive and likes to use local ingredients such as lamb, goose, and seasonal vegetables. Homemade desserts such as *torta della nonna* ("grandma's tart," made with pine nuts), *torta al cioccolato* (chocolate cake), and seasonal fruit tarts are a specialty. The decor is plain with terra-cotta accents, and there's a quiet garden for alfresco eating in warm weather. ⊠ *Via Madonetta 2/c* 🕾 *0429/602565* ⌂ *Reservations essential* 🖃 *AE, DC, MC, V* ⊙ *Closed Mon.*

$$$ 🏨 **Villa Pisani.** The spacious, high-ceilinged rooms in this enormous
Fodor'sChoice 16th-century villa are completely furnished with period furniture—
★ some even have fully frescoed walls. All rooms look out over stunning formal gardens and beyond to a 15-acre park with rare trees, a chapel, a theater, and a concealed swimming pool. You'll also have access to three big *sale* (lounges), where you can chat with the few other lucky guests and Signora Scalabrin, who shares her patrician living areas, music, and books. With breakfast served on silver platters, this is a bed-and-breakfast that outstrips almost all the competition. ⊠ *Via Roma 19, 35040 Vescovana, 11 km (7 mi) south of Este* 🕾🕾 *0425/920016* ⊕ *www. villapisani.com* 🛏 *8 rooms, 1 suite* ⌂ *Pool, horseback riding, Internet, convention center, free parking, some pets allowed; no a/c in some rooms, no room phones, no TV in some rooms, no smoking* 🖃 *AE, DC, MC, V* ⭍◯ *BP.*

$ 🏨 **Beatrice d'Este.** The statues set among the trees leading up to the entrance to this hotel against the backdrop of the castle walls make you think it's going to be rather grand. It is, but it's also family run and very good value, with quiet sunny rooms. The hotel is named after one of the most renowned women of her day (1475–97), an intelligent and cultured beauty married at the age of 16 to the seventh duke of Milan (who commissioned Leonardo da Vinci to paint *The Last Supper*). ⊠ *Viale delle Rimembranze 1, 35042* 🕾 *0429/600533* 🕾 *0429/601957* ⊕ *www. hotelbeatricedeste.com* 🛏 *30 rooms* ⌂ *Restaurant, bar, free parking, some pets allowed* 🖃 *AE, DC, MC, V* ⭍◯ *BP.*

$ 🏨 **Castello.** Some of the rooms in this centrally located hotel look out over the medieval castle walls; all are smartly furnished with style and taste. The small lobby downstairs leads straight into a busy café full of gossiping locals and serving coffee, drinks, and snacks all day. Breakfast is not included in the price. ✉ *Via San Girolamo 7/a, 35042* ☎ *0429/602223* 🖷 *0429/602418* ⊕ *www.imieiviaggi.com/hotelcastello* 🛏 *12 rooms* ⚲ *In-room data ports, minibars, parking (fee), some pets allowed* ☰ *AE, DC, MC, V* ⦿ *EP.*

Montagnana

❺ *42 km (26 mi) west of Este, 85 km (53 mi) southwest of Venice.*

You could almost be forgiven for thinking that you have been transported back to the 1300s as you approach the medieval walls and tall, crenellated towers that surround Montagnana, glowing pink against the green of the moat. Might you even hear the noise of the hooves of horses galloping past? If you're here in September, then your ears may not be deceiving you, as this is when the 10 bareback jockeys compete for the *pallium* (a red cloth), from which the name *palio* is derived. In this event the whole town celebrates the end of the rule of the tyrant Ezzelino III, who in 1242 practically destroyed the town by fire. It was thanks to the Carrara family that the defensive walls, with their 24 towers and four gates, were subsequently put in place; these now rank among the best preserved in Europe, and even boast two castles directly abutting their ramparts. One of these, the **Rocca degli Alberi**, was built in 1362 to defend the western approaches but now, functioning as a youth hostel, is only subject to invasions by backpackers.

Montagnana's eastern gate (Porta Padova) is defended by the town's oldest fortification, the **Castello di San Zeno,** a survivor from Ezzelino's time. It presently houses the **Museo Civico**, consisting of memorabilia of two famous tenors born in the town in 1885, Giovanni Martinelli and Aureliano Pertile. For a panoramic view over the red roofs and a different perspective on the walls, take a trip up the tower. ✉ *Piazza Trieste 15* ☎ *0429/804128* 🎫 *Castle and museum €2.10, tower €1* ☉ *Museum, guided tours only: Wed.–Fri. at 11, weekends at 11, 4, 5, and 6. Castle and tower: Apr.–Oct., Tues. 4–7, Wed.–Sat. 9:30–12:30 and 4–7, Sun. 10–1 and 4–7; Nov.–Mar., Tues. 3–6, Wed.–Sat. 9:30–12:30 and 3–6, Sun. 10–1 and 3–6.*

The brick **Duomo** reflects both Gothic and Renaissance styles. In its spacious nave, your eye might be caught by the altarpieces by Veronese and Buonconsiglio (died circa 1536) but will probably dwell longer on the lively painting of the decisive *Battle of Lepanto* (1571) by Vassilacchi (known as Aliense), fought against the Turkish invaders. ✉ *Piazza Vittorio Emanuele* ☎ *0429/83736* 🎫 *Free* ☉ *Apr.–Oct., daily 8–noon and 3–6; Nov.–Mar., daily 8–noon and 1–5.*

need a break? Whatever the time of year, it's worth a stop for a delicious ice cream at the **Bottega del Gelato** (☎ *0429/800855*), across the square from the cathedral. Also, don't leave town without strolling through the cobbled streets and buying some prosciutto *di Montagnana,* as sweet and tasty as any you'll find in Italy.

The Duomo is the dominant feature of the main square, **Piazza Vittorio Emanuele.** Of the Quattrocento buildings gracing the rest of the square, perhaps the finest is the Venetian Gothic **Palazzo Lombardesco,** with its balconies and five-paned windows. Notice the ornamental chimneys sprouting like flowers from the roofs.

Where to Stay & Eat

$$$ ✕ **Marco Polo.** This is a serious fish restaurant full of locals intent on enjoying their meals. It's a bit outside the town center, but worth the walk (about 10 minutes) if you're hankering for simply prepared, fresh seafood. Most dishes are steamed or boiled, then dressed with simple sauces to highlight their natural flavor. Make your way past the stacked-up piles of plates in this no-frills place and try out the risotto with prawns, scampi, or *polipo* (octopus). ⊠ *Via San Zeno 37* ☎ *0429/81509* ⚑ *Reservations essential* ▭ *AE, MC, V* ☉ *Closed Mon.*

★ **$** ✕▦ **Aldo Moro.** Pink marble, parquet floors, and polished furniture imbue this little hotel with ineffable charm. Formerly an inn, the building is steeped in style and warmth, enhanced by beamed ceilings and creaking floors. Bathrooms are pink marble, too. If you dine in the restaurant ($$; closed Monday), make sure you taste the prosciutto di Montagnana, then perhaps some *oca* (goose) or, as an extravagant novelty, tagliolini *al cacao con funghi porcini e tartufo* (with cocoa, mushrooms, and truffles). For secondi, try *filetto di cervo in salsa "mercante di vino"* (fillet of venison in a wine sauce). ⊠ *Via Guglielmo Marconi 27, 35044* ☎ *0429/81351* 🖷 *0429/82842* ⊕ *www.hotelaldomoro.com* ⊷ *29 rooms, 5 suites* ⚒ *Restaurant, bar, meeting rooms* ☉ *Closed Aug. 1–15* ⦿ *BP.*

¢ ✕▦ **Concordia.** Whether you come to eat or stay here, expect a warm welcome at this family-run establishment. You're not in the historic center, but you're surrounded by a modest, homey atmosphere with folksy furnishings to match. There are only a small number of rooms, so book ahead. A full meal ($) of traditional home cooking chosen from the simple menu might include *bigoli* (thick, whole-wheat spaghetti) *con ragù,* local prosciutto, or *pollo alla griglia* (grilled chicken). An inexpensive house wine from the Colli Euganei will set it all off nicely. ⊠ *Via San Zeno 148, 35044* ☎🖷 *0429/81673* ⊷ *8 rooms* ⚒ *Restaurant, bar* ▭ *AE, MC, V* ☉ *Restaurant closed Sun.* ⦿ *BP.*

Nightlife & the Arts

The **Palio** takes place on the first Sunday in September. Ten districts compete in a horse race around the outside of the ancient walls. You can get information from the **Comitato Palio dei 10 Communi** (☎ 0429/80448) or the **tourist office** (⊠ Piazza Trieste 3, 35044 Montagnana ☎🖷 0429/81320).

LAKE GARDA

Lake Garda is the most popular of the Italian lakes as well as the largest, spanning the borders of three regions—the Veneto, Trentino, and Lombardy. The size of the lake actually has an impact upon the climate, making the summers cooler and the winters warmer. Vacationers on packages love it, especially the German and the French, who invade the large number of hotels. If you plan to spend any time during the summer in the busiest resorts, such as Sirmione, book well ahead. Of course, if you're a windsurfer or a sailor, then this is your heaven, with breezes tailor-made for you. The funicular ride up the slopes of Monte Baldo is spectacular. You can even arrange for a mountain bike to meet you at the top or take a paragliding trip. Glorious walking can be enjoyed in the mountains that enclose the narrow northern part of the lake, tapering off to the south to give way to flatter country. On the gentle slopes are lush olive and lemon groves, oleanders and palm trees, and the vines that provide the grapes for the local wines such as Valpolicella and Bardolino. Enchanting castles and little medieval towns complete the picture.

Bardolino

❺❽ *24 km (15 mi) northeast of Sirmione, 157 km (97 mi) east of Milan.*

Famous for its red wine, Bardolino hosts the **Cura dell'Uva** (Grape Cure Festival) in late September–early October. It's a great excuse to indulge in the local vino, which is light, dry, and often slightly sparkling. (Bring aspirin, just in case the cure turns out to be worse than the disease.)

Bardolino is one of the most popular summer resorts on the lake. It stands on the eastern shore at the wider end of the lake. Here there are two handsome Romanesque churches: **San Severo**, from the 11th century, and **San Zeno**, from the 9th. Both are in the center of the small town.

Punta di San Vigilio

❺❾ *6 km (4 mi) north of Bardolino, 163 km (101 mi) east of Milan.*

Just about everyone agrees that this is the prettiest spot on Garda's eastern shore. Punta di San Vigilio is full of cypresses from the gardens of the 15th-century **Villa Guarienti di Brenzone** (⌧ Frazione Punta San Vigilio 1); the villa itself is closed to the public.

Malcesine

❻⓪ *179 km (111 mi) northwest of Venice, 67 km (42 mi) northwest of Verona.*

One of the loveliest areas along the upper eastern shore of Lake Garda, Malcesine is principally known as a summer resort with sailing and windsurfing schools. The 13 campsites and tourist villages do tend to make the town a little crowded in summer. There are, however, some nice walks from the town toward the mountains behind. The town hall was the seat of the Captains of the Lake during the 16th and 17th centuries.

Dominating the town is the 13th- to 14th-century **Castello Scaligero,** built by the della Scalas. Inside are several small museums, one of which is devoted to Goethe, who in 1786 spent a short spell in prison here—while sketching the lake he was thought to be an Austrian spy and promptly arrested. Another contains paintings of the ships being hauled to Torbole. There's a fine view from the tower. ⌧ *Via Castello* ☎ *045/7400837* 🕮 *€4* 🕓 *Apr.–Oct., daily 9–6:30; Nov.–Mar., weekends 10:30–5.*

off the beaten path | **MONTE BALDO –** If you are fond of cable cars, take the 15-minute *funivia* ride to the top of Monte Baldo (5,791 feet) for a great view of the whole lake in summer, or possibly a short ski run in winter (expect a wait). The area is also a great place for mountain biking, and you can even arrange for bikes to meet you at the top. Because of the variety of vegetation found here, from olive and lemon groves to beech woods, not to mention the profuse Alpine flowers, the mountain was once known as the *hortus europae* (garden of Europe). ✉ *Via Navene Vecchia 12* ☎ *0457/7400206* ⊕ *www.funiviamalcesine.com* 💶 *€15 round-trip* 🕓 *Mid-Mar.–mid-Sept., daily 8–6:45; mid-Sept.–mid-Oct., daily 8–5:45; mid-Oct.–mid-Mar, daily 8–4:45.*

Sports & the Outdoors

MOUNTAIN BIKING **Furioli** (✉ Piazza Matteotti 11 ☎ 045/7400089) rents bikes by the day. Contact **Funivia Malcesine-Montebaldo** (☎ 045/7400206) for mountain-bike rentals and paragliding.

Peschiera del Garda

61 *46 km (29 mi) southwest of Malcesine, 140 km (90 mi) west of Venice.*

At the southern end of the Lake Garda, Peschiera is a pleasant, old-fashioned place to wander around for a half day or so. It's less touristy than other lake towns and makes an alternative to staying in Sirmione. You can easily use Peschiera as a less expensive, more laid-back base, and drive—or, better yet, take a boat—to and from Sirmione during the day. Sports enthusiasts will find all the usual water sports on hand in Peschiera. The town is surrounded by hefty bastion walls that were begun by the Venetians in 1553 and subsequently strengthened by Napoléon and later the Austrians. Crossing the bridge from the harbor brings you through the defenses to the historic center and the *lungolago* (lake promenade) lined with villas now defended by dogs. The Roman writer Pliny (AD 23–79) noted that Peschiera was the place for eels, and indeed the eel is featured on the town's coat of arms. So don't be surprised if you see them on the menu.

off the beaten path | **PARCO GIARDINO SIGURTÀ –** Over a period of 40 years, Count Doctor Carlo Sigurtà transformed the hillside into a sumptuous garden, introducing walkways through lawn carpets, woods, canals with water lilies, surrealist sculptures in boxwood, rosebushes, grottoes, and cypresses. It's a magical place to spend an afternoon. ✉ *Valeggio sul Mincio, 8 km (5 mi) south of Peschiera* ☎ *045/6371033* 💶 *€8* 🕓 *Mar.–Nov., daily 9–6.*

Where to Stay & Eat

$–$$ ✕ **Bellavista.** Right on the lake with an outdoor terrace and view, this is a pleasantly old-fashioned restaurant and pizzeria with brisk service. Inside, the gold tablecloths and gilt mirrors give it a glitzy air. The menu includes grilled lavaret from the lake, seafood, and meat dishes such as fillet of beef with green peppercorns. ✉ *Lungolago Mazzini 1*

☎ 045/7553252 🖃 AE, DC, MC, V ☺ Closed Thurs. and mid-Nov.–mid-Dec.

$–$$ ✕ **Il Cantinone.** This quiet courtyard in the historic center is an ideal place to sample tagliolini *al ragù di trota* (with trout) or a simple and delicious *misto del lago,* an antipasto of smoked and lightly cooked lake fish. Follow with a whole fish, such as *lavarello al cartoccio* (lavaret baked in tin foil with a green herb sauce). You can eat outside in the charming courtyard (in fair weather), or indoors in the cozy dining room. The service is unusually friendly and familiar. ☒ *Via Galileo Galilei 14* ☎ *045/7551162* 🕭 *Reservations essential* 🖃 AE, DC, MC, V ☺ Closed Tues. Oct.–Mar.

$ 🏠 **Bell'Arrivo.** This family-run hotel on one of Peschiera's most prominent street corners, along the bank of the Mincio River, is an attractive place to stay in the center of town. The front rooms have big windows that look out over the lake. There's a tempting, rather grand marbled *pasticceria* (pastry shop), café, and wine bar. ☒ *Piazza Benacense 2, 37019* ☎ *045/6401322* 🖷 *045/6401311* ⊕ *www.hotelbellarrivo.it* ⤶ *27 rooms* ⚐ *Bar* 🖃 AE, DC, MC, V ☺ Closed Jan.–mid-Mar. ⊺◎⊦ EP.

$ 🏠 **San Marco.** Many of the rooms in this smart lakeside hotel have views and all guests have access to a large sun terrace. The restaurant also has a covered terrace for outdoor dining in summer. The spacious comfort and bright colors of the public areas are repeated in the rooms. It can feel a bit overdone, but in the final equation it's an appealing place, with stylish bathrooms featuring pink marble. ☒ *Lungolago Mazzini 15, 37019* ☎ *045/7550077* ⊕ *www.hotelsanmarco.tv* ⤶ *35 rooms, 4 suites* ⚐ *Restaurant, minibars, bar, free parking* 🖃 AE, DC, MC, V ⊺◎⊦BP.

Sports & the Outdoors

BOAT TRIPS **Gestione Navegazione Laghi** (☒ Piazza Matteotti 2, Desenzano ☎ 030/9149511 or 167/551801 ⊕ www.navigazionelaghi.it) runs a daily ferry to Riva del Garda from mid-March through October, costing €18.60. It takes about 3 hours each way, and there's a stopover in Riva for about 3 hours. In summer, there's an optional lunch on the boat (€15).

There is also frequent **local service** from Peschiera to Sirmione (€5.60–€8.30; 7 boats per day in summer), and all-day tickets, which enable you to get on and off the boat all over the lake for a full day, cost €22.40. The ticket office, at Peschiera's ferry dock, opens 20 minutes before each departure, and the latest schedules are posted there and on the Gestione Navegazione Laghi Web site.

If you're more ambitious about your boating, try **Peschiera Boat Rent** (☎ 349/7906599), which rents out 4-passenger, 40-hp motorboats to people without licenses, and 6-passenger, 225-hp Sea Ray 190s to people with licenses. You can take out a boat and buzz around the lake for €38–€50 an hour, four hours for €85–€150, or a full 8-hour day for €135–€220—not such a bad deal if you're in a group of four.

Sirmione

★ ⑫ *14 km (9 mi) northwest of Peschiera, 150 km (94 mi) west of Venice.*

The ruins at this enchanting town on an isthmus at the southwestern shore of Lake Garda, complete with narrow, cobbled streets that wind their way through medieval arches, are a reminder that Garda has been a holiday resort for the well-to-do since the height of the Roman era.

Sirmione is touristy, to be sure, with trinket shops and foreign-language menus galore, but as you gaze across the turquoise lake in the shadow of a 13th-century castle, you understand why. Like most of Lake Garda's towns, Sirmione is a summer place; beaches are rocky, but most of the better hotels have garden or boardwalk set-ups to enable sunbathing. If you're planning a stay in Sirmione, you'll thank yourself if you shell out the extra few euros to stay within the old town; you'll have to register with the guard at the gate to the old town, who will contact your hotel to verify your entry; next, you'll inch through a surreal obstacle course of tourists along the narrow streets and piazzas of the old town. Happily, once you park at your hotel, you can leave your car for the rest of your stay in Sirmione and easily navigate everywhere by foot. If you're considering staying along the ugly strip of hotels further down the peninsula, you might want to consider basing yourself instead in one of the towns on the lake nearby, such as Peschiera. You'll get better atmosphere and value, and you can come to Sirmione by boat or car during the day.

In the small old-town area, don't miss the tranquil **Passeggiata delle Muse,** a pedestrian boardwalk that runs along the eastern edge of the peninsula from the old town into the enormous area controlled by the Villa Cortine hotel. The path leads past the Cortine's terraced lunchtime barbecue restaurant, which is open to the public in summer, and finally to **Lido delle Bionde,** a popular rocky beach area where you can rent a chair and umbrella or rough it on the rocks. Keep in mind that unless you're staying at one of the few hotels in the old town itself, such as the Villa Cortine or Flaminia, your car won't be allowed in the old town; you'll have to park somewhere along the less charming part of the peninsula (which is overrun with budget hotels) and walk the rest of the way. Do your best to try for a spot near the base of the old town, as close as possible to the castle.

The locals will almost certainly tell you that the so-called **Grotte di Catullo** (Grottoes of Catullus) were once the site of the villa of Catullus, one of the greatest pleasure-seeking poets of all time. Present archaeological thinking doesn't concur, and there is some consensus that this was the site of two villas of slightly different periods, dating from about the 1st century AD. But never mind—the view through the cypresses and olive trees is lovely, and even if Catullus didn't have a villa here, he is closely associated with the area and undoubtedly did once plop down somewhere nearby. The ruins are at the top of the isthmus and are badly signposted: walk through the historic center and past the various villas to the top of the spit; the grottoes are on the right. The whole peninsula is best avoided on Sundays, when the huge car parks and tiny historic center are packed solid with throngs of Italian visitors. ⊠ *Grotte di Catullo* ☎ *030/916157* ▢ *€4* ⊙ *Mar.–mid-Oct., Tues.–Sun. 8:30–7; mid-Oct.–Feb., Tues.–Sun. 8:30–5.*

☺ The **Castello Scaligero,** begun in 1277, dominates the old town of Sirmione. Along with almost all the other castles on the lake, it was built by the della Scala family. As hereditary rulers of Verona for more than a century before control of the city was seized by the Visconti in 1402, they counted Garda among their possessions. Climbing to the top of the tower inside the castle is a good workout that rewards you with a nice view of the lake. Entry to all of the moated historic center of Sirmione is gained through the castle's gates, over what was originally a drawbridge (though you don't have to enter the castle itself to get into the old town). ⊠ *Piazza Castello* ☎ *030/916468* ≦ *€4* ⊙ *Tues.–Sun. 8:30–7.*

off the beaten path

GARDALAND AMUSEMENT PARK – This park has more than 40 different rides and waterslides and is one of Italy's biggest amusement parks. It is 16 km (10 mi) east of Sirmione. There is a free transfer service from Peschiera train station, less than 5 km (3 mi) up the road. In October, the park does a Halloween theme, and in December, it's a Christmas celebration. ⊠ *Castelnuovo del Garda* ☎ *045/6449777* ⊕ *www.gardaland.it* ≦ *€24* ⊙ *Mar. 19–June 16 and Sept. 12–30, daily 10–6; June 17–Sept. 11, daily 9–midnight; Oct., weekends 9:30–6:30; Dec. 1–21, weekends 10–6:30; Dec. 22–Jan. 8, daily 10–6:30.*

Where to Stay & Eat

$$$$ ✕ **La Rucola.** This quiet restaurant prides itself on attention to detail in its courteous service and impeccable food. The young chef, Gionatha Bignotti, serves mouthwatering set meals featuring either fish or meat, as well as a menu of tempting nouvelle creations that changes regularly. Preparations are rich and complex, and foie gras always works its way in somehow. The room is elegant, formally appointed, and staid—this isn't the place for a casual meal. Next door, L'Officina, La Rucola's bakery, sells pastries, bread-based snack foods, and cheeses daily until 5 PM (Thurs. until 2:30). ⊠ *Vicolo Strentelle 7* ☎ *030/916326* ⌂ *Reservations essential* ⊟ *AE, DC, MC, V* ⊙ *Closed Thurs. and Jan. No lunch Fri.*

★ **$$$$** ✕ **Vecchia Lugana.** At the base of the peninsula and outside the town, this restaurant is the standard-setter for sophisticated cuisine in the region. Adventurous diners will reap the most rewards by sampling such wonders as wood mushroom soup with river prawns or venison fillet with artichoke puree. The menu changes seasonally. There's also an elegant garden. ⊠ *Piazzale Vecchia Lugana 1, Lugana di Sirmione* ☎ *030/919012* ⊟ *AE, DC, MC, V* ⊙ *Closed Mon., Tues. and Jan.–mid-Feb. and Mon.–Thurs. in Nov.*

$$$–$$$$ ✕ **Antica Trattoria La Speranzina.** This romantic waterfront restaurant in the historic center can get pricey, but it's easily worth it if you can land one of the handful of candlelit tables that sit out on the balcony, literally hanging over the lake. The focus is on seafood, whether in the *crudo di mare* (an assortment of raw seafood), the interesting pasta creations, or the simply and excellently grilled scampi, or lake fish such as eel or trout. Wash it down with one of the local Lugana wines. Service can be slow. ⊠ *Via Dante 16* ☎ *030/9906292* ⊕ *www.lasperanzina.it* ⊟ *AE, DC, MC, V.*

$$ ✕ **Osteria Al Torcol.** What could be better than dining under a tangle of grapevines on an outdoor terrace that is tucked into a steep cobblestone walkway and peeks out onto an impossibly cute town square? On a par with the romantic setting is Osteria Al Torcol's wine list—not the longest in town, but obsessively well chosen and offered at markups that are more than reasonable. The kitchen does better work with salumi, cheeses, and pastas than with steaks. ⊠ *Via San Salvatore 30* ☎ *030/ 9904605* ▭ *AE, DC, MC, V.*

★ ¢ ✗ **Scaligeri's.** Just across the street from Sirmione's castle, this stylish, modern pizzeria has a terrace overlooking one of town's main squares. It's also home to Sirmione's first wood-fired pizza oven, returned to use in 2005 after a long hiatus. Service is quick and functional—fine for a lunch stop—and the pizzas are delicious, their crusts even thinner than the thin Italian norm. Better yet, the prices are unbelievably low, and they serve daily until 11 PM. Try the *bufalina,* with buffalo mozzarella. ⊠ *Piazza Castello* ☎ *030/916581* ▭ *AE, DC, MC, V.*

$$–$$$ ✗⌂ **Hotel Flaminia.** Since 1959, this hotel has roosted proudly in one of the choicest of old-town locations, inches from the main streets and boat landing. But a 21st-century renovation has now recast the space, from top to bottom, in a minimalist, feng-shui style. Most outlandish of all is the newest wing, across the street from the main reception, which has a bold faux-Asian aesthetic. Even if such modernity feels out of place in genteel Sirmione, the Flaminia is a refreshing break from Lake Garda's faded-old-hotel norm. Whatever your category of room, be sure you ask for a lake view; it's easily worth the extra few euros. There's a wooden terrace below, right on the lake, for sunbathing, and on the ground floor of the newer wing is Signori, a pleasantly creative restaurant (**$$–$$$**), partially in open air, guided by the same minimalist design philosophy as the hotel. Their focus is on compelling preparations of lake fish—accompanied, of course, by sweeping views of the waters from which they came. ⊠ *Piazza Flaminia 8, 25019* ☎ *030/916078* 🖷 *030/916193* ⊕ *www.hotelflaminia.it* ➶ *43 rooms* ⚴ *2 restaurants, bar, minibars, in-room safes* ▭ *AE, DC, MC, V* ⍩ *BP.*

★ $$$$ ⌂ **Villa Cortine Palace.** A formidably decorative early-19th-century villa in a secluded park taking up a good portion of the old town's island, Villa Cortine is in danger of being just plain ostentatious—but only just. The extraordinarily professional staff will leave you wanting for virtually nothing (except your wallet). The grounds—a colorful mixture of lawns, trees, statues, and fountains—slope down to a private beach with a barbecue restaurant, while the hotel's main restaurant hangs stupendously over the lake. Rooms in the original villa have old-world charm, while those in the newer wing have better lake views, and some have little balconies. Half-board is required in summer. ⊠ *Via Grotte 12, 25019* ☎ *030/9905890* 🖷 *030/916390* ⊕ *www.palacehotelvillacortine.com* ➶ *48 rooms, 6 suites* ⚴ *Restaurant, in-room safes, minibars, tennis court, pool, beach, bar, some pets allowed* ▭ *AE, DC, MC, V* ⊘ *Closed Oct. 20–Mar.* ⍩ *BP.*

Bosco Chiesanuova

63 *68 km (42 mi) northeast of Sirmione, 125 km (78 mi) northwest of Venice.*

Bosco Chiesanuova is the stopping-off point for exploration of **Parco Regionale della Lessinia** (Lessinia Regional Park). Best reached from Verona (31 km [19 mi] south), the park lies between the Adige Valley to the west and the Piccoli Dolomiti to the north. Featuring a gentle but rugged landscape, it is ideal for exploring either on foot, by mountain bike, or on horseback and, in winter, on cross-country skis. Among the cherry trees, beech groves, and meadows edged with dry-stone walls are houses made from the local *pietra di Prun,* a type of stone that, in the not-so-distant past, was used in the construction of underground ice houses where ice was stored to be sold for summer use. This is a karst limestone area, so the pastures are riven with deep gorges and sprinkled with small lakes and waterfalls. At **Ponte di Veja,** the natural attraction is the stone bridge that has been created purely by water erosion. The area is renowned for its fish fossils. The small **Museo Civico** has a nice display of artifacts and photographs of the traditions, art, and costumes of the area. ✉ *Bosco Chiesanuova* ☎ *045/7050022* 🎟 *€1.50* ⏲ *Sept.–June, weekends 4:30–6:30; July and Aug., Tues., Fri., Sat., and Sun. 4:30–6.*

Where to Stay & Eat

$ ✕🏨 **Lessinia.** This modern, functional hotel is vaguely Tyrolean in style. The plain, cheerful rooms are furnished with pine and some have mountain views. There's a big restaurant ($) downstairs (closed Wednesday), offering local specialties featuring Monte Veronese cheese, and a big billiard room in the basement. ✉ *Piazzetta Alpini 2, 37021* ☎ *045/6780151* 📠 *045/6780098* *20 rooms* *Restaurant, bar, recreation room, meeting rooms, free parking* 💳 *MC, V* 🍽 *FAP, MAP.*

Sports & the Outdoors

MOUNTAIN BIKING From June 6 until September 13 you can take your mountain bike on the special bus that leaves Verona for Bosco Chiesanuova at 9 AM, returning at 7:30 PM (€9.30 round-trip). You can get tickets from the **Verona bus station** (☎ 045/8057911) and information on biking trails from the tourist office in Verona (☎ 045/8068680).

SKIING For latest skiing information, contact **Lessinia Turistsport** (✉ Piazza della Chiesa 3 ☎ 045/7050088 🌐 www.leturispo.it).

SOUTHERN VENETO A TO Z

To research prices, get advice from other travelers, and book travel arrangements, visit www.fodors.com.

AIRPORTS & TRANSFERS

The main airport serving the Venetian Arc is Aeroporto Marco Polo, 10 km (6 mi) north of Venice, which handles international and domestic flights. A few European airlines schedule flights to Verona's Aeroporto Catullo di Villafranca, also served by charter flights.

Airport Information **Aeroporto Catullo di Villafranca** ✉ 10 km [6 mi] southwest of Verona ☎ 045/8095666 🌐 www.aeroportoverona.it. **Aeroporto Marco Polo** ☎ 041/2606111 🌐 www.veniceairport.it.

TRANSFERS From Padua, Landomas Service provides a minibus to Venice's Marco Polo airport, and SITA connects the airport with Montegrotto, Abano, and Padua. A regular bus service connects Villafranca with Verona's Porta Nuova railway station.

Taxis & Shuttles **Landomas Service** ☎ 049/8808505. **SITA** ✉ Via Pescarotto 25, Padua ☎ 049/8206811.

BOAT & FERRY TRAVEL

ACTV operates a once-daily direct boat service in the summer connecting Venice (San Zaccaria) with Chioggia and Sottomarina, along with its regular No.11 service between Chioggia and Venice's Lido via Pellestrina (an island en route).

🚤 Boat & Ferry Information **ACTV** ☎ 041/5287886.

BUS TRAVEL TO & FROM VENICE & THE VENETO

Frequent buses from Venice to the region's major cities are operated by ATVO and ACTV, both operating from the bus station at Piazzale Roma in Venice. There are interurban and interregional connections throughout the Veneto. Local tourist offices may be able to provide details of timetables and routes; otherwise contact the local bus station, or in some cases the individual bus companies operating from the station. Lake Garda is more easily explored by bus; frequent services run between the towns.

FARES & 🚌 Bus Information **ACTV** ✉ Piazzale Roma, Venice ☎ 041/2424. **ATVO**
SCHEDULES ✉ Piazzale Roma, Venice ☎ 041/5205530.

BUS TRAVEL WITHIN THE VENETO

Contact ACTV for buses from Venice to Brenta Riviera, Padua, and Chioggia; ATVO covers the Conegliano–Vittorio Veneto–Cortina routes. Contact APTV for Lake Garda, Montagnana, and Bosco Chiesanuova, including service from Venice's Piazzale Roma to Sirmione and Peschiera on Lake Garda, via Verona. In Verona, AMT gets you around; in Padua it's the APS, while FTV serves the Vicenza region. AIM takes you around the city; minibuses run every few minutes from the parking lots to the town center Monday through Saturday. Take Line A from Via Bassano, Line B from Via Farini and Via Cairoli, and Line C from Viale Cricoli.

🚌 Bus Information **ACTV** ✉ Piazzale Roma, Venice ☎ 041/5287886. **AIM** ✉ Via Fusinieri 83/h, Vicenza ☎ 0444/394909. **AMT** ✉ Via Torbido 1, Verona ☎ 045/8871111 ⊕ www.amt.it. **APS** ✉ Via Rismondi 28, Padua ☎ 049/8241111. **APTV** ✉ Autostazione di Verona Porta Nuova, Piazzale XXV Aprile, Verona ☎ 045/8057911 ⊕ www.aptv.it. **ATVO** ✉ Piazzale Roma, Venice ☎ 041/5205530. **FTV** ✉ Viale Milano 138, Vicenza ☎ 0444/223115.

CAR RENTAL

🚗 Local Agencies **Avis** ✉ Piazza Stazione 1, Padua ☎ 049/664198 ✉ Via Marzan 4, Peschiera ☎ 045/6401164 ✉ Corso del Popolo 329, Rovigo ☎ 0425/23028 ✉ Stazione FS, Verona ☎ 045/8006636 ✉ Airport, Verona ☎ 045/987571 ✉ Viale Milano 88, Vicenza ☎ 0444/321622. **Hertz** ✉ Piazza Stazione 1-VI, Padua ☎ 049/8752202 ✉ Stazione FS, Verona ☎ 045/8000832 ✉ Stazione FS Vicenza, Vicenza ☎ 0444/231728.

CAR TRAVEL

The main access roads to the region are both linked to the A1 (Autostrada del Sole), which connects Bologna, Florence, and Rome. They are the A13, which culminates in Padua, and the A22, which passes through Verona in a north–south direction. The road linking the region from east to west is the A4, the primary route from Milan as far as Trieste.

The main highway in the region is the A4, which connects Verona, Padua, and Venice with Trieste. The A13 connects Padua with Monselice and Rovigo. The A4 and SS11 pass the southern edge of Lake Garda, and the A22, which connects Verona with Trento, runs along the lake's eastern shore.

EMERGENCIES

For first aid, ask for *pronto soccorso,* and be prepared to give your address. All pharmacies post signs on the door with addresses of *farmacie di turno,* pharmacies that take turns staying open after normal business hours: at night, on Saturday afternoon, and on Sunday.

🚹 Emergency Services **Police, Ambulance, Fire** ☎ 113.

🚹 Hospitals **Ospedale Civile** ✉ Via Rodolfi 37, Vicenza ☎ 0444/993111. **Ospedale Civile e Policlinico dell'Università** ✉ Via Giustiniani 2, Padua ☎ 049/8211111. **Ospedale Civile Maggiore** ✉ Piazza Stefani, Verona ☎ 045/8071111.

LODGING

APARTMENTS & VILLAS
The Landmark Trust offers vacation rentals, self-catering accommodation in the Villa Saraceno, and a carefully restored Palladian villa in Finale di Agugliaro, south of Vicenza. It can sleep up to 16 people for minimum stays of one week from June to mid-October, and short stays of 3 nights minimum in winter. Bookings must be made well in advance.

Local agencies that rent out villas around Malcesine include La Costa Blu and Little Villa.

🚹 Local Agents **La Costa Blu** ✉ Via Gardesana 62, 37018 Malcesine ☎ 045/7400699. **Little Villa** ✉ Via Gardesana 32, 37018 Malcesine ☎ 045/7401547.

🚹 Rental Listings **The Landmark Trust** ✉ Shottesbrooke, Maidenhead, Berkshire, England SL6 3SW ☎ 01628/825925 🖷 01628/825417 ⊕ www.landmarktrust.co.uk.

TOURS

You'll find that many of the best tours begin and end in Venice because so much of the region is accessible from there. Local tourist offices will be able to provide you with a list of authorized guides, for whom there is an official tariff rate.

BOAT TOURS
Between March and November, the Burchiello excursion boat makes an all-day villa tour along the Brenta Canal, departing from Padua on Wednesday, Friday, and Sunday, and from Venice on Tuesday, Thursday, and Saturday. You can admire more than 50 villas en route and stop and visit three: the Villas Pisani, Valmarana, and Foscari. There's a lunchtime break at the Burchiello restaurant at Oriago. Contact American Express for details, or book online at ⊕ www.ilburchiello.it.

🚹 Fees & Schedules **American Express** ✉ Salizzada San Moisè, 1471 San Marco, Venice ☎ 041/5200844 🖷 041/5229937.

PRIVATE GUIDES
For an individual guide in Padua, call the Sindacato Guide Turistiche. Ippogrifo in Verona can provide escorted trips on foot, by car, or bus.

🚹 **Ippogrifo** ✉ Via Roncisvalle 76 ☎ 045/8278959. **Sindacato Guide Turistiche** ☎ 049/8209711.

SPECIAL-INTEREST TOURS
You can have a free tour of "Chioggia by Night" on Monday and Thursday, late June through early September. Get details from the tourist

office. During July and August you can take guided tours by night for "music and culture under the stars" in the towns of the Euganean Hills (Monselice, Montagnana, Este, Arquà Petrarca). Call Centro Guide Padova for information.

🎦 Fees & Schedules **Centro Guide Padova** ☎ 049/8209711. **Chioggia Tourist Office** ☎ 041/401068.

WALKING TOURS The Comune di Padova organizes nocturnal tours of Padua.

🎦 Fees & Schedules **Comune di Padova** ☎ 049/8204562.

TRAIN TRAVEL

Trains on the most important routes from the south stop almost every hour in Verona, Padua, and Venice. From northern Italy and the rest of Europe, trains usually enter via Milan to the west or through Porta Nuova station in Verona. Call Trenitalia for fare and schedule information.

From Venice, the main line running across the north of Italy connects Padua (20 minutes), Vicenza (1 hour), and Verona (1½ hours) with most routes continuing west to Milan (3 hours). From Padua, there are regular connections for Monselice, Este, Montegrotto Terme, and Rovigo, which in turn connect with Chioggia. The nearest train stations for Lake Garda are Peschiera, in the south, and Rovereto (in Trentino), from which there are frequent bus connections for Riva del Garda. Again, call Trenitalia for train information.

🎦 Train Information **Trenitalia** ☎ 892021 (no area code).

TRAVEL AGENCIES

🎦 Local Agents **A. Palladio Viaggi** ✉ Contrà Cavour 16, Vicenza ☎ 0444/546738. **Caldieri** ✉ Via Negrelli 1, Monselice ☎ 0429/783396. **Freeworld Travel** ✉ Via Carrarese 29, Montagnana ☎ 0429/804278. **Garbellini Viaggi** ✉ Via Portello 13, Rovigo ☎ 0425/361319. **Giramondo Viaggi** ✉ Via Roma 12, Verona ☎ 045/595555. **Piacere Viaggi** ✉ Viale Veneto 8/a, Chioggia ☎ 041/5500470. **Welcome Travel Group** ✉ Via Risorgimento 20, Padua ☎ 049/666133.

VISITOR INFORMATION

Italian tourist office staff all speak good English, but hours vary so wildly that it's impossible to list or describe with any accuracy.

🎦 Tourist Information **Abano Terme** ✉ Via Pietro d'Abano 18, 35031 ☎ 049/8669055. **Arquà Petrarca** ✉ Via Castello 6, 35032 ☎ 0429/777240. **Bosco Chiesanuova** ✉ Piazza Chiesa 34, 37021 ☎☎ 045/7050088. **Chioggia** ✉ Lungomare Adriatico 101, 30019 ☎ 041/401068. **Este** ✉ Via Guido Negri 9/a, 35042 ☎☎ 0429/600462. **Malcesine** ✉ Via Capitanato del Porto 6, 37018 ☎ 045/7400044. **Mestre** ✉ Rotonda Marghera, 30174 ☎ 041/937764. **Monselice** ✉ Via del Santuario 6, 35043 ☎☎ 0429/783026. **Montagnana** ✉ Piazza Trieste 3, 35044 ☎☎ 0429/81320. **Montegrotto Terme** ✉ Viale Stazione 60, 35036 ☎ 049/793384. **Padua** ✉ Stazione Ferroviaria, 35100 ☎ 049/8752077 ⊕ www.turismopadova.it ✉ Galleria Pedrocchi, 37019 ☎ 049/8767927 ✉ Piazza del Santo, 37019 ☎ 049/8753087 ⊙ Mar.–Oct. **Peschiera del Garda** ✉ Piazzale Betteloni 15, 37019 ☎ 045/7551673. **Rovigo** ✉ Via Dunant 10, 45100 ☎ 0425/386290. **Sirmione** ✉ Viale Marconi 2, 25019 ☎ 030/916114. **Verona** ✉ Stazione Ferroviaria, Porta Nuova, 37100 ☎ 045/8000861 ✉ Piazza Brà, 37121 ☎ 045/8068680 ⊕ www.tourism.verona.it. **Vicenza** ✉ Piazza Matteotti 12, 36100 ☎ 0444/320854.

Northern Veneto

Treviso, The Dolomites

WORD OF MOUTH

"Treviso is a very beautiful walled city (known as 'little Venice' because of the canals running through the center) with ample things to do and see. . . . Make sure you have a cappuccino in Piazza dei Signori, the best place to people watch and enjoy the ambiance!"

—Paulareg

"Bassano del Grappa—a lovely town on the Brenta River. You can walk the entire town in about an hour, as well as the historic Ponti degli Alpini—a wooden bridge with scenic views of the river and the Grappa mountains beyond."

—Spygirl

Updated by
Robin
Goldstein

THE REGION AROUND TREVISO called Marca Trevigiana was known by its early admirers as *gioiosa et amorosa* ("joyful and lovely"), which remains a good way to describe it today. Towns here have a quiet, canal-filled charm, and they've spawned some of Italy's supreme painters and sculptors, whose magnificent works of art and architecture are very much in evidence. Further north, the greatest creations are works of nature: the peaks of the mighty Dolomites.

The arcaded town of Treviso is dubbed "the painted city" for its prolific frescoes, and it's also home to an abundance of art by Tomaso da Modena, heir to the pre-Renaissance master Giotto. The walled town of Castelfranco has a lively vibe in summer to go with a much-admired altarpiece by the Renaissance painter Giorgione. Great art and architecture can be discovered in the same building at the Villa Barbaro at Maser, the only point where the two geniuses of the 16th century, Palladio and Veronese, coincided. Conegliano—wine capital of the Veneto—is the birthplace of the 15th-century painter Cima. The unassuming village of Possagno displays one of the largest collections of Canova's sculptures and plaster casts anywhere. Last but not least, the mountain village of Pieve di Cadore has produced yet another master, Titian, whose modest house still remains.

The Dolomites are masterpieces in their own right, particularly when the last rays of the setting sun shed their pink spell on the sheer and jagged heights. Here you can hobnob in Cortina d'Ampezzo's bars and restaurants during the ski season, or in summer experience the mountains while hiking, fishing, or horseback riding—best done on the gentler slopes of the southerly Pieve di Cadore districts. Higher up are some of the most dramatic driving routes in Italy.

The shadow of Venice, of course, is ever present, its influence stretching to Belluno, which was its northernmost ally. La Serenissima was responsible for rebuilding the town of Feltre after it was sacked by Emperor Maximilian in 1509—thus making Feltre one of the best places to absorb the feel of small-scale 16th-century Italy. The lion of St. Mark sits proudly atop a column in the piazza at Bassano del Grappa, a town made even more picturesque by its wooden bridge designed by Palladio—and enlivened by its throat-warming grappa liqueur. Marostica, famous for its human chess match held each September, was ruled by Venice for nearly 400 years and vaunts two castles with walls that tier down the hillside. Imposing defense works also gird the small centers of Castelfranco and Cittadella.

With its red walls rising above and sheltering the town within, Cittadella is perhaps the supreme example of a small fortified Italian town. It was one of the strongholds of Ezzelino III da Romano (1194–1259), a name that comes up in any account of this area. A much-hated man who terrorized the region during the 13th century, he was known as the "Son of Satan"—so monstrous and tyrannical were his deeds that he was condemned to boil in a river of blood in Dante's *Inferno*. When Ezzelino died, the remainder of his family was massacred by the citizens of Asolo to prevent his like from ever being seen again.

Exploring Northern Veneto

A half hour's drive due north of Mestre on the A27 brings you to Treviso, the chief town of the region. To its north and west, set among gentle hills are numerous walled medieval towns. The region becomes more mountainous at Bassano del Grappa in the west and at Vittorio Veneto, farther north of Treviso. From Belluno, dramatically placed on the Piave River on the edge of the Dolomites, the S51 continues north to Pieve di Cadore and Cortina d'Ampezzo in the heart of Dolomites. If you're without a car, the region is difficult to traverse, especially if you plan to make it up to the Dolomites. Buses are your best bet as an alternative way to get around.

About the Hotels

Hotels in the small towns of the region offer excellent value. Treviso caters largely to the business sector, with most hotels sited away from the historic center. If you're planning a stay in Cortina in the peak skiing season, be sure to book well ahead. The quieter resorts will have more low-key hotels, but still check on availability. Bear in mind that many hotels in the mountains and some restaurants close between Easter and June.

WHAT IT COSTS In euros					
	$$$$	$$$	$$	$	¢
RESTAURANTS	over €22	€17–€22	€12–€17	€7–€12	under €7
HOTELS	over €210	€160–€210	€110–€160	€60–€110	under €60

Restaurant prices are for a second course (secondo piatto). Hotel prices are for two people in a standard double room in high season, including tax and service.

Timing

Touring the Treviso region or the Dolomites in late spring or early summer is a visual feast, when the vines are in full leaf and the meadows lush with flowers (the cherry blossom is a sight to behold in April and May). Many of the smaller towns hold festivals in the fall, when there is much feasting and gaiety. In winter the crucial question is: snow or no snow? Snowfalls can make driving treacherous, though main roads are kept clear and tourist offices always have up-to-the-minute reports on conditions. Skiing varies wildly year by year but is almost always best in late February and March, after a full season of snow. Whatever time you plan your trip, you'll always be here at the right time for the mountains, which are stunning in all seasons.

TREVISO & ENVIRONS

The prosperous city of Treviso provides easy access to a handful of towns in the region, including the beautiful walled towns of Castelfranco, home to one of Giorgione's most famous paintings, and Cittadella, resonant with reminders of its long history. Bassano del Grappa, with its lovely Palladian bridge and ceramics, is only a hop away, as are

Marostica, known for its checkerboard square, and Asolo, antique retreat of the Venetian aristocracy. North of Treviso, the Renaissance can
be savored in the streets of Vittorio Veneto and the thriving wine center
of Conegliano. If you're a wine enthusiast, the abundant wine trails in
the area are worth exploring, and if you're interested in sculpture, you
should check out Canova's masterpieces in his museum at Possagno. For
shopping, you'll find clothes from all the internationally known Italian
makers in Treviso, as well as many crafts and ceramics shops (also found
in the smaller towns), and gourmet delicatessens selling local specialties.

Treviso

1 *30 km (19 mi) north of Venice.*

The heart of a busy manufacturing region, Treviso has been dubbed "Little Venice" because of its picturesque canals. They can't compete with
Venice's spectacular waterways, but the town has other characteristics
La Serenissima might envy, such as an authentically Italian character and
a beautiful medieval historic center, with narrow walkways and fashionable
shops, that hasn't had to contend with the effects of mass tourism. "The
painted city" is a less extravagant title for Treviso, and a more apt one:
you'll come across frescoes practically everywhere you look.

Treviso was already well established long before it came within the sphere of Venetian influence in the late 14th century, minting its own coins as early as the 8th century and becoming a center for literary and artistic excellence by the 13th. Much of the city was embellished by Tomaso da Modena (1325–79), the foremost northern Italian painter following the death of Giotto, responsible for decorating many of the Gothic churches with his frescoes.

Most of Treviso's exterior frescoes were created to compensate for a shortage in the 13th century of stone for finishing the buildings' facades. Together with the arcaded streets and mossy banked canals, where weeping willows trail their fronds in the water, they help to create an appealing town center. The area went undamaged in a bombing raid on Good Friday 1944 that destroyed about half the town. Some of the bombed structures, dating from as early as the 15th century, have been expertly restored, while others have been replaced by contemporary buildings. The damage is documented in a series of black-and-white photos that hang under the arcades in the Palazzo dei Trecento.

Treviso has early-15th-century walls, best preserved around the Porta dei Santa Quaranta, the main gate west of the center. Borgo Cavour leads past the Museo Civico to Via Calmaggiore and the main **Piazza dei Signori,** in the heart of the medieval city. Some impressive public buildings line the piazza. Behind one of them, the early-13th-century **Palazzo dei Trecento** (restored after the bombing raid of 1944), you can follow a small alley for about 200 yards to the *pescheria* (fish market) on an island in one of the canals. The nearby church of **Santa Lucia** holds frescoes by Tomaso da Modena.

need a break? Along the city's main shopping street, **Nascimben** (✉ Via Calmaggiore 32 ☎ 0422/540871 ☼ Closed Mon.) is the best *pasticceria* (pastry shop) in town. It's a good place for sampling of the local tiramisu, of which you'll see row after tantalizing row in the window.

Treviso's seven-domed **Duomo** was founded in the 12th century. Within, the Malchiostro Chapel contains fine paintings and frescoes: an *Annunciation* by Titian (circa 1488–1576) and frescoes by Pordenone (1484–1539), including an *Adoration of the Magi.* The crypt is worth a visit for its array of 12th-century columns. ✉ *Piazza del Duomo* ☎ *0422/545720* ☼ *Daily 8–noon and 3:30–7.*

Housed in the Canoniche Vecchie near the Duomo, the **Museo Diocesano d'Arte Sacra** contains archaeological material, a frescoed lunette by Tomaso da Modena, church silver, and vestments. ✉ *Canoniche Vecchie, Via Canoniche 9* ☎ *0422/416707* 🎟 *Free* ☼ *Sept.–July, Mon.–Thurs. 9–noon, Sat. 9–noon and 3–6.*

★ The most important church in Treviso is **San Nicolò,** an imposing Gothic building with an ornate vaulted ceiling. It has frescoes of the saints by Tomaso da Modena on the columns—particularly charming is the depiction of *St. Agnes* on the north side. But the artist's best work here is the remarkable series of 40 portraits of Dominican friars in the seminary

ON THE MENU

THE CUISINE OF THE TREVISO AREA combines robust country cooking and more refined dishes. Great use is made of what grows in the wild, especially in the hills. Chestnuts, berries, mushrooms, herbs, and verdure (greens) all have their place on the menu. You can't make a journey through this zone without encountering radicchio and white asparagus, the two vegetable specialties.

Game figures on the menu in the mountain zones, and in winter steaming bowls of pasta e fagioli (pasta and bean soup), creamy risotto, and polenta are staples. Don't miss the chance to try the delicious local wild mushrooms, including porcini. Treviso is reputedly the birthplace of tiramisu (literally "pick me up"), that delight composed of espresso, mascarpone cheese, sugar, ladyfingers, liqueur (usually rum), and cocoa powder.

The cattle that graze on the mountain pastures and the fertile lowlands produce excellent cheese that comes with a D.O.C.

(Denominazione di Origine Controllata) mark, a guarantee of quality. Look for Montasio and Asiago, both in mild, medium, and strong varieties. Grana Padano and Provolone Val Padana are piquant and flavorful. In summer try Morlacco, a soft, salty cheese that comes from the mountains, and Casatella, a creamy cheese made by local farmers.

Regional wine production is dominated by prosecco, the white wine of choice here (and also in Venice). Prosecco tranquillo (still) goes well with starters, spumante (sparkling) is recommended as an aperitif, and frizzante (lightly sparkling, the most popular type) is suitable for any occasion. Prosecco is often sold with a distinctive string tied round the cork, recalling the traditional means of keeping the cork in during the second fermentation. The most highly rated is Superiore di Cartizze. The Trevigiano hills also produce some nice, crisp white wines.

next door. These are astoundingly realistic considering that some were painted as early as 1352; they include one of the earliest-known portraits of a subject wearing glasses. ⊠ Capitolo dei Domenicani, Seminario Vescovile, Via San Nicolò ☎ 0422/3247 ⊙ Daily 8–noon and 3:30–7.

The deconsecrated church of **Santa Caterina,** on the east side of the city, holds more frescoes by da Modena, including his *Ursula Cycle.* The church's Cappella degli Innocenti holds other frescoes attributed to his school. Treviso's **Museo Civico** (⊠ Borgo Cavour 24 ☎ 0422/591337) is closed for restoration, and in the meantime part of its portrait collection, including works by Titian, Lorenzo Lotto (circa 1480–1556), and Jacopo Bassano (circa 1510–92), is on view at Santa Caterina. ⊠ Via Santa Caterina ☎ 0422/544864 ⊡ €3 ⊙ Tues.–Sun., 9–12:30 and 2:30–6.

Where to Stay & Eat

$$ ✕ **Antica Osteria al Cavallino.** What's on the handwritten menu tonight
Fodor's Choice is anyone's guess at this centuries-old dining mecca. Maybe it's a risotto
★ *ai funghi porcini* (with porcini mushrooms), or *tagliolini* (pasta ribbons) with lobster. And there's likely to be a fresh fish of the day. What doesn't change is the dedication to fresh ingredients, well prepared and served

with personal attention. The restaurant is located in an impressive palazzo dating back to 1540; particularly noteworthy is the outdoor terrace, which is literally built into the wall of the ancient city. Inside, dark-wood walls are adorned with old oil paintings. It's hard to imagine a better place for a meal that captures the spirit of Treviso. ⊠ *Borgo Cavour 52* ☎ *0422/412801* ⊟ *AE, DC, MC, V* ⊙ *No lunch Aug.*

$–$$ ✕ **All'Antico Portico.** This little old brick trattoria on a quiet square in Treviso's historic center is a favorite among locals and tourists alike. The menu changes daily, but always includes well-executed versions of simple local dishes; typical selections are delicious oversized ravioli with ricotta and parmigiana covered with butter and sage, and a superb salad of improbably tender *piovra* (octopus), served at room temperature, with potatoes, olives, and vegetables. The ceilings are ancient wood, the quirky knickknacks include a bicycle, and the vine-covered outdoor terrace gets at the very essence of civilized summer dining. ⊠ *Piazza Santa Maria Maggiore 18* ☎ *0422/545259* ⊟ *AE, DC, MC, V* ⊙ *Closed Tues.*

★ **$–$$** ✕ **Osteria Ponte Dante.** What could be more romantic than dining alfresco, at the meeting of two quiet canals, at a spot once immortalized by Dante? That's the setting of this osteria—and happily, the kitchen is equal to the surroundings, turning out great, simple local dishes such as ravioli *ai porcini e ricotta affumicata* (with porcini mushrooms and smoked ricotta) and a classic *fritto misto di pesce* (mixed fried fish) at reasonable prices. ⊠ *Piazza Garibaldi 6* ☎ *0422/582924* ⊟ *No credit cards* ⊙ *Closed Sun.*

¢–$$ ✕ **Toni del Spin.** Wood-paneled and styled with '30s decor, this place oozes delightful, old-fashioned character. Locals love the friendly and bustling feel as well as the wholesome food. The menu changes twice a week and is chalked on a hanging wooden board: try the filling *zuppa d'orzo e fagioli* (barley and bean soup) or the pasta e fagioli, delivered with panache and care. They also do a nice job with *branzino* (a Mediterranean sea bass). ⊠ *Via Inferiore 7* ☎ *0422/543829* ⊕ *www.ristorantetonidelspin.com* ♤ *Reservations essential* ⊟ *AE, MC, V* ⊙ *Closed Sun. No lunch Mon.*

$–$$ ✕⬚ **Locanda La Colonna.** Everything in this small hotel, set in a vine-covered 15th-century courtyard, is crisp and white. Flower-frescoed ceilings and old-fashioned washstands in the bathrooms add to the charm. It's essential to book one of the seven rooms well ahead. You can feel the history seeping through the walls in the associated restaurant of the same name ($$–$$$$), where you can dine among the pillars, beamed ceiling, and low arches of the main room or on the mezzanine floor. The chef favors fish, and beef with rosemary is a perfumey delight. There's also an old-school wine bar, Enoteca Odeon. ⊠ *Via Campana 27, 31100* ☎ *0422/544804* ᵱ *0422/419177* ⇨ *7 rooms* ⚲ *Restaurant, bar, some pets allowed* ⊟ *AE, DC, MC, V* ⊙ *Restaurant closed Sun., Mon. and 2 wks in mid-Aug.* ⦿ *EP.*

$$$ ⬚ **Carlton Hotel.** Pass the river flowing outside, walk through a lobby that's seen better days, and seek out the huge terrace right on top of the old city wall. Even the parking lot has a view from here. The hotel has that time-frozen, decades-old feel, but that's part of the charm. Above the Embassy cinema, five minutes from the train station, and five min-

TREVISO'S TOP-FLIGHT WINE BARS

TREVISO MAY BE NICKNAMED *"Little Venice"* because of its canals, but the two cities also share a tradition of excellent wine bars. They're places where you can have a quick glass of wine or stick around to sample tasty snacks and often more substantial meals. Here are some top spots:

Osteria Muscoli's is always busy, with locals popping in until 2 AM. The location—in the middle of a canal, on the same island as Treviso's fish market—also makes it a nice place to linger over savory delights, including potato-and-porcini pie, pepper cheese, and stuffed tomatoes. The menu might also include sarde in saor, the Venetian sardine specialty. ⊠ Via Pescheria 23 ☎ 0422/583390 ⊟ No credit cards ⊘ Closed Sun. Apr.–Aug., Wed. Oct.–Mar., and 3 wks in Sept.

Enoteca alla Corte Scura is a classic old place for a glass of prosecco or a cheap bite to eat, whether one of the pastas, salumi, or a platter of smoked swordfish.

Service is endearingly brusque, the crowd local, and doors stay open until 1 AM. ⊠ Via Inferiore 33 ☎ 0422/56683 ⊟ AE, MC, V ⊘ Closed Mon. No lunch Tues.

At **Cantinetta Venegazzù**, the most compelling feature is the fantastic view from the outdoor seats over Piazza dei Signori. But that's not all; here you can enjoy an impeccable platter of cured meats, washed down with one of more than 55 wines by the glass, almost all under €3. ⊠ Piazzetta Ancilotto 2 ☎ 0422/55287 ⊟ AE, MC, V ⊘ Closed Wed.

The inside of **Proseccheria Mionetto** is tackily modern, but this is where the locals go to take their late-afternoon aperitifs, for one reason alone: the little triangular piazza, which is one of the city's cutest places to sit and drink. ⊠ Via Inferiore 2 ☎ 0422/545572 ⊟ AE, DC, MC, V.

utes from the heart of Treviso, the Carlton is very convenient for touring—that is, if you're not too busy using the gym, enjoying free golf at Asolo, or tasting wines in the vineyards nearby. ⊠ *Largo di Porta Altinia 15, 31100* ☎ *0422/411661* 🖷 *0422/411620* ⊕ *www.hotelcarlton.it* 🛏 *93 rooms* ♿ *Restaurant, in-room safes, minibars, cable TV, golf privileges, gym, bicycles, bar, meeting room, some pets allowed* ⊟ *AE, DC, MC, V* ⊘ *Restaurant closed Sun.* ⧖ *BP.*

★ $ 🖫 **Il Focolare.** The spectacular location of this hotel, spitting distance from the back of the Palazzo dei Trecento in the very heart of the *centro storico*, is its best feature—precious few Treviso hotels are so well situated. But it's also a pleasant place to stay, with tidy, if smallish, rooms and a bright, welcoming reception area. ⊠ *Piazza Ancilotto 4, 31100* ☎ *0422/42256601* 🖷 *0422/4319900* ⊕ *www.ilfocolare.net* 🛏 *14 rooms* ♿ *Bar, minibars* ⊟ *AE, DC, MC, V* ⧖ *BP.*

Nightlife & the Arts

ART EXHIBITIONS   The **Casa dei Carraresi** (⊠ Via Palestro 33-35 ☎ 0422/513150 ⊕ www.lineadombra.it) hosts big, international exhibitions of 20th-century art. Contact the call center for information on current exhibits.

CONCERTS **Estate Trevigiana** (☎ 0422/547632 tourist office), a series of open-air events consisting of music, concerts, theater, outdoor movies, and dance, takes place from June to September.

BARS The piano bar **Nilo Blu** (✉ Via della Repubblica 7/c ☎ 0422/420469), 3 km (2 mi) north of the center on the road to Vittorio Veneto and Conegliano, features live jazz and rock bands most evenings but is primarily a place to lounge and talk. **Soda Pop** (✉ Via Fonderia 46 ☎ 0422/424487) has live music and a young crowd.

Shopping

Treviso is known for its wrought-iron and copper works—they might be a little difficult to transport home, but there are plenty of small shops to explore. Some of Italy's leading clothes manufacturers, including Benetton, are based in the area, and sometimes it's possible to find better prices here than in Milan or elsewhere. A general market is held Tuesday and Saturday mornings around Piazza Matteotti, known locally as Piazza del Grano.

CERAMICS For ceramics, visit **Ceramiche Artistiche di Visentin** (✉ Piazza Garibaldi 16 ☎ 0422/590990) where you can watch the owner hand-painting beautiful pieces with reproduction antique or made-to-order patterns. That said, aficionados head to Bassano.

GIFTS At **Mangiafuoco-Vecchi Giochi** (✉ Via Riccati 12 ☎ 0422/541738) you can find handcrafted puppets, models of characters from fairy tales, and handmade paper items. **De Pol** (✉ Via Calmaggiore 33 ☎ 0422/412343) sells fine leather bags, belts, and shoes.

Asolo

★ ❷ *35 km (22 mi) northwest of Treviso, 65 km (41 mi) northwest of Venice.*

The romantic, charming hillside hamlet of Asolo was the consolation prize of an exiled queen. At the end of the 15th century, Venetian-born Caterina Cornaro was sent here by Venice's doge to keep her from interfering with Venetian administration of her former kingdom of Cyprus, which she had inherited upon the death of her husband, James II Lusignan of Cyprus. To soothe the pain of exile, she established a lively and brilliant court in Asolo. In this court Cardinal Pietro Bembo (1470–1547), one of the foremost literary figures of the time, wrote the love letters *Gli Asolani,* coining the word *asolare,* meaning to while away the time in idle pleasures. Over the centuries, Venetian aristocrats continued to build gracious villas on the hillside, and in the 19th century Asolo once again became the idyllic haunt of musicians, poets, and painters. The man of letters and ideologue Gabriele d'Annunzio (1863–1938) was smitten with the beauty of the place, as was the English poet Robert Browning (1812–89). From the outside, you can see villas once inhabited by Browning and also the actress Eleonora Duse (1850–1924), called "*La Divina del teatro italiano.*" She was famous as much for her stormy love life as for her roles in Ibsen and Shakespeare. Her tomb can be found in the cemetery of the church of Sant'Anna, along with that of the English explorer and writer Freya Stark (1893–1993), who lived here for most of her life.

Asolo has not always been a scene of tranquillity. In the early 13th century it fell, like many other towns of the area, under the sway of the tyrant Ezzelino III da Romano. Upon his death in 1259 the people of Asolo made sure that his ilk was never seen again by massacring all remaining members of his family. The peaceful old-world ambience vaporizes on holiday weekends when the crowds pour in. Book your accommodation well ahead if you can.

Asolo's town center, **Piazza Maggiore,** is the site of Renaissance palaces and antique cafés. The Piazza Maggiore is also home to the frescoed 15th-century **Loggia del Capitano,** which contains the **Museo Civico,** displaying memorabilia of Asolo's dead coterie—manuscripts, Eleonora Duse's correspondence, Browning's spinet, and portraits of Caterina Cornaro. ⊠ *Piazza Maggiore* ☎ *0423/952313* 🎫 *€4* 🕓 *Weekends 10–noon and 3–7; other times by reservation.*

need a break? While away some idle moments at the famous **Caffè Centrale** (⊠ Via Roma 72 ☎ 0423/952141 ⊕ www.caffecentrale.com 🕓 Closed Tues.), which has overlooked the fountain in Piazza Maggiore and the Duomo since about 1700. They're open until 1 AM.

The **Duomo** was rebuilt in 1747 on the site of Roman baths. Caterina Cornaro donated the baptismal font, and Bassano and Lotto both painted *Assumption* altarpieces. ⊠ *Piazzetta S. Pio X 192* ☎ *0423/952376* 🕓 *Daily 7–noon and 3:30–6:30.*

Walking along Via Browning takes you past smart shops, Browning's house at No. 153, and the enoteca **Alle Ore** (⊠ Via Browning 183 ☎ 0423/952070), where you can sample the local wine and grappa. It's closed Monday. Uphill from the piazza, you'll go past Caterina's ruined **Castello** (⊠ Piazzetta E. Duse), whose theater was transported to Florida in 1930. The castle can only be viewed from the outside. As you continue uphill, you'll see the imposing **Villa Pasini** on the right, with its grand stairways—its ground floor is still occupied by the signora Pasini.

After a healthy, winding, half-hour climb uphill, you reach the medieval fortress **La Rocca.** From this summit is a view of Asolo's "hundred horizons." The site closes when the weather turns bad. ⊠ *Monte Ricco* ☎ *0423/529046 (tourist office)* 🎫 *€1.50* 🕓 *Apr.–June and Sept.–Oct., daily 10–7; Nov.–Mar., daily 10–5; July–Aug., daily 10–12:30 and 3–7.*

off the beaten path **POSSAGNO** – Just 8 km (5 mi) northwest of Asolo, this small town nestling at the foot of Monte Grappa merits a visit for its **Gipsoteca Museo Canoviano,** birthplace of the sculptor and architect Antonio Canova (1757–1822). Set in a typical Venetian garden, with vistas over the mellow countryside, the *gipsoteca* (collection of plaster casts) was built in 1836 and contains about 300 plaster, wax, and terra-cotta models that illustrate Canova's way of working. Little nails (*rèpere*) were first studded all over the plaster cast; then by means of a pantograph (a measuring device) the proportions were transferred to the final marble version. This is documented in his studio, part of his native house, alongside his charming and elegant paintings, mainly of disporting Greek nymphs. In the airy halls, marvel at the force of *Hercules and the Lion* and the beauty of *The Three Graces.* ⊠ *Piazza Canova* ☎ *0423/544323* ⊕ *www. museocanova.it* 🎟 *€4* ⊘ *Tues.–Sun. 9–noon and 3–6.*

On the other side of the road an imposing drive leads to the **Tempio,** a church—reminiscent of the Pantheon—designed by Canova as the resting place for his mortal remains. ⊠ *Stradone del Tempio* ⊘ *Tues.–Sun. 9–noon and 3:30–6.*

Where to Stay & Eat

$$$–$$$$ ✕ **Ca' Derton.** Opposite the entrance to the Castello, Ca' Derton is pleasantly old-fashioned, with early photos of Asolo and bouquets of dried flowers. Proprietor Nino and his wife, Antonietta, serve both local and international dishes, and take pride in their homemade pasta, bread, and desserts. From November through April, if you're feeling adventurous try the *sopa coada,* a local soup made with pigeon meat and bread that takes two days to prepare; the recipe is several centuries old. ⊠ *Piazza Gabriele D'Annunzio 11* ☎ *0423/529648* ⊕ *www.caderton.com* ▤ *AE, DC, MC, V* ⊘ *Closed Sun. and Feb. No lunch Mon.*

$ ✕ **Al Bacaro.** Since 1892 this osteria has been a second home to Asolo laborers and craftsmen. Whether you eat downstairs in the bar with hanging copper kettles or upstairs in the dining room lighted by lacy lamps, you get affordable wines, pastas and home-style dishes such as goulash and stewed game, tripe, or snails. You can also choose from a selection of big, open-face sandwiches generously topped with fresh salami, speck, or other cured meats. ⊠ *Via Browning 165* ☎ *0423/55150* ▤ *AE, DC, MC, V* ⊘ *Closed Wed. and 2 wks in Aug.*

$$$$
Fodor'sChoice
★ 🏨 **Villa Cipriani.** A romantic garden surrounded by gracious country homes on a hillside just below the center of Asolo is the setting for this historic villa, now part of the Starwood chain. The setting is one of the most beautiful in Italy, and the experience is opulent from start to finish, with every creature comfort and impeccable service. Past guests have included Prince Philip, Aristotle Onassis, and Queen Juliana. "Superior" rooms have guaranteed views; the two suites with private terraces are very expensive but absolutely stunning. The restaurant has its own terrace overlooking the garden and hills, a perfect place to sip an aperitif. ⊠ *Via Canova 298, 31011* ☎ *0423/523411* 🖷 *0423/952095* ⊕ *www. starwood.com/italy* 🛏 *31 rooms* ⚫ *Restaurant, in-room data ports, in-room safes, minibars, cable TV, bar, Internet, parking (fee), meeting room, some pets allowed (fee)* ▤ *AE, DC, MC, V* ⊘ *BP.*

★ **$$$–$$$$** 🏨 **Al Sole.** The smell of the polished wood floor greets you as you enter this 1920s pink-washed hotel overlooking the main square. All the rooms are large and furnished in antique style; the more expensive "superior" rooms have great views over the town, while the back rooms have leafy, rural views. The decoratively tiled bathrooms come equipped with hydro-massage showers. The hotel was once actress Eleonora Duse's preferred haunt, and her favorite room has been preserved. The summer-only restaurant ($$$; open April through October) has a pleasant terrace from which you can gaze out over picturesque Asolo. ⊠ *Via Collegio 33, 31011* ☎ *0423/951332* 🖷 *0423/951007* ⊕ *www. albergoalsole.com* 🛏 *22 rooms, 1 suite* 🖒 *Restaurant, bar, Internet station, in-room safes, minibars, cable TV, gym, massage, some pets allowed (fee)* ☰ *AE, MC, V* ᠑◯᠑ *BP.*

\$\$ 🔲 **Duse.** A spiral staircase winds its way up this narrow, centrally located building to rooms with a view of the town square. The scene gets lively on antiques fair weekends, but if the sights don't make up for the sounds, ask for the larger and quieter attic room—skylights instead of windows mean your only view is the stars. Furnishings, such as small tables with pastel tablecloths and slipcovered chairs, are simple and well tended. Some rooms are smallish, but for Asolo, the price is a real deal. ⊠ *Via Browning 190, 31011* ☎ *0423/55241* 🖷 *0423/950404* ⊕ *www. hotelduse.com* 🛏 *14 rooms* 🖒 *Minibars, in-room data ports, parking (fee), cable TV, bar, meeting room* ☰ *AE, MC, V* ᠑◯᠑ *EP.*

Nightlife & the Arts

FESTIVALS During the third weekend of September a **Palio** is held, commemorating the history of Asolo from Roman times until the arrival of Caterina Cornaro. It takes the form of a Roman chariot race through the streets and is attended by much feasting.

Shopping

An **antiques market** sets up in Piazza Maggiore on the second Sunday of the month (except July and August).

FOOD For a shop that is pure theater, visit the century-old **Ennio** (⊠ Via Browning 151 ☎ 0423/529109). Once you've ogled longingly in front of the many windows, where food is displayed in all its glory—the biggest bowls of preserves and olives you've ever seen, graceful bottles of grappa, jars of truffles, enticing pastries, formidable cheeses—a visit inside is obligatory. All of the delights will be lovingly extolled by the outgoing owner.

Maser

❸ *7 km (4½ mi) northeast of Asolo, 33 km (20½ mi) northwest of Treviso.*

★ **Villa Barbaro,** just outside the town of Maser, is one of Palladio's most gracious Renaissance creations. The fully furnished villa is still inhabited by its owners, who make you wear heavy felt slippers over your shoes to protect the highly polished floors. The elaborate stuccos and opulent frescoes by Paolo Veronese (1528–88) bring the 16th century to life. After La Rotonda in Vicenza, this is Palladio's greatest villa and is definitely worth going out of your way for. (Before making the trip, note the limited hours). On the grounds, the **Tempietto** (little church) is one of Palladio's last projects, the only church designed by him lying outside Venice. The Tempietto is currently closed for restoration, but a **cantina** on the grounds offers wine tastings. ⊠ *Via Cornuda 2* ☎ *0423/923004* ⊕ *www.villadimaser.it* 🎟 *€5* ⊘ *Apr.–Oct., Tues., Sat., and Sun. 3–6; Nov.–Mar., weekends 2:30–5 or by reservation. Closed Dec. 24–Jan. 6.*

Where to Eat

$–$$ ✕ **Agnoletti.** In the town of Giavera del Montello, about 25 km (16 mi) east of Maser, Agnoletti is an inn of a bygone era with a lovely summer garden. Historic doesn't even begin to describe it; the place has been there since 1780. The kitchen can produce an all-mushroom menu; if you order something else, at least try the mushroom *zuppa* (soup) or *tortina di funghi* (mushroom tart). ✉ *Via della Vittoria 193, Giavera del Montello* ☎ *0422/776009* ▤ *AE, DC, MC, V* ⊗ *Closed Tues., 1 wk in Jan., and 2 wks in July.*

$ ✕ **Da Bastian.** A good place to stop for lunch in Maser before visiting
Fodor'sChoice the Villa Barbaro (a 15-minute walk away), this excellent restaurant has
★ a pleasant garden for outdoor dining. Everything on the menu is seasonal; autumn and winter offerings include grilled mushrooms, homemade pumpkin tortelli, and, for second courses, baccalà, snails, and *trippa alla Veneta* (tripe cooked in a tomato and white wine sauce). The dessert trolley is laden with homemade cakes and fruit tarts. ✉ *Via Sant'Andrea* ☎ *0423/565400* ▤ *No credit cards* ⊗ *Closed Thurs. and Aug. No dinner Wed.*

Castelfranco Veneto

❹ *27 km (17 mi) west of Treviso, 45 km (28 mi) northwest of Venice.*

The stocky, battlemented walls with green banks and trees running down to the moat are not quite in the league of Cittadella's, but they nevertheless lend character to this small town. Erected in the 12th century by the Trevisans as protection against Padua, they encircle the old center, or Castello. The Castello isn't always where all the action is, though; Castelfranco is most charming when **Piazza Giorgione,** which sits outside of the Castello, becomes a lively scene on weekend nights. Outdoor cafés and the little neighboring streets buzz with activity into the wee hours.

The piazza is named for the High Renaissance painter Giorgione (circa 1478–1510), a Castelfranco native. He's something of a mysterious figure, with a sketchy biography and only six works definitively attributed to his hand, including the enigmatic *Tempest* in Venice's Accademia. What is known about him gives him the characteristics of a Romantic hero: he was handsome, with musical as well as artistic gifts, and he died young, possibly of the plague. The **Casa Giorgione** contains a small museum about the artist and, on the first floor, a chiaroscuro frieze thought to be by him. ✉ *Piazzetta San Liberale* ☎ *0423/725022* ⊕ *www.museogiorgione.it* ▤ *€2.50* ⊗ *Tues.–Sun. 10–12:30 and 3–6:30; guided tours by reservation.*

The neoclassical **Duomo,** modeled on Palladio's Chiesa del Redentore in Venice, holds frescoes by Veronese and Zelotti (1526–78). Castelfranco's greatest treasure, however, is Giorgione's altarpiece, *Madonna and Child with SS. Francis and Liberale,* known as *La Pala.* The poetic and enigmatic mood his paintings evoke is ably demonstrated here. Commissioned in 1504 to commemorate the death of a young man of 18, Matteo Costanza, it shows three figures gazing dolefully out of the picture. Mary is set apart, at one with the landscape and isolated from the two saints in the foreground. ✉ *Via Francesco Maria Preti* ☎ *0423/495202* 🎫 *Free* ⊙ *Daily 9:30–11:45 and 3:15–5:45.*

The restored **Teatro Accademico** was built to a design of F. M. Preti, also responsible for the cathedral. It's an elegant example of 18th-century work, in which concerts and theater are still performed in season. ✉ *Via Garibaldi* ☎ *0423/494500* 🎫 *Free* ⊙ *Weekdays 9–noon and 2–6.*

Outside the city walls are some fine palaces, notably the stuccoed 18th-century **Palazzo Soranzo Novello** (✉ Corso XXIX Aprile), now a bank.

The broad road Borgo Treviso leads to the **Parco Revedin Bolasco,** a tranquil garden with lakes, canals, little bridges, and hillocks. It complements a villa built in the 19th century by Giovan Battista Meduna. Here you'll find a Moorish greenhouse on an island and a circle of statues surrounding an amphitheater that was originally used as an exercise ground for horses. ☎ *337/805304* 🎫 *€3 Tues. and Thurs., free weekends* ⊙ *Mar. 21–May and Sept. 21–Nov. 2, Tues. and Thurs. 10–12:30 and 3–5:30, weekends 10–1 and 2:30–5:30; June–Sept. 20, Tues. and Thurs. 10–12:30 and 3–5:30, weekends 10–1 and 3–7:30.*

Where to Stay & Eat

$$–$$$ ✕ **Osteria al Treno.** At this well-loved place just off the Piazza Giorgione, seafood is king, whether it's the local catch of the day, impossibly sweet scampi, or pricey *aragosta* (lobster). The clientele is mostly local, and the service and ambience are comfortable, whether you're sitting at one of the four tables inside the cozy dining room or out on the much bigger tree-lined terrace in back. ✉ *Via Borgo Montegrappa 6* ☎ *0423/494802* ⌚ *Reservations essential* ▭ *AE, DC, MC, V* ⊙ *Closed Wed.*

$$ ✕ **Osteria Do Mori.** Typical dishes from the Veneto are served in this small restaurant up a little street just within Castelfranco's walls. If you've never got around to tasting *trippa* (tripe), now is your chance, but if you're not tempted by the trippa *alla parmigiana,* maybe you'll feel safer with the well-executed pasta e fagioli or one of the expertly grilled cuts of meat. ✉ *Vicolo Montebelluna 24* ☎ *0423/495725* ▭ *AE, DC, MC, V* ⊙ *Closed Thurs.*

★ $ ✕ **Pirinetomosca.** Meals at this gem of an osteria, just outside Castelfranco Veneto in the tiny hamlet of Treville, are a culinary tour through the Trevigiano countryside. In warm weather you can dine on a garden patio, enjoying masterfully delicate dishes such as the lightly fried, ricotta-stuffed *fior di zucca* (squash flowers) with a balsamic glaze, fresh tomato, and a drizzle of spicy local olive oil. The prices remind you that you're not in Venice anymore: a three-course meal runs less than €20 per person, including wine. The service is impeccable, too; the only challenge is finding the place—it's hidden next to Treville's modest cathedral. ✉ *Via Priuli 17/C, Treville* ☎ *0423/472751* ⌚ *Reservations essential* ▭ *AE, DC, MC, V* ⊙ *Closed Tues. and 2 wks in Aug.*

$$ 🏨 **Alla Torre.** The clock tower of Castelfranco's medieval castle overlooks this hotel, and the original brick wall is even incorporated into some of the suites. Rooms are modern and spacious, and the plaid carpets add a touch of hominess. A terrace gives onto the square. ✉ *Pi-*

azzetta Trento e Trieste 7, 31033 ☎ *0423/498707* 🖷 *0423/498737*
⊕ *www.hotelallatorre.it* ⇌ *45 rooms, 9 suites* ♨ *Bar, in-room safes,
minibars, some pets allowed* ▱ *AE, DC, MC, V* ⼦ *BP.*

★ **$–$$** 🖾 **Al Moretto.** In the hands of the same family for generations, this re-
fined but understated hotel offers welcoming service. The public rooms
are intimate and at the same time light, soothing, and summery, with
wicker furniture and chintz armchairs. In summer, breakfast is served
in the garden. The back section of the hotel has newer junior suites—
larger, slightly pricier rooms with beautiful, wood-beamed ceilings and
sparkling bathrooms. Ask for one of the rooms on the upper floor for
even higher ceilings. ⊠ *Via San Pio X 10, 31033* ☎ *0423/721313*
🖷 *0423/721066* ⊕ *www.albergoalmoretto.it* ⇌ *46 rooms* ♨ *In-room
data ports, in-room safes, minibars, bar, some pets allowed* ▱ *AE, DC,
MC, V* ⼦ *BP.*

Cittadella

★ ❺　*13 km (8 mi) southeast of Marostica, 61 km (38 mi) northwest of
Venice.*

Of all the walled cities in the Brenta Valley, Cittadella conveys most fully
the sense of enclosure and protection. The lofty and battlemented walls
rise up on either side as you enter through the brick arches of the Porta
Padua, painted with the red *carra* (wagon) emblem of the Carrara family. Imagine, as you pass the **Torre di Malta**, the plight of the prisoners
abandoned here to die of starvation by the tyrant Ezzelino III da Romano. The town was built on a Roman site by the Paduans as a counter
to Castelfranco, a Trevisan stronghold, and then passed to a succession
of powerful families including Ezzelino's. The lines of the streets follow
the original Roman plan, with gates at the four cardinal points. Today,
the town is pleasant but sleepy; expect simply to wander around in cu-
riosity, rather than partaking of any haute cuisine, nightlife, or famous
works of art.

Via Garibaldi leads to the main plaza, **Piazza Pierobon** and the early-
19th-century square **Duomo** with its massive columns and, inside, paintings by Jacopo Bassano, including *La Cena in Emmaus* in the sacristy.
⊠ *Via Marconi 5* ☎ *049/9404485* ⊙ *Daily 7:30–12:30 and 3–7.*

For the best view over the red-tiled roofs, pale ocher houses, and soar-
ⓒ　ing walls, climb the bell tower of the Duomo, the **Torre Campanaria**, which
doubles as a museum. As you go up, you'll see the walls festooned with
vestments, candelabra, and other ecclesiastical exhibits. ⊠ *Duomo, Via
Marconi 5* ☎ *049/9404485* ⊙ *Open by appointment only, phone for
information.*

On Via Indipendenza, the neoclassical **Teatro** has a facade by Japelli
(1783–1852). The **Palazzo Pretorio** on Via Marconi, with a fine 16th-
century marble portal and frescoes, was headquarters of whoever was
in control of the city. You can visit upon request; contact the **tourist office** (⊠ Porte Bassanesi 2, inside the Casa del Capitano ☎🖷 049/
9404485).

A pleasant end to your visit can be a walk around the exterior of the walls through the **Giardini Pubblici,** open daily 8:30–5:30.

Where to Stay & Eat

★ **$–$$** ✕ **Taverna degli Artisti.** Colorful tablecloths, ceramic dishes, and numerous paintings decorate the dining rooms of this homey restaurant, which fills to the brim with locals. Before tucking into *petto di pavoncella ai finferli e porcini* (breast of peafowl with wild mushrooms), try the *tortelli di fagiano al rosmarino e ricotta affumicata* (homemade tortelli pasta filled with pheasant, rosemary, and smoked ricotta). ⊠ *Via Mura Rotta 11* ☎ *049/9402317* ▤ *AE, MC, V* ⊗ *Closed Tues. No dinner Mon.*

★ **$** ✕ **Enoteca Bei.** This wine bar and restaurant on one of Cittadella's main squares outclasses the little old town it's in, with a very modern selection of wines by the glass, including excellent prosecco and whites from the northern Veneto. The menu is eclectic but not overambitious, with selections like *wurstel con crauti* (sausages with sauerkraut) and smoked beef with a *mostarda di verdure* (a vegetable-based marmalade) to go along with the more traditional pastas and such. Best of all is the wine-cellar-like atmosphere, which delicately balances old and new. In summer the patio is open out back. ⊠ *Piazza Scalco 10* ☎ *049/9403500* ▤ *AE, DC, MC, V* ⊗ *Closed Tues. No dinner Mon.*

$$ ▥ **La Cittadella.** The accent is emphatically floral in this beautifully decorated hotel, from the dried flower arrangements to the frescoes and wallpaper. The rooms are bright and spacious, and some have small terraces with potted plants and chairs. It's in a quiet location just outside the walls and represents very good value. ⊠ *Via Monte Pertica 3, 35013* ☎ *049/9402434* 🖷 *049/5975544* ⊕ *www.hotelcittadella.it* ⇆ *26 rooms, 9 suites, 14 apartments with kitchen* ⚐ *Restaurant, in-room safes, minibars, cable TV, indoor pool, gym, sauna, bar, babysitting, meeting room* ▤ *AE, DC, MC, V* ⦿| *BP.*

$$ ▥ **La Filanda.** A 19th-century spinning factory has been restored and adapted to house one of Cittadella's most stylish hotels. You can still see the tall brick chimney and old machinery, but the interior is now bright, spacious, and furnished to a high standard. The restaurant (closed August) serves local and national dishes, in summer under a garden gazebo. ⊠ *Via Palladio 34, 35013* ☎ *049/940000* 🖷 *049/9402111* ⊕ *www.filandapalace.it* ⇆ *70 rooms, 1 suite* ⚐ *Restaurant, in-room safes, minibars, cable TV, gym, hot tub, sauna, bar* ▤ *AE, DC, MC, V* ⦿| *BP.*

Bassano del Grappa

❻ *13 km (8 mi) north of Cittadella, 76 km (47 mi) northwest of Venice.*

Beautifully positioned directly above the swift-flowing waters of the Brenta River at the foot of the Monte Grappa massif (5,880 feet), Bassano has old streets lined with low-slung buildings flanked by wooden balconies and pretty flowerpots. Bright ceramic wares produced here and in nearby Nove are displayed in shops along byways that curve uphill toward a centuries-old square, and, even higher, to a belvedere with a good view of Monte Grappa and part of the Val Sugana. Bassano is home to the famous Nardini distillery, where grappa has been made since 1779. You can stop in for a sniff or a snifter of the liquor at any of the local cafés.

Bassano's most famous landmark is the **Ponte degli Alpini** (also called Ponte Vecchio), which has spanned the Brenta since 1209. Rebuilt countless times (floods are frequent), the present-day bridge is a post–World War II reconstruction using Andrea Palladio's 16th-century design. The great architect astutely chose to use wood as his medium, knowing that it could be replaced quickly and cheaply. For the best view, cross to the far side; then take Via Marcello and follow the *Veduta Panoramica* (panoramic view) sign. The bridge itself is named after the Alpini regiment who fought in the World War I campaigns on Monte Grappa and above Asiago and who were responsible for the present-day reconstruction. The small **Museo degli Alpini** documents this in the Taverna al Ponte. ⊠ *Via Angarono 2* ☎ *0424/503662* 🎫 *Free* ⊗ *Tues.–Sun. 8:30–8.*

★ Almost as famous as the bridge is the bar and liquor shop **Nardini** (⊠ Ponte Vecchio 2 ☎ 0424/527741 ⊗ Closed Mon. Oct.–May), right by the bridge, where grappa has been sold and served since 1779. Stop in for a taste, which you can sip in view of the bridge, or to buy a bottle of Nardini's good *invecchiata* (aged grappa). The locals all come around in the early evening for after-work aperitifs; those without a taste for straight liquor might prefer the trademark mix of grappa with the lighter *chino* (a bittersweet spirit). The place is open until 9 PM.

A few steps uphill from the bridge, the noted grappa producer Poli has set up the **Poli Grappa Museum** to accompany its shop. Most interesting are the examples of the old grappa stills, with their glass tubes twisting every which way into improbably shaped coils. Grappa was once considered by alchemists to have supernatural qualities, and its distillation techniques, you might say, were half science, half black magic. Here you can also taste almost all of Poli's numerous grappas (for free) and take home a bottle or two (not for free). ⊠ *Ponte Vecchio* ☎ *0424/524426* ⊕ *www.poligrappa.com* 🎫 *Free* ⊗ *Daily 9:30–9.*

The center of town focuses on two adjacent squares, the Piazza Libertà and the Piazza Garibaldi. Most of the buildings date from the 16th century, a period of stability under Venetian rule. Looking down on the bustle of Piazza Garibaldi is the **Torre Civica,** once part of the earlier 13th-century defense system. Also dominating the piazza is the campanile of the Gothic church of **San Francesco,** which houses an interesting 13th-century wooden crucifix, on the arms of which are carved the sun and moon. The cloister of this church is home to the **Museo Civico,** whose downstairs section is devoted to archaeological finds, notably the Chini collection of 1st-century BC vases from Apulia, a good collection of 18th-century engravings, and theatrical memorabilia and costumes of the baritone Tito Gobbi (1913–84), who was a native of the town. Upstairs, the museum features paintings from three generations of the da Ponte family, predominantly Jacopo Bassano. Note the dirty feet and wrinkled skin of the peasants in *The Adoration of the Shepherds,* a prosaic touch that heralded a new realism in Venetian painting. One room is devoted to the works of Canova; the library owns 2,000 of his drawings and 7,000 letters. ⊠ *Piazza Garibaldi* ☎ *0424/522235, 0424/ 523464 campanile* 🎫 *Torre €4.50; Museo €2* ⊗ *Torre, Apr. 6–Oct.,*

Tues.–Sat. 9:30–12:30 and 3–7, Nov.–Apr. 5, weekends 10–1 and 2–6; Museo, Tues.–Sat. 9–6:30, Sun. 3:30–6:30.

need a break? A table set outside the central **Bar Daniele** (✉ Piazza Garibaldi 39 ☎ 0424/529322) is a great place from which to watch the day-to-day life of Bassano unfold on the piazza. It's closed Tuesday afternoon and Wednesday.

The civic museum's ceramics collection is found in the 18th-century **Palazzo Sturm,** on the river's east bank. Walk through the attractive courtyard, past frescoes by Giorgio Anselmi (1723–97), to view the town's famed majolica pieces including 17th-century Manardi ware and later ware from Nove and Faenza. ✉ *Via Schiavonetti* ☎ *0424/524933* 🎟 €3 ⏱ *Tues.–Sat. 9–12:30 and 3:30–6:30, Sun. 10–12:30 and 3:30–6:30.*

Where to Stay & Eat

★ **$$** ✕ **Al Sole.** The walls of this renowned restaurant are decorated with hefty ceramic whistles in the shape of men astride animals. These oddities were typical of the area in bygone days when they were used to warn of the approach of enemies. In the two large dining areas, you can taste Bassano home cooking flirting with the international: duck ends up in pomegranate, pheasant in cognac, and cauliflower and cheese hand-stuffed into luscious pasta pillows. ✉ *Via Jacopo Vittorelli 41/43* ☎ *0424/523206* ▤ *AE, DC, MC, V* ⏱ *Closed Mon. and 3 wks late July–mid-Aug.*

$$ ✕ **Ristorante Birreria Ottone.** Excellent cuisine and a central-European beer-hall atmosphere keep the locals coming back to this old-world restaurant set in a 13th-century palazzo. It's run by the friendly Wipflinger family, headed by Otto, whose Austrian forebear founded it as a beer hall a century ago. Equally good for a simple lunch or more elaborate dinner, Ottone offers specialties that include a delicious goulash cooked with cumin. ✉ *Via Matteotti 48/50* ☎ *0424/522206* ▤ *AE, DC, MC, V* ⏱ *Closed Tues. and first 3 wks in Aug. No dinner Mon.*

$–$$ ✕ **Osteria Terraglio.** The creative, modern menu here focuses on abso-**Fodor'sChoice** lute freshness, in the wonderful array of savory snacks, the big, crisp ★ *insalatone* (main-course salads with tuna or various cheeses), and even the sliced steak fillet. Special tasting sessions of local delicacies such as asparagus, cold-pressed olive oil, and fine wines are a regular feature, and there is live jazz on Tuesday evenings. ✉ *Piazza Terraglio 28* ☎ *0424/521064* ▤ *AE, DC, MC, V* ⏱ *Closed Mon.*

$$$ ✕🛏 **Ca' Sette.** Were it not for an engraving showing Napoléon's troops massed in the courtyard, you'd never guess the great age of this hotel, which has an ultramodern interior. Each room has a different tasteful design in local wood and marble. Light sleepers should request a room that doesn't face the rather busy road. The Ca' 7 restaurant ($$–$$$) is among the best in the area. From Chef Alex Lorenzon's menu you might choose a dish in which you dig into a deep-fried, bread crumb–covered egg yolk to find it bursts golden cream over your plate of polenta, fresh mushrooms, and Asiago cheese. ✉ *Via Cunizza da Romano 4, 36061* ☎ *0424/383350* 🖷 *0424/393287* ⊕ *www.ca-sette.it* 🛏 *17 rooms, 2 suites* ⚙ *Restaurant, in-room safes, minibars, in-room data ports, bi-*

cycles, some pets allowed, no-smoking rooms ⊟ *AE, DC, MC, V* ⊗ *Restaurant closed Mon., 1st wk in Jan., and 2 wks mid-Aug. No dinner Sun.* |⊙| *BP.*

★ **$$** ⊞ **Hotel Belvedere.** This 15th-century hotel, now a member of the Bonotto chain, has richly decorated public rooms with period furnishings and Oriental rugs; the lounge has an open fireplace and a piano. Guest rooms are decorated in traditional Venetian or contemporary style. There are two rooms with facilities for people with disabilities. Two restaurants provide a choice between light, inexpensive dishes and multiple-course regional meals. ⊠ *Piazzale Giardino 14, 36061* ☎ *0424/529845* 🖷 *0424/529849* ⊕ *www.bonotto.it* ↳ *83 rooms, 4 suites* ⚒ *2 restaurants, bar, minibars, Internet, meeting rooms, some pets allowed (fee)* ⊟ *AE, DC, MC, V* ⊗ *Restaurants closed Sun.* |⊙| *BP.*

$ ⊞ **Al Castello.** In a restored town house at the foot of the medieval Torre Civica, the Cattapan family's Castello is a reasonably priced, attractive choice. The simply furnished rooms all differ in shape and size. The best ones at the front have a small balcony offering a wonderful view of the square below. ⊠ *Piazza Terraglio 20, 36061* ☎☎ *0424/228665* ⊕ *www.hotelalcastello.it* ↳ *11 rooms* ⚒ *Café, bar, Internet* ⊟ *AE, MC, V* |⊙| *EP.*

Nightlife & the Arts

FESTIVALS During July and August, Bassano stages the **Opera Estate** (☎ 0424/524214 for information and reservations), a festival of classical and jazz music, dance, opera, cinema, and theater. You can also contact the tourist office for information.

Shopping

There's a general market on Thursday and Saturday in **Piazza Garibaldi** and on Bassano del Grappa's surrounding streets.

CERAMICS Bassano del Grappa and nearby Nove are famous for ceramics. There are antiques, handmade reproductions of timeless designs, and kitschy souvenirs. Prices near the old bridge tend to run a bit higher than elsewhere in town. **Luigi Parise** (⊠ Salita Ferracina 4 ☎ 0424/228359) is a good choice for hand-painted ceramics.

FOOD Preserved foods are a Bassano specialty. **Il Melario** (⊠ Via Angarano 13 ☎ 0424/502168) has one of the best selections in town, including dried wild mushrooms and myriad liqueurs, honeys, and jams. If the friendly proprietor neglects to offer, ask to taste his roasted fava beans, a wholesome snack.

LAMPS **Lumi Vecchio Ponte** (⊠ Via Angarano 19 ☎☎ 0424/503651) is a treasure trove of copper, wrought iron, and stained-glass antique and art lamps, along with brass compasses and baroque mirrors.

Marostica

❼ *18 km (11 mi) west of Asolo, 82 km (51 mi) northwest of Venice.*

Ruled by Venice between 1404 and 1797, Marostica exudes a powerful sense of history, immediately apparent at the first glimpse of its formidable fortifications. From the **Castello Superiore,** perched on a hill overlooking the surrounding countryside, the ramparts tier down to enclose the main square and a second castle. The enclosed castle, the **Castello Inferiore,** provides marvelous views in all directions. The castle was built by the Scaligeri family in the 13th century; a guided tour will let you see the oldest and largest ivy in Europe (it's more than 420 years old), as well as the costumes used for the historic chess game on which the fame of the town rests. ⊠ *Piazza Castello* ☎ *0424/72127* 🎟 *€1* ⊙ *Mon.–Sat. 9–noon and 3–6, Sun. 3–6.*

The harmonious Piazza Castello is marked out in red and white stone checkerboard fashion and on the second weekend in September in even-numbered years is the venue for a human chess game, the **partita a scacchi.** In 1454 rival suitors for the hand of a fair maiden decided to fight it out, not by means of the sword but with chess pieces. Nowadays a set game is enacted to the accompaniment of solemn proclamations, fanfares, processions, and flag waving, with a total of 500 participants dressed in medieval garb and 20 horses in attendance, the whole thing culminating in a dramatized wedding ceremony. If you want to see it, have your tickets bought by June. For information, contact **Associazone Pro Marostica** (☎ 0424/72127 🖷 0424/72800)

After you've admired the square, drop into the nearby **Osteria alla Madonetta** (⊠ Viale Vajenti 21) to see a model of Marostica, handmade in wood by the proprietor. It looks like a bed but is in fact a seating arrangement in which to play chess, using the miniature piazza as the board. Take a seat at the long, polished wood tables by the fireplace for a glass of moscato wine, while absorbing the quaint charm of the clutter here. The 15th-century church **Sant'Antonio** (⊠Via Sant'Antonio ☎0424/72007 ⊙ Daily 8–11) contains a fine 16th-century altarpiece by the painter Jacopo Bassano.

Marostica's soil and climate conspire to produce Italy's most luscious cherries. During May and June, the square is covered with stalls selling Morello, Sandre, Roane, and Marostegane varieties.

Where to Stay & Eat

★ **$$** ✕ **Al Castello Superiore.** This place is right in the hillside castle: wind up the corkscrew road and through the gate to be greeted by stupendous views of the town and the hills behind. The castle's heyday is evoked by suits of armor and various iron implements; there's a terrace for summer dining and a welcoming fireplace for winter. Try the *tagliatelle ai torresani* (pasta with a sauce of pigeon spiced with sage and onions) or the veal with asparagus. If you haven't tasted tiramisu, here's a good place to try your first bite. ⊠ *Via Consignorio della Scala* ☎ *0424/73315* 🖃 *AE, DC, MC, V* ⊙ *Closed Wed., last wk in Jan., 1st wk in Feb., and 1 wk in mid-Aug. No lunch Thurs.*

$$ 🏨 **Due Mori.** Modern, design-conscious rooms with wooden floors and Fodor'sChoice beige marble bathrooms offer classy Italian elegance in the heart of this ★ medieval town center. Some rooms have magical views of the olive-studded terraces behind the town, while rooms 7, 8, 11, and 12 have picture-perfect views of the upper castle. With its chic, minimalist restaurant downstairs, Due Mori is an excellent base for visiting the surrounding hills and towns of the northern Veneto. ⊠ *Corso Mazzini 73, 36063*

☎ 0424/471777 🖷 0424/476920 ⊕ www.duemori.it ⇆ 12 rooms
⚂ Restaurant, minibars, Internet, some pets allowed, no-smoking rooms
🖃 AE, DC, MC, V ⊘ Closed 1st wk Jan., 1 wk mid-Aug. ⦿ BP.

Conegliano

⑧ 23 km (14 mi) north of Treviso, 60 km (37 mi) northwest of Venice.

Situated in the heart of wine-producing country, Conegliano is an attractive town with Venetian-style villas, frescoed houses, arcades, and cobbled streets. The walls that once girded the city did not succeed in repelling the series of assaults between the 12th and 14th centuries. After being subjected to Padua, Treviso, Feltre, Belluno, and the Carraresi and Scaligeri families, the city finally declared its allegiance to Venice. It turned out to be a good move: Conegliano enjoyed nearly 300 years of peace and stability after the pact.

Shops, bars, and restaurants now line Conegliano's main street, the Via XX Settembre, housed in former palaces that bear witness to the Venetian influence. As well as being known as a thriving center of wine—prosecco in particular—Conegliano is also the birthplace of the painter Giambattista Cima (1460–1518), a follower of Giorgione who enjoyed great popularity in Venice.

The **Casa di Giambattista Cima,** the modest house where Cima died in 1518, contains reproductions of his paintings and some archaeological pieces discovered when the house was restored. ⊠ Via Cima 24 ☎ 0438/21660 or 0438/411026 ⛁ €1 ⊘ Open on request only. Call for appointment.

The 14th-century **Duomo** has an arcaded facade frescoed in the 16th century by Ludovico Pozzoserrato (1550–1603/05). Inside, Cima's 1493 masterpiece, La Madonna in Trono e Santi, graces the altar, as well as paintings by Palma the Younger (1548–1628) and frescoes by Pordenone (1484–1539). ⊠ Via XX Settembre ☎ 0438/22606 ⊘ Daily 9–noon and 3–6.

The Duomo gives onto **Sala dei Battuti,** which was previously the meeting place for the Confraternità dei Flagellanti—a 13th-century brotherhood of self-flagellating mystics. It is covered with frescoes by Girolamo da Treviso (circa 1455–97) and Jacopo da Montagnana (15th century), among others. ⊠ Via XX Settembre ☎ 0438/22606 ⛁ €2, €3 in combination with Museo Civico del Castello ⊘ Sat. 10–12, Sun. 3–6, weekday mornings by appointment.

It's a steep walk up the cobbled Calle Madonna della Neve to the Castello, where you'll find the **Museo Civico del Castello** in the tower. It's full of local artifacts and memorabilia, some frescoes by Pordenone, and a good bronze by Giambologna (1529–1608). Make your way to the roof and you'll be rewarded with a fine view over the city to the gentle hills and their vines. ⊠ Piazzale San Leonardo ☎ 0438/22871 ⛁ Castello €2, €3 in combination with Museo Civico del Castello ⊘ Apr.–Sept., Tues.–Sun. 10–12:30 and 3:30–7; Oct. and Dec.–Mar., Tues.–Sun. 10–12:30 and 3–6:30.

TRAVELING THE WINE ROADS

YOU'D BE HARD-PRESSED to find a more stimulating and varied wine region than northeastern Italy. From the Valpolicella, Bardolino, and Soave produced near Verona to the superlative whites of the Collio region, wines from the Veneto and Friuli–Venezia Giulia earn more Denominazione di Origine Controllata (DOC) seals for uniqueness and quality than those of any other area of Italy.

You can travel on foot, by car, or by bicycle over hillsides covered with vineyards, each field nurturing subtly different grape varieties. On a casual trip through the countryside you're likely to come across wineries that will welcome you for a visit; for a more organized tour, check at local tourist information offices, which have maps of roads, wineries, and vendors. (If you find yourself in Bassano del Grappa, stop by Nardini distillery to pick up some grappa, the potent liquor made from grape husks.) Be advised that Italy has become more stringent about its driving regulations; seat belts and designated drivers can save fines, embarrassment, or worse.

One of the most hospitable areas in the Veneto for wine enthusiasts is the stretch of country north of Treviso, where you can follow designated wine roads—tours that blend a beautiful rural setting with the delights of the grape. Authorized wine shops where you can stop and sample are marked with a sign showing a triangular arrangement of red and yellow grapes. There are three routes to choose from, and they're managable enough that you can do them all comfortably over the course of a day or two.

Montello & Asolo Hills
This route provides a good balance of vineyards and non–wine-related sights. It winds its way from Nervesa della Battaglia, 18 km (10 mi) north of Treviso,

past two prime destinations in the area, the lovely village of Asolo and the Villa Barbaro at Maser. Asolo produces good Prosecco, whereas Montello favors merlot and cabernet. Both areas also yield pinot and chardonnay.

Piave River
The circular route follows the river Piave and runs through orchards, woods, and hills. Among the area's gems are the DOC Torchiato di Fregona and Refrontolo Passito, both made according to traditional methods. Raboso del Piave, renowned since Roman times, ages well and complements local dishes such as beans and pasta or goose stuffed with chestnuts. The other reds are cabernet, merlot, and cabernet sauvignon. As an accompaniment to fish, choose a Verduzzo del Piave or, for an aperitif, the lovely warm-yellow Pinot Grigio del Piave.

Prosecco
This route runs for 47 km (29 mi) between Valdobbiadene and Conegliano, home of Italy's first wine institute, winding between knobby hills covered in grapevines. These hang in festoons on row after row of pergolas to create a thick mantle of green. Turn off the main route to explore the narrower country lanes, most of which eventually join up. They meander through tiny hamlets and past numerous family wineries where you can taste and purchase the wines. Spring is an excellent time to visit, with no fewer than 15 local wine festivals held between March and early June.

★ **$$** ✕ **Città di Venezia.** It's no surprise to see the lions and striped poles in this restaurant, for Venice's doges liked to come here on vacation. This is the oldest eating place in the town, with a 14th-century room featuring heavy ceiling beams—but a 21st-century renovation has modernized the place. Seafood predominates, with delicacies like crab served in the shell, scallops, risotto *al nero di seppie* (with cuttlefish ink), and fillet of gilthead with capers and gherkins. The local version of *saor* sauce (onions marinated in vinegar and fried with sultanas and pine nuts) is also renowned. Reservations are advised. The adjoining Osteria La Bea Venezia is a faster and cheaper alternative, with food that's still excellent. ⊠ *Via XX Settembre 77/79* ☎ *0438/23186* ⊟ *AE, DC, MC, V* ⊘ *Closed Mon., 1 wk in Jan., and 2 wks in Aug. No dinner Sun.*

$ ✕ **Al Bacareto.** Little wooden compartments divide up this snug osteria where the jovial owner, Mario, will recite the menu (in English). Specialties include *porchetta* (suckling pig) with roast potatoes, and cuttlefish with tomato and polenta. There's also a good range of pasta dishes, open sandwiches, and pizza slices for a quick lunch, all washed down with the excellent, local Zahre beer. ⊠ *Via Cavour 6* ☎ *0438/411666* ⊟ *No credit cards* ⊘ *Closed Mon.*

$–$$ 🏠 **Canon d'Oro.** The town's oldest inn, the Canon d'Oro is in an arcaded and frescoed 16th-century building that is almost over the top—almost. It's in a central location within walking distance of the train station. The antique furniture, lovely bed linen, and terraced garden all add to its carefully cultivated charm. ⊠ *Via XX Settembre 131, 31015* ☎ *0438/ 34246* 🖷 *0438/34249* ⊕ *www.hotelcanondoro.it* ⤳ *51 rooms* ⚬ *Restaurant, in-room data ports, in-room safes, minibars, cable TV, bar, some pets allowed* ⊟ *AE, DC, MC, V* ⦿ *BP.*

Valdobbiadene

❾ *36 km (22 mi) north of Treviso, 66 km (41 mi) northwest of Venice.*

If you're following the Prosecco Wine Road, Valdobbiadene will be your end destination. As you wind your way through the hills, the vines practically creep up onto the road.

The pasticceria **Emilio Carnia** (⊠ Viale Vittoria 1 ☎ 0423/972209), established as a family-run business since 1935, doubles as a wineshop. Signor Carnia, the versatile pastry maker, not only makes excellent biscuits and pastries but chooses the grapes for the prestigious Cartizze prosecco wine. The terrace will tempt you to indulge in a breakfast croissant, a Mozart *plait* (a kind of biscuit), or an evening aperitif before continuing on your way. It's closed Wednesday.

★ **$–$$** ✕ **Cima.** A big, circular, open fire where one of the chefs performs the art of char-grilling your preferred cut of meat has center stage here, about a five-minute drive outside town. Starters reflect local produce, like gnocchi with fresh walnut sauce, while the mains delight serious meat-eaters with thick beef steaks, pork, and veal. The wine list has a concise selection of white wines and a large range of reds from virtually every region in Italy, while the house wine is prosecco from the owners' vineyards. Excellent food and service make this a great place to stop for a meal; if you want a table on the roofed wooden terrace—with its sweeping vineyard views and refreshing breeze in summer—by all means book ahead. ☒ *Via Cima 13, Loc. S. Pietro di Barbozza* ☎ *0423/ 972711* 🖷 *0423/971040* 🖃 *AE, DC, MC, V* ⊘ *Closed Tues. and Jan. No dinner Mon.*

$ ✕⌂ **Diana.** The warm hues of the exposed stone walls and tiled floors at this modern hotel are set off by discreet lighting and colorful rugs. There's plenty of comfortable space for relaxation in the large, sprawling public lounges, and some rooms have views of the surrounding hills. The large, airy restaurant ($) has an impressive trussed wooden roof under which to dine. Service is courteous. ☒ *Via Roma 49, 31049* ☎ *0423/976222* 🖷 *0423/972237* ⊕ *www.hoteldiana.org* ⇗ *57 rooms* ⌂ *Restaurant, in-room data ports, in-room safes, minibars, cable TV, bar, meeting rooms* 🖃 *AE, MC, V* ⧄ *BP.*

Vittorio Veneto

⑩ *14 km (7 mi) north of Conegliano, 70 km (43 mi) northwest of Venice.*

Vittorio Veneto owes its name to the unification of Italy in 1866 and its first king, Vittorio Emanuele II. The two towns of Ceneda and Serravalle were joined to form Vittorio Veneto, with a new town hall and train station built between them. The town extends along the main road, with Ceneda, the commercial center, in the south. To the north, Serravalle is the historic quarter enclosed within a gorge that has a more Alpine feel. After Serravalle's annexation to Venice in 1337 it became an important economic center and money market, with one of the largest Jewish communities in the north of Italy.

Although Serravalle is by far the more attractive of the two parts, Ceneda does have two sights, the first of which is the church of **Santa Maria del Meschio,** which holds a heavenly *Annunciation* by Andre Previtali (circa 1470–1528). ☒ *Piazza Meschio* ☎ *0438/53581* ⊘ *Daily 8–noon and 3–7.*

The second reason to visit Ceneda is the **Museo della Battaglia,** dedicated to the Battle of Vittorio, which in 1918 marked the final engagement of the Italian army in World War I. It is housed in the graceful **Loggia del Cenedese,** which is attributed to Jacopo Sansovino (1486–1570). ☒ *Piazza Giovanni Paolo I* ☎ *0438/57695* ⌂ *€3 includes Museo del Cenedese and San Lorenzo dei Battuti* ⊘ *May–Sept., Tues.–Sun. 9:30–12:30 and 4–7; Oct.–Apr., Tues.–Sun. 9:30–12:30 and 2–5.*

Filmmaker Franco Zeffirelli was so taken by Serravalle that he used it as a location for his 1970s adaptation of *Romeo and Juliet,* and indeed its charm rests on the fact that nothing much has changed since the 16th century. Via Martiri della Libertà leads up to the main square, lined with 15th- and 16th-century buildings and ending at the Loggia Serravalle, a fine building emblazoned with shields. The Loggia Serravalle is now the home of the **Museo del Cenedese,** a collection of local archaeological bits and pieces, minor paintings, and frescoes. ☒ *Piazza Flaminio*

☎ *0438/57103* ✉ *€3 includes Museo della Battaglia and San Lorenzo dei Battuti* ☉ *May–Sept., Tues.–Sun. 9:30–12:30 and 4–7; Oct.–Apr., Tues.–Sun. 9:30–12:30 and 2–5.*

The church of **San Lorenzo dei Battuti** houses an excellent fresco cycle painted in the mid-15th century. The damage suffered when Napoléon's men used the church as a kitchen has since been rectified. ✉ *Piazza Ve-cellio* ☎ *0438/57103* ✉ *€3 includes Museo della Battaglia and Museo del Cenedese* ☉ *May–Sept., Tues.–Sun. 9:30–12:30 and 3:30–7; Oct.–Apr., Tues.–Sun. 9:30–12:30 and 2–5.*

Crossing the river Meschio from Piazza Flaminio, you come to the **Duomo,** notable for its Titian altarpiece *The Virgin with S. Peter and S. Andrew.* ✉ *Piazza Giovanni Paolo I* ☎ *0438/53401* ☉ *May–Sept., daily 6:30–noon and 2:30–7:30; Oct.–Apr., daily 6:30–noon and 2:30–6:30.*

Where to Stay & Eat

★ $ ✕ **Locanda al Postiglione.** A post office in the time of Emperor Franz Josef, this restaurant preserves its 18th-century atmosphere with beamed ceilings and wood paneling. The menu changes daily. Regional dishes prevail; specialties include roast shank of pork, duck, and grilled porcini mushrooms. Fish is served on Thursday and Friday. Save room for the berry tarts and other homemade sweets on the dessert trolley. There are also three guest rooms upstairs. ✉ *Via Cavour 39* ☎ *0438/556924* ▭ *AE, DC, MC, V* ☉ *Closed Tues. and July 20–Aug. 10.*

$ ✕ **Taverna da Peo.** Typical Veneto cooking is served at plain wooden tables in this bustling trattoria, which stays open until 1 AM (till 2 on Friday and Saturday). The local fare is includes standards like pasta e fagioli, several varieties of seasonal vegetable risotto, *bigoli con ragù di anatra* (thick spaghetti with duck ragout), and *salsiccetta con polenta* (sausage and polenta). Service is friendly. ✉ *Via Martiri della Libertà 25* ☎ *0438/ 554930* ▭ *DC, MC, V* ☉ *Closed Tues., 2nd wk in Jan., and 3 wks in July. No dinner Mon.*

★ $ ▦ **Hotel Calvi.** Tasteful architectural and interior design have given this 19th-century inn an air of elegant comfort. The spacious lounge and breakfast room has a high, wood-beamed ceiling, big open fire, and large windows looking across the Meschio river (here just a stream), which separates the restful garden from the hills behind. Since it's handily located on the main road, about 50 yards from the north end of Serravalle, you can leave the car here and visit the town on foot, taking in its romantic lanes and medieval architecture. ✉ *Via Calvi 19, 31029* ☎ *0438/ 941682* ▤ *0438/947331* ⊕ *www.hotelcalvi.it* ⬎ *11 rooms* ⌂ *Minibars, cable TV, bar, Internet* ▭ *AE, DC, MC, V* ☉ *Closed Dec. 10–Jan. 7* ◎| *BP.*

$ ▦ **La Casa del Podestà.** An upstairs wing of this fine old patrician mansion (the podestà was the mayor) has been converted into a quality bed-and-breakfast. All rooms have their own bathrooms and feature exposed wooden roof beams and garden views. Start your day in the big breakfast room, then comfortably visit the whole town on foot. A spacious apartment is also available for longer stays (minimum 1 week) at the same price. You can use the shared kitchen. ⊠ *Piazza G. Paolo 65, 31029* ☎ *0438/53448* ⊕ *www.vittorioveneto.net/podesta/podesta.htm* ⋈ *4 rooms, 1 apartment* ⚭ *No a/c* ⊟ *No credit cards* ◯ *BP.*

Shopping
Distilleria de Negri (⊠ Via Martiri della Libertà 43 ☎ No phone), closed Wednesday, has a large stock of grappa. **Tochetti** (⊠ Via Martiri dei Libertà ☎ 0438/450025) is good for a range of fresh mountain cheeses.

THE DOLOMITES

Turn northward to enter one of Italy's grandest mountain landscapes, an exhilarating land of lush, flower-laden meadows cut through by lakes and river valleys. The towns of Belluno and Feltre lie on the mighty Piave River, the first of these a relatively neglected holiday destination dramatically sited against the jagged mountain backdrop. Feltre, a walled city perched high on a ridge with stunning views, reveals some unexpected examples of Renaissance architecture. For a more glamorous aspect of the Alps, repair to the ritzy Cortina d'Ampezzo ski resort. The scenery around Cortina is as good as anything you'll find in these mountains and can be just as scintillating in summer as in the winter months, and certainly more accessible for rambling. The rich and creamy food here, including fondues, polentas, and barley soups, reflects the Alpine climate and Austrian and Swiss influence; there are a number of dishes unique to the zone. If your doctor permits it, try the *schiz*: fresh cheese that is sliced and fried in butter, sometimes with cream added.

Belluno

⑪ *78 km (49 mi) north of Treviso, 108 km (67 mi) north of Venice.*

The Dolomites set the mood in Belluno, spread over a plateau above the junction of the Piave and Ardo rivers. It's the northernmost town of the Veneto and, given its strategic position, prospered as an ally of Venice. Now a provincial capital and busy commercial center, the city attracts a few tourists, though most prefer to stay higher in the mountains; Belluno's hotels are fairly quiet. You could spend a rewarding half day wandering around the old town, and there are some good spots for lunch. It's best to park on the lower side near the river and take the escalator up, enjoying the panorama as you go.

Take a stroll around the impressively broad main square, **Piazza dei Martiri**, complete with a grove of evergreens and bordered on one side by a unified row of arcaded palaces. To the south lies the Piazza del Duomo, where the pale-ocher **Duomo,** built in the 16th century to a design of Tullio Lombardo (1455–1532), had to be rebuilt after two earthquakes, once in 1873 and again in 1936. Inside there are 16th-century paintings by Jacopo Bassano. Next to it, topped by a green onion-shape cupola, stands the tall campanile, Belluno's most prominent monument, built in the 18th century by the Sicilian architect and stage designer Filippo Juvara (1678–1736). ⊠ *Piazza del Duomo* ☎ *0437/941908* ☉ *Daily 7–noon and 3–7.*

The **Palazzo dei Rettori,** an ornate 15th-century building with baroque touches, seat of the Venetian governors and now an administrative building, fills one side of the square. The best view of the river and surrounding countryside is from **Porta Ruga** at the end of the main street, Via Mezzaterra.

The **Museo Civico,** housed in a 17th-century palazzo, has a good collection of work by the locally born painters Sebastiano Ricci (1659–1734) and Marco Ricci (1679–1729), and the sculptor Andrea Brustolon (1662–1732). ⊠ *Piazza del Duomo 16* ☎ *0437/944836* 🎫 *€2.30* ⊙ *Mid-Apr.–Sept., Tues.–Sat. 10–noon and 4–7, Sun. 10:30–12:30; Oct.–mid-Apr., Mon., Wed., Thurs., Sat. 10–noon, Tues. and Fri. 3–6.*

Where to Stay & Eat

$–$$ ✕ **Al Borgo.** Cross the river to find this lovely rustic restaurant, an 18th-century villa in a park with views of the mountains, colored in shades of terra-cotta, green, and cream. The chef uses game like wild boar and venison, and greenery from the mountains—whatever's in season. Spring might produce risotto with wild herbs and hops, while in summer you can find gnocchi with *zucca* (pumpkin) and lamb with rosemary. On rare occasions you might be offered *pinza da noze,* a traditional wedding cake made with ricotta cheese. ⊠ *Via Anconetta 8* ☎ *0437/926755* ⏆ *Reservations essential* ▭ *AE, DC, MC, V* ⊙ *Closed Tues. and last 2 wks in Jan. No dinner Mon.*

$–$$ ✕ **Terracotta.** This small restaurant serves meat, game, and seafood, with a focus on traditional Bellunese dishes such as *formai schiz e rösti di patate* (cheese and roasted potatoes). The tiny, candlelit terrace offers intimate dining on summer evenings, with glimpses of the surrounding mountains. ⊠ *Via Garibaldi 61* ☎ *0437/942644* ▭ *AE, MC, V* ⊙ *Closed Wed.*

$ 🏨 **Cappello e Cadore.** Specially crafted wooden furniture typical of the area adds personality to the spacious, warmly decorated rooms here. There's private car parking out front, but you won't be needing your car: the hotel is in a quiet lane just a few steps behind the Piazza dei Martiri from where all the sights can be visited on foot. ⊠ *Via Ricci 8, 32100* ☎ *0437/940246* 🖶 *0437/292319* ⌁ *32 rooms* ⚬ *In-room data ports, minibars, cable TV, bar, meeting rooms, some pets allowed; no a/c* ▭ *AE, DC, MC, V* ⊙❘ *EP.*

Feltre

⓬ *31 km (19 mi) east of Belluno, 88 km (55 mi) northwest of Venice.*

Approaching along one of the river valleys below the town, you'll soon see the mellow tones of Feltre's historic center rearing above you on its narrow fortified ridge. To reach the old quarter, either wend your way up the main cobbled street from the modern zone, or opt for the steeper but more rewarding toil up one of the various flights of stone steps that thread up through the old town. Either way, you'll be stepping back into the 16th century, when Venice had Feltre almost completely rebuilt after it was sacked in 1509 by the League of Cambrai, as punishment for the town's allegiance to La Serenissima.

Via Mezzaterra, marked by gates at either end, is lined with harmonious houses, many of which are adorned with frescoes by Lorenzo Luzzo (died 1526), the town's best-known painter, who bore the unfortunate nickname of "Il Morto da Feltre" (the Dead Man of Feltre) due to his pallid complexion. Midway along, the road pans out into the **Piazza Maggiore,** the main square that holds the medieval **Castello** and the **Palazzo della Ragione,** with its Palladian portico. Here you can see the frescoed Sala Consiglio and the little wooden theater, La Scena, rebuilt in 1802 by Gian Antonio Selva, the designer of La Fenice in Venice. Call the Museo Civico for visiting hours.

Via Mezzaterra continues into Via Luzzo to the **Museo Civico,** containing a collection of paintings by Luzzo including his *Madonna with S. Vitus and S. Modestus,* as well as a portrait by Gentile Bellini (1429–1546) and a triptych by Cima da Conegliano (1460–1518). Luzzo's masterpiece, a *Transfiguration,* is housed in the sacristy of the **Chiesa di Ognissanti.** ⊠ *Via Lorenzo Luzzo 23* ☎ *0439/885242* 🖼 *€4* ☉ *Apr.–Sept., Tues.–Sun. 10–1 and 4–7; Oct.–Nov., weekends 3:30–6:30.*

In the street parallel to Via Mezzaterra, the **Galleria d'Arte Moderna Carlo Rizzarda** has wrought-iron work on display, mostly by Carlo Rizzarda (1883–1931), whose decorative pieces reveal art nouveau and art deco influences. In 1929 Rizzarda presented the town with his collection and his house. ⊠ *Via Paradiso 8* ☎ *0439/885234* 🖼 *€4* ☉ *Apr.–Sept., weekdays 10:30–12:30 and 4–7, weekends 9:30–12:30 and 4–7; Oct.–Mar. weekdays 10:30–12:30 and 3–6, weekends 9:30–12:30 and 3–6.*

At the bottom of the 16th-century stairway that leads from Piazza Maggiore you'll reach the Porta Pusterla and the **Duomo** with its baptistery. Look for the 6th-century carved Byzantine cross inside the much-altered 15th-century cathedral. ⊠ *Piazza del Duomo* ☎ *0439/2312* ☉ *Daily 8–noon and 3–7.*

Where to Stay & Eat

$$ ✕ **Hostaria Novecento.** At this restaurant in the "dress circle" on the main square, you can dine on seafood or meat dishes, including *spiedini di scampi e seppie* (scampi and cuttlefish kebabs), *petto d'oca con crostini caldi* (breast of goose with hot croutons), or a simple steak fillet with porcini mushrooms. Or you may choose just to settle in on the terrace with an ice cream or coffee and enjoy the rich surroundings of medieval architecture. ⊠ *Via Mezzaterra 24* ☎ *0439/83043* ➡ *MC, V* ☉ *Closed Mon.*

¢–$ ✕ **Osteria Mezzaterra Zanzibar.** Get a sandwich or roll made to order or sit down with a simple dish of cold cuts, pickles, cheeses, and bread in one of the growing contingent of restaurants affiliated with the Slow Food movement. The rustic, wooden decor and fine selection of wines by the glass make this an ideal rest stop after trudging up the hill to the main square. ⊠ *Via Mezzaterra 5* ☎ *0439/89020* ➡ *No credit cards.*

$ 🏠 **Doriguzzi.** The mountains are clearly visible from the windows of this modern hotel, which is near the train station and handily located a few minutes' walk from the town center. Ask for one of the two huge attic rooms with skylights that open, making you feel you could almost touch the inspiring Alpine scenery. ⊠ *Viale Piave 2, 32032* ☎ *0439/*

2003 🖨 *0439/83660* ⊕ *www.hoteldoriguzzi.it* ⬅ *23 rooms* ᗙ *In-room data ports, minibars, cable TV, bar, meeting rooms, some pets allowed* 🖃 *AE, DC, MC, V* ⦿| *BP.*

$ ▦ **Nuovo.** This is a small, modern hotel near the river in the town center. An open fireplace crackles in winter; in summer relax in the garden or on the terrace. The rooms are light and airy and full of plants; most have mountain views. The management is cheerful and hospitable. ⊠ *Via Fornere Pazze 15, 32032* ☎ *0439/2110* 🖨 *0439/89241* ⬅ *23 rooms* ᗙ *In-room data ports, minibars, cable TV, bar, meeting rooms, some pets allowed* 🖃 *AE, DC, MC, V* ⦿| *BP.*

Pieve di Cadore

⓭ *43 km (27 mi) north of Belluno, 130 km (81 mi) northwest of Venice.*

The Cadore region of the Dolomites extends as far as the Austrian frontier. Pope John Paul II vacationed in the area for years, and many other overheated city folk do so as well, though it does not have the feel of a tourist zone. The region's most important artistic center, Pieve di Cadore, is small, scenic, set on a hill, and quickly explored. A bronze statue of Pieve's most illustrious son, the painter Titian guards the **Casa Natale di Tiziano,** where he was born. It's furnished as in Titian's time but contains none of his possessions or works. ⊠ *Via Arsenale* ☎ *0435/32262* ▦ *€1.50* ⊗ *June 20–Sept. 10, Tues.–Sun. 9:30–12:30 and 4–7; other times by appointment.*

The **Museo dell'Occhiale** claims to be the only one of its kind in the world. It exhibits more than 2,000 pairs of glasses from medieval times to the present day, including the earliest French, English, and Chinese models, and the first pair of sunglasses, used by the 18th-century Venetian dramatist Carlo Goldoni. ⊠ *Via degli Alpini 39* ☎ *0435/500213* ⊕ *www.museodellocchiale.it* ▦ *€3* ⊗ *June–Sept. 10, Mon–Sat. 8:30–12:30 and 4:30–7:30; Sept. 11–May, Mon.–Sat. 8:30–12:30.*

The pretty church **Parrochiale di Santa Maria Nascente** was completed in the early 19th century and the mosaicked facade dates from 1876. Inside, the Titian altarpiece in the Cappella di San Tiziano is said to bear likenesses of the painter's family, his daughter Lavinia representing the Virgin Mary and his son Pomponio, Bishop Tiziano. ⊠ *Piazza Tiziano 41* ☎ *0435/32261* ⊗ *Daily 8–noon and 3–6.*

Where to Stay & Eat

★ $$–$$$ ✕ **La Chiusa.** It may be the secluded position in a hillside copse that entices you here, or the smell of the wood smoke in winter. Within, the ceiling beams are tree trunks and the wood paneling is imported from Turkey and Pakistan. But the star attraction is the fare itself. The genial owner, Benito Perismascietti, encourages you to linger over your victuals (the menu has a poem to this effect). Try the pasta stuffed with potatoes, walnuts, and sage, or the carrot dumplings with a cream and arugula sauce. This gourmet heaven is 20 km (12 mi) southeast of Cortina and 10 km (6 mi) west from Pieve di Cadore on the SS51. ⊠ *Località La Chiusa, Ruvignan, Vodo di Cadore* ☎ *0435/489288* 🖨 *0435/*

488048 ⩕ *Reservations essential* ☰ *AE, DC, MC, V* ⊘ *Closed Mon.,*
Tues. in spring and fall, and last 2 wks in Oct.

$–$$ ⊞ **Villa Marinotti.** This lovely wooden chalet set on a gentle slope was
once a private home, now converted into suites, and there are a pair of
bungalows on the grounds. All the accommodations are beautifully
furnished with a luxuriously light and spacious feel. In winter there's a
fogher (open fireplace). It makes an ideal center for walking, horseback
riding, and fishing. The gracious and hospitable owner speaks excellent
English. ⊠ *Via Manzago 21, Tai di Cadore, 32040* ☎ *0435/32231*
🖷 *0435/33335* ⊕ *www.villamarinotti.com* ↩ *5 suites, 2 bungalows*
♨ *Restaurant, tennis court* ☰ *AE, DC, MC, V* ⦿⎸ *BP.*

Sports & the Outdoors

BIKING   From June through September, mountain bikes can be rented from **Dy-**
namic Line (⊠ Via XX Settembre 63, Valle di Cadore ☎ 0435/519260).

WALKING   For walking trips, contact **Gruppo CAI di Pieve di Cadore** (⊠ Località Val-
calda ☎ 0435/31515).

Cortina d'Ampezzo

⑭   *30 km (19 mi) northwest of Pieve de Cadore, 155 km (97 mi) north-*
Fodor's Choice   *west of Venice.*
★

Cortina d'Ampezzo has been the Dolomites' mountain resort of choice
for more than 100 years; the Winter Olympics were held here in 1956.
Although its glamorous appeal to younger Italians may have been
eclipsed by steeper, sleeker Madonna di Campiglio, Cortina remains, for
many, Italy's most idyllic incarnation of an Alpine ski town.

Surrounded by mountains and dense forests, the "The Pearl of the
Dolomites" is in a lush meadow 4,000 feet above sea level. The town
hugs the slopes beside a fast-moving stream, and a public park extends
along one bank. Higher in the valley, luxury hotels and the villas of the
rich are identifiable by their attempts to hide behind stands of firs and
spruces. The bustling center of Cortina d'Ampezzo has little nostalgia,
despite its Alpine appearance. The tone is set by smart shops and cafés
as chic as their well-dressed patrons, whose corduroy knickerbockers
may well have been tailored by Armani. Unlike neighboring resorts that
have a strong Germanic flavor, Cortina d'Ampezzo is unapologetically
Italian and distinctly fashionable.

On Via Cantore, a winding road heading up out of town to the northeast (becoming S48), you can stop and see the **Pista Olimpica di Bob**
(Olympic Bobsled Course), a leftover from the 1956 Winter Games. The
course is open to the public, but at unpredictable times.

Where to Stay & Eat

$$–$$$ ✕ **Tavernetta.** Near the Olympic ice-skating rink, this popular restaurant
has Tirolean-style, wood-panelled dining rooms and a local clientele.
Here you can try Cortina specialties such as *zuppa di porcini* (porcini
mushroom soup), ravioli *di cervo* (stuffed with venison), and game. ⊠ *Via*
Castello 53 ☎ *0436/868102* ☰ *AE, DC, MC, V* ⊘ *Closed Nov.*

$–$$ ✕ **Birreria Vienna.** A hearty meal at a fair price is a welcome find in Cortina and, despite the name, this is more restaurant (no-smoking) than beer hall. Alpine specialties like green gnocchi with Gorgonzola and smoked saddle of pork line up alongside excellent insalatone, or single-dish salads with tuna, cheese, olives, and plenty of other goodies, and tempting pizzas with seasonal toppings. ⊠ *Via Roma 66/68* ☎ *0436/866944* ⊕ *www.cortina.dolomiti.com/aziende/vienna* ⊟ *AE, DC, MC, V* ☉ *Closed Wed. and May and Nov.*

$$$$ ▥ **De la Poste.** Loyal skiers return year after year to this lively hotel; its

Fodor'sChoice   main terrace bar is one of Cortina's social centers. De la Poste has been

★   under the careful management of the Manaìgo family since 1936. Each unique room has antiques in characteristic Dolomite style; almost all have wooden balconies. A refined main dining room—with high ceilings and large chandeliers—serves nouvelle cuisine and superb soufflés; there's also a more informal grill room with wood paneling and the family's pewter collection. Sporadic off-season bed-and-breakfast rates can be a bargain. ⊠ *Piazza Roma 14, 32043* ☎ *0436/4271* 📠 *0436/868435* ⊕ *www.delaposte.it* ⇄ *83 rooms* ♨ *2 restaurants, in-room data ports, in-room safes, minibars, cable TV, bar* ⊟ *AE, DC, MC, V* ☉ *Closed Apr.–mid-June and Oct.–mid-Dec.* �ⓄⅠ *MAP.*

$$$–$$$$ ▥ **Corona.** Noted ski instructor Luciano Rimoldi, who has coached such luminaries as Alberto Tomba, runs a cozy Alpine lodge. Modern art adorns small but comfortable pine-panel rooms; the convivial bar is a pleasant place to relax. The hotel is a five-minute walk—across the river—from the center of town, and a 10-minute ride from the lifts (a ski bus stops out front). ⊠ *Via Val di Sotto 12, 32040* ☎ *0436/3251* 📠 *0436/867339* ⊕ *www.hotelcoronacortina.it* ⇄ *44 rooms* ♨ *Restaurant, cable TV, bar, free parking; no a/c* ⊟ *AE, DC, MC, V* ☉ *Closed Apr.–June and Sept.–Nov.* ⓄⅠ *MAP.*

$$ ▥ **Meublè Oasi.** The tasteful, modern furnishings, homey atmosphere, and quiet, handy location mean you'll have to book early here. It's right next to the bus station and just a few minutes' walk from both the town center and the main ski lift. Some front rooms have big balconies and dramatic views of the Tofane peaks across town. ⊠ *Via Cantore 2, 32043* ☎ *0436/862019* 📠 *0436/879476* ⊕ *www.hoteloasi.it* ⇄ *10* ♨ *Ski storage* ⊟ *MC, V* ☉ *Closed Oct.* ⓄⅠ *BP.*

Nightlife & the Arts

At **Europa hotel** (⊠ Corso Italia 207 ☎ 0436/3221) you can expect to mingle with the couture set at the VIP disco; nonguests are welcome, but don't expect to spend less than €30 on drinks.

Sports

HIKING & Hiking information is available at the excellent local **tourist office** (⊠ Pi-

CLIMBING   azzetta San Francesco 8 ☎ 0436/3231 ⊕ www.cortina.dolomiti.com).

Cortina's **Scuola di Alpinismo** (Mountaineering School) (⊠ Corso Italia 69 ☎ 0436/868505 ⊕ www.guidecortina.com) organizes climbing trips and trekking adventures.

SKIING Cortina's long and picturesque ski runs will delight intermediates, but advanced skiers might lust for steeper terrain, which can be found only off-piste. Efficient ski bus service connects the town with the high-speed chairlifts and gondolas that ascend in all directions from the valley.

The **Dolomiti Superski pass** (⊠ Via Marconi 15 ☎ 0471/795397 ⊕ www. dolomitisuperski.com) provides access to the surrounding Dolomites (€38 per day, excluding Bromio)—with 450 lifts and gondolas serving 1200 km (750 mi) of trails. Buy one at the ticket office next to the bus station. The **Faloria gondola** (⊠ Via Ria de Zeta 8 ☎ 0436/2517) runs from the center of town. From its top you can get up to most of the central mountains.

Some of the most impressive views (and steepest slopes) are on **Monte Cristallo,** based at Misurina, 15 km (9 mi) northeast of Cortina by car or bus. The topography of the **Passo Falzarego** ski area, 16 km (10 mi) east of town, is quite dramatic.

NORTHERN VENETO A TO Z

To research prices, get advice from other travelers, and book travel arrangements, visit www.fodors.com.

AIRPORTS & TRANSFERS
Treviso's Aeroporto San Giuseppe is served by charter and commercial flights. The low-cost carrier Ryanair has adopted this airport as something of a hub, rather misleadingly dubbing the destination "Venice (Treviso)." They serve London's Luton and Stansted airports; Liverpool, England; Frankfurt, Germany; Rome's Ciampino airport; and destinations in Spain, France, and Belgium, all from Treviso. There is coach service between the airport and Piazzale Roma in Venice, also stopping in Mestre, for all flights; otherwise there is local bus service via ATVO to Treviso every 30 minutes during the day, or a taxi will come from Treviso, only 6 km (4 mi) away, to pick you up.

◪ Airlines **Ryanair** ☎ 0899/678910 in Italy (80 cents per minute) ⊕ www.ryanair.com.
◪ Airport Information **Aeroporto di Treviso** ⊠ 5 km [3 mi] southeast of Treviso, 32 km [19 mi] north of Venice ☎ 0422/315131 ⊕ www.trevisoairport.it.
◪ Taxis & Shuttles **Taxi** ☎ 0422/431515.

BUS TRAVEL TO & FROM TREVISO
Taking one of the frequent ACTV buses from Venice will get you to Treviso in a half hour. An equally frequent service runs from Padua with La Marca bus line.

◪ Bus Information **ACTV** ⊠ Piazzale Roma, Venice ☎ 041/2424. **La Marca** ⊠ Lungosile Mattei 29, Treviso ☎ 0422/577311.

BUS TRAVEL WITHIN TREVISO & THE DOLOMITES
More so than elsewhere in Italy, bus travel is a reasonable choice in the Dolomites. La Marca has connections throughout the province, including the Conegliano bus station. From Bassano del Grappa, FTV runs hourly buses to Marostica and Vicenza. ACTM serves Asolo, Maser, and

Possagno. The Dolomites are served by Dolomiti Bus. Buses run frequently between Conegliano and Valdobbiadene along the Prosecco Wine Road.

🚌 Bus Information **ACTM** ✉ Via Vittorio Veneto 13, Castelfranco Veneto ☎ 0423/493464. **Conegliano Bus Station** ✉ Piazza Fili Zoppas ☎ 0438/21011. **Dolomiti Bus** ✉ Via Col di Ren, Belluno ☎ 0437/217111 ⊕ www.dolomitibus.it. **FTV** ✉ Viale Europa 25, Romano d'Ezzelino ☎ 0424/30850. **La Marca** ✉ Lungosile Mattei 29, Treviso ☎ 0422/577311.

CAR RENTAL

🚗 Local Agencies **Ad Hoc** ✉ Via Maggio 24, Cortina ☎ 0436/868061. **Alfieri** ✉ Viale Italia 170, Conegliano ☎ 0438/32399. **Avis** ✉ c/o Garage Cima, Via Verdi 51A, Conegliano ☎ 0438/34687 ⊕ www.avis.com ✉ Piazzale Duca d'Aosta 1, Treviso ☎ 0422/542287 ✉ San Giuseppe Airport, Treviso ☎ 0422/433351. **Garage Dolomiti** ✉ Corso Italia 186, Cortina ☎ 0436/861345. **Hertz** ✉ Treviso airport ☎ 0422/264216 ⊕ www.hertz.com ✉ Via Trevigiana 1, Feltre ☎ 0439/80373. **Maggiore Budget** ✉ Via Medaglia d'Oro 46, Belluno ☎ 0437/932044 ⊕ www.maggiore.it.

CAR TRAVEL

The SS11 connects Venice with Mestre, from where the SS13 leads due north to Treviso. The autostrada A4 runs north of Mestre and continues north of Belluno. From Padua, the SS47 goes north to Bassano del Grappa.

Westward from Treviso, it's a straight run on the SS53 to Castelfranco and Cittadella. The SS47 connects Cittadella with Bassano del Grappa. Joining the autostrada A27 at Treviso Nord takes you as far as Belluno. A continuation of the A27, the SS51 heads up to Pieve di Cadore following the River Piave, and then northwest to Cortina d'Ampezzo. The SS13 and SS51 connect Treviso with Conegliano and Vittorio Veneto.

ROAD CONDITIONS Beware: wind and snow conditions in the region can be treacherous at times in the winter. Ask for snow tires and chains for your rental car if heading up to the Dolomites in winter.

EMERGENCIES

For first aid, ask for *pronto soccorso,* and be prepared to give your address. All pharmacies post signs on the door with addresses of *farmacie di turno,* pharmacies that take turns staying open after normal business hours: at night, on Saturday afternoon, and on Sunday.

🚑 Emergency Services **Ambulance, Police, and Fire** ☎ 113. **First aid** ☎ 118.

🏥 Hospitals **Bassano del Grappa** Ospedale Civile ✉ Via dei Lotti 40 ☎ 0424/888111. **Belluno** Ospedale Civile ✉ Viale Europa ☎ 0437/216111. **Treviso** Ospedale Generale ✉ Viale Vittorio Veneto 18 ☎ 0422/4281. **Vittorio Veneto** Ospedale Civile ✉ Via Forlanini 71 ☎ 0438/5671.

TRAIN TRAVEL

The Treviso train station lies on the FS line from Venice to Udine. Trains run several times an hour, and the journey takes a half hour. The FS line connects Treviso with Castelfranco, Cittadella, and Conegliano. On the Padua–Belluno line you pass through Castelfranco and Feltre. Bassano del Grappa has frequent trains to Cittadella, Venice, and Padua. Belluno connects with Conegliano and Padua. The nearest station to

Cortina d'Ampezzo is at Calalzo, 32 km (19 mi) southeast, where there are frequent connecting buses.

🚈 Train Information **FS** ☎ 892021. **Treviso Train Station** ✉ Piazzale Duca d'Aosta.

TRAVEL AGENCIES

🚈 Local Agents **Agenzia Esprit Tour** ✉ Viale d'Alviano 52, 31100 Treviso ☎ 0422/410999. **ASVI** ✉ Piazza Martiri 27/e, 32100 Belluno ☎ 0437/941746. **Giorgione** ✉ Piazza Giorgione 46, 31033 Castelfranco ☎ 0423/493601. **Grizzly Viaggi** ✉ Piazzetta Trento e Trieste 16, 32032 Feltre ☎ 0439/2222 ✉ Galleria Caffi, Belluno ☎ 0437/942726 ⊕ www.grizzlyviaggi.it. **Viaggi Montegrappa** ✉ Via Giuseppe Barbieri 40, 36061 Bassano del Grappa ☎ 0424/523007 ⊕ www.viaggimontegrappa.it.

VISITOR INFORMATION

🚈 Tourist Information **Asolo** ✉ Piazza Garibaldi 73, 31011 ☎ 0423/529046 🖶 0423/524137. **Bassano del Grappa** ✉ Largo Corona d'Italia, 36061 ☎ 0424/524351 🖶 0424/525301. **Belluno** ✉ Piazza Duomo 2, 32100 ☎🖶 0437/940083. **Castelfranco** ✉ Via Francesco Maria Preti 66, 31033 ☎ 0423/491416 🖶 0423/771085. **Cittadella** ✉ Porte Bassanesi 2, 35013 ☎🖶 049/9404485. **Conegliano** ✉ Via XX Settembre 61, 31015 ☎ 0438/21230 🖶 0438/428777. **Cortina d'Ampezzo** ✉ Piazzetta San Francesco 8, 32043 ☎ 0436/3231 🖶 0436/3235. **Feltre** ✉ Piazzetta Trento e Trieste 9, 32032 ☎ 0439/2540 🖶 0439/2839. **Marostica** ✉ Piazza Castello, 36063 ☎ 0424/72127 🖶 0424/72800. **Pieve di Cadore** ✉ Via Nazionale 45, 32044 ☎ 0435/31644 🖶 0435/31645. **Treviso** ✉ Piazzetta del Monte di Pietà 8, 31100 ☎ 0422/547632 🖶 0422/419092. **Vittorio Veneto** ✉ Viale della Vittoria 10, 31029 ☎ 0438/57243 🖶 0438/53629.

Friuli-Venezia Giulia

WORD OF MOUTH

"Trieste is a lovely city. Its history as a major trade center has left it with very interesting architecture, a very attractive fort and an old basilica up on the hill. There are many good restaurants and cafés and, of course, those glorious views of the sea."

—joegri

"Aquileia, about an hour outside of Venice on the way to Trieste, has an incredible Roman site and a basilica with the largest intact mosaic floor in Europe. This is now one of my top five favorite built environments in Italy."

—Santa Chiara

Updated by
Robin
Goldstein

TUCKED AWAY in Italy's northeastern corner, Friuli-Venezia Giulia is off most tourist tracks, and it gains as a result. Bounded by the Adriatic, a ring of mountains, and the Slovenian and Austrian borders, it's a hodge-podge of climates, cultures, and historical conflicts—in the 19th century, the great Italian novelist Ippolito Nievo described it as "a small abridged version of the universe." The capital is the old Hungarian port of Trieste, a longtime symbol of Italian nationalist aspirations that, like the medieval city of Udine, makes a perfect excursion base.

Through the ages, the region has been invaded in turn by Romans, Lombards, Cossacks, and Nazis. Venice had the most powerful influence over Friuli, with Venetian architecture dominating its capital of Udine, while the Habsburgs dominated Trieste and its surroundings, known as Venezia Giulia.

During the 19th century, Trieste was the focus for Irredentism, a movement that sought liberation from Austrian rule and ended with the arrival of Italian troops in 1918. Some of the fiercest fighting of World War I took place on the Carso hinterland near Trieste, an area now distinguished by its numerous war memorials and cemeteries containing thousands of fallen soldiers. During World War II, Italian fascism found a stronghold in Trieste, the location of one of Italy's two concentration camps.

After the war, Venezia Giulia (the eastern part of the region, including Trieste, Gorizia, and Istria) merged with Friuli (the western section that includes Udine) to form one geographical and politcal unit. As in the similarly combined northern Italian regions of Emilia and Romagna, provincial loyalties result in a (mostly) friendly rivalry between the two areas. In 1991 border posts witnessed confrontations between Yugoslav and Slovene troops in the battle for Slovenian independence. Trieste's culture and architecture remain distinctly Eastern compared with the rest of the country.

The landscape of Fruili-Venezia Giulia shows an extraordinary diversity, from the mountainous north, essentially Alpine in character, and the limestone Karst plateau around the Slovenian border, to the flat lagoons and dramatic coastline of the Adriatic. The varied topography is reflected in the patchwork past of this border zone. Whereas the palazzos of Udine reveal Venetian influence, Grado and Aquileia are strongly redolent of their Roman and early Christian past. Trieste, the capital of the region, only became Italian soil after World War II. Its peculiar frontier ambience has proven conducive to literary talent—the provided refuge for James Joyce, Richard Burton, Rainer Maria Rilke, and the native Ettore Schmitz. Joyce (1882–1941) lived in Trieste with his wife for spells before and after World War I and wrote *Portrait of the Artist as a Young Man* and part of *Ulysses* here. Sir Richard Burton (1821–90), explorer and writer, was British consul from 1872 until his death and completed his translation of *A Thousand and One Nights* in Trieste. Rilke (1875–1926) composed the *Duino Elegies* near here, and Schmitz, better known by his pen name, Italo Svevo, wrote his masterpiece, *Confessions of Zeno,* in his native city.

Exploring Friuli-Venezia Giulia

The region is easily accessed from Venice by the A4 autostrada, which terminates at Trieste. Palmanova (90 km [56 mi] from Venice) marks a crossing point for the region. From here the A23 heads north to Udine and border country with Slovenia to the east, or farther north to connect with the S52, which bisects the mountainous Western Carnia region, following the line of the River Tagliamento, the longest river of the region. Heading farther west will entail taking a tortuous mountain pass—not so easy in winter. South from Palmanova, the historic towns of Aquileia and Grado can easily be reached by the straight Roman road. All towns are well served by public transportation.

About the Restaurants & Hotels

In 1784 a decree was passed allowing peasants around Trieste to sell their own produce for eight days a year. This led to the setting up of *osmizze,* eateries where local food and wine were offered, a tradition that still continues today. Osmizze provide probably the best, and certainly the cheapest, way to experience authentic home cooking in the region—fresh cheeses, bread, prosciutto, soups, and wine in a rustic setting. Look for the *frasco,* a bunch of leaves on a post.

As this area is not very well known to tourists, apart from Austrians, it shouldn't be too hard to find accommodations. In the rural districts you'll certainly find good value. The smaller country hotels often have a restaurant with an open *fogher* (hearth), which gives an intimate and cozy air and is more than welcome in chilly winter months. Your options on the seaside vary from the plethora of hotels in Grado to tranquil spots in Duino. Trieste is busy and caters mainly to the business crowd. You'll find excellent hotels along the water here.

WHAT IT COSTS In euros					
	$$$$	$$$	$$	$	¢
RESTAURANTS	over €22	€17–€22	€12–€17	€7–€12	under €7
HOTELS	over €210	€160–€210	€110–€160	€60–€110	under €60

Restaurant prices are for a second course (secondo piatto). Hotel prices are for two people in a standard double room in high season, including tax and service.

Timing

The beauty of being in the shadow of tourist-hungry Venice is that there is never an overwhelming presence of other visitors. Any season is a pleasure here, though winter snows may make the roads difficult in Carnia, which sees a fair number of ski enthusiasts between December and March. Spring and autumn will bring walkers to this mountain zone, but never enough to spoil your enjoyment. Friuli can also be a cool haven from the heat of summer, when the coastal regions can be sultry. Tourist offices can update you about the weather and offer advice on walking conditions.

FRIULI

Infused with the spirit of Venice, the inland town of Udine holds a cluster of absorbing attractions and there are some fine sights in the vicinity, including a couple of the region's best museums. Although there are good lodgings to be found at Udine, you might prefer the quieter milieu of Cividale del Friuli, almost within spitting distance of the Julian Alps and washed through by the lovely Natisone River. Some excellent museum collections are here, particularly the Museo Cristiano annexed to the Duomo.

You don't have to venture far from Cividale to feel the Alpine earth under your feet. Carry on northward, past Tolmezzo, to enter the charmed environment of Carnia, a mountain region lacking the epic grandeur of the Dolomites but containing enough natural beauty to impress even the most jaded urban sensibility. Aside from a few larger hotels catering to skiers and hikers, the lodgings here are generally small and inexpensive. Hospitality is the watchword, and the meals are designed to cure the deep hunger induced by the clean air and healthy exertions.

To the south, the Roman population of Aquileia found safe refuge from the ravaging Huns and Lombards in the island town of Grado, whose small historic center lies adjacent to some of the region's best beaches.

There is more than a passing resemblance to Venice in the layout of this port and resort, and no lack of hotels just a short walk from the sands, not to mention fish restaurants galore.

Udine

❶ *64 km (40 mi) north of Trieste, 100 km (62 mi) east of Venice.*

Udine, the largest city on the Friuli side of the region, has a very different atmosphere than Venezia-Giulia's sprawling Trieste. Open-armed in its provincialism, Udine commands a view of the surrounding plain and the Alpine foothills. Give the old center a day of your strolling time, and you'll find unexpected charm here. The city's unevenly spaced streets burst with fun little wine bars, open-air cafés, and gobs of Friulian character, completely unaffected by tourism—or, it sometimes seems, even by modernity. According to legend, Udine stands on a mound erected by Attila the Hun so he could watch the burning of the important Roman center of Aquileia, to the south. The city flourished in the Middle Ages, thanks to its good location for trade and the rights it gained from the local patriarch to hold regular markets. There is still a distinct Venetian feel to Udine, noticeable in the architecture of Piazza della Libertà, which lies under the stern gaze of the lion of St. Mark. Like Venice, the city has a rich artistic patrimony, including a good selection of works by Tiepolo.

Udine's **Duomo,** consecrated in 1335—completed in the 15th century but much altered in the baroque period—is an essential stop for its altarpieces and frescoes by the great Venetian artist Giambattista Tiepolo (1696–1770). ⊠ *Piazza Duomo* ☎ *0432/506832* ۞ *Daily 9–noon and 4–6.*

Opposite the cathedral, the **Oratorio della Purità** is well worth a visit for more Tiepolo frescoes and, by his son, Giandomenico, grisaille (gray-toned) biblical friezes. Ask the sacristan at the cathedral to let you in; late afternoon is probably the best time. ⊠ *Piazza Duomo* ☎ *0432/ 506830* 🔲 *Free.*

The Palazzo Arcivescovile houses the **Galleria del Tiepolo,** which contains superlative examples of Tiepolo's frescoes from the Old Testament, depicting the stories of Abraham, Isaac, and Jacob and the *Judgment of Solomon* in beautiful pastel colors. In the same building, the **Museo Diocesano** features a collection of sculptures from Friuli churches from the 13th through the 18th centuries. ⊠ *Piazza Patriarcato 1* ☎ *0432/25003* ⊕ *www.museiprovinciaud.it* 🔲 *€5 includes Museo Diocesano* ۞ *Wed.–Sun. 10–noon and 3:30–6:30.*

★ Udine's large main square, **Piazza Libertà,** features the Palazzo del Comune, a typical 15th-century Venetian palace, built in imitation of the Palazzo Ducale in Venice. Opposite is the Renaissance Porticato di San Giovanni and the Torre dell'Orologio, a clock tower complete with naked *mori* (the Moors who strike the hours) on the top—another reference to Venice and the Torre d'Orologio in Piazza San Marco.

Pass through the **Arco Bollani,** a triumphal arch by Palladio, and climb the steps to the castle hill. From Udine's **Castello,** rebuilt after earthquakes in 1511 and 1976, the stunning panoramic views extend as far as Monte Nero (7,360 feet), in neighboring Slovenia. The castle now holds the city's two main museums: the Civici Musei and the Galleria di Storia ed Arte Antica. In summer, concerts are held in the gardens. The **Civici Musei** is the best place to trace the history of the area and the importance of Udine and nearby Cividale del Friuli in the formative period following the collapse of the Roman Empire. A large collection of Lombard artifacts includes weapons, jewelry, and domestic wares from this warrior race, which swept into what is now Italy in the 6th century. The **Galleria di Storia ed Arte Antica** is a wide-ranging collection of local and Italian art including canvases by the prolific Neapolitan Luca Giordano (1632–1705), the Venetians Vittore Carpaccio (circa 1460–1525) and Tiepolo, and a painting of St. Francis receiving the stigmata, attributed to Caravaggio (circa 1571–1610). Also within the castle area is the 13th-century church of **Santa Maria di Castello,** which contains frescoes contemporary with the building. It can be opened on request; inquire at the Galleria d'Arte Antica. ⊠ *Castello di Udine* ☎ *0432/271951* ⊕ *www.museiprovinciaud. it* ⊠ *€3, €1 Sun.* ☉ *Tues.–Sat. 9:30–12:30 and 3–6, Sun. 9:30–12:30.*

West of Piazza Libertà, **Piazza Matteotti,** surrounded on three sides by arcades and on the fourth by the church of San Giacomo, is the central piazza of Udine. The balcony of San Giacomo has an outside altar, which was built so that Mass could be said while business went on uninterrupted in the market below.

One of the true legends of the grappa world, **Nonino,** has been in the little town of Percoto, 13 km (8 mi) south of Udine, since 1897. The grappa giant offers tours of its distillery and tastings at its shop. Take Viale Palmanova (SS56) south out of town, bear left onto SP2, go through the town of Pavia di Udine, and continue south until you see signs for Nonino. Call in advance to schedule a visit. ⊠ *Via Aquileia 104* ☎ *0432/ 676331* ⊕ *www.nonino.it* ⊠ *Free* ☉ *By appointment only.*

Where to Stay & Eat

★ **$$$–$$$$** ✕ **Vitello d'Oro.** Udine's very elegant, landmark restaurant is the one reserved by most local people for special occasions. The big terrace in front is popular for alfresco dining in summer. The menu features both meat and fish in classic regional dishes as well as more innovative creations. You might start with an antipasto of assorted raw shellfish, including the impossibly sweet Adriatic scampi, followed by the fresh fish of the day. Service is impeccable, as is the Friuli-focused wine list. Perhaps the best way to go is the multicourse tasting menu. ⊠ *Via Valvason 4* ☎ *0432/508982* ⌕ *Reservations essential* ⊟ *AE, DC, MC, V* ☉ *Closed Sun. July–Sept. and Wed. Oct.–June.*

$$–$$$ ✕ **Senza Scampo.** The name is a rather clever pun: while the phrase means, roughly, "nowhere to hide," *scampo* is also a little-used singular form of scampi, that most prized of Adriatic shellfish, a drawing of which forms this restaurant's logo. The spectacular seafood coming from the kitchen, though, is no joke. The freshness of the fish is matched by the cutting-edge, minimalist design of the dining room. ⊠ *Via Planis 30* ☎ *0432/287151* ⊟ *AE, DC, MC, V* ☉ *Closed Sun.*

$$ ✕ **Hostaria alla Tavernetta.** This restaurant, steps from the Piazza Duomo, has been one of Udine's most trusted food addresses since 1954. It carefully blends the urban with the rustic; specialties include guinea fowl with rosemary, and sausage with local salsa of turnips and basalmic vinegar. There's a different *orzotto* (barley cooked up like risotto) daily. After your meal, have your coffee served with shaved chocolate and *cantucci* (small, hard cookies). The feeling is warm and publike. ⊠ *Via di Prampero 2* ☎ *0432/501066* ⊟ *AE, MC, V* ☽ *Closed Sun. and Mon.*

★ $ ✕ **Osteria Al Vecchio Stallo.** Hidden away in a narrow alley, this popular osteria features an interior filled with trinkets, and a beautiful courtyard shaded by grape arbors. The menu includes a bevy of the most traditional Friuli specialties with unpronounceable names, including sweet cjalzòns (ravioli stuffed with spinach, apple, pear, and cheese, and topped with melted butter and cinnamon)—and *nervetti* (gelatinous cubes of veal's knee with onions, parsley, oil, and lemon), which you won't find anywhere west of here. There's a great selection of wines by the glass, and the gregarious chef-owner is a real character. ⊠ *Via Viola 7* ☎ *0432/21296* ⊟ *No credit cards* ☽ *Closed Sun. and Wed.*

¢–$ ✕ **Al Cappello.** At this whimsical wine tavern, hats cover the ceiling, the walls are orange, and a blackboard lists 100 wines available by the glass. You can come for dinner—grilled meats are served with a splash of vinegar, and there are daily pasta specials—or stop in for a glass of wine and a snack such as an appetizer-size sandwich or *frico* (a potato-and-cheese bake). There's seating at the counter, at shared tables inside, or outside, where you're served through the open window. ⊠ *Via Paolo Sarpi 5* ☎ *0432/299327* ⊟ *No credit cards* ☽ *Closed Mon., 3 wks in Jan. and 3 wks midsummer. No dinner Sun.*

$$$ ⊡ **Astoria Hotel Italia.** The facade of this elegant, arcaded building in the heart of the old city overlooks a big plaza, providing interesting city views from many of the rooms. The spacious public areas and lounges offer contemporary elegance, while the guest rooms are individually furnished in traditional style. ⊠ *Piazza XX Settembre 24, 33100* ☎ *0432/505091* 🖷 *0432/509070* ⊕ *www.hotelastoria.udine.it* 🖵 *73 rooms, 2 suites* ♢ *Restaurant, in-room data ports, minibars, bar, meeting rooms, some pets allowed* ⊟ *AE, DC, MC, V* ⫶◎⫶ *BP.*

$$–$$$ ⊡ **Hotel Clocchiatti.** Not satisfied to rest on their laurels, the owners of FodorśChoice this converted late-19th-century mansion added the "Next" wing to their ★ hotel, with rooms that have groundbreaking modern design and comforts unequaled in all of Friuli. There are starkly angular suites with flat-panel TVs, suites with sunken Japanese baths and gardens, and rooms in which modern art is literally integrated into the beds and nightstands. A peaceful terrace overlooks a garden with its centuries-old trees, and the swimming pool is done entirely in black (which keeps the water warmer). It all has to be seen to be believed. ⊠ *Via Cividale 29, 33100* 🖷🖷 *0432/505047* ⊕ *www.hotelclocchiatti.it* 🖵 *13 rooms* ♢ *In-room safes, minibars, bicycles, bar, outdoor pool, laundry service, free parking, some pets allowed* ⊟ *AE, DC, MC, V* ⫶◎⫶ *BP.*

$ ⊡ **Quo Vadis.** A 10-minute walk from the train station, this modest, plant-filled hotel has an older part and modern annex with its own small terrace. Rooms are small but comfortable. Choose one facing away from the main road to cut down on traffic noise. Facilities are basic and there's

ON THE MENU

TRIESTE IS KNOWN for its self-service buffets, from which the aromas of cren (horseradish), paprika, capuzi garbi (sauerkraut), and jota (sauerkraut and bean soup) waft invitingly through the streets—don't be surprised to hear these Slavic syllables spoken or to find a strange dialect on menus. These dishes are what give a distinctive flavor to the cuisine of this corner of the Italian peninsula. Seafood abounds here, in some restaurants to the exclusion of everything else. Look for soups made from a diverse range of seafood—mackerel, sardines, clams, squid, and octopus to name but a few. When sated on seafood, try acclaimed San Daniele ham, either cooked or cured. In the Carnia district (and elsewhere in the region) you're sure to come across cjalzòns—ravioli stuffed with ricotta, spinach, fruits, and spices, and drowned in butter and cinnamon. Here and in other rural areas, make a point of savoring the verdure (greens picked from the mountains) and the wild fruits and berries. Sweet specialties include gnocchi stuffed with prunes and coated in cinnamon and sugar.

Friuli-Venezia Giulia produces some of the best wines in northeast Italy. The local wine par excellence is Tocai Friulano, a dry, lively white made from Tocai grapes that has attained .international stature. The red of choice is Terrano, a deep, dry, ruby wine produced from Refosco vines. Esteemed reds also come from Isonzo, Carso, and Grave del Friuli. The D.O.C. (Denominazione di Origine Controllata e Garantita) wines, which meet production and quality standards, include Malvasia Carso and Carso Terrano. The Collio designation indicates wines from vineyards in the eastern part of Friuli, near the Slovenian border. The Collio pinot bianco from here, a fragrant white, is cool and refreshing. The highly regarded sauternes-like Picolit is made in very limited quantities.

no restaurant, but Udine has a good choice of eating places. ⊠ *Piazzale Cella 28, 33100* ☏ *0432/21091* 🖷 *0432/21092* ⊕ *www.hotelquovadis.it* 🛏 *14 rooms* ⚲ *Bar, free parking* ▭ *AE, DC* ❢❁ *BP.*

Cividale del Friuli

❷ *17 km (11 mi) east of Udine, 52 km (29 mi) north of Trieste.*

For space, serenity, and beautiful scenery, venture east of Udine to the foothills of the Julian Alps and the town of Cividale del Friuli, one of the most pleasant and picturesque towns of the region. The Natisone River tumbles down from the Alps to cut a limestone swath through the town, where it is crossed by the Ponte del Diavolo (Devil's Bridge). Legend has it that the devil himself threw into the river the large stone on which the central pier of the bridge rests. The town dates from the time of Julius Caesar, who was commander of Roman legions in the area and who had it named the Forum Julii—from which the name Friuli is derived. In AD 568 it became the first Lombard duchy formed in Italy. After the demise of the Lombards, it was dominated by Franks, and the name was changed to Civitas Austriae—hence the name Cividale. Until 1238 it was the seat of the patriarchs of Aquileia, becoming a university town in 1353, though it declined from 1420 onward when it fell to Venice with the rest of Friuli and lost much of its influence to Udine. As a result, it has maintained a small, manageable size and is brimming with the impressive relics of various periods, all easily seen in less than a day. The **Duomo**, with its Gothic-Renaissance facade, contains a magnificent 12th-century silver altarpiece, a gift of the patriarch Pellegrino II (in office 1195–1204). It depicts a multitude of saints who surround the archangels Michael and Gabriel, who in turn flank the Virgin Mary. ⊠ *Piazza del Duomo* ☎ *0432/731144* ⊙ *Apr.–Oct., Mon.–Sat. 9:30–noon and 3–7, Sun. 3–7; Nov.–Mar., Mon.–Sat. 9:30–noon and 3–6, Sun. 3–6.*

Two masterpieces of Lombard sculpture are preserved in the **Museo Cristiano,** right next door to the Duomo and accessible from there. First of these is the octagonal baptistery, which incorporates 5th-century columns and capitals. This was named after Callisto, the first patriarch of Aquileia to live in Cividale (between 730 and 756). It was he who commissioned this baptistery, which is beautifully decorated with bas-reliefs, to stand originally beside the cathedral. The second piece is the altar that was carved for Ratchis, the Duke of Cividale and King of the Lombards from 744 to 749. The sides of the altar hold more bas-reliefs, depicting *Christ in Triumph,* the *Visitation,* and the *Adoration of the Magi.* Look, too, for the sculpted rhinoceros elsewhere in the museum. ⊠ *Piazza del Duomo* ☎ *0432/731144* ⊕ *www.museiprovinciaud. it* 🎫 *Free* ⊙ *Apr.–Oct., Mon.–Sat. 9:30–noon and 3–7, Sun. 3–7; Nov.–Mar., Mon.–Sat. 9:30–noon and 3–6, Sun. 3–6.*

Also in Piazza del Duomo is the **Museo Archeologico,** installed in a building dating from the late 16th century and ascribed to Palladio. It houses an important and well-displayed collection of artifacts, including Roman mosaics and bronzes, Romanesque reliefs, and the Psalter of St. Elizabeth of Hungary. Cividale was a flourishing artistic center during Lombardic times, particularly in the goldsmith's field, to which the many finely crafted and delicate pieces here attest. ⊠ *Piazza del Duomo* ☎ *0432/700700* ⊕ *www.museiprovinciaud.it* 🎫 *€2* ⊙ *Mon. 8–2; Tues.–Sun. 8:30–7:30.*

Heading toward the river, you'll soon come to the **Ipogeo Celtico,** reached by a flight of steep steps at the bottom of which are underground chambers thought to be either a Celtic place of burial or a Roman prison. On the walls are crudely carved heads possibly dating from the 3rd century BC. ⊠ *Via Monastero Maggiore 6* ☎ *0432/710360* ⊕ *www. museiprovinciaud.it* 🎫 *Free* ⊙ *Apr.–Sept., Mon.–Sat. 9:30–12:30 and 3–6:30, Sun. 9:30–1 and 3–7:30; Oct.–Mar., Mon.–Sat. 9:30–12:30 and 3–5, Sun. 9:30–12:30 and 2:30–6.*

Farther down Via Aquileia lies the river and the **Ponte del Diavolo,** the double-arched bridge crossing the Natisone. On the other side, you can browse among the stalls selling basketwork. The pretty, cobbled Via Monastero Maggiore leads along the river to one of the most evocative
★ early medieval buildings in Italy. The **Tempietto Longobardo,** a little gem of Lombard church building, stands in a perfect and peaceful location above the meandering river. Though damaged by earthquakes, there remains a remarkable 8th-century stucco procession of female figures on

either side of an arch, and lovely friezes with a vine motif. The carved and canopied wooden stalls date from the 14th century, as do the frescoes. The epiphany scene is unique in that instead of the usual three kings it depicts two kings and a queen, the last in the procession, possibly in recognition of Giseltrude, a Lombard queen at the time of the chapel's construction. ⊠ *Via Monastero Maggiore* ☎ *0432/700867* ⊕ *www.museiprovinciaud.it* ⊡ *€2* ⊗ *Apr.–Sept., Mon.–Sat. 9:30–12:30 and 3–6:30, Sun. 9:30–1 and 3–7:30; Oct.–Mar., Mon.–Sat. 9:30–12:30 and 3–5, Sun. 9:30–12:30 and 2:30–6.*

need a break?
The **Caffè Longobardo** (⊠ Via Carlo Alberto 6 ⊗ Closed Mon.) is a pleasant place to sit and sample a grappa or a slice of traditional *gubana,* a light, spongy cake filled with pine nuts and raisins, as you watch the passersby on the piazza.

Where to Stay & Eat

$ ✕ **Ai Tre Re.** Here, legend has it, three kings once divided up the countryside, and since the 1500s the Three Kings has refreshed travelers within its stone-walled garden or beside its six-foot-square wood stove. Beneath the beamed ceiling everything is homemade, including the bread of wheat and maize. Try potato gnocchi with *speck* (cured ham) and smoked ricotta, followed by sausage in white wine sauce sauce or cheese stuffed with wild herbs. ⊠ *Via Stretta San Valentino 31* ☎ *0432/700416* ☐ *MC, V* ⊗ *Closed Tues., 1 wk in Feb., 2 wks in June, and 1 wk in Oct.*

★ ¢–$ ✕ **Trattoria Dominissini.** The rustic wood furnishings and simple decor here are perfectly in keeping with Cividale's old-world charm. The menu features typical dishes of game and cheese. If you've got a soft spot for melted cheese, try the wonderful *frico di patate,* a mixture of potato and local Montasio cheese cooked in the pan like an omelet; game dishes may include *cinghiale in umido con polenta* (stewed wild boar with polenta). Asparagus is another specialty, as are desserts and excellent Friuli wines. ⊠ *Via Jacopo Stellini 18* ☎ *0432/733763* ⊕ *www.anticatrattoriadominissini.it* ☐ *AE, DC, MC, V* ⊗ *Closed Mon.*

$$ ✕☒ **Locanda Al Castello.** Set on a peaceful hillside a few minutes' drive out of town, this creeper-covered, crenellated hotel was once a monastery. Rooms are spacious and furnished in different styles, some antique, some modern, and with nice, big bathrooms. The redbrick restaurant ($–$$; closed Wed.), popular for Sunday lunch, has an open fireplace and serves national as well as local dishes, both fish and meat. Specialties include *polentina ripiena* (small rounds of polenta filled with porcini mushrooms in garlic, oil, and parsley, cooked au gratin in the oven), and *maltagliata alla lungobarda* (thinly sliced beef marinated in herbs and spices and char-grilled). ⊠ *Via del Castello 12, 33043* ☎ *0432/733242* ☐ *0432/700901* ⊕ *www.alcastello.net* ☜ *17 rooms* ♢ *Restaurant, fans, in-room data ports, in-room safes, minibars, tennis court, bar, meeting rooms, free parking, some pets allowed; no a/c* ☐ *AE, DC, MC, V* ⊗ *Closed Jan. 15–31* ◯ *BP.*

★ $ ☒ **Al Pomo d'Oro.** Pink seems to be a predominant color for little hotels in Italy, and this one is no exception, presenting a charming facade with its shutters and geraniums. It was an inn in the 12th century but has since undergone considerable renovation; rooms are furnished in a plain, modern style, some with wonderful views of the surrounding mountains. The location is excellent, a few steps away from the cathedral, and the elegant restaurant may well keep you in for the evening. ⊠ *Piazza San Giovanni 20, 33043* ☎ *0432/731489* 🖷 *0432/701257* ⊕ *www.alpomodoro.com* ⤳ *17 rooms* ♿ *Restaurant, in-room safes, minibars, bar, some pets allowed; no a/c* ⊟ *AE, DC, MC, V* ﹖⃝ *BP.*

Shopping
A **general market** is held every Saturday morning in Piazza Garibaldi; by the bridge you'll find good stalls selling wicker baskets of every description.

Aquileia

❸ *77 km (48 mi) west of Trieste, 18 km (11 mi) west of Monfalcone.*

Nowadays it's difficult to believe that this sleepy little town was, in the time of Emperor Augustus, Italy's fourth most important city (after Rome, Milan, and Capua). The patriarchate (bishopric) of Aquileia was founded here around 314, the basilica commissioned shortly afterward, and, after several centuries of decline and frequent pillaging, the town regained its prominence from the 11th to the end of the 14th century. Prominent past visitors include Herod the Great, who was received by Augustus in 10 BC; Sts. Jerome and Ambrose, who attended a council of bishops in AD 381; and Attila the Hun, who sacked the town in 452. Aquileia's magnificent Roman and Byzantine remains are strongly evocative of this patchwork past, beautifully preserved right in the middle of the serene village and refreshingly free of the mass tourism that you might expect to find given its cultural riches.

Aquileia's **Basilica** was founded by Theodore, its first patriarch, and later extended. It owes its present form to the patriarch Poppo (or Popone) who rebuilt it between 1021 and 1031, though it has accumulated different elements including the Romanesque portico and the Gothic bell tower. But the highlight of this monument is the staggering 4th-century mosaic covering the entire floor, one of the finest relics of the early Christian period in Italy and the biggest of its kind. From the vibrancy of the colors, the floor appears as if it has just been laid, and with good reason, as it was only uncovered at the beginning of the 20th century. It survived a major earthquake in 1328—just: it now ripples in corrugated waves as a consequence. Christian images combine with the pagan in this marine extravaganza of dolphins, squid, and lobsters, among which Jonah is swallowed and spewed out of an extraordinary sea monster, and cherubs fish from a boat.

Before the Edict of Constantine (the proclamation in 313 that established religious toleration for Christianity under the Romans), Christians adopted images of pagan symbolism to express their faith, some of which can be seen here. The winged figure of Victory with her laurel wreath and palm frond equates with triumph over death; the tortoise with its carapace symbolizes darkness, and the cockerel, which crows at dawn, is light. Fish, of course, represent Christ, from Ichthos—Greek for fish and an acronym for Jesus Christ, Son of God, Savior—and birds such as peacocks represent immortality. Down a flight of steps, the **Cripta degli Affreschi** contains soft-hued frescoes, among them St. Peter sending St. Mark to Aquileia and the beheading of Saints Hermagoras and Fortunatus, to whom the basilica is dedicated. The **Cripta degli Scavi** contains another huge area of mosaic paving surrounding the base to the campanile and allows you to see how the successive layers of building took place from the 4th century on. ⊠ *Piazza Capitolo* ☎ *0431/ 91067* ⊠ *Basilica free; both crypts €2.60; campanile €1.10* ☉ *Apr.–Oct., Mon.–Sat. 8:30–6, Sun. 8:30–6:30; Nov.–Mar. 8:30–12:30 and 2:30–5:30. Visits suspended during Sun. Mass (10:30–11:15).*

Beyond the basilica and across the road from it, the **archaeological site** among the cypresses reveals Roman remains of the forum, houses, cemetery, and port. The little stream was once a navigable and important waterway extending to Grado. The area is well signposted. ⊕ *www. museoarcheo-aquileia.it* ⊠ *Free* ☉ *Daily 8:15–1 hr before sunset.*

Of the town's two museums, the **Museo Archeologico** is the most rewarding, containing a wealth of material from the Roman era. Notable are the portrait busts from Republican times, semiprecious gems, amber- and gold-work—including preserved flies—a fine glass collection in iridescent hues, and miniature priapic bronzes. ⊠ *Via Roma 1* ☎ *0431/ 91096* ⊕ *www.museoarcheo-aquileia.it* ⊠ *€4* ☉ *Tues.–Sun. 8:30–7:30, Mon. 8:30–2.*

The **Museo Paleocristiano** houses more mosaics and traces the development of art from Roman to Christian times. ⊠ *Località Monastero* ☎ *0431/91131* ⊕ *www.museoarcheo-aquileia.it* ⊠ *Free* ☉ *Daily 8:30–1:45.*

Where to Stay & Eat

¢–$ ✕ **La Colombara.** The large, open fireplace in this friendly, family-run restaurant about 2 km (1 mi) northeast of Aquileia is used for cooking, and the fare is mainly fish and game. Try the stuffed calamari with artichokes or ravioli with mixed fish, or, in spring, any of several dishes based on asparagus. Everything is homemade—pasta, bread, and cakes. In August and September the restaurant organizes Roman evenings (come in a toga) when the tables are cleared for the triclinia (reclining couches). ⊠ *Via San Zilli 42* ☎ *0431/91513* ⊕ *www.lacolombara.it* ⊟ *AE, DC, MC, V* ☉ *Closed Mon.*

$ ✕🏨 **Patriarchi.** You can open your shutters onto a view of the basilica from this hotel. It's well run and very friendly, and offers good service. Colorful rugs enliven modern rooms with plenty of space. Book ahead for stays in July and August, when an umbrella on Grado's beach is included in the price. The simple restaurant ($; closed Wed.) serves its own salami or baby octopus in *salsa piccante* (spicy sauce) as antipasti on unusual glass plates. Follow it with gnocchi with salmon and cognac or *scarpena alla siciliana* (scorpion fish with black olives, tomato, and oregano). Everything is deliciously light. ⊠ *Via Giulia Augusta 12, 33051* ☎ *0431/919595* ⊟ *0431/919596* ⊕ *www.hotelpatriarchi.it* ⊅ *22 rooms* ⚘ *Restaurant, some in-room safes, minibars, bar, some pets allowed* ⊟ *AE, DC, MC, V* ☉ *Closed Nov. 10–20.* ⏹ *BP.*

Grado

4 *11 km (7 mi) south of Aquileia, 52 km (32 mi) west of Trieste.*

Grado is an island town set among lagoons and approached by cause-way from Aquileia or Monfalcone. The town has a compact and attractive historic center, but most people flock here for its 20 km (12 mi) of sandy beaches, as clean and safe as you'll find anywhere in Italy. All the usual sunning and swimming facilities are on hand, as well as thermal baths, but it's worth leaving the serried ranks of umbrellas to take a stroll round the harbor and the alleys and piazzas of the old town. This small quarter has an engaging, slightly decaying air to it and holds the best restaurants. With Grado still an active fishing port, seafood is abundant.

The old town's Venetian architecture sets the tone, a legacy of the period when Grado came under the Republic's sway in the 15th century. Its history, however, extends back further, for this was an outpost of Roman Aquileia, the place to which the inhabitants of that inland town fled in the 5th century to escape the invasions of Huns. In the 6th century, Grado became the principal patriarchal seat and grew in importance. Three engaging buildings remain from that time, in each of which you can see mosaic pavements from the 6th century.

The 6th-century **Basilica di Sant'Eufemia** has some 20 different columns with Byzantine capitals, a patterned geometrical mosaic floor, and an embossed, silver Venetian altar frontal dating from the 14th century. Remarkable, too, is the lovely 13th-century hexagonal *ambo* (pulpit) decorated with bold symbols of the Evangelists and covered by an Oriental cupola.

Next to the Basilica in Campo dei Patriarchi, the 6th-century **Battistero** (Baptistery) also has a mosaic pavement. In the same square, the church of **Santa Maria delle Grazie** displays more Byzantine columns and mosaics. ⊠ *Campo Patriarca Elia* ☎ *0439/80146* ☉ *Apr.–Oct. daily 7:30 AM–9 PM; Nov.–Mar. daily 7:30–6:30.*

Where to Stay & Eat

$$–$$$ ✕ **De Toni.** Right in the old town, this pretty restaurant exposes its floor so that you can see the foundations of the old Roman structure beneath it. Dining outside in summer is almost de rigueur. The chef has his own special recipe for fish soup; the *zuppa di vongole* (clam soup) is good, too, as is *triglia* (red mullet) in bread crumbs with vinaigrette. Reservations are advised in summer. ⊠ *Piazza Duca d'Aosta 37* ☎ *0431/80104* 🖃 *AE, DC, MC, V* ☉ *Closed Jan. and Wed. Sept.–June.*

$–$$ ✕ **Al Balaor.** As you might expect in this fishing port, seafood is the specialty. Pull up a button-backed chair in this elegant and plush restaurant with blue-green furnishings, and tuck into the fresh fish antipasti, scallops St. Jacques with polenta, *frogolezzi* (small gnocchi) with shrimp, or swordfish. As the restaurant has its own pasticceria, the cakes are superb. Reservations are advised in summer. ⊠ *Calle Zanini 3* ☎ *0431/80150* 🖃 *AE, DC, MC, V* ☉ *Closed Thurs. and 10 days in Nov.*

$$$ 🏨 **Hannover.** The best thing about this small four-star hotel is its position overlooking the tiny fishing port. Rooms are spacious and modern in a standard way, offset by the pink and green marble of the public rooms.

The beach is also nearby, and use of changing rooms there is included in the price. ✉ *Piazza XXVI Maggio 11, 34073* ☎ *0431/82264* 🖷 *0431/ 82141* ⊕ *www.hotelhannover.com* ⛵ *23 rooms, 3 suites* ♜ *Restaurant, in-room safes, minibars, health club, bar, some pets allowed* ▤ *AE, DC, MC, V* ☯ *Closed 2 wks in Jan.* ⦿ *BP.*

$$–$$$ ⌸ **Savoy.** Light and spacious, this is the only Grado hotel to offer both indoor and outdoor swimming pools. Guest rooms are elegantly minimalist. The stately striped sofas in the lobby combine with the modernistic pink and white columns to lend an almost 18th-century flavor. ✉ *Via Carducci 33, 34073* ☎ *0431/897111* 🖷 *0431/83305* ⊕ *www.hotelsavoy-grado.it* ⛵ *83 rooms* ♜ *Restaurant, in-room safes, minibars, golf privileges, in-door-outdoor pool, saltwater pool, gym, health club, bicycles, bar* ▤ *AE, DC, MC, V* ☯ *Closed Nov.–Mar.* ⦿ *BP.*

$$ ⌸ **Antares.** A pleasant, small, plant-filled hotel, it's just a step back from the waterfront in a quiet location. All rooms have a balcony and there's a terrace for sunbathing. Breakfast is served on the quiet, sunny terrace in summer and includes a range of freshly sliced cold cuts and cheeses. ✉ *Via delle Scuole 4, 34073* ☎ *0431/84961* 🖷 *0431/82385* ⊕ *www. antareshotel.info* ⛵ *19 rooms* ♜ *In-room safes, minibars, bar, parking (fee), some pets allowed* ▤ *No credit cards* ☯ *Closed Nov. 20–Feb. 10* ⦿ *BP.*

Sports & the Outdoors

BEACH   Before or after sightseeing in the old town, take a dip in the sea: the beach umbrellas are backed by cabins on lidos where you pay a small daily fee, and there's a free beach at the west end. The water is shallow and clean, making it ideal for kids.

BOAT TRIPS   The ***Motonave Cristina*** (☎☎ 0431/81412) sails twice a day from Grado to Portobuso, with a stop for lunch on the isle of Anfora.

VENEZIA GIULIA

From Trieste, the road eastward follows the coast under the shadow of the huge geological formation called the Carso, a barren expanse of limestone that forms a giant ledge, most of which is across the border in Slovenia. Italian territory extends only a couple of miles inland on this narrow strip, and Italy's small Slovene minority ekes out an agricultural existence in the region, which has changed hands countless times since the final days of imperial Rome. Forty or so kilometers (25 mi) west of Trieste, Aquileia was the principal Roman center in the region. In 313 Theodore became its first Christian patriarch (bishop), founding a basilica whose richly allegorical early Christian mosaics are among the finest to be seen in Italy today.

West of Trieste, Miramare and Duino offer more coastal pleasures but without the bustling beach culture of other resorts along this stretch. The shore here is picturesquely cliffy, the tramping ground and inspiration for both Dante and Rilke. To the north, Gorizia lies right on the Slovenian border, literally bisected by it. The hilltop castle here holds a World War I museum, recalling the conflict that devastated this region. The Slavic element is strong here; make sure you sample the local goulash.

Cormòns

❺ *14 km (9 mi) west of Gorizia, 51 km (32 mi) northwest of Trieste.*

Southeast of Udine, in the rolling hills of Friuli, Cormòns is the epicenter of the Collio region, a producer of exceptional white wine. Route 356, just west of the Slovenian border, winds through miles of vineyard-covered hills. Residents boast that Ribolla grapes have grown here for 1,000 years; the region's Tocai grapevines may be the original source for Hungary's famous Tokay wine. Local Picolit grapes are said to have been the source of papal communion wine for centuries, and it is still made here by the Sovereign Military Order of Malta.

The region has changed hands in bloody battles since the days of imperial Rome. Following World War II, international arbitrators determined whose farms would be part of Italy and whose would end up within Tito's Yugoslavia. It's no surprise that many residents here speak Slovenian in their homes and have relatives or cultivate fields across the border. In May 2004 the border effectively dissolved when Slovenia was welcomed into the European Union.

Where to Stay & Eat

$$–$$$ ✕ **Al Cacciatore de la Subida.** Set among the Collio's vineyards, Al Cac-
FodorśChoice ciatore serves food that reflects the region's Slovenian-Austrian-Italian
★ cultural blend: *zlikrofi* is a cross between ravioli and tortellini, and gnocchi are made with plum and with butter and cinnamon instead of savory ingredients. You may even find wild *sambuco* (elderflowers) and *dragoncello* (tarragon) in the desserts. The multicourse tasting menu (€48–€55) provides a consistently delicious meal. The restaurant is the centerpiece of La Subida country lodging. The simpler Osteria serves great Collio wines by the glass and bottle, along with simpler dishes. ⊠ *La Subida, Loc. Monte 22* ☎ *0481/60531* ⊕ *www.lasubida.it* ⌂ *Reservations essential* ☰ *MC, V* ⊗ *Closed Tues., Wed., and July 1–10. No lunch weekdays. Osteria closed Thurs. and Nov.*

$$–$$$ ✕ **Trattoria Al Giardinetto.** The wrought-iron gate and wide front porch make it feel like you're entering a family home, and indeed this restaurant is run by three brothers. They call their cuisine Friulian and they've come up with creative cooking techniques such as *in conserva* (steaming food with wine inside canning jars); you open your jar at the table, unlocking delightful aromas. All Giardinetto's ingredients are fresh, seasonal, and local, except for the cocoa in their desserts, such as *fondente di Araguani 72%*, a fondue of designer chocolate so rich it could substitute for a main course. ⊠ *Via Matteotti 54/56* ☎ *0481/60257* ⌂ *Reservations essential* ☰ *AE, DC, MC, V* ⊗ *Closed Mon. and Tues.*

$$$ ▦ **Castello Formentini.** Count Formentini's stunning castle has been an-
FodorśChoice cestral property for five centuries. The restored complex today includes
★ a winery, sports facilities, and superb accommodations that blend antique furnishings with modern conveniences. Not only is breakfast included, but there's complimentary wine, beer, and grappa, as well as a day-long buffet of antipasto and sweets (they boast of an anti-diet philosophy). About once a month the hotel hosts a medieval banquet in the massive hall—complete with sword fights, fire-eaters, 15th-century

recipes, and no forks. Though such events can feel contrived and tacky, here they pull it off with style; it's the closest thing there is to time travel. ⊠ *Via Oslavia 2, 34070 San Floriano del Collio, 20 km (12 mi) north-east of Cormòns* ☎ *0481/884051* 🖷 *0481/884052* ⊕ *www. golfhotelformentini.com* 🖘 *14 rooms, 1 suite* ⸝ *Snack bar, minibars, 9-hole golf course, tennis court, pool, bar, meeting room, some pets allowed, no-smoking rooms, free parking; no a/c in some rooms* ⊟ *AE, DC, MC, V* ⊘ *Closed Dec. 20–Feb.* ⦿⌶ *BP.*

$$ ⊞ **La Subida.** Josko and Loredana Sirk's painstakingly created country refuge has 13 rustic-yet-modern cottages. Wooden beams and white lace lend nostalgia to the lodgings. Wood is delivered to the rooms each day so you can enjoy the *fogolar,* a traditional Friulian fireplace. Be sure to dine in the noteworthy restaurant, Al Cacciatore (see above). ⊠ *Loc. Monte 22, 34071* ☎ *0481/60531* 🖷 *0481/61616* ⊕ *www.lasubida.it* 🖘 *13 cottages* ⸝ *2 restaurants, kitchenettes, tennis court, pool, bicycles, horseback riding, bar, some pets allowed; no a/c* ⊟ *MC, V* ⊘ *Closed 3 wks in Feb.* ⦿⌶ *EP.*

Gorizia

❻ *51 km (39 mi) northwest of Trieste, 43 km (27 mi) north of Grado.*

Like Trieste, Gorizia bears the hallmark of the Habsburgs, having remained under the control of the Austrian dynasty until 1916. After World War II, the Treaty of Paris split the town, Italy keeping the western half and Yugoslavia the eastern, which is now Nova Gorica. A quiet place, Gorizia is still imbued with a mixture of Italian and Slavic cultures, and a walk around town reveals grand streets, arcades, parks, and gardens. Don't miss the early evening *passeggiata* (a communal stroll, popular in many Italian towns) along Via Rastello, terminating in **Piazza della Vittoria,** site of a striking church, Sant'Ignazio. It has an imposing green onion dome that gives the square an Eastern European feel.

A pleasant garden surrounds the Borgo Castello, a hilltop fortified by the Venetians. Climb up the steps on the steep west side, or take the Viale D'Annunzio on the gentler south side to reach the red-roofed and battlemented **Castello.** The walls were reinforced in 1508 by the Venetians, who left their ubiquitous mark in the form of a winged lion in bas-relief over the castle entrance. In the inner court it's possible to see the original 11th- and 12th-century foundations of the keep. The rooms inside are open only during periodic art exhibitions. ⊠ *Borgo Castello 36* ☎ *0481/535146* 🖾 *€2.60* ⊘ *Tues.–Sun. 9:30–6:30.*

Within the castle complex is the church of **Santo Spirito,** built in 1398. It's notable for the hanging porch and large 16th-century wooden crucifix on the facade—actually a copy, the original squirreled away for safekeeping. ⊠ *Borgo Castello* ☎ *0481/530193* ⊘ *Daily 8–7.*

Also in the Borgo Castello, the **Musei Provinciali di Borgo Castello** houses the Museo della Grande Guerra (Museum of the Great War) and the Museo della Moda e delle Arti Applicati (Fashion and Applied Arts Museum), along with some smaller exhibitions. ⊠ *Borgo Castello 13* ☎ *0481/533926 or 530382* 🖷 *0481/534878* 🖾 *€6* ⊘ *War museum,*

Tues.–Sun. 9–7; fashion museum, Oct.–Mar., Tues.–Sun. 10–1 and 2–7, Apr.–Sept., Tues.–Sun. 10–7.

The **Palazzo Attems** is a fine neoclassical building, designed in 1745 by Nicolò Pacassi (1711–90), which stages major temporary exhibitions. ⊠ *Piazza de Amicis* ☎ *0481/531798 for information.*

Where to Stay & Eat

$–$$ ✕ **Ai Tre Soldi Goriziani.** This long dining room with plain white walls and a refined atmosphere is popular with locals on their night out. In good weather, the big garden in back is an even better place to dine. Try dishes with an Eastern European flair such as the gnocchi *di pane al sugo di goulasch* (bread gnocchi with goulash) or the Wiener schnitzel. ⊠ *Corso Italia 38* ☎ *0481/531956* ⌣ *Reservations essential* ▭ *AE, DC, MC, V* ⊗ *Closed Mon. and Aug.*

$ ✕ **Rosen Bar.** There's a predominantly dark-red tone at this restaurant with wood paneling and a copper bar. One part is more formal, the other, around the bar, less so, and there's also a garden. It's a popular spot, usually fairly lively, and with hospitable service. The small menu, equally strong in meat and fish, is handwritten and changes regularly. Try the pumpkin soup and the strudel of potato and radicchio, both delicious. Homemade puddings are a delight. ⊠ *Via Duca d'Aosta 96* ☎ *0481/522700* ▭ *AE, DC, MC, V* ⊗ *Closed Sun., Mon. and 2 wks in Feb.*

¢ ✕ **Cafè-Haus Gorizia.** Given that Italy prepares the world's best coffee, it's surprising how few places there are that offer a choice of beans. This bold, modern coffee shop is one of those few, with five varieties from gourmet bean purveyor Goppion, ranging in price from 85¢ to €1. There are basic pastries, snacks, and sandwiches, and you can sit at one of a few tables out on the sidewalk. ⊠ *Corso Italia 40* ☎ *No phone* ▭ *AE, DC, MC, V* ⊗ *No dinner.*

$ 🏨 **Euro Diplomat.** Fancy trimmings at this modern hotel right in the center of town are confined to the impressive glass chandelier in the lobby. The place is a bit tattered around the edges, and seems frozen in the modernist 1960s, but it's conveniently priced, offers standard comfort, and has surprisingly little competition in this delightful, little-visited city. ⊠ *Corso Italia 63, 34170* ☎ *0481/82166* 🖷 *0481/31658* ⊕ *www.eurodiplomathotel.it* ⏎ *70 rooms* ⌂ *Minibars, bar, meeting rooms, free parking, some pets allowed* ▭ *AE, DC, MC, V* ⦿ *BP.*

Duino

❼ *20 km (12 mi) northwest of Trieste, 12 km (8 mi) northwest of Castello di Miramare.*

The small fishing village of Duino is a picture of tranquillity, largely unspoiled, consisting of a few houses, hotels, and a police station. The contrast with the neighboring bay of Sistiana, which is chock-full of yachts and pleasure boats, couldn't be greater. You can walk the 2-km (1-mi) path from Sistiana, passing through woodland along the panoramic rocky coast, where you might even glimpse a peregrine falcon. Duino has two castles—one, the **Castello Vecchio**, is in ruins; the other **Castello** once hosted the German poet Rilke and is still inhabited by descendants of the original owners, the Della Torre e Tasso family (part of it now belongs to

CROSSING INTO SLOVENIA

IF YOU SPEND ANY TIME *at all in Gorizia, you'll find it hard not to notice the signs at every corner for its twin city, Nova Gorica, Slovenia. And if you're a wanderer by nature, you might find it equally hard to resist the temptation to pop into the former Yugoslavia for a night, or at least an afternoon.*

Hopping the Border

Getting across the border is easy—head east about 1 km (½ mi) out of the center of town, follow the signs for the Slovenian border, and show your passport at the control booth. After crossing, it's 3 km (2 mi) of rolling highway (bear left after the crossing) to the center of Nova Gorica.

Once there, it will become apparent that Italy got the better half of the bargain when the city was split after the war; Gorizia kept the beautiful castle and historic old town, while Nova Gorica is little more than bland Soviet bloc architecture. Part of town is lined with cheesy casinos, but this is also a university town, and there is an expansive main square lined with outdoor bars and cafés that gets fairly lively in the early evening. Take the opportunity to sit out on the concrete, sip a glass of Union on draft (Slovenia's pride—and arguably better than any beer in Italy), and contemplate the rise and fall of communism in Europe.

Although the Slovenian currency, the tolar (roughly 200 to the U.S. dollar) can be had from ATM machines in town, most stores, restaurants, and bars in Nova Gorica take euros, too.

Look for a local storefront selling delicious čevapčiči v lepinji, a flatbread fried on a griddle and filled with juicy, salty chunks of beef, raw onions, and bright red hot sauce. It's Slovenian comfort food par excellence.

Going Deeper

For a bigger dose of Slovenia, get on the highway toward Ljubljana and take the turnoff—after about a half hour—for **Postojnska Jama** *(Postojna Cave), an impressive set of subterranean chambers that's one of the most visited caves in Europe. A little train takes you past electrically lighted stalactites and stalagmites. There's a Vivarium where you can see cave fauna.* ☎ 386 (country code) 5/7000100 ⊕ www.postojnska-jama.si ⊙ *Guided visits only. Daily, May–Sept., every hr on the hr, 9–6; Apr. and Oct., 10, noon, 2, and 4; Nov.–Mar., 10, noon, and 2.*

From Postojnska Jama, continue a few miles further north, away from the highway, to reach the **Predjamski Grad** *(Predjama Castle), an imposing 14th-century fortress located halfway up a 400-foot cliff.* ⊙ *Daily, Nov.–Mar., 10–3; Apr. and Oct., 10–4; May–Sept., 9–7.*

You'll reap more rewards if you can make it all the way to Slovenia's capital, **Ljubljana** *(Lubiana in Italian), a vibrant city whose characteristic old town—complete with colorful onion domes—is still remarkably well preserved. The old town, sandwiched between a pretty river and a castle atop a hill, is lined with restaurants, cafés, and nightclubs.*

Ljubljana is about 100 km (65 mi) from the Italian border, and the highway is fast, making it about an hour's drive. For maps and hotel information, contact the **STIC** *(Slovenian Tourist Information Center;* ✉ *Krekov trg. 10* ☎ *386 1/3064575* ⊕ *www.ljubljana-tourism.si) or, once you're there, stop by the office in downtown Ljubljana.*

an international school). Rilke used the path for his musings and composed the *Duino Elegies*, among his last and most famous works, while staying here. This castle is not open to the public, but you can reach the Castello Vecchio easily enough, crowning an impressive headland jutting out to sea. The site is famed for the Dama Bianca (White Lady), a white rock named after a legendary episode in which the Lord Duino hurled a woman for whom he had no further use out of the castle. Before hitting the water, she turned to stone, the white rock. The locality is also said to have been a favorite haunt of Dante (1265–1321); the cliff on which he meditated bears his name.

Where to Stay & Eat

★ $ ✕🏨 **La Dama Bianca.** Right on the shore, with glorious sunset views, the balconied rooms just a few yards from the water's edge are blue, cool, light, and airy. With lush foliage and twinkling of the lights on the tables at night and on the boats out to sea, the hotel's restaurant ($$–$$$) is romantic indeed. From the catch of her fisherman husband, the affable Branca Miladinovic concocts crab served in its shell, and crescent-shape ravioli with shrimp, basil, and poppy seeds. The desserts, Signora Branca's own recipes, are to die for, and there's an excellent local wine list. ✉ *Duino Porto 61/c, 34013* ☎ *040/208137* 🖷 *040/208258* ⊕ *www. alladamabianca.com* 🛏 *7 rooms* ♨ *Restaurant, bar, some pets allowed, beach; no a/c in some rooms* 🖃 *AE, DC, MC, V* ⊘ *Hotel closed Dec. 15–Jan.; restaurant closed Thurs.* ¶⊙¶ *EP.*

$$ 🏨 **Duino Park Hotel.** This is a nice, quiet lodging a little way up the hill from the sea and run by genial management. Rooms are individually furnished, some with balconies overlooking the bay. The wicker furniture in the public area, set off by big terra-cotta floor tiles, adds to the charm. Breakfast is taken on the terrace in warm weather. ✉ *Via Duino 60/c, 34013* ☎ *040/208184* 🖷 *040/208526* ⊕ *www.duinoparkhotel. it* 🛏 *18 rooms* ♨ *Minibars, pool, sauna, bar* 🖃 *AE, DC, MC, V* ⊘ *Closed Dec.15–Feb. 15* ¶⊙¶ *BP.*

Castello di Miramare

❽ *8 km (5 mi) northwest of Trieste, 138 km (86 mi) east of Venice.*

Fodor'sChoice
★

This cliff-hanging waterfront castle in Miramare is an extravaganza of white stone, built between 1856 and 1860 for the Archduke Maximilian of Habsburg (1832–67, brother of Emperor Franz Josef). Maximilian spent a brief, happy time here until Napoléon III of France took Trieste from the Habsburgs and sent the poor archduke packing. He was given the title of emperor of Mexico in 1864 as a compensation but met his death before a Mexican firing squad in 1867. The interiors preserve much of the original fittings and ornaments: Bohemian glass chandeliers, inlaid furniture, and ornately molded ceilings, including the elaborate Gothic ceiling in the vast throne room.

Later, the castle was inhabited by the Duke Amadeo of Aosta, a military hero, and you can see the contrast between the archduke's ostentatious taste and Duke Amadeo's cleaner, simpler rooms, which are furnished in the modern Rationalist style. Virtually every room of the castle has stunning views over the open gulf. Lush grounds, which include an outdoor café-bar, surround the castle, affording stupendous views over the Adriatic. In summer, son-et-lumière shows are staged here, including a version in English. The castle is most often visited as an afternoon jaunt from Trieste, although you can stop on your way in or out of the city. ⊠ *Miramare*   ☎ *040/224143*   ⊕ *www.castello-miramare.it*   ☎ *Castle €4, grounds free* ⊘ *Castle and grounds, Nov.–Feb., daily 8–5; Oct. and Mar., daily 8–6; Apr.–Sept., daily 8–7; last entry 30 mins before closing.*

TRIESTE

Trieste is located on a mere fringe of coast, with the rugged Karst plateau above. The city is a lovely architectural melange, built on a hillside rising up from what was once the chief port of the Austro-Hungarian Habsburg Empire. Early Italian revolutionaries made Trieste their battle cry, contending it was under foreign occupation and should rightfully be returned to the motherland. The spacious streets hold a lively mix of monumental, neoclassical, and art nouveau styles, granting an air of stateliness to the city. On the downside, Trieste is also brash and clogged with traffic and can be a little overwhelming until you settle in.

Trieste was once the Roman city of Tergeste. Having chafed under a brief Venetian dominion, in 1382 the city placed itself under the protection of Leopold III of Habsburg, whose overlordship gradually developed into Austrian possession. In 1719 the city was proclaimed an imperial free port, its economy taking an upturn at the instigation of Maria Teresa, empress of Austria (1717–80), under whom a program of building started around the Grand Canal. From this anchorage for sailing ships, a regular pattern of spacious streets developed to the west of Piazza Unità d'Italia, called the Borgo Teresiano, an area still lined with grand neoclassical buildings and embellished with statues and bas-reliefs. Much of the city's pre-19th-century identity, in fact, has been submerged under this Austrian layer. The feeling of a Mittel-European city is compounded by the many cafés that grew up at the end of the 19th century. Like Vienna's coffeehouses, these are the social and cultural centers of the city, and much-beloved refuges from the city's prevailing northeast wind, the bora.

On becoming Italian in 1918, the port lost much of its business, and Trieste suffered a period of decline. After World War II, the sliver of land including Trieste and a small part of Istria became an independent, neutral state, which was officially recognized in a 1947 peace treaty. Although it was actually occupied by British and American troops for its nine years of existence, the Free Territory of Trieste issued its own currency and stamps. In 1954 a Memorandum of Understanding was signed in London, giving civil administration of Trieste to Italy and the other part of the former Free Territory to Yugoslavia, but it was not until the 1975 Treaty of Osimo that the territory was finally formally divided. The city's quays are now used as parking lots, and the container port has moved to the south side of Trieste. In recent years, the city has undergone a degree of rejuvenation and has become something of a center for science and the computer industry. Having absorbed new waves of Slavic and Eastern European immigrants, Trieste still has an international air, a tattered romance, and the offbeat ambience of a remote frontier town.

Exploring Trieste

If you're bringing a car into Trieste, find a space to park along the quay, as negotiating the city's system of one-way streets can be a nightmare. From the Stazione Centrale the Corso Cavour leads westward to the Riva, the broad quay that changes its name five times—Rivas Tre Novembre, del Mandracchio, Nazario Sauro, Tommaso Gulli, Grumula—as it skirts the seafront. The Borgo Teresiano sector of the city extends behind the Corso and the Riva's first section (Riva Tre Novembre); adjoining this area, the main Piazza Unità d'Italia opens out onto the sea. Behind the piazza, you can wind your way up through the historical center, pausing along the way at places of interest before reaching the Castello and a rewarding view of the city. On the seafront beyond the piazza, the long white building on the pier, formerly the Stazione Marittima, is now a conference center. From Piazza Oberdan a *tranvia* (cable car) runs every 20 minutes to Opicina and the Carso plateau.

If you're visiting more than a sight or two, pick up a T For You Card from the tourist information office. The €8 (24-hour) or €10 (48-hour) pass gets you free entrance to all civic museums, the Grotto Gigante, and some beach areas. You'll also be able to use all public transportation, including buses, the tram, and boats across the bay. Cardholders get discounts at some restaurants, shops, and hotels: ask when booking or ordering.

The Main Attractions

⑲ Castello di San Giusto. The Venetians, who always had an eye for the best vantage point in the cities they controlled, built the castle in the 15th century during one of their brief sojourns in Trieste. The Habsburgs enlarged it to its present size in the 18th century. Inside, some of the best exhibits in the **Civico Museo del Castello di San Giusto** are the weaponry and armor, but you can also admire an array of Flemish tapestries, a painted ceiling by Andrea Celesti (1637–1712), and period furnishings. From the ramparts, you can have a view of the area as far as the Dolomites. ⊠ *Piazza Cattedrale* ☏ *040/309362* 💴 *€2* ⊗ *Museum Tues.–Sun. 9–1. Castle Apr.–Sept., daily 9–7; Oct.–Mar., daily 9–5.*

⑱ Cattedrale di San Giusto. Fragments of Roman tombs and temples can be seen among the jumble of styles on the exterior of this 14th-century cathedral; you can see these most clearly on the pillars of the main doorway. The structure incorporates two much older churches, one dating from the 5th century. The facade has a fine and lovely Gothic rose window. The highlights of the interior are the 13th-century mosaics and frescoes, green and golden and beautifully decorated. Look up and you'll see the wooden ceiling studded with stars. ⊠ *Piazza Cattedrale* ☏ *040/309666* ⊗ *Apr.–Sept., Mon.–Sat. 8–noon and 3:30–7:30, Sun. 8–1 and 3:30–8; Oct.–Mar., Mon.–Sat. 8–noon and 2:30–6:30, Sun. 8–1 and 3:30–8.*

⑰ Museo Civico di Storia ed Arte. Statues from the Roman theater and artifacts from Egypt as well as Greece and Rome are on show at the eclectic Civic Museum of History and Art, including sculptures, glass, and manuscripts. From here you can gain access to the **Orto Lapidario** (Lapidary Garden), where you'll find classical statuary and pottery and a small

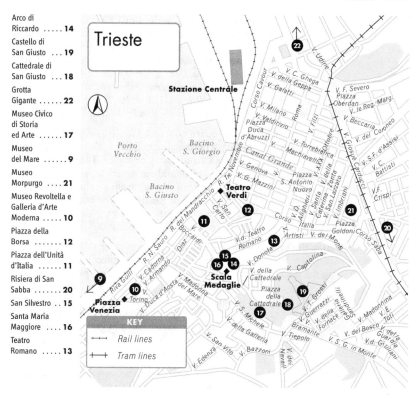

Corinthian temple that houses the remains of the archaeologist and pro-
ponent of neoclassicism, J. J. Winckelmann (1717–68). He was murdered
here in Trieste by a thief who coveted his collection of gold coins. ⊠ *Via
Cattedrale 15* ☎ *040/310500* ⌨ *€2* ⊙ *Mon. and Wed. 9–12:30 and
2–4;Tues., Thurs. and Fri. 9–12:30.*

> **need a break?**
>
> For the best ice cream in town, head for **Zampolli** (⊠ Via Ghega
> Carlo 10 ☎ 040/364868), as so many Trieste residents do, into the
> wee hours. You can identify the place by the rows of double-parked
> cars in front.

🌀 **⑨ Museo del Mare.** At Trieste's Museum of the Sea you can learn how Venetian galley rowers managed to sit three abreast and not smash one another with their oars. Displays include lots of boat models and a diorama
with *casoni* (fishermen's grass huts) and submerged *seragi* (fishnets). Outside is a park area with giant anchors and shady benches. ⊠ *Via di Campo
Marzio 5* ☎ *040/304987* ⌨ *€3* ⊙ *Tues.–Sun. 8:30–1:30.*

⑩ Museo Revoltella e Galleria d'Arte Moderna. In 1872 the Venetian Baron
Revoltella left the city his palace, library, and art collection. Original
furniture, inlaid floors, and enameled stoves set the tone in the older
part of the museum. A modern annex designed by Carlo Scarpa (1906–78),

holds one of the most important collections of 19th- and 20th-century art in Italy, including work by the metaphysical painter Giorgio De Chirico (1878–1978). On Thursday through Saturday in mid-July through August the museum is open until midnight with a bar on the terrace featuring splendid views. ✉ *Via Diaz 27* ☎ *040/6754350* ⊕ *www. museorevoltella.it* 🎫 *€5, €7 with temporary exhibits* ⊗ *Sept.–July 18, Mon. and Wed.–Sat. 9–1:30 and 4–7, Sun. 10–7; July 19–Aug., Mon. and Wed. 9–2 and 4–7, Thurs.–Sat. 9–2 and 4–midnight, Sun. 10–7.*

⑫ **Piazza della Borsa.** This square contains Trieste's original stock exchange, the **Borsa Vecchia,** a neoclassical building with a four-columned portico, now serving as the Chamber of Commerce. The statues on the top represent Asia, Europe, Africa, and the Americas, along with Mercury and Vulcan. Presiding over the square from a column is a **Statue of Leopold I** (died 994), emperor of Austria. In the same square, you can sample art nouveau style à la Trieste in the lightly decorated facade of the **Casa Bartoli,** designed in 1905 by Max Fabiani.

⑪ **Piazza dell'Unità d'Italia.** This spacious square inevitably recalls Piazza

FodorśChoice San Marco in Venice. Both are focal points of architectural interest abut-
★ ting the water. Inhabitants of Trieste, however, argue that their piazza is superior to that of San Marco, as it opens out directly onto the seafront. Imposing late-18th- and 19th-century buildings flank the square, most prominently the **Palazzo Comunale** (Town Hall) taking up the entire southern end of the piazza, designed in grand imperial style in 1877. The sidewalk cafés here have always been popular meeting places for literary and political figures and still make grand watering holes.

⑬ **Teatro Romano.** Quintus Petronius Modestus, procurator of the emperor Trajan, endowed Tergeste, as Trieste was known in Roman times, with this amphitheater in the late 1st century AD. The 6,000 spectators it once held have been replaced with grass and flowers. The statues that once adorned the proscenium arch are now in the Museo Civico di Storia ed Arte. The theater only resurfaced in 1938 after demolition work in the area. It's opposite the city's *questura* (police station). ✉ *Via del Teatro Romano.*

Also Worth Seeing

⑭ **Arco di Riccardo.** This Roman arch was built in AD 33 in honor of the emperor Augustus (63 BC–AD 14) and served as a city gate. Its name recalls the belief that Richard I of England, "the Lionheart," (1157–99) was imprisoned here after a spell in the Holy Land. ✉ *Piazza Barbacan.*

㉑ **Museo Morpurgo.** The building and its contents were left to the city in 1943 by Mario Morpurgo, a wealthy banker. It's still very much as it was in the last decades of the 19th century, and you can wander through the rooms with their glass, ceramics and porcelain, 19th-century paintings, and Japanese prints. ✉ *Via Imbriani 5* ☎ *040/636969* 🎫 *€2* ⊗ *Tues. and Thurs.–Sun. 9–1, Wed. 9–7.*

⑮ **San Silvestro.** Now used by Evangelicals, this solid little church is the oldest place of worship in Trieste. It's of plain-fronted Romanesque construction, dating from the 11th century, and said to have been erected

TRIESTE'S CAFFÈ CULTURE

TRIESTE IS JUSTLY FAMOUS for its coffee, and so it is perhaps no coincidence that Riccardo Illy, its former mayor and now president of the Friuli-Venezia Giulia region, is patriarch of the eponymous über-roaster, Illycaffè, which can be credited with supplying caffeine fixes to most Italians and much of the free world. The elegant civility of Trieste plays out beautifully in a café culture that rivals Vienna.

In Trieste, as in all of Italy, ask for a caffè and you'll get a thimbleful of high-octane espresso. Many cafés are part of a torrefazione (roasting shop), so you can sample the beans before you buy. You can taste the local brews at both the Cremcaffè and Caffè La Colombiana.

Few cafés in Trieste, Italy, and the world, can rival **Antico Caffè San Marco** (✉ Via Cesare Battisti 18 ☎ 040/363538) for its glimmering art deco style and Old World patina. It was completely destroyed in World War I, and when it was rebuilt in the 1920s, it became the meeting place for local intellectuals. On Friday and Saturday it hosts live music; it's closed Monday.

Caffè Tommaseo (✉ Piazza Tommaseo 4/c ☎ 040/362666) has been the haunt of politicians and businessmen since 1830. Sober and elegant, it has mirrors that were imported from Belgium more than 100 years ago. Weekend evenings and Sunday mornings feature live music; it's closed Monday.

Caffè Pasticceria Pirona (✉ Largo Barriera Vecchia 12 ☎ 040/636046) was patronized by the likes of James Joyce. Imagine him garnering inspiration for his Ulysses as he sipped his macchiato (literally "stained," espresso with a touch of steamed milk). Founded in 1900 by Alberto Pirona and still in the family, the place has maintained an old-fashioned look with its cherrywood fittings but has no place to sit down: it's a spot for coffee and its famously scrumptious cakes on the go. It's closed on Monday.

Cremcaffè (✉ Piazza Goldoni 10 ☎ 040/636555), closed Sunday, may not be the place to sit down and read the paper, lest you get jostled by the caffeine-craving crowd, but it's nonetheless one of the most frequented cafés in town, with 20 different blends to choose from.

For a great view of the great piazza, you couldn't do better than **Caffè Degli Specchi** (✉ Piazza dell'Unità d'Italia 7 ☎ 040/365777), where the many mirrors heighten the opportunities for people-watching.

The atmosphere is more modern than Old World at **I Paesi del Caffè** (✉ Via Einaudi 1 ☎ 040/633897), which brews and sells beans of top international varieties, including Jamaica Blue Mountain.

One of the city's finest roasting shops, **Caffè La Colombiana** (✉ Via Carducci 12 ☎ 040/370855), closed Sunday, has stood here since the 1940s—still without tables or eats, but the coffee hasn't changed since those days.

Il Gran Bar Malabar (✉ Piazza San Giovanni 6 ☎ 040/636226) is yet another wonderful stop for a coffee or an aperitif, with an excellent wine list as well and tastings every Friday.

on the site where two local martyrs, Sts. Tecla and Eufemia, once lived. ⊠ *Piazza di San Silvestro* ☎ *040/632770* ⊙ *Mon.–Sat. 9:30–12:30 and Sun. for Mass.*

⑯ **Santa Maria Maggiore.** In contrast to San Silvestro next door, this church, begun in 1627, has a square baroque facade with slender columns giving height and lightness. The interior has an altarpiece by Francesco Maffei (circa 1625–60). ⊠ *Via del Collegio 6* ☎ *040/632920* ⊙ *Mon.–Sat. 8:30–noon and 4:30–7, Sun. 8:30–noon.*

Off the Beaten Path

☾ ㉒ **Grotta Gigante.** This is the largest cave in the world open to tourists. It is more than 300 feet high, 900 feet long, and 200 feet wide, with spectacular stalactites and stalagmites. Reserve 45 minutes for the tour. It is not far from Trieste, about 10 km (6 mi) north of the city (take Bus 42 from Piazza Oberdan). ☎ *040/327312* ⊠ *€7.50* ⊙ *Apr.–June and Sept., Tues.–Sun. 10–6; July and Aug., daily 10–6; Mar. and Oct., Tues.–Sun. 10–4; Nov.–Feb., Tues.–Sun. 10–noon and 2–4. Apr.–Sept. tours leave every 30 mins; other months, every hr.*

⑳ **Risiera di San Sabba.** Originally used for the processing of rice, this building was turned into a prison and subsequently became, in 1943, one of only two concentration camps used by the Germans in Italy. A railway line ran to the crematorium, where it is estimated that 5,000 inmates were burned before liberation by the Yugoslavs on May 1, 1945. Now a museum, it serves as a reminder of the Fascist past. Bus 10 will get you here, or drive southeast out of town on Via Gabriele D'Annunzio. ⊠ *Via Giovanni Palatucci 5* ☎ *040/826202* ⊠ *Free* ⊙ *Daily 9–7.*

Where to Stay & Eat

$$$–$$$$ ✕ **Al Bagatto.** At this warm little seafood restaurant near the Piazza Unità, FodorsChoice chef-owner Giovanni Marussi will personally shepherd your meal from ★ start to finish. The best bet is his tasting menu, consisting of many little courses that might include such Adriatic wonders as *scampi crudi* (raw scampi) and delicate treatments of *aragosta* (similar to lobster). Giovanni's preparations often integrate nouvelle ingredients without overshadowing the freshness of whatever local fish he has bought in the market that morning. ⊠ *Via F. Venezian 2* ☎ *040/301771* ⌂ *Reservations essential* ▤ *AE, DC, MC, V* ⊙ *Closed Sun.*

$$$ ✕ **Hostaria alle Bandierette.** Try to keep from bumping into the tank of crayfish; then squeeze past the beds of flatfish and shellfish on crushed ice—yes, you're in seafood territory. In fact, this restaurant serves nothing else but. It's small, hectic, and full of serious eaters admiring the cooks in full view. Fish risottos, squid spaghetti, and lobsters with capers will all hit the spot. Dine on the outdoor patio in summer. ⊠ *Riva Nazario Sauro 2* ☎ *040/300686* ⌂ *Reservations essential* ▤ *AE, DC, MC, V* ⊙ *Closed Mon. and 2 wks in Jan.*

$$–$$$ ✕ **Città di Cherso.** Light, white, and restful in atmosphere, this restaurant right in the heart of downtown specializes in fish. Try the gnocchi *con seppie* (with cuttlefish, brandy, tomatoes, and cream) or the *rana pescatrice al trancio* (anglerfish steaks). Desserts are a must: there are wonderful

concoctions of chocolate and cream. ✉ *Via Cadorna 6* ☎ *040/366044* ⌁ *Reservations essential* ▤ *AE, DC, MC, V* ⊘ *Closed Tues. and Aug.*

$$–$$$ ✕ **Trattoria ai Fiori.** Fishermen still in their gum boots deliver their catch fresh off the boat to a restaurateur they've worked with for 20 years. Enjoy your fish simply grilled, or lying on a bed of wild mushrooms and truffles. Homemade pasta, bread, and gelato enliven any meal, and high ceilings brighten the dining room. ✉ *Piazza Attilio Hortis 7* ☎☎ *040/ 300633* ▤ *AE, DC, MC, V* ⊘ *Closed Sun. and 2–3 wks in Aug.*

$–$$ ✕ **Suban.** Though in the hills on the edge of town, this historic trattoria is worth the taxi ride. The rustic decor is rich in dark wood, stone, and wrought iron, and you'll find typical regional fare with imaginative variations. Among the specialties are *jota carsolina* (typical local minestrone made of cabbage, potatoes, and beans) and duck breast in Tokay sauce. Lighter fare includes *insalatine tiepide* (warm salads with smoked pork or duck) and locally smoked beef that is truly special. There are beautiful outdoor tables in good weather, from where you can watch the sunset. To get here you can take Bus 35 from Piazza Oberdan. ✉ *Via Emilio Comici 2/d* ☎ *040/54368* ▤ *AE, DC, MC, V* ⊘ *Closed Tues. and 1st 3 wks in Aug. No lunch Mon.*

★ ¢–$ ✕ **Antipastoteca di Mare.** Hidden away halfway up the hill to the Castello di San Giusto, Roberto Surian's simple little restaurant is well worth seeking out during the day and booking for the evening. You'll find here some of the tastiest of hot and cold seafood combinations, from calamari and barley salad to scallops, mussels, and *sardoni in savor* (big sardines with raisins, pine nuts, and caramelized onions). The extraordinary fish soup of sardines, mackerel, and tuna, sprinkled with lightly fried, diced garlic bread and polenta, won Roberto first prize in Trieste's prestigious Sarde Day competition. Fish is everything here, accompanied only by a simple salad, potatoes, and house wine. ✉ *Via della Fornace 1* ☎ *040/309606* ▤ *No credit cards* ⊘ *Closed Mon and 1–2 wks in Aug. No dinner Sun.*

★ ¢–$ ✕ **Trattoria da Giovanni.** The *fritto misto di pesce* (mixed fried fish) here is an elemental masterpiece, crisped by a feathery batter that preserves every drop of moisture within, casting a spotlight on the freshness of fish that flops in straight from the Adriatic. The simple side dish of chicory is elegant and acidic; don't forget to drizzle it with local oil. The space, too, is an object lesson in simplicity; familiar service and outdoor tables along one of Trieste's more evocative streets add to the effect. ✉ *Via San Lazzaro 14* ☎ *040/639396* ▤ *No credit cards* ⊘ *Closed Sun. and Aug.*

$$$$ ▦ **Duchi d'Aosta.** On the spacious Piazza Unità d'Italia, this hotel, beautifully furnished in Venetian-Renaissance style, has come a long way since its original incarnation as a 19th-century dockers' café. Each of the rooms is decorated in elegant one-off style, with dark-wood antiques, rich carpets, and plush fabrics. Down in the basement is one of northern Italy's most impressive indoor pool-spa complexes, done in the style of ancient Roman baths. Steam is scented, lights fade from one color into the next, and one gently rocking cradle even simulates weightlessness. On the ground floor is Harry's Grill, one of the city's swankiest restaurants. ✉ *Piazza Unità d'Italia 2/1, 34121* ☎ *040/7600011* ⊟ *040/366092* ⊕ *www.grandhotelduchidaosta.com* ⇆ *51 rooms, 2 suites* ⚘ *Restau-*

*Fodor's*Choice
★

rant, minibars, hot tubs, indoor pool, spa, bar, meeting rooms, parking (fee), some pets allowed ☰ *AE, DC, MC, V* ⫩◯⫩ *BP.*

★ **$$** 🖵 **Alla Posta.** The reading lounge—with its high-backed armchairs, parquet floor, and potted plants, plus a roaring fire in winter—will entice you into this elegant, central hotel. Upstairs, stylishly decorated guest rooms are outfitted with high-tech controls for amenities such as heating, air-conditioning, and wake-up calls. The spacious bathrooms are done in Italian marble. ⊠ *Piazza Oberdan 1* ☎ *040/365208* 🖷 *040/ 633720* ⊕ *www.albergopostatrieste.it* ⇰ *47 rooms* ⚭ *In-room data ports, in-room safes, minibars* ☰ *AE, DC, MC, V* ⫩◯⫩ *BP.*

$$ 🖵 **Hotel San Giusto.** Oriental rugs on the marble floor, potted palms, and chandeliers complement the elegant art deco style of this Best Western hotel. Only a 10-minute walk from the center of town, on the hill behind the castle, it's away from the concentration of hotels and restaurants downtown in a less touristy area with a mix of small shops, apartment buildings, offices, and some very good restaurants. ⊠ *Via dell'Istria 7, 34137* ☎ *040/764824* 🖷 *040/763826* ⊕ *www. hotelsangiusto.it* ⇰ *62 rooms* ⚭ *Bar, parking (fee), some pets allowed* ☰ *AE, DC, MC, V* ⫩◯⫩ *BP.*

★ **$$** 🖵 **Riviera & Maximilian's.** Seven kilometers (4 mi) north of Trieste, this lovely hotel commands stunning views across the Golfo di Trieste to Castello di Miramare. There's no sand on this stretch of coast, but an elevator leads to the hotel's own private bathing quay below, as well as a children's area. Rooms vary from modern design to vintage wood, and some have balconies and kitchenettes. The restaurant and the breakfast room also look out on the gulf. ⊠ *Strada Costiera 22, 34010* ☎ *040/ 224551* 🖷 *040/224300* ⊕ *www.hotelrivieraemaximilian.com* ⇰ *56 rooms, 2 suites, 9 apartments* ⚭ *Restaurant, minibars, in-room data ports, pool, beach, bar, Internet, meeting rooms, free parking, some pets allowed; no a/c in some rooms* ☰ *AE, DC, MC, V* ⫩◯⫩ *BP.*

$ 🖵 **Alabarda Flora.** The bright, spacious rooms in this restored, family-operated hotel have wood laminate floors and peach color schemes. The hotel is only a 10-minute walk from the train station. You can check your e-mail at the computer in the lobby and catch an English news broadcast on the satellite TV in your room. The friendly staff will offer assistance with local services, maps, and city bus tickets. Some front rooms can be noisy. ⊠ *Via Valdirivo 22, 34132* ☎ *040/630269* 🖷 *040/ 639284* ⊕ *www.hotelalabarda.it* ⇰ *18 rooms, 9 without bath* ⚭ *Bar, Internet, some pets allowed* ☰ *AE, DC, MC, V* ⫩◯⫩ *BP.*

$ 🖵 **Filoxenia.** The location on the city waterfront, and the reasonable prices, make this small hotel a choice accommodation. Members of Trieste's Greek community run the Filoxenia, and there's a good Greek restaurant on-site. The staff makes up in friendliness for what it might lack in professionalism. Rooms are simple and fresh, with white walls and two single beds covered in Mediterranean blue-stripe spreads; family rooms sleep four (€120). ⊠ *Via Mazzini 3, 34121* ☎ *040/3481644* 🖷 *040/ 661371* ⊕ *www.filoxenia.it* ⇰ *20 rooms* ⚭ *Restaurant, in-room safes, bar, meeting rooms, no-smoking rooms; no a/c in some rooms* ☰ *DC, MC, V* ⫩◯⫩ *BP.*

Nightlife & the Arts

The Arts

CONCERTS, OPERA & BALLET The concert, opera, and ballet season in Trieste runs from October through May, with events taking place in the **Teatro Verdi** (✉ Piazza Giuseppe Verdi ☎ 040/6722298 ⊕ www.teatroverdi-trieste.com). Various music and dance events are held at the **Sala Tripcovich** (✉ Piazza Libertà); for information and tickets contact Teatro Verdi. The **Festival Internazionale dell'Operetta** is held in July and August. Prices start at €7.75; for information and tickets contact Teatro Verdi.

FESTIVALS Details of events and festivals are published in the daily paper, *Il Piccolo*. The **Barcolana Autumn Cup Regatta** gets under way on the second Sunday in October, attracting more than 1,000 sailing boats. Four kilometers (2½ mi) south of Trieste, Muggia is famous for its **Carnevale,** a moveable feast in February that goes back as far as 1420, but it also has a crowd-pulling "summer edition" in July and August with music, dancing, and theater. Call the **Comune di Muggia** (☎ 040/3360340) for further information.

Nightlife

BARS **Buffet Birreria Rudy** (✉ Valdirivo 32 ☎ 040/639428 ☉ Closed Sun.), known locally as "alla Spaten," is just what it sounds like: a lively beer bar. It stays open until midnight and serves good local food, too. **Osteria da Marino** (✉ Via del Ponte 5a) has a cool, dark atmosphere, buzzing with locals at night, and serves cheap wine by the glass and good cured meats.

Shopping

You'll find Italy's biggest department-store chains, Coin and Rinascente, and most of Italy's major fashion names along Trieste's busy shopping street, **Corso Italia.** Trieste has some 60 antiques dealers, jewelers, and secondhand shops. For small items of glass and porcelain, the nameless antiques shop at Piazza Vecchia 2/c is excellent. You'll find similar shops along the Via del Ponte.

Markets

Markets are held Tuesday through Saturday. You'll find general markets in Piazza della Libertà and Via Carducci and fish, fruit, and flowers in Piazza di Ponterosso and at Riva Nazario Sauro 1. Antiques markets crowd the streets of the city's old center on the third Sunday of each month. At the beginning of November, Trieste plays host to the region's biggest antiques fair—a good opportunity to find those art nouveau pieces. Contact **Promotrieste** (Centro Congressi ✉ Stazione Marittima ☎ 040/304888) for information.

Specialty Shops

CHINA–CRYSTAL An elegant range of Venetian glass and fine china from names like Venini and Versace can be found at Orietta Spangher's **Bottega** (✉ Piazza Unità d'Italia 5 ☎ 040/366200).

CLOTHING **Alexandra** (✉ Via XXX Ottobre 14 ☎ 040/634401) has fine Italian selections of clothing. **Annamaria Costantini** (✉ Via Mazzini 22/B ☎ 040/369643) sells slightly offbeat evening wear. **Confezione Wallner** (✉ Via Roma 13 ☎ 040/631570) clothes men, women, and children.

JEWELRY For nice stocks of silverware and watches, visit **Cavallar** (⊠ Via S. Lazzaro 15 ☎ 040/630335). The proprietor of **G. Bin** (⊠ Via Giulia 10/c ☎ 040/569450) is a registered gemologist specializing in unset stones.

FRIULI-VENEZIA GIULIA A TO Z

To research prices, get advice from other travelers, and book travel arrangements, visit www.fodors.com.

AIRPORTS & TRANSFERS
There are domestic flights to Aeroporto Ronchi dei Legionari, 35 km (22 mi) northwest of Trieste, linked by regular SAF bus service to Via Flavio Gioia, near Trieste's train station. There is also an SAF connection to Udine and Gorizia from the airport.

🚹 Airport Information **Aeroporto Ronchi dei Legionari** ⊠ Redipuglia ☎ 0481/773224 ⊕ www.aeroporto.fvg.it. **SAF** ☎ 800/915303 toll-free.

BOAT & FERRY TRAVEL
Boats from Greece, Albania, Slovenia, and Croatia dock in Trieste. Contact Adriatica di Navigazione, a branch of Tirrenia, or stop at any travel agency.

🚹 Boat & Ferry Information **Tirrenia di Navigazione** ☎ 199/123199, or 39 081/3172999 from outside Italy ⊕ www.tirrenia.it.

BUS TRAVEL
Interurban and interregional bus connections serve the Veneto and Friuli-Venezia Giulia. Regular buses run from Piazzale Roma in Venice to Trieste, and there are frequent connections from Padua and Treviso. Local tourist offices may be able to provide details of timetables and routes; otherwise contact the local bus station.

The bus station in Trieste is at Piazza della Libertà; ACT operates services in and around Trieste. SAF operates services within the province and to Slovenia and Croatia, as well as between Trieste, Aquileia, Cividale, and Udine.

🚹 Bus Information **ACT** ☎ 800/016675 toll-free. **SAF** ☎ 800/915303 toll-free ⊕ www.saf.ud.it. **Trieste Bus Station** ⊠ Piazza della Libertà 11 ☎ 040/42520.

CAR RENTAL
🚹 Local Agencies **Avis** ⊠ Molo Bersaglieri 3, Stazione Marittima, Trieste ☎ 040/300820 ⊠ Aeroporto Ronchi dei Legionari, Trieste ☎ 0481/777085 ⊠ Viale Leopardi 5/a, Udine ☎ 0432/501149. **Hertz** ⊠ Molo Bersaglieri 3, Stazione Marittima, Trieste ☎ 040/3220098 ⊠ Aeroporto Ronchi dei Legionari, Trieste ☎ 0481/777025 ⊠ Via Crispi 17, Udine ☎ 0432/511211.

CAR TRAVEL
A rental car is the best way to get around the region, bar none. The good A4 autostrada runs eastward past or through Verona, Vicenza, and Venice to Trieste, off of which the A23 highway branches north to Udine; both are toll routes. The A27 links the A4 with Treviso and continues northward until it ends north of Belluno, from where you can pick up the SS51, then turn eastward on the SS52 to reach Carnia.

From Trieste the SS14 runs northwest along the coast to Monfalcone (and on to Venice), and the A4 takes the more inland route. The A23 runs from Palmanova to Udine and on to the Austrian border. The SS52 runs east from this through Tolmezzo to Carnia and Forni di Sopra. Aquileia is easily reached via the SS14, from where the straight SS352 traverses the causeway to Grado. Gorizia is accessed from Monfalcone, and Cividale from Udine along the SS54.

EMERGENCIES
All pharmacies post signs on the door with addresses of *farmacie di turno* (pharmacies taking shifts), which stay open at night, on Saturday afternoon, and on Sunday.

▶️ Emergency Services **Police** ☎ 112 or 113. **Ambulance** ☎ 118.

▶️ Hospitals **Ospedale Civile** ✉ Via Chiusaforte 41, Udine ☎ 0432/480062. **Ospedale Maggiore** ✉ Via Stuparich 1, Trieste ☎ 040/3991111.

TRAIN TRAVEL
There are 14 daily trains between Venice and Trieste and hourly service between Treviso and Udine. Trieste also connects easily with Budapest, Ljubljana, and Vienna. All towns listed in this region are connected by train with the exception of Grado and Aquileia, which are reachable by bus. Contact Trenitalia for train information.

FARES & SCHEDULES ▶️ Train Information **Stazione Gorizia** ✉ Piazzale Martiri Libertà d'Italia. **Stazione Trieste Centrale** ✉ Piazza della Libertà 8. **Stazione Udine** ✉ Piazzale d'Annunzio. **Trenitalia** ☎ 892021 ⊕ www.trenitalia.com.

TRAVEL AGENCIES
▶️ Local Agents **Natisone Viaggi Uno** ✉ Via Cividale 271, Udine ☎ 0432/582357 ⊕ www.natisoneviaggi.it. **No Stop Viaggi** ✉ Viale San Marco 38/a, Monfalcone ☎ 0481/791096. **Paterniti Viaggi/American Express** ✉ Corso Cavour 11, Trieste ☎ 040/366161 ⊕ www.paternitiviaggi.it.

VISITOR INFORMATION
▶️ Tourist Information **Aquileia** ✉ Piazza Capitolo, 33043 ☎ 0431/919491. **Cividale del Friuli** ✉ Corso Paolino d'Aquileia 10, 33051 ☎ 0432/731461 🖷 0432/731398. **Gorizia** ✉ Corso Italia 9, 34170 ☎ 0481/535764 🖷 0481/386277. **Grado** ✉ Viale Dante 72, 34073 ☎ 0431/8991 🖷 0431/899278. **Trieste** ✉ Via San Nicolò 20, 34121 ☎ 040/6796111 🖷 040/6796299 ⊕ www.triestetourism.it. **Udine** ✉ Piazza I Maggio 7, 33100 ☎ 0432/295972 🖷 0432/504743.

ITALIAN VOCABULARY

	English	Italian	Pronunciation

Basics

	English	Italian	Pronunciation
	Yes/no	Sí/No	see/no
	Please	Per favore	pear fa-**vo**-ray
	Yes, please	Sí grazie	see **grah**-tsee-ay
	Thank you	Grazie	**grah**-tsee-ay
	You're welcome	Prego	**pray**-go
	Excuse me, sorry	Scusi	**skoo**-zee
	Sorry!	Mi dispiace!	mee dis-spee-**ah**-chay
	Good morning/ afternoon	Buongiorno	bwohn-**jor**-no
	Good evening	Buona sera	**bwoh**-na **say**-ra
	Good bye	Arrivederci	a-ree-vah-**dare**-chee
	Mr. (Sir)	Signore	see-**nyo**-ray
	Mrs. (Ma'am)	Signora	see-**nyo**-ra
	Miss	Signorina	see-nyo-**ree**-na
	Pleased to meet you	Piacere	pee-ah-**chair**-ray
	How are you?	Come sta?	**ko**-may **stah**
	Very well, thanks	Bene, grazie	**ben**-ay **grah**-tsee-ay
	And you?	E lei?	ay **lay**-ee
	Hello (phone)	Pronto?	**proan**-to

Numbers

	English	Italian	Pronunciation
	one	uno	**oo**-no
	two	due	**doo**-ay
	three	tre	tray
	four	quattro	**kwah**-tro
	five	cinque	**cheen**-kway
	six	sei	say
	seven	sette	**set**-ay
	eight	otto	**oh**-to
	nine	nove	**no**-vay
	ten	dieci	dee-**eh**-chee
	eleven	undici	**oon**-dee-chee
	twelve	dodici	**doe**-dee-chee

thirteen	tredici	**tray**-dee-chee
fourteen	quattordici	kwa-**tore**-dee-chee
fifteen	quindici	**kwin**-dee-chee
sixteen	sedici	**say**-dee-chee
seventeen	diciassette	dee-cha-**set**-ay
eighteen	diciotto	dee-**cho**-to
nineteen	diciannove	dee-cha-**no**-vay
twenty	venti	**vain**-tee
twenty-one	ventuno	vain-**too**-no
twenty-two	ventidue	vain-tee-**doo**-ay
thirty	trenta	**train**-ta
forty	quaranta	kwa-**rahn**-ta
fifty	cinquanta	cheen-**kwahn**-ta
sixty	sessanta	seh-**sahn**-ta
seventy	settanta	seh-**tahn**-ta
eighty	ottanta	o-**tahn**-ta
ninety	novanta	no-**vahn**-ta
one hundred	cento	**chen**-to
one thousand	mille	**mee**-lay
ten thousand	diecimila	dee-eh-chee-**mee**-la

Useful Phrases

Do you speak English?	Parla inglese?	**par**-la een-**glay**-zay
I don't speak Italian	Non parlo italiano	non **par**-lo ee-tal-**yah**-no
I don't understand	Non capisco	non ka-**peess**-ko
Can you please repeat?	Può ripetere?	pwo ree-**pet**-ay-ray
Slowly!	Lentamente!	**len**-ta-men-tay
I don't know	Non lo so	non lo **so**
I'm American/ British	Sono americano(a)	**so**-no a-may-ree-**kah**-no(a)
	Sono inglese	**so**-no een-**glay**-zay
What's your name?	Come si chiama?	**ko**-may see kee-**ah**-ma
My name is . . .	Mi chiamo . . .	mee kee-**ah**-mo
What time is it?	Che ore sono?	kay **o**-ray **so**-no
How?	Come?	**ko**-may
When?	Quando?	**kwan**-doe
Yesterday/today/ tomorrow	Ieri/oggi/domani	**yer**-ee/**o**-jee/ do-**mah**-nee

This morning/ ternoon	Stamattina/Oggi pomeriggio	sta-ma-**tee**-na/**o**-jee af-po-mer-**ee**-jo
Tonight	Stasera	sta-**ser**-a
What?	Che cosa?	kay **ko**-za
What is it?	Che cos'è?	kay ko-**zay**
Why?	Perché?	pear-**kay**
Who?	Chi?	kee
Where is . . .	Dov'è . . .	doe-**veh**
the bus stop?	la fermata dell'autobus?	la fer-**mah**-ta del ow-toe-**booss**
the train station?	la stazione?	la sta-tsee-**oh**-nay
the subway station?	la metropolitana?	la may-tro-po-lee-**tah**-na
the terminal?	il terminale?	eel ter-mee-**nah**-lay
the post office?	l'ufficio postale?	loo-**fee**-cho po-**stah**-lay
the bank?	la banca?	la **bahn**-ka
the . . . hotel?	l'hotel . . .?	lo-**tel**
the store?	il negozio?	eel nay-**go**-tsee-o
the cashier?	la cassa?	la **kah**-sa
the . . . museum?	il museo . . .?	eel moo-**zay**-o
the hospital?	l'ospedale?	lo-spay-**dah**-lay
the first aid station?	il pronto soccorso?	eel **pron**-to so-**kor**-so
the elevator?	l'ascensore?	la-shen-**so**-ray
a telephone?	un telefono?	oon tay-**lay**-fo-no
Where are the restrooms?	Dov'è il bagno?	do-**vay** eel **bahn**-yo
Here/there	Qui/là	kwee/la
Left/right	A sinistra/a destra	a see-**neess**-tra/ a **des**-tra
Straight ahead	Avanti dritto	a-**vahn**-tee **dree**-to
Is it near/far?	È vicino/lontano?	ay vee-**chee**-no/ lon-**tah**-no
I'd like . . .	Vorrei . . .	vo-**ray**
a room	una camera	**oo**-na **kah**-may-ra
the key	la chiave	la kee-**ah**-vay
a newspaper	un giornale	oon jor-**nah**-lay
a stamp	un francobollo	oon frahn-ko-**bo**-lo
I'd like to buy . . .	Vorrei comprare . . .	vo-**ray** kom-**prah**-ray
a cigar	un sigaro	oon see-**gah**-ro
cigarettes	delle sigarette	**day**-lay see-ga-**ret**-ay
some matches	dei fiammiferi	**day**-ee **fee**-ah-**mee**-fer-ee
some soap	una saponetta	**oo**-na sa-po-**net**-a

a city plan	una pianta della città	**oo**-na **pyahn**-ta day-la chee-**tah**
a road map of . . .	una carta stradale di . . .	**oo**-na **cart**-a stra-**dah**-lay dee
a country map	una carta geografica	**oo**-na **cart**-a jay-o-**grah**-fee-ka
a magazine	una rivista	**oo**-na ree-**veess**-ta
envelopes	delle buste	**day**-lay **booss**-tay
writing paper	della carta da lettere	**day**-la **cart**-a da **let**-air-ay
a postcard	una cartolina	**oo**-na car-toe-**lee**-na
a guidebook	una guida turistica	**oo**-na **gwee**-da too-**reess**-tee-ka
How much is it?	Quanto costa?	**kwahn**-toe **coast**-a
It's expensive/cheap	È caro/economico	ay **car**-o/ay-ko-**no**-mee-ko
A little/a lot	Poco/tanto	**po**-ko/**tahn**-to
More/less	Più/meno	pee-**oo**/**may**-no
Enough/too (much)	Abbastanza/troppo	a-bas-**tahn**-sa/**tro**-po
I am sick	Sto male	sto **mah**-lay
Call a doctor	Chiama un dottore	kee-**ah**-mah oon doe-**toe**-ray
Help!	Aiuto!	a-**yoo**-toe
Stop!	Alt!	ahlt
Fire!	Al fuoco!	ahl **fwo**-ko
Caution/Look out!	Attenzione!	a-ten-**syon**-ay

Dining Out

A bottle of . . .	Una bottiglia di . . .	**oo**-na bo-**tee**-lee-ah dee
A cup of . . .	Una tazza di . . .	**oo**-na **tah**-tsa dee
A glass of . . .	Un bicchiere di . . .	oon bee-key-**air**-ay dee
Bill/check	Il conto	eel **cone**-toe
Bread	Il pane	eel **pah**-nay
Breakfast	La prima colazione	la **pree**-ma ko-la-**tsee**-oh-nay
Cocktail/aperitif	L'aperitivo	la-pay-ree-**tee**-vo
Dinner	La cena	la **chen**-a
Fixed-price menu	Menù a prezzo fisso	may-**noo** a **pret**-so **fee**-so
Fork	La forchetta	la for-**ket**-a
I am diabetic	Ho il diabete	o eel dee-a-**bay**-tay

I am vegetarian	Sono vegetariano/a	**so**-no vay-jay-ta-ree-**ah**-no/a
I'd like . . .	Vorrei . . .	vo-**ray**
I'd like to order	Vorrei ordinare	vo-**ay** or-dee-**nah**-ray
Is service included?	Il servizio è incluso?	eel ser-**vee**-tzee-o ay een-**kloo**-zo
It's good/bad	È buono/cattivo	ay **bwo**-no/ka-**tee**-vo
It's hot/cold	È caldo/freddo	ay **kahl**-doe/**fred**-o
Knife	Il coltello	eel kol-**tel**-o
Lunch	Il pranzo	eel **prahnt**-so
Menu	Il menù	eel may-**noo**
Napkin	Il tovagliolo	eel toe-va-lee-**oh**-lo
Please give me . . .	Mi dia . . .	mee **dee**-a
Salt	Il sale	eel **sah**-lay
Spoon	Il cucchiaio	eel koo-kee-**ah**-yo
Sugar	Lo zucchero	lo **tsoo**-ker-o
Waiter/Waitress	Cameriere/cameriera	ka-mare-**yer**-ay/ka-mare-**yer**-a
Wine list	La lista dei vini	la **lee**-sta **day**-ee **vee**-nee

MENU GUIDE

English	Italian
Set menu	Menù a prezzo fisso
Dish of the day	Piatto del giorno
Specialty of the house	Specialità della casa
Local specialties	Specialità locali
Extra charge	Extra . . .
In season	Di stagione
Cover charge/Service charge	Coperto/Servizio

Breakfast

Butter	Burro
Croissant	Cornetto
Eggs	Uova
Honey	Miele
Jam/Marmalade	Marmellata
Roll	Panino
Toast	Pane tostato

Starters

Assorted cold cuts	Affettati misti
Assorted seafood	Antipasto di pesce
Assorted appetizers	Antipasto misto
Toasted rounds of bread, fried or toasted in oil	Crostini/Crostoni
Diced-potato and vegetable salad with mayonnaise	Insalata russa
Eggplant parmigiana	Melanzane alla parmigiana
Fried mozzarella sandwich	Mozzarella in carrozza
Ham and melon	Prosciutto e melone
Cooked sausages and cured meats	Salumi cotti
Filled pastry shells	Vol-au-vents

Soups

"Angel hair," thin noodle soup	Capelli d'angelo
Cream of . . .	Crema di . . .
Pasta-and-bean soup	Pasta e fagioli
Egg-drop and parmesan cheese soup	Stracciatella

Pasta, Rice, and Pizza

Filled pasta	Agnolotti/ravioli/tortellini
Potato dumplings	Gnocchi

Semolina dumplings	Gnocchi alla romana
Pasta	Pasta
with four cheeses	*al quattro formaggi*
with basil/cheese/pine nuts/ garlic sauce	*al pesto*
with tomato-based meat sauce	*al ragù*
with tomato sauce	*al sugo* or *al pomodoro*
with butter	*in bianco* or *al burro*
with egg, parmesan cheese, and pepper	*alla carbonara*
green (spinach-based) pasta	*verde*
Rice	Riso
Rice dish	Risotto
with mushrooms	*ai funghi*
with saffron	*alla milanese*
Noodles	Tagliatelle
Pizza	Pizza
Pizza with seafood, cheese, artichokes, and ham in four different sections	Pizza quattro stagioni
Pizza with tomato and mozzarella	Pizza margherita
Pizza with oil, garlic, and oregano	Pizza marinara

Fish and Seafood

Anchovies	Acciughe
Bass	Persico
Carp	Carpa
Clams	Vongole
Cod	Merluzzo
Crab	Granchio
Eel	Anguilla
Lobster	Aragosta
Mackerel	Sgombro
Mullet	Triglia
Mussels	Cozze
Octopus	Polpo
Oysters	Ostriche
Pike	Luccio
Prawns	Gamberoni
Salmon	Salmone
Shrimp	Scampi
Shrimps	Gamberetti
Sole	Sogliola
Squid	Calamari
Swordfish	Pescespada

Trout	Trota
Tuna	Tonno

Methods of Preparation

Baked	Al forno
Cold, with vinegar sauce	In carpione
Fish stew	Zuppa di pesce
Fried	Fritto
Grilled (usually charcoal)	Alla griglia
Seafood salad	In insalata
Smoked	Affumicato
Stuffed	Ripieno

Meat

Boar	Cinghiale
Brain	Cervella
Braised meat with wine	Brasato
Chop	Costoletta
Duck	Anatra
Lamb	Agnello
Baby lamb	Abbacchio
Liver	Fegato
Pheasant	Fagiano
Pork roast	Arista
Rabbit	Coniglio
Steak	Bistecca
Sliced raw steak with sauce	Carpaccio
Mixed boiled meat	Bollito misto

Methods of Preparation

Battered with eggs and crumbs and fried	. . . alla milanese
Grilled	. . . ai ferri
Grilled (usually charcoal)	. . . alla griglia
Raw, with lemon/egg sauce	. . . alla tartara
Roasted	. . . arrosto
Very rare	. . . al sangue
Well done	. . . ben cotta
With ham and cheese	. . . alla valdostana
With parmesan cheese and tomatoes	. . . alla parmigiana

Vegetables

Artichokes	Carciofi
Asparagus	Asparagi
Beans	Fagioli

Brussels sprouts	Cavolini di Bruxelles
Cabbage	Cavolo
Carrots	Carote
Cauliflower	Cavolfiore
Cucumber	Cetriolo
Eggplants	Melanzane
Green beans	Fagiolini
Leeks	Porri
Lentils	Lenticchie
Lettuce	Lattuga
Mushrooms	Funghi
Onions	Cipolle
Peas	Piselli
Peppers	Peperoni
Potatoes	Patate
Roasted potatoes	*Patate arroste*
Boiled potatoes	*Patate bollite*
Fried potatoes	*Patate fritte*
Small, roasted potatoes	*Patatine novelle*
Mashed potatoes	*Purè di patate*
Radishes	Rapanelli
Salad	Insalata
vegetable	*mista*
green	*verde*
Spinach	Spinaci
Tomatoes	Pomodori
Zucchini	Zucchini

Sauces, Herbs, and Spices

Basil	Basilico
Bay leaf	Lauro
Chervil	Cerfoglio
Dill	Aneto
Garlic	Aglio
Hot dip with anchovies (for vegetables)	Bagna cauda
Marjoram	Maggiorana
Mayonnaise	Maionese
Mustard	Mostarda *or* senape
Oil	Olio
Parsley-based sauce	Salsa verde
Pepper	Pepe
Rosemary	Rosmarino
Tartar sauce	Salsa tartara
Vinegar	Aceto
White sauce	Besciamella

Cheeses

Fresh:	Caprino fresco
	Mascarpone
	Mozzarella
	Ricotta
Mild:	Caciotta
	Caprino
	Fontina
	Grana
	Provola
	Provolone dolce
	Robiola
	Scamorza
Sharp:	Asiago
	Gorgonzola
	Groviera
	Pecorino
	Provolone piccante
	Taleggio
	Toma

Fruits and Nuts

Almonds	Mandorle
Apple	Mela
Apricot	Albicocca
Blackberries	More
Black currant	Ribes nero
Blueberries	Mirtilli
Cherries	Ciliege
Chestnuts	Castagne
Coconut	Noce di cocco
Dates	Datteri
Figs	Fichi
Green grapes	Uva bianca
Black grapes	Uva nera
Grapefruit	Pompelmo
Hazelnuts	Nocciole
Lemon	Limone
Melon	Melone
Nectarine	Nocepesca
Orange	Arancia
Pear	Pera
Peach	Pesca
Pineapple	Ananas
Plum	Prugna/Susina
Prune	Prugna secca

Raisins	Uva passa
Raspberries	Lamponi
Red currant	Ribes
Strawberries	Fragole
Tangerine	Mandarino
Walnuts	Noci
Watermelon	Anguria/Cocomero
Dried fruit	Frutta secca
Fresh fruit	Frutta fresca
Fruit salad	Macedonia di frutta

Desserts

Custard filed pastry, with candied fruit	Cannoli
Ricotta filled pastry shells with sugar glaze	Cannoli alla siciliana
Ice cream with candied fruit	Cassata
Ricotta filed cake with sugar glaze	Cassata siciliana
Chocolate	Cioccolato
Cup of ice cream	Coppa gelato
Caramel custard	Crème caramel
Pie	Crostata
Fruit pie	Crostata di frutta
Ice cream	Gelato
Flaked pastry	Millefoglie
Chestnuts and whipped-cream cake	Montebianco
Whipped cream	Panna montata
Pastries	Paste
Sherbet	Sorbetto
Chocolate-coated ice cream	Tartufo
Fruit tart	Torta di frutta
Apple tart	Torta di mele
Ice-cream cake	Torta gelata
Vanilla	Vaniglia
Egg-based cream with sugar and Marsala wine	Zabaione
Ice-cream filled cake	Zuccotto

Alcoholic Drinks

On the rocks	Con ghiaccio
Straight	Liscio
With soda	Con seltz
Beer	Birra
light/dark	*chiara/scura*

Bitter cordial	Amaro
Brandy	Cognac
Cordial	Liquore
Aniseed cordial	Sambuca
Martini	Cocktail Martini
Port	Porto
Vermouth	Vermut/Martini
Wine	Vino
blush	*rosé*
dry	*secco*
full-bodied	*corposo*
light	*leggero*
red	*rosso*
sparkling	*spumante*
sweet	*dolce*
very dry	*brut*
white	*bianco*
Light wine	Vinello
Bottle	Bottiglia
Carafe	Caraffa
Flask	Fiasco

Nonalcoholic Drinks

Mineral water	Acqua minerale
carbonated	*gassata*
still	*non gassata*
Tap water	Acqua naturale
Tonic water	Acqua tonica
Coffee with steamed milk	Cappuccino
Espresso	Caffè espresso
with milk	*macchiato*
decaffeinated	*decaffeinato*
lighter espresso	*lungo*
with cordial	*corretto*
Fruit juice	Succo di frutta
Lemonade	Limonata
Milk	Latte
Orangeade	Aranciata
Tea	Tè
with milk/lemon	*col latte/col limone*
iced	*freddo*

INDEX

ABOUT OUR WRITERS

While doing physics research in the same tower where Galileo once worked, Jeff Booth felt the gravitational pull of Venice. After two years of learning to row gondolas and raise a Venetian daughter, he hasn't fallen into the Grand Canal, yet. Jeff writes for *National Geographic Traveler* and *New York* magazine, among other publications.

Although Robin S. Goldstein is trained in philosophy at Harvard and law at Yale, his heart has always been in his travel writing. His credits include not only Italy but also Spain, Mexico, Ecuador, and the Galapagos Islands. Once a resident of Genoa, he's now in almost constant motion up and down the boot, with home bases in Milan and Bologna.

Longtime Venice resident Cristina Gregorin is the author of *Venice Master Artisans,* a study of the city's traditional arts and crafts. She's worked as a guide in Venice since 1991.

Fifteen years ago California native Pamela Santina came to study art history at Venice's Ca' Foscari University, and she's still there today—though now in a teaching capacity. Her writing has appeared in *Conde Nast Traveler* and *Italy Italy* magazines, and she served as research assistant to John Berendt on his best-selling book *City of Falling Angels.* In her free time Pamela enjoys exploring new destinations with her husband and son.